More Advance Praise for
The Gunning of America

"Firearms may be instruments of death. But they are also, as Pamela Haag reveals in her thought-provoking reassessment of guns in American life, economic commodities—so much so, that it can be difficult at times to discern where business culture ends and gun culture begins."
> —Karl Jacoby, author of *Shadows at Dawn:*
> *A Borderlands Massacre and the Violence of History*

"*The Gunning of America* provides an exceptional, fresh perspective about the gun culture in America. Pamela Haag thoroughly examines the history of America's long-term relationship with guns while offering an insightful, informative philosophy as to when and how this love affair began."
> —Wes Moore, founder and CEO of BridgeEdU

THE GUNNING OF AMERICA

THE GUNNING OF AMERICA

Business and the
Making of American Gun Culture

PAMELA HAAG

BASIC BOOKS

A Member of the Perseus Books Group
New York

Published by Basic Books,
A Member of the Perseus Books Group

Books published by Basic Books are available at special discounts for bulk purchases in the United States by corporations, institutions, and other organizations. For more information, please contact the Special Markets Department at the Perseus Books Group, 2300 Chestnut Street, Suite 200, Philadelphia, PA 19103, or call (800) 810-4145, ext. 5000, or e-mail special .markets@perseusbooks.com.

Designed by Trish Wilkinson
Set in 11.5-point Goudy Oldstyle Std

Library of Congress Cataloging-in-Publication Data
Names: Haag, Pamela.
Title: The gunning of America : business and the making of American gun
    culture / Pamela Haag.
Description: New York : Basic Books, a member of the Perseus Books Group,
    2016. | Includes bibliographical references and index.
Identifiers: LCCN 2015036679 | ISBN 9780465048953 (hardcover) | ISBN
    9780465098569 (electronic)
Subjects: LCSH: Firearms—Social aspects—United States—History. | Firearms
    industry and trade—United States—History. | Capitalism—United
    States—History. | United States—Social conditions. | United
    States—Economic conditions. | BISAC: HISTORY / United States / 19th
    Century. | HISTORY / United States / General. | HISTORY / Military /
    Weapons. | BIOGRAPHY & AUTOBIOGRAPHY / Women.
Classification: LCC TS533.2 .H33 2016 | DDC 338.4/768340973—dc23
LC record available at http://lccn.loc.gov/2015036679

10 9 8 7 6 5 4 3 2 1

In memory of my brother, Stephen L. Haag

Contents

Introduction   *"The Art and Mystery of a Gunsmith"*   *ix*

CHAPTER 1   The American System   1

CHAPTER 2   The Crystal Palace   21

CHAPTER 3   "Scattering Our Guns"   45

CHAPTER 4   "More Wonderful Than Practical"   65

CHAPTER 5   Model 1866   93

CHAPTER 6   "Gun Men" and the "Oriental Lecturer"   109

CHAPTER 7   "Spirit Guns"   143

CHAPTER 8   "The Unhallowed Trade"   163

CHAPTER 9   The "Moral Effect" of a Winchester   179

CHAPTER 10   Balancing the Ledger   203

CHAPTER 11   Summer Land   211

CHAPTER 12   The Gun Industry's Visible Hand   225

CHAPTER 13   Learning to Love the Gun   249

CHAPTER 14   Mystery House   267

CHAPTER 15   "Grotesque, Yet Magnificent"   279

CHAPTER 16   Overbuilding   299

CHAPTER 17   The Soul of the "Gun Crank"   317

CHAPTER 18   King of Infinite Space   341

CHAPTER 19   The West That Won the Gun   353

CHAPTER 20   "Merchants of Death"   369
             Epilogue   389

Acknowledgments   399
Abbreviations for Frequently Cited Archives   403
Notes   405
Index   479

Introduction:
"The Art and Mystery of a Gunsmith"

T HIS BOOK TELLS THE STORY OF HOW AMERICA BECAME A GUN culture through the prism of the forgotten, unglamorous, but re-velatory archive of the gun industry—principally, the records of the Winchester Repeating Arms Company of New Haven, Connecticut.

I didn't set out to tell this story. I was drawn into the subject by a ghost story that I heard while living in New Haven. Every day, I walked past the crumbling remains of the factories built by the "rifle king," Oliver Winchester. It wasn't Oliver's story that intrigued me; it was that of his less visible, more historically numinous daughter-in-law, Sarah Winchester. According to legend, when she inherited the Win-chester rifle company's "blood fortune" in the 1800s, she took on an enormous, haunting debt of guilt, obsession, and grief along with it. Maybe this is true, and maybe it is not: a legend does not reveal its truth without a fight. What we do know is that Sarah ended up doing something enigmatic and mysterious with much of her fortune—and to this day, what she did is a compelling riddle that craves an answer.

I wanted to believe the legend of Sarah Winchester, because it spoke to something in me and planted a question in my mind. It wasn't until many years later, however, after the tragedy of the Sandy Hook Elementary School shooting in Newton, Connecticut, on Decem-ber 14, 2012, that I realized what that question was. I still wanted to know if Sarah really had felt a haunting burden of conscience for acquiring a gun fortune. But, even more so, I wanted to know why Oliver Winchester had not felt it. Admittedly, it is an anachronistic question, because it never would have been asked in his day. Oliver Winchester enjoyed an unimpeachable reputation as a minor captain of industry. Nevertheless, I wanted to know what allowed Oliver Winchester and his successors not to feel at least a small bit encumbered by the fact that they manufactured and sold millions of "fearfully destructive" guns. We hear a great deal about gun owners, but what do we know about their makers? The gun debate has been mired in rights talk for so long—what gun owners have a right to do and what gun-control advocates have a right to force them to do—that it is forgotten as a matter of conscience.[1]

I took on this question with some trepidation. Delving deeply into Oliver Winchester's world and the neglected historical archives of the American gun industry would land me in the middle of a heated debate, one that has been ensnared for decades in what one expert has described as an extraordinary degree of "polemical undergrowth." I did not want to become entrapped by that snare. I had never owned or shot a gun when I started this project; nor had I been involved in gun-control politics or advocacy. I came to this material as a historian.[2]

As a historian, I wanted to take myself back to a time when guns didn't have the freight of being malignant commodities, when they were not the muses of a disturbingly violent culture. I wanted to be able to see a gun the same way that a men's shirt manufacturer from Connecticut had when he had first encountered a "volitional" rifle in a scrappy shop on Artizan Street in New Haven in 1855. Oliver Winchester saw something in that rifle that led him to invest in it, to see if it could be mass-produced and sold. So despite my deep concerns about becoming irretrievably ensnared, I ventured into the minutiae of the industry that made the guns that made the gun culture. Once there, I was surprised by what I discovered.

The story also involves another name that later became famous: if "Pugsley" sounds at all familiar, it is because the cartoonist Charles Addams, sometime in the early twentieth century, befriended the real

Edwin Pugsley, who became the inspiration for *The Addams Family* character of the same name (the macabre son). But the real Pugsley had another claim to fame. He knew more about Winchester rifles and business than almost anyone else. He had married into the Winchester family, and he was variously the company's gun *savant*, factory superintendent, director of research, vice president, and informal but meticulous chronicler. In 1934, speaking to a prospective author of a company history, he advocated telling the story of the Winchester in the simplest, most elegant, obvious terms. His assessment has great merit: "We must go back to various types of records," he said. "In the first place . . . financial statements. As it makes money, it expands. If it loses money, it does not expand. . . . Such a tabulation will give a very graphic story." In that terse description, Pugsley distilled the ironclad equation and cold arithmetic that governed Oliver Winchester's world and the cultural history of American guns that followed.[3]

———

BY EXAMINING GUNS AS A BUSINESS, AND FOLLOWING THE MONEY, I found that some theses, counterintuitive though they may be, emerged clearly. An abridged history of the American gun culture, told from legend and popular memory, might go like this: We were born a gun culture. Americans have an exceptional, unique, and timeless relationship to guns, starting with the militias of the Revolutionary War, and it developed on its own from there. Some celebrate and some condemn this relationship, but it is in either case unique. Guns have long been a commonplace part of American life, which is why guns pretty much sell themselves. The Second Amendment, ubiquitous to contemporary gun politics, was a prominent presence historically and is a source of the gun's unique stature, while the idea of gun control is more recent. The American gun story is about civilians and individual citizens, and they are its heroes or its villains—the frontiersman, the Daniel Boone "long hunter" who trekked far into the wilderness alone, the citizen-patriot militiaman, the guiltily valorized outlaw, and the gunslinger. The gun's mystique was forged most vividly on the violent western frontier of the 1800s, and this mystique is about individualism: guns protect citizens against overzealous government infringement of liberties; they protect freedom and self-determination.[4]

This book tells the story of American guns from the perspective of what the gun was—in essence, an object, produced by businesses, to be sold. The story that highlights the Second Amendment, frontiersmen, militias, and the desires and character of the American gun owner is not to be found in the pages of this book. Or, more accurately, my work deliberately skews the story of the gun in another direction: it focuses on the missing element of the gun culture rather than reworking the familiar themes. As such, it has different characters, motivations, plot twists, highlights, and timelines, and all of these elements call into question the gun clichés that animate contemporary politics.

PERHAPS THE MOST POWERFUL CLICHÉ IS GUN EXCEPTIONALISM. Many people on both sides of the debate about guns believe that America has a unique and special relationship to guns, and that this exceptional relationship—whether celebrated or condemned—is a foundation of American gun culture. Americans have always loved guns, common wisdom holds, or, "guns are part of the American identity."[5]

A main thesis of this book is a simple but important one. We became a gun culture not because the gun was symbolically intrinsic to Americans or special to our identity, or because the gun was something exceptional in our culture, but precisely because it was not. From the vantage point of business, the gun was a product of non-exceptionalism. Perhaps not in the earliest years of its manufacture, when the government construed the gun as an exceptional instrument of war and common defense, whose more efficient production merited guaranteed contracts and markets, generous funding, protective tariffs, and a free-wheeling exchange of innovation across public armories to germinal private industry, but in the key years of its diffusion, and for many years thereafter, it was like a buckle or a pin, an unexceptional object of commerce. No pangs of conscience were attached to it, and no more special regulations, prohibitions, values, or mystique pertained to its manufacture, marketing, and sale than to a shovel. Indeed, there were no special rules concerning the international trade of guns until modest presidential embargo powers became effective in 1898. By that time, Winchester's company sat at the center of its own web of gun commerce that radiated outward to six continents. No exceptional regulations existed when Winchester and his competitors were first "scattering the guns," in his terms, to create US markets. Although the gun industry produced an exceptional product—designed to injure and kill—it followed the ordinary trends and practices of the corporate industrial economy in the nineteenth and twentieth centuries. In short: the gun was no exception.[6]

Ironically, had the gun been perceived in its early commercial years as a unique and extraordinary thing in society, we might never have become a gun culture. Under those circumstances, politics, law, and other regulatory forces might well have stepped in early on to circumscribe or shape the gun's manufacture and sale, as they did in some other places around the world. For the United States, the gun culture was forged in the image of commerce. It was stamped, perhaps indelibly, by what historian John Blum called the "amorality of business." America has an estimated 300 million guns in circulation today, but the gunning of the country started extemporaneously, and it was etched strongly by the character, ambition, and will of gun capitalists rather than by diplomats, politicians, generals, and statesmen. Gun politics today are consumed by Second Amendment controversies, but the Second Amendment did not design, invent, patent, mass-produce, advertise, sell, market, and distribute guns. Yet the gun business, which did, and does, is largely invisible in today's gun politics.[7]

In the context of business amorality and unexceptionalism, Winchester cast his industrial lot and fortune on a faster and mechanically improved rifle, and he did so not as a gunsmith or even as a gun enthusiast, but as a nineteenth-century capitalist. Others later recalled that Winchester had never personally owned a gun, had never displayed guns in his home, and had never shot a gun before he built his family and corporate fortunes off of them. He was, at the beginning, a men's shirt manufacturer. If he identified with any group, it would have been with the vanguard class of self-made men who scorned esoteric learning, but, with the help of enterprise, mechanization, and technology, took the world in hand, shattered it into discrete pieces, and then redesigned and reassembled it into more profitable versions of itself. Spellbound by the hows of industrial production, and indifferent to the whats—the industry's object—Oliver Winchester went into the gun business the way his compatriots went into corsets or hammers.

A SECOND CLICHÉ OF AMERICAN GUN CULTURE HOLDS THAT WITH guns, "demand creates its own supply," in the words of sociologist James Wright. In a nation of gun whisperers, so believers say, guns were commonplace, and their later industrial production was a reflection of preexisting demand. The view from the ledger book is different, however. The creation, discovery, invention, and reinvention of gun markets—the visible hand of the gun industrialist at work—was a recurrent, bedrock project of the gun business. It is also a recurrent theme of this book.[8]

To start at the beginning: Historians of the colonial period have stumbled into controversy when they have attempted to count guns; but studies find, in general, that guns, in various states of repair or disrepair, were neither ubiquitous nor rare. Most find a higher rate of gun ownership in the southern colonies—a few placing it around two-thirds of households—and lower rates in the northern ones—anywhere from one-third to just under a half.[9]

In the craft phase, America had as many guns as were inherited, requested, or required. In the industrial phase, after Samuel Colt and Oliver Winchester founded private armories that made six-shot revolvers and rapid-firing repeater rifles—new and patented firearms—it had as many as could be mass-produced by machine. From the gun industrialist's perspective, supply creates the need for demand: volume production required volume consumption. And the gun was no different from other commodities in this arithmetic of industry.

The US military was certainly the most convenient market. Colt wooed government support with champagne feasts at Washington, DC's, Willard and National hotels. His cousin, the company treasurer, bristled, "I have no belief in undertaking to raise the character of your

gun by old Madeira." But both Colt and Winchester struggled to acquire government contracts from the 1840s up to the Civil War, and so
they saw the wisdom of cultivating other markets. To woo a civilian
customer, Colt demonstrated his arm at the Battery Park in New York,
to little avail, since, as one gun expert noted, "multi-firing arms were
not needed by the average man." Winchester's own compatriot New
Haveners thought he had "lost his reason" when they learned that his
new manufactory "was equipped to produce 200 rifles a day." A letter
book in the archives of Colt's Patent Fire-Arms Manufacturing Company reveals detailed, fractious bickering between the company and its
favored sales "allies" over how many guns the dealers should be expected to "push." After World War I, saddled by massive wartime plant
expansion and burdened by debt, the Winchester Repeating Arms
Company (WRAC) had to push sales again, especially through what
its executives shorthanded as an ambitious national "boy plan," with a
goal of reaching "3,363,537 boys" ages ten to sixteen. "When the boys
and girls of your town arrive at the age of twelve years, they become
your prospects," the company's internal sales letter explained. It was a
new refrain in an old song. At this time the company announced the
largest nationwide marketing campaign ever undertaken for guns "in
the history of the world." As it was in the beginning, so it was in 1922:
gun markets and demand could never be taken for granted. It was the
gun business's business to create them.[10]

This example leads to another key point. Company records puncture the compelling assumption that guns just "sell themselves" in
America, or that the gun industry is fueled by a pristine demand unsul-
lied by the need for promotion, salesmanship, or marketing. While it is
true that some demand always existed, and will always exist, it is also
true that the gun industry needed to sell at adequate volumes to support mass-production, and that selling in such volumes took work.
Moreover, it took work recurrently, in different eras and under different conditions, as the gun industry grew.

This work of inventing and cultivating markets did not occur because gun titans were nefarious "Merchants of Death," intent on the
business of "Death, Inc.," as a later generation of disarmament activists

would proclaim. Rather, they were almost the opposite of that caricature: they were businessmen. Their dispassionate and ironclad gram-
mar was the agnosticism of commerce.

The exploration of gun markets fractures the monolithic idea of an
American gun culture into *cultures*, in the plural, because it reveals the
very distinct market segments that gun industrialists courted, some of
whom were barely on speaking terms. The WRAC itself was especially
proud of its capacity to recognize and stimulate desire for the thing
it made, even when that desire was dormant, insufficient, latent, or
indiscernible.

WHEN THE GUN INDUSTRIALISTS COULD NOT FIND SUFFICIENT
domestic civilian markets or secure US military contracts, they looked
far and wide to find markets and customers elsewhere. Indeed, one of
the most striking findings of this book is the degree to which all four of
the major gun capitalists relied on international markets for their very
survival in the mid-1800s. This finding points to another myth that
the business records dispel: the idea that America's gun culture is, in a
word, American, with its geography confined to the national singulari-
ties of the Revolutionary War or the frontier. Today, gun-control advocates look longingly to Western Europe, which has lower homicide
and gun violence rates than America, and Europeans occasionally puzzle disapprovingly over the American gun "obsession." But the countries that today condemn the United States' relationship with guns
kept US guns in business in the 1800s. It was very much European
bellicosity and imperial ambition by regimes and governments that
provided viable markets for America's mass-produced arms.

When viewed from the perspective of business, the American gun
culture is better understood as an international, global phenomenon on
the leading edge of the first wave of globalization in the 1860s and
1870s. Winchester survived initially by selling internationally—as did
Colt's, E. Remington & Sons, and Smith & Wesson. In the chapters
that follow, I describe the WRAC's globe-trotting "gun men" and the
expatriate American gun community in Europe. Before it was—or
could be—the "gun that won the West," the Winchester repeater was

the gun that armed the Ottoman Empire, and that traveled in an oxcart to the Juárez revolutionary forces in 1866 in Mexico. Before Remington armed sportsmen of the American outdoors, it armed everyone from the acting war minister for the papacy (5,000 sold) to various actors in Egypt (55,000) and Cuba (89,000). The Colt revolver, the "peacemaker" of the American frontier, was before that the gun of the king of Sardinia, and Smith & Wesson's contract with the Russian Empire in the 1870s to supply Model 3's kept the company afloat for five years.

———————

ANOTHER POWERFUL CLICHÉ IN TWENTY-FIRST-CENTURY POLITICS IS that gun *love* is timeless, or at least as old as American history.* To be sure, gun mavens have existed as long as guns, and there will always be anecdotal, narrative evidence to corroborate a variety of feelings toward guns, from love to revulsion, across time. But in the Winchester company's early ads, the gun comes across as closer to a plow than a culturally charged object, more on the tool tide of the equation than the totem side. For the most part, although not exclusively, the ads emphasized functionality, and gun titans sought markets in places such as the *American Agriculturalist*. Other evidence from the gun archive suggests that Americans purchased far more relatively inexpensive, secondhand, cast-off rifles that were unglamorous yet workable than they did the Winchesters or Colts prominent in legends of the frontier.

———————

* Even if every American had a gun, much as they had a shovel or an ax, the quantity of guns does not speak to gun love or to the qualitative facets of a gun culture. The phrase "gun culture" is used more than it is defined, but in this book I work on the definition that for an object to become the main component of a culture, at least two standards have to be met: diffusion and mystique. A gun culture is a matter not only of quantity but also of quality—in anthropologist Marshall Sahlins's terms, of how cultures "give significance to their objects"—and of the "social life" of a commodity. These qualitative dimensions are difficult to gauge or generalize, if they can be generalized at all, but they include the place that the gun occupies culturally as a whole and for different groups—the degree of gun affinity, love, symbolism, charisma, and totemic force and the political resonance of the gun.

The WRAC envisioned their primary customer as the "ordinary shooter"—a farmer or rural hunter.[11]

In the early 1900s, the tone of the gun industry changed. The country was more urbanized. The martial phase of western conquest was over. Logically, sales should have dropped, but the WRAC did quite well from 1890 to 1914. The company added $15.5 million to its net worth from 1889 to 1914. Its annual gun sales were almost thirty times greater in 1914, at 292,400, than in 1875, at 9,800, and eleven times greater than the 1880 sales of 26,500. Although best known for its Model 1873 of legend, the company's bread-and-butter model with much larger sales, antique gun experts will point out, was the Model 1894. Overall in the gun industry, twenty-seven gunmakers in 1910 produced over $8 million in guns and $25 million in ammunition. With less practical utility, the gun became—and to some extent *had* to become—an object with emotional value. One answer to the question "Why do Americans love guns?" is, simply, that we were invited to do so by those who made and sold them at the moment when their products had shed much of their more practical, utilitarian value. What was once needed now had to be loved. This observation suggests in turn that the notion of an emotional and political affinity for the gun was perhaps a post-frontier phenomenon of the twentieth century talking about the nineteenth.[12]

Modern advertising fascinated the Winchester executives: again, the gun was no exception to the business trends of the day in a new consumer culture, whether the product was soap or a rifle. The WRAC's internal bulletins instructed the sales force on how to seduce otherwise indifferent customers who had little need for rifles as tools. Winchester pushed the modern American gun in two seemingly opposite directions, aiming to make it an object of luxury—a nonessential but gratifying commodity like "Packards, or golf clubs, or diamonds"—as well as an object of natural or "subconscious" instinct—something all "real boys" wanted, in more modern terms of psychology. But, in both cases, the gun was an object of desire, and the customer was to be seduced to want the product. In a daily sales bulletin sent to distributors, for example, the company thought to emulate "the liquor people," who "tried to perpetuate their business by 'educating' young men to the use of their products. Very immoral of them, of course, but mighty good business."[13]

In the late 1910s, in short, the targeted customer began to shift from the "ordinary shooter" to the "gun crank." The latter, who emerged in company correspondence and the gun press, was a customer with a deep psychological bond with his gun. This was a transition from imagining a customer who needed guns but didn't especially want them to a customer who wanted guns but didn't especially need them.

Obviously, the gun industry's sales efforts did not begin in a vacuum—no good advertising does—but rode on the weedy proliferation of gun legends across popular media. Therefore, this book does not just follow the money of the gun business; it also follows the trail of the gun legends. Beginning with a largely fabricated 1867 account of Wild Bill Hickok in *Harper's*, for example, I trace forensically how this and other American gun legends took a reverse migration, beginning as fiction and hardening into fact and highbrow history as the decades progressed. On the way, they passed through scores of dime novels, movies, and fictionalized real histories. The "West that won the gun" is a collective legend of the American gunslinger that has consistently, across characters and decades, exaggerated both the quantity of gun violence in America—our ancestors were not actually as trigger-happy as twentieth-century moviegoers and readers of pulp fiction were led to believe—and the "quality" of that gun violence: in the legends, guns were tied to honor rather than intoxication, justice rather than impulsivity, and homicide rather than suicide, even though suicide for many decades has accounted for the majority of gun deaths.[14]

Above all, the West that won the gun is almost always a narrative about American individualism. Paradoxically, an industry that first perfected interchangeability and machine production, and that mass-produced its products to within 1/1,000th of an inch of each other, created one of the most enduring twentieth-century icons of this American trait.

IT IS EQUALLY PARADOXICAL THAT THE AMERICAN GUN IS ENVISIONED almost exclusively in the hands of an individual—a cowboy, a militiaman, a pioneer, or an outlaw renegade. One of the continuously overlooked facets of American gun history that I hope to restore in this book is the changing relationship—sometimes fruitful, sometimes fractious, but always consequential—between public arms, war, and the commercial gun business. For all practical purposes, the small-arms industry of Winchester, Colt, and the other gun titans that so vastly increased the volume of guns in the country started in the late 1700s and early 1800s as the war business. Winchester always envisioned his rifle as a military weapon, but before and during the Civil War, Colt and Winchester often found their new, patented gun technologies rebuffed by the military. For this reason, they sought international military contracts and civilian customers instead. Then, many decades after the fact, Oliver Winchester's early dream of acquiring large-scale US contracts was fulfilled. The World War I gun business exhibited signs of a "military-industrial complex" decades before President Dwight D. Eisenhower coined the term. The government found itself dependent on private industrial arms makers, especially Winchester and Remington, to meet war demand, including the production of more than 4 billion .30-caliber cartridges in 1918.

But war, strangely, was no longer good for the gun business by then, notwithstanding the profiteering critiques of disarmament activists. The tables had turned from the late 1700s, and the company now preferred the commercial market it had forged in its own image. Winchester's successors worried that scaling up to meet the government's needs would leave them with monstrous, even fatal excess capacity at war's end—and they were correct.

Nevertheless, in one crucial and all-but-forgotten sense, the military-industrial symbiosis between gun commerce and the common defense tacitly bolstered the case for unregulated civilian gun commerce in the crucial years of the 1920s and early 1930s. This was the era when the idea of federal gun regulation first emerged and was first debated in Congress. The War Department, gun capitalists, and others argued that if private gun businesses could not find markets in peacetime, they would not be ready to produce for the public need in wartime. This record partly explains why gun regulation was a tough sell politically, even at a time when Americans were alarmed by gangster violence and sickened by world war.

Curiously, in the 1934 hearings on the first significant federal gun legislation, the pro-gun-control assistant attorney general, Joseph Keenan, congratulated the gun industry for its "splendid spirit of cooperation" and lightly chided the "hobbyists" of a waxing NRA for their more obstreperous stance. It is a consequential irony that gun-control politics in the twentieth and twenty-first centuries would come to focus on a newly impassioned, newly mobilized, emotional faction of the gun world—the gun owners and "hobbyists"—rather than the dispassionate and rational gunmakers. The contours of twenty-first-century gun politics were beginning to take form. The modern gun might have been invented mechanically in the nineteenth century, but it was invented politically in the twentieth.

THE TRAGEDY OF AMERICAN GUN VIOLENCE EMERGED FROM THE banality of the American gun business. The forgotten but ironclad logic that gunned America was the amorality of business, not diabolical intentions of the "Merchant of Death" or the adventures of the gunslinger. The gun culture that exists today in America developed out of an unexceptional, perpetual quest for new and larger markets that had exceptional social consequences. Even so, the thrust of gun politics is toward the mystification of the gun. American gun culture is explained as a legacy of the Second Amendment, militias, Wild West gunslingers, cowboys, the frontier, American individualism, gangs, and the malignant charisma of violence, video games, manhood, and Hollywood. It is explained, in short, as the legacy of almost everything but what it always was—and still is: a business.[15]

———

THE STORY OF WHAT THE WINCHESTER FAMILY AND RIFLE DID, and what that story reveals about the making of a gun culture, constitutes much of this book. But the book is also an inquiry into an absence: a historical silence. In this book I ask questions about things not done, not said, and not, apparently, felt. I invite the reader to contemplate American gun culture from the fresh perspective of conscience rather than rights.

In this book, I treat conscience as a question of vision. The myopic conscience (in a literal rather than judgmental sense) perceives the tangible, cause-and-effect relationships immediately at hand—what ecologist and philosopher Garrett Hardin called "intrinsic responsibility" (for example, I deliberately shoot a Winchester and kill someone). When farsighted, conscience perceives more deeply across space and time (I make an enormous fortune, through marriage, off of someone who makes money manufacturing and selling Winchesters to people who kill others who may be thousands of miles away or years in the future from where I stand). Conscience is a thread that can be followed a short or long distance, depending on culture and era.

Politics in the twenty-first century is fraught with questions of conscience, complicity, and social accountability similar to those provoked by the Winchester rifle story. This second era of globalization (Winchester built his fortune during the first) fractures how and where things are made, creates complex interdependency in social and economic relations, and fosters technological advances that put distance between action and consequence. I buy a cheap T-shirt at Target, and it implicates me in the deadly collapse of a factory in Bangladesh far removed from the cash register. I drive my car and contribute to climate change that threatens the Maldives half a world away. An unscrupulous subprime lender creates a mortgage for someone in Nevada who can't afford the house, it gets bundled into an investment on Wall Street, and the global economy collapses. Today, 1 percent of Americans fight wars for the other 99 percent, in their name, and we might wonder, too, if the rest of us shouldn't see, or carry, more of that load than we do. Some are thinking anew about collective responsibility. In an essay on reparations to African Americans, essayist Ta-Nehisi Coates wrote eloquently of the "compounding moral debts" that have accumulated across the generations. These cause-and-effect relationships are often imperceptible, invisible, and remote; they are the moral analogue of chaos theory, where the fluttering of a butterfly's wings causes a hurricane halfway around the world. The long view of complicity or accountability is not, today, a politically emboldened or honored one. But as one law professor put it, if we are to understand the most challenging problems of our time—and gun violence is no exception—we must grasp the concept of indirect responsibility.[16]

If Oliver Winchester was conspicuously mute on the consequences of having been one of a handful of capitalists who created a commercial gun market, this was partly because he built his fortune in an age when the thread of conscience in economic relations was followed only a short distance. As a businessman, he didn't need to contemplate long, or far, what his doing *did* in the world. Free-contract principles didn't accommodate imprecise ideas of mutual obligation, the common good, collective interests, or accountability that couldn't be defined and de-limited on paper. This circumscribed specificity can be a source of free-dom, because it means one isn't bound by ancient, involuntary, fixed hierarchies and status relationships—but it can also lead to a foreshort-ened conscience. The corporation had been severed from its earlier presumptions of public service and was explicitly promised "limited lia-bility." While corporate accounting was punctilious, its accountability was vague. A perceptual habit of the gun industry and technology—to fracture parts, labor, and relationships into smaller pieces, to focus deeply inward, to see components over the whole—was also a habit of conscience, the innovation in technology and accountability one and the same. As philosopher Ernest Renan said of history, every nation—or, in this case, business empire—is founded upon a forgetting.

Sarah Winchester's legend speaks to my lingering question: Where did the missing conscience go? And where did the ghosts of the guns go? Sarah's story was a shadow to Oliver Winchester's light (or a light to his shadow). We know about the things they built and what they did, and much less about why they built or did them. But we do know that in her youth, Sarah was celebrated as the belle of New Haven. She had an unusually accomplished and lively intellect, and she came from solid New England stock.

After Sarah married Oliver Winchester's only son, William, in September 1862, sorrow seemed to follow her. The more the family rifle business prospered, the more she suffered. She lost several babies to stillbirth. Her only baby born alive suffered from marasmus, a gruesome, catch-all condition of "wasting away," and died after one month of heartbreaking, inexorable starvation.

Sarah brooded over her misfortunes, and this is where her legend gets entangled with one of the most beguiling and fascinating movements of her day. Spiritualism is a belief in communication with souls in the afterlife; it includes the idea that the known world and the ghostly one are overlaid and infiltrate one another. It wasn't a mainstream movement; nor was it an eccentric one. It claimed millions of followers in the 1800s, and most progressive families, from the Beechers to the Lincolns, included at least one spiritualist. A key aspect of spiritualism was that it imagined a universe orchestrated by cosmic justice. Spiritualists embraced an expansive social agenda that was antithetical to the ethics that governed Oliver Winchester's world. They sought racial and sexual equality, preferred "suffering" to the "inflicting of suffering," rejected killing and colonialism, and condemned "groveling materialism." With almost a metaphysical nostalgia, the concepts of penance, retribution, hypocrisy, wrongdoing, and other ideas then atrophying in economic life reappeared vividly in spiritualism. It was a fugitive conscience of the laissez-faire age.

I toggled between two very different archives in my research for this book—one recounting the stories of ghosts that unfolded in darkened Victorian parlors, the other displaying columns of company business records generated at the mammoth factory that was gunning America. As I did so, I came to the surprising realization that Sarah's story and Oliver's story were both governed by the same metaphor: that of the invisible hand. Adam Smith's concept of the market conveys the sense of an imperceptible but orchestrating force that knits people and actions together through unseen cause-and-effect relationships. The invisible hand imagines an economic web and a common world that is everybody's business, but no one's responsibility; in which all are implicated, but none accountable. Smith described complex interdependency, but he absolved the capitalist from conscious accountability for distant human fates beyond the narrow actions of his accounting. Orchestrated by the invisible hand, Oliver Winchester could do damage without doing wrong; he could do good without doing right. The "invisible hand" of the economy absolved him from feeling haunted by the distant consequences of his gun empire. But spiritualism's invisible hand—the ghostly hand—encouraged it.

Sarah and Oliver Winchester inhabited the same house, the same family, and the same fate, but you will not usually read about either one in the other's story. Oliver Winchester produced the rifles that contributed to many a gun legend; and, through her creation, Sarah became a counter-legend to the gun legends, and a part of our gun culture, too. Whether she intended to or not, she created an anti-memorial to the arming of America. Those who know about Oliver and his guns never write about Sarah; those who know about Sarah never write about guns. But although their stories are not interleaved narratively, Oliver's mad ambition and Sarah's mad conscience belong to the same story and culture. In some ways, they even have the same genesis. Both believed in an invisible hand. Both saw things that were not there. And it seems to me that this bifurcated estrangement—of ambition and conscience, of accounting and accountability, of the worlds of (the Winchester) men and women—is both historically and today one of the reasons that we have an intractable gun problem.

CHAPTER 1

THE AMERICAN SYSTEM

Whatever a man makes is always a thought before it is a material thing. This is true of all things—from a pin, to an empire.
—William Comstock, *Plans for Suburban and Country Homes*, 1893

WE THINK OF THE GUN OWNER AND THE SHOOTER—EITHER TO regulate or to glorify—and not of the people who make the gun. We remember John Wayne, Buffalo Bill, Wyatt Earp, and Al Capone, not the men who patented and manufactured their rifles, pistols, and submachine guns. We might think of the National Rifle Association, Columbine, or Charlton Heston, but not of the Remington brothers gathered around their roll-top desk, or Samuel Colt lobbying with champagne parties on the political frontier at Washington, DC's, Willard Hotel, or a time-motion man walking through the Winchester factory in the early 1900s, meticulously documenting the "Sum of Movements" required to make a cartridge ("place 8 trays on truck and take to machine=.013 seconds; Polish=0.140 . . . "). Insofar as the gun business is imagined at all, it tends to be imagined in its pre-Revolutionary craft phase: a gunsmith, at a bench, with an anvil. A *National Review* reporter in 2013 confessed bewilderment at the Remington plant in Ilion, New York. In his imagination, he had half expected to see a gunsmith.[1]

The gun business, as a business, remains invisible, a secret in the closet of the gun culture. Although guns are bought every day, in locations from Walmart to gun shows, we imagine a gun "owner," not a gun "consumer": In America, we don't buy guns, we *have* guns. We own them.

What sort of men made the guns that made the gun culture? Men who weren't inordinately or single-mindedly interested in guns, for one thing. The gun-industrial elite did not aspire to invent a gun, per se. Not Eli Whitney, who moved from nails to hat pins to a government musket contract that allowed him to keep his workforce employed and machines running; not Eliphalet Remington, a poet, pacifist, and a deeply religious man who would not shoot a gun on Sundays and wanted to be remembered by a tree that grew near his home; not Christopher Spencer, who went from silk to guns and back to silk; not Samuel Colt, who after his traveling laughing-gas tour and his bankruptcy and failure at making guns in Paterson, New Jersey, ventured into submarine battery prototypes before returning to the revolver. And not Oliver Winchester, who might as easily have been the men's shirt king as the rifle king. They were all, in Colt's terms, principally dedicated simply to "making something to sell."[2]

Even when they were making guns, they were not steadfastly enchanted with their product. While his letters exude feeling for the cotton gin, a lover stolen away by southern patent violators and pilferers, Whitney seemed to tolerate the musket contract as a means to an end: resolving his ever-looming "pecuniary embarrassment." He wrote to his dear friend Josiah Stebbins that he was a "poor forlorn bachelor— making guns yet." Daniel B. Wesson's future father-in-law thought little of Wesson's gun pursuits, convinced that his daughter had made a wretched match. Winchester described the rifle, with abrading empiricism, as "a machine made to throw balls."[3]

The majority of the first gun industrialists started off middling and ambitious. They had some resources, in family capital and kin, and they relied upon them for their reputations, their social and political connections, their boards of directors, their capital, and their maintenance of family control. Colt routinely pled to his father, Christopher Colt, a silk merchant, for more funds, and in 1837 Christopher advised Samuel to try another relative, his Aunt Foot, for money in exchange for stock, saying that he should "confine [the loan] to ONE of our family connections." Daniel Wesson's father was an artisan and merchant in the shoe business, and Horace Smith's father a carpenter by trade. Winchester had a long if not entirely distinguished pedigree, and it does seem as if things should have been easier for him. Oliver was descended from John Winchester, who had arrived in 1636 as a "pioneer of the new world." Six generations later, Oliver and his twin brother—the last of their father's eleven children, and the product of his third marriage—were thrown upon their own circumstances almost from birth in 1810: their father died when they were still infants.[4]

What all these men lacked in heated passion for the gun, they had for family control and ambition, self-invention, and the business of industry, whatever its object. "To do my business thoroughly is, I must confess, a passion with me," Colt wrote. Winchester asked only, of any request, "Will it interfere with Company work?" Their gun empires were at first and then for some time closely held—not only legally, as corporations, but in an almost metaphysical sense. The family name was the gun name; the family's fate and the gun's fate, the same.[5]

The American gun capitalists were a tight-knit group of competitors as well; it is curious to think how the mass production of such a culturally momentous commodity began with a small knot of intimate rivals. They sued each other, poached each other's ideas and workers, and sometimes admired each other's superior political skills (Colt praised one rival gunmaker as an "intriguer"). They were not above collaborating with each other: Winchester checked with Colt when he needed a new foreman. Colt wrote to Whitney in 1846, asking if he remembered a certain gentleman who had exhibited "specimens of a steel rifle barrel in Washington & endevered [sic] to get a contract from Government." The gentleman, Whitney responded, was Mr. "Remmington [sic]."[6]

Aside from Whitney, who attended Yale, the men who made the guns that made the gun culture had little, if any, formal education. "I wish that you would so write English that I could show the letters," his ever-censorious cousin Dudley Selden advised Colt, who was an atrocious speller. "Buy a dictionary," he added. Spencer attended formal schooling only for a twelve-week session in 1848; Wesson and Smith were apprenticed, as a shoemaker and carpenter, respectively. Corralled by dire necessity onto the family farm near Brookline, Massachusetts, Oliver Winchester attended school only during the bone-chilling winters, and only for a short time.[7]

What mostly interested all of them were manufacturing methods, mechanical elegance, and machines. They didn't love guns, but they were enamored of the machines that could make them. For the brief time that Oliver Winchester was in school, he would have learned the arithmetical art of reduction. Schoolchildren's copybooks brimmed with occasions to take a deceptively indivisible whole—a number, a unit of time, an object, or a motion—and reduce it into smaller, measurable parts, or to take small parts and aggregate them, reckoning a whole. "How many inches in 3 furlongs and 58 yards? . . . What will ten pairs of shoes cost at 25s 6 d. a pair? . . . How many seconds since the creation of the world?" Alexis de Tocqueville observed that Americans cultivated "minds accustomed to [definite] calculations." We were a zealously "guessing, reckoning, estimating and calculating" lot. If Winchester's gun had an early intellectual muse, it might have been this perceptual skill, which was also a prerequisite to the industrial age. Out of his sparse classroom schooling, the lessons of reduction must have settled deeply into his way of seeing and thinking.[8]

Like the vanguard computer-technology elite of the late twentieth century, the industrial elite of the nineteenth had a distinct worldview and character. If it could be used descriptively rather than pejoratively or diagnostically, the term "sociopathy" might apply, to connote, in its literal meaning, a disordering of social conscience, out of which a new social conscience emerged. The new order was more limited and circumscribed than the previous one. It was governed by the clean boundaries of contracts and the narrower view of empathy, mutual obligation, and accountability that contracts invited. A Whitney biographer once wondered why Whitney seemed never to take a stand on the social issues tied to his inventions, including slavery and the emergence of an industrial order with ambivalent effects on society. She concluded that Whitney had adopted a stance of "reasoned inaction," choosing not to see. Like other industrialists in the new regime, he tended to the "rituals of ethics" and the scrupulous observation of "contractual obligations," but ignored the larger, more nebulous ethical milieu. The essence of the free market, governed by contracts, is to specify obligations and relationships, not to generalize them. This specificity gave order to new obligations and new freedoms, but it also dictated a more circumscribed sense of conscientious obligation. The gun industrialists had a modern wariness, distrust, and skepticism about humanity—"Mankind generally are not to be depended on," Whitney casually asserted. It was a wariness that attuned Colt, at least, to his gun's potential market: "The good people of this wirld [sic]," he wrote, "are very far from being satisfied with each other, & my arms are the best peacemakers."[9]

Empiricists in their souls, Winchester and the other gun industrialists had little interest in the fretful tracking of spiritual consequences in their everyday pursuits. They were not bound by culture or law to ruminate on what their doing *did* in the world. Thomas Carlyle, a Cassandra against the machine and its empiricism, named and denounced the "Age of the Machine" in his influential 1829 essay "Signs of the Times." Mechanization, he said, brought detail into sharp focus, but blurred the world beyond. How would this affect a man's soul, or his perceptions? Carlyle passionately articulated the common concern that men would grow "mechanical in head and heart." The mechanical would all but eclipse the "dynamical" realm of "the spontaneous, the imaginative, the mysterious springs of love, fear and wonder." A supporter of the machine age aptly summarized its detractors' position: they saw mechanization, he said, as "circumscribing the view" and making men "insensible to perceptions of beauty and truth."[10]

But the gun-industrial elite's success began, and then persisted, on a unique double sense of sight—a sensibility that was at once intensely circumscribed and expansive. The gunmakers could "vision the future," Colt said in a letter, inventing a verb while trying to sell guns to Brigham Young. They may have had vision, but Winchester and his competitors were also meticulously empirical. Like their founder, Whitney, they did not go "quixotting" about impractically, as an 1850 advice manual put it. Whitney and the others avoided the "common failing" of inventive mechanics, that of an "ardent imagination and extravagant expectations" without pragmatism. They sought the juncture of intangible vision and tangible profit.[11]

BUT THIS IS NOT HOW THE GUN INDUSTRIALISTS ARE REMEMBERED, when they are remembered at all. The capitalists whose names the guns still bear were feverish to invent a gun, say the myths, and their guns came from the muse of artistry rather than ambition, creativity rather than the market. Eliphalet Remington "just wanted to make a better rifle" for himself when his father refused to buy him one, and then his neighbors clamored for him to make more. Remington's origin story was actually typed out laboriously in 1873 on the first Remington typewriter to be manufactured, passed down through the family, and solidified in headlines such as "Ragged Boy Wanted to Shoot Partridges: His Desire Brought World-Wide Changes in War and Peace," and "Boy's Desire for Gun Saved Ilion." Remington "was not seeking great wealth," the legend holds. Samuel Colt was seized by the image of a revolver from a ship's wheel in 1830 while sailing on the *Corlo* to Calcutta, in a kind of immaculate conception, and then "whittled his way to millions"; and Oliver Winchester is persistently misremembered as the inventor of the rifle that bears his name, rather than its financier and manufacturer, when his contribution to invention was Patent #5421 (1848) for an improved men's shirt collar that "remedied the evil" of the too-tight neck band. He never owned a gun before he made a personal and corporate fortune producing them. Had there been more future potential in it, Oliver Winchester might have been the men's shirt-collar king and not the rifle king.[12]

The gun industrialists are cast as besieged and single-mindedly obsessed. Edward Dickerson, Colt's faithful lawyer—almost more like a spouse—earned his money in Colt's patent trial against the Massachusetts Arms Company on poetic hyperbole. Here was Colt, who had toiled incessantly as the only true believer in his invention, with a passion and ambition that only a man of "ingenuity" and genius could feel. Colt "plants the seed, . . . the fruit is just ripe, he sees the market opening before him . . . he is just about to . . . take it, when the infringer steps between him and the prize," and, what is worse, the infringer is a "corporation [the Colt's company would be one, too] . . . a being that can have no merit as an inventor. They can only be purchasers of the ingenuity of others."[13]

Colt was fashioned as a lone inventor rather than a "mere capitalist," corporate warrior, savvy self-promoter, and businessman in the new order. It was not the case that Colt and Winchester invented nothing, but the invention for which they are almost never praised today is the one they truly and ingeniously came up with: the gun market, not the gun itself, which had a densely tangled provenance and many ancestors. They envisioned markets where they were currently hypothetical or hazy at best; they were on the leading edge of advertising, mass distribution, and an understanding of market segmentation (Colt probably coined the phrase "new and improved"); they established modern distribution and sales networks to move guns throughout the country; and they understood that their success depended on self-promotion. Colt's advances in machine production, and the "relentless and brilliant promotional war he waged on multiple fronts to create markets and move the product," were both more important than anything he did in gun invention, concluded a Colt expert. Other gun experts, writing largely for fellow gun devotees, have emphasized that Colt understood the "necessity of creating demand through aggressive promotion." As for Winchester, he was no "gentleman merchant," said a biographer, but "a master of product and self-promotion with a tad of flimflam thrown in," whose efforts were directed at "building up a market" for his product. He was especially skilled, as we will see, at manipulating the corporate universe, very much its maestro rather than its victim. Popular literature in earlier times tended to celebrate the marketing and promotional genius of the gun industrialists. This all changed with the emergence of modern gun-control politics in the late 1960s.[14]

Legends and partisan apocrypha are often wound around aspects of the American gun, and from any political point of view. In this case, and as this chapter and the next will explore, the image of the lone gun inventor occludes the industry's complex reliance in its founding years on federal government capital, patronage, guaranteed markets, and armories. In these collaborative contexts, at the industry's beginnings, ideas on interchangeability and design were incubated. The inventor toiling alone with his mad creation also occludes the tangled, collective ownership of gun ideas and technology that the patent system, which transformed ideas into property, could only poorly digest. The legend obscures even the existence of the gun business *as* a business, focusing instead on the creative muse.

Perhaps the most important aspect of the gun industry that the legend masks is a certain banality or unexceptionalism at the heart of the business in its formative years. The metaphor of the American gun in twenty-first-century politics is exceptionalism: guns have always had a special place in American society, they enjoy an exceptional legal status, and they are prized possessions rather than mere commodities, once and always beloved historically. We could be forgiven if we imagine that guns sprang fully formed from the head of the Second Amendment itself. But the metaphor of the gun, historically, and especially as revealed from the vantage point of the gun as a business, is more accurately a metaphor of interchangeability, not exceptionalism. Interchangeability describes the method of the gun's mass production as well as the gun industrialists' feeling toward the gun: for them, it was one thing to make, and sell, among other possibilities, a business fueled more by the inner drive of generic ambition than specific passion for firearms. And as the gun moved out of the crucible of the federal government—a martial one—into its commercial phase, the same terminology could describe the gun's status in law, policy, and economy: it was interchangeable with other commodities being produced, and treated as no more or less exceptional than the others. Much of our gun culture comes from this legacy of interchangeability—the gun's non-exceptionalism.

————

IN THE 1790S, DURING THE FIRST, CRAFT PHASE OF THE AMERICAN gun business, the United States had a gun problem, but of another sort—it did not have enough of them. It had been undergunned in the

Revolutionary War, and it was still undergunned. The Blair Report on the colonies' military preparedness in 1756 concluded that the "militia amounts to about 36,000 but not above half that number are armed." The guns that did exist were of a "miscellaneous character," a magazine for sportsmen later noted, and many were "cranky and imperfect." Many patriots had broken weapons or weapons that were nearly useless. Even the best were hard to use. They were heavy, ungainly, and encumbered by accoutrements ranging from ramrods and powder horns to bullet molds. Many were badly balanced and had to be rested on forked sticks when used. Guns were produced laboriously, one at a time, as requested. Curiously, an expert on colonial guns noted that as the Revolutionary War began, guns were especially scarce on the frontier, just where one might have expected them to be most plentiful and a household staple. The governor of Rhode Island, writing to George Washington in January 1776, said that, as for many years the colonists had "thought themselves in a perfect state of security," they had "disposed of their arms so generally" that the colony was effectively "disarmed."[15]

George Washington had noted the "scarcity of gunsmiths" as well as guns at the start of the war. In the colonial era, gunsmiths entered the trade as apprentices through one of several pathways, including family ties, indentured servitude, the Overseers of the Poor, or the Orphan's Court. The man who would become the public armorer for Massachusetts Bay during the Revolutionary War, Richard Falley, was captured by Native Americans at Fort Edward, New York, as a young man. He was taken to Montreal, where a woman purchased him for sixteen gallons of rum. She then sent him off to Massachusetts, where he became a gunsmith's apprentice. However men arrived in the gun trade, they began to learn what apprentice contracts called "the Art and Mystery of a Gunsmith."[16]

To be a gunsmith was, most often, to be other things as well. Antique gun experts have noted that there was simply not enough volume of business for gunsmiths to specialize in one gun part, or to make only guns. Most ran larger blacksmith and whitesmith cottage industries. George McGunnigle advertised in Pennsylvania that in addition to gunsmithing he made "locks, keyes, hinges of all sorts, pipe tomahawks, scalping knives, boxes and pins for vizes, grates, polished and unpolished, and iron shovels, tongs and pokers; chafing dishes, bread toasters, ladles, skimmers, flesh forks and skewers, with all kinds of iron work for a kitchen; currying combs, plate, saddles trees; . . . curbing and pincing tongs; rupture belts; grinds swords, razors, scissors, and pen knives." He later advertised in the *Pittsburgh Gazette* that he also made "bed screws and branding irons" and, apparently bored with his own list, "several other pieces of business in the white smith line, too tedious to mention." From the perspective of business, the gun belonged to the genus of other ordinary, needful domestic objects and tools that artisans could produce. Another gunsmith advertised, characteristically, that he was a repairer of "Household and Kitchen Furniture and any sort of mending in brass or iron works."[17]

These gunsmiths made guns, one at a time, for distinct markets, referred to as the "indian, civilian and publick." Meeting the demand for public arms production was a struggle in the Revolution (and the United States would find itself undergunned at the start of the Civil War, too). Renowned historian Richard Hofstadter popularized the phrase "gun culture," writing at a time of increased gun violence in 1970, and inferred its existence from the militia experience. But among the gun markets during the colonial years, one could argue that the most robust candidates for a true "gun culture" were those Native American societies that had been monumentally transformed by the lucrative fur trade. In these societies, the gun achieved diffusion, consequence, and mystique, transforming everything from gender relations to hunting techniques to spiritual beliefs.[18]

When the Revolutionary War began, "patriot gunsmiths" accepted Committee of Safety contracts to produce arms for their colonies. As for the less patriotic, Pennsylvania resolved that if gunsmiths in Lancaster County refused to make arms when asked to do so, "at the Philadelphia prices, such gun-smiths shall have their names inserted in the minutes of this committee as enemies to their country, and published as such," and their tools would be confiscated. New York was compelled to send a Thomas Blockley to England to recruit and import gunsmiths, defray the expense of their "removal," and pay their way over. They instructed Blockley to find as many sober, unmarried, and prudent men with the requisite gunsmithing tools as could fit in the small room that would accommodate them.[19]

No two guns were alike, the gunsmithing craft held, but in battle there was no advantage to uniqueness. Damage to one part of a gun made the gun useless until a gunsmith or armorer could fit a new piece specifically for it. A war chronicle describes the fractured, pokey process of keeping muskets in working condition. One county committee paid for "fetching 20 guns from John Carpenter to Waters, the Gunsmith," and then payment of 14 pounds to Waters for "repairing Guns." Other men were paid for making arms chests, or for the carriage and delivery of newly repaired arms to colonels.[20]

The continental army actually relied on commercial intrigue in Europe to arm itself. Among others who went on such expeditions, Silas Deanne, a Connecticut lawyer and storekeeper, was sent to the court of Louis XVI by the Continental Congress. The king's foreign minister, Vergennes, was secretly sympathetic to the American colonists, as was Vergennes' confidant (and France's leading dramatist), Augustin Caron de Beaumarchais, who wrote the *Barber of Seville* and *The Marriage of Figaro*. With the king's consent, Vergennes connived to have the prized 1763 pattern Charleville musket declared obsolete, so that 30,000 of them could be disposed of. At the same time, Beaumarchais and Deanne organized a firm called Hortalez & Company, favored by large loans, to buy 23,000 of the suddenly obsolete Charleville muskets for the American rebels.[21]

IN THE 1790S, WAR CLOUDS LOOMED ONCE MORE, AND THE COUNTRY still had to continue its "disgraceful resort to foreign markets" to secure guns, decried Eli Whitney's old tutor, Elizur Goodrich. Although the government did manage to secure gun shipments from some of the more advanced European gunsmiths, many were seized by ruthless privateers and pirates roaming the coastal waters. Those prized Charleville muskets were already ancient and obsolete. And the government still had only a limited number of private smiths to meet the public need. After the Revolutionary War, many gunsmiths had gone back to more profitable crafts. One man, Balthasar Smith, for example, who had run a gun-powder mill during the war, converted it into a cooper and coffin shop afterward.[22]

Congress went to work, establishing the Springfield Armory, to produce "a good and efficient magazine for the reception of the public ammunition," in Massachusetts in 1794, and Harpers Ferry, in West Virginia, in 1798. The Springfield Armory sat on an elevated plot about half a mile east of the village of Springfield. It consisted of a two-story brick building with eight rooms, which were occupied by lock filers, stockers, and finishers; a brick-forging shop; and another two-story building with storage and offices on the ground floor and a second story devoted to religious services and prayer. Armory gunsmiths were as happily irregular as their guns. They worked at their own pace. They came and went as they pleased, took frequent holidays, and kept their tools as an informal fee-simple inheritance for their work. They drank hard liquor and left their stations to gamble, gossip, and roughhouse. Harpers Ferry was a quirky, incestuous enclave where two families controlled the land and advanced their own and their friends' private interests through public funds. Armory gunsmiths produced guns just as they would in their own shops: by hand, one at a time, at a bench, on an anvil.[23]

Gunsmiths took pride in the artistic merits and individuality of their product. Henry Mauger, who worked as a stone mason in the summer and a gunsmith in the winter, advertised that he made "fancy civilian arms with a distinctive flair." Here, on the cusp of its demise, gunsmithing entered a golden age of craftsmanship. Gunmaking was similar to the high-art crafts of silversmithing and goldsmithing, clock-making and pewter works.[24]

The gun industry emerged out of the need for more domestically produced guns, especially more guns for the national defense—what the colonialists had called "public" guns—and the need for more uniform guns whose parts might be exchanged on the battlefield. For this purpose, they had to be shorn of the gunsmith's "distinctive flair." More specifically, the industry emerged out of the pit of inventor Eli Whitney's personal and pecuniary despair. He wrote to his business partner,

Phineas Miller, in 1797, "I have labored hard against the strong current of Disappointment which has been threatening to carry us down the Cataract of distruction." Unless some "speedy relief" was obtained, he would face "extreme embarrassment" financially. He was "perfectly miserable." At least Miller had a wife, and domestic comforts. But Whitney thought it better "not to live than to live as I have for three years." He wrote that "toil, anxiety and disappointment have broken me down."[25]

The South had pilfered Whitney's beloved cotton gin, and this theft was the source of Whitney's financial and spiritual angst. Because he had lost a claim on a machine that would revolutionize the South's economy, further entrenching slavery, he would invent machines that would revolutionize the North's. In 1798, a new opportunity serendipitously presented itself: guns. "I was very much embarrassed in my circumstances," Whitney reflected to his dear friend Josiah Stebbins. "Bankruptcy and ruin were constantly staring me straight in the face and disappointment tripped me at every step." At a time when he was in debt to the tune of $4,000, "an opportunity offered to contract for manufacturing muskets for the U. States," he wrote. "I embraced it." Whitney made things, but the end of a particular thing was of less interest to him than the means of making it. The point, Stebbins consoled him, was to "strike out some new invention which will astonish the World and command all their Purse Strings"—whatever that invention may be. Whitney had never made a gun before, and he had no acquaintance with the gunsmith's craft. The government issued 27 contracts for small arms in 1798, and the other 26 gunsmiths combined agreed to manufacture a total of 30,200 muskets by the old methods. Whitney contracted to make an outrageous 10,000 stand of arms (a "stand of arms" was a complete set of weapons for one soldier: for example, a rifle and a bayonet) at $13.40 each.[26]

To accomplish the task, he proposed to use "machinery moved by water," to "diminish the labor and facilitate the manufacture"; and to form "tools so that the tools themselves shall fashion the work." While gunsmiths thought of the whole, Whitney thought of the parts. It was a simple but seismic shift in vision. He took the constituent parts of the Charleville musket and contemplated them intensely. He mulled the type of mechanical operation needed to produce each part. "A good musket is a complicated engine and difficult to make," he reflected later, "difficult of execution because the conformation of most of its parts corresponds with no regular geometrical figure." (Mechanics of the time favored geometric figures over irregular forms, and could sound almost affronted when the world refused to indulge them.) The rifle, dismantled into dozens of curved, irregular parts, flouted straight lines. A fragment of the trigger resembled half a pair of scissors; another part could have been a burled coat hook.[27]

As Whitney reckoned, production of these parts involved scores of separate operations, most of them previously performed by hand. Reducing the rifle further into its minute particulars, he found that the number of operations per part, per musket, ranged from five for the trigger to twenty-four for the barrel. To reduce those functions into yet more minute operations executable by self-acting machines, Whitney thought of clothing patterns, which also presented unusually curved and shaped parts. He made a pattern, a template, for each part of his rifle. Whitney intuited that having many small machines to make many small parts was shrewder than having "one great complicated machine" that, if deranged, would halt the entire works. To grip the metal plate and further reduce deviation, Whitney employed jigs and fixtures of his own design. A chisel to follow the patterns would have required skill to operate, so Whitney invented a milling machine to cut the metal. An advocate admired the "neatness and finish" of Whitney's machinery.[28]

But everything in Whitney's life was not so neatly finished. His was an "extremely new and different business," he explained to his government patrons as he pled, repeatedly, for more time on his contract. He had to build every element of his manufactory from scratch. A snowstorm, along with the thoroughly unreliable supply chains of raw materials, delayed his progress. He had a labor shortage because he did not want to use gunsmiths, bogged down by their actual knowledge of how to make a gun. "The fact is," Whitney wrote to the secretary of the treasury, Oliver Wolcott Jr., "I have not only the arms but a large proportion of the ARMORERS to make." He had not accounted for the time it would take to make the machines that would then make the guns—focusing instead on the "facility with which I could work after all my operations [were] complete and in motion." Overhead costs, not yet named as such, were also a problem. Whitney eventually prevailed in expanding costs to include these unfamiliar concepts as well as labor and materials. He had underestimated the cost, and, quaintly, did not think it wise to take out more credit that he did not have a "fair prospect" of paying back. Manufacturing, he was realizing, was very different from mercantile transactions. "More time is required to work up raw materials and there is less certainty as to the time [to get finished products]." The point being, he needed volume. "I would not go to the expence of erecting works for this purpose unless I could contract to make a considerable number," he wrote.[29]

Whitney's letters are one of the few records of industrial production in its infancy. He complained to Stebbins of his enormous task and his life as a "solitary Old Bachelor," living constantly at the fledgling manufactory, with only his workers for companionship, and cursed the stars that had led him down this daunting path. Whitney was inventing invention, in a sense: he was trailblazing an idea of machine production that was the crucible not only of the gun industry, but also of industry generally.[30]

Peculiarly, Whitney could be making progress but not have made a single gun. A government inspector arrived at Whitney's manufactory after the two-year contract had expired and was appalled by the jumble of machinery. "Instead of making guns," according to a later assessment, "he was making machines."[31]

It was a difficult but foundational riddle of the coming industrial age: How could the production of one single gun take years, but the production of 10,000 only a little bit longer? The government treated the experiment with attitudes ranging from anxious support to jittery skepticism. Even Whitney's stalwart allies, including an inspector of small arms, Captain Decius Wadsworth, thought that in Whitney's plan there was "more to please the imagination than of real utility."[32]

Whitney pled successfully for more time at the end of the two years. Despite a persuasively painstaking recitation of his production hurdles and his not-yet-in-motion waterworks, his confidence was growing. Tenaciously, he knew he could bring the work "fairly into operation . . . to a profit to myself—and avoid pecuniary embarrassment," which was the ever-fixed mark of his gun ambition. Treasury Secretary Wolcott insisted that he at least produce a "number of compleat arms" so that he could give a positive report at the next session of Congress.[33]

In early 1801, Whitney arrived at the muddy, unfinished White House with a mysterious black box. He was ready to exhibit its contents to the president, the heads of departments, and others, and he proclaimed confidently to President John Adams and his advisers that he was now as ready to produce 10,000 muskets as to produce one. Before their astonished eyes, Whitney placed ten of each part of a musket on the table and proceeded to assemble ten rifles out of them. Thomas Jefferson wrote an introductory letter to the Virginia governor, James Monroe, saying that Whitney had made molds and machines "so exactly equal," that one could "take 100 locks to pieces and mingle their parts and the hundreds locks may be put together . . . without employing a smith." Jefferson had assembled pieces himself, as he described earlier, in 1785, and found that "taking pieces at hazard as they came in hand, they fitted in a most perfect manner."[34]

Whitney envisioned an ongoing, symbiotic relationship between the government and fledgling manufacturers like himself for the production of public arms. The public, he wrote, was getting a domestic source of guns, not work "done by vagabond, worthless foreigners," and they would be produced "for the interest of the public" at as "low a RATE as possible." Whitney had the "vanity to suppose" they would be the best in America and equal to any in the world. He shared technology, such as milling machines, with the armories. By the same token, Whitney requested and received special protection from competition in his gun business. He wrote to Wolcott in July 1798 pointing out that Wolcott's notion of establishing other armories in Whitney's region, akin to England's gunsmith's row in Birmingham, would "occasion such a competition it would be ruinous to both." It would "raise the price of labour" intolerably, not to mention the price of charcoal. "These are the considerations which materially affect the

Contractor," he explained, "and are not uninteresting to 'The Public.'"
Nor did he think that blending his contract with another was wise. If
he could barely make 10,000 stand of arms in time, with labor and materials shortages, it was "folly to think of making double the quantity in
the same place." Wolcott readily acquiesced to Whitney, despite a
number of competitive proposals for public arms, and agreed to "guard
by all means in my power . . . against the mischiefs of too great a
competition."[35]

Fully eleven years after he signed the contract, in 1809, Whitney
delivered the last of his 10,000 stand of arms. It was doubtless a relief,
but Whitney was anxious about the future. He would not—could not—
have built his manufactory without federal patronage, and he would
not—could not—occupy his machines, the new imperative of industrial production, without yet more public contracts, indefinitely. Other
aspiring gun manufacturers agreed that they required and deserved special government support. There were no other sources of continuous
and adequate demand at the time to justify the initial outlay of capital.
The Ordnance Department explained in 1823 that no gun manufacturer would have survived, or attempted, industrial production without
assurance of the "steady support and patronage given by the Government," because no other market assured the volume of sales that machine production required. All but Whitney himself who attempted
to participate in the gun industry "were either ruined by the attempt
or found the business so unprofitable and hazardous" as to make it undesirable. Even after Congress approved a permanent appropriation for
arms in 1808, most fledgling gun industrialists failed. In the gun business's infancy, Colt expert William Hosley wrote, military contracts
amounted to "government supplied venture capital," by which industrialists honed their manufactories, machines, and knowledge. This
process was the beginning of what would become known as "the American system" of manufacturing. The gun industry did not begin as a private commercial enterprise, but as a chimera composed of private
enterprise and the common defense. It had one guaranteed market, and
it had a permeable boundary between the gun entrepreneur and the
government armories, through which innovation flowed easily. Gun

production was very limited in the United States outside of government contracts. Notwithstanding popular ideas of a timeless civilian market—or demand—Whitney's lifeline was the federal government and public arms.[36]

At this time the gun was occasionally seen as an exceptional object, but only because it was chiefly a "warlike good" and a weapon for the public defense. Tench Coxe, who prepared the 1810 census, thought it best to put the manufactures that were "useful or necessary to the defense of the United States," and were "requisite for war," under a separate category. Their manufacture had been "encouraged . . . by high duties, and by advances in specie, or . . . raw materials." These measures overcame the "want of capital" that otherwise hobbled industrial gun production. Coxe proposed that the sale of guns be more strictly inspected to prevent potential fraud.[37]

In this phase of the gun business—the forgotten public foundation for the later commercial success of Winchester, Colt, and others—the gun business was largely the war business; the US government was the guaranteed customer and market, and a collaborative rather than a proprietary attitude toward innovation, design, and technology prevailed. The federal government, wrote a Colt expert, had a "nearly messianic zeal for system and uniformity," that is, concision, elegance, and interchangeable production, that amounted to a war on idiosyncrasy. The 1810 census rhapsodized the dawning industrial age, praising "these wonderful machines," that were vastly easier and cheaper to employ than humans, "working as if they were animated beings, . . . laboring with organs that never tire, and subject to no expence of food, or bed, or raiment, or dwelling." Nor did they gamble, drink ardent spirits, "scuffle," fist-fight or lollygag during the workday as the artisan gunsmiths of Harpers Ferry and Springfield did. The artisan who regulated size and proportion "by his own Eye," as Whitney wrote, invariably fell short of machined uniformity.[38]

Roswell Lee took over the Springfield Armory in 1815, intent on extending Whitney's work. In a prototype of factory management, each worker received a day's worth of supplies out of which to make guns, and the foreman recorded these amounts precisely on the debit side of a ledger. The credit side constituted the parts or units produced that day. In this way, Lee wrote, "complete accountability is established and enforced." Springfield was no longer "a disorganized collection of craft workers," but "a disciplined assemblage of industrial workers." Lee had broken the artisan. He had "subdue[d] the refractory tempers of work people," an Englishman noted approvingly.[39]

Commander General Callender Irvine—Whitney called him "a poor, pitiful villainous piece of a thing in the place of a public officer"—had doubts about the intimacy of enterprise and the public arms business. Why should the United States rely on private contractors who wanted only to get "public money" to build massive facilities for their own commercial pursuits? "Better to increase the number of our public establishments," he argued, dispense with private gunmakers, "and bring the whole under the superintendence of one judicious and independent man." Irvine imagined himself that man, although independent he was not: he had an interest in a rival gun, the Wickham rifle.[40]

Irvine harassed Whitney, whom he considered "not a practical Gun Smith," with dubious complaints over the quality of his muskets (although Whitney had produced more guns than any other American, he was, in fact, not a gunsmith). Irvine refused to pay him without changes to the bayonet and barrel. In Whitney's response one hears the emboldened, intricate language of contract and an emboldened gun manufacturer beginning to chafe against the presumptions of the government as a customer. He would make no alterations to his gun unless he received "suitable remuneration . . . but I think it should be done by AGREEMENT, and not ORDER." To Whitney, his contract with the government was akin to one "between two private individuals," no more or less sacred; to Irvine, the government and the commonweal's interests put a thumb on the contractual scale and tacitly gave him more power to bully if not dictate the terms. Almost imperiously, he responded to Whitney, "I have neither leisure nor time to spare for an epistolary controversy with you or any other man," and he expected Whitney to make alterations. "Altho it is a trite remark," Whitney retorted, "it is nevertheless true that there is always two sides to a contract."[41]

Whitney mourned to Stebbins that Irvine had managed to ruin such a large portion of "the little patch" that constituted his life. In his fairly accurate assessment, Irvine's intention was to "break me up in the Manufacture of Arms" and to "ruin every private manufactory" of arms in the country. Irvine tried and failed to pass legislation in 1813 to have both public armories and private manufacturers under one superintendent.[42]

Whatever his personal interests, or animus, Irvine had raised a core problem of guns in America: How could the common good be reconciled with commercial imperatives, and should an object so critical to the public's well-being be entrusted to private entrepreneurs? This tension between commerce and commonweal, differently articulated and usually eclipsed, was a part of the American gun legacy from the start. Over the next decades, from the 1820s to the early 1840s, it would grow more extreme. As we will see, the first generation of gun industrialists would replace the gunsmith's craft; then the collaborative spirit of the gun business as the public defense, war business, always an anxious alliance, would defer to the patent wars, a competitive spirit among private manufacturers, and a quest for new, non-US-military markets that led in surprising directions.

CHAPTER 2

THE CRYSTAL PALACE

I N 1836, TWO OF THE PEOPLE WHO ARE NOW MOST INDELIBLY associated with the guns of the Old West were in Baltimore, Maryland, scraping out a living at the intersection of magic and technology.

Samuel Colt was a public showman of the amusing wonders of nitrous oxide—laughing gas. Traveling as "Dr. Samuel Coult," not the last of his largely fabricated honorifics, Colt provided "Scientific Amusement" to audiences from Quebec to New Orleans by demonstrating the gas's "singular and amusing effects" on "menageries" of volunteers, sometimes placed in cages and nets, who inhaled it. Dr. Coult elicited hilarious bouts of dancing, singing, wrestling, boxing, and fantastic feats from the volunteers through "the witchcraft of the gas."[1]

Oliver Winchester first embarked on his business life in Baltimore with a brief stint as a master builder. Then he appears, fleetingly, in the city directory as a daguerreotypist, forerunner to a portrait photographer. As his clients perceived it, Winchester made people appear by supernatural conjuring. The daguerreotypist's tools so frightened one farmer, according to an 1849 magazine article, that he "dashed down the stairs as if a legion of evil spirits were after him" before the portrait could be taken. The daguerreotypist moved from "surface to depth, . . . conscious of something besides the mere physical," in a way that felt supernatural, ghostly. At its leading edge, technology seemed to blur into magic—it was incomprehensible, haunting, and, for all practical purposes, produced mysterious phantasms.[2]

Colt enlisted a local mechanic in Baltimore, John Pearson, to pro-totype his pistol in 1836. He envisioned a multi-firing arm, a revolver, with multiple chambers discharged through one barrel by use of a lock and spring design. It was, his first biographer wrote, a "new tool," a "miracle of much in little." The collaboration with Pearson did not go smoothly. Colt routinely disappointed Pearson—and others—by refus-ing to pay them on time, or at all. An increasingly bitter Pearson wrote Colt in the spring of 1836 that he was out of "patience and money." Colt had promised payment, but Pearson suspected that he was "very likely not one foot nearer than you was when you last wrote." He wasn't. Pearson had worked faithfully night and day, and although he had two small pistols ready for forging, he would not do so until he had his money. He could think of many other places to work where he could "get my pay every week." "You are in a devil of a hurry. But not to pay your men."[3]

Samuel Colt meanwhile was busy advancing his understanding of industry, especially processes applicable to gun manufacture, by inter-viewing personnel at iron mines, an ax factory, a sword factory, "all parts of the US Armory," and a gun manufacturer's operations in Mid-dletown, Connecticut, where owner Simeon North was using a ground-breaking model of interchangeability. The government had been, and still was, a flourishing incubator for gun innovation and industrial ad-vances in general. At Springfield, fledgling capitalists, technologists, and employees of the Ordnance Department worked toward a shared goal of interchangeability and machine production as well as toward their own individual goals. The federal contract system fostered—even demanded—cooperation and collaboration. By an open-door policy, any aspiring entrepreneur or mechanic could wander in, sketch, ask questions, and leave with new, potentially profitable ideas to apply to textiles and other vanguard industries. The collaborative advance of interchangeable production and the demise of the gunsmith—related processes that unfolded throughout the 1820s and 1830s—cleared the path for the commercial gun industry.[4]

Harpers Ferry put up the strongest fight. Lieutenant Colonel George Bomford, head of the Ordnance Department from 1821 to 1842, wanted to introduce efficient, rational production to Harpers Ferry and bring the armory up to Roswell Lee's standard at Springfield. Government representatives from the 1820s on descended upon the armory, emboldened by six shiny sets of gauges to keep rifles true to the template. They were devoted to what one self-proclaimed "soldier technologist" celebrated as "a knowledge and love of order and system." Bomford dispatched Thomas Dunn to Harpers Ferry in 1830, intent on the enforcement of the work regulations established in 1827. Dunn vowed to eliminate loitering, drinking, gambling, absenteeism, and other staples of the gunsmith's workday, pledging to enforce industrial discipline at any cost. And it was any cost that he paid: after six months, an outraged ex-employee named Ebenezer Cox marched into Dunn's office and shot and killed him. Other armory employees embraced Cox as a folk hero and told Dunn's tale in ominous, cautionary tones for any superintendent who might think to reform them.[5]

Undaunted, Major Henry Knox Craig next tried his hand. He was unpersuaded by armorers' protests against working on the clock, a reviled symbol of the regime of industrial discipline that deprived them of their freedom and spontaneity in movement, work, and play. In March 1842, the Harpers Ferry gunsmiths walked off the job. A delegation chartered a boat to sail down the Chesapeake and Ohio Canal to Washington, DC, to appeal directly to President John Tyler. They were reduced to slaves, they pleaded, "mere machines of labor."[6]

As the Harpers Ferry gunsmiths fought for their way of life and livelihoods, a figure who would loom large for both Colt and Winchester was appointed superintendent of the Springfield Armory. James Wolfe Ripley, who took over the armory in 1842 and who would eventually head the Ordnance Department, was a humorless, dour, deeply religious man, hell-bent on furthering the industrial gun regimen. He was burned in effigy from the Springfield Armory flagpole three times for his trouble. Ripley threatened to fire anyone who subscribed to the *Independent Democrat* newspaper after it criticized his work at the armory—and yet, impervious to his hoard of enemies, he also hoped to convert all of Springfield to the Episcopal faith. During Ripley's tenure, gun expert William Hosley writes, the "open door" of public and private innovation and exchange began to close, and the quasi-public character of the fledgling gun industry faded. It was replaced by proprietary competition among fledgling gun industrialist-capitalists, who had availed themselves of armory ideas, and enjoyed the armory's development of uniform production, but now wanted to make money by keeping their own innovations secret and patentable. The gun industry was beginning to attract private capital, and its patented designs failed to impress the US government, which tended now to view the innovations as mere passing "novelties." The once cooperative bond between government and gunmaker was decisively severed by the late 1840s. Apparently, this shift embittered Ripley against the first group of gun industrialists—consequentially, as we will see—for years to come. The gun was being reconceptualized subtly from an exceptional martial tool, uniquely supported by the US government, to an unexceptional commercial commodity, whose makers, moving forward, would have an awkward relationship to the military and the imperatives of common defense.[7]

Meanwhile, established gunsmiths from the early 1800s were going extinct as a class, their disappearance traceable in the New Haven city directory and the US Census of Industry, whose tally moved over time from the number of "gunsmiths" to "arms manufacturers." The craft way of life, with gambling, drinking, and spontaneous production, had been replaced by the 1850s at the E. Remington & Sons manufactory with "work rules," such as: "Godliness, cleanliness and punctuality are the necessities of a good business. . . . [C]lothing must be of a sober nature. The staff will not disport themselves in raiment of bright colors," and "The craving of tobacco, wines or spirits is a human weakness and as such is forbidden." The modernization of arms production—the key shift from the craft to the industrial phase of the gun business's biography—would be complete by the 1850s. One gunsmith who still had "the machinery for making swords . . . rusting on [his] hands" correctly intuited that the emerging manufacturing system would spell a protracted but "certain death" for him. An observer of the process noticed the effect of interchangeability on men. "Each workman becomes adept at his part. . . . The consequences . . . to the workman is that not one of them becomes a finished armorer." Although he makes firearms, "he cannot make a fire-arm." The gun's manufacture became a more fractured, microscopic process with each generation, and the totality of the gun, and its consequence, became harder to see.[8]

STANDING ON THE SHOULDERS OF PEARSON'S SPOTTILY REMUNERATED ingenuity, public armory advances in interchangeable, uniform production, and the ruins of gunsmithing as a craft, Samuel Colt established his first factory in Paterson, New Jersey, in 1836. Early on, Colt had a few thousand dollars' worth of guns out on consignment in the commercial market. He had intended originally to produce for both the US government and civilian markets. The main problem—and historical curiosity—is that Colt couldn't make a profit off of his gun. The civilian market was there to be created, not taken, as Colt, along with Smith and Wesson and Winchester, would soon discover.[9]

When his cousin and treasurer, Dudley Selden, asked about the price for guns in November 1837, Colt responded, "It is my opinion that the rifles now finished for market will readily sail [sic] in New York or Washington (if exhibited by a proper person) for $100 per peace [sic] wholesale and $125 at Retail. . . . Either of which prices will yield a handsome profit for the first lot," judging that they would not cost more than $50 apiece to produce.[10]

Colt placed his first advertisement on December 22, 1837, in the *New York Courier and Enquirer*. Flyers promised a public exhibition of the "Patent Repeating Rifle" at the Battery on a Monday afternoon. Colt, who called himself the "patentee," promised that the rifles were "eight times more effective and very little more expensive" than any other rifle. He quickly discovered that he had over-"visioned" his market. Only the very wealthy had any interest in considering his gun. The Paterson factory was equipped to produce a large quantity, but "they could not sell as much as they could make," a Colt biographer wrote. Of the first lot of two hundred rifles and five hundred pistols, not even one hundred pistols had sold. The problem was a complicated production design—and the simple fact, as a gun expert noted, that "multi-firing arms were not needed by the average man." The American commercial market was not the place to find the needed volume. Two years after he placed his first ad, Colt placed another in the *New York Times*, on May 21, 1839, to tell of a variety of rifles and pistols available at his New York depot "at greatly reduced prices."[11]

There was another possibility. Colt's father, Christopher, advised him not to "go west young man," as Horace Greeley famously advised, with his invention, but in the opposite direction, to Europe. Trying to win sales through the US government in 1837, Christopher advised, would "keep back your European interest much to your disadvantage." Samuel's father speculated that dealers in England, France, and Germany would be of more help to get the business going. When Samuel went to Washington to seek a patent for his "idea of a gun revolving by the operation of cocking the lock," a patent expert advised him to go to Europe, as well, "where he thought these arms were more wanted than here."[12]

But for now, as commercial demand failed him, Colt sought a market in the bewildering world of Washington, a minefield of alliances, patronage, and personal interests. Colt sensed them keenly. He sprinkled his letters with references to colonels and rival gun entrepreneurs who were "great personal friends." Some were in alliance with one another or "close cronies"; some he called his avowed "enemies"; and some he recognized as superior "intriguers." Newspaper reporters and other writers conspired in the tangled political alliances by writing on favored patent arms. "The editor of the Georgetown Papers deserves to have his ____ kicked," C. F. Pond wrote to Colt after Colt's gun was passed over for another design, the Sharps rifle, supported by such sympathetic coverage.[13]

Purists such as Christopher Colt and Dudley Selden imagined that guns could be sold on technological merits. Steeped in the ethics and character of the honorable gentleman merchant, they struggled to understand influence-peddling and corruption, or even the creation and manipulation of customer demand. Their point of view resembles the twenty-first-century assumption that the market is a disinterested judge of gun appetite, and that the gun business is only delivering what its customers have: a spontaneous, prefigured desire to own, a "build it and they will come" approach. Selden felt that if Colt's revolvers were as good as he promised, the orders should come pouring in. Colt, in contrast, realized he would need to create his market, give out pistols, demonstrate the gun, dispatch salesmen, and advertise: techniques that to Selden smacked of lowbrow medicine shows. Without eager customers asking for the product, lamented Selden, "I have not faith in [the Company stock]. Years will go by, I fear, before it will make any adequate returns to a purchaser, if ever. All your promises have proved illusory."[14]

Christopher Colt hoped that the newspapers in Washington might "puff the invention a bit," but he generally thought like Selden. "Your success," he wrote to his son, "depends on the simple matter of fact which is the best invention in the opinion of the Commission, [and] as they decide, so will public sentiment go for or against your Patent."[15]

But the visible hand of Samuel Colt sat heavily on all the gun markets he endeavored to cultivate. Christopher had strongly advised his son to "LAY ASIDE every amusement" until "your arms [are] in the Market and Profit realized." Actually, Colt perceived that on the hidden frontiers of the gun business—the Willard Hotel of Washington and the halls of government—business was best navigated precisely with parties, liquor, gift guns, amusements, and bribery, what Colt called, in one case, a "substantial gift of cash." A month of lavish entertainment cost the flailing Paterson company hundreds of dollars: "You use money as if it were drawn from an inexhaustible mine," Selden complained. "I have no belief in undertaking to raise the character of your gun by old Madeira."[16]

Colonel Bomford, head of the Ordnance Department, had wanted to replace muzzle-loading with breech-loading rifles early in his tenure. It was suspected in the 1830s, however, that he had a personal stake in the success of another model, the Hall rifle, and Christopher Colt warned his son against the man. "With a little 'Legerdemain' (keeping out of Col Bumferds way [sic])," Samuel thought he might be able to snag an order from the US Navy, Samuel wrote to Selden. "I am

confident that the officers would be glad to use arms of my construction to protect their cowardly selves at the Government Expence." Or,
if he could not circumvent Bomford, then he could "help" him with a
bribe, just as he assumed that Bomford had been "helped" by John Hall
and Simeon North, who had large contracts for public arms. Selden
was outraged. "I will not become party to a negotiation with a public
officer to allow him compensation for aid in securing a contract," he
wrote. "The suggestion with respect to Col Bomford is dishonorable in
every way and if you write me [again] I trust it will relate to other
topics."[17]

Colt had not found a civilian market, nor was he having success
with Washington, owing, he felt, to prejudice among army officers
against any innovations on "old and well known implements of War
fare." He decided it was time to bypass the federal government—the
"perfectly imbecilic" chief of the Ordnance Department and an "old
fogey" colonel, among other foes—and take the guns straight to officers in the field. So he traveled in 1838 to what a Colt historian from
the 1950s called the "festering protuberance on the bottom corner of
America," the "stinking morass" known as the Florida Everglades. The
eternally damp skies, rain dripping on leaves, moss-hung cypress trees,
and dense marsh were as far from the arid Old West of tumbleweed as
one could imagine, but this was another forgotten frontier for Colt and
his revolver. Here, Colonel William Harney was fighting the Semi-
noles, skilled and tenacious warriors who knew the land and out-
maneuvered the colonel's troops. He wanted to arm his men with
Colt's rifles, convinced they were "the only things that will finish the
INFERNAL WAR."[18]

Colt traveled a miserable passage of ten days, with five hundred rifles and a few pistols, through the canals and out to the Chesapeake
Bay to Charleston. When he received Harney's $6,250, he left for
St. Augustine to deliver the goods. "I reached this place last evening,"
he told Selden, after having spent fourteen more days traveling from
the Charleston location. "God only knows when I shall reach [New
York]," he complained, "for bad luck seems to have been on my side
since I started this cursed adventure." His yawl to get from the ship to

the meeting spot in Florida was swamped one mile from shore in the breakers. Colt was in the water for four hours, and the luggage, including Harney's payment, never washed ashore, which further incensed Selden. Colt had tried unsuccessfully to dump shares of his stock to clear his debt, and without the Florida money, Selden had to carry the burden longer.[19]

Harney later credited Colt's guns for his victory. With dispassionate brutality he described shooting Seminole warriors and placing them at "conspicuous places on the trees as a warning to others." "I honestly believe that but for these arms, the Indians would now be luxuriating in the everglades of Florida."[20]

The war left a haunting question, for those who cared to contemplate it: what to think about the souls and ghosts of those killed, the deaths that the new technology of multi-firing guns had so efficiently and gruesomely wrought. For his part, Colt thought of his gun's casualties from a market calculus. They were fodder for one of his first advertising letters in the *New York Evening Star* in January 1841, akin to an advertorial (Colt would testify in 1854 before a British Parliament committee, exploring small arms production, that "all new mechanics think that Government patronage is valuable to them. It is an advertisement, if nothing else"). "The results of [Harney's movements] with Colt's Repeating Rifles in the everglades . . . is alone the reason why the Indian warriors are pouring in as if by magic [to surrender]"—not diplomacy or negotiations, as had been rumored. But Harney's military success in the Florida swamps, Colt told a London society of civil engineers, "though very glorious for the government, was exactly the reverse for [me], for by exterminating the Indians, and bringing the war rapidly to an end, the market for the arms was destroyed." It was a breathtakingly frank statement of the sharpening antinomy between commercial and public markets and aims. Colt's lawyer, Edward Dickerson, agreed that Colt's revolver had shot itself in the foot: "The thing was so good that it ruined itself, or it killed all the Indians. . . . If it had been a slower process, the . . . Company would have prolonged their business; but the moment the Indians were extirpated, there was no market for their guns." There was a blasé utility and steely calculus to

Colt's thinking that constituted a new kind of character. It contrasted not only with the attitude of the Dudley Seldens of the world, who were preoccupied with reputation, honor, good credit, and fair dealing, but also with the military and martial ethics of public culture and defense.[21]

As the gun market and the Paterson enterprise failed, Selden's successor as treasurer, John Ehlers, fought a bitter custody battle over finished guns. Colt requested many guns to give to influential people and requisitioned them as security against his loans. This ploy had outraged an uncomprehending Selden, who saw the guns as company property: "I know not what you may think of the morals of this business, but it seems to me not much better than putting your hand in a man's pocket." In August 1841, with the feeble commercial market ostensibly dead and the government uninterested, Ehlers tried to seize Colt's patent rights to settle the debt that Colt personally owed to the company. Then Ehlers absconded with the company's finished arms. The Paterson company ended in bankruptcy in 1842, but not before Colt contemplated posting a runaway ad in the New York newspapers: "AB-SCONDED: A German calling himself John Ehlers . . . the upper part of his head [bald] . . . face round, figure stout and vulgar looking," who had run off with $50,000 to $70,000 worth of guns.[22]

Ehlers may have had guns to sell, but he did not have anything more. He did not possess what Colt possessed: the intellectual property of the idea of the gun, nourished by the close-knit, nonproprietary exchange of technological ingenuity in federal armories, which had been transformed into a species of private property through a patent. Colt knew that patent rights, the most insubstantial, numinous kind of property—invisible and contrived by law—were also the most valuable property he owned.

———

AFTER DAGUERREOTYPIST, WINCHESTER NEXT APPEARS AS THE proprietor of a men's clothing shop. With a shirt-collar patent in hand, he and his new business partner, John Davies, moved to New Haven in

1848. There, they introduced a manufactory into a town that was, according to a local historian, still "small, self-contained, self-satisfied," and nearly "homogeneous," and that "had the character of an overgrown village." The scale of business for an early manufacturing company tended to be small and geographically circumscribed. Distribution posed such challenges that goods tended to be sold only through regional merchants.[23]

The early gun business was no exception. When Eliphalet Remington began making guns, there was no railroad system, and trade was largely local. He did have the Erie Canal, however. His orders tended to be small, so he shipped the guns by bundling them tightly, putting a tag on the package, going to the nearby humpback bridge over the canal, lifting a board from the floor of the bridge, and dropping the gun package into the bullhead freighter as it passed underneath. Remington then mailed the customer a letter saying that his guns would be arriving on that boat.[24]

Antebellum merchants mostly had limited knowledge of distant regions even within the country. Not Oliver Winchester. Looking beyond New Haven, he reckoned that each American man could wear out an average of two shirts a year, so that, potentially, thousands of men would buy that many shirts from him. It was a strange idea, the conjuring of a larger, blurry aggregation of customers than any he'd physically seen. The inner engine of Winchester's ambition appears inevitable and obvious retrospectively, but in his moment, Winchester was catching something on the periphery of cultural vision, neither unprecedented nor entirely familiar.

Winchester and Davies built a four-story, 118-foot-long, T-shaped manufactory near Court Street. Winchester installed his family—his wife, Jane; two daughters; and one son, William—in a home right next to the factory. New England was falling in love with what one admirer of mechanization called "self-acting machines," believing they would replace skilled human labor. But Winchester still practiced the "putting-out" system: He employed some workers in the New Haven plant, who cut one piece of a shirt, according to pattern. Then, Winchester sent the pieces to the homes of workers, mostly women and girls, for hand-sewing. At the peak of his putting-out system, Winchester employed 800 in the plant and another 5,000 scattered in homes throughout Connecticut, Massachusetts, and Long Island. Davies sold the shirts at a New York City depot on Warren Street.[25]

When Winchester's fortune still appeared to be securely fated to men's shirt collars, its true genesis in guns was being conceived elsewhere, by inventor Walter Hunt, from Martinsburg, New York. Hunt's most enduring invention was surely his humblest—the safety pin. Even when he didn't intend to, Hunt ended up tinkering useful things into existence. He had irrepressibly abundant ideas and no facility with money. Protective tariffs, generous patent laws, and other incubators of American industry could only do so much for him. The safety pin came about while Hunt fidgeted a piece of wire into an intriguing twisted shape as he tried to conjure a way to pay off a $15 debt. He perceived mechanical utility as a habit. He invented a knife sharpener, a streetcar bell, a fountain pen, a nail-making machine, artificial stone, road-sweeping machinery, a precursor to the bicycle, an iceboat, and a sewing machine, which ensnared him in a losing patent war with Elias Howe.[26]

Hunt was a Quaker pacifist. When his son George Washington Hunt declared his intention in 1846 to enlist in the army to fight in Texas, Walter managed to dissuade him. But the turmoil got Hunt wondering if a more efficient firearm might end wars sooner, and thereby save lives. He speculated that the time-consuming, dangerous process of hand-loading cranky muskets and rifles with human fingers, from an upright position in the midst of battle, might be done faster and better mechanically. He envisioned two things: a breech-loading rifle, and a repeater mechanism.[27]

Gun historians consider Hunt's final product "brilliant" and "original in the extreme." In simplified terms, he had conceived of the first partially automatic rifle.

Hunt won a patent in 1848 for a rifle with a tubular magazine that sat just under the long barrel, equipped with a spiral-spring firing pin that advanced his patented "rocket ball" bullets automatically. His repeater mechanism to replace hand-loading proved too complicated in practice. Still, Hunt's Volitional Repeater had shown that an action of the most mortal consequence could be done by mechanical means. The volitional rifle was aptly named.[28]

As was often the case for Hunt with his inventions, he had to sell the patent for this audacious rifle—this time to model-maker George Arrowsmith. He needed the money desperately. From there, Hunt lost sight of it. Decades later, Hunt's great-grandson, Clinton Nottage Hunt, would found a World Peace Foundation, through which he proposed a "Five Year Plan for Disarmament" and a US secretary of peace in the presidential cabinet.[29]

COLT WAS DEMORALIZED—AND, SEEMINGLY, OUT OF THE DISMAL gun business. If America was born a gun culture, it was not reflected on Colt's bottom line. He fashioned himself to Texas senator Sam Houston in 1847 as a "poor devil of an inventor," adding that he was oppressed by military officers "who have the power to promote or crush at pleasure all improvements in fire arms for military purposes." As he was leaving Washington one day, Colt encountered a Texas Ranger captain, Sam Walker. Walker had seen that dealers would take a loss on Colt's overpriced and under-desired pistols just to get rid of them. Walker believed in the gun, however, and shared Colt's view that government officials were a "set of asses." Colt persuaded Selden, somehow, to have the factory produce 1,000 of them, to be sold to Walker at cost.[30]

Colt "visioned" all of Texas armed with Colt revolvers, overlooking the fact that 1,000 guns, coupled with those on hand with dealers, would saturate the sparsely populated republic. Selden suspected as much and voiced his objections. "It is poor business to sell your product without making a profit," he wrote to Colt. "If the purchaser wants it he will pay you a fair price. If he does not want it and there is a demand for it, sooner or later someone will pay you enough so that you can make a profit."[31]

Colt conceded that the first Walker contract might bring him "out at the little end of the Horn" financially, but he was gambling that the product's exposure would elicit heftier US government sales.[32]

Colt borrowed equipment from Whitney to tool up; as part of the agreement, he would keep the equipment after the order was completed. Colt faced the familiar production delays and the frustration of having to pay what he considered exorbitant wages, three or four dollars a day, to "entice" workers. By early March 1847, Walker was sending Colt increasingly frantic letters. He needed to start drilling his regiment on horseback in Kentucky. Send the pistols "as rapidly as possible," he implored. "There is nothing now not even a Female gives me so many thoughts." Colt finally filled the order by May, but in this case Selden's characteristically gloomy prophecy proved correct. The small volume of orders from Texas never justified Colt's waiver of a profit for that sale.[33]

As Winchester was establishing his shirt factory in New Haven in 1848, Colt was resurrecting his gun business thirty-eight miles to the north, with a Hartford factory that the *Daily Courant* called a "museum of curious machinery." Colt was becoming a hardened man against the US government market he had so energetically courted. A few years after begging for a government appointment out of desperation, when he was as "poor as a churchmouse," Colt advised his half-brother, William, to avoid government work entirely. "Don't, for the sake of your own good name think again of being a subordinate officer of government. You had better blow out your brains at once and manure some honest man's ground with your carcass than to hang your ambition on so low a peg." Colt wrote to Mormon leader Brigham Young in the Utah Territory to interest him in the Colt revolver as protection against "raids of savages" or "white marauders." Colt sympathized with Young's various legal conflicts with the federal government over land and sovereignty, as if a man who had "wrested an empire from wilderness and savages would tolerate interference from pettifogging politicians who begged the appointment because they could not make a living in any other way."[34]

But where to find markets, and customers, to pace his machinery that could turn out five hundred pistols and rifles a month, since Colt had erred in thinking that after Texas, the "government [would be] disposed to encourage me." It wasn't.[35]

In Hartford, Colt's Armsmear mansion provided one answer to how Colt navigated the gun business in the late 1840s and 1850s and continued to innovate it. Armsmear was built in 1856, and it was Colt's residence until his death in 1862. One of the more interesting and elaborate features of the home was a large room, given pride of place, that housed a walnut Cabinet of Memorials. The cabinet contained many eclectic items, including early forms of the revolver, like gun embryos preserved in formaldehyde. Mostly, the cabinet housed exquisite presents and offerings of appreciation to Colt from around the globe. One of the earliest, given to Colt in 1850 from the sultan of the Ottoman Empire, was a gold snuff box, with scores of diamonds in a floral pattern on the top. The cabinet also displayed a ring from the Russian grand duke, Alexander Alexandrovich, given to Colt in 1854, with the imperial cipher in tiny diamonds and "the whole surrounded by six brilliants of goodly size," as Colt's first biographer put it. Another ring was given to Colt by the king of Sardinia, in appreciation for his revolver. The cabinet contained a tea-caddy and cigar case from Siam, a Koran with extensive gold illumination, a medal from London, and a medallion from Italy. The memorials came from all corners of the world and from places with different religions, creeds, cultures, and forms of government. But all the gift-givers had one thing in common: they all bought Colt's guns.[36]

The Cabinet of Memorials held tangible mementoes from a gun business and reputation first built outside the United States. It was in international sales that Colt found his early success and wealth. No objects are more indelibly associated with the American West than the Colt revolver and the Winchester rifle, and yet no objects relied more heavily for their survival—before, but especially after, the Civil War—on non-US, global markets. Namely, it was the European regimes of the mid-1800s, embattled with each other and brimming with imperial ambition, where the demand for guns ran highest. Insofar as America has an exceptional gun pathology or culture, it is more accurately understood as one facet of an international pathology or culture, as it is in the international arena that the American gun business first survived.

In 1849, Colt trailblazed the path that the other gun industrialists—Remington, Smith and Wesson, and Winchester—would follow: they went abroad, to Europe, South America, Asia, and the Middle East, to sell their guns. Colt began "visioning the world as his arms market." The making of the American gun culture was a global phenomenon. As an American in Vienna later advised gun inventor Hiram Maxim, "If you want to make a pile of money, invent something that will enable these Europeans to cut each other's throats with greater facility."[37]

Colt divined the European war clouds from the limited information on foreign developments in American newspapers and from his agents and collaborators. George Landers, a shipping merchant and global entrepreneur, enticed him with news of "revolutionary times in Europe." In March 1848, Landers set sail on the *Cambria*, but before he left, he wrote to Colt for a pistol to take along. "Now is your time for Europe," he said prophetically. "I may have a chance to make your eternal fortune, besides profiting something clear myself."[38]

Colt himself made the first of his many forays to Europe and the Middle East in 1849. He gave clandestine assistance to Narcisco Lopez, a soldier of fortune trying to conquer Cuba; he shipped guns on the *Hydron* for British officers in South Africa; Landers met a Sardinian agent in the Astor House in New York and delighted him with Colt's pistol; and Colt sold to the "men of brains in Mexico" who had a high opinion of his gun. His Mexican agent learned his trade in the "gentleman's after cabin" on the steamer *Zavela*. He had gone "across the Rio Grande only in shorts to a small town called Randillo del Fortune," two hundred miles from Chihuahua, he reported to Colt in 1849. He "was much pleased with the country," and he would return with pack mules to seek the governor of Chihuahua, "to try to have his troops furnished with [Colts] to fight the Indians." He would also sell pistols at good prices to ranchers. Colt gifted profligately abroad. He sent two pistols and two rifles to the imam of Muscat. After a shipment of his arms smuggled illegally in bales of cotton to Russia was confiscated en route, in Prussia, he had his Berlin agent send one of his revolvers to Wilhelm IV to facilitate a resolution. The 1856 *Hartford Courant* attributed much of Colt's success internationally to his gifts:

"As Europe's sovereigns received presents of costly pistols," the newspaper wrote, "these presents were productive of magnificent gifts and orders for arms." Colt's fame, and the market for his guns, grew internationally more than in the United States.[39]

For Samuel Colt and the American gun business, 1849 and 1850 were watershed years. Colt, testifying in London in 1854 before a committee on small arms production, said that until that time, he had not been "successful at all." His business "was not profitable, [and] it did not make any money till lately." But he was turning a corner, abetted by foreign markets. Although he never abandoned the quest for military sales, he was fulfilling an earlier prophecy he had made: that soon, "the Government may go to the Devil and I will go my own way."[40]

COLT ALSO TRIUMPHED ON ANOTHER FORGOTTEN GUN FRONTIER: the courtroom. The American gun shows up often in stories of claim jumping and land settlement in the West, but more than in these stories, America's gun culture was developed largely through patent litigation. (Over five hundred patents were taken out for breech-loading guns alone from 1800 to 1871.) In the courtroom, the ethereal property of the idea of the gun, which Colt had never relinquished, was claimed, contested, and counterclaimed, and its borders were fiercely patrolled against infringement.[41]

To make an idea qualify as property through a patent—perhaps the most important prerequisite for the momentous shift that took the gun from its collaborative martial phase into its commercial phase—the gun inventor, or, more often, his capitalist adviser, had to claim originality of design. *Armsmear*, Henry Barnard's hyperbolic, posthumous homage to Colt, conceded that there had been a notion of "pepperboxes" before, a gun design precursor to the revolver, but then noted that "such an unwieldy arm . . . contrasts with the real revolver" as much as an alarm watch compares to "the rooster the Mohammedan pilgrim to mecca carries . . . to wake him up for nocturnal prayers." The boundaries of intellectual gun property were murkier than that, of course. Experts in gun technology and design rarely see a pristine singularity or novelty, without mechanical precursors; designs tend to be cumulative and characterized by small but crucial refinements on existing designs, bearing fingerprints from multiple inventors and mechanics. The patent provided deceptive certitude of ownership, when in reality an idea was usually claimed by more than one inventor—like Melville's Moby-Dick, stuck with multiple harpoons—each of whom declared clear and sole possession. Most gun capitalists, especially Winchester, spent a great deal of time and energy in the courts, mired in patent litigation.[42]

At an 1851 trial, the Massachusetts Arms Company defended itself against Colt's claims of a patent violation with the testimony of six men, who said they had invented a revolver in the 1830s on their own. The Massachusetts company also marshaled descriptions from foreign publications. In each of these cases, it argued, the revolver "had passed from a conception to a machine, from an idea to an embodiment; that it was embodied and used." Massachusetts Arms asserted that, however ingenious Colt's own revolver was, he had not therein exhausted the "mechanical diversities" of gun design, and that its gun differed from the plaintiff's just as much as Colt's gun differed from the six or more revolver designs that preceded his own. In the commercial gun culture, industrialists—especially Winchester, who made generous use of the courts—routinely designed guns with the same goal: to steer their way safely and without litigation through the design maze of an existing patent. Gun genius was in ongoing, deferential conversation with the more profane matter of patent boundaries and law.[43]

Colt's dogged and faithful attorney, Dickerson, argued that the Massachusetts Arms design was substantially the same as Colt's, and he knew that if he could convince the jury of that, Colt could use the courts to shut down the company's revolver production, effectively killing the competition. Considering the high stakes, Dickerson used all the legal and rhetorical arrows in his quiver, fashioning a patent-friendly biography of Colt as the lone, suffering inventor, a "poet in wood and steel," who saw the "golden apple" finally ripening for him, when Massachusetts Arms had violated his patent and "invented the *same* thing." Like other beleaguered inventors, Colt had to "enter on that field of strife and litigation, of unfair and unjust competition," at just the moment that he began to "reap the fruits . . . of success."[44]

Colt's moves cut a template for Winchester and for the American gun industry. Colt had finally made a profit. He had nurtured his (foreign) market, and he had emerged rebaptized from the 1850 patent trial, which he won as the lone inventor, driven by his incandescent gun brilliance. He was shorn clean of intellectual and political debts to government, politicians, family resources, mechanics, and other inventors, as if it had always been Colt, alone; as if his revolver had always been a success.

———

INTERCHANGEABILITY HAD GERMINATED IN BRITAIN AND LAID DOWN roots in New England. It had been perfected on guns. And then it returned home like the prodigal son at London's celebrated Exhibition of Industry in 1851. Joseph Paxton had brilliantly, if accidentally, designed the Exhibition Hall to fulfill Carlyle's gloomy prophecy that mechanization would "encircle and imprison" the world in a "glass bell." Paxton enclosed the machinery under a giant glass roof supported with iron beams. *Punch* magazine immortalized it as the Crystal Palace. Some Londoners called it the fairy palace: it sparkled in the sun from half a mile away.[45]

Sir Henry Bessemer described a London astir with excitement. Six million visitors formed a "solid mass of carriages, horses, policemen and pedestrians . . . [and] hundreds of ladies in their satin shoes" flashed tickets from their carriage windows and descended delicately onto the streets in beautiful dresses. Crystal Palace exhibitors had divided all matter into ten realms with thousands of subdivisions. The Machinery Hall presented a deafening, imperious menagerie of machines in motion to awed, often mystified human onlookers. Queen Victoria found it "beautiful, bewildering and enchanting." She marveled that "what used to be done by hand and used to take months doing is now accomplished in a few instants by the most beautiful machinery." All of it, she confessed, did leave her mentally exhausted. Charles Dickens felt overwhelmed, too. "I have a natural horror of sights, and the fusion of the many sights in one has not decreased it," he wrote. Enthralled visitors maneuvered Dickens into lying when they would ask, "Have you seen? . . ." Because, he said, "if I don't [say yes] he'll explain it, and I can't bear that."[46]

The Machinery Hall intermingled the absurd and the revolutionary, a hodgepodge created when the manner of producing something transfixes people more than the thing produced. An "Ottoman Coal Sarcophagus," which answered the desperately needed "purpose of an ottoman and a coal receptacle in one," shared space with the McCormick reaper. A dual "lady's parasol driving whip" was of the same genus as the "interchangeable systems" for guns—on display from America.[47]

The Vermont "precision manufacturers" firm of Robbins & Lawrence demonstrated interchangeability by disassembling whole rifles into parts and reassembling them. Most visitors had never seen such a thing. Any part fit any rifle. It was almost magic. But Colt stole the show. He displayed five hundred machine-made guns artfully in a spiral pattern inside a glass case, and served free brandy from a bottle he kept stashed under the counter. The *Daily News* of London reported that "the click of Mr. Colt's revolvers [was] unceasing," as he demonstrated his wares. *Gleason's Home Companion* raved that Colt had "actually revolutionized" arms.[48]

The Crystal Palace was a fairy-tale portal into European markets for much of the American gun industry. This did not go unnoticed by the European press, which, amid encomiums for the "most perfect uniformity of design" in Colt's pistol, also noted its "murderous task," and criticized the American gun industrialists as mercenary and ruthless. A French report on the Crystal Palace found the revolver especially loathsome. It was a weapon "abused by all: filibusters, travelers, and friends of violence." Although they were more rhetorically florid and pointed in their critique, some Americans viewed the repeater technology with similar aversion. The report claimed, dubiously, that revolver owners "under the slightest pretext . . . kill each other with incredible fury."[49]

Under the circumstances, Colt never pursued the French market. But elsewhere in Europe, the nations that today are appalled at the American gun culture were the ones that kept the American gun business solvent for many years. "American industry is profiting largely by the belligerent propensities lately developed in the East of Europe," the *London Magnet* wrote bluntly. "Russia and Turkey are outbidding each other in the markets of the world for the implements . . . of slaughter, and it is in the United States alone that they find the means of gratifying their wishes promptly available." A small knot of New England manufacturers would arm almost the whole world in the next thirty years. As revealed from the vantage point of business, the development of the American gun culture was very much a non-American, global affair. Without the thirsty markets of imperial Europe and other belligerent regimes abroad, which created a kind of expatriate American gun culture, the business would have struggled to stay afloat in the mid-1800s. *Scientific American* noted the tectonic shift in the gun business. The United States before the 1860s had imported almost all of its guns, but by 1881 leading authorities estimated that "with the single exception of the needle gun, every arm on a breech-loading system used in Europe is of American origin."[50]

Simultaneously, the great gun shops of Europe—the famed "Gunsmith's Row" of Birmingham, England, and the illustrious gunsmiths of Leige, Belgium—began to recede in the shadow of American interchangeable production. *Scientific American* noted that they had scoffed at the idea of "making each arm a perfect pattern," and through commercial "survival of the fittest," the United States had leaped ahead. From this point forward, the directives and pressures of finding markets for mass-produced guns would fall most heavily on the country—the United States—that developed the gun industry and technology. European and other international states would excel as the most coveted consumers for mass-produced guns in the 1800s, but not as their producers.[51]

An international arms race had begun, radiating outward from Connecticut, the new gun basket, to the world. The Duke of Wellington frequently visited Colt's exhibit, where he proselytized the merits of repeater guns to British single-shot devotees. Catching the new rhythm of industrial manufacturing, the English realized that Colt would maintain a permanent advantage and be in a position to "undersell any imitators that may appear," having already made the initial, extremely heavy outlay of capital to produce the machines to produce the guns. In this new gun calculus, the ten thousandth gun was vastly cheaper and easier to make than the first, as Whitney first understood—but only made sense if the ten thousandth could actually be sold.[52]

Colt's and Robbins & Lawrence's prize-winning gun exhibits were also the sensational international debut of interchangeable parts and the "American System of Manufactures." This term would be shorthanded within the decade to "The American System," which would be shorthanded again later simply to "manufacturing."

———

OLIVER WINCHESTER BECAME A TRUE BELIEVER IN THE AMERICAN System early in 1852, when a partner of the New Haven Wheeler & Wilson manufactory took one of his Howe sewing machines to the nearby Winchester shirt establishment, hoping to drum up business.[53]

At first, Winchester wasn't enthusiastic about the sewing machine. Skeptical, he refused to try what he called the "contrivance." Wheeler persisted, and when he actually "caused a shirt to be made with the machine" in Winchester's presence, his "skepticism gave way to wonderment." Winchester was not himself a mechanic, but a seer of mechanical things. New and large systems, systems of industry and economy, emerged out of thousands of small choices and ways of seeing. Others in his day worried about the social reverberations of the sewing machine and "mechanical cunning"—but evidently not Winchester. For him, the sewing machine was a source of awe and beautiful, dispassionate precision as much as profit. He admired not only its speed, but also, as he told the dealer, its "perfection."[54]

Within two months of taking sewing machines on a trial basis, Winchester had converted entirely to machine production. In 1853, he decreased his workforce by 4,500.[55]

A few years later Winchester produced an advertisement for his shirts. The factory on Court Street anchors the page proudly, and five smaller images radiate from it. In his first gun ads, Remington, too, opted to illustrate the factory itself. Winchester's ad displays no men's shirts, no customers purchasing shirts, and no models wearing them. Instead, it shows off the factory itself and its mechanical configurations. Imagine if a J. Crew catalog today featured photographs of the places where the company's clothes were manufactured, instead of artfully modeled finished products.[56]

The machine, with an attendant, would "do the work of five hand-sewers, at least, and do it *better*," as well as cheaper, Winchester deposed in a lawsuit between warring inventors Walter Hunt and Elias Howe. Winchester's thinking was minutely precise. He reckoned his savings per each item, per each week, and concluded that, cumulatively, the sewing machine "shows a saving in this single manufactory of $240,000 a year." In the mid-and late 1850s, Winchester's half interest in shirt manufacturing amounted to $200,000 (about $4,350,000 today). In this way, he began to become wealthy.[57]

Winchester and other entrepreneurs were amassing into an industrial elite. The prominent lecturer and essayist Oliver Wendell Holmes begrudgingly admired their success, "though its origin may have been in . . . unctuous commodities." Having become prosperous on the not especially unctuous commodity of a shirt collar, Winchester apparently wanted to satisfy his yen for enterprise and find a new investment through which to funnel some of his capital.[58]

Winchester's office stood near Artizan Street, and in the 1850s he liked to prowl the scrappy, industrious neighborhood. He visited from time to time in the workshop of Benjamin Tyler Henry, a brilliant gunsmith from New Hampshire. There, he found Henry tinkering with a dauntingly original project that he'd inherited, circuitously, from Walter Hunt's prolific imagination. It was the volitional rifle.[59]

CHAPTER 3

"SCATTERING OUR GUNS"

A T THE POINT WHERE MECHANICAL CUNNING INTERSECTED WITH human desire, the idea of arms mass-produced by self-acting machines baffled many of Oliver Winchester's contemporaries in the 1850s. For the first time, the milling, edging, and other key gun machinery existed on a scale suitable to outfit large private armories. But guns were still frequently imagined in martial terms. The *Hartford Courant* named them "deadly implements of war." A writer for *Harper's* magazine, touring the Springfield Armory, hoped that only a small number "of these terrible instruments of carnage and destruction . . . [were] destined ever to be used." Aside from "peaceful drilling and parades," certainly the greater portion would remain "stored in the nation's arsenals, where they lie, and are to lie, as we hope, forever, undisturbed." As for guns and violence, most murders at this time involved not guns, but weapons of opportunity, such as fists and bricks. These weapons outnumbered guns and knives combined.[1]

Of the eighty-five murders committed in the 1850s that were mentioned in popular books and pamphlets, twenty-four (29 percent) involved a gun. Interestingly, the percentage was similar in the 1860s (23 percent) and 1870s (25 percent). The number of gun homicides written about in these publications cannot be equated with the actual percentage of gun homicides (national data are unavailable on this point), but the percentages are an important reminder that the problem of

45

American violence was not synonymous with the gun. Poisoning, especially with arsenic, along with throat-slitting, stabbing, and beating with fists, or with objects such as pump handles or hammers, were some of the common non-gun methods of violence. In this set of eighty-five murders, the largest category was that of intimate, domestic homicide: out of thirty-six of these (42 percent of the total), there were seventeen murders of wives by husbands, five murders of husbands by wives, nine involving mistresses or lovers, and five involving miscellaneous family murders (murder of a father or brother-in-law, for example). Of the twenty-five murders committed with guns, seven (28 percent) involved the fatal shooting of someone involved in a lovers' quarrel or spousal murder. Many of the remaining gun homicides occurred in disputes over gambling debts, gold watches, inheritances, or other types of property or money matters.[2]

As for sporting or hunting, the rifle's prospects seemed limited. Henry William Herbert, perhaps America's first sporting writer, predicted that before the century ended, rifles would be "obsolete" in the United States and lose both their "utility and honor." In 1848, wrote Herbert, rifles were rare on the East Coast. Interest in rifles, befitting their association with war, fluctuated apace with armed conflict, and the 1850s were comparatively peaceful.[3]

Americans had complex and not overwhelmingly positive feelings about the new semiautomatic guns, which contributed to sluggish demand. The view from the business ledger reveals these years to be challenging ones for the gun industrialist. Winchester and Colt could not create a civilian market in a vacuum, and the American consumer was not rushing to meet them halfway. Those who saw guns as implements of slaughter would have agreed with British poet John Milton's observations about the cannon, that the idea came from Satan himself: "In future days, if malice should abound, / someone intent on mischief, or inspired / with devilish machination, might devise / like instruments to plague the sons of man." Admirers of Colt's revolver countered with an exculpatory 1850s precursor to mutually assured destruction in war. The *Hartford Daily Times* praised Colt's "moral importance" for humanity in "adding to the efficiency of warlike weapons." In his patent lawsuit against the Massachusetts Arms Company, Colt's attorney thought it prudent to defend the gun's very existence by making reference to armies. He conceded that "peaceful citizens of Massachusetts, perhaps not one of you has ever owned a pistol," but said that "when a man can invent a process by which a whole army can be killed . . . the millennium will arrive, and the lion and the lamb will lie down together." The "peacemaker," as Colt himself coined his six-shooter, was by this logic a "humane improvement" in the world.[4]

The gruesome carnage of these new "destructive weapons of war" was widely noted in the 1850s, whether to condemn or to praise, yet an emerging aesthetic ideal simultaneously saw the guns as "perfect" because they had been produced by the exacting, impartial precision of the machine. The new gun often stimulated an adjectival mix of barbarity and perfection: the former applied to its use, the latter to its manufacture. The aesthetic equation of beauty with the sameness that only a machine could achieve began to predominate. The *Daily News of London* captured the duality. A writer visiting a revolver factory became transfixed as he observed the metamorphosis of huge bars of iron into guns. He described the bars before the process began as "ugly . . . in their shapelessness and dusky asperity." In the basement, noticing more of the raw materials, he said that if someone was "philosophic or imaginative," he might "speculate on the amount of death and bloodshed which is to be elicited from all that harmless looking metal and timber." The "rude and sullen iron" began to acquire its sinister purpose at the furnace. Here, the "sinewy Vulcans in attendance"—the actual human workers—fashioned barrels and triggers. Yet this ugly and "complex life of wheels, rods, shafts and levers" yielded a finished product that seemed nothing short of a "perfect weapon." In the coming years, no adjective would attach itself more closely to Winchester's repeater rifle than "perfect." Colt testified in London that the gunsmith's eye "cannot control the hand sufficiently to imitate" the perfect uniformity of a machine. In a few short decades, the machine had gone from an imitation of the human hand to the ideal against which the hand faltered.[5]

In America, the late 1850s were lean years for the gun's industrial vanguard. In 1857 the fledgling Smith & Wesson would produce only

four handguns. Remington, which had always focused on military orders, turned to the production of other commodities. Eliphalet Remington traveled widely to find customers for his guns, with important papers
tucked into his silk hat. He wrote to his son Philo in 1857 from the
road, saying he had "thrown away two days and about ten dollars in pursuit of our lame ducks at Joliet, as there is but little prospect of getting
anything out of them." It seemed noteworthy when another customer
agreed to buy six pistols. Eliphalet was on the lookout for a potential civilian product, however, and experimented in several directions "The
Remingtons are making a lady's pistol," a local newspaper reported in
1859, "so look out ye burglars of houses and of hearts." They also tried
to manufacture a gun the size of a pocket comb that would function like
a "burglar detector" and explode when a burglar tried to open a door or
lift a sash. In 1858 Remington patented a "gentleman's cane gun." This
was a cane that could also shoot a bullet, to keep stray dogs and ruffians
at bay. Fewer than 2,000 were ever produced, and sales were disappoint-
ing, although Remington sales agent F. E. Spinner did manage to sell
four of them at the 36th Congress in Washington in 1861.[6]

Samuel Colt assessed the sales prospects to be poor. "There has not
been so dull a time in years for my business as just now," he wrote to
R. W. Latham in December 1858—although he remained dubious that
demand truly could be sagging as badly as it was. "In careful consideration of the real *and supposed* causes of the great falling off" in business
with his key dealers—whom Colt always suspected of being lazy gun
hucksters—he proposed "greatly reduced prices" to them, but insisted
that any dealer with a commission above 10 percent sell no other revolving breech firearms but Colt's (italics added). As for rifles, he wrote
to his employee William Hartley, "we may find it desirable to resort to
our Italian friends." Colt had sent an agent out to California to tap
into the gold-rush market in 1853, but he found the market saturated.
The new crop of settlers was more interested in agriculture than gold,
and they had little need for the guns.[7]

Colt had not given up on the "larger quantities" of guns that might
be sold to the US government, despite his bitterness, but he had no
luck. Colt told Latham in July 1858 that he had returned home from

Washington "without one single order for my arms . . . and now I am without scarcely anything to do with my large armory." Colt worked through his agents to get orders for state militias. Latham wrote him in August that he should dispatch his secretary with an appeal for an order for 10,000 revolvers to the Honorable B. R. Floyd of Virginia. "Write it in your best style," Latham implored, "and give some 'Indean War' reason for it," and hope that he would order at least 5,000. A few days later, Colt penned the letter, marked private and confidential, dutifully mentioning the "recent Indean outbreaks in Washington territories and elsewhere," and explaining that he had to appeal directly to states—and governors—owing to a colonel's strong "personal feelings" against the Colt revolver and his unwillingness to stock them in the "publick stores for infantry." He instructed Floyd to destroy the letter after he read it.[8]

With inauspicious markets and politics at home, Colt redoubled his attention to Europe. Here, the gun business was as fruitful as it was challenging in the United States. The fever for the new American-made guns raged hot, fueled by an imperial and martial sense that the guns were needed. The military publication *Colburn's United Service Magazine* confessed in September 1859 that despite the efforts at peace congresses and conferences in the 1850s, "it is now universally admitted that the time has not arrived when we may turn our spears into pruning-hooks. On the contrary, there never was a period when men were so bent upon applying them to deadly use, rendering them still more destructive, and giving them the keenest edge that steel will take. . . . We are really puzzled to know what weapon is the best. . . . How shall we arm?"[9]

Colt delighted in the Continent's bellicosity. "The demand for arms here [in Europe] is unabating," he wrote in 1852, "and I am dubling [*sic*] my facilities to make them for this market." Colt sold to all belligerents abroad, including Turkey, Austria, and Russia, the latter through Tsar Nicholas, whose arms inspector traveled back to Hartford with Colt, disguised and smuggled in as his valet. He sold to a soon-to-be unified Italy. Gino Garibaldi thanked Colt for his arms in 1860, calling them a "subsidy of moral potency from a great American nation." He sold to

England. Lieutenant Hans Buck, in London, wrote to Colt in 1859 that it seemed Europe was on the brink of a "long and sanguinary war" (although which imagined war he might have been referring to is not entirely clear). The "sad lot of incapables" would probably make a mess of things, but Buck and a few others "place[d] their trust in their 'Colt.'"[10]

Colt reasoned that Europeans would encroach on Asia, and the Asians would want to resist with the best guns they could find. He furnished Commodore Matthew Perry with sample rifles. "It has occurred to me that they would be invaluable in the expedition to Japan," Colt wrote in 1852, as Perry endeavored to "open" Japan to US trade. Colt happened to have five hundred pistols on hand, because he had contracted with General Juan Manuel de Rosas to supply the "Brasilian government . . . but Rosas having been defeated and fled the country," the guns might as well be sent with Perry to Asia. Years later, Perry reported back that the second king of Siam had praised the revolver. "He is well educated and a great lover of the arts," Perry wrote. "If you desire to present him a pair of your miniature pistols, in a pretty case, I will forward the gift." Perry had also stirred interest with "several of the princes of Japan, the governor of Shanghai, and the king of Lew Chew.[11]

So brisk were Colt's sales abroad that an 1858 advertisement included a back page devoted entirely to foreign notices and testimonials. Colt even opened a London factory in 1854 with the help of engineer Charles Manby, who assured him, "I am quietly working to produce the impression that your manufactory is to be established under government auspices and to work entirely for the trade of the army and navy. This impression must be made so as to disarm competitors." As Colt waited for the cunning Manby to close the deal on his London land, he worried that valuable time was being lost, and that "no such hoorah for Colt's arms can again be raised without grate [sic] efforts." To his representative abroad, Charles Dennet, he said, attuned as always to the marketing imperative, "You must keep the thing as much before the public as possible." He urged him to "have some of the arms at different publick [sic] places and occasionally get short spicey notice in the papers of some extraordinary performance by someone of Her Majesty's officers with one of them."[12]

IN THIS COMMERCIALLY FLINTY CONTEXT, WINCHESTER PONDERED inventor Benjamin Henry's rifle in the Artizan Street shop. It was mechanically possible to mass-produce rifles, but where was the point, profit, or logic in it? Henry's novelty, a self-acting repeater, able to mechanically reload, had been variously possessed, tweaked, and sold like a valuable but inscrutable treasure. The idea, now property, had first been sold by Walter Hunt to George Arrowsmith; then from Arrowsmith to inventor Lewis Jennings; then from Jennings to capitalist Cortlandt C. Palmer, a man who knew nothing about guns. Palmer had enlisted manufacturers Robbins & Lawrence, in Vermont, to try to produce a repeater—and Henry was the superintendent of the shop at that time.[13]

Palmer was interested in the idea of this new gun, but he needed mechanical help to develop it. In the complex but incestuous family tree of American gun design, orchestrated through patents, the story of Oliver Winchester's gun business begins with Horace Smith and Daniel Wesson. Palmer turned to Smith and Wesson. For some time, Smith had been working the mechanical Lorelei of how to design a gun that could function like a repeater—and his ideas came close to infringing on the Hunt and Jennings gun patents that Palmer now owned. When Palmer approached them, Smith and Wesson had only expenses, two patents, and depleted finances to show for their inventive efforts, and Palmer might have used the threat of patent infringement to pressure them to collaborate with him—or, more charitably, Palmer offered to finance them with $10,000 in desperately needed cash. Whatever the case, Smith and Wesson joined Palmer in a partnership on June 20, 1854, in Norwich, Connecticut, to see if they could mass-produce a repeater firearm. Henry continued to work on the riddle as well. The venture failed after one year. Smith and Wesson sold their assets— namely, their patents—to a group of New Haven investors, who founded the Volcanic Repeating Arms Company in 1855.[14]

A year earlier, Colt had established himself as the main stockholder of his new Colt's Patent Repeating Firearms corporation, the largest private armory in the world, so as to avoid being "subject to the whims of a pack of dam fools and knaves styling themselves as a board of directors," doubtless recalling his Paterson debacle. The Volcanic Repeating Arms Company brought together forty damn fools, otherwise known as New Haven men of property and influence. They included seven clock makers, three carriage makers, two bakers, two grocers, and representatives of shipping. Shareholders exchanged control for protection from responsibility and for limited liability. They met for the first time on July 3, 1855, in New Haven, to pay the first installment on their shares and to elect directors.[15]

The company had been named not by Smith and Wesson or any other inventor but by *Scientific American*, because the rapid firing power of the gun had reminded one of the magazine's writers of a volcano's fiery eruption. Harnessing Henry's inventive talent and the valuable patent, the company intended to mass-produce the repeater firearm. That year, Oliver Winchester made his first modest foray into the arms business, buying 80 shares of the Volcanic Repeating Arms Company, valued at $25 par, out of 6,000 shares, for a corporation capitalized at $150,000.[16]

The American System involved making real people—craftsmen— disappear through mechanization, but it also involved making false people appear, through what historian Daniel Boorstin has called "a new mystery, a new unintelligibility," at the leading edge of the economy, to which we've long grown accustomed. In 1837, Connecticut had passed the prototype Incorporation Act. The corporation took many people—stockholders—and melded them into one legal "fictitious person" endowed with the real and true rights of an individual before the law. "A corporation," Supreme Court Chief Justice John Marshall had written in 1819, "is an artificial being, invisible, intangible, and existing only in contemplation of the law." Perhaps not unlike a ghost, or a spirit, the corporation was supernatural, unseen, and conjured only by the law as a medium. Others gravitated to the same vocabulary to describe the ghostly, immortal nature of the corporation, referring to the "romantic mysteries of high finance" that replaced many face-to-face methods of exchange in the early 1800s, or the "magic" of stock, which could alchemize to money. There was a core inscrutability in the corporate system and in the emerging industrial economy—a contrived idea of property made real by social consensus and embodied in law. The willingness to believe that became normalized only with time.[17]

For as precise, empirical, and tangible as their methods of production were, the fortunes of the gun capitalists rested on the most fantastic, mysterious, and incorporeal of things: a corporate charter, a patent, an imagined market, and their own capacity to "vision the future." Like Colt, Winchester understood that his fortune depended on these most ethereal holdings, not the more concrete assets of a building or a set of gunsmith's tools, or even an invention that he had conceived himself. The two men with actual firearms backgrounds—Smith and Wesson—sold out and abandoned their patents to a man—Winchester—who knew nothing about firearms and yet who had an inexplicably perseverant faith in the patent's value.[18]

Why Winchester became so interested in the gun business is something of a mystery. He had no personal or abiding interest in rifles previously. Surely, he knew of Whitney's operations, and of Colt's enterprises, but the Colt's archive contains no correspondence between Winchester and Colt from the 1850s, and the Winchester letter book contains only a query from Winchester to Colt's foreman about a potential employee. Winchester had never shot a rifle, displayed one, or even owned one before starting his gun business, and even after entering the business, he only personally owned two—a pair of engraved, ivory-gripped pistols, numbers 1401 and 1506, from the early Volcanic days, kept in the family as heirlooms. By investing in the Volcanic gun, Winchester was venturing into an industry that had barely begun, to create a product that had yet to be perfected, about which he knew little, to be sold to markets that did not clearly exist, by the "fictitious person" of a corporation. On the surface, it wasn't a wise idea.[19]

The Volcanic plant occupied an unprepossessing building at the corner of Orange and Grove Streets. Compared to Winchester's shirt empire, this must have felt like a regression—perhaps thrilling, perhaps dispiriting. Winchester employed fifty men, mostly of English or Scottish descent, and four girls who made ammunition exclusively. When one of his customers complained that cartridges had been filled with tobacco by mistake—or as a time-saving measure—Oliver dismissed the statement, "as none but girls fill them," and they did not use tobacco.[20]

At the beginning, the company would get a gun order, blow a whistle to call the help in, and send the help back to the farms after the order was completed. Volcanic pistols sold for $11.50 each at a time when city directories sold for $1. Following the breathless, self-interested journalistic hyperbole of the 1850s, which often merged advertisement and news, the *New Haven Palladium* touted the Volcanic pistol as "one of the most perfect things in the shooting line that we ever took into our hands," a gun that made Colt's pistol a mere "distortion," some "clumsy, uncouth and ridiculous affair of a fire-arm." Not to be outdone, the *New Haven Journal Courier* extolled the Volcanic as "the very perfection of firearms," certain to attract orders from all quarters.[21]

That didn't quite happen. As was evident with Colt, there was a perhaps immovable ceiling on what gun capitalists could sell in the United States in the mid-1800s, notwithstanding their energetic efforts to craft the market. The gun did not sell, and the chief investors and original founders withdrew from the company in 1856 and 1857. In one year, Winchester moved from a minor shareholder to a major investor and the president of the ailing corporation. He continued to loan the company his personal money to keep it afloat, acquiring more of its property, patents, and machinery as collateral.

Winchester was stubbornly obsessed by his idea of what the repeater might become. Intending to mesh the mechanically possible with the humanly desirable, he deepened his involvement as others fled. In 1857, with its cash down to $97.38, the Volcanic company had no choice but to sell its mortgages to pay Winchester back to cover his loans.[22]

Winchester's actions combined courage and rapaciousness: most likely, in calling in his mortgages, Winchester was making a play for nearly complete control over the company's fortunes. He knew, with the split consciousness of an individual and a shareholder, that the company couldn't cover his loans without forfeiting its collateral.[23]

After Winchester secured majority control of the company in 1857, he rechristened it the New Haven Arms Company. The name Volcanic still enchanted him, however, and he retained it for marketing purposes. Winchester held exclusive ownership of the patents, and he held 800 of the 1,900 shares issued. The list of stockholders included some of New Haven's most venerable founding families. One of them was Leonard Pardee, scion of one of New Haven's founding fathers, George Pardee. Leonard was a partner in a prosperous carriage manufactory. He was the father of just one son and five living daughters: Estelle, Isabelle, Mary, Antoinette—and Sarah.[24]

As president, treasurer, and chief stockholder of the New Haven Arms Company, Winchester set out to collect debts, no matter how small. In September 1857, he had his secretary write to the very first Volcanic dealer, F. G. Wheeler, "We are much in want of funds, [so] we take the liberty to call your attention [to an] account showing a balance in our favour of $202.50."[25]

The company then began to "turn out finished arms, and put them into the market," as Winchester put it in a letter to a stockholder. Americans reacted to the repeater with curiosity and guarded approval. Frank Leslie's *Weekly Illustrated* in October 1858 praised the Volcanic's pride of execution and "really marvelous rapidity." The *Milwaukee Daily Sentinel* called it a great "organ of destructiveness." To Winchester, who had embraced the industrial aesthetic, the Volcanic was a "beautiful and very effecting weapon."[26]

Winchester worked tirelessly to create a market for the Volcanic (because he had to) and began to build a dealer network. The energetic dealer Joseph Merwin established himself in New York City; in the next two years, Winchester found dealers in Philadelphia, Boston, New Orleans, and San Francisco. He circulated broadsides to agents and friends, and he posted advertisements that tended either toward effusive triumphalism or desiccated mechanical tutelage. Merwin advertised the Volcanic Repeating Fire Arm as "A TRIUMPH OF AMERICAN INGENUITY" in the *New York Times* of August 1859. He tried to appeal to the gold-rush customer, not realizing, as Colt had, that this gun market was saturated, with another *New York Times* ad: "HO! For Pike's Peak, no mother's son should be allowed to go to the Gold Diggings without one of these Volcanic repeating rifles or pistols. . . . With a good conscience and a Volcanic pistol, you may sleep soundly and safely, with your hard-earned nuggets by your side. My friend, if you have regard for your life or your scalp, do not fail to get one or more of these invaluable weapons." Another ad dispensed with drama. It read: "Directions: Push the spring up in the tube, by the knob A, till the . . . cap B can be turned to the left, then put the cartridges . . . in the tube, replace the cap B, when the spring will allow the cartridge down, raise the hammer C and swing the lever D. CLEAR forward, which will elevate the carrier E with pin F, when the arm is in condition for discharge." Then, "in case of misfire, bring up another ball."[27]

The weapon might have been perfectly ingenious—arguably the "parent of all American magazine guns," reflected *Frank Leslie's* in 1878—but in practice it was not in fact perfect. Writing to a stockholder, Winchester had to concede that, "after a few months of vain efforts to sell them," he had found there were "radical defects" in his repeater that seriously dampened sales. Faulty ammunition diminished the gun's power and lethality, and was the primary technological hurdle to a repeater rifle. Whatever the reasons, the gun fell "dismally short of developing its potentialities to the fullest." As a company memoir recalls, "output soon exceeded demand." Other multi-firing gun ventures had fallen into bankruptcy, and Colt was also complaining of the stagnant market.[28]

Even in St. Louis, the most robust gun entrepôt in the nation, with six gun merchants in the late 1850s, the Volcanic had no luck. Nonetheless, it did find some customers. The New York City police used it in 1858 to quell riots on Staten Island against a yellow fever hospital. The Volcanic #704, the only one inscribed to a woman, found its way to Lizzie Tomlinson in St. Louis, who may have been a madam (the gun was discovered in 1937). The adventurer William Cowper Prime introduced the Volcanic to Egypt but explained, in his 1857 volumes *Boat Life in Egypt and Nubia* and *Tent Life in the Holy Land*, that guns were "useful only for show in Egypt." And yet, confronted by a stone-throwing mob while on horseback, Prime drew his Volcanic, and a "shudder of fear" and "terror" rippled through the mob. King Farouk, an antique firearms enthusiast and known kleptomaniac, had two Volcanic pistols in his possession when he took the throne in 1936.[29]

Winchester's gun sales to these and other customers were remarkably casual and haphazard. When a customer's name was not known, the Volcanic sales ledger recorded, "Sold To a Stranger." Customers sometimes simply wrote directly to Winchester to order guns. Winchester responded to one customer: "In your letter you say 'send us more rifles and ammunition immediately.'" Apparently there was nothing else to go on, for he added: "Please send us a *definite* order stating number wanted . . . and how many cartridges." Samuel Colt's sales could be casual, too. He received a letter from one customer who tersely implored, "Please send me by express tomorrow without fail one of yr. Pistol with box and appendages," and another from a customer in Kentucky, who wrote saying he desired a "pair of your newly modelled repeating pistols, of a size not too large to be carried about one's person yet large enough to be relied upon in any emergency." He added, "Do not send me articles that will sometimes fire and sometimes fail. . . . I have any quantity of such pistols on hand already."[30]

The first and most basic problem for Winchester and his company was volume. He needed it. This was the transformative facet of the gun business as an industry rather than a craft, and arguably a prerequisite for a true gun culture. Gunmakers were no longer producing the guns that were needed, when they were needed, and supplementing their incomes with other crafts in between, but trying to sell all the guns that could be produced by machines that were tooled up to produce one design. When a customer in 1857 requested a "Navy" pistol (a Colt's model), Winchester responded frostily, "You do not seem to understand that to manufacture each different size of firearm involves a very large outlay of capital, which cannot be . . . entered upon but by degrees." The dynamic between gunmaker and buyer shifted from "I, a customer, need a gun, to my specifications. Make me one," to "I, an industrialist, have made many guns, to my template. I will sell them to you." Sociologist James Wright has stated as a truth of American guns that "demand creates its own supply," but supply creates demand, too—or the economic imperative to find or invent demand for a product. Dealers and merchants needed to move more guns more quickly.[31]

In the 1850s, the Volcanic factory had limited production capacity—not even two hundred rifles a month—but it was still a daunting quantity. To encourage bulk sales, Winchester devised discount schemes for his merchants and dealers that were determined by volume. He wrote to one prospective dealer that he would offer a 20 percent discount on purchases of over $100, 25 percent on those over $1,000, and 30 percent on those over $5,000. The more the dealer sold, the larger his profit margin. In case the concept was unclear, Winchester explained, "We will leave with you to do the best you can for us in making a sale so far as to make the largest discount." Winchester insisted that his price lists be adhered to, and he emphatically avoided consignment as much as possible in favor of "absolute sales," which, obviously, increased the dealer's incentive to sell as many guns in stock as he could.[32]

Working through a third party, Winchester proposed to sell to one dealer all the "arms"—a novel abbreviation, requiring quotation marks—he could sell "at a discount of 20 percent . . . or 5 percent additional discount for CASH." In addition, the dealer could have exclusive rights to sell in his area if he agreed "to use all due effort by advertising, etc., to give them a *thorough chance to be known* and sold." To establish a depot in New York City, on Broadway, Winchester reached out to Smith and Wesson, in the gun capitalists' intimately competitive fashion, to propose that they sell their guns together.[33]

Colt pushed volume as well. Revolvers didn't just sell themselves, and it was the gun capitalist's ordinary, repetitive task to roll the boulder of demand up the hill, cultivate a market, and then do it again. Eventually, the companies would succeed in building their domestic markets, but at this time, even their best marketing and sales designs struggled against demand and price. In 1855, Colt was offering dealers a 25 percent discount for sales of under $3,000 a month, and a 30 percent discount for sales over that amount. If a dealer achieved a very high volume of $30,000 net and in cash, he provided an additional 5 percent discount. "But no such terms or discount will be given when there is a combination of parties for such purchase," he warned, "with a view of dividing the Arms between them."

Dealers quickly caught on to the volume-driven arithmetic of industrial production. A Philadelphia dealer in 1850 asked Colt if "by ordering a considerable lot of your guns . . . the prices and terms will be put low so as to be advantageous." In the early 1850s, cranky dealers wrote to Colt to plead their cases and complain of the lethargic gun business. "I should be entitled to a larger discount," reasoned a Boston dealer, "than parties who order but a few of [the revolvers], and not as I sell them." Demand was not so great that the market could sustain Colt's prices. Like others among the gun elite, Colt tended to overestimate the market. "Cannot you reduce your prices?" a Philadelphia dealer asked. "We think if your Pistols were lower there might be more sold." Another Philadelphia dealer bluntly informed Colt that he wanted only four pistols, since "the extra discount . . . I do not consider a sufficient inducement to give larger orders; and I prefer getting just what pistols I want for present orders." The problem, said a New York dealer, was that "the profit on your goods is so small . . . there is but little encouragement to order largely." Other dealers rightly questioned whether they were getting the very best discounts from Colt and Winchester. "You will be kind enough to let us know," wrote one to Colt, "if the prices that you charge us are as low as you sell to others."[34]

Winchester had what appears in hindsight an ingenious if counterintuitive gun marketing strategy. While he coveted US government contracts, he realized that there was potentially more to gain in selling guns to individuals through dealers rather than in bulk to larger entities. He needed a high volume of sales, but, absent government contracts—surely the most elegant solution to the volume problem—he preferred that orders accumulate through small sales on a dispersed market. "We must advise against any efforts to sell to clubs at present," he wrote to an Indiana dealer, "unless small ones of ten or so. . . . We decline all large orders and give the preference to small ones, for the express purpose of *scattering our guns as much as possible*" (italics added). To another retailer, he likewise advised, "Do not sell to clubs if you can take single orders," and to a lieutenant colonel he explained that he had declined "most orders for three hundred to a thousand" because, given the company's limited production, it could only fulfill them by "cutting off smaller quantities" that would be more beneficial in terms of promotion and sales. The strategy was attuned preternaturally to the civilian, commercial gun market—which was more about individuals than about governments, units, regiments, or clubs. It would prove crucial to sales years later.[35]

FOR NOW, IT SEEMED THAT WINCHESTER HAD OVERREACHED. BETWEEN 1857 and 1858, his company produced about 3,200 flawed Volcanic repeaters, because they had "no way but to finish up those we had commenced." To do otherwise, Winchester explained, "would have been a total loss," although it was close to a total loss, anyway. Most of the 3,200 repeaters collected dust for many decades until they were placed on planks laid over sawhorses at the company's employee entrance and sold for fifty cents apiece.[36]

With newfangled machinery churning out near-useless guns, the New Haven Arms Company lumbered heavily in the red, and Winchester continued to bail it out by loaning it more and more capital, as an individual, to keep it afloat as a corporation. Even his feistiness for the enterprise faltered. Winchester contemplated abandoning the whole project. "I have repeatedly offered to give all of my stock to other stockholders, if they would reimburse my advances," he explained, as it would "relieve me from my responsibility for the Company, which covers its whole indebtedness." Unsurprisingly, the offer didn't tempt investors, and Winchester continued to carry the weight of what must have seemed a costly phantasm of a perfectly-functioning, multi-firing gun and a gun-loving country and world hungry for as many as he could produce.[37]

It looked like the foray into mass-producing guns would end in bankruptcy for Winchester, as it had for other players in the business. This had been Samuel Colt's fate with the Paterson company in 1842, it had been the fate of the Wesson Rifle Company in 1849, and it might have been Remington's fate, had he not diversified to non-gun production at perilous moments of peace. Neither the gun market nor industrial production had proven to be as seamless as they'd imagined it.[38]

The bad luck continued in 1860. In order to raise desperately needed operating capital for his company, Winchester contracted to produce 3,000 revolvers for Cyrus Manville of New York. Unfortunately for him, the revolvers never found their way into circulation. "We calculated to clear some eight thousand upon the sale," Winchester lamented, but when the pistols were finished, Manville "failed to respond," and "we now have them on hand, and the capital they cost locked up in a lawsuit" against him.[39]

As the company produced defective weapons, Winchester did have the consolation of time and experience to perfect certain improvements on the repeater—and patent them. The new design features "obviated the objections to the old arms." Winchester convinced his board of directors to drop the Volcanic line and cast the company's fate with the Henry rifle and cartridge. He enlisted Benjamin Tyler Henry to resolve two problems with the repeater: one with the cartridge, the other with the bolt and firing pin mechanics. Winchester continued to advance large funds to the New Haven Arms Company, became a cosigner for its debts, and took over Henry's house mortgage to ensure his loyalty until he could solve the mechanical riddle.[40]

That would take three years.

At the end of that time, Winchester wrote, they finally and truly had "made a perfect thing as applied to a rifle." The Henry was an "utterly revolutionary" weapon, according to a military scholar. Other gun experts have called it a "winner to begin with" and the most "technically advanced" gun to emerge in the Civil War years. It was streamlined, with a magazine beneath the barrel that had the huge capacity of fifteen rounds. The shooter did not have to manually cock the hammer, which increased its killing speed. Winchester called the Henry the "coming gun"; it was endowed with lethal "simplicity" and "not at all liable to derangement," a reviewer said in praising it. Winchester saw Henrys as "peculiarly adopted for cavalry and for picket and scouting purposes, and very efficient for all infantry uses. . . . They will put twice as many balls in a target of any given size and distance as any other rifle in a given time, which we consider the true test of the advantage of Accuracy and Rapidity combined." In one of Winchester's advertising circulars, the rifle appears alone. No one holds the weapon. It floats, elegant and mechanically pristine. Perfect.[41]

To earn his patent, Henry had to carefully illustrate his improvements. The rifle doesn't appear in its entirety, but in sixteen fractions. Out of context, they are boxes, cones, and triangles on the page. When the pieces were assembled, the rifle worked like this: The magazine sat below the barrel. A spring forced the cartridges toward the breech, so that there was always a cartridge ready to fire. By "means of a mechanical arrangement," a reviewer explained, the breech was opened, the old cartridge extracted, and the rifle cocked. The fresh cartridge was forced into position once the trigger guard was brought back to its original position—all in one motion, and with a horrible delicacy. Henry's painstaking work had created an invisible hand to simulate the shooter's hand. The lever action freed the shooter from having to load and reload. A reviewer marveled that "in much less time than I have taken to describe the process . . . the whole contents of the chamber might be discharged by even an inexperienced [shooter]."[42]

Self-acting machines had created self-acting rifles.

THE 1860 VOLUME OF SCIENTIFIC AMERICAN, A PROUD "CELEBRANT of the machine," included a back-pages advertising section. In this cluttered emporium capitalists with money and mechanics with ideas found each other. An agent advertised the territorial patent rights for "Fox's 'Excelsior' Cracker Machine," in full operation at a New York bakery, that was "doing the work of 90 men, with only 10 operatives employed!!" Five thousand agents were wanted to sell "five new inventions—all very recent, and of great value to families." An advertiser hawked an "improved jouval turbine water wheel" to move machines. Portable steam engines, stationary steam engines, and a *Steam for the Millions* pamphlet promised to bring steam malingerers into the quickening industrial mainstream.[43]

In this context of fertile and eclectic invention, a fearsome new gun rubbed elbows with the cracker machine, a combination smoothing iron and lamp, an improved threshing machine, and improvements on hay elevating forks. On October 16, 1860, inventor B. Tyler Henry was granted US Patent #30,446 for a "magazine fire arm," which he assigned immediately to the New Haven Arms Company and its principal stockholder, Oliver F. Winchester.[44]

Winchester had already been heavily ensnared in arms production for five dramatically unprofitable years. "Too much exhausted" by the follies with the Volcanic repeater, he explained, the company would postpone manufacture of the patented Henry rifle until early 1861. When 1861 arrived, it began to make the tools and fixtures that would mass-produce the rifle itself.[45]

Winchester wasn't inclined toward coyness, and he outlined the company's affairs bluntly to investors. "From the commencement of our organization, there has not been a month in which our expenditures have not exceeded our receipts," he wrote to E. B. Martin, a timid stockholder eager to dump his shares. "Consequently we have accumulated a very large indebtedness"—almost all of it to Winchester personally. He had loaned the New Haven Arms Company $22,000 (the economic status equivalent of $6,730,000 today, or a standard of living equivalent to $534,000); the company owed one bank $36,687, and another $10,000; it owed inventor and superintendent Benjamin Tyler Henry $2,500; and it had borrowed from stockholders other than Winchester another $6,250, for a total debt of $77, 437 (the economic status equivalent of $23,700,000 today).[46]

In characteristically unsparing language, Winchester spelled out Martin's options for him: "The assets [of the company] cannot be sold for enough to pay its indebtedness," he explained. "So much for the present value of the stock—which, you will see, is nothing."[47]

Still, Winchester did not really believe this. What was a share, except a kind of invented property, like a patent, with invented value, based on what people decided to see, and believe? He emended: "The stock, however, has a value, but it is entirely prospective. It arises from the fact that our new rifle is a success [mechanically], and will, in time, if pressed with vigor, retrieve our past losses."[48]

"Press with vigor" understated the matter. Having solved a mechanical problem of how, Winchester needed to crack a riddle of why. Just as crucial as the mechanical invention of a mass-produced repeater was the invention of a world in which it would be mass-purchased. Winchester asked Martin to take a leap of faith and support the company through a loan. "There has been but one sale of the stock, to my knowledge, and this was made recently upon this prospective value, at 25 cents on the dollar. . . . We should prefer to have you hold on, and help us. If you sell, however, it will help us indirectly, as the parties offering to buy do so with the purpose of seeing the thing through, if money will do it." As for himself, Winchester had reached a point of no return. He was seeing the thing through.[49]

CHAPTER 4

"MORE WONDERFUL THAN PRACTICAL"

Before it killed the gun industrialists (or many of them), the Civil War saved them. The New Haven Arms Company was tottering on bankruptcy, again, before the war. Remington's company had converted much of its manufactory to non-gun items during the comparatively halcyon 1850s: had the war not intervened, the company might well have failed. The war created the demand that gun capitalists desperately sought—and then abruptly withdrew it at war's end, while also leaving thousands of surplus rifles drifting through the country in its wake to depress commercial demand. All of this revealed the inherent pitfalls for the gun industrialist of construing the gun business as the war business.[1]

Abolitionist and famous clergyman Henry Ward Beecher animated the rifle, nicknamed a "Beecher Bible," with a "truly moral agency," giving it a reputation as the righteous instrument of a just war. Otherwise, he preached, you might as well "read the Bible to buffaloes" as try to persuade slaveholders to change their views. Winchester described himself and his outfit as "unconditional unionmen in every sense," refusing to sell to southern sympathizers, although Confederates acquired Henrys through indirect sales and thefts. Remington was a pacifist: he agonized over the drift toward war, and his worries were exacerbated by his foreboding about the war's burden on his manu-factory. Among the gun-industrial elite, however, it was Samuel Colt who perhaps best epitomized the American gun industry's future as it moved even more decisively from a government phase to the non-exceptionalism of the commercial phase, in which gun sales, especially internationally, were untethered to belief, creed, politics, patriotism, or partisan agendas. For Colt, according to a biographer, "making and selling munitions was a business like any other"; and as Colt himself put it, guns were just something to "get out and sell." Although Colt was not a southern sympathizer, he "was busy shipping arms to the South up to the last possible moment" in crates vaguely marked "Hard-ware." Writing to his superintendents on the brink of war, Colt said, "Run the Armory night & day with a double set of hands. Make hay while the sun shines." Amos Colt, a company representative, departed from Washington, DC, in early January 1860 to go to Richmond, Vir-ginia, and "thence to North and South Carolina, Georgia, Alabama, Louisiana, Mississippi, Arkansas, and Tennessee" to sell Colt's guns. About a year later, the *Sunny South*, a newspaper in Aberdeen, Missis-sippi, featured an ad for Colt's Patent Firearms at "GREAT REDUC-TION IN PRICE," in "packages of 5, 10, and 20 each."[2]

Colt's letters detail his interest in establishing a gun factory in Rich-mond or elsewhere in the South. Toward the end of 1859, he dis-patched his loyal representative William Hartley to Richmond to "convince them that we will do everything in our power to carry out [the governor's] designs, whether it is by creating a manufactory of arms . . . at Richmond or employing my armory here in his service." With the Virginia governor, Hartley surveyed the state armory and the adjoining penitentiary and grounds to estimate the costs for Colt to equip the place to make 5,000 rifles a year. The site had enormous wa-ter power, and Hartley surmised that the land would "increasing[ly] be of great value." He proposed that Virginia sell the old state armory to a company to be "incorporated with a capital of $500,000 to $1,000,000" at the site's present value of $150,000 or $200,000. The availability of "penitentiary labor of 200 men and the fine granite found here," he wrote, would make it possible to build a "fine arsenal" that was more easily defended than the current installation.[3]

Hartley reckoned that the company's stock could be sold in Virginia, and that a gun factory would get a good "southern trade." He was willing to "head the list with a subscription of say 9/16th of the stock." Hartley followed up in January 1860 to say that there was a "great deal to be made out of the armory at Richmond. . . . You may look upon it as settled fact that they will erect and put in operation an armory in Richmond which will command the support of the southern states for their military arms." Hartley qualified this statement, saying that the arms could be made elsewhere and simply "assembled and marked" at the Virginia location. He estimated that "a cheap rifle should be made for the militia at 10 to 15 each." Colt also sent a gift pistol to the Georgia governor's son, as he was considering the establishment of an armory there. "I have no doubt that the understanding would result in mutual profit," he concluded, "to my state and yourself."[4]

The *New York Times* accused Colt of treason on the eve of the Civil War, noting that he was "incessantly occupied" in making arms for the South, an effort he made "no attempt to conceal." The *New York Daily Tribune* decried him as a "traitor," a man "base enough to sell arms" that would be turned against him. The paper proposed that "so bad a citizen," who would not work for a "fair share equivalent for the government" (instead abiding by the commercial muse and getting as much money as he could from whomever he could), should have his factory seized. Domestic peace eclipsed the tense antinomy of commerce and commonweal, but it was always there, waiting to be seen.[5]

Meanwhile, the Union was undergunned, having not tooled up in 1861 for a protracted war. "We must have arms—any arms, no matter what," wrote officer John Fremont, in command of the Department of the West, immediately after Bull Run. Rifle fluency was not much better. Historians of militia culture and gun experts have noted that militias were "virtually untrained," with activities limited by law to one-day musters, and sometimes even these were "devoted to getting drunk together." The North anxiously looked to the small community of hobbyists, many of them of German and Swiss descent, for instruction in rifle use.[6]

Europe was a forgotten commercial frontline in the early Civil War. Marcellus Hartley, who would cross paths with Winchester and the WRAC several times, is recognized by gun experts as perhaps the most ingenious of American arms entrepreneurs. In 1854 he was just establishing his own shop on Maiden Lane, in lower Manhattan. Hartley was the eldest son of a religious man who was inspired to battle the vice and suffering that he saw around him in New York City. His most important work was an "Essay on Milk," against the "evil conditions" of milk production. Growing up in the glow of moral zealotry, Marcellus pivoted to commercial agnosticism. Beginning as a clerk with "no connections or capital," he learned a great deal about guns. But, like gunmakers who happily made other things, Hartley would sell whatever he could sell. On a trip to Europe, knowing that coral ornaments were in demand in the United States, he cornered the market on coral in southern Europe; on another trip, to Florence, Italy, a display of copies of the old masters intrigued him, so he bought the entire stock, filled a small vessel with his new cargo, and sold all of the paintings in the American West and South for a good profit. But guns interested him the most, and in the 1850s Hartley began taking trips out West, according to his memoirist, "for the purpose of creating a market for his wares."[7]

The secretary of war gave Hartley's partner, Jacob Schuyler, a secret assignment in July 1861 to buy guns in Europe "on the very lowest terms compatible with the earliest possible delivery." Two months after that, he reiterated loudly "the URGENT NECESSITY . . . for the IMMEDIATE delivery of all the arms" he could buy. Next, Hartley was dispatched to buy guns. He reported that Europe was crawling with southern agents, and they were purchasing generously and covertly shipping arms to the United States via Nassau in the Bahamas. Hartley worried that they would "clean the market out," but if he could corner the market, the South, with no means to produce its own guns, would have to "succumb." He succeeded in controlling almost all gun production on the Continent in 1862, purchasing over 200,000 stand of

arms, while also tracking down and undermining Confederate contracts by offering "unscrupulous manufacturers" somewhat higher
prices to break their existing contracts and sell to the Union instead.
Years later, Hartley rued these tactics: most members of the gun elite
were fastidious about the trees of contractual ethics, if not the forest of
their gun enterprise.[8]

Winchester had always envisioned his rifle as a military weapon, and
with guns in short supply, the government tantalized him with the prospect of a guaranteed market. He provided the Ordnance Department
with his Henry in 1861. Colonel George Talcott in the department rejected breech-loading weapons. To the secretary of war, he wrote, "There
are now Colts, Jenks [the Remington design], Hubbels, Nuttings—and I
know not how many other kinds of arms—that they will ultimately all
pass into oblivion cannot be doubted."[9]

General James Ripley of the Ordnance Department especially
loathed the patented repeater guns, although he endorsed single-shot
breech-loaders. He called the repeaters a "great evil" and believed they
were a fad. In an 1862 congressional investigation of the nebulous
means by which small arms contracts were granted, Ripley elaborated
disdainfully that each of the "vast variety of new inventions [has], of
course, its advocates, insisting upon the superiority of his favorite
arm, . . . and urging its adoption." The doors of the Ordnance Department had been slammed shut on gun inventor Christopher Spencer,
who decried Ripley as "the fossil of the Ordnance Department" who
was irrationally opposed to all "newfangled Jim Crack" guns. They had
been slammed on Winchester, too, who raged against the "immobility
of prejudice" toward his repeater, and protested in a letter to his favorite journal, *Scientific American*, under the name "O.F.W.," that "General Ripley . . . has recently said that he prefers the old flintlock musket
to any of the modern, improved firearms." The only reason, "or excuse," given for his opinion, he continued, was that the arms would
waste ammunition. "The saving of life does not appear an element
worthy of consideration," Winchester said. He accused Ripley, not in-
accurately, of being a gun fogey. "Where is the military genius to grasp
[the repeater rifle]," he fumed elsewhere, "and . . . best develop the

capacities of this terrible engine, the exclusive control of which would enable any government . . . to rule the world?"[10]

That military genius was not Ripley. And, in fairness, other tacticians worldwide also failed to understand the advances that had been made. One confessed on the pages of the influential *Field* magazine in Britain that "this most murderous weapon" puzzled him. And in advance of the illustrious Swiss munitions trials just after the Civil War, an international showcase for the exhibition (and sale) of new gun models, the Henry was much spoken of, but it was seen as both too delicate and too deadly, "more wonderful than practical."[11]

Ripley loathed the new semiautomatic weapons for several reasons. He thought them too complicated, too heavy, and too costly in comparison to the entirely adequate and lighter single-shot breech-loaders, and apt to waste ammunition. This last objection was a source of ridicule in the halls of the Winchester company decades later, when resistance to faster and more automatic assault weapons that "used too much ammunition" seemed "odd" and quaintly preposterous.[12]

Some of Ripley's resistance was more heatedly personal. He hated the inventors of the new repeater guns as much as he hated the guns themselves. He commented, accurately, that their inventions "owe many of their modifications and much of their successful working to the ingenuity and skill of the mechanics in government employ, for which the inventor obtains all the compensation and lays claim to all the credit." It must have been even more galling to see how Colt, especially, had described himself as a "poor devil of an inventor," a tenaciously abject figure of individual brilliance, when what he accomplished by way of invention owed so much to the freewheeling exchange of innovation about guns in the public armory system—and to what could arguably be described as his own poaching of earlier revolver designs from shop windows in Calcutta, and from those whom a lawyer in a Colt patent case had dismissed as "obscure men in obscure places." It is precisely the dense, tangled threads of gun technology and ideas that the narrative of the Lone Inventor, parallel to the Lone Gunman, obscures.[13]

Ripley stood at the juncture of the military-centric gun culture of the early 1800s and the civilian-centric one of the late 1800s. In a broader sense, he loathed the patented guns because he did not seem to "vision" the new realities of the gun as an industry and a commercial business. He did not understand the new guns themselves—he insisted, for example, that they should have bayonets, when, as Winchester countered, "we do not consider it necessary for the reason that a body of men armed with the rifles would never get within forty rods of any enemy." But also he didn't understand the soul of the gun capitalist. Some were partisan, but their business was not, and followed its own commercial algorithm. Ripley wrote that the "many people urgent and clamorous" for gun contracts, with their eclectic "propositions to sell new and untried arms," were introducing a heterogeneity that undermined the uniformity of arms that defined the military and the idea of a soldier as part of a cohesive troop. But it was only by new-fangled design—the glint of originality patentable into a piece of property—that the business now survived. John Gallagher and Company was incredulous that Ripley reserved the right to annul its entire contract for 20,000 rifle muskets if the order was late. Military contracts generically stipulate a hard deadline for delivery, more exacting technical tests and measurements, and definite, usually large, quantities. Ripley believed that armaments were valuable if delivered on time, to support a military mission, but this idea chafed against "capital," as Gallagher explained: the gun industrialist's expenses and risks were frontloaded, and such a clause would deter "the outlay of from one to two hundred thousand dollars, which capitalists are supposed to embark with us." When Ripley refused to remove the clause, Gallagher tried again to explain industrial capitalism. The clause "embarrasses" us, he wrote, as the gun industrialists could suffer "loss of both capital and labor" if it was enforced.[14]

The gun industry and government, with their respective directives of commerce and common defense, were put in the awkward position of being codependent but irreconcilable. For example, Winchester tended to imagine military trials to test new weapons largely as occasions for the government to give advice to private gun capitalists and manufacturers on how they could "perfect weapons of self-defense," as Winchester called them, but the government used trials to make more practical, limited decisions about purchases and contracts. The interests of Winchester's bottom line and the requirements of public defense were not always the same, or in harmony.[15]

The shimmering military market that should have been so easy for the modern repeaters would have to be approached stealthily. After butting heads with Ripley, the gun manufacturer could appeal to political allies and collaborators. This meant getting a "reachable" politician, of whom there were plenty, and working the gun frontier of Washington's Willard and National hotels, where gun lobbyists and capitalists congregated. Patronage and bribery were ordinary facets of conducting any business and politics at the time. Gun lobbyists in the late 1900s and early 2000s are most identified with legislative campaigns against gun control, but there was no federal legislation in the mid- and late 1800s for the gun capitalist, or his lobbyist, to worry about. Instead, the first generation of gun lobbyists went about the business of business: they worked to secure federal government contracts and, in Colt's case, argued for invaluable patent extensions that would all but ensure gun market domination.[16]

In 1854, Congress had held hearings on whether Colt had bribed members of Congress or used other "illegal or improper means" to obtain the plum prize of a seven-year patent extension. Ultimately, the committee was divided on Colt's guilt, but the hearings are useful for what they reveal about the banally crooked practices of the gun business. Colt had lobbied with his usual ingenuous audacity. He wrote to a General Kingman, "I send by express today a half dozen boxes of champagne . . . with the compliments of the season and the cause of Patent Extension." David Augustus Wright of the *New York Day Book*, a weekly paper, testified that there had been a "good deal of gossip around the hotels" in Washington. On the piazza of the National, Wright chatted with Colt's brother, who said that Colt must have spent over $60,000 on "feasts, presents, etc.," to secure the patent. On another occasion, the Honorable G. Dean excused himself from Wright's room at the hotel, saying that he had to go down to one of the nightly suppers of persuasion hosted by Colt's devoted lawyer, Edward Dickerson. When he returned, he told Wright that a "dead set [i.e., a strong sell] had been made at him to go for the renewal of Colt's patent." An unidentified lady next to him at the table had promoted Colt's cause because Colt had sent her two boxes of kid gloves from Paris. Others testified that one of Colt's opponents had made this or that congressman a large offer to help defeat the Colt extension. Dickerson had to pay off Horace Day, who controlled a group of "low letter writers" who were threatening to slander the Colt patent extension in the newspapers. Day chided Dickerson that he "was a fool not to have bought up all the correspondents at a thousand dollars a head for the purpose of writing the matter up"—presumably the going rate for DC journalists.[17]

On this frontier, Christopher Spencer had a substantial lead on his chief repeater rifle rival, Winchester. The secretary of the navy, Gideon Welles, wrote to Commodore John Dahlgren in 1861 saying that he would consider his attention to the Spencer rifle a "special favor" on behalf of his "special friend," silk manufacturer Charles Cheney, who was financing it. When the navy order was too small to justify an extensive retooling, Cheney and Spencer hired a lobbyist, Robert Denny, who worked out of the Willard to promote the rifle. A Spencer biographer thinks it most likely that James Blaine, Speaker of the House of Representatives, and possibly Welles were unpublished stockholders in the Spencer company, but this was never proven, and their confidential dealings never revealed whether this was true. Indisputably, however, Welles and Cheney had a close friendship, and Secretary of War Simon Cameron was reachable, to say the least, according to a gun historian. His cronies obtained and then resold gun contracts without competitive bidding.[18]

Spencer next took his case to President Abraham Lincoln, who was more broad-minded about the new patented guns, but disappointed in the Spencer. Spencer's repeater rifle had gotten "so out of order as to have been entirely useless in battle," Lincoln thought. Word of Lincoln's displeasure reached Spencer, who traveled to Washington on August 18, 1863, to demonstrate the rifle to the president personally. He arrived at the White House with rifle in hand and was ushered right in—with remarkable nonchalance—to the president's inner chambers.

Lincoln looked it over carefully and asked Spencer to take it apart, as he wanted to see "the inwardness of the thing." The next day, Lincoln and Spencer went to the spot where the Washington Monument now stands, with Lincoln's son Robert and his secretary, John Hay, to set up an impromptu shooting range. Lincoln did well with the target, hitting close around the bull's-eye. Hay, whose shooting that day was "lamentably bad," recalled Spencer, in the style of the day, as a "quiet little Yankee who sold himself in relentless slavery to his idea for six weary years before it was perfect." With such powerful allies, Ripley was overruled and an initial 10,000 Spencers were ordered by the Ordnance Department.[19]

Winchester worked the Willard, too, but not with Spencer's success. Despite good reports on the Henry from navy tests, and shipments of complimentary rifles to influential military officers bivouacked at the hotels, Winchester had no contract. He finally received a very modest one through Colonel Lafayette Baker, a well-connected, mysterious, self-impressed figure with a vivid imagination and a penchant for grandiosity. Baker might have been a claim jumper in the gold rush, but by the outbreak of the Civil War he had achieved an influential position in Washington as the leader of spy-detectives against the Confederacy. Later he became the provost marshal of Washington, DC.[20]

Time obscured the lobbying, cronyism, kickbacks, bribes, and dumb serendipity that defined the US military gun market. The gun industry in the 1900s found it good advertisement to point to arms contracts in the 1800s as certification of the quality of their guns, not their connections. "The selection of a fire arm by a government," Colt's company advertised, "is never based upon sentiment"—only on the arm's objective reliability and quality, and rigorous tests of the same. In another it assured, "You make no mistake, when you follow the government's example."[21]

———

WINCHESTER'S DREAM OF LARGE-VOLUME MILITARY SALES FADED early. Military indifference, if not hostility, drove him deeper into the arms of the civilian or paramilitary commercial market, out of necessity if not preference.

If the army would not come to the newfangled guns, then the guns would go to the battlefield tents. First-generation gun capitalists were peripatetic—roaming the country in search of their markets. Spencer journeyed with rifle samples and ammunition to the frontlines of Murfreesboro, Tennessee, in February 1863. He kept a meticulous account of his frugal journey by horseback and train. He skipped breakfast, allocated fifty cents for lunch, and spent a dollar a night for a sleeping car. In the way that myths attach to American guns like tarpaper, Spencer recalled of his journey, years later, that he had dined with a Nashville woman after the Battle of Stone's River, and although his rifle was "dealing death to the innocent boys of the South," she bore him no animosity, only "wish[ed] that I had never been the cause of the invention." His biographer pointed out that he left Tennessee months, not days, after this battle, and that no Spencers had yet been used in combat, so his hostess most likely had no particular idea who he was, how his gun worked, or how many southern men it could kill. Curiously, in his recollection, Spencer interjected a voice of conscience against himself.[22]

For Winchester, the infamous "dark and bloody ground" of Kentucky beckoned. It was a state of divided loyalties on the near frontier, gripped by fear and danger, and in need of guns. Winchester made a pilgrimage there in 1863. Essentially, Kentucky was a paramilitary market, a place where civilians might be called upon to act as soldiers in personal self-defense against raiding Confederate rebels. The ideal customers in Kentucky, as Winchester envisioned them, were "substantial farmers, and good men," who "design to whip 'guerillas'" in defense of their homes and land, and to fight those whom Winchester chillingly described as "Indians or other varmint." This new kind of gun customer, not a soldier but a citizen-defender, was taking form in the shell of the old. He was an individual with a force of some fifty men, embattled on his home turf.[23]

Winchester had a powerful, garrulous ally in George Prentice, the pro-Union editor of the *Louisville Journal*, who was known as "The

Annihilator" of rebel interests. Winchester's traveling sales agent, William Stanton, had sold Prentice a Henry, and he extolled it in an editorial as "the most beautiful and efficient rifle we ever saw." On his pages Prentice vividly conjured a land of imperiled citizens and foreboding times. "Rebel outlaws are becoming more common in Kentucky," he said. "Guerillas are scouring different counties nightly and practicing the most atrocious outrages, . . . and . . . it is understood . . . that secret companies are on foot for a sudden and general insurrection. . . . It behooves every loyal citizen to prepare himself upon his own responsibility, with the best weapon of defense." The Henry was so perfect, he said, that there was "nothing left for inventors to do," ever, to improve guns.[24]

Stanton, working hard to cultivate the Kentucky paramilitary market, established three Winchester dealers. Each of them heavily advertised the Henry in the *Journal*. Then, Prentice decided to become a Winchester dealer himself. In the same office that housed his *Journal*, in which he touted the Henry so vigorously, he opened his own gun depot with $7,000 worth of Henry rifles (about 280). The other dealers abruptly stopped advertising in the paper, and Prentice became the sole Louisville agent for Henrys. Of the 900 Henrys produced and sold by October 1862, almost one-third had gone to Prentice. He was, single-handedly, a large chunk of Winchester's market. Confederate forces invaded Kentucky in the early fall of 1862. "Under the influence of panic"—as well as copious quantities of alcohol—Prentice then frantically sold his entire supply of Henry rifles below wholesale cost.[25]

Almost overnight, Prentice had glutted Winchester's once-brisk gun market in the region. Prentice explained that he had only wanted, patriotically, to arm Kentuckians with the very best rifles. Indirectly, he armed Confederates, too, in a state with such divided loyalties (Henry #165, for example, was hastily inscribed, "5th Tenn Cavalry"). Prentice ruined Winchester's fledgling market and infuriated other dealers, who were suddenly deprived of customers and convinced that Prentice had gotten preferential prices. Winchester was a "unionman," but commerce, not patriotism, was his prime directive. Defiant commercial agnosticism was more pronounced in Colt, but it was very much part of Winchester's character, too. He reassured an angry Indiana dealer that "there is not one [Henry] in Louisville for sale . . . nor shall we send any more to that market until we can place them in the hands that will maintain the price." Winchester promised that Prentice had indeed paid the same price for the rifles as other dealers, but said he had "fooled them away" in a silly panic. In another letter, Winchester explained that "regular dealers who do *business* for a living" could not afford to sell rifles for less than cost, however patriotic their motives. To his Ohio dealer, he promised that he would "send no more guns to Louisville until they become so hungry for them that some responsible house will guarantee to abide by the prices." He appealed to a potential dealer's "sense of justice" to maintain regular prices, "so as not to kill the goose that lays the golden egg."[26]

After having made such a mess of things, Prentice audaciously requested yet more guns in late October 1862. Winchester implored him not to sell at cut-rate prices again: "We perfectly understand that you pursued the course you did . . . from purely disinterested motives," he wrote, "but the result has proven very injurious to us . . . financially and morally." Especially financially: "You made nothing and we made but little more."[27]

Winchester was learning a nerve-wracking lesson about the martial market for guns that would further nudge him toward both civilian and foreign markets: "The demand" for guns, he found, was "very spasmodic." American gun demand is sometimes imagined today as a robust, stable line, like a steady heartbeat, but it was more the jagged arrhythmia of a cardiac arrest. The military was the most efficient source of high-volume orders, which were necessary in order to make good on the capital outlay in machines for industrial production. But the gun capitalist who relied on military markets was lashing himself to the boom and bust of war—bouts of frantic production and backlogged orders followed by potentially deadly peacetime doldrums.[28]

Even without large contracts, Winchester was finding that the Civil War itself was a series of small spasms of demand within the larger spasm of war. "Trade rather follows with the advance of our armies," he wrote to an Ohio dealer, "and is and will be most stirring near the scenes of active movements and hostilities." On October 18, 1862, Winchester's orders were "one month ahead of supply." On November 4 they were "backed up for four months." By December 1, while orders were still "far in advance of supply, . . . lately we have gained on them." Sixteen days later, however, Winchester wrote that several orders had been "countermanded"; suddenly, they were "accumulating stock so fast that we cannot take back the rifles we sold you." But that could change any day, should a major order for a regiment come through, or if the army got paid. Two weeks later he pleaded to an important dealer, John Brown, "we have refrained from reading extracts from western papers, fearing that we might find an obituary notice of you among them. . . . We write to inquire if you are alive? We otherwise cannot account for your long silences. If you 'still live' can you not tell about the rifle business?"[29]

In April 1863, the market was brisk again, with sales several months ahead of supply, and Winchester had to tell Brown, whose business had suddenly jumped, that he had no extra rifles to send him. When a customer complained that the rifle was "worthless," an emboldened Winchester responded that, given "sales several months ahead of supply," he found the accusation "annoying." The idea might well have germinated in Winchester's mind that continuity in a steady nonmilitary market would be more valuable, and more compatible with industrial production, than spasmodically plentiful volume in wartime.[30]

WINCHESTER'S EFFORTS TO BUILD A MARKET FOR RAPID-FIRE GUNS was surprisingly close in, small scale, and intimate. This is one of the more striking themes of the company's archives from the 1860s. The individual dealer was as much a gun ambassador as a merchant before national advertising closed the gap between consumer and manufacturer. The commercial gun market was small enough that one dealer could sway gun tastes and sales.

In the early 1860s, gun merchant B. Kittredge in Cincinnati had a financial investment in the Wesson rifle, and he considered the Henry a threat. Winchester appraised Kittredge as a man of "large means, great energy and pertinacity of purpose, and entirely regardless of the means he uses to attain his ends." In short, Kittredge was ruthless. Winchester explained to his loyal Ohio wholesaler John Brown that Kittredge had tried to prejudice customers against the Henry to "foist some other arm on the public" by "pointing out imaginary defects and flaws," including the gun slander that Winchester made "the meanest cartridges in the world." The thirst for gun business was such that Winchester both noticed and cared about this, and he refused to fill orders for Henrys from Kittredge. "We understand HIM," Winchester explained to Brown in November 1862. He closed his letter with a pep talk, as he often did, against poor sales. Kittredge persisted in trying to place an order, so a few days after writing to Brown, Winchester wrote directly to Kittredge: "We have reason to believe that your interest in another rifle has led you to use your influence to injure the sale of ours by means which appear to us at least unfair, if not dishonorable." Even worse, Kittredge seemed to be aiming to "monopolize sales" by offering extravagant discounts and forcing other dealers to do the same, "thus driving them out of the market." "Our purpose," Winchester admonished him, "is to guard our rifles from becoming a football in the market." And "for this purpose, we shall confine our business to fair business men who are willing to 'live and let live.'"[31]

In March 1863, Winchester dispatched Brown to buy all the Henrys already at Kittredge's store. With the rifle's serial numbers in hand, Winchester could "trace out" that a Kentucky wholesaler had sold the Henrys to a dealer in Cairo, Illinois, who then slyly sold them to Kittredge. Winchester wrote to the Kentucky dealer saying that he would rather pay the dealer a profit on the Henrys and take them back than have them used by Kittredge to corrode the rifle's good name.[32]

Thwarted, Kittredge suggested that perhaps there should be a public exhibition of the Henry and the Wesson. Winchester took the idea personally and saw the proposal as a "rather amusing, and hardly excusable" act of "egotism" on Kittredge's part. His and his rifle's honor were getting entangled (so much so that he interpreted employee errors as nothing less than acts of "faithlessness" against him). Winchester would have found it more "manly" had Kittredge simply admitted that his assessment of the Henry was wrong. But if he wanted a public competition between the Henry and the Wesson, Winchester was prepared to wager "not less than $5,000 or over $10,000" that the Henry would win. Winchester's letter seems to have put an end to the idea.[33]

Indirectly, the Ordnance Department's resistance to the Henry and other patented repeater arms encouraged a quasi-military, private arming of soldiers who bought their own Henry rifles, produced by a business that was slowly but methodically shifting its eggs from one basket to another, envisioning a future market of "scattered" guns more than military contracts. At the end of 1863, Winchester wrote to a General Alfred, 1,500 Henrys had been made and sold, "none to the government, or to any organized body," except 104 furnished to a Kentucky company of sharpshooters. Most of the other Henrys had been sold to individual officers in the army and navy, or to soldiers. Winchester usually declined orders for 300 to 1,000 rifles to continue what would prove a prescient strategy of dispersing the rifle in small numbers, but widely. "We cannot fill [large orders] in time without cutting off calls for smaller quantities which scatter the goods and are more for our benefit," he explained to Lieutenant Colonel A. C. Ellithorpe (although he made an exception in this case, since Ellithorpe, who wanted 400 rifles, was a prominent politician-soldier with valuable connections).[34]

Gifting guns to influential figures was always an important part of seducing demand and building a market. Guns sometimes had to be given away before they were bought. Colt sent a pistol to a US captain to woo the elusive US military. The captain confessed that he "felt a delicacy about accepting it, as I presume having no claim of acquaintance or friendship, or services," with Colt whatsoever. Ultimately, however, he chose to accept it, and hoped that it was in his power at some future time to repay the favor "in any way that I can *legitimately* serve you" (italics added). But in 1862, gifts were a marketing luxury Winchester could ill afford. As he explained to a Judge Williams of Mayfield, who was enlisted to sell his guns in Kentucky, "our profits do not allow us to be as liberal as we could wish in the way of presents; notwithstanding, when judiciously made, they are good investments." So in this case he agreed to add one gift gun to every 100 that the judge

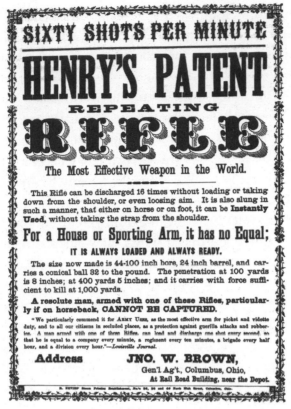

Early Henry's Rifle ad. *Courtesy of the Buffalo Bill Center of the West.*

ordered, "to be used as presents, as in your discretion it may seem best" to stimulate demand.[35]

By the end of the war, the majority of the 8,500 Henrys used in the conflict had been purchased privately, compared to the 106,667 Spencers mostly purchased through the government. What seemed like Winchester's gun misfortune during the war—his small orders to individuals, his focus on "guerillas" and citizens, his finesse with advertisement and marketing (which did not go unnoticed by rival firms), and his cultivation of a vexatious, dispersed group of dealers who could "scatter" his guns far and wide—would prove his good fortune afterward.[36]

For the gun capitalist, the Civil War (or any other war) was a peculiar new thing: an advertisement. Winchester aggressively sought "narrative," as he called it, from the (comparatively few) officers who were
using Henrys. He wrote to the chaplain of the 12th Kentucky Cavalry,
which he had furnished with Henry rifles, saying he had "heard that
some very remarkable feats [had] been accomplished with them by
the brave men of your Regiment." He implored that the reverend write
"an authentic narrative" of "these stirring events as a just tribute to
courage"—and, of course, as valuable advertisement for his gun's
"power and efficiency."[37]

In the 1850s, Colt's had benefited from a fabular account of a mirac-
ulously efficient weapon that inspired sales-quickening awe in those
who heard it. A Lesghian chief in the Caucasus armed with a Colt's
revolver had slain several Russians, an English newspaper had said,
and the Russians thought him "the prince of darkness himself, out on a
sporting expedition for the express purpose of bagging Russian soldiers" with his magical "Devil's Pistol." Winchester's equivalent came
with a thrilling story of a battle in southern Kentucky between a band
of seven mounted guerrillas under "Tinker Dave's" leadership, and one
man sympathetic to the federal government and armed with just one
Henry rifle. James Wilson, the Unionist, was known to have a large
amount of money in his house, which attracted the attention of the
marauding, disloyal thieves.[38]

One morning, while Wilson's family sat at breakfast, the outlaws
suddenly approached. Wilson seized his money box and his Henry rifle
and stashed them outside. Then he returned to the table as the members of the gang began shooting their pistols. One shot "struck a glass
of water his wife was raising to her lips, breaking the glass," a Kentucky
newspaper reported. Wilson sprang to his feet and declared, "For God's
sake gentlemen, if you wish to murder me, do not do it at my own table
in the presence of my family!"[39]

In a fateful concession to honor, the gang consented to kill Wilson
outdoors. As soon as he reached his front door, Wilson sprang into action, running for cover—and his Henry. Several shots passed through
his hat as he ran. Wilson managed to kill five of the marauders in five

inexplicably quick shots. The other two, understandably, lunged for their horses, but the sixth shot took off the fingers of the sixth man's hand. The seventh shot killed him. With just one rifle and no help, Wilson, the "plucky defender," had killed seven (or eight . . . or nine . . .) of the gang, and had wounded others, sending Tinker Dave into a hasty, frightened retreat.[40]

Although the story appeared to come out of nowhere—an authentic, spontaneous account of the Henry's perfection—it was first published in Prentice's newspaper. On December 30, 1862, Winchester wrote to Prentice that he had "heard some marvelous stories in connection with the name Capt. J. Wilson of the 22nd Kentucky cavalry." Winchester admitted that he did not have "full confidence in their accuracy." The same day he wrote directly to Wilson: "I have heard a detailed and thrilling account of your adventures with Guerillas, in which your coolness and courage were conspicuous, aided by a skillful use of Henry's Rifle. I do not know how true the account is," he conceded, "but feel a great interest in obtaining a reliable statement." None was forthcoming. In March 1863, Winchester replied to a letter Wilson had sent him to complain about a glitch in the Henry's breech pin. "In your letter you omit to give me the particulars of your encounter with the 7 Guerillas," Winchester implored. "I presume the omission arose from a disinclination to repeat your own exploit," rather than, perhaps, that the incident never happened as told. "But incidents of this kind make up the romance of war," he argued, "and should be preserved." Winchester promised to rewrite the incident in the second or third person, to preserve Wilson's modesty in not wanting to boast.[41]

He never received a statement of the facts, or a confirmation, but the story was too tantalizing to relinquish. Once it was printed in the Winchester dealer-editor's paper, "naturally, the account of this remarkable fight spread quickly all over the country," the *New Haven Register* reminisced, and so did demand for the Henry, "a firearm which made every man a host in himself."[42]

In the fall of 1862, Winchester was optimistic. "Our progress in the last three months has been entirely satisfactory," he wrote in a shareholder letter. "Our rifle has, during that time, acquired a high reputation in Kentucky, and other western states. We have been obliged to decline many orders; for what few our facilities enable us to make, we have finished and sold about 900 rifles, and hope to average 10 per day after this."[43]

In another letter, he complained that "there are few in this neighborhood [New England] who have tested the rifle" or "know even of the existence of the weapon." Indeed, the Henry gun customer identified by Winchester would have been almost unintelligible in a New England of steady character and temperament. "Yet the border states" were now giving him more orders than he could handle. Confederates were bewailing the Henry as "that damned Yankee rifle that can be loaded on Sunday and fired all week." Winchester said, "We must creep a little longer. By and by we hope to walk and then we shall soon be in a position to drive."[44]

———

FORTUNES WERE CHANGING IN THE PRIVATE WORLD OF THE Winchester family as well. Oliver's only son, Will, married Sarah L. Pardee on September 30, 1862, in the shadow of the Civil War's bloodiest battle, Antietam, which had occurred thirteen days earlier.

Few records remain of Sarah's early life. We know that the Pardee women of New Haven had always been renowned as spinners, weavers, and knitters, even from the first generation. When the Pardee women gathered on winter evenings, knitting was always part of the sociability. They couldn't resist creating things, even in leisure—that momentous, first casting off, and the appearance of something out of what had been nothing more than a bundle of yarn. They were single-minded in their industrious concentration. "Wait until I knit into my needle," they would say, to stave off distraction.[45]

By the time Sarah Pardee was born in 1840, the family had accumulated a long and unblemished record of New Haven citizenship, and the women were known to be "strong, lively, and spirited." According to genealogist Aaron Pardee, "they were married and were given in marriage, but were, so far as it appears, faithful. We do not find them in the divorce courts, or in other courts. . . . They seem to have been quiet, exemplary . . . citizens." To date, the Pardee women had left no ostentatious historical footprint.[46]

Leonard Pardee, Sarah's father, ran the City Bathing House until 1847. After that he started a prosperous business as a highly skilled craftsman, a finish carpenter who produced the architectural details and woodwork embellishments that fed the Victorian design trends of the mid-1800s. The Pardee and Winchester families lived near each other on Court Street in the early 1850s, and presumably Sarah and Will had known each other. However their courtship began, Sarah would have been a suitable and impressive prospect for a rising potentate like Will. She was feted as the blue-eyed "belle of New Haven." The Pardee strain was of medium build, but Sarah, at four foot ten and just ninety-five pounds, was extremely petite and attractive. She was highly accomplished, well educated, and an avid, eclectic reader. Leonard Pardee took uncommon pride in his daughter's uncommon genius and intellectual sophistication. He boasted of Sarah's success in musical composition, the arts, mathematics, sciences, and her mastery of four languages. The Pardee family was intensely progressive; their household visitors included prominent abolitionists, freethinkers, and the controversial founder of the American Society for the Prevention of Cruelty to Animals.[47]

Despite Sarah's intellectual refinements, curiosities, and aptitudes, the canvas of a woman's life, at least prescriptively, was confining. Affluent women had two purposes by the ideology of separate spheres that animated middle-class life at the time, and in the 1860s, Sarah seemed to follow them dutifully. While husbands fought tenaciously in the sphere of the competitive economy, wives were to soften the blows and nurture the distinct sphere of the home. One wifely purpose was to tend to a husband's moral and spiritual well-being by sweetening his home life. The middle-class home—and wife—was a haven from "amoral" competitive ruthlessness. Sarah and Will might not have spent a great deal of time together, or ever shared anything about Will's business. Historians have described a "veritable abyss" that separated the worlds of husbands and wives in affluent marriages—the former were engaged in their professions and businesses, and the latter were almost "passive witness[es]" to the same; nonetheless, they shared intimately and inescapably the same fate. Sarah's other role was to have and nurture children. These were the "essentials of women's being," W. R. Greg famously wrote in his 1869 essay, "Why Are Women Redundant?" He suggested that single women be deported to Australia or to colonies with a favorable excess of men to solve the inconvenience of their existence and give them purpose.[48]

At this moment, in late 1862, as Winchester perfected his repeater rifle and Sarah and Will married, they were, all of them, locked into their fates, although they would not reveal themselves for years, even decades. It was as a captain described of his Henry-armed troop: "the boys had 'wound up' their repeaters." They were waiting only "for an opportunity to touch the magic spring" to set them into deadly and semiautomatic motion.[49]

THE REPEATER COULD CHANGE THE NATURE OF WARFARE, THE GUN business, and even the psyche of the shooter—and not everyone saw this as a positive, technological immanence. Some tacticians (as best articulated by M. M. Dragomirov, a Russian professor of military tactics, but applicable to other contexts) rejected the "fire-worshiping" idea of rifles that could shoot rapidly from a distance, because they believed, philosophically and metaphysically, that bravery won battles, not firepower. This belief, incidentally, echoed Cervantes' observation, expressed centuries earlier, that the "diabolical invention" of artillery must have sentenced its inventor to hell, as it empowered the "infamous coward" to deprive the valiant cavalier of his life, with nothing more than a "random ball" fired into the "gallant breast . . . , from whence no man can tell shot off." The Henry rifle would change not only tactics but also the psyche of the shooter and society, said critics. It would corrode bravery and even martial imagination by encouraging stealth sniper shots from behind cover, as well as a preoccupation with individual action and safety. Furthermore, it would advance individualism and independence over the collective courage, mass move-ment, and blind obedience of the troops.[50]

The repeater rifle did indeed begin to change the character and psy-che of both regiments and individuals in subtle and not-so-subtle ways. Winchester understood this. In a *Scientific American* article of 1863, he mused, not for the last time, on what he called the "moral effect" of a rapid-firing gun. Imagine being a foot soldier in battle with a muzzle-loading rifle. Encumbered with cartridge and percussion pouches, and a nine-pound rifle, you would load your weapon on a firing line, as mil-itary historian William Hallahan vividly described the scene, "while facing, amid ground-shaking roars, enemy cannon balls . . . followed by a charge of enemy infantrymen, bellowing and firing, as officers on both sides shouted orders and the wounded men cried out with pain." Another gun historian imagined the musket shooter delivering per-haps a few shots before "all were swallowed up in a vicious melee of stabbing bayonets and clubbed muskets amid the horrible, deafening screams and curses of the wounded and the dying." That soldiers en-dured this agony was due to the stigma of cowardice and the worse fate of the lash or firing squad.[51]

To be a shooter was to be a target—but the Henry made killing more remote than it had been previously. Sharpshooters could remain concealed while reloading, rather than standing to face an enemy bar-rage. And with the speed of fire, enemy troops had little chance to charge and get close to the Henry-armed soldier. A combatant re-ported that "no line of men who came within fifty yards of another force armed with the Spencer . . . can either get away alive, or reach them with a charge, as in either case they are certain to be destroyed by the terrible fire poured into their ranks." Ironically, Sarah Winchester's brother-in-law Homer Sprague described similarly the "steady stream of lead," and its "prolonged and tremendous roar"—but with reference to the Sharps repeater, not the Winchester.[52]

To be a muzzle-loading shooter was to be deliberate and slow. He had to be. Withstanding the deafening melee of battle, the soldier with a muzzle-loader would have to stand erect and exposed, pull a paper cartridge from his pouch with bullet and powder, pour the powder down the barrel, draw out a ramrod from the gun's tube, and ram the ball and powder down. Then he'd prime the gun, replace the old cap with a new one, fully cock the rifle, and fire. A skilled shooter would fire perhaps two shots a minute, but almost never achieved that mark in the heat of battle. The repeater was a revolution in speed and rapid fire. The killing got faster—from a possible two to twenty-five shots a minute—and the soldier acquired a new feeling of omnipotence.[53]

As the semiautomatic ancestor of automatic machine guns, the Henry performed "a terrible work of death," Civil War regiments reported, opening an "astonishingly rapid fire." One private with a Henry said he could fire ninety rounds so fast, without having to stop, that his barrel was too hot to touch. "I spit on it and it would sizzle," he reported. At the "army of the Tennessee's Waterloo," the last great Confederate charge at the end of 1864, 20,000 rebel infantry advanced with bands playing "Bonnie Blue Flag." They charged into Henry-armed soldiers of the 65th Indiana Infantry, Company A, and a 12th Kentucky unit armed with Colt revolving rifles. The rebel major general recalled that the Yankee line "spit out a continuously living fringe of flame," the most deadly fire he had ever witnessed. Some rebels "pulled their hats over their faces as if to shield from a storm of hail."[54]

The soldier armed with a muzzle-loader often missed his mark, even if he did not misfire. The new repeaters were not only faster but also deadlier. A Texan recalled "men staggering to the rear covered with blood," shocked by the carnage and feeling as if "the world was coming to an end then and there." The 8th Michigan Cavalry, using Spencers, inspired "terror"—a recurring description—in the rebel soldiers, who thought them "a much stronger force than we were," an officer reported. "This was the first instance during the war," he said, "where the proportion killed was greater than the wounded." The ratio of killed to wounded was three to one, owing to the repeaters.[55]

The soldier with a muzzle-loader was not so omnipotent that he could imagine himself, or act, as an individual in battle, or stand alone. He was an armed but vulnerable figure with a killing capacity limited by accuracy, speed, and gun design. Soldiers fired their muskets on command, en masse, within fifty yards of the enemy. As Winchester energetically explained to promote the Henry, his repeater magnified the power and lethality of the individual. Some tacticians worried that rifles would unleash individualist, "egotistical impulses" in a shooter. Semiautomatic repeaters made every individual, in a twenty-first-century phrase, an "army of one." The math was almost exponential, or, as the first Samuel Colt biographer described it, "geometrical." The revolver, he said, "cannot but 'demoralize' antagonists. Each fresh chamber . . . resembles a new head of the multiplying hydra." The *Louisville Journal* enthused that one man "armed with one of these rifles can load and discharge one shot every second, so that he is equal to a company every minute, a regiment every ten minutes, a brigade every half hour, and a division every hour." Reports from the battlefield praised that a command "armed with this rifle and possessed with a proper spirit to use it, could . . . defy ten times their number." Another officer, using Spencers, put the multiplying effect at five or six, and yet another estimated that a lone Henry shooter had a four-to-one advantage. During the Atlanta campaign, a swap of 2,000 Spencer-armed horsemen for 11,000 infantrymen was judged fairly equal. By its technology alone, the repeater invited and emboldened the individual, lone gunman, whether guerrilla, soldier, or civilian—and Winchester sensed this early in his gun enterprise.[56]

In terms of tactics, the Ordnance Department and others had worried that patent arms, so much faster in their action and more lethal, would corrode troop discipline with indiscriminate shooting, in contrast to the more plodding and deliberate tactics associated with single-shot rifles. Instead, Winchester retorted, his repeater allowed the shooter to hold fire, without fear of not having time to reload, and thus "make every shot count." Right after the war, still courting the military market, albeit not the American one, Winchester wrote to the British secretary of state for war to dispel objections voiced by a special committee on breech-loading and repeater rifles. "A gun is a machine made to throw balls," he wrote. "The one, then, that will throw the most in a given time, with equal accuracy and labor, everything else also being equal, must be the best gun," QED. The objection that his "fast firing" guns would waste ammunition "seems to have been based upon a vague idea that because a gun could be made with which it was possible to fire very rapidly, it was impossible not to do so, that it must be a sort of self-acting machine, uncontrollable by the human will," Winchester wrote. Instead, a soldier would have "consciousness of reserved power that keeps him cool, and self-possessed." "Time spent in loading is time lost," he firmly concluded.[57]

The Civil War did show that such discipline was possible. The soldiers of a Spencer-armed Connecticut regiment fired their repeaters for a minute or two but ceased immediately at the bugle call. At the same time, Winchester's gun was to some extent a "self-acting machine" that inflected, even if it did not dictate, the psyche of the shooter. Guns would seem to move almost by teleology toward greater rapidity, faster killing power, and more indiscriminate shooting, with less ammunition held in reserve.[58]

Armed with such a fiery hot weapon, ironically, shooters became "cool men," as several commented. The obverse of "coolness," as Winchester often described the repeater-armed man, was terror at the other end of the barrel. Ohio governor John Brough fantasized in 1864 that thousands of "Henry-armed pro-Southern draft dodgers" would rise up against him. In the grips of Henry terror he frantically telegraphed the US secretary of war, Edwin Stanton, to get him to halt the sale of Henrys in Ohio (since the government had not contracted for Henrys, however, Stanton could not control their distribution). The repeater soldier had newfound "feelings of invincibility," and, according to another frequent description, "confidence." One invincibly cool soldier or guerrilla could become many. In his first advertisements, some written in his own hand, Oliver Winchester introduced a Henry-owning American who lived on the wire, with precipitously changing fortunes and imminent danger. The Henry was "always loaded and always ready" to fire sixteen cartridges in a few seconds; it was the perfect "house or sporting arm," especially for "citizens in secluded places," Winchester said. It could be "'INSTANTLY USED,' with . . . force sufficient to kill," even at 1,000 yards. "A resolute man, armed with one or more of these Rifles, particularly on horseback, CANNOT BE CAPTURED."[59]

The Henry was a momentous step in a journey toward an embold-ened individual shooter capable of more automatic, rapid, and remote shooting—which as a general rule tends to make killing easier. The Henry shooter, in other words, was a distinctly modern character.[60]

AND YET THE NEW REPEATERS WERE TO THE CIVIL WAR WHAT THE American rifle was to the Revolutionary War—important, but over-estimated and scarce. Most of the Civil War fighting still occurred with ungainly muzzle-loaders. By the end of the war, however, breech-loaders had shown themselves to be the weapon of the future and consigned the muzzle-loader to the dustbin of gun history; the breech-loading repeater, specifically, had begun its ascent. During the war, Winchester had learned what must have been hard yet invaluable les-sons about the gun business. Out of the misfortune of not getting a large military contract, as we have seen, he came to appreciate instead the marketing benefits of scattering his guns as widely as possible. He had learned that the war's casualties, for the gun capitalist, provided "narrative" and could be sources of advertisement to reach individual customers. While he would continue to seek military business, Win-chester could not have helped but appreciate that reliance on war business was a "spasmodic" and jagged enterprise in terms of demand—ill-suited to the new economy of commercial industrial production, which favored a constant, steady supply and distribution. Immediately after the war, as we will see in the next chapter, he would learn yet more lessons: about first-generation corporate warfare, the price of am-bition, and the imperative that his fate, fortune, and business always remain within his family. Out of this process, the Henry rifle would fi-nally become the Winchester rifle.[61]

CHAPTER 5

MODEL 1866

WHEN HE SHOULD HAVE FELT PROSPEROUS, FETED, AND ingenious, Benjamin Tyler Henry felt bitter. Winchester had branded the rifle with an "H" as homage to the inventor, and it bore Henry's name, but Winchester hadn't been generous in the more tangible homage of money. Henry couldn't accept or perhaps comprehend how the man who had conceived the gun got less than the man who capitalized and manufactured it.

Winchester's contract system baffled Henry. Winchester executive Edwin Pugsley recalled the impressive prosperity that the few successful and skilled gun foremen like Henry could reach: "These men would drive in to work in a flashy buggy behind a fancy pair of horses," he wrote, "wearing a high hat and frock coats, put the horses in the stable, take off their finery, put on overalls and be a foreman for the ensuing ten hours, only to repeat the process at the end of the day."[1]

Henry resented the contract system all the same. He produced his rifle using machinery that Winchester owned, in the New Haven Arms Company manufactory that Winchester owned. Unlike the gunsmiths before him, Henry couldn't even claim an informal title to the gunmaking tools, since they were now manufacturing machines—not tools—which Winchester owned. Nor did Henry own his own idea. He'd converted the idea of the repeater into property when he had patented it, and he had assigned the patent to Winchester (not that he'd had any choice, because he had lacked the capital to "get up a machine" to produce it). Henry was caught between the old gun ways and the new, in which capital triumphed over craft. As a superintendent, Henry paid all of his employees, and he kept the difference between employee costs and the contract price to the company as his income. He might make around $15,000 over five years, but he was working to earn that. Winchester didn't give royalties to inventors of the patents he held, so Henry was not really making anything for having conceived the repeater rifle.[2]

Instead, the person who knew the least about the gun was profiting the most off of it. Winchester seemed to hold all the cards. Gun inventors, heirs to the gunsmiths, who knew how to make guns, were in many ways getting marginalized from the gun industry. When Henry's contract expired in 1864 and he left the New Haven Arms Company, he was bitter. Winchester simply engaged new superintendents and increased the workforce from thirty-seven to one hundred. Henry seemed to have little recourse—except that he was a stockholder in the New Haven Arms Company. The most tangible power he had lay in the most intangible leverage that he owned: his name and his stock. Henry saw his chance for justice when Oliver Winchester left in April 1865 on a long-awaited journey to Europe.

When he left on his tour, Winchester and his business partner John Davies had just retired from the shirt business and cast their lot entirely with rifles. Winchester traveled first to sun-washed Naples, and then planned to take in the Rheine Falls at Schauffhausen and the rejuvenating waters of the Baden Baden resort in Germany, a station of the cross for ambition-weary men. On his European journey, where others took in spectacular scenery, Winchester peered deeply into the guts of a rifle. He wanted to tinker with the mechanisms in the Henry magazine that had caused the rifle to clog with mud during the Civil War.[3]

Judging from his agenda, Winchester was thinking of his rifle's post–Civil War future in foreign markets. He intended to enter the Henry in the Swiss munitions trials in Zurich to create interest and sales. He made valuable personal contacts for European markets, including Baron von Nolcken, his future German agent, and the French gun dealer François de Suzanne, who brokered a deal to send 1,000 Henrys to the French forces in Mexico serving Emperor Maximilian. Suzanne shipped them via Cuba to preempt any potential US objection about the French, with Winchester as their commercial conduit, violating the Monroe Doctrine. Winchester also intended to talk with a Swiss arms maker about designing a rifle that would solve both the crankiness of the Henry repeater and the crankiness of its inventor: Winchester wanted to commission a rifle with Henry-like action but a different magazine—a magazine so different from Henry's that it would avoid patent conflicts with him. At least in part, and sometimes large part, gun designs reflected the constraints imposed by the labyrinth of existing patents.[4]

In his 1865 catalog copy, Winchester deployed his reckoning skills to tout improvements to the Henry. A gun "requiring NO TIME to load," he wrote, "would be the perfect weapon." He compared the Henry to the Spencer. The latter required "three motions, and is good for twenty shots per minute, while the Henry rifle requires but *two* motions and is good for thirty shots per minute." And, he couldn't help but parse further, the Spencer "actually requires a compound motion" that the Henry did not, "and, if so counted, it would make the difference as four to two, instead of three to two [motions]." He had thus "mathematically demonstrated the theoretical superiority of the Henry." Winchester was still looking wistfully toward the military market, and he concluded that improvements made the Henry particularly adaptive "to cavalry and infantry service" and "military men."[5]

Winchester had planned to be gone for several months, so before he set sail he assigned power of attorney for the New Haven Arms Company to its secretary, Charles Nott. Winchester hadn't been in Zurich long when he received a telegram that he must have read with stunned, infuriated disbelief. Henry and some sympathetic stockholders had made a move for control of the company. Nott was a traitor. In collaboration with Henry, he had used his power-of-attorney authority to petition the Connecticut state legislature to have the stockholders turn control over to him—and to change the name of the New Haven Arms Company to the Henry Repeating Rifle Company. Henry was trying to maneuver Winchester out of the gun business.

Winchester headed back to New Haven immediately. Then he went to war, of the bloodless corporate style. He called in all the mortgages that he and his son Will held, for immediate collection. This essentially deprived Henry of the factory—at that time located in Bridgeport, not New Haven—which crippled Henry's chance to attract capital or begin gun production. It also gave Winchester a new factory site to make an "improved" repeater that would tweak Henry's design just enough to outwit patent litigation.[6]

Next, Winchester dispatched with the company's traitorous stockholders who had followed Henry by forcing an unwanted vote on Nott's role as secretary and his own role as president. Winchester won and Nott lost, since Oliver and Will Winchester and John Davies controlled a large chunk of the stock. Winchester maintained operational control over the remains of the company, but, in July 1865, he also signed articles of association with his son Will and John Davies to establish a Winchester Arms Company.

Henry's move to strip Oliver Winchester of control of one arms factory had instead put Winchester and his family in complete, direct control of two, and laid the groundwork for a rifle empire in Winchester's name, not the inventor Henry's.

Just as Winchester had intended, the deftly gutted Henry (née New Haven) Arms Company starved. Orders, revenue, and the workforce dropped precipitously from July to December. At a stockholders' meeting on December 31, 1865, Winchester essentially offered a takeover. He would assume all the credits and liabilities of the foundering New Haven company, either by the outright purchase of its existing stock, or through an exchange of company stock for stock that he would issue for the new corporation that he would create in 1866, the Winchester Arms Company.[7]

Stockholders with only a commitment to profit and none of Henry's added incentives of personal dignity or revenge didn't have the stout hearts for this. The fact that Henry filed a breach of contract suit against Winchester in January 1866, while seemingly a bold move, only revealed to stockholders how desperate things really were for the company. Reading between the lines, the majority voted to accept Winchester's offer at their meeting on February 3, 1866.[8]

The incident must have affirmed Winchester's fierce lifelong resolve that control and leadership remain always with the family men—the only men, along with Davies, whom he could trust. On February 1, 1869, out of 4,500 shares issued, he personally held 2,040, and his immediate family owned another 450. The industrial economy was feckless. Only family and land last.[9]

Winchester decided to move the works from Bridgeport a few miles up the road to New Haven, and he laid the cornerstone for the New Haven factory that would bear his name in May 1866. He chose farmland, just north of New Haven proper that was approached by ordinary country roads, convenient to the Northampton canal, and surrounded by cow pasture. In the next few years, Winchester employees would test their rifles informally by firing randomly out of second- and third-story windows onto these pastures, occasionally killing a stray cow in the process.[10]

Gun manufactories of the 1860s were disorienting, clamorous caverns that smelled of machine oil, gas lamps, tobacco, and sweat. Great water wheels (Colt's had a one-hundred-foot circumference and ran half a mile in a minute) or coal-powered steam engines rumbled deeply; metal machines cutting metal screeched loudly. E. Remington & Sons had a steam engine with 150 horse power and a series of water wheels moved by steam, and the welding and forge rooms, where future guns underwent trials by fire and hammer, sent "the clang of [their] incessant industry throughout the village" of Ilion. Mark Twain toured Colt's factory in 1868 and found "every floor a dense wilderness of strange iron machines that stretches away into the remote distance and confusing perspective—a tangled forest of rods, bars, pulleys, wheels and all the imaginable and unimaginable forms of mechanism." Colt biographer Henry Barnard marveled at how "bewildered in wild-eyed wonder" the

Puritans would be if they could walk among the machines of Colt's colossal armory, filled with more than a thousand machines. The factory itself was a mystery, created out of "processes new, secret, or patented." Barnard also gravitated to the metaphor of a wilderness, contrasting the Puritans' natural wilds to Colt's transfiguration, so strange that it would have appeared like something conjured by Aladdin's magic lamp. Somehow, from out of Colt's "forest," Twain mused, a finished, "deadly 'Navy' [pistol]" emerged out of the other side, but it was a "confusing perspective," indeed, because the casual visitor could have no concept of how the gun got made.[11]

Around the same time, Horace Smith and Daniel Wesson formed their Fire Arms Company in Springfield, Massachusetts, as a joint stock concern, closely held by the two of them. From their new business, calved from the earlier Volcanic partnership, Smith and Wesson felt that Winchester was manufacturing under a patent for a gun design by W. C. Hicks that they controlled. They handled the matter with aplomb, writing that perhaps Winchester would like to possess their patents, and if so, they would sell them to him. Winchester threatened to take them to court, but quite cordially offered them hospitality should they have to travel to Connecticut to adjudicate the case. Smith and Wesson hoped to avoid the "annoyance of litigation"; Winchester agreed, admitting that altering tools and machinery enough to avoid patent infringement entirely would involve "no inconsiderable expense and time." Smith and Wesson contemplated placing all of their interest in the Hicks patent at Winchester's disposal for a royalty of 12½ percent—but their contemplations did not involve any conversation with Hicks himself, and they feared that it would be "no little effort on their part" to secure the inventor's consent. Those with the most intimate craft or mechanical knowledge of guns were more distant from the levers and gears of the gun industry.[12]

Where did Henry, Hicks, and Christian Sharps—who was also outraged that his patent rights had been violated by the company that bore his name—or any other gunsmith or inventor belong in the new mechanical wilderness? The American gun business had started as a craft, by gunsmiths, and had been nurtured as a fledgling industry in a quasi-public crucible, supported by US government funds and policies, but now it had moved decisively into a commercially focused phase characterized by heavy investments in machine production by private capital, legal battles over the peculiar property of patents, and fierce competition to sell the gun as an unexceptional commodity not unlike others. Benjamin Tyler Henry had the soul of a genius, not a capitalist. He had envisioned a factory that would produce the rifle he had conceived, but found himself bankrupt, without a source of capital. Instead of creating his own corporation, he had set in motion the birth of Oliver Winchester's. Decades later, Winchester, the gun's capitalist, would frequently be misremembered as the gun's inventor.[13]

Henry died in June 1898. "He had been wealthy several times," his obituary notes, and poor just as often. He left no heirs, and no will, and only the property of two patents, for a trolley car wheel and a carriage axle. "If only he had lived," the obituary concluded with inextinguishable, posthumous ambition, "he could have made and sold" both inventions, but it was not to be.[14]

———

IN THE MONTHS THAT OLIVER WINCHESTER FOUGHT FOR DOMINION over the New Haven Arms Company, Sarah Winchester became pregnant. Hers was in many ways an inauspicious, unforgiving era for motherhood. In 1866, infancy was still "a time to die," wrote one historian, and yet the resigned, providential Puritan attitude toward infant mortality had been replaced by a more exalted—or accusatory— view of the mother as the force whose devotion could keep babies healthy. Mothers were to be as self-made in their success as their male counterparts. The fledgling field of pediatrics cited fatalities caused by "the ignorance and false pride of the mothers," one doctor wrote. "Children are killed," he added, "by the manner in which they are dressed, and then by the food that is given them as much as any other cause."[15]

Annie Pardee Winchester was born on June 15, 1866. Sarah and Will remembered death when they named Annie after Will's sister, who had died three years earlier while her husband, a pastor, was serving as a missionary abroad.[16]

Annie was not a healthy baby, and she did not thrive. The impulse at first must have been what it would still be today when the most feared nightmare and the most cherished dream of motherhood collide—to normalize, and to look for the most benign, least heartbreaking explanation. Perhaps Annie would come around of her own accord, and show the effects of nourishment.

Annie had been born at the wrong time and in the wrong place. Infant deaths rose with the temperature in July and August, with the summer heat exacerbating infant maladies of the digestion and nerves and producing a badly tolerated "languor." Infants in northeastern cities got the worst of it. Some physicians attributed the summer spike in mortality to inborn frailties that were merely exacerbated by the heat; others blamed the deaths, in the judgmental tendency of the day, on inadequate nursing or careless hand-feeding—"the wicked act of luxurious and licentious" mothers, devoted to fashion over maternal duty.[17]

In the first week or two, as Annie wasted away, she would have shown uneasiness and attacks of pain, in which she would cry and suffer. Sometimes Annie might have recuperated and remained still in the intervening hours, or seemed drowsy, but other babies with stomach or intestinal disorders appeared to be in constant discomfort, with no respite from a cry that devolves from a wail to a whimper of desperation. A diligent nurse or another woman might have tested to see if Sarah or a wet nurse was producing milk by trying to draw it forth themselves. If they could get a "good mouthful," then they would know that the supply was adequate.[18]

Transformation from death to life could still be almost magically instantaneous, once nourishment was provided or adequately absorbed. Although Annie was languid and pale, and her belly distended, she could still, perhaps, survive.[19]

The summer heat enveloped the tiny world of the Winchester family home where Sarah and Annie struggled. On July 8 the thermometer climbed to almost 100 degrees, and the *New York Times* recorded more than twenty deaths from sunstroke in the urban inferno. On July

14 the deaths continued. It reached 98 degrees in Hartford on July 16. The next day New Haven grew hotter than it had been in eighty-nine years, reaching a high of almost 103. At 104 degrees, it was the hottest day ever in New York. Twenty-three more northeasterners died. It wasn't weather; it was more like a malevolent force.[20]

———————

ON JULY 7, 1866, AS HIS GRANDDAUGHTER'S HEALTH DETERIORATED, Oliver Winchester closed the books of the feeble, atrophying New Haven (Henry) Arms Company. Winchester gave the stockholders a choice: they could cash in their shares or exchange them for stock in the new Winchester company. Most chose the second option. Holders of 1,190 shares exchanged them for 2,170 newly minted shares of WRAC stock, valued at par $100. Some diffident or disgusted stockholders opted to take the cash and close out their gun folly. New Haveners commended Winchester's offer to buy their stock to a generous total of $136,500, and to give stockholders an option to stay or to sell. Winchester had starved the upstart company to death. Now he could complete its resurrection as an immortal corporation in his own name.[21]

Under a special act of the assembly, the Connecticut legislature granted Winchester a charter to incorporate the Winchester Repeating Arms Company in the summer of 1866. The WRAC was born into the status and privilege of personhood before the law. The repeater rifle would not become famous under the gunsmith or inventor's name, but in the name of its industrialist and capitalist.[22]

When New Haveners learned that Winchester's new plant "was equipped to produce 200 rifles a day," they were "aghast at the incredible folly of anyone thinking that a production of 200 guns a day could be sold. It was freely said that Mr. Winchester had entirely lost his reason and should be confined to an insane asylum; that the plant would not run more than three or four days a year and would be shut down the remaining time," to wither and die by stagnation from lack of demand. Winchester executive and informal chronicler Edwin Pugsley reflected, decades later, that it might seem laughable in retrospect, but people did not yet have the "mass consciousness" of the large numbers—or large numbers of guns—that Winchester himself helped to create.[23]

———————

ANNIE HAD GRAVE INANITION AND MALNOURISHMENT, THE catch-all condition of marasmus. We don't know what happened to her, only that this is what it looked like: the gradual and progressive withering and wasting away of the body. Few things are as horribly incongruous, or as clinically obvious, as a starving baby, the spectacle of an infant who has become a miniature old man. There were two, equally tragic, possibilities: either Annie could assimilate nourishment but wasn't receiving any, or she was receiving nourishment but couldn't assimilate it. If the latter, she might have lacked a functioning liver; she might have had twisted intestines; she might have had a metabolic affliction; she might have been infected by syphilis. Annie fell into a more ominous, resigned silence as her body unraveled into death. Debilitating weakness overcame her most basic instincts. As her body filled with bile and her stomach shut down, Annie would have had the dark, yellow-orange hue of severe jaundice.[24]

Dr. Charles Ives was thirty-five, and in his ten years in practice he had built up a considerable client list among New Haven's elite families, who preferred to be tended to by Yale men. Ives was a man of science and faith, and he was writing a book on the dynamic of the two. He might have contemplated the effect on Sarah of seeing her baby's starvation. Doctors agreed that only consumption—tuberculosis—ravaged the body as savagely as the atrophy of young children.[25]

In the last moment, Annie would have simply grown too feeble to breathe. Ives recorded marasmus as the cause of death on Annie's death certificate on Tuesday, July 24. Annie had lived for forty days in inexorable decline. It was almost as if she had been born to die. Doubtless, Sarah next began the business of grief and the intricate rituals of Victorian mourning.

Perhaps she had done something wrong; perhaps she had done absolutely nothing wrong. Perhaps she imagined culpability where none at all existed. Whatever the case, and whatever the source of Annie's marasmus, the baby had died because Sarah could not nourish, nurture, or nurse her.

In the hours after Annie's death, lethal heat produced extremely violent thunderstorms in New Haven. Then the thunderstorms gave way to ice—a freakish hailstorm that damaged crops throughout Middlesex County. This is a part of Sarah's legend—the backdrop of her tragedy—that the historical record can confirm.[26]

Sarah's was an empirical, problem-solving age, even in its habits of grief. Likely, she didn't resign herself entirely to divine will in Annie's death. She might well have assumed instead that things happened by the gearings of cause and effect. Some call it karma and others the gambler's fallacy, psychologist Stuart Vyse has explained: the belief that one random event is affected by another one, and that "the universe is founded on a . . . homeostasis"; thus, said Vyse, it is "a balance sheet view of the cosmos in which no good deed goes unrewarded, and no cruelty goes unpunished." Others know it as cosmic justice. Whatever the case, Sarah's legend holds that she had a lifelong, violent aversion to thunderstorms. Perhaps this diabolical thunderstorm had seared both a tragic moment and an accusatory, unforgettable question into her mind: What had she done, and why had this happened to her?[27]

A life, like a rifle, had hundreds of component pieces, and they all meshed together, in perfect, delicate concert, for a purpose, even if we can't see the small parts, or understand the mechanics. The pieces fit together.

———

THE SAME WEEK THAT ANNIE DIED, THE WINCHESTER REPEATING Arms Company gave birth, in the peculiar fashion of corporate bodies, to the improved rapid-fire repeater rifle. These rifles, and designs to follow, would proliferate and carry the Winchester name forward intergenerationally, whereas Sarah's womb had failed in the task, and would fail again.

WRAC superintendent Nelson King had designed the most important, and quickly patented, improvement to the Winchester repeater, known as the Model 1866—or just the Model 66: a tweaked, more rugged loading system. The WRAC 1867 catalog advertised that the design improvement achieved the coveted but rare gun conjunction of "stronger, yet lighter." With a side-loading attachment, "the whole 15 cartridges can be fired in 15 seconds," Winchester boasted, "or at the rate of sixty shots a minute, or in double-quick time, in 7½ seconds, or at a rate of . . . two shots per second." The mathematical reckoning of the gun's power (how many shots fired per second . . . per minute . . . per hour) was dizzying. An expert who kept a box of cartridges on his right hip could fire fifty shots if he used the side-loader, and began with the rifle fully loaded with its first fifteen shots—and all of this "without taking aim."[28]

The Henry was rebaptized the Winchester and rebranded with the letter "W." Winchester's stalwart partner, John Davies, traveled to New York City the first week in September, where he had heard that a crumpled Henry was likely to pursue a claim against the WRAC, but he was optimistic that it was a last-ditch, desperate move that required little comment. Davies casually toted a few of the repeater rifles along on his sojourns around New York, handing them out to acquaintances to stimulate interest. In these informal ways, patent guns diffused through the country.[29]

The first batch of 3,211 Winchester Model 66s left New Haven not for the western frontier, but by boat, on September 15, for what Winchester called the "romance of war" abroad, to a dealer in Paris. These were the first of over 8,062,000 guns, excluding substantial World War I production, that Winchester would sell by 1930.[30]

Paul Jenkins, an ex-Union soldier, also had one of the first Winchester repeaters. With it, he intruded into the heart of Blackfeet Indian territory after the Civil War to mine borax, 2,300 miles from New Haven. Blackfeet had observed that it took miners several seconds to reload their single-shot weapons, during which time they were essentially unarmed and helpless. While a few dozen surrounded the miners, the tribe would offer up one or two braves as decoy targets. Invariably, the white man would shoot the brave, stop to reload his rifle—and then find himself ambushed and easily overtaken by the entire tribe.

But not this time. Two miners in Jenkins's crew saw about forty Blackfeet creeping toward an approach in hopes of drawing fire. Armed with repeaters, the miners fired their Winchesters once. Just as they'd anticipated, the puffs of smoke from their rifles cued the entire tribe to charge, following rules of engagement that the Winchester had just rewritten. Inexplicably, though, the guns kept firing, to the baffled horror of the warriors.[31]

For emphasis, the miners riddled the corpses with bullets and arranged them "so that the survivors might . . . contemplate the fatal results of their terrible encounter with weapons that obviously appeared never to need to be reloaded at all," according to a gun expert who later wrote about the incident. After the massacre, the Blackfeet told of a terrifying weapon so supernatural that it must have come from a malevolent deity. The Blackfeet called the new Winchester rifles "spirit guns."[32]

———

IN HIS *THEORY OF MORAL SENTIMENTS*, ADAM SMITH CRITICIZED the "man of system," who believed in the visible hand of a planned economy. This was not Oliver Winchester's belief, or his world. Like Smith, he tended to his parts, and to the short view of his business at hand, and probably trusted in the anodyne economic order that would emerge spontaneously out of many millions acting on their own momentum. "In the great chess-board of human society," Smith wrote, "every single piece has a principle of motion of its own."[33]

As the first batch of Winchesters made their way from New Haven to France, and as Sarah Winchester grieved Annie hard, Elizabeth Colt was building a church in Hartford. Elizabeth was Samuel Colt's widow. She had her own principle of motion. Samuel's—and Oliver's, and Will's—stories could be told, and almost always are, without much reference to their wives. Samuel married his in 1856. On the surface, the most intimate figure in Colt's life was the most irrelevant to the story of his life's work, or to the American gun culture. When in 1998 the city of Hartford undertook an exhibition on the Colt gun industry and home, including Elizabeth's collection of memorabilia and art, organizers struggled to harmonize these two realms. Reviewers sensed their loose-jointed connections and the "complicated, divergent histories" the objects evoked.[34]

Samuel Colt's enterprise was none of Elizabeth's business, but it was her responsibility. This was true of Sarah, too, and all the gun wives. After Samuel's death in 1862, Elizabeth became the keeper and heir of Colt's legacy, and his memorialist. She carried the multifaceted inheritance of a name, a blood fortune, and a social reputation. Elizabeth was well aware of the ambivalence in his character—perhaps even in his life's work. In addition to his business and his business tactics, Colt's life contained its share of sordid mystery and murky family drama. In 1841, his brother John got into an argument over a debt with a printer and murdered the printer with a hatchet. He passed a pleasant evening before returning the next day to stuff the corpse in a container and ship it to New Orleans. Hot weather betrayed the decomposing corpse, and John was sentenced to hang for murder. Although Samuel Colt's brother had committed a strange kind of faux pas by not using a Colt to commit the murder, Samuel seized the occasion of the trial to demonstrate his revolvers in the courtroom. The day of his execution, amid the sounds of the gallows being hammered, John committed suicide. He had married his lover, Caroline, earlier in the day. The murder alone was the news sensation of the year, but the story contained more mysteries: some claimed that Caroline had borne not John's illegitimate child, but Samuel's; in any case, Samuel supported the child after John's death. This was part of what Samuel had wrought—visionary acumen, business success, and tenacity, as well as family murder, bribery, deceit, broken promises, and a world transformed by his ruthlessly elegant "implement of slaughter" and an equally ruthless—i.e., modern—approach to selling them. With all of this looming behind her, Elizabeth made it her mission to "see that the world remembered only the good," a Colt biographer later said. She crafted a triumphalist narrative, and she made sure it would last by commissioning a piece of biography-hagiography called *Armsmear*, after the Colt homestead, known for the "witchery" of its extravagance. She might have intuited that with gunmakers, as with gunslingers, the first telling of the myth imprints indelibly on the culture. *Armsmear* idealized Colt in dramatic shudders of hyperbole.[35]

Then, as one of the most prominent citizens of Hartford and a deeply religious woman, Elizabeth built a church. She placed it halfway between Armsmear and the Armory, the two poles on the Colt axis. Edward Tuckerman Potter (who built Mark Twain's home) designed her Church of the Good Shepherd. The edifice was startling, to those who looked at it closely: in lieu of cherubs, gargoyles, or saints, its door, known as the "Armorer's Door," is decorated with small parts of a Colt's revolver. In an astounding, yet ingenuous, architectural conjunction of the sacred and profane, Colt's Navy revolvers brace the column capitals; crosses commingle with bullet molds, pistol hammers, and barrels; accents of revolver cylinders entwine with ivy, the gun commingled with and infiltrating the divine. Inside the church, behind the altar, is a stained glass window with Joseph of Egypt, holding grain. The face of Joseph, standing next to Jesus, strikingly resembles Samuel Colt. The countenance of a baby, being elevated to heaven, resembles portraits of the couple's firstborn son.[36]

Elizabeth, the widowed keeper of the Colt legacy and fortune, built and memorialized her late husband's legacy in a disturbing excess of homage to ambition. Before too long, Sarah Winchester, too, would interpret, memorialize, and build, but with a very different hyperbole. As the two rifle widows told it, the legacy of the gun business is one or the other, nothing in between: it is Colt, inscribed for eternity among the angels, or it is Winchester, trapped for eternity among the demon spirits.

CHAPTER 6

"GUN MEN" AND
THE "ORIENTAL LECTURER"

G OOD AND BAD FORTUNE TENDED TO WORK INVERSELY FOR
gun capitalists. The Spencer's good fortune in war turned to bad
fortune in peace. Despite the Ordnance Department's endorsement
(indirectly, because of it), and despite encomiums such as one from a
soldier who said, "I have got Spencer on the brain," the Spencer firm
failed in 1868. The post–Civil War glut of Spencer rifles sent prices
plummeting and the company went bankrupt. Spencer reminisced
that "when the war was ended, motives of patriotism were no longer an
incentive to continue making the weapons of warfare, and the return
to the peaceful industry of silk was hailed with delight." Guns did not
enthuse him commercially as they did Winchester (although eventually he did devise new gun designs).[1]

On April 1, 1867, Winchester's corporate war was over, and he
opened the Books of Account for the Winchester Repeating Arms
Company with the subscription to stock. The WRAC assumed the liabilities of the New Haven Arms Company, which amounted to precisely $188,493.59. The new company took over the accounts
receivable, which amounted to precisely $183,608.85. Winchester had
no glut of rifles or a contraction of government orders to contend with.
Still, he faced the same existential dilemma that had ruined Spencer.[2]

Experts agree that the American gun market for years after the Civil War was "abysmal." Demand had "fallen off drastically" for Smith & Wesson, which made only 15 guns a month in 1867, and for others. The American gun business was "fighting to stay afloat." Colt's leased out some of its factory space. Winchester sold just 308 Henrys in the first six months of 1866, and employment at the factory declined from 72 men during the war to about 25 afterward. What followed was a "great struggle to survive," a Remington family member and executive recalled in the early 1900s, as the company had "more than a million dollars' worth of products on hand and no adequate market for them. . . . Nearly every additional production added to the financial burden." The Remington brothers huddled anxiously around their roll-top desk when the government's abrupt cancellation of wartime contracts silenced the gargantuan furnaces of the Ilion factory. In the early 1870s, they would handle the all-but-dead gun market by diversifying, as they had in the 1850s, to make "sewing machines, horse cars, cotton gins, bridges, plows, mowers and reapers or anything else that strikes their fancy," *Scientific American* reported. The gun legacy of the Civil War contributed to the stagnation for the commercial gun industry, as the Ordnance Department sold unsuitable arms "uninterruptedly" from March 1865 through June 1871, with net proceeds into the US Treasury of $17 million. Half a million men went home from the war with guns, which obviously dampened demand, but helped make America one of the most heavily armed nations in the world. This happened not through gun sales, per se, or exclusively, or even principally, but through the informal gun inheritance of a civil war. A lethal peculiarity of this civil war was that men on opposing sides returned to the same homes they had left, in the same reconstructed country, but now with guns in their hands.[3]

Productive capacity was "far greater than necessary to satisfy demand," particularly in a "gun weary nation," a Connecticut historian wrote. Without strong sales volume, overhead costs in the gun industry were crushingly heavy after the war.[4]

Gun dealer Marcellus Hartley reasoned that the problem with the gun business was the erratic nature of demand, contingent as it was on

Winchester cartridge board. The Winchester Repeating Arms Company, like other gun titans, would make much of its profit in the late 1800s off of the ammunition to feed the modern repeater rifles. *Courtesy of the Buffalo Bill Center of the West.*

the tripwire of war. Hartley figured that a hunter might buy two guns in his entire lifetime, if that, and they would rarely wear out. But that same hunter would buy ammunition every year. With gun demand inherently constrained by need, desire, and durability, he reasoned, then perhaps the future for the arms industrialist lay with bullets instead, which might at least stabilize the boom-and-bust gun cycle so incompatible with industrial production. Great demand and profit would come from ammunition. This was a lesson that all of the gun industry would embrace by century's end, as a larger share of profits would come from the sale of ammunition to feed rapid-firing guns, rather than the guns themselves. Hartley bought two small New England cartridge companies, moved the entire ammunition works to Bridgeport, Connecticut, in 1867, and formed the United Metallic Cartridge (UMC) Company. He hired as his superintendent a versatile mechanical genius named A. C. Hobbs, a wood carver and carriage and lock maker who had won a $1,000 prize offered to anyone who could pick the lock of the Bank of England. He accomplished the task, with picks, after fifty-one hours of work.[5]

Other gun industrialists found themselves seeking new markets for their wares. It is not that they abandoned the quest for US contracts. Alexander Gorlov, a Russian artillery expert, visited the United States in 1867 and noted the "desire of successful inventors to make a big profit all at once," which had stimulated what he took to be a characteristically American fervor and excitement. "Many people from all walks of life, who frequently have little understanding of firearms, and even a few personages of the female sex," he wrote, "have applied their effort to create a firearm for the Army," and to slurp around Washington, DC, hotels for contracts. Nor were gun capitalists overlooking the thus far challenging US civilian market. Winchester intended to exploit "whatever American civilian market existed," the company archives recall. He cultivated his first seventeen dealers, from New York to San Francisco and New Orleans, sometimes in a disastrously casual fashion. The mysterious General Lafayette Baker, from the war, became a dealer in the Northwest. Baker worked up a debt to the company, offered mortgages on a hotel as collateral, and then defaulted on payments. Winchester sued him, to no avail—Baker's mortgages proved worthless—and the company lost thousands. Winchester faced similar difficulties with his Brownsville, Texas, dealer.[6]

Primarily, however, gun industrialists from the mid-1860s to the early and mid-1870s relied on foreign, international markets and consumers to stay alive. An 1880 US Census Bureau review of the firearms industry noted succinctly that the "civil war gave tremendous impetus to arms manufacture, . . . and after its close, the capital invested sought a foreign market, and millions of arms were exported." The number of gun capitalists who failed after the war because of their lack of international contracts and markets attests indirectly to their vital importance in the creation of an American gun culture. Robbins & Lawrence, whose founders were pioneers of interchangeable production; the Spencer Company; and the Sharps Company all failed owing to lack of adequate foreign contracts. Christian Sharps had first sent a representative to the southern states to see if he could "drum up" demand, which he found, instead, to be "dismal." Next, a representative sailed to Europe, but failed, and nothing could stave off the Sharps debts and creditors.[7]

The arms industrialists who survived, and those who became synonymous with the American West, thrived first in, and because of, non-US markets. The post–Civil War phase of the American gun business is characterized most dramatically by market difficulties at home and with the government, and the consequent widespread and intense cultivation of foreign markets for survival, by all of the gun titans. The gun industry was on the leading edge of the first wave of economic globalization, and from the perspective of guns as a business, it is clear that the development of an "American" gun culture was bound up inextricably—and quite necessarily—with non-US, international markets and commerce in firearms.

Colt's company trailblazed the path abroad: throughout the late 1860s, it simply continued its focus on international markets that founder Samuel Colt had pursued in the 1850s. Its 1869 Russian contract, for example, made "business lively" for many years at Hartford, according to a historian of Russia.[8]

Horace Smith and Daniel Wesson joined the parade of American gun capitalists traveling to Europe, Arabia, and Asia to present gift guns to despots, tsars, officers, revolutionaries, and other individuals, and to sell guns wherever they could. Smith & Wesson made its foreign debut at the 1867 Paris Exhibition. It meant everything to the company to have a postbellum Russian contract, and the latter was the only thing that got Smith & Wesson out of financial duress. Foreign sales saved the company up until 1874. The Russian contract came about after the Grand Duke Alexei Alexandrovich went on a buffalo hunting expedition with "Buffalo Bill" Cody in the summer of 1869. Colonel William Cody had ridden the pony express in 1860, had been a civilian scout in the Civil War, and was involved in sixteen battles with Native Americans afterward. He became famous as a hunter for the Union Pacific, killing buffalo to supply meat to railroad workers, and in Wyoming he once killed sixty-nine buffaloes in a single day. He always used a Winchester for these tasks. But the grand duke went straight from the hunting trip to Springfield, where he contracted for a modified revolver that would take a special cartridge requested by the Russian Army. Before long, Springfield was swarming with zealous Russian technicians, whom Daniel Wesson eventually sent home in exasperation.[9]

Smith & Wesson delivered over 250,000 of its Model 3 Army Russian gun, which kept the factory occupied for almost five years. It also sold a Model 3 Turkish model, and a model in 1878 to the Japanese navy, Australia, Cuba, and Spain. Smaller lots sold to England, Europe, and Asia—all told, 40 percent of the model sold to non-US customers.[10]

Remington, the legend holds, was at a disadvantage because the founder, Eliphalet Remington, and his sons did not believe in bribes. Alas, "it may be said with absolute confidence that no big arms contract has ever been given in Eastern Europe without some sort of graft attached," a disarmament activist recollected in 1934. As the 1870s progressed, and it became impossible—if it had not always been so—to make foreign arms deals without bribery, the Remington company fell on even greater difficulty. In 1866, however, the Remington brothers had dispatched to the European courts Samuel Remington, whom they deemed to be the most amiable, polished, and charming salesman among them. A Remington descendent recollected that Samuel was an "ambitious man," with a "greater desire to make money for personal ends than either of his brothers."[11]

Samuel established his headquarters in Paris, where he lived opulently. He regularly graced the best royal palaces of Europe, including attending the soirées of Napoleon III's wife at the Tuileries, and socialized at the finest clubs of London. He demonstrated the very successful Remington "rolling block" (an action design) single-shot rifle before royalty, armies, and dignitaries, arriving in Potsdam on a beautiful charger, wearing a Prince Albert coat and silk hat. The king of Prussia wanted to try the rolling block personally, but the gun had a dud cartridge, and the enraged king threw the gun to the ground.[12]

Although it did not win the Prussian market, E. Remington & Sons survived after the war on sales of its rifle to non-US markets. Sales to foreign governments brought the company to unimagined prosperity and spurred massive expansion of the Remington factory. Remington sold 145,000 of the rolling block to France in 1870 and 1871 in what was believed to have been the largest scale of production ever realized in any public or private arms factory. It also sold to Puerto Rico (10,000), Cuba (89,000), Spain (130,000), Egypt (55,000), Mexico (50,000), and Chile (12,000), and a quantity unknown to the Chinese Army, via Marcellus Hartley's gun business in New York. It sold a breech-loading rifle to Denmark, Sweden, Norway, Luxembourg (5,000), Cuba and Spain (8,000), Japan (3,000), Greece (16,000), Peru (5,000), and Argentina. It even sold to the Papal States. The acting war minister for the papacy, Ermanno Kanzler, ordered 5,000 Remington rolling-block rifles, underwritten by a French Catholic organization, for the Zouaves Pontificaux armed forces.[13]

In Egypt, Isma'il Pasha, the great khedive of Egypt, wanted to equip his army with the latest guns. Samuel Remington set sail for Cairo, and a deep friendship developed between the two. The khedive was so impressed by the timely delivery of the rifles that he gave Samuel a plot of land in one of Cairo's poshest neighborhoods. Samuel gratefully accepted the gift, not realizing that it would have been an unspeakable discourtesy if he did not build a house on the lot. So he built a beautiful marble palace, and then left it empty and silent, as he never had any occasion to live in it. As for the Remington order, it proved disastrous. The company manufactured a good number of the 10,000 Model 1875 revolvers, but did not ship them because Egypt was still behind on its payments for its first rifle order. Samuel Remington's fabulous mansion in Cairo sat like a marble mausoleum to a gun infatuation gone bad.[14]

"The sun of happiness has beamed upon the town," the *Ilion Citizen* effused when Remington secured another international contract for 15,000 Spanish model rifles for the Argentine Republic. Tiny, improbable Ilion, a town whose fate was thoroughly inseparable from the Remingtons', was a vector for international arms commerce. It hosted a delegation of "several prominent Mexicans" in May 1874, including the son of the ex-emperor Augustin de Iturbide, in town to purchase cartridge-making machinery; it got to know well a "Colonel Minnie" who lived in town for several years as the inspector of Egyptian arms; it prepared "in lavish profusion" an elegant supper in appreciation of visiting members of the Spanish Ordnance Commission, replete with music, "gaslight, tapers, flags, evergreen trimmings," and fancy carriages for use by the visiting Spaniards; in the other direction, highly skilled Remington workers set sail for Cuba in 1881, as guests of the government, to help construct a new armory there.[15]

Marcellus Hartley likewise brought the world to his Bridgeport ammunition factory in the early 1870s. Alexander Gorlov, the Russian artillery expert, encamped at the factory as a representative to oversee Russia's substantial order for metallic cartridges. He demanded an almost "impossible standard of perfection." The Grand Duke Alexei Alexandrovich visited the Bridgeport factory in 1871, and the young women of the town were deliriously excited over a royal visit. The imperial standard of the black eagle of the house of Romanov flew over the factory. Gorlov took the duke on a tour of the factory—which was impressive in itself—but even more impressive to the duke were the young women working the machines, who were wearing beautiful silk dresses for the occasion. They had decorated the "grasshopper machines" (so named because they had long rods) with flowers and ribbons. The duke apparently was shocked by the matter of how working girls could afford silk dresses.[16]

The archive of surviving sales records from Hartley's giant gun business, Schuyler, Hartley & Graham (SHG), although most likely only a partial record, nevertheless attests to the firm's brisk international business from 1868 to 1880; more specifically, to its arming of regimes, governments, or individuals in South and Central America and the Caribbean. In each of these cases, SHG's—and the gun industry's—commercial transactions may or may not have overlaid with the US government's diplomacy and its desire to prevent European regional involvement under the Monroe Doctrine, but, whatever the case, international arms commerce proceeded independently of US diplomatic or political considerations. Although their sales certainly inflected and influenced international affairs, the gun titans could choose themselves whom to arm, why, and at what price.[17]

The majority of SHG's international shipments in these twelve years went to Havana. Cuba was engaged from 1868 to 1878 in a Ten Years' War for independence against Spain, a development that the United States studiously ignored, but not so US gun dealers and makers. SHG made thirty-six shipments to Cuba from 1869 to 1874, including 140 Spanish-design Remingtons to a Sir Don Gabriel de Amenabar, of the 2nd company of the 5th Battalion of volunteers; numerous shipments to Colonel Enrique Barbaza, who was fighting for the Spanish; and a shipment of 130 .43-caliber Remington rifles to a mysterious "E.M." in Havana in June 1871. SHG might have shipped only to the Spanish or to both sides during these years.[18]

SHG sold and shipped arms frequently to Mexico as well, with twenty-three recorded shipments in the 1870s, one composed of 1,000 Enfield rifles sent "in the cheapest kind of boxes" possible to Mexico's minister of war, as well as a large number to an A. Hoffman, presumably an arms dealer, in Veracruz, and others to murkier recipients in Mexico such as "E.G." and "C.M." The company made eighteen shipments to the Dominican Republic, and sixteen to Panama. It also made seven shipments to the Dutch Caribbean island of Curacao, five each to Guatemala and Costa Rica, three to Haiti, and three to El Salvador. From 1868 to 1880 the SHG account records also show one shipment each to the Latin American and Caribbean countries of Honduras, Bahamas, Brazil, Ecuador, and Chile. In other regions of the world, SHG shipped liberally to Liberia (ten times), made at least two shipments to a dealer in Japan, and one each to "Gaboon" (Gabon, perhaps), Hong Kong, and Paris.[19]

OLIVER WINCHESTER SURVIVED ON NON-US MARKETS, TOO. He didn't invent the gun that bore his name, or the machines that made the guns, or the parts that made the machines that made the guns. But he did invent (or find) their market. He reached many of the foreign markets through ads in *Army and Navy Journal*. The influential journal,

founded in 1863, was mostly read by American and foreign military officers. Winchester, Remington, Sharps, Whitney Arms, and Gatling
placed a flurry of ads in the *Journal*, often on the same page. They included detailed technical drawings, usually of specific gun parts, data
on sales to governments, and results from shooting matches. They did
not require any seductive appeal to the mystique of the gun, or narrative. Revealing gun capitalists' deep dependency on foreign markets,
some ads offered pamphlets in French, German, or Spanish. In the
same spirit, Winchester promptly translated his older catalogs into
German and French in the late 1860s.[20]

To his advantage, Winchester and the other gun capitalists faced no
restrictions on gun sales. The gun was treated as another commodity
whose manufacturers, in the words of two experts in the field, "took
advantage of laissez-faire economics and sold weapons to interested
customers, no matter who or where they might have been." The president acquired a first, limited right to embargo arms exports only in
1898. So gun titans were in the peculiar position of making and selling
a commodity far and wide that exceptionally inflected wars, expeditions, conquests, and other matters of great public and political interest, but operating unexceptionally in this phase of the gun industry
as autonomous commercial agents, independent of public oversight.
Episodically—but rarely—this peculiarity did come into worried congressional view. In 1870, the US government offered guns deemed obsolete or unsuitable for sale to arms dealers at public auction, as had
been the custom since 1865. Gun dealers and capitalists Schuyler,
Hartley & Graham and E. Remington & Sons bought roughly $9 mil-
lion of these arms on a 20 percent margin, with the intention of selling
them for much more. "It is a speculative trade," testified Colonel Silas
Crispin. "We even had women make applications for arms." At this
time, France was on the cusp of war with Germany, and this provided
an obvious market.[21]

The trouble began on October 13, 1870, when Secretary of War
W. W. Belknap discovered a telegram that Watson Squires, the E. Remington & Sons salesman and secretary, had sent from Washington back
to headquarters in Ilion. "If you have not yet bought for the [French]

government," the telegram read, "you will now be able to do so on better terms." This language strongly suggested to Belknap that the company was an "agent" of the French government. It is important to note
here that had E. Remington & Sons simply been selling arms made at
Ilion, through private contracts, they would not have attracted attention, but, in this case, they were selling arms purchased from one government, the United States, to another, France, in plausible violation
of the United States' status as neutral in the Franco-Prussian conflict.[22]

Secretary Belknap got in his carriage and rushed over to the Ordnance Department, where he insisted "over and over and over" again
that no sales of consigned US arms be made to France or Germany via
Remington. Two years later, Congress held hearings on this incident to
ascertain, among other questions, whether these sales truly comported
with neutrality; who, specifically, had actually purchased the guns; and
for whom. What became clear in the testimony from US military and
ordnance officials and E. Remington & Sons is that the situation defied any tidy definitions and revealed the awkward quasi-public consequences of the private, commercial gun business. True, all of New York
knew that the arms purchased from the US government by Remington's sales representative were being loaded almost instantly onto
steamers at Pier 50, known as the French pier, and marked "R.F.," for
"Republic of France"; and, in any case, even without such evidence
and gossip from the port, it was a truism of the gun industry that guns
sold abroad, naturally, at places in conflict or war. "Nobody buys from a
government on a large scale except for the purpose of being in war
somewhere," Secretary of the Navy George Robeson explained.[23]

The abridged chain of possession, from the US government, via
E. Remington & Sons, to the French government, was quite obvious,
but elicited no curiosity, interest, or opprobrium from the Ordnance Department or military officials or E. Remington & Sons. This despite the
efforts of suddenly incredulous congressmen concerned about "national
honor," who prodded their witnesses to transliterate commercial transactions into political ones and see them as violations of neutrality.[24]

When asked if he knew that the Remingtons were "French agents,"
the shipping merchant responded, characteristically, "No. My idea was

simply that Mr. Remington, as an arms-dealer, was purchasing arms here and selling them there." S. V. Benet, a major of ordnance, echoed this view: "I supposed that these dealers were purchasing on speculation, to sell again wherever they could get a market." Nor did Robeson evince concern when asked if he had any knowledge of "what became of the arms" after the government sale. "Not the slightest," he answered. "I never thought of it before until this question was brought up." The commodore of the US Navy, Augustus Case, stationed in the navy's Ordnance Department, answered with the same spare, unyielding elegance: When Representative Ephraim Acker asked Case, "It was the business of the government to sell arms, and it was not its business to inquire where they were going?," he answered, "I think not. We sell arms to arms-dealers, . . . and they dispose of them to their own advantage." Case was further questioned about whether he thought it the "duty of the government" to know such things, and he responded, "not at all." Still, Acker continued, did he not draw a "reasonable inference" that "they calculated to sell these arms to one or the other belligerents?" Case answered, "The inference was that they wanted to sell them to somebody who would pay for them, and give them a profit."[25]

Despite strenuous efforts to construe E. Remington & Sons as a covert agent of the French government, and a minority report that decried the obvious "*pretext*" of the company's impolitic role as an agent, the majority of the committee members concluded that even if the arms were quite obviously going to France, this was a commercial transaction, and they saw no grounds "in international law, or morals" to "repudiat[e] its contract" with one of its own citizens—the Remington company—when they had sold them guns at auction, any more than a private citizen could break an agreement. A contract was a contract. If, in an earlier, germinal phase of the gun industry, the gunmaker was very much at the mercy of the US government and patronage, the shoe was now decisively on the other foot of laissez-faire commercial enterprise, and the sanctity of contract won over murkier considerations of "national honor."[26]

A momentous thing—the arming of America's civilian population— in one respect began indirectly, in far distant, international locales, and haphazardly. For as entrenched as the armed world is today, it couldn't have started in a more improvisational fashion. It is imprinted strongly and perhaps indelibly by the character, ambition, and will of gun capitalists rather than of diplomats, politicians, generals, rifle-carrying pioneers, or statesmen.

Oliver Winchester needed salesmen to find customers and redeem the "incredible folly" of his gun manufactory, to recall New Haven's earlier assessment that Winchester was deranged to think he could sell as many guns as he could make in a factory. A keen judge and exploiter of other people's talents, Winchester plucked his first regular arms salesman out of the primer shop of his manufactory. There, Thomas Emmett Addis worked at a bench and delighted his coworkers with Irish jigs. Winchester must have sensed that this man possessed the "nerve" required, above all else, to sell repeater rifles.[27]

Addis had had an unhappy childhood. He ran away from home at the age of thirteen and never returned, and he harbored a lifelong, intense bitterness toward the Roman Catholic Church for reasons unknown. His family name was O'Connor, but it was easy to change names in the mid-1800s, so he renamed himself after an Irish patriot (a transcription mistake must have occurred, as the patriot's name was Addis Emmett). "He was truly a self-made man," a company memoir said, and in the age of self-made men, one's name and identity constituted another kind of frontier to be cultivated and manipulated.[28]

Addis was remembered by Winchester employees as a very peculiar man. He chose to invent himself as a scrupulously mannered, fastidious gentleman whose style "bordered on affectation." He dressed meticulously, with a black cutaway jacket, a dark tie, shoes neatly polished, and a high-crowned derby hat. Addis sported a flamboyant, thick handlebar mustache, and he never left home without a gold-headed cane, not because he needed one, but because he felt it conferred dignity. He might have felt the same about his fabricated military title. By the late 1860s he'd acquired the title "Colonel," but no one had any idea where it came from.[29]

Winchester sent Addis on his first of many missions in 1866. It was a life-or-death one for both of them. The WRAC was tottering on bankruptcy, and a sale to Mexico would keep it going. Don Benito Juárez was waging a revolutionary battle in Mexico against Napoleon III's appointed regime of Ferdinand Maximilian, the archduke of Austria. Juárez had heard rumors of these wondrous, unstoppable Model 66s, and he sent Winchester an order for 1,000 repeaters and 500,000 rounds of ammunition, to be delivered to a border town.[30]

Deliver the cargo in Brownsville, Winchester instructed Addis, but under no circumstances whatsoever relinquish it before you've received payment. Although Winchester had an order from Juárez, he would sell to "either warring party" (and, indeed, already had: the first Model 66 order had been shipped to France for Maximilian).[31]

Addis dutifully went to Brownsville, Texas, and waited a month with no sign of the Juárez forces. Then he received word that he would be paid if he brought the guns to Monterrey, in Mexico. Making the trip violated Winchester's literal instructions, but Addis took matters into his own hands, following the advice of an ex-Confederate officer he'd met in Brownsville. He kept a few Winchesters close by, loaded the rest onto oxcarts, traveled 240 miles, and crossed the Rio Grande toward Monterrey, where he hoped to close the deal with Juárez.[32]

When he arrived, Addis rented a ramshackle one-room store, draped American flags over the guns, the door, and himself, and announced that he would only relinquish the goods when he had the silver coin in hand. "I am an American citizen in charge of that property," he declared unwaveringly to Juárez's representatives, "and you will not get those munitions until they are paid for and I will remain in this store until they are paid for, and anyone who attempts to take them away will be shot."[33]

Clear enough. The Juárez forces connived for four months to secure the guns without paying for them anyway. When Addis finally gave notice that the rifles could be had by whichever side would pay (US government sympathies be damned), and that he would gladly sell them to Maximilian's forces, Juárez settled up.

Now there was only the matter of transporting the profits through the bandit-infested Mexican countryside when everyone for miles around knew that the Colonel had a fortune in silver on him. Honorably unpersuaded by advice that he stay in Mexico and live like a grandee off of Winchester's pilfered profit, Addis hired a Diligence stagecoach with a driver, armed guards, and a team of four horses, packed his coin in the boot of the coach, and left Monterrey at 2:00 A.M. for the 240-mile trek back to the border.

In addition to run-of-the-mill bandits, Addis realized that the Juárez forces had no intention of paying for weapons that they could get for free, simply by robbing him on his treacherous journey out of the country. Addis trusted no one, not even his driver. After traveling dusty back roads for several hours, Addis suddenly stopped the coach, took out his pistol and a rope, and put a slip noose around the driver's neck. He bound him hand and foot and stuffed him in the back of the coach. Then he rigged the rope to his own leg, so that if the driver became "rebellious" he could jerk his leg to tighten the noose around his neck and choke him.

Addis drove the coach to Brownsville, stabbing himself in the thigh with a large scarf pin to keep himself awake and vigilant. When they arrived at the Rio Grande, he removed the driver's noose and released him with heartfelt apologies for his rude but prudently cautious treatment of him. He told him that he could trust no man in Mexico, especially as no one in Mexico seemed willing to trust him.

Addis was through the most dangerous part of the journey, across the mountains, and would go it alone from there. He dismissed his guards, paying them double what they'd agreed upon, and dropped their money in a bag from the rear seat of the coach. He told them to remain standing until the coach was out of sight, and that he'd shoot them if they moved before then.

When Addis finally arrived at the other side of the river in Brownsville, he took the coin to the Wells Fargo office for immediate shipment to the WRAC representative in New Orleans. Then he made contact with Oliver Winchester by telegram for the first time in nine months. Winchester's friends had long given up on Addis and counseled Winchester that he'd probably never hear from him again. He would skip the country with the $57,000.

The Addis affair was of great—indeed, mortal—importance to the company in 1867, when its accounts receivable amounted to $183,608, of which $57,000 came from the Mexico sale and $58,000 from a sale to the Chilean-Peruvian government (one government at the time), and just $1,374 in cash. Meanwhile, the 1,000 guns that Addis delivered had killed a share of the 50,000 war dead from the conflict and helped Juárez and his people vanquish Prince Max, who was executed in July 1867. (The city named after Juárez had the highest homicide rate per capita in the world in 2010. Mexico has strict gun-control regulations, but that has not deterred homicide and gun violence related to drug cartels. As in 1866, guns come across the border from the United States, among other sources of supply.)[34]

Addis had found his calling. A peculiar one, but a calling. He sought war and tinderboxes the way others sought gold. He was part of the fraternity of first-generation "gun men." That is what Oliver Winchester's son-in-law and future company president, T. G. (or "TG") Bennett, called them. They were the men who indirectly built the American gun culture by operating internationally in a milieu of intrigue, bribery, dissemblance, cutthroat competition, self-invention, and makeshift interpretations of honor in regions of the world that most Americans knew nothing about, but whose purchase of Winchester guns would begin an arms diaspora radiating from Connecticut outward.[35]

Bennett had been born in New Haven and attended the Russell school until he was sixteen, when he enlisted with the 28th Connecticut Volunteer Infantry for the Civil War. After the war he attended the Sheffield Scientific School at Yale, so he had much more scientific education and mechanical training than Oliver Winchester. He joined the WRAC in 1870, right after Yale, and surveyed the land for the New Haven plant construction. He solidified his position the old-fashioned, continental way, by marrying Winchester's daughter Hannah Jane, who went by Jane, in 1872. Bennett was a big man with a handlebar mustache and an austere, patient, quiet demeanor. He had piercing grey eyes but otherwise conveyed no aura of power. Like Winchester, he was almost single-minded about business.[36]

Throughout the 1870s, without restrictions on the gun market, and planted firmly in the saddle of commercial agnosticism, Winchester representatives jockeyed to sell everywhere. Bennett and Addis crossed paths and rendezvoused at Winchester's orchestration to make sales to foreign dealers, despots, monarchs, revolutionaries, and governments; to secure non-US patents; and to track down counterfeit Winchester producers ("These parties have learned better than to pay for what can be stolen," Bennett wrote home). "I have a letter from your father by which I am to see Mr. Addis somewhere, perhaps at Turin. I am also to go to Constantinople. It will turn out however that neither of these trips are necessary . . . of course you won't mention my having said so," wrote TG Bennett to Jane. From Hungary, he bemoaned, "I shall take the first passage possible home . . . staying only until I can find out where Mr. Addis is."[37]

A Colt's agent decades later rued that "the whole process of selling arms abroad has brought into play the most despicable side of human nature: lies, deceit, hypocrisy, greed, and graft occupying a most prominent part." Bennett's descriptions of the gun business, however, were more tedious than ominous, more *Death of a Salesman* than *Day of the Jackal.* Typically he vacillated between ennui and bemusement, tinged always with homesickness. Often he sounded more like a world-weary, droll Continental tourist than a trailblazing arms dealer. He wrote to Jane from Bucharest: "The encyclopedia lied." He found no "plague" or "bazaars" there. A "Roumanian dresses like ordinary people except that he leaves his shirt outside of his trowsers. . . . This to an American is quite picturesque. But aside from this one thing there seems to be nothing characteristic or peculiar or interesting. In such a land one looks for something new and exciting in dress or life—broiled missionary on the bill of fare, or something like that. But you don't find it here."[38]

To summarize the European-American gun world, he wrote: "Everything is just the same without variation." And yet he did not mean that it was boring: "We excite ourselves with supposed intrigues against us dropped by one friend or another, discuss counter plots of fearful vengeance and sure ruin to our foes." The American gun men in Europe were intimately cutthroat. Bennett continued, "all . . . have each recounted the private swindles of the others. . . . A miserable business is it not. It amuses me, however, not a little."[39]

Typical of the milieu was a man named Broadwell, known as "the General." Bennett encountered him in Bucharest and described him as "the first, so far as I know, of that class of gun men Americans who came out to skim these ignorant European nations" in the 1860s. Broadwell had paid $6,000 for the rights to a very flawed gun, but he grossly overestimated its appeal to foreign governments. Even worse was the wretched gun itself. It blew up in his hands and occasionally "blackened his face beyond all possibility of blushing, to say nothing of explanation."[40]

Chagrined but not vanquished, Broadwell went to St. Petersburg, hoping to secure an order from the tsar, but had no luck, and not even enough money to get home. But the gun's notoriety preceded it. "You will guess from what I write," TG lamented to Jane, "that I am not very pleasantly surrounded."[41]

Like Benjamin Tyler Henry, gun men were a tenacious breed; many of them became "wealthy many times," and theirs was often a rags-to-riches-to-rags story. "It is to be remarked of these men that they . . . burn their hands in the same fire again and again. They might end up depleted in purse but never ruined. This is to such men impossible," Bennett wrote, adding that he and Broadwell "talked guns" and "ideas for cities and oceans of money," over dinners in Bucharest, Paris, or wherever political turmoil and intrigue lured them.[42]

Bennett found his work occasionally tedious, but overall these were "stirring days" for the globe-trotting gun men who served the rifle kings. One of SHG's international agents, W. W. Reynolds, having negotiated an arms deal with the French in the early 1870s, managed to escape in a balloon over the German lines, although he was shot at repeatedly and his balloon's gas bag was pierced. Another Remington agent burrowed into Chinese culture, thoroughly "adopted the native costume" and customs, and gained the trust of the general and diplomat Li Hung Chang, who embraced the Remington breech-loader over the old muzzle-loaders still in use at the time. Watson C. Squires was a poor Ilion schoolteacher when he fell in love and married into the Remington family and business. He promptly went abroad to sell guns to the Russians, Turks, Austrians, and Egyptians. On his way home, he traveled through Mexico and South America, and sold there as well. When the gun trade "stagnated," and the company was left with a large, unsellable stock, Philo Remington offered to give Squires a tract of land in what would become Seattle. Although Squires was gloomy about leaving the gun business, he made millions off of the land and became the governor of the Washington Territory and then a US senator—all before the age of forty.[43]

Inventors were also part of the American gun expatriate community. They hoped to secure patents in Europe, or felt that their genius was undervalued in the United States. Benjamin Berkeley Hotchkiss was born in Watertown, Connecticut, and worked in his family's hardware manufactory, which produced everything from buckles to oxbow pins. His brother Andrew, an inventive genius, was crippled and couldn't walk, so he devised a cart for himself to get about the office and trained a large dog to drive it. Benjamin and Andrew thrived during the Civil War on government orders for rifle shells. As with the Spencer, however, peace curdled Hotchkiss's good fortune to bad. Seeking new markets and fortune in Europe, he set sail in 1867 and established an office in Paris and a manufactory in St. Denis.[44]

Another brother, Charles, recalled Benjamin's early travails abroad. He had "not money enough to buy anything more than a crust of bread," but felt that if he could only "hold out," his gun inventions would make him rich. He was in such dire straits that even his wardrobe of clothing was claimed by creditors. To get his clothes, he had to climb into the wardrobe from the back, so as not to break the creditors' seal. One day Hotchkiss was traveling from Vienna to Bucharest with his wife. On the train he started talking to a Romanian army officer who wanted a magazine rifle. Hotchkiss's imagination started churning. The train stopped at a station for the passengers to dine, and Hotchkiss requested that the officer escort his wife to dinner. Having gotten rid of his distracting companions, he frantically sketched a detailed gun in the margin of the Paris *Figaro*. Underneath, he wrote "This is a magazine rifle. Make it at once. BBH," and mailed it back to his St. Denis shop. After its random conception on a European train, the rifle emigrated back to the United States and was shown at the

Philadelphia Exposition of 1876. Winchester bought the patent, after a furious competition, and promoted the "Hotchkiss Repeater" as "the most promising gun yet made for army use." At the Exposition, he wrote, "it . . . was at once recognized by all gun makers as most probably the 'coming' gun," using one of his favorite phrases.[45]

It was coming, perhaps, but it never arrived. The gun, after improvements, was called the Winchester Model 1883, but it wasn't a commercial success. Theirs was a tricky business of accurately gauging—or creating—new fashions in death.

ON HIS OWN GUN-SELLING EXPEDITIONS THROUGHOUT THE 1870s and 1880s, Thomas Addis would mysteriously "depart without ceremony, disappear for a time, but return with his object successfully completed," recalls the company archive. He prided himself on being ready to start for the most remote corner of the earth on a moment's notice. Addis kept his luggage ready and a full supply of linen and clothes to pack, including twelve laundered shirts. TG Bennett once asked Addis how fast he could prepare for a European trip. The Colonel picked up a New York paper, turned to the shipping news, and said that he'd be ready to board a steamer scheduled to sail that evening.[46]

In his gun dealing, Addis followed scrupulously what George Bernard Shaw's character Undershaft described as the arms credo: "to give arms to all men who offer an honest price without respect for persons or principles: to aristocrats and republicans, to Nihilist and Czar, to Capitalist and Socialist . . . to burglar and policeman, to black man, white man, and yellow man, to all . . . nationalities, all faiths, all follies, all causes and all crimes." The gun men took the 1870s "amorality of business," as historian John Blum termed it, to an extreme, selling their lethal commodity with the commercial equivalent of agnosticism.[47]

Reputedly, Addis would visit every part of the "civilized world" in his lifetime. He asked that his gravestone identify him only as "Thomas Emmett Addis—Traveler." Over the decades he sent concise and candid dispatches back to the company on his expeditions to find markets, written in barely legible hand on his knee, from a moving pony carriage or train.[48]

The United States treated the gun as an unexceptional commodity, but some other countries did not, which complicated Addis's sales efforts. In Saurebaya, Java, he lamented, "dealing in arms is attended with some difficulties, [since] authorities will not permit more than ten guns . . . to enter the city in a month." Bangkok, Siam, too, would "be a grand market for our goods, were free importation permitted," but, as it was, "the regulations are practically prohibitive, as a permit must be obtained from the King himself who will only grant a permit where he is satisfied the arms will not be used against him." Nevertheless," Addis admitted, "arms were arriving from time to time without permits, but it is extremely risky business and the profit is not large enough to warrant any risks," although he implied that if it were otherwise he might assume the risks.[49]

Singapore, the Straits Settlement, tantalized, and would be a "grand market for arms were it not for the fact that their exportation is absolutely prohibited to all those countries whose inhabitants desire to purchase them," he wrote. "The natives of Java, Borneo and Sumatra desire arms, but no arms of any sort" were allowed to go there from Singapore. Smuggling was always an option. Singapore was a "'free port,' [and] considerable smuggling is done; the penalty in cases of detection is a fine of $5,000 and imprisonment." The benefits would have to outweigh the penalties.[50]

Addis dismissed Western Australia as not worth the trouble—"no town of 5,000 inhabitants, and would require months' time to make the trip." In New South Wales, there was one dealer—only one—with whom Addis had "no success": "Will have nothing to do with us," he reported, as he "feels very sore on account of our making no allowance for the rifles which were stolen [en route] and replaced by New York papers and bricks" (pilfering was always a problem). In other places, such as Japan, there was, quite simply, "very little demand."[51]

Addis traveled hundreds of miles across the desert to the city of Fez, with assistance from the US vice consul at Casablanca, to negotiate a contract with the sultan of Morocco for 1,000 muskets and 1 million cartridges. As part of the deal, several Moroccan gunsmiths visited New Haven. The city had never seen such an exotic entourage. A

Winchester storekeeper housed them near the factory, and company workers recalled that they "created great consternation . . . by the practice of their daily religious rites . . . —ablutions, chicken killing, and so forth." They were sent immediately to a clothing store to replace their native garments from Fez with American clothing, but whenever they could, in the evenings, they would put on their flowing robes and go downtown, where they elicited great curiosity. Their costumes "flit[ted] about like bats" in the semidarkness, as they insisted on walking down the middle of the street.[52]

Addis sold 300,000 carbines and 100,000 cartridges to the government of "Hayti" for $25,000 ($610,000 worth of arms today). He enjoyed unlimited territory and power, and he was allowed to accept lumber, crops, or other commodities in exchange for guns. For Haiti, Addis sailed down with the guns and returned with negotiable bills of lading for coffee, which the WRAC sold in a makeshift arms-for-coffee deal.[53]

Addis haphazardly and serendipitously picked up business on his way to business. The London agent for Winchesters first handled the guns because of a chance meeting in 1875 between Addis and the president of the agent's company. They were both traveling to Turkey on business, and they became friendly on the journey. Addis persuaded the president to try out a case of Winchester repeaters on the English market.[54]

Addis and Bennett traveled far and wide, but their biggest, most momentous deals in the early 1870s were the ones that led them to Constantinople. Addis, who picked up foreign languages easily, went there so often that eventually he could understand Turkish. In 1870, the fate of the "gun that won the West"—and America—hinged precariously, halfway around the world, in Turkey, on the whims of an egomaniacal, deranged sultan known as the Madman of Dolmabache.[55]

———

IN THE LATE 1860S, CONSTANTINOPLE WAS CALLED THE "THRESHOLD of happiness." Americans' knowledge of Turkey usually extended no further than *Arabian Nights* and tales of white slavery, abductions, and, in the words of British journalist Noel Barber, "harem maidens, ravishings, eunuchs, and slaves with their tongues slit guarding abominable secrets." Reality was somewhat different. Abdul Aziz was the sultan of the Ottoman Empire from 1861 to 1876. He decided to visit Europe, to showcase his Western sensibility. No prospective visitor had inflamed the French imagination more. Newspapers tantalized readers with the prospect of the sultan traveling in a "solid gold coach, with a retinue of concubines and a trail of elephants led by negro slaves chained in gold." In reality, Aziz arrived a "portly gentleman in a plain frock coat." It must have been quite a disappointment.[56]

Christopher Oscanyan was an Armenian Turk by birth and a naturalized US citizen. He had been educated in the United States and was the consul general of the Ottoman government in New York City during the 1860s and 1870s. This was an honorary position. Oscanyan made his living by charging brokerage fees for shipments from the United States to Turkey. He "cut quite a dash" in New York, a Winchester company memoir said.[57]

For many of the self-fashioned identities of the day, duties were largely unspecified. As later court testimony revealed, this was true of Oscanyan's position as consul general. "No one knows precisely what he [did]," according to court documents, although he was definitely "some sort of representative of the Turkish government."[58]

Oscanyan was, however, an informal cultural ambassador of the Ottoman Empire. Billed as "the Oriental Lecturer," he had an illustrious reputation as a speaker and author on Turkish life. He lamented "the difficulty of finding *authentic* sources of information" about "the affairs of the orient," as there were so few American travelers, beyond the small number of traders and missionaries. He informally tasked himself with disabusing Americans of their silly, fabulous legends of the Turks.[59]

His task must have been complicated by the inconvenient fact that Sultan Abdul Aziz was a silly, fabulous figure. Aziz was a "vast hulk of a man," wrote Noel Barber. He looked "every inch a Sultan, with a full face and large staring eyes and a beard streaked with grey." Aside from his physical grandeur, Aziz was a vacuous, extravagant, and increasingly deranged ruler. He had 900 concubines guarded by 3,000 black eunuchs, and a staff of 5,000 servants, each with a precise task. One was to put the royal backgammon board in its proper place; another was to trim Aziz's toenails. His megalomania only added to the empire's notoriety of being both morally and financially bankrupt. The Madman of Dolmabache either committed suicide or was murdered in 1876, having dragged the empire into great debt with his bouts of maniacal extravagance.[60]

Whatever the sultan's madness, at least the Ottomans didn't have taxes or excessive regulations. European businessmen who felt burdened by both in their own countries were flocking to Constantinople, a dynamic, cosmopolitan city with vast untapped potential to make money. And this was the point that the Oriental Lecturer needed to emphasize to secure US-Turkish business—and his brokerage commissions. Far from being a place of "perpetual stagnation," Oscanyan reassured businessmen, there were no obstacles to commerce in Turkish waters, and the port would gladly remove any commercial hindrances. True, at the time, Turkey was "notorious throughout the world for its corruption," as a 1930s disarmament activist wrote. Bribes were the unavoidable lifeblood of business. But here, gun industrialists could capitalize on Ottoman-European conflict.[61]

Rustem Bey, a Turkish army officer, was sent to the United States in May 1869 by the sultan's war department to recommend and purchase arms and ammunition. Bey spoke little English, so he relied on his old friend Christopher Oscanyan to be his guide and interpreter. Oscanyan thought of the Winchester rifle, and his commission opportunities. At the time, Oliver Winchester was working in a small office on New Haven's Chapel Street, with a handful of men under his direct guidance who were beginning to build a rifle empire. His office staff consisted of his son Will, the vice president; a bookkeeper; and a porter named Al Harris. The shop superintendent, Nelson King, employed three clerks. In 1869, the factory, headed by Winchester's seven-person staff, sold about 10,930 guns. Oscanyan met with Winchester, who urged him to call Bey's attention to the wonders of the repeater rifle. Oscanyan promised to do so—for a commission on any sales that were "affected through his instrumentality."[62]

This was neither a transaction between governments nor an illicit, covert, black-ops enterprise. It was simply business, on a frontier, like any other business with any other commodity, and it is how modern firearms reshaped the world: ad hoc and fortuitously, in a brief laissez-faire heyday, with deals hanging on idiosyncrasies of character and circumstance along with bribery, occasional swindling and dissemblance, and the gun men's mettle. The private interests of the gun capitalists and the gun salesmen shaped matters of public interest.

Assured of a piece of the profits, Oscanyan displayed the Model 1866 to Bey, who didn't like it at all. He thought it was too complicated for the Turkish soldier. In January 1870, the sultan seemed to be leaning toward the Spencer. He'd heard of the post–Civil War glut of Spencers that the US government would gladly sell to other governments. Thinking of his commission, however, Oscanyan exerted his influence with Bey to have the Spencer derided and the Winchester extolled. Bey obtained an order for 1,000 guns, to please Oscanyan. He also dissuaded the Ottoman Empire from dealing through the US government.[63]

Meanwhile, Winchester worked every angle. Early in 1870, the WRAC made an agreement with Azarian, Pere et Fils, a Constantinople company, to act as the WRAC's official representative in all transactions with the Ottoman Empire. TG Bennett described the Azarian firm as "a very curious one." It was composed of Aristakes Azarian; his two sons, Pier and Joseph; and his brother Joseph. Azarian himself, around sixty years old, was very short, very fat, and so frenetic that he barely seemed to ever eat, drink, or sleep. Owing to its confidential business, Azarian kept no clerks in the office, and every decision, including the wording of telegrams, was arrived at collectively. Bennett said, "They shout, stamp, gesticulate, *solo, uno, trio, quarto*, and just as you expect to see them punch each other . . . the noises cease and the point is settled," and "with the most astonishing judgment and cunning." The Turkish government ministers deferred to Aristakes, who was even allowed to walk into the War Department in muddy boots, when all others had to take off their shoes and wear special slippers.

The government hung on his every word. Azarian had visited Marcellus Hartley's United Metallic Cartridge factory in Bridgeport in 1872. He took a courtesy tour without identifying himself and was thought to be simply a "strange Armenian man." After the tour, he revealed himself to be a representative of the Turkish government and ordered 10 million rounds of ammunition on the spot.[64]

In the spring of 1870, Winchester sent sixteen guns, including one that was gold-plated and five silver-plated ones, to Azarian for Turkish officials. Then the Winchester underwent trials before the sultan, with Addis as a representative. The Winchester and other rifles passed all the tests, until the dreaded sand test. Rifles were placed in a blanket and shaken in sand until the rifle's action was clogged. Using only tools carried by an ordinary soldier, the rifle salesman then had to put the rifle into action.[65]

Rifles from other companies failed all around him, but Addis was undaunted. He asked for water, and was told that a canteen wasn't part of the soldier's equipment. Because Addis had been drinking heavily, as was his custom, he was equipped to solve the problem: he urinated on the rifle to clear sand out of its action. Competitors fumed, but every soldier had a bladder; hence, Addis argued, he had complied with the test's requirements.[66]

Evidently, Addis' ingenuity impressed the sultan's representatives. With an order imminent from the Ottoman Empire, Winchester now realized that he might have to pay a double commission, one to Azarian and one to Oscanyan, so in mid-July he began talking exclusively with Azarian.

Oscanyan was furious. He wanted to claim a commission for his services in persuading Bey to pursue the Winchester. As Oscanyan petitioned for a share of the gun-trade bounty, Azarian wrote that he, too, wanted to be promised a commission on *any* sale to the sultan, regardless of whether it came through him. Winchester rejected both proposals. If he promised to pay a commission to all of the agents who had slyly peddled their influence on his behalf, "it would break us," Winchester concluded with his usual candor. It was out of the question.[67]

(Around the same time, E. Remington & Sons was dealing with the same dreaded prospect of paying a "double commission" on sales to Cuba. Remington had contracted with Samuel Norris in 1868 to sell arms for a 10 percent commission on orders with "any European countries, or any associations . . . contracting for European powers." Norris did quite well in his international sales, earning roughly half a million dollars in his first years. The company's protracted conflict with its gun man ultimately had to do with the vagaries of colonialism and the difference, if any, between a European "country" and a "power." Norris contended that he should have a commission on sales to Havana, Cuba, because Cuba was a colony of the European country of Spain, and hence loosely part of his territory. For the purposes of not having to pay the double commission, Remington's lawyer had to argue that Cuba was its own "country" even if it was not recognized as a "power" or government, whose purchase of the Remington rifle was not at all dependent on the "parent country" of Spain doing the same. For the gun industrialist, an entity's independence was tacitly determined by its capacity to buy its own guns. Foreign sales in the 1870s presented all sorts of dilemmas of nomenclature, since gun industrialists, although private commercial agents, operated on a global, imperial stage. "Suppose a European country [was] at war with an Asiatic power, say, France with China," the Remington lawyer hypothesized, and "arms had been sold to parties in New York with the intent that these arms should be furnished to France for use . . . in China." If the arms had been shipped by way of San Francisco, directly to China, but for use by French troops in China, then by the strict construction of sales to "European countries," Norris would not be entitled to his commission. For that reason, Remington had used two terms, country and government—and by that distinction, Cuba was certainly a "country" even if not recognized as a "government," and not a European one, at that. Hence, Norris was not entitled to his 10 percent commission.)[68]

In late September, negotiations between Winchester and the Turks lurched along. Winchester complained to Azarian that "there is much want of clearness and much confusion of ideas." Ahead of his time, in tone and entrepreneurial style, Winchester prized clarity to the point of brutality. "I now write for the purpose of trying to state clearly what I am willing to do," he said. "I should be pleased to sell the Turkish government five, or fifty thousand of our guns, if I can make anything on them." He had already offered the lowest price, and the sultan's bargaining left him unimpressed. "The offer made us by the Government was simply ridiculous," Winchester stated with unsparing candor. "Your Government does not seem to understand the method of doing business in this country. We are not in the habit of asking twice as much for our goods as we expect to get. We ask only a moderate profit."[69]

Winchester was also contending in his negotiations with counterfeiters who would stamp a **W** on a rifle and claim that it was an authentic Winchester. (Likewise, Colt's ads routinely warned the customer against "counterfeits and patent infringements.") "The party who made the proposition to furnish our arms [at less than price] is a swindler," Winchester wrote decisively to Azarian. Even if European armorers could ensure the "great exactitude and perfect workmanship" of a Winchester, they could never get up to speed with New Haven's humming machinery, which could "make and deliver [20,000] guns before anyone in Europe" could finish one. Belying none of his precarious footing in the gun business, Winchester warned Azarian, "We are now turning them out every day, increasing the quantity"—with more business than they could handle.

Winchester delivered a bravura P.S.: "You have only to telegraph to us, when you shall have arranged a contract, thus: 'Yes, for fifteen thousand' (more or less, as the case may be); or 'No.' This I shall understand, and will reply, 'All right,' or 'Too late,' as the case may be."[70]

On November 9, 1870, Winchester and the sultan's minister of war sealed their momentous contract. Winchester would sell 15,000 muskets and 5,000 repeating carbines for $28 and $20 each, respectively, with a discount of 5 percent, "payable ready money in gold," deliverable to the wharf at New York no later than January 1, 1871, and shipping at a rate of at least 1,000 arms a week.[71]

The Turkish order was marvelously audacious and ambitious when Winchester had relatively few years of experience. An employee recollected that in the winter of 1870, the "shop was running on the

Turkish contract" almost nonstop, with two ten-hour shifts a day. In the midst of the contract, Winchester was also moving the factory from Bridgeport to New Haven. The Turkish inspectors insisted that production not be affected. Winchester operated the most important machines up until the very last minute, and then their belts were cut and they were loaded onto flatcars for the short journey to New Haven. This happened around noon, and production would start promptly again at 7 A.M. the next morning in the new factory. When the cargo was ready, five steamers and seven sailing ships, including the *Daisy*, the *Henry Knight*, the *Americus*, and the *Mindota*, transported it to Turkey. This was how international gun commerce typically worked. Mortimer MacKenzie ran a shipping business in New York and regularly shipped arms, which he treated "just as any other merchandise." He shipped often for Smith & Wesson, E. Remington & Sons, and Schuyler, Hartley & Graham (Austin Baldwin & Company, another gun wholesaler, actually had its own steamer). The gun industrialist would come to his office and tell him how many hundreds or thousands of cases it needed to ship and make a "regular freight engagement for so many cases. . . . The whole thing was managed much the same as our ordinary business," Mortimer concluded.[72]

Including ammunition, the Turkish contracts brought the company a gross income of over $1,360,000 for the 1870 contract and a similar 1871 agreement for additional arms. It could not have arrived too soon, as Oliver Winchester was hanging by a thread. As he awaited final payments on a subsequent Turkish contract, he wrote to the Malleable Iron Fittings firm of Branford, Connecticut, to beg its forbearance. "We are very short," he wrote, "but we may be relieved at any moment by remittance from abroad, [and] ask your patient indulgence."[73]

Oscanyan wanted his share, the promised 10 percent commission, for his labors of persuasion. Winchester flatly refused. Oscanyan sued in 1875 in New York to enforce the agreement. The service in question, which the plaintiff had stated "so baldly and clearly," the court ruling summarized, was to buy and sell "official influence" over the sultan on Winchester's behalf, and "personal influence over Rustem Bey." The court concluded that "the benefit which would accrue to the government of which [Oscanyan] was the commercial representative . . . does not seem to have entered into his mind" at all. It hadn't. The "public good," as the court recognized, had little to do with this or any other gun sales, even those to another government. Oscanyan was thinking of his commission and private agreement with Winchester.[74]

Obviously, the Oscanyan ruling declared, the courts do not exist to enforce or recognize a contract that is "tainted with . . . vices," "corrupt in itself," and "repugnant" to the idea of public service. The accounting worked entirely in Winchester's favor. He had secured for free all of Oscanyan's influence, which was all Oscanyan had to sell.[75]

Everyone had an angle. In February 1877, as Oscanyan's case wended its way through appeals, the New York Times reported on "The Adventures of a Turkish 'Nobleman' in New-York," and how a "social fraud [had] imposed" himself on the city, a "dashing naval gentleman . . . known to his friends as 'Edinboro' Bey, captain in the naval service of his imperial majesty the Sultan." Presumably, since he told New York society that he was on a vital mission connected to the pending war between Russia and Turkey, authorized to charter shipments of guns to Constantinople, and an important witness in the contentious Oscanyan suit, "Edinboro" Bey was pretending to be Rustem Bey. Or was Rustem himself, reinvented. Prominent New Yorkers introduced him into society, where he dazzled the elite with his "audacity, wit and consequential bearing."[76]

The Times couldn't know precisely what happened when "Bey" and Winchester met in New Haven, except that Bey had left New York broke, without paying his hotel bill, but returned flush with money. A Winchester agent in New York cashed for Bey a draft for $600 in gold on the Bank of New York. Then Bey left the city, and was not heard from again. The Times reported rumors that Winchester was willing to "bleed liberally" by way of cash to secure Bey's loyalty, silence, or disappearance in the Oscanyan lawsuit.

Even though they were duped, New York's elite had to admire the show. Dissemblance was part of doing business, and a business in its own right. "He has proven himself one of the most adroit and accomplished *adventurers* that the metropolis has ever entertained," wrote the *Times*. "Even the gentlemen who have suffered most by him cannot help expressing their admiration of the fellow's insinuating address, . . . and *Arabian Nights*–like imagination."

WINCHESTER CONTINUED TO DO BUSINESS WITH THE TURKS throughout the 1870s. In the first weeks of December 1877, TG Bennett was in Constantinople to seal another contract, with another sultan. This sultan, Abdul Hamid II, was thin, sallow, and, according to Bennett, "stupid in appearance." The Ottoman Empire's last despotic ruler, Hamid turned the empire into a parody of its former grandeur, squandering the empire's wealth in random extravagance.[77]

By the time of Bennett's visit in December, the Turks were mired in one of their thirteen wars with the Russians, who aspired to conquer Constantinople. As early as June, the *New York Times* reported that a "body of Christian volunteers armed with Winchester rifles" was leaving to join the fray. Bennett reported home to Jane, "we have no news of the war here, as it is not considered best to give it. . . . The people of Constantinople will know when the Russians come but nothing before."[78]

Bennett intermingled arms negotiations with tourism and expeditions to find decorative goods for Jane. After inspecting a cartridge factory (Winchester had sold cartridge-making machinery to Spain and Turkey) and finding it thoroughly wasteful, with good brass getting thrown out and no good bullets being produced, he set out with an English-speaking tourist to find the howling dervishes in a dark, small mosque on the outskirts of Pera.[79]

Through it all, as he often did, Bennett pined for home. "You don't know how I long to see our house," he told Jane. Still, he mused, "It is curious to think that while this is going on here, the Russians are surely grinding upon [the Turkish] armys [sic] beyond the Balkans."[80]

It was curious, and more so because the Winchester was in that conflict changing European warfare. The Winchesters were actually devastating the Russians, in one of the most tactically brilliant maneuvers of the nineteenth century, by which the Turkish field marshal Osman Pasha managed to hold up a massive, 40,000-strong Russian force in a five-month siege. Osman's army at Plevna, now part of Bulgaria, was a small one of 10,000 at the beginning of the siege. But it was equipped with a strange new firepower—at least 8,000 and perhaps as many as 12,000 of the Winchester 66s that had been sold in 1870 and 1871. Through long periods of constant firing, the repeater rifles would dispatch a total of 40 million to 60 million rounds of ammunition on the Russians.[81]

The Russians, led by the Grand Duke Nicholas, Nikolai Nikolaievich, had walked surely into town on July 30—and into a trap. They expected to face a smaller army, and not the Peabody-Martinis and Winchesters—both models of repeater rifles—which unleashed a constant, infantry-decimating "wall of hot lead," as a gun expert wrote. In this first assault, the Turks lost only 12 killed and 30 wounded; the Russians lost 74 officers and 2,771 men in a firefight that lasted no more than 20 minutes. "What the Russians didn't know," the *New Haven Register* recollected in 1971, "was that the Turks were firing a repeater rifle that cut the enemy soldiers to ribbons as they reloaded their single-shot weapons." The *Register* called it a "hero rifle"—"part of 100 years of U.S.-Turk military 'aid' as the term is used today." But the US government's aid had had nothing to do with Osman's guns: Winchester had armed the Turks, for his own profit, in improvised collusion with the mysterious Bey and Oscanyan.[82]

Subsequent attacks were just as horrific. A fully loaded Winchester lay next to many of the Turkish soldiers at trenchlines hidden in the undulating terrain. Death with the Winchester was loud, fast, and relentless. What the US government saw as a liability—the potential waste of ammunition with a repeater, and profligate shooting—Osman saw as tactically effective. He issued soldiers with repeaters 500 cartridges, and instructed them to shoot as much and as fast as possible. They unleashed an unheard of 20,000 shots per minute in one battle. Russia's coalition lost 14,000 men and 356 officers. Reporters wrote of the Second Battle of Plevna that it would be difficult to recall "another instance of a corps being so rapidly destroyed" as this "frightful slaughter."[83]

Disease and dwindling supplies were more effective against the Turks than the Russians' small arms, rendered impotent by the Winchesters. When Osman finally surrendered, the grand duke took him prisoner at a huge breakfast gathering, congratulated him on his brilliant defense of Plevna, and returned his sword as a tribute. It was a ritual of more intimate warfare, on the cusp of the new.[84]

Word of the horrendous casualties by this fearsome new repeater spread through Europe, which had been following the "Plevna Delay" incredulously. How could such a small Turkish force be thwarting the Russian juggernaut? Journalists didn't recognize the significance of the rapid-firing Winchesters at the time, but war rooms around the world did. A lieutenant colonel in London urged the adaptation of the Winchester repeater, based on its "deadly effect" at Plevna. A vice admiral concurred, saying, "I have been for a long time a consistent advocate of the magazine gun known as the Winchester, or the Winchester-Henry as it is also called: for there is a gentleman of the name of Henry who has been connected with it." Henry might have been pleased to be remembered, as few did remember him anymore.[85]

Winchester's foreign sales thrived. Nations and tribes raced to acquire this new weapon of mystery and near supernatural power. Eventually, Fiji replaced its boomerangs with repeater rifles. From Bangkok, King Rama V of Thailand bought Winchesters in the 1880s to combat French aggression in Laos and Cambodia. People who had never met an American had met the American gun. "Eskimos and South Sea Islanders" bought the rifle, and it was known on "the African veldt and the Australian bush," according to a company retrospective. Isolated Arab tribes scattered in African deserts began to demand Winchesters from secondhand dealers.[86]

As part of the ongoing gun evolution to faster shooting, practically every European nation replaced outdated and single-shot rifles with rapid-fire ones. Gun innovation moved almost invariably in the direction of greater speed, lethality, and power in the commercial arms race. The Plevna Winchesters had inaugurated irreversibly the age of the semiautomatic rifle.[87]

BACK IN NEW HAVEN, THE IRONCLAD ACCOUNTING OF THE GUN business held true: death and commercial fecundity were linked. Because of the sultan's business, Oliver Winchester was turning the corner to profit and expansion. The Turkish contracts (international, not domestic, sales) "put the Company on Easy Street," the company archive recalls.[88]

In April 1871, a once timid, now giddy board presented Oliver Winchester with a letter of appreciation, praising his "most untiring perseverance . . . under every discouraging circumstance imaginable," and his "consummate financial skill and inventive genius" that allowed stockholders to enjoy "very handsome financial returns."[89]

Since April 1, 1867, the net worth of the company had increased by $727,105, to $1,177,105 (the economic status equivalent of $324 million today). A letter from Winchester to the stockholders on March 6, 1872, described the liabilities and assets with which the Account Books were opened for the year beginning in February 1872. The company now had a surplus of "reliable assets" of $510,797.76, which did not include the assets of the Patent Right account—the most important but intangible asset. Its profits in the year 1872, Winchester reported, had increased by $60,659.94. Sales for 1872 were $1,015,652.20, an increase of $206,258.56 over the year before. The Imperial Ottoman government had contributed $333,172.12 to those sales. The 1870s were a decade, the company archive recalls, "when the rewards to our Company were rich, and the money poured in."[90]

TG Bennett felt flush in good fortune, too, despite his complaints about the European arms-trading life of travel, all the swindles, and the insufficiently dazzling natives in the company of gun men. "The [new summer] leads me to consider how short our lives really are," he wrote to Jane from Romania in 1879, "and to feel rebellious that two months of mine should be spent here so far away from you. And yet, who have had as much to be thankful for as we. I cannot think of anyone with whom we could advantageously change. Can you?"[91]

CHAPTER 7

"SPIRIT GUNS"

We all walk in mysteries. We are surrounded by an atmosphere [and] we do not know what is stirring in it, or how it is connected with our spirit.

—Goethe

Sarah Winchester's bad fortune didn't end with Annie's starvation. The record is unclear on how many failed pregnancies and stillbirths she experienced—death certificates didn't consistently include or exclude stillborn infants. Her thwarted reproduction was more private and shrouded than Oliver Winchester's meticulously accounted production. But she apparently had no surviving babies from 1866 to 1879.[1]

Unusual but plausible hearsay comes from a social column in a local newspaper from November 1969. It says that a Mrs. Charles H. Merrill had donated an exquisite, flared, black silk and lace coat for a charity auction. In the 1800s it was a Victorian jacket, the columnist noted, but, in 1969, it made a cute minidress. The jacket had been in Sarah Winchester's maternity wardrobe. When Sarah died in 1922, Mrs. Merrill had helped Sarah's niece sort things. Sarah still had two complete baby layettes, decades after they would have been of any use, intended for babies that she lost before or at birth. Mrs. Merrill, a collector of antique clothing, had bought the maternity jacket and skirts. She learned from Sarah's niece that Sarah wore them "during three pregnancies, all of which ended in stillbirth." Three is probably a minimum.[2]

While she tried in vain to have a child, Sarah fulfilled the venerable role in the 1860s and 1870s of tending to the men and children in her extended family. Poet Emily Dickinson did the same in her cloistered, creative life, as did other "barren" and spinster women in New England families with intergenerational households. She doted on Will. "Sallie [Sarah's nickname] is extending herself to have things nice for William and we come in for our share," wrote TG Bennett to Jane while she was on holiday in September 1876. "Showers of pansies are heaped upon our heads." While Jane was away, their baby went to sleep with Sarah, and the baby ate better for Sarah than for anyone else. Before dinner, Sarah prepared tea for the Winchester men; if it was raining, she fetched the coach to spare them the steep walk from the Winchester factory back home. The larger and more prolific the Winchester rifle's world became, the smaller and more stunted Sarah's became.[3]

As she contended with the loss of successive infants, Sarah was suppressing what was to the rest of the family evidence of Will's deteriorating tuberculosis. In the summer of 1878, TG was in New Haven and Jane at the shore. He wrote that Will had stayed only a night at Martha's Vineyard because "the air there seemed to afflict him very violently, giving him a fearful cough." He concluded, "I cannot understand why Sarah does not feel alarmed about him. He seems to me much more worn and thin than last year," when, in a reaction of paranoid doting, Sarah had tried to keep Will away from his ailing father.[4]

At the end of July, Sarah and Will took the clear, restorative air in the White Mountains and stayed at the posh Sinclair House in Bethlehem, New Hampshire. Built by ale tycoon Frank Jones for his daughter, the Sinclair was a haven for wealthy asthma, TB, and hay-fever sufferers. Sarah and Will spent their days on the stately wraparound porch, or playing croquet and bowling on the lawn. Evenings were devoted to elaborate meals, dancing, orchestras, and card-playing. They enjoyed the company of one of the "generals" from TG's expatriate society of gun men, and regaled TG with stories when they returned. But the air did nothing to improve Will's health.[5]

SARAH'S BAD FORTUNE DEEPENED—AND WAS ENCLOSED—WITHIN A beautiful mansion that displayed Oliver Winchester's growing good fortune with guns. Sarah and Will lived in Oliver's mansion while they were building their own. Flanked by magisterial elms, pines, and oaks, Prospect Street had New Haven's most palatial residences and rose to one of the highest points of the city. The homes were praised for their dignity and privacy. It begins in the center of the city with the Grove Street cemetery, known for its Egyptian gate that looks like something from the set of *Aida*. A partisan 1966 retrospective compared Prospect Street to the most influential streets in the world: it may not have been "as spacious as the Champs-Elysees," or "as ugly as Park Ave.," but its "influence on the world has been quite incalculable," the retrospective said, with its important men of affairs as residents.[6]

Winchester and John Davies built mansions next to each other, and in the same style, at the center of Prospect Street. Like the Davies house, the Winchester mansion was brick, three stories high, stuccoed, with a mansard roof. Looking out from the mansion's broad windows, to the west and south, the Winchester family saw the rugged face of West Rock, but nearer, they could keep the outline of the WRAC just in view, a brick behemoth within the shadow of Prospect Hill. Other gun capitalists also kept their family homes visually tethered to their businesses. Samuel Colt's florid mansion, Armsmear, sat within eyeshot of the Russian-inspired blue onion dome with gold stars that crowned the Colt's factory. The Remington family built an extravagant Italianate mansion on Armory Hill, overlooking their factory.[7]

Winchester had a fairly large domestic staff, so others handled seamlessly the small labors and repetitive chores of life. He employed six female domestics; one gardener, who lived on the estate with his wife; and a coachman, who lived there with his wife and son. The house was valued at $150,000 ($2,810,000 today).[8]

When construction was finished on the Davies mansion, Davies invited the fifty workmen who had built it for a special dinner. After assembling them in the grand lower hall to thank them, he recounted his life's story—which, like their houses, was almost identical to Winchester's. He'd "commenced his struggle in the world with a capital of

only $150," he told the workers, "but through economy, strict atten-
tion to business, and integrity, he had amassed a competence for life."
This was how you built a house, a fortune, and a family name. Everything had worked as it should, laid brick by brick.[9]

Winchester was celebrated, in the approbation of his day, as a "man
of capital and character" in New Haven. He enjoyed the elusive status
of goodness in society. As for his own conscience, he was typical of
other gun capitalists in not expressing any concern about the nature of
his enterprise: gun industrialists, wrote a historian, placed "a gun
within the reach of every American and urged him to buy it—without
any discernible qualm of conscience." To inquire after that sort of conscience in the industry's formative years, and in its own habitat, is to
investigate a silence, or the null set of an anachronism.[10]

Winchester performed generous deeds as he industrialized New Haven through guns. Other captains of industry weren't so civic-minded,
so New Haven found much to applaud in his success. He served as
lieutenant governor for Connecticut, and was nicknamed "The Governor." He was known to assist workers as much as he could in their
own careers and education, but he was single-minded about business.
His only question was, "Will it interfere with Company work?"[11]

The most famous photograph of Winchester was taken in a gallery
on Chapel Street. The sitting had finished, and Winchester got up
restlessly to put on his hat and the long military cloak that he always
wore in winter. As he was leaving, the photographer asked to take his
picture, "just as you are." His motion seemed more authentic to his
character—in movement, and ambition—than the repose of the formal portraits.[12]

Throughout the 1870s, Winchester donated land to Yale University,
including a thirty-six-acre plot on Prospect Street for the main building
of the university observatory, with its heliometer and an equatorial
telescope. Will loved astronomy, pomology, and the cultivation of hothouse orchids. A century later, the private residences of New Haven's
vanguard industrialists were mostly sold to Yale. The Winchester estate
no longer exists; the Divinity School occupies its grounds and the

Davies mansion, which still stands. The irony wasn't lost on a divinity student in the 1960s. "It is our business ultimately to put the armaments division of Winchester out of business lock, stock, and barrel," he wrote. By this point, a conscientious qualm about the gun industry had developed, but so, too, had the iconic legend of the Winchester. Without it, the student shadowboxed, "how could we have won the west, or maintained our freedom to watch television today?"[13]

THOSE ARE AMONG THE SPARSE FACTS OF SARAH'S LIFE ON PROSPECT Street. She had a baby who died. She tried to have others. Her husband was grimly ill in the 1870s, and she didn't want to confront what that might mean for his future, or to anticipate another layer of grief. A morose mood descended over Sarah and Will as the losses accumulated and the illness worsened. A Yale student who researched Sarah's life in 1951 noted that her friends knew well about her "hopeless search for what you're not supposed to know": she harbored a dream of communing with the dead, and piercing the veil between life and the afterlife.[14]

Was it during this dark time, as legend holds, that Sarah first visited a medium?

We cannot know for sure that Sarah believed in ghosts. She never stated it directly in her own words, at least in anything we still have in writing. Most of her correspondence is lost, and she left no diary, so this book provides a speculative answer to a genuine mystery. The first mention of Sarah as being compelled to a fabulously strange mission by "superstition"—but not ghosts—appears on March 29, 1895, in a San Jose paper, in an article that was reprinted soon afterward in a national journal. The term "spiritualist" is then explicitly applied to her in print in a California newspaper from January 1909, in an article on a court case that declared her to be a "Stanch [sic] Spiritualist." Sarah's spiritualist convictions were asserted confidently in a *New York Times* article from 1911. That same year, the rumors around Sarah and her spiritualism had weedily grown, to the extent that a columnist tried to dispel some of the more outlandish ghost stories of the "woman of mystery," including rumors that she was performing diabolical rites with her Japanese servants. Clearly, in between 1895 and 1911, the strange story of Sarah Winchester as a spiritualist had solidified.[15]

But we're getting ahead of the story. There are things we know about Sarah, as fact; there are other things said about her, as fiction; and there are things that can be gleaned and riddled out from the tangible clues Sarah left us. She is a haunting enigma, and this is speculative work.

Today a belief in ghosts is tied dishonorably to insanity or gullibility, and those who rightly defend Sarah Winchester against spurious accusations of madness do so partly by rejecting the idea that she believed in spiritual communion. But actually, it would have been unusual if Sarah *hadn't* at least explored spiritualism in the postbellum years, especially since she came from a prosperous and exceptionally progressive family. In New England, Sarah was living, curiously, at the center of both the gun industry and spiritualism, and she belonged to the class most spellbound by it. Her region's towns and cities were "strongholds of the faith," according to spiritualist leader and former actress Emma Hardinge Britten. On Sundays, anywhere from 500 to 1,000 people attended spiritualist lectures and séances in places like Willimantic and Norwich, Connecticut. They tried to make contact with the "excarnated" (the politically correct term for the dead) with Ouija boards, spirit-writing, chair-thumping, object-throwing, or inner sight. The illustrious Mrs. Fanny Conant drew hundreds to her triweekly séances at the Banner of Light circle room, where "agreeable social reunions" were said to occur with spirits.[16]

————

THE SPIRITUALIST MOVEMENT, THE LOOM ON WHICH SARAH'S LEGEND is woven, began in the late 1840s and flourished in the 1850s. It was on the wane and might have run its course naturally—until the Civil War. The almost ubiquitous family loss and mourning wrought by war revived the movement. Spiritualism tantalized those mired in grief with almost irresistible consolations, especially in comparison to the vague, figurative solace of the soul's immortality offered by orthodox religion. Spiritualists believed that the afterlife seamlessly extended earthly life. The worlds of the living and the dead commingled, and ghosts walked all around the living, unseen, all day long. "Our departed friends," the prominent spiritualist Robert Dale Owen wrote, are not "impalpable shades," but recognizable, intact people, albeit invisible to most of us, with all of their senses, memories, thoughts, and affections. Other well-known spiritualists compared death to walking into a new room, "a journey from one place to another," or simply the "next phase of life." The realm of spirit existence was real and tangible, "a daguerreotype of earth," only better.[17]

"Summer Land," a popular spiritualist term for the "spirit world" overlaying our known and visible world, was a well-lit place. Spiritualists described ghosts living in magnificent, shimmering mansions that glittered as if made of pure gold and precious gems. Spirits even organized themselves into familiar class hierarchies. An article on how to form spirit circles advised readers about how to use tricks to "attract a higher and more pleasing class of spirits." Claiming the persistence of ego, appearance, homes, class distinctions, thoughts, and feelings in death, spiritualism amounted to a hubristic nullification of death—it made death, effectively, a moment of resurrection. Hardinge Britten proclaimed it defiantly: "THERE ARE NO DEAD."[18]

These were such gorgeous *desiderata* that spiritualists saw, or thought they saw, or said they saw, or dreamt and imagined they saw, with such a quality of verisimilitude, and the feel of prophecy, that it would have taken an act of disenchanted willpower not to believe, when belief would have felt so good, and been so easy. True, the idea had its skeptics (some, including Judge Jon Worth Edmonds of the New York Supreme Court, became converts), but it also had hundreds of thousands of indisputably sane believers, some of them from the most prominent, illustrious American families. The *Spiritual Telegraph* newspaper dismissed criticism easily enough as the "insensate bigotry" of a few groups: the "pious pulpit and sanguine press," the Harvard "phillipic," and the "fine gentlemen of the 'Dundreary' class"—amiable but brainless aristocrats.[19]

But spiritualism was a philosophy as much as a salve. Its followers wove their ideas into a national ghost story—and, as with any ghost story, the spirits came with a message that had been forgotten, flouted, or repressed in the world of the living.

That forgotten message, in broadest strokes, was about conscience and accountability. Spiritualist Dr. P. B. Randolph of New Orleans powerfully summarized the message at the movement's first camp meeting: "All that . . . has been wrong, must be atoned for. We must, in some way, make atonement for every thought, word and deed which has wounded, wronged or injured a . . . fellow being." True "peace of conscience" could be obtained only by this exacting standard of accountability. On this point, spiritualists widely quoted spiritualist Henry Wright: "You will find what you carry with you, wherever you go." Spiritualism insisted upon a collective fate: that we were all in an indiscernible and mysterious web of relationships. The cosmos, as one spiritualist described it, was the "most sensitively attuned harp." Notes, movements, and actions in one place had distant reverberations in another. In other words, to borrow a metaphor from the contemporaneous economic world, spiritualists believed that a society's conscience was orchestrated by an invisible hand, and they believed it as sincerely as others believed that an invisible hand orchestrated the economy.[20]

In practical terms, spiritualists, from this foundation, envisioned an accountability that extended far beyond the short-sighted, delineated obligations prevalent in contracts and economic life. Spiritualism was a counterculture to the mainstream culture of industry, empiricism, competition, individualism, and laissez-faire economics. Each year in the 1860s and 1870s, spiritualists held a national convention and passed resolutions. They resolved, in 1867, to "each honor ourselves and our profession by suffering rather than inflicting suffering, by dying rather than by killing." At their Providence convention in 1866, they agreed that it was "an imperative duty for all to give a full and just equivalent for all they may consume," essentially predicting carbon offsets and the zero carbon footprint. In 1870, they said that the "earth, like the air and light, belong in common to the children of men. Each child by virtue of its existence, has an equal and inalienable right to so much of the earth's surface as is necessary . . . to support and perfect its development"; therefore, laws of private property were unjust. The convention also deplored the injustice of "existing relations between capital and labor," and predicted that the country would become an "oligarchy" of nobles and paupers. The "object of life is not to make machines of men," they stated, "but to cultivate all their faculties." Year after year, spiritualists resolved to combat inequalities between the sexes and races. They supported universal suffrage, but they opposed tobacco and liquor, the compulsory reading of the Bible in schools, "groveling materialism," the discouragement of immigration, and unhealthy "fashionable" dress. In 1867 they condemned the "sickness, suffering, and poverty" throughout American society, resolving to form "moral police societies" to "search out and relieve the poor and needy . . . and extend to them sympathy." They were committed to "universal righteousness." And, almost every year, they approved resolutions against "the wickedness of war," on which Winchester was building his empire. "All preparations for war tend to develop and strengthen the animal passions . . . at the expense of love, justice, truth, mercy, forgiveness," said the spiritualists. They cast their eyes westward and saw the Indians as the "original inheritors of the Western continent, which the whites have cruelly and unjustly usurped."[21]

The *New York Times* scoffed that the 1866 platform was "laughable" and a "bunch of nonsense." It continued, "Was there ever such a conglomeration of subjects," or such "doubtful, strange and dreamy theories . . . just about such as one would expect from that class of people whose brains are addled with fancies of intercourse with spirits in the other world." Although, by 2015, the spiritualist resolutions would more or less comprise the core beliefs of the progressive and liberal readers of the *New York Times*.[22]

There are fashions to conscience. Oliver and Will Winchester didn't tend to the why of things, only the how, as the Scottish philosopher Thomas Carlyle had foretold, and feared. He wrote, "Our grand business is not to see what lies dimly at a distance, but to *do* what lies clearly at hand." The mindset and worldview of science and industry were minutely focused, technologically enthralled, and empirical.

Winchester and his class had the same positivism, and triumphalism toward industry, that Silicon Valley has today for computer technology. Spiritualist Elizabeth Phelps challenged this blinkered view in *The Atlantic*. She worried that in the empirical age of the machine and science, humans were getting dangerously literal-minded and narrowly focused. It could hardly be wondered at, she concluded, that such a person "failed to see" the marvelous. Will Winchester might have illustrated Phelps's point. He focused minutely on one part of a part of the Winchester rifle, a reloading tool, losing himself in a maze of mechanical detail so that he could patent his improved design; he would then assign the patent as property to the company.[23]

Spiritualism elaborated a conscience at odds with that of the Winchester men and other industrialists. True, accounting, in the most punctilious, financial sense, was meticulously ironclad in Will's world at the Winchester factory. The careful accounting in the gun industry, initiated in the 1810s, had only grown more precise. Only Eliphalet Remington had never bothered to systematize. He dutifully entered transactions in leather ledger books, but "a ten thousand dollar payment for one thousand tons of steel might be on the same page as an item of three and a half dollars." He kept the financial status of the company in his head.[24]

The more precise the gun industry's accounting, however, the more vague and nebulous its accountability. There was no accounting of what every rifle did once it left the factory. For the spiritualists, this would have seemed a disastrous oversight. They imagined an expansive standard of accountability of conscience. Inclined to describe the fantastic in terms of the literal, they spoke of how everything from a ghost's life was instantly transcribed from his memory to the ledger—or "memorandum books"—of his follies and sins, and "all the particulars are then revealed." One spiritualist imagined that the accounting books of the soul would be "opened and read before them, page by page," with exquisite, torturous verisimilitude. According to another, ghosts would act out and dramatize the moral perfidies that the recently deceased had committed in life. As elder spirits recited one's crimes, the faces of the victims would appear—all the virgins enticed to dishonor, all those swindled and deceived, all the victims of "back-biting" that a spirit had not even "accounted" as evil during his life-time, but just part of doing business. He was wrong. The backbiter was forced to listen to all the words he'd used, in painstaking order and accuracy.[25]

With conscience made transparent, even noble deeds ignobly in-spired provided no absolution. Swedish mystic Emanuel Swedenborg told of a spirit who had acted "justly and sincerely" toward his neigh-bors in life, but for dubious motivations, perhaps because he feared the loss of reputation, hoped to profit from his behavior, sought a reward, or acted only "out of regard for himself and his own honor." But weren't these the ordinary—indeed, righteous—motivations of the industrial world, where people acted this way, out of regard for self, and in quest of profit, and that seemed sufficiently virtuous behavior, each individ-ual act contributing to a cumulative social good? By spiritualism's scru-pulous accountability, a just action performed for selfish intention was still evil.

Imagine that you had no sanctuary from these disquieted ghosts and their clairvoyant, flawless accounting. Neither in the dark recesses of your home, its "silent chambers or secret closets," Hardinge Britten warned, nor on the "city streets . . . thronged with unseen people who flit about us," could you escape the spirits' "piercing" but invisible eyes. They were "scanning all our ways," she continued, like an omniscient, discorporated conscience. One anonymous spiritualist imagined an al-ternative Crystal Palace: no matter how "thick the walls, or how many doors were locked" between us and the spirit realm, he ominously in-structed, everything was on view in the sight of the angels, "just as though all dwelling-houses were transparent crystal palaces." Some-day, somewhere, as Hardinge Britten put it, "the wrong doer and his victims [come] face to face; earth's murdered ones in life."[26]

Spiritualism delivered this horror of accountability—along with the ecstasy of reunion.

ALMOST CERTAINLY, SARAH KNEW OF SPIRITUALISM, GROWING UP in her place, time, and class, and in a progressive family engaged in the intellectual life of the day; it is likely that, after Annie's demise, she was among the millions who explored spiritualism, although we cannot know that for a fact. If she did, she might have started out craving the emotional consolation of Summer Land, feeling that she would do anything, anything at all, to have another chance, a reunion, more time. Sarah might have yearned to have the spirit world that hovered all around her made visible, so that she could see Annie and her other babies growing up in a parallel but perfected version of the corporeal world. There was a metaphysical ambition and hunger in spiritualism that the skeptics couldn't budge, and anyone in the depths of grief could be forgiven for seeking the comfort of a plausible, if not mainstream, movement that promised an ecstatic, tangible reunion.

But one can speculate, given her keen intellect, that she might have followed the thread further, too, and contemplated the idea that ghosts of the departed returned for a reason. They offered a master key to the cosmic riddle, a key that might help her decipher the meaning of her tragedy. Sarah loved playful allusion and riddles. At a party she created place cards that symbolized guests by appropriate flowers. Guests had to solve the riddle of what flower corresponded to their personality and circumstances to find their seat. The encryptions of nature and coincidence might not be that different. Spiritualism proposed that the "deepest truths are vailed [sic] in obscurity," spiritualist Andrew Jackson Davis wrote, and formed a kind of "mysterium magnum—immensely incomprehensible." At the intersection of two very different trends of her day—the empirical and the ghostly—Sarah might have become engrossed in that inscrutable, baffling riddle of why. Was some "deeper truth" blighting her and making her barren? Why did the accounting of her life not balance out?[27]

———

SPIRITUALIST LECTURERS WERE DOUBTLESS AS SINCERE AS ANY OTHER people of faith, but they taught a philosophy that fed the hunger for ghostly proof. As spiritualism gained millions of receptive followers, some mediums learned to commodify grief in the same way that Winchester commodified guns.[28]

"It was suggested that Mrs. William W. Winchester fell under [a medium's] spell." This is what a Winchester descendent wrote to an archivist in 1980. The identity of the medium is unknown: sometimes an Adam Coombs is named; in other versions, the medium is unnamed, but described as a woman and a "seeress." Often, Sarah's medium is said to have been based in Boston.[29]

Sarah might never have visited her—but an Ada, not Adam, Coombs did exist. She appears in the 1880 federal census as a clairvoyant, also known as a seeress, along with her sister, Adelade. Ada existed at the right time and place to be Sarah's medium. Furthermore, although she was living in Hastings, Minnesota, in 1880, Ada was born in Massachusetts in 1859, and her father still lived there. As for her activities, skills, and motives, it is a matter for informed conjecture.[30]

Ada Coombs might have been a fraud, or she might have been a "white medium"—that is, honest. Some psychics today have finely attuned, supernatural acuity to perceive things that others cannot, claiming to detect auras and to intuit and sense more than they could possibly know by reason. Being a clairvoyant meant that Ada presented herself as someone with second sight, able to see the invisible, ghostly world and convey messages.

Ada would have worked and traveled in a mysterious world of sleight of hand, illusion, and instantaneous perception fed by a voracious hunger for miracles and ghosts. She would have practiced her trade in private, dimly lit parlors and at some of the dozens of mass spiritualist camp meetings that convened in New England's groves and woodlands, the largest of which attracted 20,000 people. They were festive and haunting affairs, with dancing, speakers, and social outings. At the first meeting, in Joseph Lynde's woods in Massachusetts in 1866, the horse- and steam-car companies ran extra cars on the Boston and Maine Railroad for a 20-cent fare. Signs were specially painted for the occasion: "To Spiritualist Camp."[31]

At summer meetings, the white tents that mediums, slate writers, seers, and amateurs pitched for a dollar a day cut tidy, impromptu avenues through the camps. Inside these tents, festooned with flowers, painted figures, designs, and emblems of magical power, a sitter could see the trajectory of her entire life. At others, for a quarter or a few dollars (mediums tended to adjust fees based on what the sitter could afford), she could converse with a departed lover. It was a small price to pay.[32]

Spiritualist leader Emma Hardinge Britten saw the camp meeting as a counterpoint to what Oliver Winchester would have called the "romance of war." The camp resembled a martial camp, Hardinge Britten wrote, but its tents were adorned with flowers and wreaths rather than the war's grim paraphernalia. "Instead of sheltering the fever-racked forms of mailed victims, only waiting for the shrill cry of the bugle to marshal them to murder or death, [it] shades the peaceful slumbers of those who know no death."[33]

Threading through the tents, merchants provisioned the camps, trading in more reliable goods than the mediums'. They delivered fish, meats, lobster, and oysters fresh daily; local farmers sold berries, vegetables, milk, and ice. After morning meals and before the keenly awaited evening lectures, illuminated by starlight and thousands of lanterns, spiritualists disappeared into their tents for private sittings, or visited around campfires, where they talked "metaphysics" and discussed their "experiences with Mediums."[34]

Mediums learned early that people needed to *know* what they already believed. The majority did not want faith, but proof. Like a midwife, the medium brought forth and materialized the things her sitters knew were there but were not yet visible. It was her business to give substantiality to an idea that was already prefigured, crystalline, within the client.[35]

The world of the medium had its embattled realist critics, but an anonymous medium who revealed tricks of his long trade in an 1891 book scorned the scientists, preachers, and reporters who tried from their different perspectives to debunk spiritualism. Their expertise and scientific mindset didn't equip them to unravel the medium's art. In what way was the chemist better suited to discover her techniques than the perceptive, ordinary clerk or day laborer? The skeptics deployed far too complicated methods and explanations.[36]

Popular accounts imagined the medium as primitive—attuned to the supernatural—and this perception served the seer well with skeptics and believers. Skeptics were disarmed by it. They developed attacks based on intellectual superiority, rather than their observational powers. Believers were enchanted by it. Reporters in the 1800s were undecided as to whether mediums were beautiful or grotesque as a class, but they were always seductive.[37]

Mediums talked of "paralyzing" the sitter in astonishment. Full-form séances were the most prized of all spiritualist feats and the ones that fetched top dollar from wealthy clients. The art was perfected in Boston, San Francisco, and New York. It was usually performed with a "spirit cabinet," a four-by-six-foot space specially constructed with a disguised trap door on the ceiling and two thick curtains as doors. Spiritualism held that ghosts preferred to enter and exit a séance through hidden spaces such as this. Any observant carpenter—rather than what a medium dismissed as "top heavy investigators," loaded down with degrees—might have gleaned from the presence of ceiling panels in the cabinet that it had been added on to the corner of the room with a lath and plaster partition, and he might have investigated further, but skeptics thought along the explanatory lines of swamp gases, neurasthenia, and the physics of light. An accomplice would lower himself by a ladder inside the spirit cabinet that the sitters had declared empty and normal fifteen minutes before. With the mood and veracity established, the accomplice had only to slip out of the spirit cabinet a white handkerchief draped over a wire mask, and then quickly pull it back so that it would appear to vanish. It seemed such an obvious deception that one medium was startled when sitters claimed that the handkerchief in the fading, dim light was a human head, and even distinguished its features. They proclaimed it a case of "etherealization," since they swore they could look right through it. One gentleman, a doctor, said that he had even seen the convolutions of the brain.[38]

They were sure they had seen this. A good medium would have learned early that her clients' aching hunger for proof made them her allies, and that proof of the supernatural, certainly the most incorporeal and fantastic of products, was among the easiest to sell. Even resistant sitters, to say nothing of the receptive, sought the *gestalt* that would make suggestive fragments cohere. We can imagine that Ada looked on in bemused but sympathetic astonishment at the susceptibility that desire kindled, as a handkerchief and wire mask got recognized emphatically by dozens of paralyzed sitters as beloved fathers, mothers, wives, and husbands.[39]

But most of a medium's illusions were crafted out of research. Mediums traveled. Their professional success depended on this wandering: they established credibility in a new town, with a flourishing spiritualist community, by performing at a spiritualist hall or other location in which they revealed intimate details about strangers' deceased loved ones. Everywhere a medium traveled to ply her trade, a resident medium or an agent had a card index of prominent spiritualists in the region and the minutiae of when and how their loved ones had died, their heartaches, their business failures, and so on, and the mediums, to varying degrees, would share information on their marks. Skeptics had rumored for years of a blue book that contained all of this information. Notebooks existed for some places, like Boston, but cards were more common. In exchange for information in the visiting medium's home town, the resident medium provided detailed information about the town's believers who were likely to appear at a public "test" for the visitor.[40]

For Cincinnati, mediums had a sixty-three-page book of more than five hundred spiritualists and séance regulars. From it, a seer could learn that S. O. Wilson was a shoe dealer, whose "spt. [spirit] son Albert" had died of lung fever when he was nineteen years old, and had been an only child. "Parents kept his books and clothing," she would learn, "and he is always described as a student, with book in hand. Good mark for private settings."

Other entries included:

R. B. Young, rich.

Remarks: a good mark for private seances at his home, and will pay well. Dead gone on physical manifestations and materialization. . . . Agree with everything he says and you are all right.

Spt. Dau. [daughter] Alice, aged 19, pneumonia, upper front teeth gold filled, extraordinarily long hair. Quite an artist, and one of her landscapes hangs in parlor in gilt and flush frame. . . . Spirit painting of her in the sitting-room that is kept curtained. She is an artist in spirit world. Supposed to have a son in spirit that had no earth life named Egbert O.

The spirit son Egbert was an "inventor in spirit life and supposed to work through Thos. Edison. Is especially interested in electrical work."[41]

Good mediums studied funeral notes in local newspapers and followed the "Movements of Lecturers and Mediums" column in the *Banner of Light* newspaper. A medium's ear was open to the small details that constitute the illusionist's art.[42]

Revelations of a Spirit Medium describes an event attended by a man listed in the local card index as a very "comfortably fixed" hop raiser. He'd had trouble with his last crop, because he had not sold it to a buyer he knew and had shipped it to a merchant in England instead. His spirit daughter Clara had died at the age of twenty-two after being thrown from a horse. She was a fine pianist. His spirit son Albert had drowned at nineteen.[43]

This man was in the audience at the test meeting, and a fellow medium helped to spot him. Approaching the man, the visiting medium raised his hand solemnly and portentously to his ear. "I hear beautiful music about you," he intoned. "It is made on a piano. And I hear the name Clara." The receptive audience began to murmur and hum. "Now I hear Albert. He is your son and was drowned while away from home on a visit. He says you had best sell your hop crop to the home buyers this year." The audience was satisfied; awed, really, especially when the medium elicited sincere confirmation that the farmer had never seen him. It was elegant advertising for the medium, and his parlor was soon crowded with customers wanting private, quarter-hour sittings, desperate to believe in and see ghosts. As for the farmer, the ecstatic, thrilling epiphany probably kept him up that night, and maybe it changed the arc of his life. He now *knew* what he knew before. The medium had transposed a desperately beautiful belief into a cosmic truth.[44]

Even today, belief in the supernatural is widely—but furtively—held. Three out of four Americans believe in some aspect of the paranormal—and more believe than confess to believe. One-third believes specifically in ghosts, or in angels who punish the wicked and reward the righteous where law and society do not. For these Americans, the supernatural is still a fugitive conscience, where messages unheeded elsewhere are materialized and voiced, often literally—for example, in electronic voice phenomena (EVP) sessions between ghosts and ghost hunters. For Sarah, and millions of others devastated by the Civil War (some at the hands of Henry rifles)—or suffering the banal calamity of a child's death—the implications of these beliefs, which were then far more mainstream than they are today, must have been breathtaking—inexpressibly sublime or immensely horrifying. Or both.[45]

———

DOCTORS FELT THAT NO DEATH WAS AS BAD AS MARASMUS, OR A baby's wasting away. Except for tuberculosis. Sarah contended with both: a baby who could not nurse, and a husband who could not breathe. By the most elemental indicia of life, she had failed at the womanly sine qua non. Will was the only son in Oliver's family. The Winchester name would die if she didn't produce a child, even as the eponymous manufactory was churning out thousands of heirs and namesakes in guns.

In September 1878, Will's deteriorating health was obvious to TG Bennett. He wrote from New Haven to Jane, who was traveling: "Will does not find himself much better, I fear. And from something he said I conclude that he has been revolving in his own mind the idea of going away again. It really seems as if he ought to do so."[46]

The next letter on family matters comes after a seven-month gap, and leaves the historian craving some explanatory note in between. On April 1, 1879, in response to a letter that Jane had sent on March 12, TG wrote to his wife from Romania: "I suppose Will is entitled to a letter of congratulations, but I don't know what on earth to say in such a case," leaving the "case" unelaborated. "Please tell him that I rejoice with him in the matter. I don't suppose the baby is very dear to him yet but it will be before long."[47]

Sarah might have had a baby with calamitous deformities that were obvious at birth, although birth records show nothing for the spring of 1879. By April 13, the news had gotten worse. The baby most likely had died. "Remember me to your brother," TG wrote, "whom I have perhaps failed to mention in my late letters but who has been often in my mind."[48]

Sarah must have added to the ledger book of her grief and her body's lifeless offspring. Now, the reality she had tried to suppress began to be foisted on her more forcefully as things got worse, and as others noticed the decay: Will was dying, too.

CHAPTER 8

"THE UNHALLOWED TRADE"

THE GUN FACTORY IN NEW HAVEN WAS GROWING. BY THE END OF the 1870s it had expanded to five acres of floor room with machinery praised in the term of the day as perfect, and the company had produced 207,429 rifles in a few different models. The gunsmith would not have recognized a gun in the tessellation of industrial production. The business had moved from one man making one gun to more than 150 men each making one part of one gun.[1]

Oliver Winchester's sales to the sultan had spared the company the death sentence of other arms manufacturers, and in an 1875 advertisement Winchester could boast, of his repeating rifles, "about 200,000 now in use in all parts of the world." (The same year, E. Remington & Sons calculated that it had sold almost a million rifles worldwide.) But the Winchester ascent in the 1870s had not been smooth. The company's internal newsletter, the *Winchester Record*, reminisced that in these years "the Governor [Winchester] used to go to the various dealers in New York for orders for cartridges and was happy when he returned with an order which a present-day salesman [in 1919] would hardly consider." New Haven newspapers treated shipments of 10,000 cartridges as print-worthy business. The 1879 report to the board of directors explained candidly that the company faced "strong and growing competition," and that "the decrease in the amount of business for the past year is attributable to the fact that all of our foreign contracts were

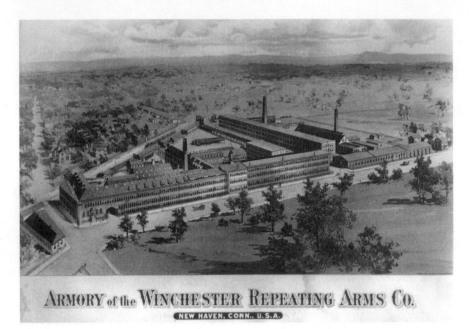

ARMORY of the WINCHESTER REPEATING ARMS CO.
NEW HAVEN, CONN., U.S.A.

The Winchester Repeating Arms Factory. Oliver Winchester and other gun cap-italists liked to feature their factories on letterheads and advertisements. *Courtesy of the Buffalo Bill Center of the West.*

completed. . . . We have [since then] depended entirely on our domestic trade." The domestic trade was "constantly increasing," it reassured the board—but, without the international contracts, it was still not enough.[2]

To make mass-produced repeater guns profitable, Winchester could shrink the number of competitors fighting for their share of the gun market, or he could grow the pie by finding, or inventing, bigger markets. He'd do both. Of the 239 firms in 1860 that produced small arms, only 26 survived to 1900. Of those 26, only 2 would become American icons of the West: Colt and Winchester. Although the fabled western outlaw and the fabled eastern captain of industry seemed like opposites, they were close kins in conscience. By "frontier justice" and "root, hog, or die" laissez faire, respectively, each maneuvered in a relatively unregulated world of valorized rugged individualism. Writing in 1919, New

Haven journalist Burton Hendrick observed that "the industrial warfare of the sixties was a free-for-all," calling it a "frontier business"
world. Historian Roger Burlingame, discussing the postbellum era, later
referred to the "lapse of public conscience" in the business world—and
the gun business was no exception to the larger economic mood of the
day. From 1866 to 1870, 27 New England gun-manufacturing firms disappeared, 18 in the Connecticut Valley alone, an extraordinary attrition rate, reflected also in US Census data on manufacturing.[3]

A good number of the disappeared ghost firms ended up absorbed by
the WRAC. Winchester zealously took over, bought out, and elimi-
nated rivals. Other gunmakers lacked this drive to acquire and absorb.
They might not have had the prescient audacity to see how the purchase
of a company that they didn't want could benefit them. Winchester
bought rivals, (including, eventually, Eli Whitney's armory, at the armory's request—the genius behind Connecticut gun manufacturing absorbed into what a New Haven historian called its "mammoth spiritual
descendent"), not because he wanted their assets, but to kill them and
the competition they represented. He perceived the value of something
that was not there, or the rival idea, being deliberately blighted. Sometimes Winchester moved an acquisition's machinery to New Haven,
where it sat idle, and fallowed their patents. In other cases he sold the
machines. Winchester bought the American Repeating Rifle Company
(which had earlier bought the Spencer Company) in 1869 for $118,000,
then sold its machinery at a Boston auction that drew more than 1,500
bidders. To dispose of the rival Spencer rifles themselves, Winchester
simply placed an ad in Scientific American on December 11, 1869, "Repeating Firearms for Sale," that listed (actually, exaggerated) his Spencer inventory.[4]

In the post–Civil War years, for industry generally, smaller and less
efficient firms that "could not reap the sweet harvest of economies of
scale," in business historian Glenn Porter's terms, "were pushed steadily
toward the grey subservience of marginal production." Winchester's
high-volume production required high-volume consumption. Eventually, Winchester and Colt, and the 26 firms that survived the transition to an arms industry, would succeed in making Americans the

highest gun-owning civilian population in the world. But they were not there yet.[5]

It is telling that someone as entrepreneurially prescient as Winchester did not first prefer the civilian US market over government sales. From 1879 until World War I, with the exception of the Spanish-American War, his priorities changed, and the US military market comprised only a small share of the company's business by the end of that period. During this phase of the American gun industry the domestic markets, from sporting to frontier warfare to home defense, were cultivated and nourished. Likewise, Winchester's reliance on foreign markets declined, falling to no more than 10 or 15 percent of total sales by 1890. (However, Winchester did arm one of the most brutal colonial forays. Thomas Addis traveled through the Amazon River Valley—where he created a "great market" for the Model 73 rifle among rubber gatherers, who exploited and almost wiped out the indigenous people of the Amazon. For the colonialists, "no other gun has seemed to take its place.") The imperial Europe that had indirectly armed America by sustaining its gun industry did not translate into gun-friendly European civilian markets or laws.[6]

Winchester had envisioned and would now develop what Remington did not grasp: the potential of a "scattered" civilian American market. If Winchester couldn't arm the American government, he could arm America. Despite the drawbacks of "fickle tastes," a gun historian noted, and limited demand, this was plausibly a steadier market than what could be had with the spasms of war-driven military contracts. The civilian market needed to be invented and shaped as much as the rifle, however. While not strangers to firearms, neither were Americans just waiting for an arms industrialist to churn out guns. Winchester himself understood this reality, and understood it better than any of his rivals except for Colt. The WRAC retrospectively took pride in its advertising and marketing acumen, as did the Winchester (and Colt) company archivists and historians—particularly before post-1968 gun control made these admissions impolitic and before gun advocates began to mystify America's affections for guns as culturally innate and a priori. WRAC archives singled out the company's advertising in the early 1900s as a key to Winchester's success, noting, "In years gone by, this Company did everything to advertise the gun and make it popular." But it's a tendency with any product, whether mouthwash or a gun (only more so with the gun), that if the author of the market is successful, then his authorship is erased, and the desire for the product appears obvious, as if it had always been there.[7]

From the vantage point of business, gun cultures are better understood as gun markets. Remington, Colt, and Winchester understood market segmentation, and they understood the gun's distinct potential uses and customers. Robert Henning, a historian of marketing, has noted that the firearms business was an early, enthusiastic pioneer into advertisement to find and develop civilian markets, and that during the industry's most expansive period of growth in the years after the Civil War, ads shaped the gun culture, though they have received almost no attention. The gun capitalist's understanding of different gun markets reflects a larger segmentation in Americans' relationship to guns—the distinct ways that groups give significance and deeper meaning, or not, to distinct kinds of guns.[8]

In addition to reaching a military market through *Army and Navy Journal*, gun industrialists advertised energetically to one segment of the civilian market in the *American Agriculturalist* and publications such as *Rural New Yorker* and, for the mechanically inclined, *Scientific American*. With a circulation of 100,000, the monthly *American Agriculturalist* was the leading farm publication of the day. Here, Winchester and others touted their guns' "simplicity of mechanism," reliability, and "ease of manipulation" for a nonmilitary, rural customer. For this commercial customer, the gun was still very much a tool, like a plow.[9]

But the gun industrialists began to advertise in general-interest publications to a very different market of civilians: a mostly urban population. They were not farmers, soldiers, or sportsmen, but customers who might purchase a gun for self-defense. Winchester advertised heavily in *Harper's* from 1868 onward, promoting the Winchester's power, its accuracy, and, as always, its killing speed. Even Remington, who was less interested than Winchester in civilian markets, advertised a Vest

Pocket Pistol for "personal protection." "In these days of Housebreaking and Robbery," the copy read, "every House, Store, Bank and Office should have one of Remington's Revolvers." Colt's appealed early on to self-defense, advertising an array of pistol designs in 1875, including the "little Colt," the "pony Colt," the "ladies' Colt," and the "pet Colt." Colt's ads warned that "if you buy anything cheaper, your life . . . may balance the difference in cost. If you buy a Colt's . . . pistol, you feel certain that you have one true friend, with six hearts in his body, and who can always be relied on." The guns would not "stick fast . . . as do the guns which open like molasses gates or nut crackers."[10]

There was also the sportsman, reached through journals such as *Forest and Stream, Turf Field and Farm,* and *Shooting and Fishing* (first published in 1885 as *The Rifle*). This market and gun subculture included Americans interested in rifle range shooting and recreational hunting. A paramilitary "cult of accuracy" around rifle target shooting flourished briefly between 1870 and the early 1880s, partly as an effect of the Civil War, and predominantly with war veterans and National Guard members. The target-shooting competition, the *Schuetzenbund,* was an import from Europe, where shooting festivals had been held for six hundred years in Germany and Switzerland (first with bow and arrow). Shooting clubs, with women's auxiliaries and benefit societies, spread along the current of ethnicity, flourishing in cities such as Milwaukee, Buffalo, Cincinnati, and Chicago with substantial German populations. The social features of the *Schuetzenbund* were as important as the shooting. Thousands mingled and socialized, listened to Tyrolean singers, gambled at lottery booths, imbibed from beer kegs, or exchanged secret club handshakes, while a few hundred actually shot. This gun subculture had an obvious martial element and owed its character more to Europe than to the western frontier: Americans in the first year of the illustrious Creedmoor competition worried over their poor scores and gun fluency vis-à-vis European shooters. The shooting match, as a gun ritual and "miniaturized" war, appealed to nationalistic rivalries with European powers.[11]

The elite gun industrialists still hoped for military contracts, but they were now also prioritizing the cultivation of a civilian market.

Some civilians still saw the gun as a tool for agriculture and needed one for the farm; others could be persuaded to buy a revolver or a rifle for protection at home, or tied rituals of marksmanship to national pride and warrior culture, or bought rifles for hunting, recreational or otherwise. Still other customers, on the country's edges, constituted a market that was distinct from the others yet overlaid with them: these customers envisioned a kind of paramilitary use for the rifle, appreciating how it made "every man a host," as Winchester said, or an army of one. They had rifles for hunting, protection, and the paramilitary project of western conquest. Winchester reached this last group in local western newspapers such as the *Omaha (NE) Republican* and the *Leavenworth (KS) Times and Conservative.*

These civilian gun markets constituted distinct gun milieus with customers who had different reasons for buying, wanting, loving, or using guns. When guns are approached from the path of constitutional law or the Second Amendment, or constellated into one "gun culture," the gun achieves a deceptive political and artifactual unity: the differences among guns or gun owners become less important than the similarities, or obscured, and the gun is treated as a generic object. But when the subject is approached from the path of the business strategies that drove the dissemination of guns, the heterogeneity of gun markets and guns becomes more obvious and meaningful. The Winchester, Remington, and Colt companies were well aware of the segmented gun markets that they sought to reach, cultivate, and expand, and the farmer's relationship to the gun was not the same as the urban marksman's.

Oliver Winchester and his contemporaries are largely responsible for establishing the basic structure of the commercial gun market, and experts cite this as a particular aspect of Winchester's entrepreneurial genius. The number of Winchester jobbers—middlemen who sold to gun retailers—expanded sharply in the United States and Canada during the period, to more than 150 by 1880. The points of production and purchase—one and the same, or close to it, in the gunsmith days—were now several steps removed from each other, and distant.[12]

Stories of the gunslinger migrated in reverse of people and actual guns, from West to East. But seen from the perspective of business, the armed "Wild West" was very much a product of the eastern, corporate industrialism and vanguard technology that the West is imagined to oppose. Historian Patricia Limerick has noted the ways in which frontier mythology, mystification, and even history obscure the deep commercial foundations of the West, presenting the western frontier as an antithesis to eastern culture. In reality, the frontier was ensnared in the northeastern octopus of the gun industry—one of the "high-tech" enterprises of its day. From the Colt and Winchester factories in the Connecticut Valley, and the Remington factories in New York, guns moved through the arteries of the major wholesalers. They included some that Oliver Winchester had solicited in the late 1850s—Cooper & Pond, JP Moore and Sons, and A. W. Spies. Winchester accepted orders from parties "not known to us" if they had references—or, better yet, cash in hand. The largest and most influential of these was Schuyler, Hartley & Graham (SHG) in Lower Manhattan's financial district—seemingly a world apart from the frontier gun culture, but actually close to its heart. The largest percentage of arms went to Missouri and then moved west and north to the Dakota Territory and the northern plains. Dealers in Natchez and Vicksburg, Mississippi, and in New Orleans were transit points for arms moving into the southern plains and Texas, respectively. Part of the civilian domestic trade was international: many of the weapons SHG shipped to California ultimately went to Mexico or to Central America, via San Francisco dealers such as AJ Plate. WNL Barnes, also in San Francisco, was thought to deal guns to Hawaii. Likewise, shipments to Texas might easily have ended up arming Mexico.[13]

The veins of the gun market ran through retailers such as the McAusland Brothers in Montana and Omaha, Nebraska; Freund and Brothers, with depots in Salt Lake City, Laramie, and at the "terminus of the U.P. railroad"; and Simmons Hardware in St. Louis, which had its own network of traveling salesmen. Its capillaries were all the individuals who variously traded, gambled away, lost, gifted, or sold their guns.[14]

Turf Field and Farm noted in an 1875 article on the gun trade that B. Kittredge and Company, the largest gun merchant in the world at that time, had far exceeded the "mere shops" of the old gunsmith powerhouses in Belgium and Britain. The article also cited some of the more obscure, business-related reasons why civilian gun markets thrived in the United States but waned in Europe. The gun trade had proliferated at Kittredge (and other houses) in the heady American brew of risk, anonymity, distance, and credit. But manufacturers and merchants in Britain were "far more rigid in the scrutiny of the character of their customers than American dealers and manufacturers." Prissily, and foolishly from a business perspective, they would not accept an order until they were "satisfied of their customer's responsibility and honor." And, unlike American houses, where credit was easy, the once-dominant European houses still wanted cash only. (Smith & Wesson was similarly hidebound in its "strict Yankee attitude" toward customers. It required payment in gold before shipment.)[15]

In retail transactions, the "Sold to a Stranger" anonymity of the 1850s continued, reinforcing the gun's unexceptional, ordinary status as a commodity. Many decades later, when gun-control advocates started to make their voices heard, they had to combat a long and deeply entrenched tradition of unexceptional anonymity and informality in the civilian gun market. It was a difficult task to transform a gun sale from an unexceptional to an exceptional commercial transaction, and therefore worthy of different treatment or regulation. SHG, for example, shipped twenty cases of Winchester .44 carbines on November 8, 1871. The rifles had come from the WRAC, and they were going to a customer entered in the SHG ledger only as "B," in Corpus Christi, Texas, and from there most likely to arm fighters somewhere in Mexico. In addition to initials, SHG sometimes used casual, coded descriptors. Their records reveal that in 1897 they shipped arms to "our Cuban friends," and one hundred Remington rifles from "the lot belonging to our friends." In the early 1900s, a Baldwin and Company dealer who sold Winchesters and Colts described the process "when a man comes into our store and wants to buy a . . . revolver": "We do not ask him his name when he pays. . . . Tomorrow, if [a] gentleman came into my office and handed me the money for 1,000 Colts . . . I would grab him in my arms and be glad to see him. What he was going to do [with] them, of course, would be none of my business."[16]

Colt's company archive includes an Allies Letter Book, spanning 1873 to 1880, which offers a rare glimpse at the visible hand of the civilian gun market. The letters puncture the notion that in America, guns "sell themselves." The market was there to be invented, not found; cultivated, not claimed. These were unexceptional machinations of business, applied in this case to a commodity of greater consequence than men's shirt collars. Colt's "allies," sometimes called "our mutual friends," included the pantheon of gun dealers: Schuyler, Hartley & Graham; Kittredge; Spies, Kissan and Company; Henry Folsom of New York and New Orleans; and John P. Norris and Sons. With the exception of Norris and Kittredge, these firms were among the first Winchester wholesalers as well. "The Allies" formed a gun dealers' "combination," in Colt's terms ("wishing . . . the members of the combination much success," the company signed a letter), which was conceived in the late 1850s. They negotiated prices, volume, and discounts directly with the company; acted in unison, through a contract; and split the gun profits among themselves. They had exclusive sale of all pistols, except those sold to the government, and were entitled to an extra 10 percent on guns sold above the contract number. Colt, like Winchester, gave discounts for dealers who found ways to move more rifles. The dealers' contract stipulated that Colt's would not sell at less than a set price to anyone except the Allies, to whom the idea of "clashing prices is greatly depreciated [sic]." The Allies, in turn, agreed not to sell rival guns at anything less than the retail price. Conversely, they would never sell Colts at less than a minimum price, and they would not engage in direct or indirect bartering. They purchased the guns, which tended to "urge their sales much more rapidly" than selling on consignment.[17]

In the Allies' dealings with Colt's, they worried about a few chronic problems with the American civilian gun market. One was volume. Usually, the Allies had too many guns to sell, and Colt's wanted them to take on yet more inventory. The depression of the 1870s only exacerbated the problem. "The trade for pistols is very dull and the lookout for the future does not look so favorably as it did last year," wrote Allies representative SHG in June 1875. Yet, "even with a surplus on hand,"

Colt's still wanted the Allies to "bank up" and take more inventory. The Allies were being asked to "push" too many 7-shot pistols (more than 42,000) through the sludge of a too slow market. If Colt's wanted the gun dealers to take more, it would have to offer them a discount of 10 percent. "We . . . think our look is very unsatisfactory for the sale of pistols," SHG wrote. "You may not be aware of it, but the Allies have a very large number of your NEW line on hand UNSOLD, and this crowding pistols on them beyond their judgment may result in YOUR disadvantage." SHG reminded Colt's, subtly, that the Allies would benefit from having a "great incentive to take and sell the pistols" at the higher volume, but it would injure Colt's if the "pistols would be made without any market for the new." Ultimately, the Allies agreed to take 42,000 of the 7-shot pistol at $2.99 apiece, with a discount of 10 percent should they agree to push an additional 30,000. "The object of this arrangement," the Allies wrote, "is, as you will see, to make each party interested until the entire lot is sold."[18]

Another problem was prices. The Allies routinely urged Colt's to lower them, as they thought the guns would sell better at lower prices. They made this plea in December 1874, saying, "it will be necessary for you to reduce the price of your new .38 and .41 Revolvers, for they move VERY slow since the reduction of . . . other manufacturers." Two years later, Colt's wanted to make a new stock of .38 and .41 rimfire pistols "at prices to suit the times"—which, for the gun market, were inauspicious. But it debated whether late 1876 was the proper time to put them on the market. Times were hard. But Colt's also consistently envisioned its market ambitiously, as its founder had, and it also consistently surmised that the problem was poor sales effort rather than overpriced or underwanted goods. In a common refrain, the company mused that sales of the new .30, .32, .38, and .41 "might be increased largely if they were properly *pushed*," implying that the Allies were listless gun hucksters. They had been given a lot of time to "work off their stock," after all, and they should have done better.[19]

The 7-shot sold badly, and the Allies conveyed to Colt's that they "UNANIMOUSLY think that the company ought not to ask at this time to put the [Old Model] 7-shot on the market." They had been assured that if the new 7-shot "were not selling well enough, they would be put at a price that WOULD sell them! They are moving now more fairly than for some time past, if not fast enough to meet your views." The Allies wanted until January 1 to "work off" the surplus gun stock, and then they would be ready for a fresh start. They proposed that Colt's reduce the price of the new 7-shot, so that they could increase sales and reduce their stock before the introduction of the Old Model (7-shot) on January 1, 1877. They thought it "injudicious" for Colt's to "press" them to take the OM, especially at a price higher than $1.75 each. Colt's refused to lower the price, because the company could not afford to do so. Besides, Colt's executives were convinced that "price is NOT the obstacle or impediment in the way of its success." Uninspired sales efforts were. But in order to give the Allies an "opportunity to show their zeal and relieve themselves of any surplus of stock," said Colt's, "we have decided to withhold the old model 7-shot from the market for the present."[20]

In February 1877 the market was worse. The Allies agreed to take the balance of the rimfire .38 new line revolvers, for example, but only if Colt's would turn off the spigot and agree to "produce no more of these pistols." By October, given the "depressed state of the pistol market," and the Allies' overstock, they were imploring Colt's to reduce the number of pistols being made. They had put in their "best efforts," they wrote, eager to deflect blame away from insufficient "pushing" of the product. But they had to report that sales, alas, had decreased.[21]

THE ALLIES' BICKERING AND TRAVAILS UNDERCUT TODAY'S POPULAR images of the ubiquitous Colt revolver and Winchester rifle. As vigorously as the Winchester and Colt companies pushed their dealers and advertised, the guns were expensive for most settlers. (On the frontier in 1872, a Henry might cost $30 to $37, depending on finish, and a Winchester 66 $45.) Or, even if they could have afforded them, they preferred cheaper, functional, yet unglamorous guns to the new patented models.[22]

Gun curator and historian Herbert Houze reviewed an important and overlooked archive—the surviving business ledger, from 1868 to 1886, of Schuyler, Hartley & Graham's military sales depot—which he claimed reinvents the idea of the "Western gun." While it is partly true that Colt's and the WRAC relied on frontier sales, Houze argued that the notion of the Winchester and the Colt as iconic frontier guns is "as much a fiction as the sources from which it is drawn." Guns were diffusing across the country in these years—but which guns, and from what sources? SHG shipped 5,567 US Model 1842 percussion muskets, the most widely sold general-purpose arm; 4,005 Prussian .69-caliber Model 1839 percussion muskets; 3,594 British Enfield .577-caliber Pattern 1853 percussion rifles; 2,105 French Chausseur de Vincennes .69-caliber percussion muskets; 2,083 US Allin .50–70CF-caliber breech-loading rifles; 1,080 Austrian .69-caliber Model 1854 percussion rifles; and smaller numbers of other eclectic types. SHG shipped only 414 Winchester Model 1873 carbines and rifles west, and 709 Winchester Model 66 carbines and rifles from 1868 to 1886 (similarly, it shipped only 178 Colt's pistols or revolvers, although this figure might reflect Colt's' covenants with dealers). Given the number of European model guns and rifles sold by SHG, the American western gun "culture" is revealed here, once again, to be part of an international commerce in arms.[23]

Even a number of guns shipped west by SHG actually went into international markets. SHG shipped 7,183 firearms to California between 1868 and 1885, over 70 percent of them rifles, which probably reflects that from California the rifles were shipped to Mexico and Central America. Houze found that handguns were a "distinct rarity" among California dealers.[24]

Viewed from the gun merchant's account ledger rather than Hollywood's silver screen, the gun market's tastes and preferences, owing to frugality or indifference or both, leaned toward cheaper, mechanically more dowdy, but still functional cast-off weapons, legacies of the antebellum or Civil War years, including single-shots and muzzle-loaders, rather than the (post facto) glamorized Winchester and Colt's patented arms. The gun's simple functionality as a tool prevailed over the mystique of the newer models. Seen from the commercial perspective and the eastern industrial economy to which it belonged, gun diffusion preceded mystique, and not vice versa, and even the American western gun market was indirectly bound up with international commerce, insofar as many of the most popular models were old European models. Accounts of the "Prussian percussion musket" or of US Model 1822 may not have much panache, but they may be more accurate than popular legends of "the gun that won the West."[25]

No federal laws delimited Winchester's cultivation of a gun market, although the West was a crucible of thousands of state and local gun-control laws concerning pistol-toting and gun etiquette. The gun today is mired in political fetishization, but the Second Amendment was a slumbering giant during the years of the gun's most intense diffusion. The gun was an ordinary, unexceptional object of commerce, treated unexceptionally.[26]

When it came to conquest—and race—the gun did, however, become more exceptional. In August 1876, after George Armstrong Custer's shocking demise at Little Big Horn, the federal government passed two resolutions that for the first time attempted to control gun commerce. These resolutions prohibited the sale of arms or ammunition to "hostile Indians of the northwest" and called for the confiscation of guns from "any Indian who may be proven to have committed any depredation on the white or friendly Indians." Before passage of the resolutions, Native Americans were able to acquire the latest patented Winchesters and other guns easily enough, if they could afford them, through licensed Indian agents who ran reservation trading posts, using government vouchers for hardware, through treaties that swapped Indian land for guns, or simply through traders. Custer and other officers had long been convinced that Native Americans were better armed than their own troops. A fur-trade expert noted that traders were first and foremost merchants, and their desire to sell trumped whatever "slight qualms" they might have felt in selling weapons to hostile Native Americans. Indeed, Oliver Winchester saw irresistible advertising fodder in the Native Americans' fascination with guns. He promoted his rifle by saying that, among the Indians, "possession is a passion." Buffalo Bill agreed that "an Indian will give more for [a Winchester] than any other gun he can get."[27]

The arms trade and traffic went on after the 1876 resolutions pretty much as they had before. The Indian agent for the Apaches in New Mexico reported, characteristically, that he had "the power to order obnoxious persons off the reservation, [but] they can go to one of [the] ranches right under my nose and laugh at me with impunity. They can carry on their trade with the Indians, and . . . they are as completely beyond my control as if they were in New York or Washington." The Ute had plenty of Winchesters, another agent reported, with traders "everywhere doing a thrifty business."[28]

The tenacity of this gun business disturbed the commissioner of Indian affairs, who concluded, "At least with some traders, the accompanying horrors of a war with savages have not always been sufficient to overcome their greed for gain" and "self-aggrandizement." The Indian agent for the Ute reservation shrilly condemned the trade and articulated the basic but unstated fact that the gun industry was selling a lethal commodity. "There is no offense against the commonwealth showing greater moral turpitude than the crime of those persons who recklessly place in the hands of savages all the improved pattern of arms, which they know will be used to destroy the lives of innocent white citizens." The 1876 resolutions were inadequate to stem the "murderous traffic" to "non-civilized Indians" and the "unhallowed trade in implements of death."[29]

In few other contexts at the time was the arms merchant or capitalist's "greed for gain" criticized, or the amoral gun business transmogrified into an immorality. In the darkened parlors and séance tents of spiritualism, the age's fugitive conscience, such distant connections and accountabilities might indeed be vividly perceived, but not in the empirical, laissez-faire world of the gun industrialist, with his narrow business accounting. The idea of the arms dealer or profiteer as "no better than a murderer," an abridgement of cause (selling a gun) and effect (killing a person), and an expansion of gun accountability was almost unheard of. The longer view of what the gun economy did in the world, how the commerce of one arms dealer could rend the social fabric by a murder elsewhere, was always there to be seen—even if, in the 1870s, it was seen most often through the lens of conquest and racism.

CHAPTER 9

THE "MORAL EFFECT"
OF A WINCHESTER

THE WINCHESTER MODEL 73 BECAME A SORT OF GUN CELEBRITY—but mostly in the 1900s, looking through a glass darkly at the 1800s. Like other celebrities, it eventually went by only one name: Winchester. Like extremely successful celebrities, it then went by just one letter, a red, thunderous *W*. The family name, which became the rifle name, eventually stood for the genus, becoming a synonym for repeating, semiautomatic rifles. "The model '73 is the first rifle which went into every corner of the world and is still being used by every race of mankind," the company boasted in 1920.[1]

When considered from a business perspective, however, it becomes clear that the quintessential frontier rifle flourished later, in the "post-frontier" early 1900s. Its celebrity biography backdated its diffusion and even its popularity.[2]

Winchester production figures show that the Model 73 of legend was barely in circulation in 1873. Numbers #1 through #126 were manufactured in 1873, but only 18 shipped in this first year. In 1874 Winchester produced 2,599, but shipped only 108. The WRAC produced 41,515 Model 73s in the 1870s, or 5.7 percent of the total produced. The company produced two other gun models in the 1870s, and the Model 66 was by far the decade's staple Winchester, at 122,675 produced, with the Model 76, introduced in 1876, adding production of 8,968. In the 1880s, Winchester produced over half a million guns (524,555) in seven models, and the Model 73 was the most heavily produced model, at 282,426 total for the decade, or 54 percent of all Winchesters produced in the 1880s, and 39 percent of all Model 73s ever produced. Only 55,015 were made of the decade's second most heavily produced Winchester, the Model 1885.[3]

Although it was the biggest seller in the 1880s (but not the 1870s), viewed in terms of the history of the model, it is interesting that roughly equal numbers of Model 73s were produced in the 1900s (234,050) and 1890s (217,362). Even though the company produced no Model 73s in 1907 or 1908, it still produced one-third of its Model 73s in the 1890s, and another third from 1900 to 1909, with the single highest yearly production ever (149,996, or 21 percent of the total) in 1904. Thinking in terms of per capita production, the WRAC produced one Model 73 per 547 Americans in 1904 (although it is, of course, not the case that all of the guns produced were sold domestically), and 1 per 5,116 Americans in 1875.[4]

Why did the Model 73 take off in the 1880s and 1900s? Technologically and materially, it was, quite simply, a better gun, and this certainly contributed to its (retrospectively enhanced) fame and stature. The Model 73 was identical to the Model 66 in mechanical principles, but with improvements in accuracy, power, and handiness. The cartridge was changed to center fire, and it held a charge of 40 grains of powder instead of 25. This capacity increased the gun's initial velocity from about 1,125 feet per second to 1,325. Winchester, still thinking, albeit with waning zeal, of martial use, touted two other mechanical improvements that prevented premature explosion or accidents and made the 73 "especially suited to Military Arms."[5]

The gun performed almost every operation automatically. Winchester wrote, "All the operation of loading and withdrawing the empty shell, in short, every function of the Gun, except pulling the trigger, is performed by two motions of the operating lever; vis., forward and back"—and he could not help but specify that this was "substantially *one* motion."[6]

The lever performed five functions in one: it opened the breech of the gun, extracted the shell of the fired cartridge, advanced the next cartridge from the magazine to the barrel, cocked the gun, and closed the breach. The entire process, from the loading of a cartridge from the magazine to the firing of the gun, could be executed in half a second, and repeated just as rapidly, delivering eighteen shots in nine seconds. Axiomatically, the more mechanically ingenious the gun became, the less skilled, gun-smart, or ingenious the shooter needed to be. Winchester assured potential customers that "a child ten years old can with half an hour's instruction load and fire it with perfect safety." And, if one cartridge should misfire, another was easily and quickly advanced.[7]

Speed (not power) and accuracy from a distance were the mechanical soul of all Winchesters. With each design advance, the volition of the rifle became more volitional. Small, mortal operations of armed conflict occurred through the technological ingenuity of the mechanical hand, and the confrontation became less intimate or physically immediate. The gun "did" more of the motions and actions of killing.

The trajectory in guns was toward faster shooting and more reflexive operation for other gun capitalists as well. The *Sunday Herald and Weekly National Intelligence* compared the Smith & Wesson Schofield pistol favorably to Colt's. It could discharge empty shells "all at once. . . . You grab a handful of cartridges, fill the chambers without looking at them." What a contrast, this "easy and, above all, rapid, proceeding," in comparison to Colt's suddenly "slow and . . . tedious" reloading process.[8]

In a broadside, Winchester promoted the character capacities elicited by the repeater's technological ones. And this was a second component of the Model 73's gun celebrity: although Winchester still mostly promoted his rifles for their functionality and mechanical virtues, he was also deepening his feel for a gun's aura, sensing a competitive advantage in imbuing the rifle with character, or, more often, ascribing character attributes to its user. This tendency would only grow stronger in the twentieth century. "The great advantage of this rifle over all others consists in the *moral effect* it has . . . ," he wrote, "for if there is anything that will make a party of men, or one single man, stand up and fight to the last moment, it is the knowledge that he has a gun in his hands that will not fail to do its duty just at the time when it is most wanted" (italics added). Winchester here elaborated the "coolness" of the semiautomatic shooter, earlier noted in the Civil War, and the Winchester as a boost of courage in the face of lopsided or insuperable odds. Its rapid fire and reliability made the 73 "an ideal arm for . . . the kind of mobile warfare that was typical of Indian-white man fighting" and for those threatened with "sudden attack." Colt, likewise, once described his revolver as perfect for conflicts of a "special and brief character, [when] it be desirable to throw a mass of fire upon a particular point for a limited time." In a sense, the Winchester rifle and Colt's revolver both promised the advantage of overkill. Winchester's advertisement imagined the rifle as protection for women and children in a jittery, dangerous world, "as it is at times necessary for all men to be away from home, consequently leaving [them] to fight for themselves."[9]

For the first time in the 1870s, Winchester stressed the rifle's non-military attributes in his advertisement and promotion. He now shared testimonials and stories from civilians. For example, one concerned the Model 73, #289, which found its way to the Antelope Station in Cheyenne, Nebraska, where its owner proclaimed it the "BEST GUN" he'd ever used, saying, "I have often got from four to seven antelope out of a herd in less than a minute, where, with any other gun, I could not have gotten more than two shots." Then there was the route superintendent for mail coaches at a station in Texas who killed "three or four of the enemy [Indians], and as many of their horses, with [his] Winchester rifle."[10]

One of the most obvious but significant aspects of these stories is that they're usually about a lone gunman—one armed individual, in private battle against beast or man. In this sense, they are unlike tales of wartime bravery. Rebuffed by the US military and courting a civilian market, Winchester now self-consciously conflated the two, writing of the gun's moral effect "either upon an army or an individual"; either upon "a party of men or one single man." His testimonials routinely equated the firepower of a "single man" with the firepower "of an entire regiment of soldiers firing muzzle-loaders." Before this time, the use of guns against humans was predominantly a social or national act, inspired by patriotism, or *esprit de corps*. It would prove one of Winchester's deepest but subtlest legacies: he conceived of the lone civilian, "scattered" throughout the country, as his customer, a figure who became the iconic twentieth- and twenty-first-century American gunman.[11]

Winchester's approach meshed with the hard paramilitary realities of conquest and settlement. Indeed, it is worth contemplating how much America's heavily armed civilian population owes to the peculiarly domestic nature of both the most cataclysmic nineteenth-century war, the Civil War, and its most violent conquest, of Native American cultures. Unlike in Europe, which kept the US gun business alive, but does not today have our civilian gun violence, in America war and conquest were both domestic, and the guns deployed stayed put within American borders. Western emigrants, de facto, were somewhere between soldier and civilian, their everyday existence to some extent militarized in a land in between battlefield and settlement. In Europe, conquest involved imperial expeditions; America's conquest blurred settler into soldier—and the Model 73, in both design and germinal mystique, suited that hybrid environment.

Military aims infiltrated nonmilitary sport and landscape in the West as well. The government supported a "martial ecology" after the Civil War that merged the agendas of rifle hunting and conquest, according to one historian. Plains Indians clashed with settlers for rights to the rich hunting ranges and game trails. In this context, the army encouraged sporting as an instrument of conquest: the more buffalo killed by sport hunters, the more endangered the Native American food supply became. The army gave rifle hunters logistical aid, hunting tips, protection, and ammunition. The only biography of Buffalo Bill written by a family member recounts how he guided three companies of the 5th Cavalry, along with some personal friends of General Emory from New York and England, on a twenty-day scout. "The expedition had two objectives," wrote Julia Cody Goodman, Buffalo Bill's older sister: "To hunt for game and to find hostile Indians." Game they found, but none of the other prey. The New Yorker was disappointed. He wanted to "see action," so Bill invented some. His Wild West show was a show before it was a show; the West and its gun were postmodern before postmodernity, in the sense that stories and narratives of the West constructed the lived experience and reality of the West. Buffalo Bill "prevailed upon Pawnee scouts to disguise themselves as hostile Indians. When [the New Yorker] saw the 'enemy' warriors charging down upon him, he turned tail and galloped towards camp."[12]

There is a blasé seamlessness here and elsewhere between human and animal "prey." Indians were "all too often regarded by American frontiersmen as another breed of wild animal," historian Richard Hofstadter observed in his signal essay on the "gun culture." Colonel George Schofield, for whom the Smith & Wesson revolver was named, wrote to the company in 1875 to report his great success during his "second expedition against hostile Indians, . . . having killed almost everything—but an Indian—with [the Smith & Wesson gun]." Chillingly Schofield commented, in another context, "I want no other occupation in life than to ward off the savage and kill off his food until there should no longer be an Indian frontier in our beautiful country."[13]

The same gun worked for war and the hunt, and it was advertised as such. Oliver Winchester advertised the Model 66 as the ideal weapon for "Indian, Bear or Buffalo hunting," blurring lines between the prey, and advertised its rifles "For Military and Sporting Purposes" in the *Army and Navy* journal. "For general hunting or Indian fighting," Buffalo Bill pronounced Winchester "the boss." In its 1877 catalog, Remington promoted the hunting or sporting rifle as the "frontier rifle," saying it had "furnished the interior department for arming the Indian police." Colt's condensed these markets into one ad on the pages of *Turf Field and Farm*, promoting the "Peacemaker" as a pistol not only for "officers of the army and navy" but also for "all who travel among dangerous communities." The weapon was good, Colt's advertised, for "public or private service."[14]

Winchester began to individualize the gun. He had to. This was the market he had, if not the one he had at first imagined or preferred. In this phase of the gun business, Winchester and other gun titans cultivated the US civilian market of individual customers. He needed to untether his rifle from formal war and the military market, and think about the private army of one, in a kind of military-civilian market in-filtration not evident in other contexts. To the extent that the rifle had a moral effect, it was an intricate one. For the Winchester customer, a life is lived alone in both self-reliance and vulnerability. It achieves heroic transcendence through speed, in fight and flight, and in the always-imminent "moments of emergency." Winchester's world, in his coinage, was one of "single individuals, traveling through a wild coun-try." His gun business would prosper to the simple, elegant extent that he could convince other Americans that this was their world, too.[15]

FROM THE VANTAGE POINT OF THE GUN INDUSTRY, THE ASSOCIATION of Winchester's rifle with individualism was paradoxical. When Rem-ington had embarked on the gun business in 1816, he had made guns on a customized and individual basis for customers, as gunsmiths had, on demand. W. W. Greener, one of Britain's foremost gun experts, opined in an 1881 opus that newfangled repeater rifles would fail com-mercially precisely because they were mass-produced. He saw as folly "the assumption that one type of gun will suit . . . everyone. . . . As no two persons are exactly alike," each would have his own gun prefer-ences. Interchangeability worked fine for military purposes, Greener speculated, where the homogeneity of the mass over the individual soldier was essential, but for civilian arms, the "*sine qua non* that all will be alike" of mass-produced guns precluded the true individualizing and value-creating "fancy of the workman, [the] incentive to produce a better arm" and preferences in ornamentation. The machine-made repeater was just an "assemblage of various synoforms, neither artistic nor symmetrical . . . at best only a mediocre production."[16]

In the 1870s, guns were being mass-produced, in the hands of the industrialist and not the gunsmith, in a more complex corporate econ-omy; each Winchester was machined to within 1/1,000th of an inch and made with interchangeable parts by machine, and rifles achieved unprecedented diffusion. But the Winchester's diffusion and its germi-nal mystique were at odds. To some extent, the mystique relied, tacitly, on obfuscating the ties between the world of the gun business—eastern, industrial, corporate, and driven by interchangeability—and the aura of the gun. In gun ownership, the feeling of individualism, or of secure autonomy for "single individuals," was—and is—an anxious, if not untenable, form of self-sovereignty, because everyone for whom the gun is mass-produced and sold has the same gun and the same idea.[17]

Winchester's "One of One Thousand" campaign in 1875 romantically elaborated this core gun paradox of mass-produced individualism, vividly demonstrating Winchester's growing feel for the gun mystique. Winchester had a strong self-conscious hand in making the Model 73 a gun "celebrity." One of a thousand rifles were promoted as the very best and the most "super accurate" of all 720,610 Model 73s made between 1873 and 1924, tweaked with set-triggers and extra finishing. The company sold them at the higher price for a Model 73 of $100— roughly $2,200 today. Gun mavens today consider these the most glamorous of the Winchester family: they were used by Billy the Kid and Buffalo Bill—celebrity guns owned by celebrities. A Winchester 1 of 1,000 sold in 2013 for $95,000, and antique gun collectors surmise that other guns of this model could sell for substantially more than that, perhaps even $200,000 or $400,000.[18]

Much of the American gun culture was built out of profitable malarkey—and the 1 of a 1,000 campaign was another example. In 1936, Winchester executive Edwin Pugsley wrote to a Winchester admirer that "there is a great deal of mystery and hokum still clinging to the gun business." The "atmosphere of mystery" had been even worse in the days of gunsmiths, Pugsley felt. Still, the idea of a Winchester barrel with extraordinary mechanical properties, as with the Model 73, was a bit of hokum. One can readily see "that a part of a billet of steel might be made into a gun part and another part of the same billet into a mowing machine, and the part which went into the gun barrel would have no more mythical properties than its brother in the mowing machine," Pugsley said. "I realize that this is not good sales talk," he conceded, "for, unquestionably, we could charge many customers $10.00 extra for a selected barrel," as the company had in the 1870s and 1880s, he recalled, with barrels "engraved 'one in a thousand' and sold at an extra price."[19]

Whatever the case, a mass-produced, mass-marketed object was to become an enduring idiom of American individualism. The earliest

striation of this mystique was laid down by Winchester's own advertisements and testimonials, the most indelible of which were generously fabularized (recall Captain Wilson's Civil War battle in Kentucky
against bandits, for example). The next layer consisted of stories written by others: journalism that blurred fact and fantasy, for example,
and dime novels of the West published in the early decades of the commercial gun business. This layer wasn't any more true or accurate than
others, but it and the gun industrialists' advertisements were there first
and formed the bedrock, and would appear most proximate to historical fact as more layers of myth were piled on top of them in the twentieth century.

In February 1867, journalist George Ward Nichols published an article in *Harper's* on "Wild Bill" Hickok that became a trope for the
western gun hero. Nichols told of Dave Tutt, a professional gambler
and rebel scout during the war. Tutt arrived in Springfield, Missouri,
intent on picking a fight with Hickok. There was an "undercurrent of a
woman" involved, Hickok told Nichols, and he faced off against Tutt
in the town plaza. The men fired, and the ball went through Tutt's
heart. In a scene restaged into perpetuity, on silver screen and in back-
yards, Tutt "stood stock still for a second or two, then raised his arm as
if ter fire again, then he swayed a little, staggered three or four steps,
and then fell dead." Hickok didn't even need to look back to know
Tutt was dead. He said, "I knew he was a dead man. I never miss a
shot." Hickok distilled the code of the gun: "He tried to degrade me,
and I couldn't stand that, you know, for I am a fighting man, you
know. . . . A man must defend his honor." Nichols concluded his piece:
"I have told this story precisely as it was told to me . . . and I have no
doubt of its truth."[20]

Perhaps not, but Nichols's local readers recognized it as hooey even
in 1867, and their criticisms sent Nichols fleeing back to writing about
music. The *Springfield Patriot* wrote that some citizens were "exces-
sively indignant" at the outrageous fabrications in *Harper's*, and what
they perceived as slanderous "caricatures" against their city that all of
the fools of New England were gullible enough to swallow as gospel
truth, but the "great majority [were] in convulsions of laughter." All

agreed that the piece should have been published in the company of "other fabricated more or less funnyisms," and not as the lead article. Some in Springfield remembered Nichols's stay there, and his "splurging among our 'strange, half-civilized people,' seriously endangering the supply of lager and corn whisky, and putting on more airs than a spotted stud-horse in the ring of a county fair." As for the portrait of Wild Bill, none in Springfield had suspected that he had dispatched "several hundreds with his own hands," as the article claimed. The editors of the *Leavenworth Daily Conservative* in Kansas opined reservedly that the article sounded "mythical."[21]

Nichols's article included an account of Hickok's 1861 shooting of David McCanles and two others—a gang of "murderers and regular cut-throats," as Nichols had it—at Rock Creek Station in Nebraska, a stagecoach and Pony Express post where Hickok was employed. Another writer, Ramon Adams, a foremost expert on westerns, noted that Hickok and an accomplice had killed three men, including McCanles, in cold blood, with Hickok shooting from behind a curtain, and that McCanles had never pulled a gun. The "Wild Billians," as one review of gunfighters calls them, had Hickok as the valiant stagecoach defender of "government property" (the US mail) against thieves, but the consensus seems to be that McCanles, the owner of the Rock Creek property, went over unarmed to collect overdue rent, per a contract, and that tensions between the men might have been exacerbated by the fact that Hickok had made overtures toward McCanles's mistress.[22]

The McCanles gunfight was to become the core of the Hickok legend. The larger the legend, and the more it defines a culture, the more difficult it is for historians to trace its concrete production. But the story of the American gun culture is constructed in some part of the story of gunslingers and gunfighters, and as loamy and encompassing as these stories became in the 1900s, their tangible, literal origins are not impossible to trace forensically. The iconic American gun stories, like the iconic guns themselves, came from the Northeast. The guns came from the factories of New Haven and Hartford; and the dime novels that told of the gun's adventures came from what a *Ladies Home Journal* editor aptly named the "literary factories" of New York. One dime novelist writer recalled that in a "little den on an upper floor" of the "worm-eaten old building" of publisher Beadle & Adams, he would "grind out dime novels day after day with the steadiness of a machine."[23]

Dime novels were not the only means of transmission for the first generation of gun legends—the sensationalist pink newspaper the *National Police Gazette* wrote luridly of the West's gunmen—but they were the most widely distributed and powerful. "Beadle's dime novels," roughly 100 pages, were sensational stories, but they were generically presented as real, thrilling, authentic, and true tales of the West. They flourished in the 1860s and through to the early 1890s. Beadle & Adams would publish 3,158 titles, mass-producing the story of the mass-produced Winchester rifle. Dime novels, one of the authors told an interviewer in 1902, required "only three things—a riotous imagination, a dramatic instinct, and a right hand that never tires." As scholar Michael Denning explained, dime novels followed interchangeable stock plots and characters and could be churned out by anonymous writers. Another dime novel author described the basic template of the tale: "Virtue must triumph, vice and crime must not only be defeated, but must be painted in colors so strong and vivid that there is no mistake about it." Owen Payne White, who wrote stories of "gun fighting murderers" for *Collier's* in the genre, recollected in his autobiography that, while the stories claimed to be "true and vivid," his editor encouraged him to write about topics that he hadn't researched and knew nothing about. He promoted "the sale of the magazine by killing someone in almost every paragraph."[24]

And it was through these dime novels and similar works that the 1867 Wild Bill story from Nichols's pen and imagination began its long reverse migration, from fable and legend into the more solid stature of history and settled wisdom by the mid-1900s. Other characters—Buffalo Bill, Billy the Kid, Belle Starr, Calamity Jane, and the California bandit Murieta, contrived out of whole cloth—would follow the same path—from lowbrow fiction into highbrow historical fact—and from there would be summoned either as a condemnation or as a celebration of America's gun culture.

In 1881, *Heroes of the Plains, or Lives and Wonderful Adventures of Wild Bill*, authored by James Buel, was published by "Historical Publishing" in St. Louis. Ramon Adams has noted that although this book wasn't a dime novel, it read like one. Its formidable length and large circulation encouraged readers to treat it as factual—and it replicated the false Nichols story. The next year, one of the most prolific of the dime novelists, Prentice Ingraham, penned *Wild Bill, The Pistol Dead Shot*, which, according to Adams, "made [Wild Bill] a superhuman, engaging in exploits with no semblance of truth to them." The same year, a book on the history of Nebraska tried to present a more realistic account of Wild Bill's Rock Creek fight, noting that he killed only three men, and that, far from demonstrating courage, he had simply displayed "skill in the use of firearms"—and cowardice. Nevertheless, Wild Bill was becoming a dime-novel favorite, and the "false true" story drowned out the modest and rare attempts at history. Ingraham reprised Nichols's narrative again in 1884, but embellished Hickok's gun lethality, in the predilections of the genre, by describing him as "one man [who] whipped ten desperadoes, killing eight of them." Subsequent stories did likewise: they took the core of the Nichols account and exaggerated both the number of gun victims and the atrocities of the McCanles "gang." Ned Buntline's 1886 dime novel had McCanles killing Hickok's father in front of the entire family, and an 1890 account, *Wild Jim, The Texas Cowboy*, had Hickok disemboweling his antagonist in retaliation.[25]

Hickok himself, like Buffalo Bill, must have been at least instinctively if not explicitly aware of the benefits of self-commodification, and he, too, exaggerated stories of his gun violence and its righteousness. He was fond of "loading easterners" with tall tales of his gun exploits, and he appeared in Buffalo Bill's Wild West show. He told author Henry Stanley (*My Early Travels and Adventures in America and Asia*) the malarkey that he had killed "considerably over a hundred" white men. It all started when he was twenty-eight years old and was robbed at a hotel in Leavenworth. He stabbed one man before using "his revolver on the others left and right," killing four more. He then fled, he said, but returned with soldiers to capture the entire villainous band of fifteen thieves. Hickok told the story of the McCanles fight to

General Armstrong Custer's impressionable wife, years after the fact, as a heroic stand against a ferocious gang of horse thieves and killers, and this account, too, accreted into fact.[26]

In the 1890s, the dime novels of the 1880s, which had drawn on Nichols's fiction of 1867, became the basis for stories of gunfighters that claimed authenticity. An anonymous 1893 account, *Buffalo Bill and His Wild West Companions*, used Ingraham, who drew on Nichols, as an authority; a 1901 book, *History of Our Wild West and Stories of Pioneer Life*, followed the false Buel narrative as fact. Another author, Emerson Hough, wrote an influential account in 1907, *The Story of the Outlaw*, that replicated the Nichols legend. Hough dignified Wild Bill by promoting him from a stable hand to agent of Rock Creek Station. The same year, an author considered "an able historian," according to Adams, repeated the Nichols fable in *The Great Plains: The Romance of Western American Exploration*, and embellished the gunslinger story in the typical fashion by having Wild Bill getting attacked by ten men, and then wiping out the entire "M'Kandlas" gang.[27]

Wild Bill stories published in the first decade of the 1900s would have more gravitas and authority than the dime novels of the 1880s, but would still draw on the Nichols core. *Famous Scouts . . .* , published in 1910, dignified Buel and Hough as authorities by writing that Bill had dictated the "true" story to Buel. In 1911, a political science professor at the University of Wyoming perpetuated the Nichols-Buel-Hough legend as fact. A year later, another serious book, *Pioneer Tales of the Oregon Trail*, decried the "wide variance between the truth and fiction told by Emerson Hough," but the next year, the publisher L&M Oppenheimer, notorious for its wildly fictive "true" accounts of the West, published perhaps the most fabularized version ever of Bill's conflict: it confused Wild Bill with Buffalo Bill, and had him kill ten men single-handedly. One effort at history contended against a dozen narratives that took Nichols as bedrock, settled as fact, and told the fiction anew. It was an error written in 1867 into the DNA code for the marrow of America's "gun culture" that was replicated through the decades, with narrative mutations almost invariably in the direction of exaggerated lethality and greater moral righteousness.[28]

The Hickok story of Rock Creek illustrates a larger pattern. Gun-men began as legends, and their stories tended to burnish the impulsiv-ity and stupidity of gun violence into an epic, scaffolding it with a purpose and a code: the Hickok origins story takes a mundane, ambig-uous property dispute without a clear villain or hero, armed impulsiv-ity, and banal but combustible sexual tensions and refashions them into a fable with an excess of both gun-riddled corpses and meaning.[29]

More than five hundred dime novels were written about Buffalo Bill Cody alone, and he became literally the most storied Winchester man. Like Hickok, Buffalo Bill did not become a myth so much as he began as one. His founding mythology was that he had killed and scalped the Cheyenne chief Yellow Hand in revenge for Custer's death. Julia Cody Goodman, his sister, recalled that from the Yellow Hand tale forward, the "hacks and historians, the myth makers and malingerers, the sugar-coaters and scandalmongers" all got in on the action, to write "panegy-rics and diatribes" in which Bill was presented as "god or devil," early examples of the Manichean narrative style of the American gunman. Buffalo Bill's sister recalled that he only occasionally discovered the "skeleton of himself under the purple prose . . . outlandish adventures and superhuman feats" that, for example, dime novelist Ned Buntline concocted.[30]

Hickok's story, Buffalo Bill's story, and the story in general of the gun and the frontier got abbreviated into a few familiar plots and phrases: its morally stark narrative pitted the lone, repeater-armed gunman, equal to many, against a horde of desperados and bad men, as in this dime novel:

> Nearer and nearer came the rushing band of Indians, for what had two hundred mounted warriors to fear from one man?
>
> Nearer and nearer until presently, Buffalo Bill was seen to raise his rifle and a perfect stream of fire seemed to flow out of the muzzle, while the shots came in rapid succession.
>
> It was a Winchester repeating rifle, and Buffalo Bill had been test-ing it thoroughly.

And the result was such that . . . down in the dust had gone several of their number. . . .

With a wild, defiant war-cry, Buffalo Bill wheeled and rode away, loading his matchless rifle as he ran.[31]

The dime western put Winchester, if not the rifle itself, in the back pockets of boys who repeated its catechism of the frontier, perhaps without knowing exactly what it meant: "Crack crack crack went the Winchester and fifteen Indians bit the dust."[32]

Buffalo Bill himself invented fabulous stories, or sometimes had them ghostwritten to be published under his name. He once wrote to his publisher: "I am sorry to have to lie so outrageously in this yarn. My hero has killed more Indians on one war trail than I have killed all my life. But I understand this is what is expected of border tales. If you think

Buffalo Bill illustration for the cover of a dime novel. More than five hundred dime novels were written about Buffalo Bill. *Courtesy of the Denver Public Library, Western History Collection.*

the revolver and bowie knife are used too freely, you may cut out a fatal shot or stab whenever you deem it wise."[33] He also self-commodified with his Wild West show. The show was atrociously written, by Buntline, and wildly successful. The *Chicago Times* said in a review that "if Buntline had actually spent four hours in writing this play, it would be difficult to ascertain what he had been doing all that time." But the audiences loved it, and Buffalo Bill wrote home to his sister in 1886 saying that the public "looks upon me as the one man in my business. And if they will only think so for a year or two I will make money enough for us all for our life time." The Wild West show was a strange ritual of conquest: Bill slayed the Indians in a putatively authentic reenactment of the already mythic Yellow Hand tale, and the Native American actors, who restaged their own demise at the hands of Winchesters and Colts, left to thunderous applause—and then returned, resurrected with ghostly immortality, for the next performance.[34]

If the Winchester 73 rifle had been a book, it would have been a dime novel: mass-produced with interchangeable plots; mechanical, predictable, requiring little exertion by the user; and delivering its conclusion efficiently and precisely. Like the Winchester rifle, the dime novel was semiautomatic. It did more of the work for the reader. It was molded, "machined," and produced in much the same way as the rifle. The interchangeable, machined story, like the rifle itself, had a mystique based in heroic individualism. As society became less individualistic, the gun promised individualism; as Americans became less democratically equal in terms of wealth, the Winchester equalized them; as the world and economy became more complex and interconnected, the mystique conjured the lone gunman. The generic rifle and its owner were *sui generis*, in a class of their own. The reader gloried in the violent, triumphant life of a character who was just like the others in hundreds of dime novels with millions of readers—but entirely his own man.[35]

The gun mystique would gain momentum because, like any legend, it resolved contradictions that history could not manage. It is often said that Americans "love their guns" because of our tradition of individualism, but the gun's seduction involves a dual heritage: an ideal of individual equality, and a reality where it sometimes falls short. The gun had a kind of narrative firepower to resolve this tension. It could transliterate the subjugated into the powerful lone gunman, and this aspect of the gun mystique was germinal in the 1800s.

For example, as it became clear during Reconstruction that southern blacks would not enjoy the benefits of free citizenship or the protection of law against white mobs and lynchings, the appeal of the Winchester grew stronger for black leaders, such as scholar and activist W. E. B. Du Bois and journalist Ida B. Wells. Wells, who on another occasion bought a pistol after a lynching, wrote, "The Winchester rifle deserves a place of honor in every Black home."[36]

On a July evening in 1892 in New Orleans, Robert Charles, a black man, was sitting with a friend on a rowhouse stoop when the police approached and asked what his business was. The confrontation turned violent. The police grabbed Charles and wounded him, but he managed to return to his room, where he grabbed his Winchester and shot and killed the police captain who had pursued him. A mob descended on the city to attack the black community. The next day, the police found Charles hiding in a friend's home. He took his Winchester and let loose a barrage, but eventually realized that he was surrounded. Charles was shot and killed. In her telling of this story, Wells characterized Charles as a valiant gunman—or the Alamo, as historian Nicholas Johnson writes. "Charles made a last stand in a small building," she wrote, "and fought a mob of twenty thousand single-handed, and alone." The mob set fire to his building, but even then, "Charles was shooting and every crack of his death-dealing rifle added another victim to the price which he had placed upon his own life." The *Times-Democrat* of New Orleans noted Charles' acumen with his Winchester. "He worked his weapon with incredible rapidity," the paper said. "His wonderful marksmanship never failed him for a moment." When the fire was too much to endure, he appeared at the door, "rifle in hand, to charge the countless guns that were drawn upon him. . . . He raised his gun to fire again, but this time it failed for 100 shots riddled his body." Wells's narration of Charles's demise was the gunslinger story, complete with its exaggerated, individual omnipotence, transliterated to the side of the racially oppressed, a feat achieved through the gun. For Wells and other African Americans, the Winchester was an extemporized steel bridge to get from the reality of racial subjugation to the ideal of equality.[37]

A popular inscription on the Winchester 73 read: "Be not afraid of any man, no matter what his size. When danger threatens, call on me. And I will equalize." Colt's first biographer believed that the firearm was a "blessing to mankind" because it gave protection to "the weak against the strong," the "dwarf some superiorities over the giant." Echoing Samuel Colt's promotional copy of the 1850s down to the 1870s, the *New Orleans Republican* predicted that the shotgun would become a "famous peacemaker" when juries and justice failed the black man. This idea became prominent again in the late 1960s, when a young black man in Chicago, for example, claimed the gun as "status," adding, "That's why they call it an equalizer. What's happening today is everybody's getting more and more equal because everybody's got one."[38]

"God made man, and Colt made them equal," one adage held. Of course, making men equal is presumably what the institutions of American law and democracy were supposed to do. For African Americans, Native Americans, and other groups, including women, who were disenfranchised or vulnerable, the Winchester promised a self-sovereignty and individual power that had not been achieved by institutions or law. If war is diplomacy by other means, then the Winchester was equality by other means: the gun, rather than being interpreted as the apotheosis of American individualism, could be seen as the individual's tool of last resort when the social contract has torn and the work of equalizing has fallen short: the dream that has deferred to the gun.[39]

It must be the American gun's most enduring and satisfying seduction: the notion that a gun can equalize—that the abused spouse, for example, can arm herself and be powerful and safe, her finger on the trigger razing years of degradation. Who can dispute that in the face of the institutional failures of injustice and indifference, the brandishing of a gun, even if it is never shot, would feel like, and *be*, a form of empowerment?

But it still matters who is at which end of the barrel. As dominant as constitutional debates are to gun politics today, the Supreme Court's first Second Amendment case, *United States v. Cruikshank*, was only heard in 1876, the same year the federal government restricted the gun trade to Native Americans. It emerged out of the single bloodiest day of violence during Reconstruction, and it tested the South's black codes—state legislation that, among other things, prohibited African American gun ownership in the most heavily armed region of the country. Colfax was the county seat of Grant Parish in Louisiana. The massacre that happened there on Easter Sunday in 1873 did not resemble the heroic narration of Robert Charles's last stand. The Radical Republican sheriff of Colfax had deputized 150 African Americans to defend the town against white Democrats who were outraged over a community of freedmen's efforts to assert and use their new political rights. For three weeks, the hastily drilled and armed men managed to hold off more heavily armed whites who surrounded the brick stable that served as the town's courthouse. On Easter Sunday, whites shot most of the town's black defenders dead as they tried to surrender.[40]

The defendant in *Cruikshank* was a member of the Colfax mob. Among other things, he'd been charged with restricting blacks' rights to bear arms. In this ruling, the Court upheld the right of states to pass civilian firearms controls and legislation. In other words, the justices found that the federal government did not have the power to restrict or limit state gun legislation, which meant that the racist agenda of effectively disarming African Americans through state gun laws would be permitted. (Subsequent laws in the early 1900s in the South were blatant in their intention to selectively limit gun ownership according to race.) In what seems like a negative image of twenty-first-century gun politics, the ruling supported state legislation—gun control—to limit African American citizens' access to the gun market as against the northern liberal campaign to protect emancipated slaves' unrestricted right to bear arms for their own protection and the protection of their families.[41]

As for the gun violence itself, it is more often intraracial than heroically deployed against inequalities or the oppressor. Renowned sociologist Gunnar Myrdal observed in the early 1940s what more conservative black leaders, such as Booker T. Washington, had already feared, that the "custom of going armed" in the South, which was "taken over by negroes during Reconstruction days," and the "dangerous pattern" of having guns around "undoubtedly contributes to the high record of violent actions, most of the time directed against other negroes." The African American homicide rate in US cities by the mid-1920s was between seven and eight times that of whites. In practice, the philosophy of the gun deferred to the stupidity and impulsivity of its use. A gun imagined against a white mob gets used against a lover or neighbor, instead, or by the mob against the oppressed. We might love the gun for the lure of last-ditch individualism and equality, but that doesn't mean the gun loves us back.[42]

IF THIS GERMINAL GUN MYSTIQUE EXAGGERATED THE "QUALITY" of gun violence—tying it to values of individual agency, justice, and equality—it also exaggerated the quantity of gun violence. Tales of gunmen imagine America as more gun-violent than it was, when it would seem that bias should lean in the other, exculpatory direction. This gun overkill was evident early on in Daniel Boone's legend, and it persisted up to and beyond the Hickok story. We wrote, staged, advertised, filmed, debated, and televised our way into a gun culture more than we shot our way in.

Billy the Kid's story did not fade from fact into legend, but from legend into fact. Two years before the Kid's death at age twenty-three, the wife of the territorial governor of New Mexico wrote to her husband the false legend that he had killed a man for every year of his life, when it is doubtful that he killed more than eight. According to historian Gary Roberts, many old-timers spoke of how they knew Billy the Kid, and recounted stories of him as if they were their own eyewitness memories—but these stories were so similar to a *National Police Gazette* story that there could be no doubt as to their provenance. The Kid's overkill, like that of other famous gunmen, began immediately after his death with the publication of dime novels, including John Woodruff Lewis's *The True Life of Billy the Kid* (1881) and a serial account in

Las Vegas Optic. Subsequent accounts exaggerated the number of people he killed and injured, although he was portrayed as more sociopathic than other gunmen. Works concluded that he killed "just for the sport of it," "went about shooting folks just for the fun of it," and had "more individual killings to his credit" than any other. A very rare book prepared for each member of the Livestock Association in 1905 repeated the story that had been told by the New Mexico governor's wife, describing the Kid as an "infamous cutthroat" who had killed one man for each year of his "horrible life."[43]

Other narratives of the western gun followed the same pattern: The Johnson County "War of Wyoming" involved nothing more than "two inconspicuous ranchmen . . . over a line fence quarrel." Sam Bass had "not a few murders" to his name, it was said, when in fact he had none, and so on.[44]

These legends were to become a gun culture archive in the 1900s, but the forgotten archives of the gun culture, including the dispassionate figures of Marcellus Hartley's business ledger books, tell a different story about the quantity of gun violence. What American gun critics and lovers alike tend to take as a given, whether as a tool of condemnation or praise—that the United States is a "nation of cowboys"— gun devotees who know the most about the material world of nineteenth-century gun production cast into doubt. Herbert Houze's study of the Schuyler, Hartley & Graham ledger book, for example, reveals that SHG's earliest shipments to Missouri, the hub of the gun trade, consisted of large-bore hunting rifles and carbines suitable for self-defense. But "consumer demand for such arms rapidly decreased" from 1868 onward, replaced by demand for arms suitable for small game and bird hunting. Likewise, in Nebraska, the transformation from "a frontier state to a settled society," said Houze, is charted in SHG's arms shipments from Lower Manhattan, which shifted from personal defense weapons in the late 1860s to farmers' guns by 1879 and a substantially decreased volume in guns overall. The absence of carbine shipments, he argued, "indicates that settlers no longer perceived the native population as a threat." The gun depot A. D. McAusland, in Miles City, Montana, had been a major transit point for gun commerce to buffalo hunters. By 1882, however, the area "had been tamed to such an extent" that SHG was shipping plain amber glass target balls for recreational trap-shooting instead of guns. Even in Texas, the dealer Comminge & Geisler ordered 3,040 Lagousky Patent Clay Pigeons in 1885 as gun orders decreased.[45]

In her groundbreaking work on western history, Patricia Limerick brilliantly revised the idea of an 1870s and 1880s frontier of adventuresome gun violence in a place of "free" land to be taken. "The events of western history represent not a simple process of territorial expansion," she argued, "but an array of efforts to wrap the concept of property around unwieldy objects." The battles in this jagged, complex process of conquest happened in the more quiet ellipses of the dime-novel plots. They happened in offices, over deeds, and through barbed wire and agriculture.[46]

A body of scholarship about gun violence on the "frontier" has found that gun violence and its historical consequences have been overestimated, not underestimated. Some of the scholarship on gun violence in the West, although not all of it, has questioned its assumed ubiquity while recognizing a core of truth. The West was more gun-violent than other places—but not as violent as we think. Law professor Adam Winkler noted that gun violence wasn't common on the frontier. We remember the Gunfight at the O.K. Corral in Arizona because it was an infrequent event. Historians Robert Dykstra and Eugene Hollon revisited frontier violence and couldn't find evidence that there had ever been shootouts in the five most important Kansas cattle towns. There were only 45 homicides overall in the 15-year span from 1870 to 1885, for an average of 1.5 homicides per cattle-trading season. Even when cowboys and range riders used guns, they almost never used them in Hollywood-style gunfights. "Getting the drop on"—that is, eluding and avoiding—rivals and enemies was more conducive to survival than shooting.[47]

As for guns and interpersonal violence, Roger Lane, a crime historian, found the mining country mountains far more murderous in the 1870s and 1880s than the plains. Bodie, California, which experienced a mining boom in the late 1870s, recorded 29 murders in a town of only 5,000. When we talk about gun violence in America, we are often talking about booze, bachelorhood, and racial-ethnic strife. Shootings happened impulsively because of lethally obstinate notions of offense and honor among intoxicated, socially unattached men living in close quarters. The incidents often lacked the narrative intricacy or moral gravitas common to legends of gun violence.[48]

But the mystique would transform—or inflect—an older and larger tradition of American violence as it evolved from the late 1800s to the 1900s. The extraordinary violence of the gunman, American studies scholar Richard Slotkin brilliantly argued, masked the ordinary violence of the ages. That ordinary violence might include deadly clashes between capital and labor in the age of the robber barons, and the nonphysical brutality of conquest—the systematic unraveling of indigenous cultures to hew survivors, in the language of the 1800s, to the ways of "civilization" as opposed to "savagery."[49]

The cowboy's actual life embodied this ordinary violence as vividly as his mythic life embodied the extraordinary violence of the gunslinger. Cowboys, historian David Cartwright observed, "were lower-class bachelor laborers in a risky and unhealthful line of work" who lived in a disreputable "subculture" ravaged by whiskey. Novelist and historian Wallace Stegner depicted the true cowboy as almost entirely opposite of his mythic avatar—not the autonomous, armed hero of his own life in the wide open West, but an "overworked, underpaid hireling, almost as homeless and dispossessed as a modern crop worker." Through "moral surgery," Cartwright noted, the cowboy became an American icon of rugged individualism and risk taking, but dismounted from horse and myth, he was a "drunk sleeping it off on the manure behind the saloon."[50]

The cowboy was no more the product of American individualism than the Winchester rifle itself, although both were becoming its icons. The legends that would become "facts" about the American gun culture made gun violence both more common and more coolly righteous than it was. The violence of the lone gunman was not the violence we most had, but it was, apparently, the violence we most preferred.

CHAPTER 10

BALANCING THE LEDGER

On December 11, 1880, Oliver Winchester died at his Prospect Street estate. He was sixty-nine, and he had been ill and infirm for a few years before he finally succumbed to an unspecified affliction, perhaps heart failure. "Winchester's career was in the best American tradition," obituaries said, of the self-made man.[1]

Eulogies praised Winchester's imagination, for he had been able "to see the red and golden streaks of sunshine where to others it was cloudy and overcast." He had had the unique ability to see "future possibilities." It was true that much of Winchester's genius as a gun capitalist was creative, not mechanical, and rooted in his skills as a salesman and entrepreneur—to "vision" a gun market. His "fearfully destructive inventions and fabrications," noted a nineteenth-century biographical entry, might have done more good than anything else by "circumscrib[ing] the ravages of war, . . . reducing it to the absurdities of comparative suicide." It was an exculpatory idea, although there is no evidence that the repeater rifle stimulated a pacifism of mutually assured destruction. Instead, people and animals were shot faster, at greater distances, with a more mechanically volitional weapon.[2]

Oliver Winchester's motives for his life's work are elusive and conjectural. There were as few stories or legends about Winchester the man as there was a surfeit of them about Winchester the rifle. But from murky and even bland motives, Oliver and the other Winchester men created a deeply consequential legacy.[3]

His accounting was deeply in the black. Winchester had emerged the preeminent name for semiautomatic rifles. He had helped mold a commercial market and a civilian-armed society. He and a handful of others had made the mass-production of arms plausible and profitable. Winchester's corporate value went from the red to the black of $3 million in 1880 (the economic status equivalent of $783 million today).[4]

Winchester's keenest—or at least clearest—ambitions were in the private realm. His business machinations unwaveringly revealed his family devotion and pride. His business was a family dynasty, an uncommon accomplishment, and he took steps to ensure it stayed that way. Before Winchester's death, his son Will was in management, although hobbled by his health, and his son-in-law TG Bennett was secretary. Winchester had further tightened family control in 1878 by appointing W. W. Converse, who was married to Sarah Winchester's sister, Mary, as treasurer.[5]

Before his death, Oliver Winchester chose Converse as president. When Converse died in 1889, TG Bennett finally became president. John Browning, a gun *savant*—known as the Thomas Edison of guns—and the inventor of most of the company's patented designs in the 1880s and 1890s, recalled that Bennett presided over the WRAC like a "high priest." Others saw him as the "god" in the Winchester temple. Browning recalled, "He looked so solid in his chair that I had the feeling I could come back year after year, find him there, make a deal without any wasted words, and get back to work. It was a comfortable feeling." Winchester had also kept his family in financial control. Wives were useful for that task. The majority control of the 10,000 shares of stock outstanding was held by his wife, Jane (4,400 shares); his son's wife, Sarah (777 shares); and his daughter, Hannah Jane (400 shares).[6]

Oliver Winchester felt this was a good decision. When he died, the fate of the family, the fortune, and the gun was annealed—just as he had always wanted. For Sarah, in the calamitous early 1880s, the fate of the family, the gun, and the fortune was just as strongly tied, as we will see.

WILL WINCHESTER WAS FORTY-THREE YEARS OLD WHEN HIS FATHER died, and he rapidly failed in health in the months that followed. He had suffered gruesomely, and when he died four months after his father, he did not have a gentle passing. In the midst of "terrible exhaustion and debility" from a deeply seated case of tuberculosis, Will had taken up residence at the Windsor Hotel in New York City, hoping to benefit from cutting-edge tuberculosis treatments. He returned home to New Haven by train on March 5. He graciously but bluntly informed his train conductor that he was taking his last trip, and returning to New Haven to die. He died on March 7, and just two months later, Sarah's mother also died in New Haven.[7]

Sarah's story pulls us back to a much smaller space but within the same saga—a brooding, grief-shrouded world in a mansion on Prospect Street. Even by nineteenth-century standards, death had stalked her remorselessly. Another spiritualist, Richard Frothington, wrote in *The Galaxy* of his relentless pursuit of his wife through spirit land. "Do not tell the world-weary wretch who has caught a glimpse of the 'summer land' to turn away his gaze and look again . . . on this cold and wintry earth," he pleaded. Summer Land was too beautiful to relinquish. Grief is a peculiar kind of luxury. Others would have been prodded out of it, and away from spiritualism's consuming ecstasies, through work, exigency, or others to care for. Sarah had no such impediments; her wealth permitted, perhaps invited, her obsession.[8]

We do not know whether Sarah and the medium Ada Coombs ever met, and if they did, we can only imagine what might have transpired. Perhaps Sarah was in one of the one thousand carriages that brought curious but discreet day sojourners to the charming two-month Niantic, Connecticut, spiritualist camp, forty miles from New Haven by the sea, a place known as a city in the pines. Or she might have "made a sneak," like other women of wealthy families, who left their carriages around the corner and arrived heavily veiled, coming in disguise to hear ghostly messages.[9]

The first time Ada met Sarah for a sitting, if it was unscheduled, she wouldn't have had time to prepare, and couldn't have drawn from her book. Doubtless, Sarah conveyed a "good condition," with an electric intellect and keen credulousness. Under these circumstances, clairvoyants usually confined themselves to anodyne, breezy imprecisions about fields of flowers in Summer Land—but in this case Ada might have made more effort. An impressive technique that only a few mediums mastered was to have the sitter write the spirit she wanted to reach just one question, a simple one, and seal it in an envelope. When Sarah finished, Ada would take the envelope in her lap, quickly go to the thick folds of her dress (female mediums had an advantage because their clothing and long hair provided more hiding spaces for accessories), and retrieve a small sponge saturated with alcohol, which she rubbed over the envelope. The alcohol dried almost instantly, left no trace, and made the question visible. Nothing else worked like this, especially not water, which wrinkled the paper. Before answering the question, she would stare fixedly into vacant space for a minute or so, and then appear to be seized by a mysterious power—shuddering, lifting her eyes, closing them, and snapping back to attention with a bewildered look. Whatever the mode of ghostly communication, Sarah certainly would have wanted to see Will, and to hear a message of what he'd learned in the afterlife.[10]

Clairvoyants like Ada usually claimed to see a "beautiful spirit light" above the sitter's head, and would reassure the curious and grieving that the "spirit comes to you."

For a first visit, that might have been miracle enough.

On Sarah's next visit, Coombs would have been ready. The name "Winchester" is simple as far as research goes. Ada could have easily excavated Sarah's common but profound sorrows, and been able to conjure up an image of Will. An infant daughter, dead, no other children, a husband lost to the agony of tuberculosis, and a rifle fortune. Skeptics imagine that the intellectually feeble make the best marks for the medium, but it isn't so. The heartbroken and rich are the best sitters, the ones who have prolific, receptive minds capable of understanding and the leisure to pursue it, and are arrogant enough to read coincidences of the universe as personal inscriptions. That hubris requires power, not gullibility.

Slate-writing was a popular technique. With enough time, and her notecards on Sarah's bad fortune, Ada could have prepared slates. The best result came from muriatic acid, mixed with half an ounce of pure zinc shavings. Ada would have dipped her quill pen into the mixture and pondered a good long while on what Will should say, something marvelously specific but not refutable. Working on intuition, Ada would have made much out of a detail, perhaps the fact that Will and Sarah had been building their own mansion, at 194 Prospect Street, when Will died. The house was never completed.[11]

When Sarah arrived, Ada would have made a flourish, before Sarah's eyes, of wiping the slate clean with a damp rag. It is easy to imagine that a medium would revel in this trick, which enlists the skeptic's undeluded request to *see* the slate being cleaned as part of her deception: the zinc-mixture writing would not show up on a wet slate, so the skeptic's skepticism itself facilitated deceit. Sarah would have seen with her own eyes that the slate was perfectly clean, free of writing.[12]

Ada would have then contrived the beginning of a trance. She would have massaged her eyes, then snapped her fingers to throw off distracting earthly conditions from her inner sight. She might have thrown her head back and rolled her eyes until only the whites were visible—to have a better view of the ghost. Then she might have spread one hand across her forehead and raised the other high as if grasping for an object or spirit. She could have fallen silent for a few pregnant seconds, and then begun to speak.[13]

She may have described the gentleman standing by Sarah as a "very near relative," with gray eyes and a beard, and asked Sarah if she recognized him. Of course, Sarah would have recognized the ghost as Will.[14]

Most likely, Ada would have conveyed a dispatch that Will was watching over Sarah, and was *right there*. She would have mixed fantasy with factual detail to authenticate her vision. "From the influences that come over me," she may have said, she perceived that Will died in pain, strangling with consumption. This she would have known from newspapers.

By this time the slate would have been ready, and dry, revealing its message from Will. The slate would convey in beautifully legible pen just one statement: Will wished that, before he passed, he had finished their house on Prospect Street.[15]

After Sarah left, astonished, Ada would have had to smash the slate before her next sitting. Once the zinc writing was on the slate, there was no such thing as getting it off.

AFTER SEVERAL SITTINGS, ADA MAY WELL HAVE BECOME THE VICTIM of her own ingenuity and persuasive skill. There are only so many fragments of information one can glean from notecards. The miracle, a medium's product, was finite. At the last sitting, Ada would have to claim that Will's spirit had "disintegrated." Mediums would say that a spirit was no longer in a favorable condition for communication. Then they moved on.

If legend is true, what Ada did next might have had a few motivations. Fulfilling a grieving person's deepest yearning and resurrecting the spirit of a loved one would tend to build intimacy, even if it was humbug, and who is to say that it entirely was, or that the creation of this illusion, and this ghostly hand, was any more grievously counterfeit than other inventive illusions of the age in Will and Oliver's world.

Maybe Ada felt a peculiar alliance with Sarah. They were more like conspirators than predator and prey, colluding to create the world that Sarah wanted to have, and could afford to contrive, where there was no death and Will and Annie existed, overlaid invisibly with her world but not apart from it. Many got paid to help wealthy people like Sarah enjoy the world that they wanted, whether as domestics or gardeners, and that tangible world, too, was a tissue-thin illusion, spun out of beautiful, audacious incongruities and improbabilities—like Will's prize hothouse orchids in the middle of cold, flinty New Haven. When Ada had to dig deeper to contemplate something for Will to say, it might have felt closer to a gift than deceit, and perhaps what she eventually devised to say was correct. An aura of private anguish hung around Sarah, who was haunted before she had ever arrived at Ada's tent. At séances, novelist Nathaniel Hawthorne wrote, "the whole material is . . . in the dreamer's mind, though concealed at various depths below the surface."[16]

A full materialization would have been challenging and would have required too many assistants, but let's say that Ada wanted Sarah to see Will. To perform a materialization, she would have placed a large table near the spirit cabinet, ostensibly to lay a candle and instrument upon, but really so that if Sarah made a rush or a "grab" at the materialized form, the table would slow her progress. It is hard to imagine the enthralled Sarah making a grab out of skepticism, but perhaps she would have out of yearning. Before they began, Ada would have had Sarah make a thorough inspection of the cabinet. The ceiling panels always looked unremarkable to the amateur eye, or even to the scientist-investigator who had never himself built a corner cabinet. As the trap door, practically silent, opened in the darkened room, Ada would have had a music box play lightly, to mask any slight sound of her assistant descending down the ladder. He would likely have worn a suit of black tights, except for his right arm, which would have been bare up to his shoulder: his hand needed to be made visible.[17]

The most essential thing was to find the right paint for the ghostly hand. One medium swore that he never found it anywhere except at Devoe and Company of New York. You bought it in six-ounce jelly glasses and pulverized it to powder by thinning it with a pint of turpentine. Then you soaked strips of muslin in the mixture. When they were dry, you shook the powder from the cloth and used it as a powder puff on the accomplice's bare arm and face. He would earn a few dollars for his work. The only drawback was the odor of the turpentine, which always lingered to some extent, but could be masked.[18]

In this dark, heavily draped room, a luminous arm and the glimpse of a hand and face would appear, and then quickly disappear. Sarah's belief was underwritten by a tremendous force of longing, guilt, grief, and obsession. When Will's ghost disappeared and evaporated, she would have known, again, what it meant to say that your heart had broken.

What Ada told her, and that the legend tells us, Sarah might already have feared and intuited. But supernatural terror, like tragedy, begins with the full force of self-recognition. Sarah may have heard the cogs of justice click into place. The spirits had exacted retribution against Sarah—and the Winchester name—by taking Will's life, and Annie's, and the lives of all her babies, to atone for those killed by their rifles. Annie's and Will's deaths were acts of cosmic accounting. The greater the profits, the greater the debt; the deeper Oliver's ambition, and Will's, the heavier her conscience. Oliver's fondest dream had been to create an intergenerational, immortal alloy of the Winchester business: rifle, fortune, and family. It stands to reason that if this was plausible as a dream, it was plausible as a nightmare—that the web of complicity would be a family one along with the fortune. The 371,250 Winchester guns sent into the world by 1884 alone, guns that bore her husband's name, her daughter's name, and her own name, had sown a blood fortune for her that she would reap somehow, in some way—even if she herself hadn't killed with a gun; or designed, manufactured, circulated, or marketed guns, or perhaps ever touched one; or financed or built a gun factory.[19]

The sacrifice of her family would not end the curse. Sarah, and Will, and Annie, and the others would continue to be haunted and terrorized by the ghosts who had been killed by Winchester rifles unless she made particular amends.

One telling of the legend has it that Ada told Sarah she could "balance the ledger." Then, through Ada, Will outlined an urgent, astonishing, and fantastic mission for Sarah: a mission of both evasion and atonement.[20]

THE SPIRITUALIST EMANUEL SWEDENBORG WROTE, "THE RULING . . . love of every man remains with him after death, and is not extirpated to eternity." We know that on the third anniversary of Will's death, Sarah left a commemorative flower vase at his grave in the Evergreen Cemetery. Once she left, she would never see New Haven again. The vase read, "In Loving Remembrance—March 7, 1884. IF LOVE LIVES IN THE HEART IT IS NOT DEAD."[21]

Then she lit out for The Territory.

CHAPTER 11

SUMMER LAND

Sarah Winchester's weeklong train journey west in 1885 along the Southern Pacific Railroad made almost three hundred stops, just from Chicago to California. In a way, the journey was her autobiography. Sarah retraced a land razed and "upbuilt" by her name. The railroad had transported the guns and cartridges west, and the Winchesters had trailblazed the railroads, fending off attacks and supplying workers with buffalo meat. It must be odd to have your name change from a family to a thing, the people you love conjured by a gun. When Americans heard it, they imagined a rifle, and the two words had become interchangeable: the Winchester now connoted a rifle in the generic. If she looked closely, Sarah could have seen Winchester cartridges gleaming along the railroad's path.[1]

Her brother-in-law, TG Bennett, thought little of the upbuilt results. His December 1883 cross-country journey had made him grumpy. "Our country is I regret to write a hollow sham gilded at its outer edges with a few places like New Haven and New York and perhaps San Francisco on the other side and within, a vast plain of mud and rocks completely indescribable in its unattractiveness." He found the West that Winchester had famously won aesthetically deficient: "Nebraska is a sea of mud and the rest are worse," he wrote. "The Rockies are a sham. . . . We saw no herds of bison and antelope as are shown in the guide books" (Winchester rifles had helped to kill them off), and they had seen only one small wolf. And yet, Bennett conceded, "it is provoking to see that all the pleasant places and in fact many unpleasant ones are settled up and fenced in with wire fences."[2]

When Sarah reached Omaha, Nebraska, and headed farther west, she would have seen newly prosperous farmers' homes with straight, symmetrical fences, just as TG had said, as well as windmills and red barns. Lucrative herds of cattle, horses, and sheep had usurped the buffalo's land.[3]

Then she arrived at Kearney, a town of a few thousand, settled and quiet by the 1880s. Kearney earlier had been the scene of "hair-raising adventures," according to a Union and Southern Pacific guidebook. This was where Major Frank J. North, with his four companies of Pawnee Indians, had made history "in the early days of progress," defending the overland route against hostile Indians during the construction period. "As an Indian fighter he had no superior," said the railroad company narrative. He cleaned out "whole tribes of hostiles," and "his name became a terror to the Indians." And, earlier still, as an 1882 dime novel told it, Buffalo Bill had killed and scalped his first Indian with his trusty Winchester at Fort Kearney.[4]

Sarah reached Plum Creek about two hours after Kearney to discover a prosperous town of 2,500 people. It was more famous for its great irrigation system than for the Cheyenne wars that underlay its prosperity. Crops of grains and vegetables were shipped from Kearney across the country.[5]

Through Echo Canyon, Utah, the shriek of the locomotive ricocheted off of cliffs like an explosion. When she reached Nevada, Sarah would have seen how "capital, [and] new railroads," had "torn the mask off the face of this treasure land," the railroad guidebook said. This "land of mystery" had only truly been revealed when fortune-seeking pioneers had cracked open her riches in ore, which had previously been hidden by nature's disguise of "barren mountains" and "lusterless sage."[6]

The hundreds of stops and towns on a railroad that the Winchester rifle had trailblazed all blurred into one legend of the frontier that piled striations of upbuilding on top of conquest. A deceptive nature had been fractured to reveal its riches. This is what Winchester had wrought, ambition braided with violence. It was the family business.

Sarah traveled until she could go no farther, pursued—or compelled— to the edge of America. She arrived finally in Santa Clara, California, just south of San Francisco, known as the Valley of Heart's Delight.

This was the most fertile valley in the world, and the most equitable climate in the world, next to Aswan, Egypt, and physicians extolled it for its healthful benefits in the 1880s. Its Edenic bounty dazzled travelers habituated to the stern cragginess of New England. In June, the "floral wealth is abundant beyond description," westward traveler Caroline Churchill wrote home. Santa Clara often inspired galloping hyperbole from travelers, who were overwhelmed by the colors and by the taste of floral perfumes that settled on their tongues. The Santa Clara Valley was fecund and green all winter, but in June, the climbing vines brightened, violets and carnations perfumed the air, and clusters of small roses of "snowy whiteness" appeared everywhere. It stirred Churchill to magnanimous "feelings of gratitude to the great creator that he has thus beautified and adorned bounteous Mother Earth."[7]

The valley was a fairy tale that nature told about itself. Delicate pink roses blossomed an astonishing six inches across; fantastically, the yellow, flowering tops of mustard plants grew as high as the heads of the men who passed them, mounted on horses; pioneers named streets such as Moorpark in gratitude for the divinely unrivaled sweetness and juiciness of a variety of apricot.[8]

An occasional white farmhouse punctuated the otherwise uninterrupted, luxuriant undulations of meadow and orchard. Peaches, apricots, almonds, and grapes that grew heavy on deep green vines flourished almost without effort. Nothing came easier to the valley than fertility.[9]

San Jose, the seat of the county, is cradled by mountains, which form an unbroken chain extending from east to west, while to the north and south the valley is bounded by foothills. One visitor sensed a poetic tension between mountain and valley, a landscape of both "sterility and fertility, like the characteristics of life." Attuned to the matter as she was, perhaps Sarah sensed that same bewitching tension between the two.[10]

Whatever the case, this was where she stopped.

———

HISTORIAN PATRICIA LIMERICK HAS WRITTEN THAT IF THE REAL western movie was made, it would be a less thrilling but more accurate story than the westerns we know. It would tell the story of property—the "drawing of lines and the making of borders," and tireless efforts to make others respect those borders as true. This is how Sarah, the other Winchester, built and won her west. The frontier's most violent conflicts happened not with the gun, but in showdowns about property in land offices and courtrooms, with the weapons of deeds and lawsuits.[11]

The discovery of gold in California in 1848 sparked a "mania," not infrequently described by Californians as the "beginning of our national madness—our insanity of greed," or a "mental illness." It was said that "the lower order of San Franciscans puts his trust in men unknown and builds his hope in things unseen." At the stock exchange on California Street, small grains of truth were spun into rumors of mountains of gold: "A rush for shares takes place," said one observer. "In six weeks, everybody in San Francisco is rich and mad. Their mouths are full of wondrous tales." A baseline of hallucinatory insanity was the norm for the Santa Clara Valley. Everyone "aims at emphasis" and exaggeration, a British traveler and historian wrote. "An actor rants, a preacher roars, a singer screams."[12]

A rage of land speculation followed the gold rush. "At every opening on the way," a speaker at the Pacific Club lamented, "you see these visionary towns, with phantom streets and squares." Wobbly grandiosity appeared seemingly out of nowhere, from nothing. Northern California was a place to make a fortune. Also, it was a place of eccentric exile—and expiation—for fortunes and lives made elsewhere. In the

1870s, enigmatic figures came here and built pretentiously, largely, and fantastically, driven by mysterious longings, grief, and secrets.[13]

The valley's flagships, the Lick Observatory and Stanford University, are also both mausoleums and monuments to grief. Leland Stanford made his fortune selling goods to gold miners in California—a surer profit than hunting for the gold itself. He was also the president of the Central Pacific Railroad. In 1884, his fifteen-year-old son died, and in his memory, the grief-stricken parents laid the cornerstone for Stanford University on their 7,200-acre vineyard and horse ranch. Santa Clara's "shabby millionaire" James Lick was famously enigmatic—either "avaricious, unwashed, and unsocial," as a local history described him, or industrious, intelligent, and sober, depending on whom you asked. In 1858, he built a florid, baronial mansion in the memory of his lost love, the daughter of a wealthy Pennsylvania mill owner. The mansion had twenty-four rooms and just as many fireplaces, and cost him $300,000 ($8.9 million today). Lick drew eclectically, if not haphazardly, on any and all architectural styles, creating an aesthetic dream state in which an Italianate aspect competed with a pillar porch reminiscent of the plantation South. This extravagant architectural fugue was not unusual in the valley. As soon as Lick completed his building, he inexplicably tired of his own grandeur, and moved to a shanty near the mill.[14]

Perhaps driven by fears of death, and eager to perform good deeds, Lick turned his attention to charitable donations. In October 1873, he announced that he would fund an observatory at the summit of Mount Hamilton, southeast of San Jose. The county supervisors agreed to build a state-of-the-art road leading to the observatory. By the time Lick died in 1876, he had donated almost $1 million to the observatory project, equipping it with a telescope more powerful than any other of his era.[15]

By the end of 1886, Lick Observatory was almost complete. The twenty-mile road leading to the observatory, with hundreds of turns, had been open for almost a decade. The observatory was ready to become the most "illustrious mausoleum that the hand of man has constructed," a local historian wrote, just as Lick had intended. In 1887, his casket was moved from the cemetery and placed in the foundation of a pier that supported the telescope.[16]

The dome held the thirty-six-inch telescope lens, the world's largest, designed by William Malcolm. Malcolm was independently wealthy and could devote himself fully to his passion: optics. He liked to experiment in a small room that commanded a broad view of Syracuse, New York. From this room he could see for miles across the country. His obituary noted that "distant objects serv[ed] him as targets on which to align each new glass as it was turned out." The farther into the distance he saw, the better. His greatest ambition was to design a lens that adjusted its sight automatically, just like the human eye, to perceive distances both near and far.[17]

But, mainly, rifle owners knew and revered Malcolm. This is because he became famous perfecting a rifle telescope, one that bore his name. He equipped riflemen everywhere—and, occasionally, an observatory.[18]

Traveler Loraine Immen praised the observatory itself as a "marvel of solidity." But for the last seven miles up the road, even this monumental, "far-famed crown of astronomical research" seemed "as evanescent and unreachable as a rainbow's pot of gold." It was a trick of the eye, like others in the valley.[19]

———

PEOPLE CAME HERE TO CRACK OPEN THE EARTH AND FIND GOLD, buy plots in an almond grove, or get rich on land speculation and schemes. Rumors (and acts) of madness wove seamlessly through Northern California's development.

As for Sarah, there might have been several motives for relocation. Her sister Isabelle had preceded her to California with her rancher husband, and her sister Nettie had relocated there with her husband, Homer Sprague, who was beginning what would prove a disastrous tenure as president of Mills College. But Sarah shunned her rightful position in the "San Jose 100," a makeshift aristocracy of the Santa Clara Valley, and through her mysterious reclusiveness she violated the neighborly, disarmingly informal social code among California ranchers. By the enigma of silence, she became an object of speculation, as did her intentions.

Some Californians said that Sarah Winchester had fled New England and chosen the valley because of her morbid fear of thunderstorms. Those who speculated could not have known the meaning encrypted in thunderstorms for Sarah. Other locals gossiped, along the same lines, that she had come (along with at least one-fourth of California's other settlers) in search of the famed, salubrious climate of the state. She had read a book back East, and learned of the climate's miraculous healing properties, and considered it "providential" that she come here.[20]

Spiritualists praised the climate, too. They considered the dry air of the West most conducive for making contact, since "wet, damp, and foggy weather is bad for the production of physical phenomena," as one spiritualist opined. Also, California was a frontier of the mind, the spiritualist wrote, free of Puritan laws that said "thus far, and no farther." This freer land accommodated prophetic dreams and visions— and ghost stories. In California, wandering souls were comforted. They hoped, and waited, for signs from the spirits.[21]

Others, taking notice of Sarah's incongruous mourning attire, speculated that she had come simply seeking "travel's assuagement of sorrow." How could Sarah or anyone be haunted here, in this new geography, among people who came here to resurrect themselves?[22]

In early 1886, Sarah and Isabelle traveled by carriage along the sparsely populated, dusty Santa Cruz–Santa Clara road outside of San Jose. If she looked up toward Mount Hamilton, she saw the nearly completed Lick Observatory. The country had only fifty observatories then, and one of them sat close by the Winchester homestead in New Haven, a fixed reference point for Sarah's world on Prospect Street, and a gift from her family to Yale. William had donated additional land to the Yale Observatory in his will, in recognition of his love of astronomy and celestial mysteries. Gazing to either side of the road, Sarah saw for miles only grain fields and flora, gradually yielding to orchards.[23]

On this trip, when the carriage reached a spot in the road, four miles outside of San Jose, the legend holds that Sarah had a stirring feeling that she should be here. She called excitedly for the coachman to stop, and stepped out of the carriage. Sarah had spotted an unremarkable, almost finished five-room wooden farmhouse being built by Dr. Augustine Caldwell. It sat on a knoll on forty-five sunny acres of land alongside the road. A local recalled that the doctor's isolated cottage originally sat "in an island of tall trees rising above the level of a . . . mile of orchards."[24]

Whatever her motivations—a supernatural vision, or something worldly, or a combination of both—Sarah had chosen her land oddly, and even, seemingly, at random. The land wasn't uninhabited. The doctor had almost completed his house, and none of it was for sale. Sarah had a fortune, and the means to purchase land anywhere in the valley. This particular acreage had nothing especially practical about it; in fact, it was quite impractical.

To look at it, the place was as far away from Sarah's past as anyplace in America could be. Nothing looked less like Prospect Street. Nothing could smell or feel less like New England. Even on sunny days, the cliffs surrounding the Winchester homestead and the street's sentry of oaks and elms had fended off the sunlight that drenched the Santa Clara Valley. Sarah had journeyed from a gray, cold, and barren hill to a golden, warm, and fertile valley. Hail, heat waves, and violent thunderstorms had harbingered tragedy for Sarah, and now she had managed to find a place in America without weather. Maybe Sarah perceived this knoll on the very fringe of America as a fitting place of refuge, in a valley already teeming with heartbroken exiles, grieving eccentrics, and millionaire, guilt-ridden expatriates. Certainly, it would be easy to forget here, and California had seduced others with more quixotic dreams than blissful amnesia. The valley might have promised Sarah a future without a past.

Or, it could be that the land's hypnotic enchantment to Sarah was more ambivalently coy than that, wavering between memory and forgetfulness, exile and homecoming.

An 1883 guidebook reported that the Santa Clara Valley, this "health-giving Eden," was located in the ideal state for "Fruit Growers and Consumptives"—and Will had been both.[25]

The floral perfumes must have been familiar to Sarah from the award-winning gardens at the Winchester mansion and its exquisite hothouses. In October 1854, New Haveners delighted in the horticultural tent at the first Connecticut state fair on the Green. Will loved pomology, as did Oliver, and they'd contributed their own carefully cultivated varieties of grapes and roses to the botanical feast, the perfume of the flowers overwhelming visitors. It was magic to see such exotic creatures on the cusp of a New England winter, in a tent on the Green in New Haven. Here, in the valley, they tumbled forth carelessly and effortlessly.[26]

And there was Will's other love, of the stars. The observatory on Mount Hamilton stood just as Will's beloved Yale Observatory presided over Prospect Street. There is no reason to believe that Sarah knew that the lens in the observatory came from the genius behind the rifle telescope, that even this fantastic new spectacle had ties to the rifle that made the world that she had left behind . . . that the rifle was all but inescapable.

What other spot in America could simultaneously be so new and strange and so old and familiar, suitable both for exile and reunion?

"I have the strangest feeling," Sarah told her sister. "This is the house I must have."

"But you haven't even seen the inside," Isabelle protested. "It's being built to order for someone."[27]

Undeterred, and like another westward pilgrim before her, she declared to herself that this was the place.

SARAH'S LAND HAD BEEN CLAIMED FIRST BY THE KING OF SPAIN, under the Laws of the Indies in 1769, and last by a John Hamm. As far as Santa Clara titles went, hers was an unusually tidy and unbroken one. Sarah paid Hamm $12,750 in gold coin for the plot with the unfinished Caldwell cottage on the knoll that held magnetic attraction for her.[28]

The surveyor of the land marked the center point with a corner rock. He ran chains around it and sank redwood stakes deep in the ground to define it, with deceptive certitude. The surveyor had done his work with perishable precision. The title bounded her estate by "two rows of prune trees," a corner rock, and fences, seemingly eternal but long ago obliterated. Sarah wanted a "perfect" title that would give her undisputed, absolute claim to her land. E. B. Rambo, the Winchester representative in San Francisco, was tasked with helping her in these transactions. He explained to her brother-in-law W. W. Converse, who was now WRAC president, that although Sarah had asked the lawyer to "pronounce the title perfect," "no title is absolutely perfect," especially not in California.[29]

California settlers named what they claimed. The names, according to a British traveler, "tell a story of ascent and ownership." Sarah called her land "Llanada Villa," which means "house on the plains" in the obscure dialect of a Northern California tribe—or, as others translate it, the "plain house."[30]

ALMOST AS SOON AS SHE HAD PURCHASED HER FLAGSHIP LOT, SARAH cast her eye on more land, to accommodate her sister, and perhaps other family members who might migrate west. She wanted more land, secured by perfect titles. Whatever Sarah and Isabelle saw in the new land, Rambo saw much less. On April 16, 1888, Isabelle drove Rambo over to 140 acres of land near Mountain View that she and Sarah were determined to purchase.

"I walked pretty much all over the place," Rambo reported back to Converse, who wondered what sort of an investment it would make. "The whole place has been allowed to turn down very much. The present crop is very, very thin and poor," and in rye, no less. True, there were some "old vines, and some apple trees; however, neither of much value," he continued. The dwelling houses disappointed as well, "habitable and good enough for tenants or help, perhaps," but "ought not count much as money value." Sarah might not lose money but wouldn't make a profit, was his view. It might "sell some time for $200.00 or $225.00 per acre, perhaps, but in my opinion only when cut up in small tracts."[31]

San Jose invited big vision, not Rambo's peevish literalism. Sarah and Isabelle had pointed to future railroad growth to make their case to Rambo. They also predicted that Stanford University would attract residents, as if that made sense. Rambo didn't warm to either argument. Who would want to buy land in San Jose, and the fringes of San Francisco? He put little stock in the new railroad ever being built, and could not imagine an influx of residents and buyers on account of the fledgling university, which would never amount to much, he thought. Rambo advised Converse against making an investment in the land himself.[32]

Still, none of this really mattered, because Sarah and Isabelle had a plan, or several of them. Rambo gestured at it in his correspondence to Converse, referring elliptically to "their standpoint" and "their plans." Sarah had already bought more than 10,000 acres near the land that they now intended to purchase, including Sarah's own Llanada Villa property. "They have set their hearts on this scheme," he wrote. Sarah and Isabelle wanted to buy the acreage in question so as to avoid buying land farther away and having to "run two establishments" instead of one. Tantalizingly—and strangely, in light of what was to follow—Rambo wrote that Sarah and Isabelle "do not want to live out of the world, even if they can make more money."[33]

Part of the "establishment" they envisioned would be entrepreneurial: Isabelle had deeply impressed Rambo that she was nimble enough with worldly matters to succeed in raising crops as well as breeding coach or large carriage horses, and he felt confident that they would pay a "handsome return," since California sported "lots of fools to buy stylish carriage horses."[34]

As for the rest, Isabelle's part of "THEIR plans" over the coming decades would prove less cryptic than Sarah's. While her husband worked the land that Rambo found to be stingy into a vineyard,

Isabelle devoted herself to causes that were extremely progressive in her time. Both sisters would prove in many ways to have consciences ahead of their times. Isabelle was known as a "friend of the helpless," and she was devoted to "humane work for man and beast." She was active in the NAACP, and her particular concern was the plight of abandoned, abused, homeless, and illegitimate children. Isabelle eventually converted several rooms and two carriage houses on this land into a haven for homeless and abandoned children, until Sarah sold that land, including the ranch, to the University Land Corporation in 1907, which promptly subdivided it.[35]

Rambo concluded that although Isabelle's husband would probably fail to turn a profit, under "THEIR circumstances, think purchase would be a fair business." In another letter, he echoed that view: "It will not be a bad purchase from *their* standpoint. I see no reason why they should be advised to the contrary. Others go into more hazardous ventures daily."[36]

Converse instructed the dyspeptic Rambo to "understand that Mrs. Winchester has made up her mind to take the property at a price not to exceed $25,000," and to act as her agent.[37]

In May 1888, Sarah proceeded with the purchase of the land called Diel Ranch, after a prior owner. A year later, Sarah still had not taken possession of this new land, but had received two title documents. She had divined, purchased, titled, circumscribed, and named her world. Now she could commence with her plans.[38]

———

HER NEIGHBORS WHISPERED ABOUT THE INSCRUTABLE LIFE OF THE "millionaress." A few years after Sarah arrived, the *San Francisco Examiner* wrote that "Mrs. Winchester in appearance is attractive and scarcely beyond the prime of life. In business she is shrewd, and socially very exclusive."[39]

The rifle heralded her like a grim ambassador. A neighbor who arrived in the valley after Sarah recalled, "My first recollection of the

Winchester name was when I purchased a .22 caliber Winchester rifle . . . from Sears, Roebuck and Company for $3.75 (no tax)."[40]

French traveler Amaury Mars, an excitable, aspiring Alexis de Tocqueville, journeyed to Santa Clara Valley in 1901 to cover a visit from President William McKinley. Sarah had been asked to extend the president an invitation, but she had declined. Mars took a carriage ride from Alviso toward San Jose along an enchanting road. First he and his traveling companions passed an asylum for the insane, which stirred him, coincidentally, to contemplate on themes deeply relevant to both Oliver and Sarah Winchester: how "wars, this slaughter of fellow human beings," that came from "brains that are disordered," could only bring a terrible "expiation."[41]

Continuing down the valley road, Mars happily turned his thoughts from expiation and madness to beautiful country homes shrouded in leafy foliage. Six miles or so out of San Jose, he drove in front of gates that reputedly led to one of the "finest pieces of real estate in the Valley." They "were informed that it was the property of a lady who resides there. A lady? How delightful! Is she amiable, intellectual, accomplished, handsome?" Since the passage to the mansion was shrouded so heavily all around with flowers, climbing vines, and cypress trees, Mars could catch only a glimpse of Sarah Winchester's estate, and the beginnings of her mystery, inside.[42]

However, Sarah did make an appearance in 1890, in the San Jose city directory listed as an orchardist—"Winchester, Mrs. SL., fruit."[43]

CHAPTER 12

THE GUN INDUSTRY'S
VISIBLE HAND

A s Oliver Winchester and the founding generation of gun industrialists passed away, the second generation faced a gun economy of greater speed, size, and volume. Gun manufacturers were churning out more guns every year, in the tens of thousands annually. Like other industries, they were contending not only with more efficient industrial production—machines were in the saddle—but also with more stable, if not sated, markets and with smaller profit margins. The gun capitalist faced the same riddle as his kin in the stove business: "It is a chronic case of too many stoves and not enough people to buy them." The WRAC's profits were 41.9 percent of net sales in 1875 (the highest pre–World War I year), 28 percent in 1892, 16.4 percent in 1904, and 9.4 percent in 1907 (the lowest pre–World War I year). The price index for all commodities had fallen (the dismay is palpable in an 1881 Winchester ad that touted breech-loading rifles, "all of which we sell at astonishingly low prices"). A Winchester 73 sold for $50 in 1873, but $25 in 1879. In 1880, the WRAC sold 26,500 guns, or 1 per 1,893 Americans, and produced 34,224 (1 per 1,466 Americans); in 1890, it sold 79,100 (1 per 796 Americans) and made 66,057 new guns (1 per 953). Colt's made 25,943 revolvers and pistols in 1880 (1 per 1,934). Industrialists saw the advantage of modifying brutal competitive capitalism with monopoly capitalism—in the form of pools, trusts, holding companies, associations, and mergers—and the gun industry was no exception.[1]

If Oliver Winchester's work had been to build the gun industry and markets, his son-in-law TG Bennett's task was to manage and control them to maintain profit. In the 1880s and 1890s, the visible hand of the gun industrialist sat heavily on the gun market and orchestrated it. In this and other moments the gun business was a business, and acted like one, which is neither shocking nor diabolical, but it does demystify assumptions about gun demand and desire. The arithmetic of the gun industry at this critical juncture was not "demand creates supply" and profit, but closer to a less elegant truth: that trusts, associations, and price-fixing preserve profit.

THE WRAC'S MAIN COMPETITORS INCLUDED COLT'S, MARLIN, AND Remington. Had Colt and Winchester competed on the same terms in both rifles and revolvers, the commercial gun market might have been dangerously diluted for both of them. Instead, they became brothers of arms, to tweak the cliché. Each company threatened to produce the other's signature gun. In the 1880s, Colt's wanted to bring out a repeater rifle, and even completed some 6,400 of them. Winchester immediately began experimenting with revolvers. TG Bennett recalled that in 1883 the WRAC took several revolver models to Hartford to "get the advice of the pistol experts" on mechanics and marketability. It was a subtle brandish, but effective. With only a gentlemen's agreement to divide the market, something mentioned a few times in the WRAC archive, Colt simply discontinued rifle production, and Winchester never produced revolvers. After Winchester released the Model 73, with its famous "40–40–40" ammunition, Colt's began to chamber its six-shooter to take the Winchester ammunition. The corporations softened their rivalry in guns through collusion in bullets.[2]

As for its second chief rival, E. Remington & Sons, Winchester had long had its eye on this giant in repeater sporting arms, and the sporting market was now one of the WRAC's priority segments. Founder Eliphalet Remington was sometimes recalled as the gunmaker with a heart of gold. Remington was a pacifist poet who loathed war. He debated whether to take up the "quill or the hammer" early in life, and, after the War of 1812, penned that even peace could not "disabuse the gloom / that reigns within the warrior's tomb / or . . . assuage the widow's grief / or to the orphan speak relief." One myth, which Dimitra Doukas described in an economic history, was that he and his sons (Eliphalet died in 1861) were simply "too good" to compete. The myth is partially true, if lack of foresight about gun markets might be considered a corollary of goodness.[3]

E. Remington & Sons was in deep financial trouble as early as 1882. The cause of its trouble, wrote the local press, was "various," and is still not entirely clear. At this critical juncture, the Remington sons seemed both too focused and not focused enough on guns. They were too focused on them in that they sold off the company's promising typewriter business, because they thought they should put all their eggs in the gun basket and save their flagship product. In 1882, the typewriter captivated their employee Henry Benedict, who urged Philo Remington not to sell it for quick cash. When Philo felt that he should save the gun business instead, he sold the typewriter business to Benedict for $186,000—which provided a meager two months of working capital for the flailing gun company. Before long, the typewriter business was worth $186 million. At the same time, the company ventured into an eclectic panoply of other non-gun products, such as the sewing machine, that became catastrophic drains on their profitability.[4]

The Remingtons wanted to maintain their gun focus, but they hitched their fortunes to the wrong gun market: the martial, military world of government contracts. Remington anticipated keen international demand for their Lee rifles, which never materialized, and by the obverse logic of the 1880s gun industry, they suffered while—and because—South America was enjoying a peaceful interlude and in a "waiting" rather than a buying mood. Other military contracts in the 1880s were canceled. And in this respect, the Remingtons had not focused on guns enough: they missed the wave of various commercial markets that the Winchester and Colt's companies had caught. The Remington centennial history in 1916 reflected on the matter, with surprising candor, saying, "An entirely new type of customer for fire-arms was [emerging]: the American consumer." But the Remington family had "lacked the imagination to see possibilities in millions of such customers, served through thousands of merchants, for John Jones' purchase of a single shotgun seemed insignificant beside Jean Crapeau's contract for a hundred thousand army rifles." The history added, "Even if the vision was clear, not many men of the passing gen-eration had the knowledge [to build that market]." Winchester had scattered his guns to individuals as widely as possible years before oth-ers had really seen the potential of this market; Remington had not. How could it be better to sell to a few here and there, through jobbers and retailers, than to many? This inability to "vision" the civilian mar-ket was slowly killing the company and draining much of the Reming-ton sons' personal fortunes.[5]

Others pointed in 1888 to bad financial decisions and investments by the Remington brothers. During the boom years, the "money came easily and was spent foolishly," and the company had been securing loans on unfavorable terms and kiting its debts to stave off bankruptcy for some time.[6]

Whatever the various causes, by 1886 the factory was almost dor-mant and the company in its death throes. The Remingtons were fiercely loyal to their town, and their employees, reciprocally, loaned money to keep the operation going. Remington began paying employ-ees on an "order" system that promised compensation in a few weeks or months against future orders. It amounted to not much more than a system of IOUs—basically, company scrip. In 1872, E. Remington & Sons' yearly statement had shown a modest debt of $75,037.21, and in 1886, it showed an immodest debt of $860,318.33.[7]

On what became known in Ilion as Black Friday—April 28, 1886—E. Remington & Sons filed papers in the county clerk's office to dis-solve the insolvent company and place it in the hands of receivers, a small group of Ilion town leaders. This had a "very depressing" effect on the townspeople, the local paper said in an understatement. The exact amount of the company's debt was unknown, and its affairs too "highly complicated" to tell for certain. About eight out of ten citizens of the village were creditors of the corporation, and several merchants holding worthless Remington scrip failed. Two local grocers, for example, held about $16,000 each in paper orders for reimbursement from Remington. Larger creditors included iron, steel, and brass works. Estimates of the debt at first ranged from $600,000 to $1 million, and the receivers' accounting of the debt was close to that. They found that the defunct Remington company was in debt to "actual employees" by $65,000; to those with "old wage and labor claims" to the tune of $125,000; to the largest bulk of creditors, with unsecured debt, to the amount of $635,000, and to creditors who mistakenly thought they had secured debt, but now found it inadequate, to the amount of $75,000.[8]

In past years, there had always been relief from bankruptcy and distress from creditors and loans. Up until Black Friday itself, Ilionites had hoped that Marcellus Hartley would come around and save the firm, as he always had. But, this time, he might have had a different agenda, or so speculates Doukas, who wonders if he was the one who leaked news to the New York attorney general of Remington's reckless insolvency. "People [in Ilion] have hoped all along that the loan of $500,000 from New York parties would be effected and this would tide over all difficulties," the *Ilion Citizen* wrote, but the negotiations failed. Likewise, from 1886 to 1888, the receivers had arranged to have Hartley negotiate a Turkish military contract for 600,000 stand of arms, which would have revived the company's fortunes. But, this time, Hartley's efforts failed.[9]

At least as early as 1887, Hartley might have begun to pursue his own agenda concerning the flailing Remington company. It is reasonable to imagine that Hartley, thinking of a trust with competitor-ally WRAC, had ambivalent interests in the fate of Remington's Turkish deal, and it is quite clear that, whatever his motives, he was not going to bail it out this time. Once Hartley's loan negotiations fell apart, and once Hartley's negotiations with the Turks failed as well, there was nothing left for the Remington family or the receivers but to "wind up the business" of the company, and for the receivers to put it up for auction.[10]

Hartley proposed a gun trust to control the Remington company with Winchester, and it was a topic of conversation at the WRAC board meeting on January 24, 1888. The board discussed Hartley's suggestion that a syndicate be formed to produce a controlling interest in Remington. Hartley proposed that the Winchester bid to achieve this objective not exceed $75,000. The WRAC directors agreed with Hartley's proposal and authorized company president Converse and vice president Bennett to bid on behalf of the company at the Remington auction on February 1. If all went according to plan on auction day, then Hartley & Graham would own E. Remington & Sons, but they would be in a syndicate with the WRAC, which would actually own half of the Hartley & Graham interest.[11]

Sixty mechanics and workers from Ilion, an unwitting David against the Goliath of the collusive Hartley and WRAC, had their own ideas after the auction was announced. They had taken pledges and pooled their capital to purchase Remington themselves. They intended to win the company at this auction. Ilion wanted to fight to maintain the works locally, with local ownership.

Ilion was on "the tiptoe of expectation" on the very cold February auction day. In addition to the local Ilion group of bidders, some thirty businessmen, variously flocked, including a group of "Boston capitalists" and another of "New Yorkers," were present to bid in the company office. Outside, a large crowd of villagers gathered to view the sale "from a respectable distance." Hartley's man, W. W. Reynolds, had already become familiar in Ilion for his "Anglican face and . . . pugnacious bearing" and his habit of grasping an unlighted cigar tightly in his teeth. He was bidding for Hartley & Graham. The wily "New Yorker" knew all the tricks, Ilion surmised, such as planting spies in opposing camps at auction to "run them ashore." Another tactic was a shocking last-minute announcement: just before the auction began, an attorney from New York City suddenly appeared. He claimed to represent a creditor, and announced to the crowd that Remington owed $750,000, and that whoever purchased the company would be held responsible for that debt.[12]

Ilion was stunned by this news. The auction began promptly as scheduled, at noon, then broke for lunch from 12:30 to 1:30, and then resumed afterward outside, on the office steps. Reynolds, suspiciously unperturbed by news of this new debt, dominated the bidding. The WRAC dropped out (a ruse, given its intent to collude with Hartley & Graham) at $150,000, and Reynolds won the bidding for E. Remington & Sons at a mere $152,000.[13]

After the auction, Ilion was preoccupied with just two matters: that the armory had sold "for a song" ("a property costing a million and a half, insured for $600,000, selling for a cold $152,000—Whew!"), and that they were unsure precisely "who it was that really bought" it. Ilionites observed that Converse's and Reynolds's bids were never far apart; that they were "in consultation, both before and after the sale"; that Converse, Bennett, and Reynolds were all present, oddly, when the papers were signed after the auction; and that the three had left Ilion together on the train for New York City after the auction. It all gave the vivid appearance, another local paper concluded, of a "good understanding" between the WRAC and Hartley & Graham. "Monopoly is the order of the day and the Winchester Arms Co. are by no means backward in their desire [for one]."[14]

Mr. Reynolds assured Ilion that Winchester was "in no way interested" in the purchase, but the *Citizen* concluded diplomatically that "appearances are exceedingly strong against Mr. Reynolds' veracity." The village was at first relieved that Hartley & Graham had purchased the factory, but deeply feared any involvement by the WRAC, which they suspected would shut down the works and move its equipment, as the company had done many times before, to equip a new five-story factory in New Haven. The mood darkened at the prospect of a gun trust. "The lord help Ilion now," a citizen said. "Pack up your grip and dig out," said another; it was "the coldest day Ilion ever had." They had one last resort, however: the courtroom.[15]

Instead of stipulating a minimum bid, Judge P. Williams of Watertown had reserved the right to review and set aside the Remington sale, and he did just that in a special session after the auction, with lawyers for three parties represented: E. H. Risley, for Utica creditors; Arthur Beardsley, for Hartley & Graham; and A. M. Mills, for the Ilionites who had hoped to buy the company.

Mills pled strenuously for the court to set aside the sale. He made much of the false mortgage claim at the auction, saying that the bogus debt had served its purpose of "frightening bidders" and caused the Ilionites to withdraw, convinced that "whoever bought the property would have a law suit." He further argued that the works had been gotten "for a ridiculously low sum," when an intelligent mason swore that $152,000 would not even build the stacks. And impassioned, life-time Remington workers valued the "name" and reputation of Remington itself as worth "half a million."[16]

Risley countered that the mystery mortgage claim had been "laughed off" at the auction itself, and the potential bidders reassured that the bonds had already been canceled. Judge Williams confessed that he was "disgusted" by the last-minute debt announcement, but he did not seem as exercised over that as the low sale price.[17]

The sixty-five Ilionites and the Hartley-WRAC gun trust were arguing in different economic universes. To Mills, and the court, the sale price seemed shockingly low. Judge Williams had hoped that the plant would sell for at least $400,000. In contrast, the "capitalists," represented by Beardsley, reckoned the economics of the gun business differently: the economy had gotten larger, and corporations, behemoth. It was not that E. Remington & Sons was "too big to fail," but that it was, quite simply, too big to run—unless by what Beardsley baldly described as either "a very rich individual or by a combination of individuals" or concerns. If the people of the town got the company, he argued, "it would be dead." It was certainly true that the Ilion group could afford to buy the Remington property, but could they afford to *have* it? It would require from $200,000 to $400,000 net cash simply to run the plant—and run it must, as "idle machinery" deteriorated quickly. The payroll alone required $3,000 to $7,000 a week, and it took "considerable capital to buy material and hold the manufactured stock until sold," to say nothing of paying the creditors. Doubtless this explained why the property had been advertised nationally for six weeks and attracted only four or five serious bidders.[18]

Judge Williams mulled his options and ruled that a second auction should be held. But this time, "bidders must take care of themselves," he warned. He did not want to set a precedent for dismissing valid auctions simply because the bids did not satisfy, or the Ilionites were outwitted on auction day. There would be no third chance to increase the sale price.[19]

THE SECOND AUCTION TOOK PLACE ON A BRIGHT DAY IN MARCH, which the village took as an auspicious omen. The streets were thronged with spectators; the 9:45 A.M. train from New York brought bidders, including TG Bennett; and the Osgood House hosted a motley group of "anxious creditors" and capitalists, whose pedigrees were discreetly "speculated upon" by the locals. Inside, the E. Remington & Sons company office was "packed with usual suspects, and also with reporters, lawyers, capitalists, creditors, and hundreds of others."[20]

Ilionites had vowed to go out on the warpath to secure their company, with subscriptions equal to $300,000, or double Hartley & Graham's first winning bid. The spirited bidding quickly came down to a contest between US senator Warner Miller, from New York, who represented the Ilion group, and Reynolds, for Hartley & Graham. It then advanced in $100 increments until suddenly, and inexplicably, Senator Miller left the auction and immediately boarded the "Flyer" train bound for Chicago. Miller's replacement for the Ilion interest raised the bid to $199,800, and then "unaccountably, fell silent." Reynolds bid $200,000. The auctioneer lingered on the bid, but to no avail. "Spoils to the Victors," the *Citizen* headlined. "Hartley and Graham Get the Property, Again." More accurately, Hartley & Graham and the WRAC got the property. The WRAC's archives recorded that the company paid $100,000 for its purchase of a half-interest in Hartley & Graham's ownership.[21]

What had happened? The Ilion group easily could have bested a $200,000 bid. The Ilion people understood that the "bottom [had] dropped out of their syndicate, or that combinations were made." The *Citizen* asked, almost rhetorically, "Is it a gun trust?" but was fairly certain that it was. "That the Ilion syndicate was in power to raise the price much higher than they did can not be disputed," opined the *Citizen*, so why did it not bid more, or at least compel Hartley & Graham (and Winchester) to pay more for the company?[22]

The answer arrived at the *Ilion Citizen* after the auction, in the form of a letter from Hartley to Senator Miller that had been sent before the auction: it reassured Miller that Hartley & Graham would run the Remington works, in Ilion, on "business principles, and to make money, and [had] no intention whatever of dismantling . . . them." Based on this letter, and perhaps Miller's own conviction that the company would require far more capital to run than the Ilion group could muster, he had declined to bid aggressively on Ilion's behalf.[23]

The contents of this letter improved the mood in town, and a local paper, for its part, applauded the outcome, saying that Ilion was better off with such men of "push and enterprise" in place to run the company, rather than the inadequately shrewd or ruthless Remington generation. But the reassuring letter still did not explain why the Ilionites had let the plant go so cheaply, or why news of this promise from Hartley had not been made public earlier. Doukas speculated that Miller might have gotten other considerations for trying to keep the price low by abruptly hopping on a train and not bidding, but we do not know, and the gun monopoly "covered its heavy tracks" very well.[24]

Whatever the case, the octopus of gun monopoly was too mighty to combat, and the sheer bigness of the company, and its appetite for operating capital, too great for the Ilion group of mechanics and merchants. "We are frequently asked if we are opposed to monopoly," the *Citizen* said, and "almost invariably we answer yes, unless we are in the monopoly. . . . And hence when it was told here Wednesday after the sale that there was or was not to be a gun trust and that this was to be a big end in that trust, it was difficult to find a man who was opposed to trusts (do you catch on?)." This was the gun business of the 1880s, to which Ilion, and the rechristened "Remington Arms Company," were now firmly lashed.[25]

In May, Hartley legally transferred ownership of Remington to a syndicate of the WRAC, Hartley & Graham, and a few Chicago capitalists. For its half-ownership, the WRAC received a valuable concession that trimmed the competition and managed the gun market tightly in its favor: "It was understood that the Remington would not place upon the market a repeating arm in competition with the Winchester gun," the WRAC archive explains. If the WRAC had begun the 1880s with at least three main repeater-rifle competitors, they were beginning the 1890s with one: Marlin. Loyalties were fragile in the gun industry, however, and even during the years of Winchester's half-ownership—before Winchester and Remington-Hartley became bitter rivals once more in the 1900s—the works did propose to market a repeating gun similar to a Winchester design. When the WRAC "desired to protest," the company archive says, "a concerted search was made, for some document [stating the agreement of 1888]." And, unsurprisingly, none was found.[26]

AROUND THE SAME TIME, GUNS JOINED A NUMBER OF OTHER commodities that were starting to be produced through cooperative agreements of some kind, including steel, salt, petroleum, rubber, tobacco, window glass, nonferrous metals, sugar, leather products, cottonseed oil, nails, thread, bicycles, rope, paper, whiskey, starch, soda fountains, wallpaper, grass twine, wringers, buttons, glue, and novelty toys. Guns were not exceptional, but another item on a long, eclectic roster.[27]

At this perilous juncture, the industry orchestrated the market with maneuvers that "by modern standards would be illegal," gun historian R. L. Wilson noted, but that were legal at the time. The Ammunition Manufacturers Association (AMA) was incorporated in New Jersey in September 1883, a product of the new idea that a corporation was an "entity in itself" and not just a "legal fiction." As such, it was entitled to do what other individuals could do, including owning stock in other corporations through holding companies, as New Jersey had concluded. The AMA was a chimera—a corporation born of bickering, hostile corporate parents who still constituted the organization's membership. The Winchester company was a founding member, along with Hartley's United Metallic Cartridge, US Cartridge, Phoenix, and a lawyer named Horace Fowler, who held just four shares. A Winchester executive ingenuously summarized the logic behind the AMA: "There had been very serious competition among the larger ammunition manufacturers, and they thought it would be much better for all hands to get together and make some money, rather than spend their time and money and energy cutting each other's throats."[28]

The AMA's purpose, according to the certificate of incorporation, was to "buy and sell ammunition of all kinds and to act as agents for others," to prevent "serious competition between [the members]," and "to settle differences between those engaged in the manufacture of or in dealing in ammunition, and to devise and take measures to foster and protect their trade and business." This was not the first time that Winchester and Hartley et al. had cooperated. They had colluded earlier, in 1879, to split the gun markets in Romania and Morocco, and to seek contracts with the Romanian government and divide the profits and expenses equally, with Aristakes Azarian brokering the deal.[29]

The AMA controlled half the ammunition market. It deterred competition and entry into the business, and it fixed prices and dealer discounts. Members pooled and split profits based on the percentage of stock held by each company.

The AMA, and the US market in bullets, thrived from 1883 to 1890, when the Sherman Antitrust Act went into effect. The total value of ammunition produced in the United States was $1.9 million in 1879 and $6.54 million in 1889, almost a threefold increase. Winchester's ammunition sales from 1883 to 1889 totaled $4.9 million and returned an "Association profit" of $1.2 million. Hartley's insight after the Civil War—that the ammunition to feed rapid-fire guns, more than the guns themselves, might be the lasting key to profit—had proved to be prescient: in these years, ammunition generated more than half of the WRAC's net profits. The robust ammunition returns for the association might have been driven purely by an increase in total demand, by the strong degree of control exercised over the industry that the association achieved, or, most likely, by a combination of both: gun profits accrued from market orchestration as well as demand.[30]

After the Sherman Act went into effect, TG Bennett had a conversation with an old colleague on "the state of the country." "Like me," he wrote to Jane, "he is for the straight slaughter of every present authority—the wiping out of the Sherman law, and feels that there is very little that should be spared in getting back to the old state of things"—which, with the AMA, had been profitable for the company.[31]

The AMA went about its business in the 1890s, after the Sherman Act went into effect, assured that the law was sufficiently ambiguous that the association might conform to its letter if not its spirit. But the AMA parties did adjust their practices. Instead of giving a basic percentage rebate to dealers on the association list, they offered these favored houses salaries based on the average volume of orders. This arrangement allowed the association to treat each jobber individually: it could modify a dealer's discounts or privileges to secure his loyalty. It also offered larger discounts to large houses that pushed greater volume—which, from the moment gun production became an industry rather than a craft, was the prime directive.[32]

The visible hand of the market in this case was H. S. Leonard, a Winchester vice president of sales. His one surviving letter book in the archive provides a rare glimpse at the quotidian workings of the association. Whatever their content, Leonard's letters about association business began and ended the same way: he stamped them as "Confidential" at the start and ended them by admonishing the recipient that he was to treat the information in "STRICTEST CONFIDENCE." The recipient, he said, must be very careful not to lose the letter itself. In another note, Leonard said he "strongly advised that you do not carry [the letter] about in your pocket, so that by any possibility it could be lost or mislaid. It would be very damaging to have this list [of association houses] escape." The recipient was also to be "very careful not to allude to [the letter's content] in conversation with any customers NOT ON THIS LIST." Leonard was somewhat more wary about association letters than he was about actual Winchester demonstration

guns that he shipped to salesmen, including the company's new automatic rifle in 1903. He did instruct the salesmen that he wanted to
avoid "having [guns] float around the country for a long time before
reaching you," telling them they should be at their addresses when the
automatics arrived. But he had greater capitalized and underscored urgency regarding the letters.[33]

In his dispatches, Leonard also conveyed instructions from association commissioner William Odell. Sometimes they involved inviting
salary houses on to, or culling them from, the association list, an extremely touchy matter. Leonard wrote to a trusted Philadelphia jobber
that the "task of weeding out the Association salary list" would soon
begin, and "a number of houses will be dropped." He wanted to know if
any other dealers in the jobber's territory were not entitled to be on the
list and to report on them fully. The association worried about "notorious price cutters," or those who were "keeping the trade generally, for
one reason or another, in a state of turmoil" (others would call that
turmoil competition). Such a house was a *disturbing element that should
be removed*."[34]

Leonard sometimes informed salesmen of measures to "equalize
profits" among association members, or to divert purchases from one
business to another. Odell wrote to association salary houses to say that
"with the object of equalizing sales between our members, we desire to
divert a certain amount of business for Loaded Paper Shot Shells to
[the WRAC]." Leonard emphasized to company jobbers "the importance of cooperation . . . in adjusting sales amongst ourselves." For
each carload shipment of ammunition, the retailers on the special association list would get the preferred carload rate, and an extra salary
allowance of 5 percent rather than 2.5 percent. In other cases, similar
discounts were offered to "equalize sales" on Hartley's United Metallic
Cartridge (UMC) ammunition, or to divert sales to Winchester. In
May 1903, the "diversion of Association business" concerned the
UMC and the United States Company, association members who had
fallen behind in their sales quotas. In January 1903 Leonard wrote to
salesmen that all AMA houses were to receive the same proportion of
ammunition: 60 percent Winchester and 40 percent the UMC. "This

special proposition," he wrote, "is made with the view of equalizing sales between the two companies."[35]

Association houses enjoyed dating privileges: to manage seasonal demand, they could place orders before March 15 but pay for the order in September, at the same discount they would have received if they had paid cash on delivery. The association also used its market muscle to thwart non-member competitors and entrepreneurial gun upstarts. "In your work among the dealers, large and small alike, we wish that whenever you find a house that is endeavoring to push Peters [Cartridge Company] goods," Leonard wrote, "that you make a special effort to swing them over to our side." Leonard told salesmen that they could "knock out a lot of demand for the Peters goods" in this way.[36]

More intense scrutiny of antitrust violations and the consolidation of interests between the WRAC, the UMC, and Remington, as well as competition from ammunition manufacturers outside of the association, finally led to the AMA's dissolution in November 1907. Winchester revisited the AMA era in 1951, however, when it reviewed a company history it had commissioned from Yale economist Harold Williamson. Company executives disliked the first draft. For the public relations director and lawyer, the biggest objection was Williamson's inclusion of material on the AMA, which would "only focus attention upon acts . . . which now are deemed illegal." The public relations director was of the mind that "it was necessary for Winchester to 'confess' its sins against the Sherman anti-trust act," but wondered whether the "continuance of alleged illegal practices beyond the dissolution of the AMA in 1907" should be alluded to, especially since the confessional strategy did not have the blessings of other erstwhile association members—and, evidently, continued beyond 1907.[37]

Sidney Kay, another company reader of the draft, agreed that in at least some cases, it was the better part of gun-industry valor to make the visible hand invisible again. He worried about a description of "discounts given a few large customers which were in excess of those given other groups." "I think it is bad strategy to bring that up," he concluded. "It doesn't help anybody to know that somebody else got the better of them—even though it was a long time ago."[38]

Winchester did indeed treat dealers preferentially, based on volume of sales, zeal, and fidelity to the company's minimum retail prices, which led to what the company archives call a "muddled" and sour relationship with some of the dealers. The company referred in correspondence to A, B, and C houses, and discreetly offered different discounts to each. A September 1905 draft letter offered a 5 percent discount to one group of dealers, so long as they maintained the company's minimum retail prices, and "[did] not sell our guns in a manner deemed detrimental to the best interest of the trade or ourselves." A draft letter the next month offered a 10 percent discount to other jobbers who sold to "LEGITIMATE DEALERS." The WRAC confidentially invited some retailers who were known to "regularly stock and push" Winchester guns to participate in a "profit sharing scheme" with other select dealers who were placed "on the most favorable basis."[39]

Sears & Roebuck had ideas about pricing and profit sharing, too. Sears was an Amazon.com of its day—a vast, eclectic emporium of discounted commodities that utilized the cutting-edge technology of the mail-order catalog. The catalog advertised pages upon pages of guns, to be ordered and shipped through the mail. The first federal gun-control legislation, passed in 1927, targeted this anonymous mail-order market, by which six-year-olds and lunatics alike, legislators noted, could easily purchase guns.

Sears ignored the WRAC's minimum pricing policy. In 1911 and 1913, two Supreme Court rulings would hold it to be illegal for manufacturers to control selling prices, but for now, the matter was undecided and controversial. The impulse among retailers generally, the company archive suggests, was toward gun price-cutting to attract customers. Sears also offered the take-down shotgun (designed to be taken apart for easier transport and storage) as a premium for customers who spent over $300, strange as it is today to imagine a gun as an added bonus, tossed in for buying a sewing machine or shoes. Because of what the WRAC called Sears' "demoralization of prices" and flouting of "the maintenance of fair profits," TG Bennett absolutely refused to send it guns. The company applauded dealers who could charge above the minimum prices, but insisted on a floor, if not a ceiling. Its executives argued that once Sears "offered to give away part of their profit," so would other retailers, and they would all be on a slippery slope of unprofitability.[40]

Remington had the same concerns about the "demoralization of the trade" that the "wrong channels of distribution" could cause. When it sold its shotgun trade in 1910 to another concern, Remington reiterated that the new owner would distribute only through "retail merchants" and keep the gun merchandise "out of the hands of the catalog and mail order houses." The new owners reassured Remington that there would be only "one fixed price for these goods and far from being a trust we will in reality be a benefit to the small retail dealers. . . . We are not going to cater to catalogue or mail order houses in any way, shape or manner."[41]

Sears dug in. When a customer attempted to order a Winchester in November 1905, it responded petulantly that it could not fulfill the order because the WRAC "consider[s] our profit sharing plan . . . as being a cut in price on their line of goods." Winchester had "considered it advisable to sacrifice our business to further the interests of the other dealers who are almost universally in favor of large profits," Sears explained. "The factory is trying to prevent our getting [guns] from wholesale dealers."[42]

After Bennett cut off Sears' supply, Sears continued to advertise what the WRAC decried as "cut" prices. He suspected that Sears would next try to purchase guns covertly, to secure a few guns at a time from the trade or from jobbers by "using the names of houses which in fact have no existence except upon the letter head"—a kind of straw purchase. The WRAC urged jobbers to strenuously scrutinize orders for "abnormally large quantities" to ensure they were not directly or indirectly intended for Sears, however artfully convoluted or disguised the supply chain.[43]

Fred Biffar was the head of Sears' gun department, and he was scheming exactly as Bennett suspected. He had "strictly confidential" plans, he explained to two dealers. Biffar sent an order for Winchesters, one among many, to a Georgia dealer and suggested that he "buy these goods in small quantities from your local jobbers . . . and when you have accumulated about ten guns, pack them carefully and ship them to us." They were "receiving thousands of cases" with similar small amounts daily. Biffar recommended that the retailer "take one or two . . . guns and put them on your show window, to make it appear you are selling this line of goods." "You will have to work cautiously on this business," he warned, to "not arouse suspicion, and by all means do not attempt to buy many of these goods at one time from any one house." Biffar instructed another retailer to buy small orders of Winchesters from dealers in Omaha, Council Bluffs, St. Joseph, St. Louis, and Des Moines, "without arousing suspicion. . . . Ship them to Nebraska City, . . . then reship them to us."[44]

The WRAC had conceded at the start that it would be a "difficult" task to prevent "Sears from getting the goods," and it could be "only partially accomplished." But even a partial success would sufficiently impede the "Messrs. Sears et al. from making a profitable business." Actually, the task was not impossible. Leonard compiled a meticulous list of 110 gun houses that were covertly supplying Sears, and he discovered another four houses in the process that "advertise and sell Winchester arms over the counter at cut prices, and whom we consider undesirable to supply."[45]

THE WRAC WAS ALSO TAKING THE INITIATIVE IN ITS FOREIGN SALES to impose order and control over distribution. That initiative revealed precise knowledge of how retailers connected to other retailers, and even to the now-distant terminus of an actual customer. In May 1910, the company wanted to direct "the traffic in our goods as far as possible through the jobbing and commission houses that push our lines and make a specialty of them." It compiled a detailed list of houses that should be included, and smaller houses that wholesalers should avoid because of insufficient volume. The latter included Dillemna Fils & Cie in Paris, which had "clients in Buenos Aires." "Were quoted years ago," the archives noted, "and in 1902 bought $484 worth of guns. Have bought nothing of us direct since." Winchester also removed from its list firms such as Ad Jansen, in Liege, Belgium, which had "never bought anything of us direct. Obtain their supplies from Rick

Freeres, through Andre Schaub & Pioso." The company would still do business with Marius & Levy, also in Paris, as they knew that it was a generous buyer for its house in South America, as was Zeller, Villinger & Company in Antwerp.[46]

Gun deals, and dealers, could be nebulous, but they were not beyond the sales department's purview when commercial interests were at stake.[47]

Noncommercial interests were different. In 1898, Congress granted the president his first authority to control the international gun market, by banning arms exports during the Spanish-American War. Arguably, this was a historically perishable remedy that had already passed its prime by 1900, since the WRAC in New Haven sat at the center of its own web of arms dealers, regimes, governments, and individuals that radiated outward to these, and other, locations: Sweden, Norway, Italy, Holland, Greece, France, Denmark, England, Newfoundland, the West Indies, New Zealand, Nicaragua, Australia, the Philippine Islands, Japan, India (Calcutta), Siam, Java, East Africa, West Africa, South Africa, Trinidad, the Canal Zone, the Virgin Islands, the British West Indies, Tasmania, Korea, Mexico, New Caledonia, Brazil, Spain, Portugal, Arabia, Ceylon, Sumatra, Cuba, Belize, Republica del Salvadore, British Honduras, Fiji Islands, New South Wales, Switzerland, Scotland, Ireland, Peru, Ecuador, Uruguay, Chile, St. Johns, Bolivia, and China. William Sherer Jr., known as the "Dean of the Winchester foreign traveling force," joined the company in 1898 and made twenty-two trips around the world in as many years to introduce Winchesters to countries on six continents. A confidential British report estimated that there were 10 million to 12 million "spare arms" sloshing about the world in the 1910s, a percentage of which would be trafficked by secondhand dealers. The Winchester "ruled the destinies of the mushroom monarchies south of the Caribbean," and from the plateau of Tibet to Cape Town, an employee's poem said in celebration of the rifle.[48]

After a complaint to President William Howard Taft from his ally Francisco Madero, the Mexican president, Congress extended the president's 1898 embargo authority on March 14, 1912, with legislation that empowered him to forbid American firms from exporting armaments to "any American country where he finds conditions of domestic violence existing, which are promoted by the use of arms and munitions of war procured from the United States" (although historian Alexander DeConde noted that no comparable standards applied to domestic sales). Taft prohibited gun sales to Mexico, aside from the selective export of arms to Madero.[49]

In September 1912, a Senate subcommittee on foreign relations was interested forensically in just the sort of question, politically, that had preoccupied Winchester, commercially, with Sears: whether US corporations had found illicit paths to arm the rebellion against Madero, and if so, how. The Winchester archive notes that the WRAC voluntarily refused to make deliveries of goods to firms with Mexican affiliations, and the government commended it for this—although congressional testimony made clear that Winchesters went across the border anyway. Winchester dealers and others testified to their code of studious incuriosity, sleight of hand, and innuendo. Waldo Pitkin, a Winchester dealer at the New Orleans gun wholesaler A. Baldwin and Company, hadn't done any business with "Mexican revolutionists that I know of as revolutionists." Then again, they didn't come wearing labels, and he'd sold "rather large" orders of ammunition to parties for "spot cash," which was the standard for all sales. Some took orders by phone and payment by messenger, and never actually saw the customer.[50]

The archive of gun merchants Schuyler, Hartley & Graham includes an 1895 order to ship rifles in cases "disguised as much as possible" to a port in North Carolina. The firm shipped rifles, discreetly—as was common practice for gun industrialists, to ward off poachers and inspectors, or as an act of subterfuge and disguise against corporate rivals—some marked only with "to Chemulpo, Corea [sic]"; 1,000 Remingtons marked "GS" to Guatemala; and 10 Lee rifles in a crate "M&C., L," to Hong Kong. Scores of other examples could be given.[51]

Dealers enjoyed some of the same anonymity in their transactions with Winchester. A few dealers testified that they never carried an account with the WRAC, but paid with cash, and that the company, "with the war business," in fact insisted on cash, for obvious reasons. The head of Krakauer, Zork & Moyer had purchased 150,000 to 200,000 Winchesters from 1909 to 1912, but he had "no book accounts with the Winchester RAC." Instead, Adolph Krakauer had "an arrangement by which [the WRAC] presents the bill to our banker in New York, and he pays it, so we have no account with them at all" (or record—Krakauer immediately added, "This testimony is not for publication, is it?").[52]

In August 1912, Pitkin fulfilled an order for $118,000 for a large quantity of Winchester rifles and cartridges and some Colt's guns to a man by the name of Segura, clearly a Mexican of some political stripe. Pitkin had no idea how the Winchesters would be used, but "the extent of the order," he testified, " . . . made me suppose it was not intended for domestic consumption." Pitkin had fulfilled another large order in December 1911 through a straw purchaser, a "man by the name of Jon Cash—a good deal like John Doe—for a quantity of ammunition." Pitkin felt that he had "a perfect right . . . to sell any kind of goods for cash, and we have done nothing wrong, so long as we do not attempt to make any delivery" (the customer was responsible for the actual delivery, usually to a spot along the border). A Los Angeles dealer said he hadn't armed revolutionists "collectively." Of course, he qualified, "some people may have come in and outfitted, but we would never know what they were doing."[53]

William Fitzpatrick, with A. Baldwin and Company, testified that from 1909 to 1912, "various parties" had come to his store to buy arms and ammunition, "in some cases in abnormal quantities," using the language that Winchester deployed as a flag for covert Sears purchases. "One of those Spanish-looking chaps; I never knew him from the man on the moon," he said, wanted to buy $40,000 worth of arms ($1,010,000 today). Fitzpatrick assumed they were intended for the "present revolutionists," because "I could not think of anybody else that would use such a quantity."[54]

"Of course I never at any time made any inquiries," Fitzpatrick continued, "because I did . . . not want to know about their business. We wanted to sell everything that we could sell. . . . We would not make deliveries at all, but we would simply put the goods on the sidewalk," as was customary. Fitzpatrick recalled that he made a "beautiful profit" from another sale of 3 million rounds of ammunition and $60,000 worth of Winchester rifles.[55]

ALTHOUGH THEY MAY HAVE BEEN MORE INGENUOUS THAN TWENTY-first-century gun dealers, these Winchester salesmen sound distinctly modern in attitude, if not particulars: the gun market was a chaotic space beyond the control of a dealer, or arms maker, or law. Ironically, in years when the gun industry orchestrated the market for profit, a mood of chaotic resignation emerged around the orchestration of the market for the common good, however interpreted. The web of gun sales comes across as mystified and ineffable. Dealers and opponents of gun control today claim likewise—that they have no real control over where guns end up or how they are used, that a determined individual, whether a revolutionary or a criminal, will always be able to get a gun, and that attempts to regulate the flow of guns are naïve—the main difference being that in 1912, Winchester's dealers felt little compunction about straw purchasers or about the freewheeling nature of their business.

To some extent, history supports skepticism about how the circulation of guns, once made, can be controlled. Still, it was not entirely a question of what couldn't be done with or to dealers, but of what was chosen to be done. For example, dealers and the WRAC used "abnormal quantities" as flags to illicit gun activity with Sears, and this approach today—the management of gun dealers rather than gun owners, and forensic attention to patterns of gun commerce—characterizes successful Virginia legislation, in effect from 1993 to 2012, to clog the pipeline of guns from South to Northeast through prohibition of bulk gun sales. In a 1999 lawsuit, a retired Smith & Wesson executive stricken with conscience testified that the gun industry was "fully aware" that its guns seeped into and fed illicit markets, but did nothing to try to supervise or correct that.[56]

A visible hand, in New Haven, sat heavily on Winchester's network when it came to the directives of commerce—the retail price battle against Sears, or the support of high-volume international dealers, or the AMA. But on imperatives of the commonweal—in this case, the enforcement of an arms embargo—the fatalistic metaphor of the invisible hand and an inscrutable gun market of mystery prevailed. Any control over such a web seemed futile.

CHAPTER 13

LEARNING TO LOVE THE GUN

O<small>N PAPER, THE 1890S AND EARLY 1900S SHOULD HAVE BEEN</small>
lean times for the Winchester Repeating Arms Company. Population growth had slowed, the country was more urbanized, and the "closing" of the frontier logically should have led to a decline in demand for firearms.[1]

Postbellum interest in the martial-militia world of marksmanship and shooting competitions had been pronounced "practically dead" by *Shooting and Fishing*. A reader wrote in 1896, "You might as well be in the desert of Sahara as at a rifle range." The National Rifle Association had been founded in 1871 after alarm arose over the poor marksmanship of National Guard members who had been tasked with defending citizens in the Orange Riots, the ethnic-religious strife between New York's Catholics and its Protestant Irish population. The NRA died in obscurity in 1892, but it did not stay dead. In 1904, the resurrected NRA and the National Board for the Protection of Rifle Practice met in Washington, DC, with an agenda to bolster Americans' atrophied rifle skills. Only one-third of the states had ranges or "made any pretense of training national guardsmen as riflemen," the NRA found. Another third of the states had no range whatsoever, and the final third had "really bad ones." The NRA figured that only about 36,000 men in the regular army and 40,000 of the "citizen soldiery" of the guard would have been trained with a rifle in the event of war. The American male's skill was poor, despite the presumption that the United States was a nation of gun whisperers, rifle-wielding frontiersmen, Colt's lovers, and militia patriots. The NRA appointed a committee to secure appropriations from the federal government for rifle ranges and military arms for use by clubs, and it worked hard to revive state and local rifle associations. In 1905 and 1906—in an early example of gun "lobbying"—it helped pass legislation to allow the secretary of war to sell surplus rifles to NRA-affiliated clubs, an example of the ongoing, overlooked interaction of military and commercial arms enterprises.[2]

With rifle clubs moribund, marksmanship low, and the West "gone, gone with the lost Atlantis," Theodore Roosevelt mourned, Winchester sales grew over three and a half times from 1890 to 1914. The net worth of the company increased from roughly $1.3 million to $16.8 million, even after taking into account depreciation. "For a quiet, peace-loving nation," a commentator observed in 1892, "it is surprising how many firearms are sold in this country every year." In 1892, 500,000 rifles (1 per 130 Americans), 750,000 pistols (1 per 87 Americans), and 400,000 shotguns (1 per 163 Americans) were added to the cumulative gun "load." These are impressive sales figures, given that guns were made to last. Winchester reached its pre–World War I peak production figure in 1904, with 286,089 guns made. The US Census Bureau reported the value of products in the firearms industry (ammunition and guns) at $12,748,419 in 1870 and $34,111,564 in 1910. Nationwide, approximately 223 million guns—evenly divided among rifles, shotguns, and handguns—were legally manufactured domestically or imported from 1899 to 1993. Paradoxically, Americans were gun thirsty when on paper they should have been waterlogged.[3]

In this post-frontier gun economy and society, the Winchester had to make a transition from being considered a tool to being seen as something with richer qualitative value in order to attract what a Winchester historian called the average, prospective shooter. In the social life of the gun, and the history of how Americans gave significance to it, this was a critical moment and a new, modern phase of the business in which gun mystique deepened. The gun began a metamorphosis to become a thing that served psychological needs more than the pragmatic ones of war, ranching, the conquest of Native Americans, or the rural economy. Strategically and materially, this meant greater emphasis on sales, marketing, emotionally resonant modern advertising techniques, and an infrastructure within the company to support those efforts. What was once needed now had to be loved. When the gun's history is told as a story of business, a timeline emerges for its cultural and political life. The gun's mystique was elaborated in the post-frontier America of the 1900s even more than in the 1800s. It developed at least in part out of the gun industry's adaptation to business realities and its desire to promote new values for its product. The self-conscious promotion of the gun's intangible emotional values was not a product of villainy or any inordinate effort at manipulation, but an unexceptional function of the consumer economy at a time when guns had to compete against other discretionary, leisure, and luxury commodities.[4]

THE GRADUAL TRANSITION BY WHICH THE GUN HEART BEGAN TO prevail over the head was evident in gun advertisement. The golden age of color lithography in advertisement coincided with the growth in Winchester gun net sales, from $1.8 million in 1885 to $11 million in 1912. And the firearms industry made especially heavy use of lithographic advertisement. Forbes Lithograph, in Boston, was the largest of more than thirty-six lithograph houses that served the WRAC and other gun titans. Western artist Frederic Remington—Eliphalet's cousin—was commissioned for a large number of these ads. Like the dime novels that served up gun narratives, the lithographs were sometimes sold for a dime as their own objects of gun commerce. The Remington company marketed "Cowboy Watering Geraniums" by Philip Goodwin as a jigsaw puzzle.[5]

Gun advertisements developed what Richard Rattenbury, curator of the National Cowboy and Western Heritage Museum, calls a "distinctive visual vernacular" in that they are intended to "incite the viewer's imagination" by telling a narrative. The lithographs conveyed some "feeling, be it excitement, nostalgia, humor, suspense, romance, adventure or even serenity," said Rattenbury. Artists most often created a "predicament scene": a hunter or scout finds himself surprised by an adversary, whether man or beast, an Indian or an enraged moose, and the lithographic advertisement depicts the man poised on the brink of action. The lithograph offers no resolution to the momentous predicament, but is frozen in the moment of tense uncertainty.[6]

The WRAC was one of the most prolific users of color lithography among gun manufacturers, and it was the first gun business to distribute full-color lithographic calendars in the 1880s. A 1950s collector of Remington memorabilia and literature wrote that the "dream of going into an isolated antique store and finding a 1920 Remington calendar in the original mailing tube is still what makes me drive ten miles off the highway to 'Granny's Antiques.'" In their day, Remington wholesalers looked forward to the ten calendars that Remington allotted "to each one of our good friends of the wholesale trade" (its 90,000 retailers got one calendar each). Sportsmen looked forward to the Winchester promotional calendar so enthusiastically that *Shooting and Fishing* reviewed it each year, like a book. The reviewer found the 1896 calendar's lead image, "The Finishing Shot," to be, in most respects, excellent. The moose and the hunters' costumes were well-drawn. But he noted that the artist had misplaced the rear sights of the rifle. Likewise, the picture "Aim Low" featured a man poised to take a shot at a mountain goat. The picture satisfied overall—except that the rifles, the promotional centerpiece of the calendar—were very "poorly drawn," and the shooter's position was conspicuously inaccurate.[7]

Inaccuracies with the guns and the featured predicament were not unusual, even though gun companies reviewed and edited the ads. Goodwin's "When Action Counts" was unrealistic as a hunting scene, as "the swift moving rifleman could not easily place a lethal shot in the retreating grizzly bear." A Smith & Wesson–commissioned image, "In the Gallery or in the Woods," which evocatively shows a man in a business suit and then hunting in the woods, suggests that he might have been better off staying in the office, since a Smith & Wesson .44-caliber revolver would not likely "discourage a pugnacious moose." A 1911 Winchester image, "Confronting a Bear," pits two hunters armed with .401-caliber ammunition and Model 1910 semiautomatics, which would have been barely adequate for the predicament at hand.[8]

Winchester promotional calendar. The gun industry made enthusiastic use of color-lithography advertising at the turn of the century, and these calendars were eagerly anticipated by gun consumers. *Courtesy Tom Webster Family Collection.*

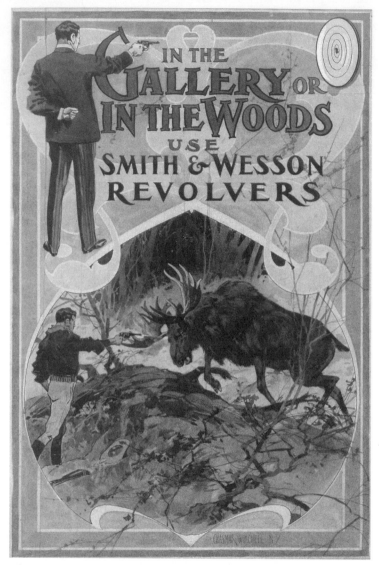

The American gun consumer at the turn of the century, shooting in a gallery in his business clothes and enjoying a weekend hunting in the woods. *Courtesy Smith & Wesson.*

Why the mistakes? Color lithographs allowed for meticulous detail—but accuracy and detail were not really the most important feature of the ads. Their mood, atmosphere, and emotional charge were. The earliest gun ads in the 1850s had featured dense text on the weapon's merits, but only rudimentary woodcuts, if that, to illustrate the gun itself. The gun's practical and mechanical virtues, not the tableau, or emotion, had been the stars of the advertisements. With lithographs, context prevailed over text, and mystique over pragmatism. The calculation that a gun would have to elicit imagination, gripping emotion, or the adrenaline of battling a truculent grizzly to sell is, itself, a change in the business. Indeed, the depiction of a predicament *in media res* rather than a predicament's successful resolution (for example, an image of a man bestriding a bear carcass, the Winchester triumphantly aloft) privileges emotion even over visual evidence of the rifle's efficacy.

Around the turn of the century, as another marketing initiative, Winchester began to deploy gun "missionaries." So did the Remington Arms Company, which appointed missionaries—known as "business getters"—to work as "advance men ahead of salesmen, making appointments and meeting the *consuming public*" (italics added). Remington retired the term in 1913, as the functions of the missionary became simply those of sales and salesmen in general. The deeply evocative term speaks to the zealous, heartfelt sell, and the urge, like that of other missionaries, to entice new converts. The gun missionaries were skilled marksmen, trick shots, and "expert entertainers." They did not make direct sales, but appealed to the public, representing Winchester and stirring up demand.[9]

The gun missionary, like any other, led a peripatetic, far-flung life. *Shooting and Fishing* described one who was "known from the Bay of Fundy to the gulf, and then across the country to San Francisco and along the Pacific Coast, from there to Sitka, Alaska." He made friends and stimulated sales interest wherever he went. Winchester's missionaries received and spread the word as handed down from New Haven's H. S. Leonard, Winchester vice president of sales, who urged them to aggressively "push" some products over others—the term of art for early 1900s advertisement ("It pays to push COLTS because they are the BEST KNOWN, [and] BEST ADVERTISED," Colt's told dealers). In May 1905, Leonard wrote to twenty-two gun missionaries saying that the company's wishes "were as follows: NEW RIVAL shells

ONLY to be pushed in all sections where they are selling well, and NO EFFORT WHATEVER MADE to change dealers over to NUBLACKS . . . in territory where NEW RIVALS are selling freely."[10]

Leonard worried that the gun missionaries who enjoyed too much freedom were sales slackers. He expected of his missionaries the evangelical emotion, fervency, and "energy" of any other missionary, scolding those who padded their hours, or who "strolled in" late at tournaments, when "the other fellows who were on the ground early . . . had been hustling like beavers." While it was important that the missionary "avoid making [himself] obnoxious . . . by over-zealous actions, good missionary work and banker's hours . . . can by no possible means be coupled together." Selling Winchester guns wasn't a job so much as a belief. Leonard also noted "a strong tendency to carry the 'entertainment' feature of the work altogether too far," but at the same time, he recognized that, in the twentieth-century gun business, the gun needed to tap into deep emotions and increase customers' zeal for the product through entertainment.[11]

Similar shifts toward gun affinity over utility occurred within the hunting community. The passionate animosity toward the "market hunter," who killed game to sell, reveals the gun's developing mystique as an object removed from commerce and the business that produced it. Before he was the reviled, greedy market hunter with a rifle, he was the picturesque, rugged "mountain man" with a rifle, a free trapper in the Rocky Mountains of the mid-1800s who traded his pelts at annual rendezvous gatherings with Native Americans. Armchair frontiersmen today stage meticulous reenactments of these trading events. Or the market hunter was the "buff runner" who slaughtered buffalo to provision the railroad after the Civil War and—in what was almost interpreted as a public service—to "passify" the Indians by depriving them of their food supply. Or, earlier still, the market hunter was the lone hunter of masculine prowess, who trekked into the wilderness with rifle in hand, returning to resupply and sell furs. By the 1890s, the market hunter, who did much the same thing, traipsing out to kill animals to sell on the market, as his own agent, without regard for regulations, had metamorphosed to a materialistic, craven figure.[12]

The hunting world consisted of "two distinct classes," *Shooting and Fishing* asserted in 1896: "One is represented by the marketmen's association, composed of gentlemen whose interest is solely a pecuniary one. . . . The other . . . is composed of sportsmen." In 1890, *Shooting and Fishing* decried the "professional slaughterers" who hunted for profit as, curiously, effete and emasculated. They should relinquish their "miserable, shiftless existence and support themselves and their families by other and more honorable means," the magazine said. The market hunter, himself emasculated by avaricious killing, in turn fed, literally, an effete market: the sedentary urban bourgeoisie and "city epicures" who clamored for exotic wares hanging in city shop windows and served in high-end restaurants.[13]

Worse, the indiscriminate profit-driven killing deprived the urban office worker of the new economy: more dependent on pen than gun, he wanted access to the emotional asylum of recreational hunting—to become that shooter depicted in "In the Gallery or in the Woods" who sought rejuvenation away from the office economy. Should the market hunter roam unimpeded, the "outlook will be very dreary to many a man who looks forward to a few hours spent away from the dusty office with breech-loader . . . as a period of rest and recuperation," said *Shooting and Fishing*. Under the new metaphysic, it was more honorable to do other work for profit and hunt for none; the purpose of hunting was emotional, not culinary or economic, sustenance.[14]

The market-hunter backlash went deeper than protests against the violation of gaming laws. Its incandescent rage was directed against the conjunction, now morally repugnant, of the market and the hunt. The market hunter equipped himself with "first-rate guns" and the best provisions for his "business," *Shooting and Fishing* inveighed, but "not a spark of any feeling, save a grasping avariciousness, enters into the market hunter's microscopic soul." The market hunter spoke only of how much he made, the only "standpoint" from which he thought about hunting. Whereas "the pulse of a true sportsman would bound and throb with excitement, the market hunter remains stolid and unmoved." His offense was his dispassionate, "cunning" approach to the gun and the hunt; the sportsman, in contrast, had a mystified if not mystical view, the heart ruling over the head. He killed for emotion over reason, love over profit, den wall over market. It was an arbitrary absolution, perhaps, whose moral coordinates plausibly could have been reversed (non-market hunters often killed large quantities of animals, too), but a powerful and new one that calved two "gun cultures" out of one, each with proponents who had a distinct view of why they had guns, which guns they should have, how they used them, and why they loved them. The essence of the critique was less about the quantity of animals killed than about the quality of the killing—how riflemen felt about shooting. The gun appealed precisely insofar as it offered an alternative to the sedentary, urban office life of the new economy and the market, such that the confounding of the two felt antagonistic and unseemly.[15]

Critics of the market hunter provide another example of a moment when big-picture connections between commerce and the commonweal can be suddenly perceived. In an editorial called "Marketing Game" in 1894, *Shooting and Fishing* disagreed with a reader who argued that any free-born American should be allowed to "buy and sell any articles of food" without limitation. "The average man cannot afford to buy it and the average man cannot afford to hunt it," the editorial said. "But it is the average man who kicks the hardest about having his rights taken away." He did not realize that he was "working against his fellow average man" who went out to shoot recreationally. Only dealers benefited from market hunting, but too many were "blind" and failed to see the connection.[16]

Two points seem especially relevant in the calving of one gun culture from another. First, the sport riflemen were not rallying against gun-control advocates or the government but as one gun subculture against another. The "gun culture" was not one unitary phenomenon. Gun cultures are formed, shattered, transformed, and reconstituted over time. Gun interest waxed and waned, chose new objects and inspirations, and sometimes flared up, and then died down. The sportsmen loathed the market hunters, and so on. The discussion of guns today is typically categorical (we either were or were not a gun culture), rather than dimensional (there are degrees, and different kinds, of gun attachment). It is valuable to parse the matter, and to ask questions—which guns, how were they made, why were they made, how are they used, by whom, and why do these users love them—rather than to simply compress all gun milieus into one American gun culture. At the least, the gun "culture" might need to be pluralized into "cultures." The consolidation of "The Gun" as a unified political or cultural object is a creation of the earliest stirrings of the gun debate, as we will see. Second, and as evident in earlier and other examples, eastern gun capitalists created a myth and a product whose very appeal was that it provided a sharp alternative to—or even repudiated—the corporate industry and the rationalized, sedentary urban life that produced it. Part of their success relied implicitly on obscuring the web that connected the corporation to the consumer, the business to the product, or the commercial market to the gun.

WINCHESTER'S MOST FAMOUS CUSTOMER, THEODORE ROOSEVELT, knew how to love a gun. He deepened its emotional valence beyond its practical value, speaking of the gun as an object of sentiment and sentimentalism. As the "wilderness warrior" and the most powerful conservationist of his day, Roosevelt did not have the market hunter's heart. He imbued his Winchesters, whether used in war, self-defense, or sport, with all the passion that the reviled market hunter lacked, and with all the adrenaline-fueled thrills that Winchester predicament scenes conveyed; indeed, he lived the Winchester calendar. From safari in Nairobi, Roosevelt once compared the choice of a rifle to the choice of a friend. On another occasion, in 1885, he praised the Winchester as "by all odds the best weapon I ever had." He wasn't monogamous to it, but he was deeply partial. It consoled him in 1884, as he grieved his first wife's death on a long hunting trip; it saved him from a grizzly attack in 1889. Roosevelt's Winchester 76 would have saved him or, more likely, been his stout companion in death, had he been forced to duel his rancher-neighbor, the "crazy Frenchman" the Marquis de Mores, who planned to get insanely rich out West and stage a coup d'état in France. The marquis was a great marksman who also preferred a Winchester, with which he had already killed two men in duels, and "countless prairie chickens." The Winchester .30-caliber 1895 lever-action rifle was there on July 1, 1898, at the charge of San Juan Hill, which Roosevelt came to see as "the great day of my life." When he embarked on his famous African safari in 1909, he had a Winchester representative personally board his ship at the American Hamburg pier in New York with his guns, hermetically sealed, and each in its own leather case, so that Roosevelt could keep them close by in his cabin. The company archive includes letters from Roosevelt to Oliver's grandson, Win Bennett, in which Roosevelt emerges as a fastidious, occasionally peevish gun customer with exacting standards.[17]

Roosevelt saw a fine rifle as a "bundle of incompatibilities," an ongoing design trade-off between power and other desired qualities. He saw modern politics much the same way, he told an audience in 1893. His political and hunting lives converged on the matter of unfair competition, manliness, and the tricky equipoise of freedom and regulation. It was a reciprocal lesson of Roosevelt's politics and the hunt that fair competition and free citizenship ironically required regulation of the wild spaces. Winchester the company was thriving in a world of trusts, syndicates, combinations, and pools that crushed individualism and fair competition, as Roosevelt saw things. Winchester the gun thrived in the Dakota Territory, a sentimentalized "land of vast silent spaces," Roosevelt wrote. The world of these vast spaces was antithetical to the corporate world, a place where ranchers "led a free and hardy life, with horse and with rifle."[18]

Roosevelt returned consistently to the idea that the rancher, the rifleman, and the Winchester-armed Rough Rider of the Spanish-American War had "the mind and soul of the average American of the right type" and the "average American citizen." This hunter-citizen was "hard" (ethically, Americans seemed to exist for Roosevelt on a spectrum from hard to soft, with Henry James, that "miserable little snob," anchoring the soft end), filled with "virile virtues" and "virile vigor," and endowed with an embodied heroism, by which "a man pays with his body" when he takes a position. The world of the rifleman and the cowboy had always been masculine, by default (although, as historian Laura Browder noted, the nineteenth century celebrated gun-toting Prairie Madonnas as heroic, individualist defenders of the family). But in Roosevelt's telling, it was more self-consciously, deliberately, and passionately so. Historian Kristin Hoganson and others have illustrated the anxieties around gender at the turn of the century that stimulated an interest in the "manly" life, bringing about the rise of boxing, football, and romantic views of war that "provoked" actual military conflict. The gun was another site for this elaboration. Roosevelt's contribution to the modern gun mystique was to interweave explicitly the qualities of the rifleman with those of virile masculinity, and then to typify and generalize these emotional qualities as those of the average American. He gave the gun a modern, recognizable soul, and he sensed how it could help to resolve, or palliate, the "bundle of incompatibilities" of modern life. When he imagined an American of the right type—still hardy despite urban life; still a free individual despite the octopus corporate economy, with its unfair associations and monopolies; still hard despite the softening forces of modernity—that American had a gun. Winchester manufactured the commodity that Roosevelt envisioned as a remedy for the modern corporate economy in which Winchester manufactured it. The deepening, modern mystique of the gun subtly relied on the obfuscation of the tie between the world of the gun industry and that of the gun.[19]

From Nairobi, Roosevelt wrote to the company, "In *Scribner's* magazine you will see how well I have done with your .405, against lion, giraffe, and other game." These accounts, "African Game Trails," ran in 1909 and 1910. Biographer Desmond Morris wrote that Roosevelt "professed to love the things he killed." While on safari, he collected specimens for the Smithsonian, including a fleeing giraffe, whose back he broke with a long shot from four hundred yards.[20]

The modern associations that Roosevelt elaborated between the gun, the hunt, individualism, and masculinity are such ironclad clichés today that it's worth noting that others in the gun community saw things differently, and that social meanings were not as obvious as they have come to appear. Shooting with the latest small-bore (referring to the size of the interior of the barrel) Winchesters was an even less intimate form of killing than achieved with earlier models, because it made distance shots easier; by that standard, it struck some sportsmen as unfair, cowardly, and unmanly. An editorial from Calcutta in 1902 blamed much of the extermination of wildlife in Uganda and Somaliland on small-bore rifles. It recommended that no rifle under .500- or .450-bore be allowed for sporting. A "modern gunner" could "pump lead at his unsuspecting quarry, with a minimum of noise," and from hundreds of yards away, before the animal even had cause to be alarmed. Big game shooting, the editorial argued, "has . . . become a mere mechanical operation, calling neither for skill . . . nor any great exertion." In earlier times, the hunter had been required to "strain every nerve" when approaching his prey, and exhibit great skill to land a shot. No more.[21]

The quantity of killing was, as the editorial worried, enormous and profligate. The Winchester company archive includes a letter from a Belgian customer, a hunter on safari at the same time as Roosevelt, who reported back that in seventy days, with his Winchester .405, he had killed 94 animals, including 11 elephants, 10 rhebok, 5 rhinos, 3 hippos, 9 antelope, and 3 warthogs. He could have gotten many more, "but found it unnecessary, having good head shots" already—unmarred animal heads to mount.[22]

––––––––––

THE MYSTIQUE OF THE WINCHESTER GUN COULD NOT HAVE BEEN more removed from the Winchester gun business, and in a way, that was precisely the point, and precisely the gun's quickening seduction. As was true in the 1800s, in the early 1900s the ways of the gun economy and the gun mystique diverged. As hunters dug bullets out of the carcasses of hippos in Africa or spent weekends in recreational hunting, the Winchester factory and its workers were coming under the punctilious, soulless regime of scientific management.

Springfield Armory colonel Roswell Lee and the gun industrialists had pioneered the American System of manufactures in the early 1800s, and their intellectual heirs had refined it toward scientific management by century's end. Henry Metcalfe, Lee's intellectual progeny, had run several arsenals. Metcalfe published the first book on cost ac-counting in manufacturing. He and other engineers delivered papers about "indirect expenses"—the hidden costs, burdens, and liabilities of manufacturing things.[23]

As Andrew Carnegie explained in *North American Review*, when artisans or small manufacturers produced goods, a businessman could easily "limit or stop production" as demand changed. But, in "enor-mous establishments with five or ten million dollars of capital in-vested," it cost less to run at a loss than to "check his production." The basic algorithm of the gun business in the new century, and this new phase, was that even as gun need, and markets, became somewhat harder to define, the quantity of guns produced was ever greater as fac-tories moved toward continuous-process production. Colt's made the most pre–World War I pistols and revolvers in 1911 (152,644; 1 per 614 Americans) and 1912 (137,342; 1 per 694). Winchester made over a quarter of a million guns in 1911 (256,834, or 1 per 365 Ameri-cans) and achieved its highest prewar sales in 1912, with 324,500 (1 per 293 Americans). Winchester sold an average of over a quarter of a million guns (269,783) annually from 1904 to 1910, and Winchester sales from 1911 to 1914 averaged 300,000 guns a year. Military and foreign sales alike had receded, and the bulk of the increased produc-tion was sold in the domestic market.[24]

Frederick Winslow Taylor delivered his first paper on the scientific management of the factory in 1895. He proposed meticulous time-motion studies of each action involved in the production of each part of each item produced. The goal was to keep an order flowing continu-ously and smoothly through the production process, without costly lulls, gaps, hiccups, or idle time. In this way, too, each factory could assign an optimal unit cost for each commodity.[25]

Robert Werle, a Yale Sheffield School graduate, was the time-motion man of guns. He conducted scientific management time stud-ies at the Winchester and Colt factories in the 1910s. Werle and his team meticulously observed and parsed each operation in the making of a gun. Eli Whitney's founding logic of the gun industry, to fracture the process into small parts, had been taken to its desiccated extreme.

The Winchester drill press involved 11 discrete movements per operation by one workman. "Placing piece in jig (15 seconds); Spot (3 sec.); Remove to Drill (1 sec.); Drill (16 sec.); Insert bushing and move to 2nd Drill (3 sec.); Drill (10 sec.); Remove bushing, clean jig and place under reamer (15 sec.); Ream (5 sec); Remove to Second Reamer (7 sec.); Remove from Jig (8 sec.); Wash Chips from Fixture (3 sec.)." The "Sum of Movements" was 87 seconds. From this, the Gauging Allowance came out to 60 seconds for 10 pieces. Gross production per hour per machine was figured at 38.7 pieces. Production Lost to Fatigue and Contingencies, 10.7 pieces.[26]

Out of these observations, Werle prepared an "instruction card" for each gun operation, showing how it could be performed most efficiently for the ideal "production per day." He figured production per day through a formula: Production/Day=R.P.M./1.05 (600–1.25 H.T.-W.A.-P), where RPM was "production per minute or revolutions per minute times." The figure 1.05 was 105 percent of machine time, with a 5 percent allowance for belt slipping, power variation, etc.; 600 minutes represented a 10-hour workday, minus H.T.—the "sum of all adjusting, oiling, tool setting, etc . . . per day"; W.A. was the daily wash-up allowance per employee, and P., the "personal allowance" per employee. With this formula Werle determined the maximal production, or base rate, by the machine (and worker) per day, and determined a piece rate for payment.[27]

The production of one .30-caliber cartridge required six parts. The six parts required precisely 94 discrete operations, with 351 tools and 108 gauges to ensure the cartridge was precisely and exactly correct and true. Werle's instruction card for the Cartridge Department, which, before long, would produce 700 million bullets for World War I, detailed each large operation for each part, and each element that made up that operation, and the amount of time each element consumed. "OPERATION A—ROUGHING" alone had six suboperations:

Place 8 trays on truck and take to machine = .013
Put Belt on Pulleys = .025
Pick up Piece and Apply to Belt: .025

Polish: .140
Place Piece in Tray: .020
Set Aside Six Trays: .005

The company decided after this time study that "the output of gun parts will be treated as though divided up into comparatively small separate orders, each of these being ordered and kept track of independently." A Planning Division would ensure continuous production by managing the flow of parts through the factory, each part its own "product." The Remington Arms Company, like Colt's and the WRAC, likewise moved toward strict economy of space and flow. A visitor noted, "Everywhere there are machines, set in serried rows so close that you wonder how the operators find room to work, until you see that there are no wasted motions." When journalist and novelist Theodore Dreiser visited the Winchester factory in 1898, he wrote that, "so distinct [were] the processes," that people who were employed to perform one operation on one part of one piece of a rifle had "never even seen other parts manufactured," and knew nothing of the process.[28]

Modern accounting was both more precise and more mysterious than it had been before, as it was now attuned to the hypothetical, indirect waste of less than steady, constant production. Dreiser marveled at the minute accounting, which augured Werle's time-motion efficiency: "Nothing could be more admirably planned, or more completely and precisely executed, than the system of accounts kept at the offices, by which not only every pecuniary transaction, but also, as would seem, almost every mechanical operation or act that takes place is made a matter of record. Indeed the whole history of every workman's doing, and of every piece of work done, is to be found recorded."[29]

The newly professionalized accountant had a loftier view of his task. He was, as one described, a creative "reader of hieroglyphs, . . . for every erasure, altercation [*sic*], dot, dash or character may have a meaning," however obscure. Accounting was a mystery, encoded in the dry balance sheet. When a factory did not produce at standard volume, this inefficiency increased the unit cost. Scientific management had a term for this: it was called a business's "unabsorbed burden." Sarah Winchester might have understood the phrase, but by a very different accounting. The solution to the unabsorbed burden was a regime of continuous production—insofar as possible, to produce with no costly lulls in the process.[30]

CHAPTER 14

MYSTERY HOUSE

*All things are engaged in writing their own history. The air is full
of sounds, the sky of tokens; the ground is all memoranda and
signatures, and every object is covered with hints, which speak to
the intelligent.*

—*Spiritual Republic*, January 1867

On May 14, 1898, Sarah Winchester sat in a second-floor
conservatory, one of her favorite rooms at her estate, Llanada
Villa, shrouded behind a tall cypress tree hedge. Ingeniously, she had
designed the conservatory floor so that it could be lifted up to expose
zinc panels that drained the water used for plants into a barrel below.
Sarah was San Francisco before it was San Francisco: she believed in
water conservation when resources seemed boundless; she made herb
soups using only ingredients from the grounds of her estate.[1]

Sarah had unanswered correspondence before her. She had to
tackle a letter to her sister-in-law Jane. On this day, as she wrote, President McKinley was ordering a military expedition to occupy the Phil-
ippines. In a few weeks, on July 1, Theodore Roosevelt would lead the
attack to take San Juan Hill and open the strategically critical route to
Santiago de Cuba, with a Winchester rifle tucked under his arm. Roosevelt had tried to pay a courtesy call on Sarah in 1897 on a California
trip, as homage to the rifle he loved, but she had managed to thwart his

plans, explaining to the San Jose Chamber of Commerce that she never received guests in her home.[2]

New Haven had greeted the Spanish-American War with zeal. Some of the Yale men had organized a horse battery; others had found places with Roosevelt's exotic unit of Rough Riders. Still others had flocked to the volunteer army. One platoon was composed entirely of Yale men, including popular athletes. The WRAC had hired hundreds of new workers for the war and was running at full tilt, operating around the clock with 3,000 employees—a new record. By the middle of May, Winchester's auxiliary buildings at Lake Whitney were humming with activity after several idle years.[3]

But Sarah did not share New Haven's—or her late father-in-law's—affection for the "romance of war." "War is now a sad reality," Sarah lamented to Jane in her letter. "Although it seems more remote from me than from my eastern friends, I hope none of the experiences which seem to be a possibility will come to them."

"I am going to try to get sufficiently awake to reply," she cautioned. "For years I have been more or less troubled with insomnia but for two or three weeks I have been so sleepy all of the time that I find it difficult to summon energy enough to do anything. At the same time I am continually very tired and listless. I don't know to what to attribute this very somnolent condition, unless it is the result of having left off drinking coffee. In some respects I think I am better for the abstinence but it is horrible to be so dull and good for nothing."

Judging from Sarah's response, reading Jane's letter had put her in a reflective mood and deepened her melancholy. The year before, Sarah's mother-in-law, Hannah Jane Winchester, had died. One effect of her death was to transmit yet more of the rifle fortune to Sarah's purse, or shoulders. Four thousand shares had gone to Oliver's wife when he had died in 1880. When Will died, yet more shares fell to Sarah directly, whether she desired them or not. Hannah Jane Winchester's shares were now divided between Sarah and Jane, which meant that Sarah held just under half (48 percent) of the Winchester stock. Each received an additional 2,000 shares; for Sarah, that was in addition to her existing 777 shares and several million dollars she had inherited earlier. The dividends paid on these stocks were impressive, and accumulated yet more fortune around Sarah. From 1869 to 1914, the percentage of profits paid out in dividends to stockholders was, aside from six years, never less than 21 percent, and in some cases as high as 79 percent. Through another death—a particularly heartbreaking one for Sarah—she had been catapulted passively and without any intention from wealthy to flamboyantly wealthy.[4]

In her reply to Jane, Sarah wondered how "mother" had been robed for burial, and whether she appeared lifelike. She wondered about others from New Haven, too, especially Jane's son, Ollie. She shrewdly advised Jane to put money in trust for him, rather than putting an ungainly fortune in his "actual possession."

She asked about the house on the hill—Prospect Street—and whether it was closed or occupied, before cutting her reverie cleanly and abruptly short, as she found it better not to think much about New Haven: "There is so much of sadness inseparable from thoughts of all these things that I try not to allow myself to dwell on them long." That sadness had happened decades ago, but it still felt so poignantly immediate.

Jane had asked in an earlier letter if Sarah wanted mementos from Jane Winchester's belongings, and Sarah didn't feel she had any claim, really, on any sort of gift. She thought it would be nice to have something that had been very closely associated with Jane—something intimate that had touched her body and that still resonated with a part of her—so long as it was not anything of value. As she mused on Jane's pins and familiar objects, a painful memory seized her. Before Oliver's death, Will had presented his father with two paintings of Oliver and his wife. Sarah did not want to think of this. The circumstances were all so "unutterably sad," she wrote, that it still pained her deeply to remember them.

But she did recall the conversation with Will about the paintings, so acutely, maybe, that it seemed to exist in space and dimension as well as memory. Will had told her that he was giving his mother and father a lifelong interest in the portraits, but that when they expired, the pieces would return to him. Sarah had never gotten the paintings back, but a lingering fidelity to Will prodded her to ask after them. Maybe Will's spirit would be restless and upset if he knew that the paintings had been neglected. Perhaps it was important, in ways she couldn't fully appreciate or understand, that she fulfill this deferred promise. She asked after the paintings—then she was interrupted from her task.

She resumed writing the letter the next day. Her family back East seemed to be growing restless and impatient for a visit. She had been out West for over a decade now. Jane had inquired after a visit, too, and Sarah hastened to explain that she was "not yet situated to give a *pressing* invitation." The farm consumed her energy and she had no time or stamina left for getting the house finished up and settled. "Even when I do try, it is much like the old horse on a treadmill—I end up about where I started," she wrote.

Plaster, for example, bedeviled Sarah. "I have such dreadful luck with plaster." She had tried so many plasterers, and none had met her standards. "They excuse the defects in all sorts of ways, an occasional earthquake serving them well," she wryly noted. The room she wanted to use for guests had been poorly plastered, and "[as] soon as I can feel equal to the disagreeable task, I shall have it all removed from the walls and replastered, and this is about the way I progress." The plumbing system vexed and enervated her. "Nothing but a radical change can make my plumbing beyond reproach," she explained to Jane. She had been working so very hard, but perfection eluded her, always.

On June 11, 1898, as US Marines landed at Guantanamo, Cuba— and President McKinley spurred congressional debate on Hawaii by arguing, "we must have Hawaii to help us get our share of China"— Sarah sat down once more to try to write to Jane in reply to her letter of May 29, and to finish that letter, once and for all.[5]

Jane had asked her to provide the dates when she had purchased pieces of silver, including a tea strainer, a reading glass with a handle of iridescent pearl, a salad spoon and fork, and, in 1890, a silver berry or bonbon dish—so that Jane could have them engraved as heirlooms for her children. The circulation of small objects of silver and ivory knitted the Winchester family into one. Sarah had sent other small silver gifts to nieces and other relatives, engraved with their dates and "gift of Mrs. William W. Winchester." She remembered sending her mother-in-law an 1897 Christmas gift of a silver vase, and regretted that she hadn't done so with an intuitively sad heart, she reflected, since it would prove to be Jane Winchester's last holiday.[6]

Sarah's task was time consuming. She explained that she kept many boxes and baskets of letters but had not yet sorted them out. And, in the course of her search for acknowledgments of her various silver gifts, she became, she apologized to Jane, "so interested in reading over old letters that I lost much time in this way, and continually found myself forgetting my object in looking them over. I must have other boxes put away somewhere, as I have as yet found no letters dated previous to eighty-nine."

This dispirited her. Sarah had risen in the morning, firmly resolved to work her way through a pile of unanswered letters, but she had not even finished the letter to Jane, and the late afternoon sun had already slanted into the room. She attributed some of her dilatory, meandering efforts to the illness of her little dog Snip, which had distracted her attention from everything else. And she invariably left the letters to which she was replying in her room. To "be economical of strength and energy," she would try to remember their contents by heart rather than retrieve them. But that effort, too, took diligent attention and time, and she ended up back where she had started.[7]

Sarah recalled that Jane had asked her about the sights of California. "I have not seen much of it outside of this valley. I am not very enterprising as traveler or sight seer," Sarah had to confess. "Every day, I look up and see the Lick Observatory glistening up on the top of Mt. Hamilton, but I doubt if I ever get any nearer to it."

Jane had inquired about visits to California again, which might well have filled Sarah with some longing, overwhelmed by a cold finger of dread, because she thought it best to qualify her enthusiasm about a visit, as the home was nowhere near ready to receive family. "I hope someday to get so situated that I shall feel that it would not be an imposition on my friends to invite them to visit me," she told Jane.

Sarah interrupted her thoughts and reread the sentence about the Lick Observatory. She must have thought better of it, so she typed out a parenthetical correction a few lines below in the typed letter; but then she must have thought better of the correction, because she scratched out the qualifying codicil with a pen.

She explained her misgivings about a visit, presumably to stave it off, and strengthened the urgency of her first warning. "For one reason and another since I started in to make alterations in my house," she wrote, "I have not been able to get anything like settled."

"It would make a long story to tell all about it," Sarah added.

Jane, accustomed to the sober industriousness of New Haven, would not understand how much more difficult it was to get competent work done in California than back East. "I am constantly having to make an *upheaval* for some reason," Sarah explained. Always, one project seemed to create two or three more in its wake. "For instance," she elaborated, "my upper hall which leads to the sleeping apartment was rendered so unexpectedly dark by a little addition that after a number of people had missed their footing on the stairs I decided that safety demanded something to be done so, over a year ago, I took out a wall and put in a skylight; then I had to have plastering done," and the plastering created new problems to be resolved. Then, over the winter, "such little rain as we had revealed to my dismay leaks in the new skylight so that it must be reconstructed, and so it goes."

Heating systems exercised her. "The house is very rambling," Sarah wrote, "and to keep it properly warmed is a problem but I hope it will be solved before next winter." All problems had their solutions—any inventive, enterprising Yankee understood that—so Sarah worried about leaving Jane with an impression of sloth. "If I did not get so easily tired out I should hurry up things more than I do," she elaborated. She apologized, and then added that just the visit from the furnace man had "used me up completely for a day or so."

Evidently Sarah had regretted writing candidly in her last letter about the two portraits that Will had commissioned, and she wished to redo or undo that passage of the earlier letter: in the midst of a paragraph on the lack of rain and the condition of the local foliage, she abruptly switched course to try to explain that it was only "loyalty to William" that had inspired her to mention the paintings so boldly.

She was gratified to learn that she would be receiving a silver thimble and pin as mementos of "the dear 'little mother' who has passed from mortal vision." The phrase is telling. To Sarah, Jane Winchester was not visible—but neither was she gone. Sometimes mysteries reveal themselves in very small but spontaneous details and archival fragments. Of all that was written about Sarah, and the exceedingly smaller amount written by Sarah herself, this phrase, singularly, suggests that Sarah Winchester really did believe in ghosts, after all.

Sarah realized that this was the longest letter she had managed to write in some time. There were four others that she thought it imperative to attempt. She had to respond to a telegram about the division of the Winchester estate that Jane's husband, TG, had sent her. That telegram had given her second thoughts about her first missive, so she had felt it necessary to write and send a second letter to untangle the first and straighten things out. She hadn't yet gotten to her response to the telegram. But now, it was already after five in the evening, and to lift the morale of her cook, Sarah was trying hard to be prompt for her meals. She mentioned to Jane by way of self-reproach that she usually retired for her night's rest almost immediately after dinner, while it was still light outside. She might have found it necessary, and safer, to attempt sleep at that early hour for her own reasons, but she did not explain that to Jane.

At precisely midnight, the story goes, a Japanese caretaker would ring a huge, sonorous bell at Llanada Villa. The bell rope hung down from inside the smooth, unscalable walls of the bell tower, which could not be accessed from the outside by any stairs or walkways. Only the Japanese caretaker and his understudy, who was entrusted to take over the task should the caretaker perish, knew how to find the end of the rope. They came to it through a tunnel in the cellar—the caretaker having thoughtfully drawn his apprentice a map. Sarah had given this caretaker an expensive pocket watch so that he could perform the bell-ringing function precisely at midnight. But as the pocket watch might be imperfect, she bought him a "chronometer"—a clock—for his quarters. She chose the most expensive and exquisite one she could find. By this chronometer, he could set his pocket watch to within a fraction of a second of perfection.

Then, Sarah thought to buy a second, and then a third, chronometer, to keep the first one true, which the caretaker also kept in his quarters.

But even fine chronometers might fail, and lose a fraction of a second or two of time, which would transmit an error to the other chronometer, and to the expensive pocket watch. So Sarah asked that the caretaker consult the Lick Observatory each day. Precision of time had mattered so much to Will and Oliver. In 1879, and then after Will's death, they had endowed a heliometer at the Yale observatory to ensure "uniformity of time," the "object being to furnish an accurate time device, and give the local watch industries the advantages afforded by similar observatories elsewhere." Checking with the observatory, the caretaker at Llanada Villa could check the integrity of the first chronometer, from which he could check the second, and then, in turn, confirm the accuracy of the pocket watch, and ring the bell precisely at midnight.[8]

Following the ritual so closely must have mattered deeply to Sarah.

Most likely, she would be up for much of the night despite retiring earlier, but she didn't share her nocturnal schedule with Jane. Instead, she concluded her letter on a hopeful note: soon she would "feel more wide awake and develop more energy and enterprise." Sometime, she said, "I hope to get all straightened out [on the house]," so that she could "say with confidence" that she wanted them all to visit.

When she finished the letter, Sarah probably placed it carefully on a pile for her niece and secretary; then maybe she straightened the pile, just one more time. Then perhaps she gazed out of her conservatory's large windows. The room sat somewhere near the original core of the eight-bedroom cottage that she had bought, unfinished, from Dr. Caldwell in 1886. But maybe she herself was not entirely certain of where those eight rooms were now.

From her conservatory, to the left, she saw her Palladian and bull's-eye windows, so popular in San Francisco at the time, and part of her

Sarah Winchester's Llanada Villa, before the 1906 earthquake. At this time the estate was at the peak of both its size and eccentricity. It was reputed to be the most expensive private residence to build in the world. *Courtesy of the Bancroft Library, University of California at Berkeley.*

front porch. Another room sat over it, which had a balcony on top of it. Just behind that balcony she had added several other rooms and sections, each growing progressively higher until they reached a seven-story tower, just behind her and out of view. The shingled roofs fought for air with their competing towers and cupolas, and she could not see the end of the house from her vantage point, but she could not see it from any vantage point, so she looked out upon a sea of minarets, belvederes, turrets, widow's walks, towers, skylights, ridgepoles, dormers, and pediments winding to no particular destination, without motive, aesthetic, or end, in a maze of wood and shingle that spilled forth like a fugue, or a dream.

There were problems, as she had explained to Jane, and so much building and rebuilding and unbuilding to come. But she was feeling a bit more industrious today, and perhaps she allowed herself some satisfaction in her progress.

FROM THE OUTSIDE PEERING IN, SANTA CLARA COULD SCARCELY ignore, and could not decipher, the noise and activity behind the cypress hedge in front of the Winchester estate. Signs warned: "No Admittance Except for Business." The view from the outside was still breathtaking. The estate had a beautiful lawn. Fountains threw spray onto statuary, including an Indian brave that seemed almost human. Lilacs, trees, vines, pampas grass, and rare plants and flowers grew everywhere. Even the summerhouses and conservatories had charming pinnacles, and unexpected niches revealed clusters of hidden statuary.[9]

The *San Jose Evening News* on March 29, 1895, took notice. This was the first-ever published recognition that Sarah was up to something fantastic, and strange, in the valley. *American Architect and Building News* reprinted the San Jose story in February 1896, with the headline, "Superstition in Building." "The first view of the house fills one with surprise," said the story. "You mechanically rub your eyes to assure yourself that the number of turrets is not an illusion, they are so fantastic and dreamlike. But nearer approach reveals others, and still others."[10]

The estate, pre-1906 earthquake, resembled a German castle with its strongholds: "From every point-of-view new towers appear. . . . For every addition of the many that have been made has one or more separate roofs, and every roof is elongated into a tower or rounded into a dome. Not everyone created is sure to remain, though. The main cupola was pulled down and rebuilt sixteen times before it pleased the taste of the owner and was allowed to stay."

Even as the article's author wrote, workers were "sawing and hammering in the work of constructing another turret on the Winchester mansion." Shrewdly, he noted that "even the barns and granaries are built in L's and T's, which suggest that they were made in parts and are ready at any time to have the work continued."[11]

In 1905, before the San Francisco earthquake, Sarah Winchester's estate would have the distinction of being the most expensive residence to build in the country—$130 million in 2015 dollars. Sarah lived alone here with her niece—Isabelle's daughter, Frances—in almost complete solitude, aided by a "staff of loyal, closemouthed

Oriental servants." A pack of bloodhounds roamed the property behind the high, impenetrable hedge to ward off nosy visitors, and the
doors were "closed to all but a favored few," a *San Francisco Chronicle*
article noted. The mansion had 200 rooms on seven stories, 10,000
windows, and 2,000 doors, trap doors, and spy holes. In 1905, Llanada
Villa was as enigmatic and enormous as it would ever be, stranger inside even than from without.[12]

The "rifle widow's" estate was described in its day by the *New York
Times* as a "vast, complex edifice, reared upon the compelling fantasies
of an aged, wealthy recluse . . . and representing in truth a stranger
blend of romance and philosophy than fiction tells."[13]

Sarah built. She built with what a contemporary called "inexplica-
ble ceaselessness." For over three decades she built constantly, employing sixteen carpenters at three times the going wage—she paid a living
wage decades before its time—to work in shifts, twenty-four hours a
day, to build additions, towers, or new rooms that made no sense and
had no obvious purpose, sometimes only to be torn down the next day,
or plastered over.[14]

The *San Jose Mercury News* in 1911 called Sarah's colossus a "great
question mark in a sea of apricot and olive orchards." Over a century
later, the Santa Clara Valley still felt compelled to riddle out Sarah's
designs and intentions. Wrote the *San Francisco Chronicle*, "the Mansion is an ornately complex answer to a very simple question: Why?"[15]

CHAPTER 15

"GROTESQUE,
YET MAGNIFICENT"

Oh mad Arachne,
so did I see you already half spider,
wretched on the shreds of the work, which
to your own hurt was wrought by you!
— *Dante, Divine Comedy*

"SHE WAS NEVER DISCUSSED TOO MUCH IN MY IMMEDIATE FAMILY," STG and Jane Bennett's granddaughter Susan recalled of Sarah Winchester in 1971, "even though my grandfather and grandmother certainly corresponded with her. No one ever went out to visit her . . . though I know my father and mother asked to see her, after finishing up a fabulous trip to Baja in the fall of 1906. They were told she couldn't see them." Susan "got the impression that she was not too well thought of by her eastern connections . . . because she was considered a bit too eccentric by her in-laws." Susan better understood the "rebuff" after visiting Sarah's house in San Jose for the first time in 1968.[1]

Things might have developed differently and less bizarrely. Sarah might have built nonstop, forever, in orderly, straight lines, on all the land she bought in the Santa Clara Valley, and she would have been called a developer instead of a lunatic.[2]

279

In April 1906, Sarah caused the cataclysmic San Francisco earthquake. Of the thousands killed and the miles razed by the great shock and subsequent fires, legend holds, Sarah knew that the message was intended for her and sent by vengeful spirits. Sarah had requested perfect titles to her lands, and total privacy, and dominion over her world on the estate, but she could always be found. Emissaries of rough cosmic justice could send a world of brick, stone, and glass crashing down on her. From Texas, TG wrote urgently to Jane, "The news from San Francisco is terrible and I wonder if you have telegraphed Sallie [Sarah's nickname in the family]?"[3]

It is unclear whether Sarah was actually at Llanada Villa when the quake struck, but as it is most commonly told, she was sleeping in one of her many bedrooms toward the front of the house when the calamity occurred. Her servants escaped unharmed, but since Sarah so often switched bedrooms, they couldn't locate their frantic mistress for an hour. When they finally found the right bedroom, they discovered that the door frame had partially collapsed, along with the room's chimney, jamming the door shut. Sarah's self-enclosing labyrinth had collapsed on her. Some say the marks on the door frame, still visible today, are from the crowbar used to free her.[4]

Whatever the case, Sarah's castle was heavily damaged. A seven-story tower had pancaked and collapsed; several chimneys had tumbled to the ground; turrets had broken apart; third- and fourth-floor additions were devastated; and, as a local historian put it, "twenty years of meticulous wood and tile craftsmanship were destroyed" in an instant.[5]

Sarah ordered the damaged front of the house boarded up, never to be repaired. Her niece's husband later reported that Sarah said of her house that "it looked as though it had been built by a crazy person." Apparently, she did contemplate the abandonment and sale of her Llanada Villa creation. Already, the ghost story of Sarah Winchester and the American gun was woven into print. A San Francisco Examiner headline from April 1908 read, "Woman Defies Ghosts in Selling her House."[6]

She roved farther westward, but ran out of West.

She could go no farther than the San Francisco Bay. Among her more than a dozen real estate holdings, she owned thirteen acres of marsh land by the bay that hugged the shore next to a eucalyptus forest and a polo field, with stables for ponies, and there she planted a houseboat. There was nothing for her but to move to an ark. In the spiritualist tradition, this made sense. Restless spirits and ghosts were either afraid or incapable of crossing water, so by this logic the ark was a home security system. It made sense in the seismological tradition, too, as the houseboat, being on water, was the thing least likely to be damaged by earthquakes.[7]

Sarah began work on an immense concrete seawall to hold back the bay. Then, she envisioned ambitiously the creation of an elaborate network of canals, waterways, floodgates, and boathouses to run the entire span of her land. Then, she could maintain a whole fleet of yachts, and what one article called "rescue arks," to wend their way through her watery labyrinth. Then, if she had a private fleet of yachts, she would want to admire her empire, so she intended next to build on land "the finest country home in the west," a Palo Alto newspaper said. To build the finest country home, the article continued, she first had to build a mountain high enough to "preside over the entire Bay," and her canal system, and her fleet, so she had workers create huge mounds of earth to build the mountain that nature had neglected to provide.[8]

For six months Sarah lived on her hastily constructed houseboat, a refuge after the earthquake, and the modest beachhead of her grandiosity. Then, as impulsively as it had begun, Sarah's work on the nautical country estate stopped. By 1909 she had wearied of the "new toy," the newspaper explained. She left the manmade mountain where it was, abandoned the construction to the fog, and gave the houseboat to her niece Sadie Rutherford. "It was beautiful inside," a longtime resident of nearby Burlingame recalled. "It had all different kinds of hardwood floors and different fireplace mantels. . . . It wasn't locked up and kids loved to play in it." Hoboes used the ark as a waystation until it burned down in 1929.[9]

For whatever reason, ghostly or worldly, Sarah steeled up her courage and returned to Llanada Villa. Whatever she wanted to say, or do, it was about a house—*this* house—not a boat, or more land, or random, perpetual building on more land. Whatever she wanted to do, she would do it here.

SARAH LEFT NO DIARY OR BLUEPRINT OF HER WORK AT LLANADA Villa. She scrawled turrets and additions on napkins or brown paper, and tore down the turrets and additions as casually as she destroyed the sketches of them. Ralph Rambo, son of the Winchester agent who had helped Sarah buy her land, recalled that "some days she sketched plans on the spot using a sawhorse drawing table and any handy material, often brown wrapping paper (and she used both sides)." Sarah had no training in architectural design, and in any case architecture was in its infancy as a profession. Her bank receipts show that she subscribed to the *Architectural Record*, however.[10]

Her creation, a "monstrous" design, visitors called it, made no more sense than her methods; which is to say, they were not profitable, purposeful, linear, coherent, or functional. "The house is like a problem in mathematics with faulty figures cropping up again and again," a visitor later observed. "As architecture, it is unique, improper and illogical." Nothing could have been more perfect—interchangeable—than the Winchester rifle, each varying no more than 1/1,000th of an inch from each other; and nothing could have been more idiosyncratically singular than the Winchester estate built with the Winchester rifle fortune.[11]

But it did seem to represent a morbid introversion. The first thing to hypothesize is that she was mad—although clearly she wasn't. Sarah was obsessive but competent, sometimes brilliant, in many respects, including her business acumen. She ran a large, functioning orchard, was fascinated by the high-tech machinery of her day, and was a prolific amateur inventor. She designed a servant's call box and intercom system; a needle-point shower; window shutters that opened from the inside; wool insulation to control room temperatures; and metal plates for stair corners to prevent dust accumulation. She was among the first to use hinged fireplace trap doors to allow ashes to drop to one central location in the basement. Sarah also invented burglar-proof window latches: they resembled the Winchester rifle trigger and trip hammer.[12]

In 1906 she wrote to her lawyer Samuel Leib to establish trust funds for her sisters and their husbands, to painstakingly dissect an ambiguous deed for fifty acres that she wanted to purchase, and to fight what she called the "Railroad Invasion" of a portion of her land. (Though she fought feistily, she was ultimately unsuccessful.) Sarah's perspicacity, lucidity, and legal fluency was punctuated by the occasional cryptic reference to distractions that pulled her away from the business at hand. "I have had an unusual degree of perplexity and annoyance with other matters," she wrote to Leib in November 1905, "which have required all the thought and attention that my limitations would allow." She was frequently ill, and serious arthritis occasionally limited her stamina. With intriguing ambiguity, she wrote, "I occasionally have no respite from the suffering, which seems is impossible for me to get entirely free from."[13]

Sarah wanted to systematize her regular monthly payments to several people, and so she wrote to Leib reasonably in December 1908, "I think it would be better to buy bonds which have a long period to run before maturity." In July 1909, Leib executed her impulsively unequivocal wishes, writing to the Union Trust Company that "Mrs. Winchester desired this money paid monthly, for certain reasons of her own, I imagine, although she did not explain that part to me." When Sarah next wrote to Leib almost a year later, in November 1909, she reported that since last communicating, "I have not been able to give very close attention to anything," although she didn't elaborate why. She clarified that she wanted any adopted children to be encompassed by the term "children" in her trusts (Isabelle was planning to adopt a baby she was caring for)—and that she wanted to "reserve the right at any time to modify the terms of the trust or to revoke it all together." Then, she did just that. "For good reasons I am very anxious to have the check, which should come on or before the first of Feb. [to Isabelle] sent to me. For reasons which I cannot explain, I know that this would be the best disposition."[14]

Here, and in the artifact of her house, Sarah comes across as lucidly cryptic—not mad, but not predictable—and not without a purpose. Like a black hole, the Mystery House, as Sarah's estate came to be called, collapses a tremendous force and energy into one concentrated space.

Hundreds of thousands visit the Mystery House every year. If it seemed only an architectural landfill of madness, or the soullessly random sampler of a lively hobbyist, then it wouldn't compel; if it seemed an obvious, legible message of a predictable, orderly mind, then it wouldn't fascinate. Sarah's magnetism is that of an artist more than a lunatic. The house is a derangement with intention, in which you catch a glimpse of an insight on the edge of intelligibility, expressed in the medium of architecture and the style of a fading Victorianism. It is the sense of the riddle that compels the visits—the sense that Sarah wanted to tell us something, and that what we need to know to solve it is encrypted in the house itself.

Sarah was certainly not insane, and perhaps not even "eccentric," as one of her workers described her. It was just that, to her, "the spirit world was very real."[15]

————

IN THE DEAD OF NIGHT IN THE WILDS OUTSIDE OF SAN JOSE, SARAH's castle, surrounded by acres and acres of orchards, was illuminated only by stars and moonlight. It was quiet—aside from a few carpenters, somewhere, working the graveyard shift, tearing down or rebuilding something on the estate.

For Sarah, there must have been consolation for grief in this perpetual doing and undoing, building and unbuilding, weaving and unweaving. Ulysses' Penelope staves off suitors by promising that she will choose one only when she finishes weaving Ulysses' burial shroud. She is loyal, and she knows in her bones he is not dead. Penelope locks herself in her tower and weaves and then unweaves each night, working constantly and never finishing. Her fidelity to the (presumed) dead was preserved by interminable but pointless industriousness.

There are possible ghostly explanations for everything that Sarah did and created, the two worlds, sacred and profane, interleaved. In the ghost story, perpetual building was the directive, conveyed from Will through the medium Coombs, to atone for wrongs and protect her beloveds' souls. A 1911 *New York Times* article contains the first, and only, purportedly direct statement from Sarah about why she did what she did, although, by this point, conjectural rumors had solidified into fact, just as in the Winchester rifle legends. Sarah had told the "few friends who persisted in visiting her despite their brusque reception that [she] had received a message from the spirit world warning her that all would be well so long as the sound of hammers did not cease in the house or on the grounds."[16]

Sarah was an insomniac, and she never slept well, or long. She wore a black veil, lingering in a liminal, suspended state of mourning decades after Will's death. Harry Borchers was a tile setter at the estate. "I rarely caught more than a glimpse of her," he recalled. "Sometimes she'd suddenly appear out of nowhere, and then I'd get the impression that she'd been standing there for *some* time, watching us work." On any given night, she meandered awake in a labyrinth of her own inscrutable design, "a veiled little figure flitting through the halls."[17]

She was preoccupied with means of entrance, and escape, and points of transition. A staircase, one of forty, goes nowhere and ends at a ceiling. Cabinets and doors open onto walls; halls wind back to the beginning; rooms are boxes within boxes, small rooms built within big rooms; balconies and windows are inside rather than out, and some balconies only inches wide; chimneys stop floors short of the ceiling; floors have "skylights." A linen closet as big as an apartment sits next to a cupboard less than an inch deep. Sarah had doors that open onto walls. One room had a normal-sized door next to a small, child-sized one; another had a secret door identical to one on a corner closet—it could be opened from within the room, but not from without, and the closet drawer didn't open at all. Connections and paths from one point to another appear to be made, but are thwarted. Like Daedalus's "dark, inextricable" maze, commissioned by Minos to hide the family secret, the "monstrous offspring" of the half-human, half-bull minotaur, Sarah's labyrinth tricks

A Winchester Mystery House staircase that goes nowhere, one of many enigmatic architectural features of the estate. *Courtesy of the Winchester Mystery House.*

the eye. The passages are disorienting, and details are designed to confuse. In one room, Sarah designed the parquetry in an unusual pattern. When the light hit the floor a particular way, the dark boards appeared light, and the light boards, dark. Bull's-eye windows give an upside-down view of the world. Even these basic truths, of up and down, and light and dark, could be subverted, and played with, to disorient. Like Daedalus, who designed so ingeniously that he could barely retrace his own steps out of his maze, Sarah was both the inventor and prisoner of the world she built.[18]

If a mind were a house, it would look like this. Ideas, memories, and guilt occur to us, all day long. They come to consciousness. If they displease or terrify, we brood or fuss over them for a while, then revise them to make them manageable, or we plaster over them and suppress them, or refashion and displace them into another idea. "Glaring mistakes failed to discourage her," the younger Rambo said of her building. "Sarah simply ordered the error torn out, sealed up, built over or around, or . . . totally ignored." The mental and architectural processes of revision, destruction, suppression, and creation were each ongoing, and eternally self-perpetuating. Sigmund Freud wrote that the mind resembled architectural ruins; specifically, he thought of Rome. Striations of past traumas and events layer the unconscious and never disappear. Llanada Villa was not a place to live so much as a rich "psychical entity," in which "nothing that ever took shape has passed away"; all ancient struggles and notions existed concurrently with the modern.[19]

Sarah remodeled some rooms ten times or more, and one worker spent an entire year laying by hand the flawless parlor floor, an interlocking davit parquet of ash, oak, and mahogany. She created gorgeous rooms, perhaps for ghosts, at their direction, or perhaps for her own pleasure or consolation; appointed them with the best luxuries and the latest conveniences; and closed them off, never or rarely to be used. Workmen restoring the estate in 1975 discovered a previously unknown room. It had two chairs, an early 1900s speaker that fit into an old phonograph, and a door latched by a 1910 lock. Her estate is purported to have a long-ago buried and never re-excavated wine cellar with a gritty handprint on its wall. Interpreting the handprint as an evil augury, a personification of unclean hands, Sarah had the wine cellar sealed shut. Then she moved on to a new project and apparently forgot all about it and built over it—or chose to forget, because it was too terrifying to be remembered.[20]

In the ghost story, Sarah built her home like a maze to trick and confuse the spirits of Winchester rifle casualties—at least the evil ones, who were clever, and wanted to hurt her. "They must never be able to find their way through my house," she is quoted as saying to a friend. "Each year I will add new rooms so that the spirits will go weary of trying to get me." In a house of nothing but tangents, you could always run somewhere and arrive nowhere.[21]

Escape is futile—but relief is to be found in more building and in movement.

Scattered through the dark labyrinth are small, allusive clues. Sarah left them everywhere in the details of the mansion. She liked to work in groupings of thirteen, the favored occult number. She had thirteen sections to her will, which she signed thirteen times, and thirteen-hole overflow drains in a sink. Thirteen hooks hang on one wall, and thirteen transparent stones are embedded in a Tiffany window. The daisy, which was Sarah's favorite flower (and the name of one of her nieces), recurs on everything from windows to bathroom tiles, and cleverly plays on thirteen, because a perfect daisy has thirteen petals. A daisy stained-glass window has nine small daisies, with thirteen petals each.[22]

Perhaps her favorite motif was the spider web. It appears on everything from a bamboo cabinet in one of scores of bedrooms to windows and ceiling panels. Sarah's most stunning spider-web window embeds thirteen blue and amber stones. The spider web is a feminine symbol, tied to spinning and weaving. Like Daedalus and his maze, the spider spins her own world—and home—and then resides in the center of it, the web radiating outward, a creation encompassing many auxiliary spirals and threads into one fabric. The spider is the skilled, ingenious weaver, but she is also the captive of her web. Alfred Tennyson's "Lady of Shallot," one of the most widely read and memorized pieces of Sarah's youth, tells of the heroine who lives alone, imprisoned in a tower and laboring under a curse. She must "weave both day and night," without stopping. Then one day, Lancelot's voice seduces her into the world. When she leaves the loom, the curse is upon her, and she dies ensnared in her own threads, both the master-inventor and the slave of her own making.[23]

One can imagine Sarah wandering through the encrypted labyrinth in the night, perhaps pursued and terrified by the ghosts she knows are real; perhaps simply restless and perpetually disquieted by her anguished, sad thoughts, the drama of her interior life. She makes her way to the grand ballroom through a stunning entry hall never used by living human visitors; it is festooned with silver, gold, and hundreds of prisms, so that in daylight, all the colors of the rainbow dance across the walls, the ceiling, and the floor.[24]

The ballroom never hosted any guests, but by late Victorian custom it was the most public room in a mansion, a portal to the interior spaces. It's one of the most dazzling rooms, and the only one that she had an architect design, which suggests that it was either more or less important than the others. When the 1906 earthquake struck, Sarah was undoing the labors of the architect and the craftsmen: she had just begun to frame out and expand the space, haphazardly, so that it would reach farther out into her front lawn. The twenty-by-forty-foot ball-room cost her over $9,000 ($244,000 today). Artisans painstakingly laid the floor of bird's-eye maple by hand, without nails, with an exqui-site diamond pattern inlay. Sarah ordered a few of the ballroom floors redone because of slight flaws and imperfect acoustics, to the disgust of her workmen, who couldn't discern either.[25]

The ballroom's ceiling is a delicately hand-carved white ash, and altogether in the room Sarah used nineteen different kinds of rare wood. This room had one of the house's only three mirrors, placed over the mantel. On one wall of the room is a fireproof safe, protected by four heavy doors.[26]

The ballroom's two meticulously crafted Tiffany art-glass windows to the right of the organ are the closest things to the eyes of the house. Here, Sarah left her most self-conscious clues, or at least the only ones in words rather than allusion. She had two quotations embedded in the windows. For the first, she selected, "These same thoughts people this little world," from the prison soliloquy in Shakespeare's *Richard II*, one of the bard's most accomplished, and unusually interior, passages. Richard II delivers the soliloquy shortly before his murder. He's been deposed and imprisoned in a small, windowless room by his cousin, the usurper Bolingbroke, with no chance of escape or reprieve. Narcissistic and spoiled, Richard self-consciously "watches himself think" in this soliloquy, wrote Shakespeare scholar Stephen Greenblatt. He tries to forge a link between his prison and the world ("I have been studying how I may compare / This prison where I live unto the world"). But he arrives at dead ends each time.[27]

The insurmountable problem is that the world beyond Richard's prison cell has people in it, and, in his cell, "here is not a creature but myself." Still, Richard vows to begin the effort anew, and "hammer it out." He has an idea. He'll create his own world within the prison, and use the "intercourse" of his brain and his soul to populate his imagined world with "a generation of still-breeding" (stillborn) thoughts. "These same thoughts people this little world," Richard says. They perform in his mind's inner theater, continuously, the same tormenting scenes of his fall from power and grace. In this little world, Richard II can play different roles, but only to meet the same tragic ending, to arrive at the same obstacles, futility, and solitude—in the same imprisoning, contained place.

Sarah drew from *Troilus and Cressida* for the quotation in the second window, which says, "Wide unclasp the table of their thoughts." It's an unusual choice, and it shows Sarah's progressive intellect, since the play was considered so salacious and unsettlingly *sui generis* that it only made its US debut in 1916, in New Haven. Many scholars consider *Troilus and Cressida* to be one of Shakespeare's least satisfying works. It hovers between tragedy and comedy in its bleak, almost postmodern pessimism and refusal of expected resolutions and endings. The play subverts the heroism of love and the romance of war (as Oliver Winchester called it), and suggests that truth and valor are uncertain. Morally deceptive, unfaithful women such as Cressida will "wide unclasp the table of their thoughts" to any "ticklish reader" who comes along, Ulysses inveighs against Cressida's lusty, seductive behavior. The two quotations, from two plays, evoke perfectly a solitary kingdom built entirely of thoughts, and rich with stunted, awry reproduction. Sarah's cloistered inner theater is peopled only by "stillborn" thoughts of a blighted union. In the medium of these thoughts, she tells us, she will "hammer it out," even if it is a perpetually futile project.[28]

The organ sat against the back wall of the ballroom, next to the windows. Before Sarah left New Haven, she had paid a worker two dollars to move the organ back to its original spot after Will's death. She might have had it relocated to play for him in his last days. When she moved to San Jose, the reed orchestral organ came with her.[29]

And here, deep into the San Jose night, servants could hear Sarah playing opera pieces furiously. She played under the light from a chandelier from Germany that has thirteen bulbs (although legend holds that the last bulb was grafted onto the original, which arrived with only twelve); it is suspended from one of thirteen ceiling panels, with thirteen smaller boxes within them, and the room is further illuminated by thirteen candelabras of solid silver. Playing her organ to no one of the visible and known world, Sarah sought that respite from suffering that it seemed "impossible" for her "to get entirely free from," as she wrote to Leib, the attorney. What suffering we do not know. Her crippling arthritis, certainly, and the organ playing might have relieved her pain as it loosened up her fingers and joints. But the legend endures because we do not really want to believe the smallest, most profane explanation—and, more importantly, Sarah's house does not invite us in that profane direction. Instead, it invites us to be playfully imaginative. We want to tell the ghost story, and perhaps we need to tell it, as the necessary fiction. It is the American counter-legend to the gun legend. And in the ghost story, Sarah plays the organ, and builds perpetually, in order to placate and please millions of ghosts and atone for her blood fortune. She is not alone, but surrounded by the souls of those who, like her mother-in-law, had not actually died, but had merely "passed from mortal vision." It may have been the literal project of a spiritualist or the figurative impulse of an artist, but ultimately, Sarah built a place for all of the ghosts wrought by the guns to go, and be thought of.

As Sarah hammered it out in San Jose, Captain E. Crossman, who wrote something of a gun gossip column, toured the "big Winchester factories" in New Haven and described the labyrinthine WRAC in terms quite similar to Sarah's Llanada Villa. He, like novelist Theodore Dreiser, was disoriented by the gargantuan, chaotic buildings. Even after gaining admission to the main factory, he said,

> you are not a bit nearer to gaining entrance to the inner mystery of mysteries than when you stood outside. The Winchester plant is not a . . . symmetrically disposed group. It is merely a great huddle of buildings of all shapes, ages and sizes, smeared out over most of that part of New Haven, a plant too immense in size to grasp by one trip through. . . . You're lost in that huge collection of large buildings. Comes a faint impression of many stairs climbed and others unclimbed again, fireproof doors opening and closing, wheels running round and

round, and miles of machines that cut and chewed and stamped and did things less apparent. It is a simple matter, going through one of the great arms plants like Winchester, but *seeing* it is quite another thing.

Colt's factory was called "a mighty maze" as well. Unlike Sarah's maze, which would eventually be deemed a "Victorian acid trip" and a "fungus" lacking "all rhyme and reason," the "seeming chaos" of the great Colt's gun factory was actually "a cosmos," one of grand design and logic. In 1866, New Haven had considered Oliver Winchester quite mad to believe that he could sell so many guns, but by the 1910s, Americans had stopped asking seriously whether the enterprise was madness.[30]

Sanity relies, to some extent, on narrowness of vision, on foreshortened complicity. The gun industry reverberated widely and with lethal consequence in the world, but it was expected and permitted to tend only to its own parts, which became ever more minutely fractured, almost to the point of invisibility, into the thousands of movements of Robert Werle's instruction cards. It wasn't that Sarah saw a different world, but that, like someone standing on top of a very tall building and gazing outward, she was seeing much farther down the road.

The Winchester family business was guided by the accepted, settled logic of one kind of invisible hand. As for the other invisible hand— the ghostly kind, another style of conscience altogether—it now belonged to the Victorian world of spiritualism or its successor, the modern world of madness. A triumphant worldview usually comes to appear natural and inevitable; a vanquished one, deranged and "crazy." As Sarah frantically built in San Jose, Freud was interpreting ghosts clinically as examples of the uncanny and the return of the repressed. The uncanny introduces ambivalence. It makes the "homely" and familiar things of life suddenly "unhomely" and unfamiliar—which is precisely what Sarah's construction did. It took the familiar space of home and made it "unhomely" and deranged. It was not the gun business's business to contemplate the effects of the product, or what "every workman's doing" did in the world, or the ghosts of the victims of the guns it produced. But legend tells us that it was Sarah's business, and her legend would grow, not coincidentally, as Americans became more ambivalently gun conscious in the twentieth century.

For his part, however, Theodore Dreiser did sense queasily the larger Winchester web, the *gestalt* of the thousands of small processes connected to the great "system of railway tracks" at the factory "connecting the works with the great metropolitan centres of the world," and from there, with places as far-flung as Alaska and Panama, all armed with Winchesters. He also intuited how the paradox of the gun factory's precision and enormity obscured the web. When Dreiser left the factory and returned to the "simple world, where there is no roar of countless machinery, no hurry of thousands of hands, no evidence of a careful and exact system, the memory of the great plant with its floors and dark shop and thousand noises becomes a strange evil, making for war." The evil was modified, Dreiser concluded, by a more optimistic idea that Winchesters might compel peace—but it was a burden all the same. In accounting terms, an unabsorbed burden.[31]

———

IT IS THE GENIUS OF SARAH'S ENIGMATIC RIDDLE, WHETHER intuitive or ghostly, to point the why question back to that exquisitely rationalized factory in New Haven. If Sarah had only wanted to spend down and expiate her blood fortune, she could have become a philanthropist of great renown and impact. She quietly performed charitable deeds in California, as did Isabelle, so this was part of her life's work, but not the most conspicuous part. She could have been like Leland Stanford, who built a university to assuage his grief. But in some ways, the conversion of a blood fortune into philanthropy would have defeated the message, or at least one message. It would have morally whitewashed Sarah's blood fortune and converted it into something unimpeachable. The rifle fortune would have yielded something good, that goodness becoming the final, exculpatory link in an otherwise grisly chain.[32]

Maybe she didn't want to rehabilitate the fortune, but to show instead the immutable deformity at its heart. Her anti-memorial still bears stubborn, cryptic witness to "monstrous offspring." Had she built Winchester University next to Stanford, no one would think a century later about a haunting conscience, accountability, and the long view of cosmic justice. They would not have seen a house stubbornly and immovably bound in by an eight-lane road, the I-280 freeway, and the Winchester Mobile Home Park, along with the remains of a vintage space-age Century 23 movie theater, in what we know as Silicon Valley—still a place of fantastic creations, mad, brilliant enterprise, and make-believe worlds. They wouldn't have been forced to ponder the virtue, and the terror, of feeling more conscientiously or spiritually complicit than is required by contract, economy, law, or society. They wouldn't be moved to contemplate what vastly distant fates touch our own, or that we touch, through the remote consequences of our life's work. They would not start to imagine what their doing did in the world.[33]

The house, a counter-legend to our gun legends, conveys a restless, brilliant, eminently sane if obsessive mind, and, I think, the convolutions of an uneasy conscience, whatever the source of the unease. Perhaps Sarah recognized that unease, as a believer in ghosts, or perhaps she only dimly perceived it, and then wove it into her creation, just as any artist pours into her work unarticulated impulses. Sarah feared that the rifle blood fortune had cursed and deformed her family and her home. Wittingly or not, at whatever level of rational volition or self-consciousness, she brilliantly illustrated that deformation in her labors, converting a vast rifle fortune into a monstrous, distorted mansion designed to be both haunted and haunting. Sarah's house is also something that Winchester built, as lasting as the rifle.

IT'S FEASIBLE TO POISE (MALE) AMBITION AND (FEMALE) CONSCIENCE against each other along a fault line of American character. Sarah Winchester's estate could be seen as Oliver Winchester's portrait of Dorian Grey, silently absorbing the American gun horror. Sarah's is an extreme case of empathy; Oliver's, perhaps, an extreme case of sociopathy. In one other way, Oliver and Sarah were kindred spirits, the two

Winchesters consumed by an enthralling, mad vision. Sarah pursued a "career of pathological self-perpetuation," her creation a "product of wealth and abnormality," said later observers. Sarah's work was, as one visitor put it, "grotesque, yet magnificent."[34]

Sarah's achievement was outwardly grotesque, but inwardly magnificent. You could argue that Oliver Winchester's was outwardly magnificent, but inwardly grotesque. Spiritualist Emanuel Swedenborg said that a long time ago, the spirits named the ages of man, from gold to silver to brass, to correspond to our understanding of the moral universe. They assigned to Sarah and Oliver's age the name of iron. It signified the age of a "hard truth without good."[35]

Oliver's world was indeed a hard one. It had logic, but no truth. Sarah's had truth, but no logic.

———

IN FEBRUARY 1914, ON THE EVE OF A WORLD WAR THAT WOULD prove fateful for the company and for the Winchester heirs, the WRAC inventoried its annual consumption of resources. This resource footprint, what a corporation would hide today, attested to the stature of the company and so was worth bragging about:

Engine horse power, steam, 2,400
Engine horse power, gas, 3,000
Coal: 40,000 tons
Oil: 450,000 gallons
Steel: 5,000 tons
Copper: 2,600 tons
Lead: 12,000 tons
Employees: 6,000
Models made: 19
Styles of guns made: 450
Varieties of cartridges: 639
Floor space: 36.5 acres[36]

It took millions of feet of lumber to construct the gun's shipping cases alone. When the company tried to substitute paper cases, poor customers in the South complained because they had been using the wooden crates to make stools and furniture.[37]

Simultaneously, Sarah had been on a voracious real estate binge, decades before the Santa Clara Valley was famous for its property fetish. With a fortune built on the global diaspora of a rifle heading outward to every corner of the world, Sarah drew raw materials and precious objects inward from every corner of the world, like Samuel Colt's wife, with her indiscriminately stuffed Victorian parlor. It was a convention of bourgeois femininity, as cultural critic Walter Benjamin explained, to create "phantasmagorias of the interior," a "private environment that represents the universe" and "gathers remote places and the past"—although Sarah's was a darkly puzzling subversion of Elizabeth Colt's efforts in Hartford. Special agents bought items for Sarah around the world. An inventory of the Sarah Winchester house and her resources would have included:

2,000 doors
150,000 panes of glass
47 fireplaces
Rocking horse, purchased from a Brooklyn junk dealer for $300
7½ miles of pipe in the sprinkler system
48 H.P model B4 Suburban with extra air springs, $7,230
Lincresta wallpaper, $2.00 a yard, France
Hand-painted tiles, Vienna
Fawn and Indian lawn sculptures, New York
16 solid gold nails
Yew and sweet olive trees, West Asia
Hand-painted wallpaper, Japan
Bamboo for fireplace mantel, Japan
Embellished mirrors, France
Ceramic tiles, Sweden
Rosewood, Mexico
Cherrywood, Japan

24 acres, Burlingame

35 acres, Oak Grove Ave.

2.16 acres, Hillsborough, San Mateo

37 acres, bound in the south by the Southern Pacific Railroad, in the east by the lands of Winchester and Burlingame Villa Park, and in the north by Grand Line

6 acres, Valpariso Park

28.24 acres, by the "lands of Slade and Winchester"

5 acres, east of Atherton Ave.

5.96 acres, adjacent to the "lands of Winchester"[38]

The accounting was impressive. The WRAC had an uninterrupted record of dividends from 1868 to 1915. During that period, sales increased from $324,000 to $11.5 million, and net profits averaged over $800,000 a year.[39]

Sarah's accounting was equally impressive. She had an uninterrupted record of spending down from 1886 to 1915. Her house alone would draw down $5 million, and she spent more on land, furnishings, flora, and the opulent interior.

Even so, she accumulated more wealth from rifles faster than she could shed it. However impetuously she spent, it was never fast enough.

On the cusp of war, the Winchester stories had moved in opposite directions, like two elements of the same mobile, each following its own principle of motion. On the East Coast, the Winchester Company had built the largest private arsenal in the world. On the West Coast, Sarah Winchester had built the largest private residence in the world. At war's end, their fates would converge once more as the Winchesters got mired in webs of their own creation in both New Haven and San Jose.[40]

CHAPTER 16

OVERBUILDING

"I T WOULD SEEM THAT ALL THE EARTH WOULD LIKE TO FIGHT BUT have not the money or gun to do it with," TG Bennett wrote to his wife, Jane, in early 1915. For a gun potentate he was surprisingly glum about the war. It is "too much for me," he continued. "I wish some overwhelming disaster to all the combatants might force an immediate peace. . . . Had we a million guns, we could sell them at once."[1]

In 1917, the company secured what Oliver Winchester had most coveted in his lifetime: massive US government contracts to arm World War I. New Haven was awed and self-impressed by its factory. Winchester was called a city in itself, and "buildings were erected almost as if by magic," the *New Haven Register* wrote. Its floor space doubled, to 3,250,000 feet. The company had long ago swallowed up the cow pastures around it. Now, the factory "mushroomed out and soared into the air." The "sign of the big red 'W' recalls to . . . mind a plant . . . with massive buildings stretching a half-mile in either direction, . . . with innumerable chimneys, reaching far into the sky," a Yale student recalled of the early 1900s. Observers gravitated toward lurid metaphor to capture the poetic mystery of such colossal growth and building. The Remington factory in Ilion "blazed with light in the hours of darkness," a reporter marveled, and "mighty steel spider webs" arose. "There is an air of mystery about the big works enhanced by the guards, the high fences, and the locked gates. . . . Wood and iron become cases of rifles as if by magic. Would you walk in the places where the outside world does not see? Would you look behind the scenes of this mighty steel drama?"[2]

Wartime production created a constant, deafening roar. From the WRAC shot tower, the tallest building in Connecticut, in which molten lead was dropped to form shot balls, the "hum of industry" rose up, a cacophony of "the turning of countless shafts and the productive efforts of thousands of men and women." A New Havener waxed rhapsodic that "night and day . . . night and day the mighty machines thundered—rumbling, roiling, fulminating—their various bellies tended by an army of 475 rollers, shearers, cleaners, annealers, packers, and . . . others." And, still, "the expansion went on."[3]

The WRAC started 1914 with just under 6,000 employees and had almost 20,000 by war's end in 1918. Employees and their families now constituted a remarkable one-third of New Haven's population. Each day, it hired scores of new employees. On November 12, 1917, alone, the company hired 135 new employees—including 70 to make guns and 48 to make bullets. To transport its 20,000 workers, Winchester ran 30 special trolley cars (Remington did the same in Ilion, New York, with the "Remington Arms Special" trolley that transported desperately needed workers from other regions into town).[4]

Each of these employees made a small part of a gun or cartridge or performed a small operation, following Werle's "instruction card" for the task. They were not makers of guns, but of small parts of guns made by the machines they tended. Now, the company itself had to remind employees of the long and deep view, that they were all making guns, here, for soldiers to be killed several steps removed in dismal trenches, there. The connections were never removed from view entirely, although it was often a distant view. "Each operation is a link in the chain of production," the company warned employees during the 1918 influenza epidemic. "Your responsibility to the boys at the front is personal and direct." One slipup on one part, and the "boys in France have lost just that many guns and cartridges."[5]

World War I contracts added the equivalent of five years of orders onto the factory's monumental but still inadequate capacity. TG

Bennett and his son Winchester (Win), the successor as WRAC president, hoped that night shifts and the decline in commercial demand would clear space to produce Model 1895s for the Russians, but they had accepted a hefty contract to produce Enfields for the British. It is noteworthy that the burden of producing a British rifle fell so heavily on the Winchester factory, in Connecticut: it speaks to a decades-long transformation by which the mass production of guns, with its attendant pressures to mass-sell the guns, had shifted to the United States. For as strained as US wartime capacities were, they exceeded those of Western Europe.[6]

After the British contracts, the WRAC would be moving toward fulfilling the once-coveted US contracts exclusively—contracts for service rifles, government cartridges, Browning machine rifles, Colt automatic pistols, gallery practice muskets, rifle and hand grenades, mortar propellant shells, 12-gauge shotguns with sawed-off barrels that were known as riot guns (the Germans threatened to execute Americans found with them, owing to the grisly casualties and unnecessary suffering they caused, in violation of article 23 of the Hague [II] Convention), and, Winchester concluded, other "etc.s" of war.[7]

This was a military-industrial complex decades before President Eisenhower introduced the term. The Small Arms Division of the Ordnance Department met on September 27, 1917, in Washington, DC, to discuss with commercial arms makers how many .30-caliber cartridges it would need for the war. It was estimated that they'd need 4 billion in 1918. Almost all of these cartridges were to come from commercial manufacturers, including Winchester, Remington, US Cartridge, Maxim Munition, and National Brass. At maximum capacity, these companies could produce an estimated 2,692,000,000 cartridges, and they could fairly easily make up the shortage of 1,308,000,000 through additional building and retooling. Winchester was good for an estimated 26,000,000 a month, and US Cartridge could increase to 125,000,000 a month "if the Government is willing to finance increase in plant."[8]

A colonel involved in these discussions stated that the military would meet its production needs "from the private industries"; it planned to use the one public arsenal on the list for experimental development rather than manufacturing. The vitality of public, common defense tacitly relied on the vitality of the private, commercial gun market—and this tense interdependency is a largely forgotten part of the story of how America's civilian gun culture emerged.[9]

Likewise, the standard army rifle, the Springfield, was produced meagerly at the Rock Island and Springfield arsenals. US Representative John Tilson of Connecticut recollected in a postwar commendation of the gun industry that the country had only 700,000 Springfield rifles at the start of war, "but even that was not the weakest point. . . . The supreme difficulty was that we were not prepared to make any more." The proto-industrialists, such as Whitney, had relied on US government contracts, innovation, tariffs, guaranteed markets, and capital to build a commercial gun industry; now the US government relied on the commercial gun industry for public defense.[10]

The wartime revival of patriotic codependency was not welcome news for the Winchester family. TG suspected that the WRAC would simply be taken over by the government if it defied or fell short of orders. In 1917, Smith & Wesson won several US government contracts but it was in disarray, with Daniel B. Wesson's sons Walter and Joe alternating leadership, and both in failing health (Daniel Wesson had died in 1906). The company could not tool up to accelerate production, so the government took control of the Smith & Wesson plant in September 1918, and federal agents managed it until the war's end.[11]

The military-industrial collaboration irritated Winchester in ways large and small. The War Department divided the country into thirteen ordnance districts, and the gun valley fell under the Bridgeport, Connecticut, office's domain. Former commercial rivals shared (had to share) production secrets. The government honeycombed the company with its own punctilious auditors, who at one point accused the company of "fake [accounting] procedures." At a meeting of the ammunition manufacturers' committee, Remington complained about visits from the "Efficiency Men," and warned Winchester against the Industrial Services officials, who were stirring up "industrial unrest" among workers. The company should be on guard, in particular, against a Mary Van Kleeck. When visiting Remington, she had "raised a particular bog with the girl employees." "Remington," said a note, felt that when she visited Winchester, "she will be on the war path."[12]

To deal with unionization efforts, which Winchester management loathed—and since it was performing as an ad hoc public utility—the company asked the chief of ordnance to help suppress Winchester strikes as dangerous "insurrections." Win Bennett also wrote a confidential letter to the secretary of war to argue that the government should provide plant protection. Stating the military-commercial interdependency baldly, he wrote that, "in the last analysis, [the government] must [rely] upon [private industry]." He then pointed out, accurately, that "in the present crisis these special industries are in the nature of government plants." But while the military protected its own plants, it had taken no steps to protect "privately-owned plants of even greater military importance." Likewise, the Remington Arms Company at its own expense erected an eight-foot iron fence and an elaborate pass system for employees to move even from one department to another, to guard against espionage and bombs in "the great game of war and life" that ensnared them.[13]

Ostensibly, this military-industrial relationship produced a great macabre windfall for the gun industry. Critics would increasingly denounce it as such, indicting "war-profiting corporations" and likening the profiteers to "a school of sharks" upon a whale carcass. The popular "devil theory" held that arms manufacturers, and the glamorization of weapons, had caused World War 1, in part because the system made "warfare a direct occasion of private gain." "War is to [the gun business] what milk is to a baby," *Harper's* opined. "They fatten on it." The critique eventually culminated in hearings led by progressive Republican senator Gerald Nye in 1934 and 1935 to investigate small arms and other industries of war.[14]

TG and Win Bennett, two of the sharks, should have realized great fortune, yet they embraced the business uneasily. They were snagged in an unprofitable paradox. A world unhinged by violence and ravenous for guns of the company's own invention endangered the company. Money spent for the frenzied building spree to fulfill government contracts in the short term could kill the company in the long term. Even a US auditor stationed at the WRAC conceded that the government had "pressure[d]" the company into building, and that the expansion would eventually be "valueless in a commercial sense." In a letter to Jane in 1916, before the United States entered the war, TG predicted that the war might "mean great harm to the WRAC." He was right, counterintuitive though it sounds. In the past half-century, things had changed for the gun capitalist. The preferred market was commercial, not martial. The gun culture of the early 1900s was not the gun culture of the early 1800s; despite what disarmament activists assumed, the best gun business wasn't really the war business anymore. During this phase, the gun industry, which had been cultivating a commercial market for decades, was thrust back uncomfortably into a quasi-public role, with massive expansion and conversion imperatives.[15]

Oliver Winchester had dreaded a spasmodic gun market, and nothing would prove more spasmodic and slyly destructive to business than world war. Winchester executive Edwin Pugsley recalled the company's wartime travails in a 1921 internal memo. As he saw it, Winchester had started 1914 as an "old fashioned New England institution" that had had little to do with US government contracts; it had shaped itself instead to the commercial market. Upon this institution was "thrown the burdens of [the] sudden and . . . enormous requirements of both cartridges and guns" in a massive war. "In order to produce these the plant had to be entirely made over physically, requiring the erection of new buildings . . . new machinery; new tools; fixtures and gages."[16]

The proud Oliver Winchester had never relied on banks for financing; nor had TG. During his tenure as president, TG boasted "that the Company had not borrowed a cent for forty years." Now, ironically, at the time of greatest gun demand, in order to get the money to build maniacally to fulfill the contracts, Win Bennett, like Remington's leaders, would have to borrow—over $10 million. In 1915 the WRAC borrowed first from J. P. Morgan. Then, in March 1916, Win sought financing from investment bankers Kidder & Peabody of New York and Boston. The plan proposed that the company issue notes to be bought by Kidder & Peabody, and that the proceeds of this issue—over $8 million—be used to retire the earlier debt to Morgan.[17]

The burdensome successes, if not sins, of the grandfather fell on the third generation's shoulders. Win staggered under the company's gargantuan size. TG Bennett lamented that his son suffered terribly over the business, "so used up by the anxiety and the burden of uncertainties as to be near a breakdown." Win even resigned temporarily during the war, and went to bed with a months-long liver illness. Toward the end of an unprofitable, unsettling year in 1917, TG Bennett temporarily returned to his accustomed throne in "the temple," as the ingenious gun inventor John Browning had called the factory, to take his son's place and anxiously await the turn of global events.[18]

———————

COLOSSAL AS IT HAD GROWN, THE COMPANY STILL HAD TROUBLE sating the war's demand in 1918, so the US government hectored them all to work harder. A War Department telegram on April 9, 1918, declared, "EXISTING CONDITIONS MAKE it imperative that you accelerate production in every way possible."[19]

This included minimizing or eliminating paperwork and actual contracts. The company embarked on $20 million worth of US government business for which it hadn't received a contract or even a written procurement order. It began production of a machine-gun part on the strength of one telegram; in another case, it churned out 27 million .45-caliber cartridges based on a letter. The company had rifles and cartridges ready for delivery before the government had the gauges to inspect them. Other work, the company recounted, began based on the wisp of "a verbal order placed by telephone," little more than Sarah's impulsively issued building orders, hastily sketched on napkins, paper bags, and tablecloths.[20]

By the spring of 1918, overall wartime production was soaring, and turning out rifles for fourteen army divisions a month. The criticism that American forces would be "compelled to use broomsticks for lack of rifles," as a wire article reported, deferred to concerns that rifle production would swamp storage facilities, although the "stream of war supplies . . . has not yet attained full flood and will not for several months." The combined output from Winchester, Remington, and other private armorers was more than 250,000 rifles a month.[21]

Great as the flood of rifles and bullets was, by mid-April 1918, the government was pushing Winchester toward continuous operation, including twenty-four-hour shifts, even on Saturdays and Sundays. Urgent letters and correspondence flew between the company and various war departments. Winchester wrote that it was eager to help, but the government would have to cover the time-and-a-half labor increases for weekend shifts. Women would be working fifty-one hours a week. The government would also have to purchase all the necessary raw materials. On July 16, 1918, the WRAC learned that "the government has approved a plan for continuous operation. . . . That is to say, day and night operation, every day, and Sunday."[22]

"THE ENTIRE WINCHESTER PRODUCTION IS AT THE DISPOSAL OF THE GOVERNMENT FIRST," said a confidential Winchester sales bulletin for July 2, 1918. But it reassured salesmen that the company would be tending to the commercial market as soon as it could. Another bulletin, sent to distributors, looked wistfully ahead to the commercial trade: "As fast as it is practical, it is our purpose to . . . enjoy again as promptly as possible the reputation which Winchester had for prompt service, before the war needs arose."[23]

The war commandeered Winchester's domestic commercial business and clipped its international one. When the country joined the war, the Trading with the Enemy Act greatly expanded the federal arms embargo power. Winchester applied diligently for clearance to resume business with eclectic foreign dealers and individuals, and throughout 1918, government agencies rebuffed it. "It has come to our attention that you have been having business communications with a concern outside of this country who is on the enemy trading list," a terse letter reads, referring to a firm in Chihuahua, Chile. The WRAC was "well advised to have no dealings" with a V. Vidaurazaga in Ariquipa, Peru, or with the Aziz Alabi Brothers in El Salvador, as they were on the "suspicion" list. Winchester was denied permission to send arms to Switzerland, Brazil, Guatemala, and Haiti. It had been getting orders from Mexico, and the Mexican government, but the United

States would not allow shipments there, perhaps because Mexico had been approached by Germany to attack the United States.[24]

The navigation of foreign sales now required more finesse with bureaucrats than bandits. A company representative pleaded to New Haven headquarters, "For some reason all of our applications are being turned down by the War Trade Board. Will you kindly . . . ascertain what the prospects are of accepting business from merchants in Spain?" The government explained to Winchester that company officials had allowed "private orders to interfere with government requirements," and "it is suggested that your office invite their attention to this reason in order that they may see the error of their ways."[25]

TG Bennett needed only to gaze out of his office window onto the Winchester city that engulfed him, with its own circulatory system of trolleys and its labyrinth of frantically constructed buildings, to sense other errors, if not of his own volition. With world peace ominously on the horizon, Bennett and the Winchester family would be left with a rifle kingdom that had been grossly overbuilt.

When he looked around, the plant must have seemed like a strange dream whose inner logic evaporates the instant the dreamer awakes. The deferred fulfillment of Oliver's deepest ambition—substantial US government contracts—could dash his fondest dream—the family's immortal control of the business.

A company memo to an assortment of vice presidents anticipated the postwar problem of "unabsorbed capacity" and "the actual burden costs" it would create. "The cost of running the plant when it is not producing" would hurt, obviously. Win Bennett faced the same problem in 1918 that his grandfather had in 1868: too many guns and too much capacity for too little demand. In its infancy, productive capacity had been 200 rifles a day, and New Haven thought Oliver quite mad to believe that he could sell that many. In the spring of 1918, it was at least 2,100 a day—2,000 rifles and 100 machine guns.[26]

Bennett must have asked himself now what Oliver had asked himself in 1866: Who would buy all of these guns?

By Armistice Day, November 11, 1918, the Winchester Repeating Arms Company had completed 292 contracts, on 114 kinds of articles, to furnish Allied forces with almost $100 million worth of arms and ammunition, for a war in which over 16 million soldiers and civilians were killed. It had produced, for the US government alone, 545,000 rifles, 47,000 Browning machine rifles, 31,600 "various rifles," 524,500,000 .30-caliber cartridges, 58,000,000 .45 automatic Colt cartridges, and 18,700,000 "various other cartridges."[27]

Sympathetically, the US auditor assigned to the WRAC had recommended that the government accept a claim to cover at least a token share of the costs of plant rearrangement and expansion, but it was less than half, and far from enough.[28]

In the spring of 1918, Bennett took to describing the company as a ditch through which massive amounts of money flowed: it flowed in, but it flowed right back out, along with the "full flood" of rifles the newspapers had extolled, all without accruing benefit to the company itself. "With deep banks and high fillings with cement and steel," wrote TG, "while the water runs and the land is irrigated, the building is of value, but as soon as the water stops, and there remains only the cement and embankments and fillings, the ditch is of no value to its owners, and is a target only to the tax gatherer."[29]

TG's son Win was still in touchy, precarious health—he had "lost his health carrying on this business," TG had concluded—and, in any case, his son could not do what needed to be done next. The sight of Win consumed by nerves over the factory expansion and debt might have prodded TG toward a consequential truth.[30]

The mad architecture of the frenetically expanded WRAC in New Haven could only be resolved by making contact with the mad architect of the frenetically expanded House of Mystery in San Jose.

––––––––

AS THE WINCHESTER WAR FACTORY BELLOWED AND CHURNED, Sarah continued her parallel project of overbuilding. Her home, like the gun company, "mushroomed." It was almost as if she were keeping pace with the company. She went about the task in an equally manic manner, but she was on an antithetical mission. "Day and night, the work continued," the *New York Times* had reported in 1911, at a "place where construction never ceased." The ghost story of Sarah's labors found surer footing in history, and fact, with each year, such that the *San Francisco Examiner* called her "The Spirit Saver of the Carpenters' Union." This 1915 article was chiefly about Isabelle Merriman's bizarre abduction of an unknown fugitive with "lost mentality" from a local hospital, for his protection from pestering "vultures" who wanted to figure out who he was. The article said that Isabelle had recently spent time in Gardner's Sanitarium for Mental and Nervous Diseases, in Belmont. As an aside, Sarah Winchester was described as the widow of the "famous gun inventor" (Oliver Winchester was now often misremembered as the gun's inventor rather than a capitalist, and Sarah as his wife rather than his daughter-in-law). In an amusing endorsement of the labor movement, the *Examiner* recounted that the spirits had told Sarah "she would die if *union* carpenters stopped work on her home." (italics added) so "she got busy." "For more than eight years," the reporter wrote, "her San Jose home has been in the hands of carpenters. They remodel and rebuild, they reconstruct and replan and always there is activity in the house." Another article noted that the place had seen "continuous growth . . . from a tiny cottage . . . to a rambling castle of a hundred towers." The "work went on, year in and year out, until at the present time it is doubtful if anyone but Mrs. Winchester could pick out her original . . . rooms."[31]

By 1914, Sarah's estate, like its estranged parent (or doppelganger), the WRAC, was more like a small, self-contained city. "As the house grew," an architect noted, "a self-sufficient little town grew up around it." This town had its own sewage system, pump house, gas and electric system, and annunciator speaker system with over 150 boxes so Sarah's servants could determine their mistress' whereabouts in the labyrinth. It had a water tower and a sophisticated French drain irrigation system for both the mansion and the orchards. It was "best described as something like a little village," another critic said, "a village of odd, connected houses, all built for a single tenant," that amounted to an "extensive pile" of oddity. It qualified as folly by architectural critic Barbara Jones's definition: "a folly may be fashionable or frantic, built to keep up with the neighbors or built from obsession." But "always at [its] heart stands disquiet." "Wings were extended in all directions from this original building, and then stories were added," the *Mercury News* reported in 1911 with an interesting double entendre, since stories were added to decipher Sarah's motives as well.[32]

On April 4, 1918, TG and Jane attended the dedication ceremony of the W. W. Winchester tuberculosis ward at what is now the Yale–New Haven Hospital. Sarah had sent her lawyer Samuel Leib across the country to New Haven in 1911 with $300,000 in cash to establish the ward in Will's honor.[33]

Sarah, the benefactor, did not attend the dedication ceremony herself—she didn't travel to her bank, much less to New Haven. When she wanted a safe deposit box for her will and deeds, Sarah dispatched Leib, her faithful ambassador to the world, to find one that met her exacting specifications. He proudly reported back that in his scavenger hunt he had discovered one at the San Jose Safe Deposit Bank, "the size being 8 inches deep by 10 inches wide and 18 inches long." The bank "could not ALONE open the box," he emphatically reassured Sarah, "nor could the holder of your key so do ALONE." Most important, "the bank building has a side entrance, permitting you to have a perfectly quiet and unobserved access to the private room next to the boxes." Sarah had self-entombed in the web she had spun. Even Leib conducted most of his business on Sarah's behalf through letters. Sarah found writing a painful task, due to arthritis, but preferred to convey her wishes about her trusts to Leib through correspondence, which he found admirably "clear and concise." Leib volunteered to meet her in person, but it was unlikely to happen, so he swore by his stenographer's ability to keep things "absolutely confidential."[34]

Merchants continued their thriving practice of bringing the world to Sarah. Or, Sarah had her chauffeur drive her into town, and she stayed in her carriage, or her luxury Renault with a Rothschild limousine body, while merchants brought goods out for her to inspect. Sarah had a long-standing dispute over payment with a dentist, and years later, the dentist's son recalled stopping by the house with his embattled father. Sarah, heavily veiled in black, terrified the dentist—he was afraid "the old coot" would bite him. Sarah had become spooky, in the way that living anachronisms often are.[35]

Exiled from the world as she was, Sarah would not attend the dedication in New Haven. But she had crafted an invitation list for the event. The day after the event, TG Bennett sat at his typewriter to make contact with Sarah. He reported that the ceremony had been "appropriate, graceful and dignified," and well attended. Sarah had asked that he find people in the WRAC who remembered Will. Most likely, her sense of time was skewed. "Thirty-seven years seems to have taken all but ourselves," her brother-in-law apologized wistfully, as no one "could think of anyone left at the shop who knew Will." Sarah's invited guests had attended, along with many soldiers, the new patients, who enjoyed the Winchester ward's luxuries of "electric lighting, ventilation, sterilizing [equipment] . . . washing and iron machinery." In "my time [the Civil War]," wrote TG, "soldiers were not so well taken care of."[36]

TG reassured her that the newspaper's transcription of the Yale dean's address, where in one sentence the name Bennett was used instead of Winchester, was wrong, and that the dean had made no such error. He anticipated that Sarah would notice any imperfection, and anticipated that she would care.

"It is a long time since I wrote you about the *shop*," TG said. Perhaps as he underscored that word, he was reminiscing on a more manageable day back in 1870—his sense of time as suspended as Sarah's—just after he had married into the family business, when the sprawling Winchester city might have been called something as cozy as a shop.[37]

"The year 1917 was a terrible one," he wrote her, venturing into the heart of things. The problem was, quite simply, the accrual of debt. "We were all the time facing large debts and handling what for us were enormous sums which came and went, leaving little with us." The WRAC had only been able to pay half of its debt, and it was having trouble "piling up" any gains. TG viewed himself more as a war hostage than a profiteer. Those coveted US government contracts, he wrote, "are as it were orders to do so and so. To decline [them] would probably mean [the government] taking over our property." This coercion came also with profits taxes, which took 60 percent.[38]

None of this would have been entirely new to Sarah. She had stayed scrupulously apprised of stock value, as well as Winchester wartime contracts and orders, with her business acumen in full force. Although she might not have bothered to do so, it was important to her to follow the story, in a sense, of the Winchester stock.[39]

TG was maneuvering around one inviolable, unstated truth: Sarah would need to be involved in any resolution to this crisis. She and his wife, Jane, were by far the largest stockholders in the company. This was not by plan so much as by attrition. The Winchester fortune had over the decades fallen to the women. By 1918, Winchester stock and dividends had accumulated value and rolled downhill to Sarah, the survivor and heir of the men's business.[40]

Jane held about the same amount as Sarah, but neither had voted or made decisions directly as shareholders. Their stock was held by the Winchester Purchasing Company and voted by TG Bennett. In 1905, TG had written to Jane from London about the holding company plan: "I feel that it will be very greatly to the WRA Co. interest and advantage. Also it would recombine the Winchester stock as in your father's time, and keep its voting power." Tactically, the holding company protected the Winchester family sovereignty that TG was now maneuvering to relinquish, as it guarded against hostile takeover. It also made it impossible for Winchester family members to withdraw their stock individually. As always, the family was in it together.[41]

The holding company, a fabricated entity to vote the fortunes of another fabricated entity, controlled Sarah's 2,777 shares in the WRAC, worth an estimated $6,248,250 (the economic status equivalent of $583 million today). Before TG could sever the Winchester family's ties and sell the Winchester majority to investment bankers—the future of American capitalism—he would need Jane's and Sarah's assents. His wife posed no difficulty. But in the months ahead, with TG committed to a once-unthinkable course, the fate of the Winchester Company, after five decades, was in her hands.

On August 18, TG wrote to Sarah again. The year had ended well. "We shall probably make $8,000,000" on US government contracts, he said, and that money, along with the company's cash, should have gotten them clear of their Kidder & Peabody debt. Should have. But new "tax laws" for which TG Bennett had deep contempt were chewing into that profit, and would "leave us quite poor, our indebtedness being considered." The company hadn't even paid off half of its loan from the bankers.[42]

TG next understated something momentous: "It seems to me dangerous for the family to keep the control longer." He reminded Sarah that he was seventy-three years old, and that Win "at a vital time was unable to do much." The problem of debt was a large matter, he concluded, and he could not advise Sarah or Jane to put more money into it. He was proposing that, for the first time, the fates of the Winchester rifle and the Winchester family part ways.[43]

TG proposed that Sarah and Jane deposit nearly all of their stock—at least 90 percent—with Kidder & Peabody. In return, these old stockholders, the Winchester family, would get seven and a half shares of a new first preferred stock for every old share. That would amount to 20,827 shares for Sarah, valued at under $3.75 million, diminished alarmingly from its earlier value. A local historian noted later that Leib might have been more disturbed by this drastic devaluation than Sarah. The reorganization would give the company much-needed cash, free the family from responsibility, and in effect sell control of the stock to investment bankers at what TG reckoned to be a fair price. If Sarah agreed to the plan.[44]

"Think it over," TG concluded. "I should be glad to have your favorable telegram."

Throughout September, Leib communicated with Winchester vice presidents A.W. Hooper and TG Bennett to hammer out the reorganization and the demise of the family control that had been Oliver's compelling, intergenerational ambition. "Considering the peace of mind and quiet which those who are part of the Winchester family are entitled to enjoy during the latter part of their lives," Leib wrote, he had recommended that Sarah acquiesce to the proposition in broad strokes, though he feared that Sarah would be parting with her stock at much too low a value.[45]

TG's response hints at the family's view of Sarah's eccentricities, and how they sidestepped them like a creaky stair: "It is very fortunate for Mrs. Winchester that she has your advice," TG wrote, "as I would hesitate to commit her property, under the circumstances in which she finds herself, without counsel other than her own." The circumstances are unelaborated. Bennett dusted off the ditch analogy he had used earlier—that money flowed through the factory without accumulating value—to disabuse Leib of his notion that the company had as much value as the lawyer had surmised. "A good deal of the property concerned in this transition . . . will be valuable if business is found for it," TG said, and he was hopeful that the bankers could find business, but otherwise, it was valueless. "Since the first of the year I have seen immense sums of money flow through our particular ditch," he continued, "and very little of it has been gathered to us."[46]

TG's was an unromantic analogy—Oliver's castle in the air had become TG's ditch—but it was trenchant. The WRAC building and expansion only had logic, or made sense, in one context, that of war production. In peacetime, it, too, looked like architectural folly.

Unequivocally, Sarah wanted to be free of the business. Leib was negotiating only to make sure that she received fair value. Leib conveyed one thing emphatically: "Whatever happens she absolutely cannot put any more money into the concern." Sarah's preoccupations and firm preferences were clearer still in letters from 1921, in which Leib fought with Sarah over compensation for his work in the reorganization that had taken a year and a half to finalize. Sarah had apparently accused Leib of overcharging her. A mannered but incredulous Leib expounded on the advantages he had secured for Sarah. "I wish to state that I remember that you *very strongly* objected to being made responsible *as a stockholder* for any of the debts then existing or in the future corporation to be formed," he reminded her in the course of defending himself. Sarah would not bear the burden of the Winchester debts or imperil her California estate in its service. She had already spent down a huge portion of that fortune on her home, including over $1 million on materials alone.[47]

TG approached Sarah with anxious solicitude as he negotiated with Leib and waited to see what she might do with her newfound omnipotence over the Winchester family fate. She might insist that the family fight to maintain control; she might insist upon a higher value for the stock, as Leib seemed to prefer; she might do nothing, and delay the entire deal through inaction, or obsessive repetition. TG had confidence in Leib, but Leib's signature couldn't close the deal.

Throughout September, TG waited apprehensively for the crucial telegram to inform him of Sarah's consent. He dispatched Jane to make a wearying cross-country journey to San Jose, presumably to help the cause, as Jane had maintained at least a tenuous thread of communication with her sister-in-law. Sarah lived in a 160-room mansion. Nevertheless, Jane stayed at a hotel in San Jose, an uncomfortable one that she complained about bitterly to TG. She apparently never went inside Sarah's house or even visited with her.[48]

In the end, Sarah didn't fight for more power, money, or time. There is little to suggest that she would have been interested in any of those things. On September 20, TG wrote excitedly that Western Union had just "squealed a few words indicating the assent of S.L.W. is obtained." With this cheery news, TG urged Jane to "stay in bed a lot, and don't get too gay," and to head home as soon as she could.[49]

By the end of September 1918, the Winchester family was disentangled for the first time from control of the Winchester rifle. Sarah had disowned the original WRAC stock, and she was unenthused about claiming its offspring, the lion's share of her fortune. The new stock sat in Leib's office vault for over a year after the reorganization. Sarah would not receive him to complete paperwork, because of her "physical suffering," and she would not venture out to his office. She was content to keep the stock in limbo, much to the panic of Kidder & Peabody, as she had not signed the stock over to the new holding company. Eventually, in February 1921, a Winchester executive appeared at Leib's doorstep to handle the matter of Sarah's stock once and for all. The executive was to get Sarah to sign the certificates and return them to New Haven in order to complete the reorganization. A month later, Sarah did just that, and the deal was complete.[50]

Sarah had held over $6 million worth of Winchester Repeating Arms Company shares before the proposed reorganization. Afterward, the value was drained, and closer to $3 million. This meant that more had been spent down and expended in the ceaseless construction of her fantastic estate than had accumulated in the value of her stock.

The company's accounting book, after many prosperous decades, had finally gone into the red, but Sarah's private accounting book, after many debt-burdened decades of another kind, had finally gone into the black.

Sometime after the reorganization, TG told Leib that "without our arrangement with [Kidder & Peabody] we should, today, be in bankruptcy, or so near it as to be helpless." TG had had to destroy Winchester as a family concern in order to save it, but it was the best option. "Now," TG concluded, "all of our debts are paid." Perhaps Sarah's were as well.[51]

CHAPTER 17

THE SOUL OF
THE "GUN CRANK"

THE WRAC, NOW UNDER THE DIRECTION OF INVESTMENT
bankers Kidder & Peabody, faced a devastating 75 percent reduction in business and a 70 percent workforce reduction. As an internal
memo bluntly concluded, the company was finding it difficult to "get
business to fill up our idle machinery" or make "arms and ammunition
on a profitable basis."[1]

This was true for other gun capitalists: a crushing bust followed the
boom of world war. Remington carried an extraordinary burden of
weedy overbuilding. It had quadrupled production capacity, with more
than a million feet of new floor space. Ultimately, Remington produced 69 percent of the rifles shipped to US forces in the war. United
Metallic Cartridge (UMC) produced 28 million cartridges a week,
adding 24 acres of floor space and 160 new buildings. To meet wartime
demand, the plant sprawled down Bridgeport's main street, and UMC
built overhead bridges to connect one building to another. When this
did not suffice, it rented a factory in Hoboken, New Jersey, under the
leadership of a motor company executive, Harry Pinney, who promised, "With a year's time and two million dollars, I'll have a plant turning out two million cartridges a day."[2]

Then, as quickly as the grim extravagance had materialized, it vanished. Remington lost its substantial contracts with Russia's Nicholas II after the 1917 revolution, and the armistice abruptly ended the war business. The effect of the Russian cancellation was "like an automobile hitting a telegraph pole at sixty miles an hour," wrote Remington historian Alden Hatch. President Marcy Dodge—Eliphalet Remington's grandson, like Win Bennett to Oliver—remembered of 1917, "Each night . . . I lay there thinking that I had nothing left of all I had once owned, and that I had no further employment [for thousands of men]." Remington was informed on December 23, 1918, that the US government was immediately suspending all contracts and operations in the factory as well, which dismayed several thousand workmen who remained at the factory.[3]

Among the major gunmakers, only Colt's was an exception to the counterintuitive arithmetic. Colt's had expanded like the others, but in 1920 its president proudly reported to stockholders that the "company doesn't owe a dollar to anybody," although even this company's surplus shrank in the 1920s as Colt's fulfilled backlogged commercial orders for handguns at perilously low prewar prices.[4]

This was not how war profiteer theorists and gun critics imagined things in the postwar years. "The mighty stream of supplies flowed out and the corresponding stream of prosperity flowed in," inveighed Walter Millis in his bestseller, *Road to War*. In Winchester's case, specifically, the prosperity also flowed right back out, through TG's ditch. In its 1921 catalog, the WRAC took pride in its war effort as patriotism, not business. It had produced an "uninterrupted flow of 700,000,000 cartridges," without the rejection of even a single lot by the government. "We have kept the faith in time of stress," it concluded. A key popularizer of the devil theory scoffed at this. "They could hardly complain of bad business," he wrote, but "there is no mention of war profits" in the catalog.[5]

The company had anticipated the postwar crisis: "On the cessation of the war, we should have to begin again to build up our commercial business, which today is almost literally nothing," one letter to the government revenue agent said. In 1919 and 1920, the company inaugurated the "Winchester Plan" to enlarge its commercial business in order to increase income and pay off debts, the two immediate post-war imperatives. The company newsletter explained that the end of the war contracts had left the WRAC with a "great deal of building space, machinery, etc., which was no longer needed." While sales of guns and ammunition had been greater than ever before, they were "not great enough to occupy all this space and equipment." So, the company decided to manufacture new products that would use the same kind of machinery. It hoped to be able to stop laying off men and employ as many returning soldiers as possible in the gunmaker's most harrowing hour: the transition to peace. The year 1919 began a spree in which the company cannibalized almost a dozen corporations. It developed a cutlery division to make knives, and it took over two pocket-knife concerns. As it bought more companies, it introduced a bewildering array of new products: axes, fishing rods, batteries, skis, baseball bats, paints, household brushes, gas refrigerators, and flash-lights. The company produced roller skates through the acquisition of the Barney and Berry plant in Springfield, Massachusetts. The WRAC planned to establish its own retail stores in major cities, along with a network of warehouses to distribute new product lines.[6]

Other gun giants pursued a similar solution to the same problem. Smith & Wesson branched out into handcuffs, razor-blade sharpeners, washing machines, and a Swedish-designed toilet flush valve, to the amusement of the gun competition. Remington tried to diversify by pursuing cash-register and cutlery manufactures. Colt's, although anomalously debt-free, was still left with 100,000 square feet of excess factory space; it diversified by manufacturing adding machines and ini-tiated a terrible venture into commercial dishwashers.[7]

IN WINCHESTER'S GUN MERCHANDISE LINE SPECIFICALLY, A FIGURE was materializing in the company and in the American lexicon: the "gun crank." The concept was not entirely new. An 1888 *Shooting and Fishing* article defined the rifle crank as someone who was enamored with the novelty of new guns, and a great quantity of them. Annoying the often less knowledgeable clerk with questions on gun "technics," the gun crank sought "all the various new things which are constantly coming into the market, numbers of which are of but little value." The ways of the gun crank were "peculiar." Some bought but never used their guns; another would incessantly "talk and ventilate his views." The promise of the next, new gun mesmerized the gun crank.[8]

In 1889, a letter writer to *Shooting and Fishing* identified himself as "what may be called a 'crank,' that is, eccentric, or out of the central portion of riflemen's ideas in general." Winchester vice president Henry Brewer thought the gun crank was "the trend" of the day, although he still felt he "represent[ed] a small percentage of the buyers and does not represent the everyday shooters—the farmer's boy and the ordinary shooter." The *Winchester Herald*, a company newspaper exclusively for Winchester salesmen, defined the crank as the fellow "who is particularly and peculiarly interested in shooting (this applies to shot-gun as well as rifle)," adding that he existed in "every community." A November 1917 daily sales bulletin featured a letter from a Winchester customer who boasted that his town of Yakima, Washington, had "the most gun cranks of any." While the gun factories "may consider [the gun crank] a pest," the *Winchester Herald* opined, with a little imagination, they could potentially use them to boost their bottom lines. "Take the trouble to turn him around and examine him from all angles," it advised, "and it will possibly develop that you can, by turning the crank in your direction, cause him to increase your gun and ammunition turnover."[9]

Although the WRAC did not yet completely get it, the *Herald* was right. The gun crank who sought gun novelty for its own sake, and ever more guns—who loved not only a gun but a lot of them—was close to its ideal consumer in an age of faster production and dwindling practical need for their product. "Modern labor savings devices," *Shooting and Fishing* accurately noted, produced guns "at prices which bring them within the reach of all," though with a "small margin of profit." More goods produced in less time to get maximal production and use out of the factory required more consumers, so sales and marketing became a new front for scientific management theories.[10]

WRAC EXECUTIVE EDWIN PUGSLEY CONTEMPLATED MARKETS and "future product lines" on a quail hunting trip in the South in 1919. He observed a bias against the automatic that had inspired only the second attempt by Congress to restrict hunting arms the year before. Mr. F. S. Bright, a Winchester representative, was part of what the company called the "shooting fraternity in Washington." Bright had sent a dispatch to Win Bennett apprising him of legislation "which is antagonistic to automatic rifles and shot guns," and "the best way to stop such legislation," he suggested, "will be to talk with Congressman Meechers, who introduced it." In other words, to lobby. Likewise, at its 1911 sales convention, Remington's executives urged their salesmen to wire to headquarters information on state firearms legislation against autoloader and pump-action rifles, and to assuage worries in the field about the "dangers of guns" by saying, "Each and every shot must be fired by the man behind the gun." Executives instructed salesmen to "personally speak to the clerk of each state's House of Representatives and be sure that they realize that it is 'misguided people who condemn the autoloading and pump guns.'"[11]

At this moment, gun "lobbying" began to acquire more familiar twenty-first-century meanings. Gun lobbyists had worked the Washington, DC, hotels in the 1850s and 1860s, especially to secure federal government contracts, but in the early 1900s, Washington representatives of the gun behemoths started to put a new item on their lobbying agenda: they now began to argue against legislation injurious to their business, which had not been an issue in the 1800s. Simultaneously, as we have seen, the National Rifle Association in the early 1900s lobbied for legislation to support marksmanship and the creation of rifle ranges and clubs nationwide. In this early example of industry lobbying, Bright had misremembered the name. Representative John Meeker of Missouri had introduced a bill in 1917 that "frankly states as its purpose," worried *Forest and Stream*, "the prevention of excessive killing" of migratory game birds. Meeker proposed, among other things, to make it unlawful for hunters to use the repeating gun or automatic pump. The "feeling against the automatic seems to me much more apparent," Pugsley confirmed, "especially among . . . hunters who up to the present time have had no scruples whatsoever about the amount of game they killed or [that] was killed. . . . This same class of people are now actively condemning the automatic and are beginning to question the pump." The newfound qualms about the faster weapons surprised Pugsley, who was raised on a pump and had shot one his entire life without criticism.[12]

Pugsley "was impressed by the large number of single-barrel, cheap shot guns, 12 [gauge], which I saw everywhere": "Almost every darkey that we met in the field had one of these guns with him. They were the gun most in evidence in hardware show cases." Perhaps the company could capitalize on this, make use of its machinery, and consider "the manufacture of a cheap single barrel gun." If it took this route, Pugsley candidly proposed quantity over quality. "I do not believe that we should attempt to maintain Winchester quality," he recommended, "but should make as cheap a gun as possible." In fact, they should quarantine it from higher-quality rifles "in a separate part of our factory, keeping its components separate from our . . . standard product during its manufacture." Pugsley observed the considerable amount of ammunition used in the Deep South and thought the company "should go after that business very strongly."[13]

The WRAC also marketed the notorious riot guns that the Germans had protested for their brutality ("American Shot Gun Gets Fritz in a Rage!" the *Winchester Record* had written). Before the war, Winchester executives felt that this gun was underperforming its market, with "traffic . . . far short of what it should be. . . . We believe, properly worked up, there can be created a good demand," they told their salesmen, and urged them to push the gun, which sold for $25. It was advertised as "indispensable for banks, watchmen, express messengers, prison guards, sentries, train hands, and home protection." It shot nine times more bullets than a revolver in the same amount of time, and when loaded with buckshot covered an area nine times greater. A WRAC engineer had tested the '97 riot gun and found that an ordinary shooter probably wouldn't hit his target more than half the time at seventy-five yards, so the gun was better for short range. It was ideal for "shooting in the dark, where aim is uncertain . . . and at moving objects." With the riot gun, "marksmanship is not necessary."[14]

This kind of gun could be advertised as protection for businesses as well as homes. Guns could protect businesses against "disturbances, either racial or political," one sales letter said. "Employing as they do a large mixed population, racially, of unknown political leaning and of unknown status from other standpoints," companies were in need of guns; there was a need to protect the "general industrial life of the nation." Winchester could, and did, manufacture a variety of guns of different quality. This is still true, although contemporary gun politics occasionally draw distinctions between the junk gun manufacturers of Southern California and more respectable ones. As Matt Bai of *Newsweek* concluded in a 1999 investigative piece, gun companies don't make dangerous pistols or weapons by preference or fiat, per se—"they do it to survive."[15]

The gun industry, not for the last time, also courted women, especially as trap shooting at country clubs became popular. The company enlisted a Mrs. "Ad" Topperwein, of their famous husband-and-wife missionary team, to promote the idea that shooting instilled confidence for self-defense: "How often has it happened . . . when you were obliged to be alone at night . . . and fretted all through the night? What a wonderful relief it would have been if you had a gun or pistol with you." Marlin, Winchester's rival, ran ads featuring women holding sporting rifles and shotguns with captions such as, "Buy a Marlin and Be Happy!" and, "Isn't it a Beauty? This neat little, sweet little pump gun adds zest to the sport of shooting." Smith & Wesson appealed to home defense and advertised to women the "Thorough-Bred of the Revolver World." "No woman now a days need be without protection," an ad said in *The Outing* magazine. "Any woman can learn how to use a Smith & Wesson in a few hours, and . . . she will no longer feel a sense of helplessness when male members of the family are absent."[16]

"American Girls Shoot Their Way into Albanian Hearts!" the *Winchester Record* announced, in a quirky celebration of the gun's global diaspora. As two female Red Cross workers waited in Kopliku, Albania, for the arrival of relief supplies, they had sauntered over to watch the target practice "of a group of fierce looking Albanians." They set up an empty milk can, and although neither "had ever handled a gun of the weight or length the Albanians used," they "acquitted themselves creditably," having already trained with Winchesters.[17]

(Annie Oakley was the most famous Winchester markswoman, but a company executive had to confess later that although he wanted "no part in shattering any illusion that may be held about Annie Oakley," her shooting was rudimentary and unimpressive, and her success "simply the result of hi-power circus publicity." Oakley's husband was one of the Wild West show's press agents, and Annie was his "meal ticket." "The boys would round up the News Paper men with a copy of the show program together with a lot of passes which were called Annie Oaklies, and to this day they still call a free pass to a circus an Annie Oakley," the Winchester executive explained. As surprising as his information was, and although "few people would believe the truth," especially in "the shooting public," it was nevertheless "the gospel truth.")[18]

The centerpiece, and the most energetically pursued market, was the company's "boy plan." The WRAC prepared a direct-mail typewritten letter about the .22 caliber to send to boys between the ages of ten and sixteen. It urged its retailers to "send us a list of names of boys in your town, so we can send this illustrated letter under your own name." The company planned to reach 3,363,537 boys this way. "Prepare for sales," the company enthused to its sales force. "Read this letter. Put yourself in the place of a boy of 14. Would you let another day go by before calling on your dealer?"[19]

Another sales letter began, "Picture a red-headed boy in the front row of the movies. He's on the edge of his seat, eyes still popping out of his head as the end is written across a big game film where Winchester rifles were the star speakers. Up flashes your 'ad'—boys earning Winchester sharpshooter medals. What's the next thought in that boy's mind? What's he going to save up his quarters for? A Winchester of course."

The company hoped that the government might support its Junior Rifle Corps, a club to promote marksmanship that was part of its marketing campaign. Captain E. Crossman, a gun gossip columnist of sorts, wrote in the gun press that "one of the greatest movements to popularize rifle shooting in this country—even though it be from a purely business standpoint—is the Winchester junior rifle corps movement. Most dealers know that it has stimulated shooting among boys in their vicinity." The Remington Arms Company also pursued boys as the market of the future. They produced advertising pamphlets for "Boys' Rifle Clubs" with instructions on how to "Build Your Own Range Easily," and penned feature articles such as, "How a Boy Made the First Remington," and "Four American Boys Who Are Famous Rifle Shots."[20]

On December 16, 1918, the WRAC's vice president, Henry Brewer, sat down in Washington with a lieutenant colonel named Townsend, whom he described as an "old standby" in the shooting community and a prominent member of the National Rifle Association. After the war, with more surplus government weapons to offer members, NRA membership rose steadily. It is worth noting that as much as the NRA and the gun industry are assumed to be in lobbying lockstep today, that is not, and was not, entirely the case. In this example, the WRAC worried that the NRA's desire and ability to deliver surplus government weapons to members would cut into the company's commercial business and bottom line, although, on the upside, it would stimulate greater interest in rifle shooting overall, which could help sales. Although the NRA had advocated for rifle ranges and clubs in the early 1900s, the organization was not involved heavily in political lobbying at the time. Brewer reported back to New Haven that he had learned that

> there were two ways in which the government could stimulate rifle shooting at a very low cost to the government. One way was to cooperate through manufacturing concerns . . . that were reaching the small boys. The other was to work through the associations such as the NRA, thus stimulating rifle shooting among civilian adults. . . . [Townsend] wishes to know how many boys we are stimulating, how many are in [the Junior Rifle Corps]; in other words, to what extent is the nation,

from a military point of view, profiting by the result of our stimulating the youth of the country in the use of a rifle. He will use this as an argument.[21]

"We understand that in some [sales] territories," Brewer went on, states had "an age limit for boys who can buy Guns and Ammunition," and urged WRAC jobbers to "write us a full detailed report outlining the law, its provisions and penalties," if this was so. Dealers were also reporting resistance from parents. "I could sell a thousand rifles to boys if it weren't for the parents," a retailer complained. He was catching the leading edge of maternal opposition to guns. Senator Arthur Capper of Kansas wrote gun-control legislation for Washington, DC, after a senator was severely wounded in the crossfire between police and bootleggers, that passed in 1932, following years of hearings. In a radio address, Capper chided parents who thought it "cute" to have their children play even with toy guns, to say nothing of actual ones. "I do not think this is 'cute,'" Capper averred. "I think it is the real American tragedy."[22]

Inside the company family, Winchester urged retailers to appeal to the source, not to the parents, and tell their "boy customers" about their rifles. A March 1921 ad in the internal sales publication assured them that "there isn't a boy in your town who doesn't want to own a Winchester rifle!" The retailer's task was to "Put a Winchester into the Hands of Every Youth in Your Town. When the boys and girls of your town arrive at the age of twelve years, they become your prospects."[23]

REGARDLESS OF WHICH MARKET IT WANTED TO REACH, WINCHESTER embraced mass advertisement, as did the rest of corporate America, with an almost religious zeal. "We know there is a whole lot of gun and ammunition business, a world of it, within the reach of every dealer selling Winchester goods," a letter to the sales force said. Winchester didn't want for confidence. In 1920, as the Winchester Plan proceeded, the company told its sales force, "I don't want to brag about what we have in mind but I want to make this statement. . . . *We are engaged at the present minute in the greatest commercial venture in the history of this country, probably in the history of the world.*" Gun columnist Crossman confirmed that "the Winchester company has a well-organized and most efficient advertising and publicity department. It is whispered that Winchester will spend not far from a million in advertising this year."[24]

In a confidential letter to all jobbers and salesmen in 1917, the WRAC sketched out its postwar marketing and advertising ambitions. "You are going to sell more guns this year than you ever sold before!" the company promised. "The need today [as always] is for more gun business. The best way to make . . . ammunition business is to put more guns into hands of shooters."[25]

First, Winchester would initiate "the biggest and most carefully planned national advertising campaign ever undertaken by any firm of gun makers in the world." Second, the company would work on direct-mail solicitation and supply its missionaries and jobbers with "interesting, handsomely illustrated booklets" for counter and window displays. (Remington also shipped "window material" to key wholesalers and retailers and elicited their opinions, in 1917, on the quality of the displays and lithography, which Remington thought was a "decided advance in this valuable form of advertising" from previous years.) Finally, the company would work with its sales force to organize new gun clubs or to revive old ones that had languished. The world war had shown the importance of having civilians who knew how to shoot rifles.[26]

To give demand a boost and "get the full benefit . . . from this great advertising campaign," the WRAC deployed over one hundred of its special missionary salesmen in a coast-to-coast campaign to spread the word about Winchester guns. This time, it planned to leave no "large gaps or bare spaces" in its advertising. Its "whole aim from now on is a uniform distribution [of "advertising matter"] over the entire country."[27]

This marketing campaign was an inflection in the ongoing challenge of gun demand and stagnation. The company needed to "push sales" in order to grow enough to maintain its market position, and it recognized that "quality alone" was "insufficient to build and maintain customer interest." In this as in other moments, Winchester was a business acting like any other business in the early 1900s. Manufacturers of all stripes were trying to reach a mass audience through national advertising. At the same time, the gun industry began to exercise more control over its sales forces and even to apply modified principles of scientific management to sales. The 1913 Remington Arms Company sales convention took a sullen turn when management began to lecture about the importance of timely and very detailed sales reports from the field. Headquarters had been receiving unacceptably sketchy weekly reports lacking data on the specific names of towns, numbers of sales calls, and results. Executives proposed that salesmen complete these forms on Sunday mornings, when they weren't making sales calls.[28]

National advertising and tighter control over jobbers and retailers closed the gap between manufacturer and consumer. The middlemen—wholesalers, jobbers, and retailers—no longer controlled the message or decided which products they wanted to push. Winchester made this point all but explicit in its confidential correspondence to jobbers about its epic national campaign, which reassured them—or warned them—that "our advertising will CREATE the demand." Selling a gun, or any nonessential commodity, was a ritual of seduction. The president of Rub-No-More soap was no different than Winchester executives in a modern belief that advertising was key: whether it be for soap or gun, "we create the desire for our product through advertising," to "burn" demand into the consumer's mind.[29]

In a letter to dealers, the Colt's company explained the new advertising realities: "WE advertise to create a demand on YOU for our Arms; when that result is produced, it's YOU who can obtain direct benefit by making the SALE." Colt's provided local dealers with free advertising templates, to which they only needed to add their name and address. Likewise, Remington and Winchester prepared national advertisement material, homogenizing the more idiosyncratic messages and wiles of jobbers and missionaries. The scale of advertising was getting larger, and the company was thinking big. It prepared Winchester-embossed envelopes for missionaries to give to dealers and others, but it berated the missionaries for leaving them in "little houses in towns of not over . . . five hundred people who would not use 1,000 envelopes in almost as many years." They should be more particular

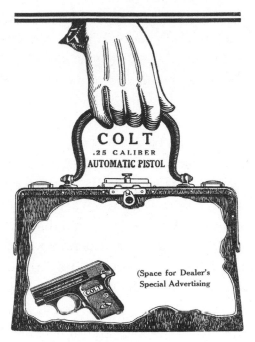

Colt's ad template. In the early 1900s, the gun industry, like other industries, moved toward national advertising and templates that local dealers could customize. *Courtesy of the Connecticut State Library.*

about who received them: "We do not wish to have them . . . given to a lot of little men who have no occasion to use them."[30]

National ad templates for Colt's "told the COLT story," Colt's explained to its dealers. Mass advertisement did indeed allow the gun manufacturer to tell, and control, the narrative and message about its product. During and after the world war, the story that Colt's told to itself, about itself, was one of individual Americans besieged and embattled in their most sacred places. The war had been brought home, and in this tenebrous, anxious reality, Americans faced danger at home and in their automobiles; there was a "threat at every curve, crossroad, and hill." The war, with its combative, bellicose "spirit of restlessness," would "beset us for a time," Colt's warned. Ingeniously, it seized on the growing popularity of the automobile and the makeshift new frontier of the parkways and roads. It warned "automobilists": "Be Prepared Against Country Hold Ups." "Suppose your car is held up by thugs tonight, in some lonesome country spot, how would you fare?" With a Colt slid "between the cushions, in the tool box, or in your pocket," at "hands up," you "can fire the first shot first." If the automobilist encountered no hold-up man, he could always "pull up on the road to have target practice—keeps a crowd happy." Colt's advertised a revolver in *National Sportsman* with a scene of three men, in suits, and the text: "One of the enjoyable features of a well-spent summer outing is the pleasure of living it over again around the fireside. 'Do you remember that night,' young Bob said, 'when that bunch of thugs held me up as I set camp waiting for you to return?'" His companion recalls the Colt revolver and responds, "They found you ready for them, didn't they!"[31]

In the Colt's story, as told through its ads, the responsibility for protection against these urban, modern equivalents of the "predicament scenes" featured in the hunting and sporting calendars rested with the individual, not the government or the police, in a deepening of the paramilitary mood that Winchester had conveyed in the 1860s. "Responsibility for the protection of your property, your home, your loved ones is too serious a matter to be entrusted to an arm of doubtful lineage," it warned. In *American* magazine, Colt's blurred war and peacetime. "Homes must be guarded as well as fought for. . . . Each one is responsible for the preservation of that ideal, to give the utmost in protection for his home." Another ad template said, "It's YOUR Turn Now": "We have made your home safe against the dangers of the Hun. Now, keep it safe against the dangers of the unprotected. Get a Colt." The Colt was a "tangible bulwark" against "lawless intrusion"; it was the modern equivalent, Colt's wrote, of an ancient talisman, the carving of a "winged disk about the doorway" to signify safety.[32]

On this frontier, and in contrast to sporting rifles, which emphasized acumen, the best gun "Works Automatically—Requires No Thought!" So Colt's stated in a 1912 *Everybody's* magazine ad that featured a

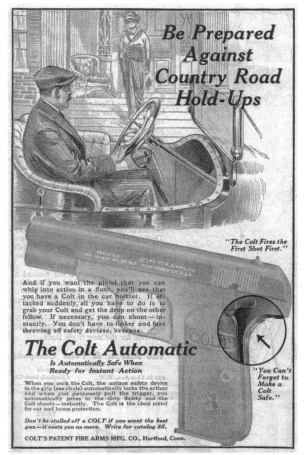

Colt's company ad from the early twentieth century.
The company imagined its revolver in more spaces
of everyday life, including cars and vest pockets.
Courtesy of the Connecticut State Library.

husband and wife talking guns with a dealer. With the automatic .45, "when you pull the trigger you automatically (without thought) press in the grip safety and the Colt shoots." Self-preservation came from speed over skill, the ability to "fire the first shot first" on the hold-up man. No gun could be "brought into action" faster.[33]

The ease of use was especially important, because Colt's ads conveyed a sense of the gun casually infiltrating new places and dimensions of everyday life, making it seem almost ubiquitous. Colt's conceptualized its markets both more precisely and more numerously than before. The ads promoted a Colt's tucked between the seat cushions of an automobile; a revolver that fit snugly in a "ladies' muff or handbag"; a gun that "just fits in a man's vest"; and, by the 1960s, a revolver that came in a book, "bound to fit the finest collection," with a personalized book mark included.[34]

For Winchester, much of the story the company told about itself, which its national ad templates cloned, had to do with the gun's emotional resonance, and especially the manly emotions it stirred. One could argue (although it is not my argument) that the gun had always traded on these emotions, or always quickened them; but from the vantage point of business, they are a much stronger, more deliberate, and more self-conscious invention of the 1900s than of the 1800s, when the Winchester sold itself on pragmatic, utilitarian terms. Advertisement had come a long way from the 1857 ad for Winchester's Volcanic pistol: "Directions: Push the spring up in the tube, by the knob A, till the top or cap B can be turned to the left, then put the cartridges (ten or less) in the tube . . . " Gun marketing had moved from narrative—a description of how guns worked—to lyric—a description of how they made you feel.

This inflection is neither diabolical nor surprising. It was a business acting like a business, and beginning to find new ways to create value for its product—an intangible value—as other uses became obsolete. Necessity was the mother of a gun mystique.

To pursue its boy plan, Winchester advertised expansively in *American Boy*, *Boys' Life*, *Youth's Companion*, the *Saturday Evening Post*, and other national magazines. Today, there is a popular sense that the deep association of guns and masculinity is almost inborn to the nation's collective unconscious. Seen from the archives of the gun business, it is something energetically invoked and defined on ad copy for weekly magazines, and then amplified and duplicated thousands of times over with other forms of mass advertisement. While most gun users and customers were male in the 1800s, the emotional ties of guns to masculine qualities, desires, and virtues, or those of the "average" American citizen, is a more modern aspect of gun advertisement and culture. In other words, the gun was changing from being a male tool to being a male totem. "Every real American father or mother is proud these days to have a boy who can place five shots straight in the bull's eye and wear a Winchester sharpshooter medal," said one ad. In the campaign of "winning over the parents," the company emphasized that all boys should know how to handle guns safely, as well as less tangible benefits, such as that a gun would "make a man of any boy," and teach him self-reliance.[35]

The Winchester company touted the gun as a masculine *bona fide*, much as Theodore Roosevelt did as he shaped his image. These ideas cut a template for the gun mystique of the twentieth and twenty-first centuries. The Industrial Manufacturer news bureau promoted the pistol as an antidote for the "soft" and effete "slick-haired sheiks and flapping flappers" of the 1920s. The "red-blooded individual" and the "wholesome young Americans" with an enduring interest in the "primitive things in life—camping, hunting, fishing . . . "—showed that the country was not "degenerating into a nation of lounge lizard anemics." The notion that every "real boy" wanted a Winchester rifle became a prominent ad slogan in the late 1910s. A gun would develop the "sturdy manliness that every real boy wants to have," and nothing was closer to a "real boy's heart" than shooting. "Every real American mother and father" could see that he should have one. "The kid you're so proud of has been wearing knickerbockers long enough now to make it natural for him to want a rifle"; after all, he had "grown up on countless boys' adventure stories." (Of course, the source of the natural desire, in this example, was fiction.)[36]

With expanded marketing personnel, Winchester refined the art of the gun sale. It treated the moment of salesmanship as an improvisational theater of small gestures and brilliant moves to seduce the customer. Dealers and retailers shared tricks of the trade in confidential sales bulletins, which are preserved in the Winchester archive. The company admired, for example, a "crackerjack idea" from a Mr. Reddington of Indiana to "quote prices of Guns in bushels of Corn and Wheat instead of dollars and cents," especially in rural districts. As objects of salesmanship, guns were unexceptional, no different from

Winchester Herald ad from 1921. The company appealed to boy consumers and tapped into the language of natural, in-born desires and instincts. *Courtesy of the Buffalo Bill Center of the West.*

shoes. "Let us suppose you have a dealer who says, 'I have had two of your guns in stock for two years and haven't made a sale,'" a sales role-playing exercise proposed. The WRAC urged the distributor to question, "If you only had two pairs of shoes in stock, and you kept them covered up with other goods in an out of the way place, you couldn't possibly expect your shoe sales to hold up, could you?" The salesman concludes, "Selling guns is like selling shoes—you have got to carry the assortment and let people know it. Your trouble is not that you are overstocked, but that you are . . . understocked."[37]

The point in this and other lessons was to push the sales force beyond the natural inclinations of the customer or market demand. "Remember that the one single aim of the Winchester sales force just now is to sell Winchester guns—plenty of them." As it was in the beginning, volume was imperative. The numbers changed, but not the algorithm. A June 1917 bulletin for distributors instructed them that "your aim should be to sell your customer quite a bit more than he can sell without effort or, to put it the other way, ALL he can possibly sell with his best personal effort backed by ours in the way of the big advertising campaign." Moreover, "when a dealer has on hand only a stock of guns that he is confident will 'sell themselves,' that is an unhealthy condition for Winchester." But "when a dealer has on hand so great a stock of guns as to arouse in him a determination to push their sale *hard* . . . and keeping everlastingly after every prospective gun buyer, he is IN A HEALTHY MERCHANDIZING CONDITION for himself and for Winchester."[38]

Distributor Guy Harrison in Texas agreed that "need" had to be coaxed. If he had listened to the objections of retailers and dealers, he would not have sold 30 percent of the guns he had turned over. "It is a matter of grind it out in ninety-five cases out of a hundred," said a bulletin. Jobber Walter Scott, also from Texas, worked the Corpus Christi territory that he'd been warned off of as unpromising, because a drought had restricted stock purchases to necessities. Scott "convinced some of [the Corpus Christi dealers] that they were 'compelled to have' Winchester rifles and guns in order to keep up with the extensive advertising campaign."[39]

Winchester encouraged impulse, spur-of-the-moment purchases, too. Retailers "should have on hand a well assorted stock of arms . . . so as to be prepared to close the sale while the buying impulse is on the customer." Imagine, the company continued, "if, when a buyer comes to you all ready to buy a Winchester . . . , you are prepared to put it into his hands—let him feel it—handle it—heft it—monkey with the perfect mechanism of the Winchester action . . . feel its comfortable cuddle to his shoulder, its smooth brown stock to his cheek and see the almost effortless way in which vision accurately adjusts itself to the sight—right then and there you close the sale. If, though, you have to dig around for a catalog and show him a cold-blooded cut, all enthusiasm will cool and the sale is lost."[40]

The company archive reveals an emphasis on getting a rifle into a potential customer's hands as soon as possible, because there was no surer way to "make a man want to own a gun quicker." Once he had the gun in his hands, "he likes to think of it as his." This desire, kindled on emotion, impulse, and the gun's sensuality, quieted the "High Price talk" that otherwise stymied sales. "The first operation in selling a gun at retail is to place it in the buyer's hands so he can 'feel' it—impress him with the balance. . . . Sidetrack the price until the customer insists on knowing. . . . Have the prospective customer worked up to the point where he is pretty likely to BUY regardless of the fact that the price is a little higher than he expected to pay."[41]

Winchester perfected the best ritual to "get the gun in the customer's hands the right way to stimulate desire": "Be sure you hand it to him with the gun pointing to his left, so that he will not have to change it end for end. Your left hand should be at the butt plate of the stock and your right hand at the end of the magazine. He will then grasp it at the pistol grip and action slide handle, the correct holding points."[42]

The Winchester's appeal in the twentieth century had less to do with the utilitarian or martial promotion of the 1870s than with how the gun *felt*—and the feelings about self that its balance, graceful lines, and finish could evoke. "The love of fire arms is strong in the American heart," the Industrial Manufacturer noted. More to the point, the gun industry was learning to kindle that love and inspire a sentimental attachment in the customer.[43]

Advertisement drew on the modern psychological vocabulary of desire and tied gun love to subconscious instincts. The marketing naturalized the male desire to own a gun at just the moment when guns were less imperative or intrinsic to an American man's life. "A boy's *natural interest* in a gun is going to make him get his hands on one sooner or later," so it was better to teach him how to shoot correctly (italics added). In the *Literary Digest*, a company advertisement said, "You know [your son] wants a gun. But you don't know how much he wants it. He can't tell you. It's beyond words." A boy's "yearning for a gun *demands your attention*," fathers were told in another ad. "He will get hold of one sooner or later. It is his natural instinct." Ads said that "the pulse of any red-blooded man quickens when the thought strikes home that the Winchester is all his own," and that men "in all walks of life never cease to feel a thrill when they get their hands on a Winchester shotgun." Sometimes the company interpreted the natural desire to include females as well: "Every man, woman or child has an inherent desire to own a gun," the *Winchester Herald* proclaimed. "Translate that desire into the sale of a Winchester. . . . A display of guns and ammunition always arouses interest, for it appeals to an *inborn trait* of human nature" (italics added). In the *Winchester Record* of December 1919, the WRAC naturalized "the shooting instinct which is present in most boys and girls," and hoped it might be "easier for our young people to indulge [it]."[44]

Modern advertising thickened the mystique of the American gun. If the first guns belonged to the genus of household tools, and were produced by smiths who typically made a range of similar tools, from pincing tongs to hinges, the modern gun belonged to the genus of discretionary commodities. A vanguard scientific management marketing expert in the late 1910s proposed that a product contending with saturated markets could "be helped remarkably in its distribution by developing an entirely new use." With guns, these new uses could be emotional and psychological as well as practical. Earlier, sales had meant "satisfying wants"—wants that existed independently of advertisement—but in a consumer culture where demand ideally kept pace with faster production, sales meant "the actual creating of wants in the minds of the purchaser, and the building up of desires." To do this, the capitalist needed to know something of "practical psychology," and the ways in which modern advertisement appealed to the "emotional over the rational." His analysis of national advertisements found that emotional appeals—to emulation, pride, and social achievement—outweighed rational appeals 535 to 342. Appeals to utility and thrift were replaced by the manipulation of the "psychological attitudes of consumers" and appeals to "status, sex appeal, achievement . . . pride, prejudice, [and] fear." Perhaps the very decline in pragmatic need for a gun could encourage more sales, not fewer—at least to the twentieth-century gun cranks, who valued guns for nonutilitarian reasons, as objects of desire and affinity. From the gun industry's perspective, it was just as valuable to sell many guns to one customer as to sell one gun each, as a tool, to many. Indeed, of all the markets Winchester pursued after the war, the soul of the ideal modern gun customer was closest to that of the passionate, eccentric, gun-loving—not gun-needing—crank.[45]

In the creation of desire and want through advertisement, the Winchester company was no different from Quaker Oats, whose ad man recalled that his goal was "to awaken an interest in and create a demand for cereals where none existed." The WRAC's strategies conformed to the larger trends of the day, whereby "advertising aims to teach people that they have wants, which they did not realize before, and where such wants can best be supplied," the 1901 *Thompson Red Book on Advertising* explained. Obviously, desire for rifles or revolvers did not have to be conjured out of thin air, or nothing, any more than desire for breakfast cereal did. The point is that modern advertisement in general began to think about creating want, need, and desire, rather than simply advertising products to fill preexisting and predefined needs.[46]

"Desire does not grow in a day," a Winchester sales bulletin instructed its representatives in 1921. "If you are a merchant you will early remind the hunter and shooter of the lure of the woods, the fields, the trap, and a desire in his mind becomes action in his purse. You will be the merchant who has the goods to satisfy the desire for a gun." Winchester thought to emulate the liquor industry: "The liquor people tried to perpetuate their business by 'educating' young men to the use of their products. Very immoral of them, of course, but mighty good business. . . . How would you get at the boys [to buy rifles] and what with?"[47]

Or, the gun was like a diamond. The company advised its sales force to counter objections about high prices by going "ahead with your sales talk just as you would if you were selling Packards, or golf clubs, or diamonds, or any other article that was not primarily intended to appeal to the man who cannot afford to indulge himself in a little mild extravagance."[48]

There was competition not only within but across industries, and the gun industry and the WRAC were well aware of this new landscape. Winchester sporting rifles now competed for the leisure dollar with nonessential commodities spawned by other industries, including liquor, radios, golf clubs, and phonographs. The gun was being reoriented in two antithetical directions: as a commodity of instinct, and as a luxury—and, in both cases, an object of desire.[49]

One answer to the nebulous but compelling question of why Americans love guns is simply that the gun industry invited us to. As an unexceptional, agnostic imperative of doing business in the early 1900s, its marketing and advertisement burnished the gun as an object of emotional value and affinity. Eventually, it would become one of political affinity as well.

CHAPTER 18

KING OF INFINITE SPACE

I could be bound in a nutshell, and count myself a king of infinite space, were it not that I had bad dreams.

—William Shakespeare, *Hamlet*

IN THE EARLY 1920S, THE LIFE'S WORK OF SARAH AND THE Winchester men was winding down. Sarah's crippling arthritis had worsened and her overall health had declined since the WRAC's reorganization. She couldn't monitor her staff's activities as assiduously as she had before. Locals gossiped that half of Sarah's carpenters would make a loud bustle to satisfy the bedridden Sarah's directives for continuous production, while the other half found a secluded spot on the fourth-story widow's walk, the tallest spot still standing after the 1906 earthquake, where they played poker and smoked.[1]

Sarah's gardeners must have sensed the lassitude settling over the estate, and quietly stopped taking their mistress's instructions earnestly: the ash bin for the estate's boiler was discovered almost full when the remodeling finally ended. Clearly, Sarah's directive that it be continuously emptied to fertilize the gardens had been ignored.[2]

The gardeners might have been slacking in their duties, but not around Llanada Villa's front lawn. Here, they dutifully spread potash, pruned, and weeded. This spot could still betray their sloth, because the window of a second-floor bedroom was Sarah's favorite place to repose in her last years.[3]

341

Some of the horticultural features on the front yard only make sense from above. Looking down from Sarah's window, you see a front hedge meticulously crafted into the shape of a crescent moon, green shrubbery filled in with hundreds of yellow chrysanthemums, the gardener's house that she'd designed in a keyhole shape.[4]

The crescent moon symbolizes resurrection and life eternal in the Islamic tradition. Just as the two points of the moon are about to close in on each other, they stop, promising a free and boundless space beyond. The Ottoman Turks, to whom Oliver Winchester owed his business's survival, used the crescent moon on their flag and tombs. The keyhole, for Dante, connoted admission to heavenly and earthly paradise. Janus, one of the most ancient Roman gods and the conductor of souls between worlds, held a staff in his right hand and a key in his left, his one face gazing earthward and the other heavenward.

Follow your eye outward, from the crescent moon to a path, which is flanked by thirteen towering California palms leading to the estate's front entrance: here, statues of Demeter and Hebe, made in New England, once stood guard.[5]

Hebe was the goddess of eternal youth, blessed with powers of rejuvenation. She was born to Zeus and Hera, and given to Hercules in marriage after his apotheosis. Demeter ensured the soul's survival in the kingdom of the dead. Her story is told in a splendid early Greek poem. The goddess of the harvest, she had only one daughter, Persephone, the goddess of spring. No divine messenger would tell Demeter the truth, that Hades had abducted Persephone and made her his bride. But, as Persephone descended in Hades' chariot to the underworld, her mother heard her weeping. Demeter grieved so intensely that famine beset the earth, and Zeus had to intervene. Hades agreed to free Persephone for six months of the year, when she has a joyous reunion with her mother, and the fertility of spring returns, "[making] the fields once more rich with abundant fruit and the whole world bright with flowers and green leaves." Demeter and Persephone share an eternal bond between mother and daughter that is interrupted, but not severed, by death.[6]

Sarah's allusion, here as elsewhere, was exquisitely crafted. For decades, Sarah had lived in her own labyrinth, suspended between the living and the dead, perhaps in horror. But also, perhaps, in yearning. After all, if Sarah really did feel tormented by malevolent ghosts, then it would have been easy enough to design a ghost-proof estate, by the axioms of Victorian spiritualism. Ghosts prefer chimneys for entrance and exit, are afraid of water, and avoid mirrors and light, because they cast no reflection, and find this humiliating. Rather than building a mirror-laden, chimney-free house surrounded by a moat, Sarah built a moat-free home with one mirror and forty-seven chimneys, some of which stop floors short of the roof.[7]

Her design was a reasonable compromise, if your deepest terror is conjoined to your most sublime dream. As she looked down on her horticultural encryption of death and resurrection, after so much building, and with her life's work and legacy nearing an end, Sarah might have permitted herself a cautiously pleasant reverie of Summer Land, and reunion.

———

ON OCTOBER 22, 1920, THE WRAC CELEBRATED "BENNETT DAY" to mark TG's half-century of service in various capacities. He had toiled his whole life to "[extend] rifles to every race of mankind." After Oliver, TG was the man who had most imprinted his character on the Winchester enterprise. At noon, the plant enjoyed a special Thomas G. Bennett Concert, followed by a banquet. TG spoke appreciatively and praised Oliver's founding wisdom. He concluded with a modest, even wary, assessment of his own legacy: "I simply did the best I could."[8]

Years earlier, in 1905, Bennett had feared he would not survive at his job. He had exchanged pensive letters with Jane as he took a cure for an unknown affliction at the Hotel Bristol, in Geneva. Momentous as the Winchester legacy already was, he accounted his contribution more as one of dutiful male routine. "I didn't work because it seemed necessary but because it was interesting and my place in the world," he mused. Jane had reproached herself in an earlier letter for not having taken adequate care of her mother, or of TG himself. It was a glum contemplation inspired by the "bunching" of three death anniversaries in early spring, including her mother's and Will's. Jane and TG had fulfilled their prescribed places, and Jane had lived, TG reassured her, a "most useful and dignified life, . . . wonderfully without mistake." TG reaffirmed his debt to her, noting that his professional destiny was partly of her making: "You have probably helped me to all I am and to my record, which should have been a more distinguished . . . one, the aid being what it was." What he offered as marital praise—one shared destiny within two dramatically separate spheres—Sarah might just as logically have imagined as the premise of a marital curse. Any thought to the contrary, TG concluded, came only from a "distorted view of life and the past."[9]

Still, TG's comments and a disquiet about a life's work, dutifully executed, seemed mildly to haunt them both, even if it had no particular object or correlative. Some of the distant legacies of what our doing does, for which neither TG nor anyone else would ever be held culpable in a court of law—things we would never be considered personally accountable for—are too enormous to see—and too terrifying, on the rare occasions when they are seen.

———

At its January 1920 sales convention, the company put a cheerful face on its wavering fortunes. In the early 1920s, sales conventions with elaborate banquets, revues, and speeches spread the new corporate gospel of sales as a "moral crusade" and way of life. At the Winchester convention, seventy sales representatives paraded from their hotel to the company to hear the opening session, the building's entrance flanked by display windows from the "advertising" department—a newly minted concoction, requiring quotation marks—of the Christmas and hunting season promotions. Sales reps heard inspirational addresses and sessions on "selling the hostile dealer," "sales talk," "psychological tests," and "the power and personality of advertising." They enjoyed dance performances by girls from the factory shops.[10]

The convention cheer belied a dire accounting. When Sarah's lawyer Samuel Leib inquired on her behalf about the company's health in March 1921, he heard from a vice president that business had "fallen off sadly" since 1920. The company had had to lay off many employees. "The force has been cut to the limit, wages reduced, and no overtime." The cash required to build more and acquire new lines had hardly been realized in sales.[11]

In his New Year's message for 1922, company president J. E. Otterson promised not to waste employees' time recounting the woes of the Winchester Plan. Although the "so-called sales and advertising service" of the plan to promote non-gun products had developed encouragingly, it had been discontinued in 1921 as a result of bad business conditions. The company's domestic business had been only 80 percent of its 1920 business, and its export business an appalling 20 percent of the previous year's, although this was common among exporters. Otterson couldn't deny that the company had been "chastened by adversity." The turn in fortune owed much to what Edwin Pugsley described as "extremely extravagant postwar building"—to correct for the wartime overbuilding. The plan was failing, except with fishing tackle as well as guns and bullets: there, "consumer demand had been abnormally large."[12]

At the end of August 1922, the company shouldered a crushing debt once more. It merged with the Simmons Hardware Companies, at the latter's request, to become a new chimera, the Winchester-Simmons Company. The Winchester Repeating Arms Company, an artificial person before the law, was born unnaturally in the sweltering summer of 1866. It died an equally unnatural death, of a sort, on August 22, 1922, by way of merger, taking on a new name.

Just two weeks after the WRAC died as an autonomous corporate entity, so did Sarah, by way of heart failure, in her sleep. The *San Jose Mercury News* discreetly eulogized her as "a woman of the most retiring nature, extremely sensitive and opposed to publicity of any character," who never let her good charitable deeds be known. Judge S. F. Leib, for many years "her counselor and friend," said with a perhaps unintended ambiguity that Mrs. Winchester was "as sane as any woman I have ever known" and "all that a good woman should be. . . . If there is a heaven, there she must surely be."[13]

Since the early 1900s, Sarah had been habitually honing and revising her trust funds and will before they finally satisfied her. Significantly, although she organized her estate with painstaking logic and care, making sure to leave trust funds to beloved teachers, employees, nieces, and nephews, she made no specific instruction for her most flamboyant legacy, the palace on which she had spent down the bulk of her rifle fortune, except that it and the furniture should be sold off. It is as if she left it to no one and everyone—much like a myth, or a work of art. Of her original fortune, only $4 million remained, and Sarah left most of that to the New Haven Hospital Society through which she had established the tuberculosis ward in Will's name. San Jose reacted to news of Sarah's diminished fortune with "considerable surprise."[14]

Whatever else it was, Sarah's 1918 decision to relinquish her WRAC stock, and her long-awaited consent by signature in 1921, had severed for the first time the bond between the Winchester Repeating Arms Company and the Winchester family. Maybe after this quietly momentous act, Sarah finally felt on some level that she was ready, and that it was safe, to die.

———

NEITHER THE WRAC NOR SARAH'S BUILDING MADE MUCH SENSE, after their idiosyncratic purposes expired—to arm an unimaginably grisly world war, or to protect two long-departed spirits and evade millions of vengeful ones.

In March 1922, as movers emptied the hundreds of rooms in Sarah's mansion, the Winchester company produced a key list that inventoried each of the 213 rooms at the main factory, presumably as part of its merger with Simmons. Size was a crushing financial liability for the WRAC. An auditor had predicted correctly that once Winchester completed its government orders, the plant's costly sprawl to accommodate such production would be "valueless to the Company in a commercial sense." Leib described Sarah's mansion at the same time, and in almost the same language, as having been "appraised as of no value." Idiosyncratic overbuilding had rendered it—them—monstrous, and therefore worthless. Official documentation understated the mansion as "a large frame dwelling in bad state of repair, and outbuildings." T. C. Barnett first bought it and A. P. Marston, a fruit dryer in Santa Clara County, leased it for ten years from Barnett on behalf of the J. H. Brown Amusement Company. John Brown had grown up in Pittsburgh and, intrigued by mining boxcars, had invented one of the first roller coasters. When the Browns moved west, they operated beach rides in Southern California—and his Crystal Beach resort had included a "House of Mystery" attraction. In 1932, after having rented it for a decade, the Browns bought a house that reputedly cost over $5 million to build and appoint for $20,000.[15]

At this moment, Sarah's ghost story became a commodity. The Browns saw a tourist attraction in the castle's eccentricity and let the estate deteriorate to accentuate a haunting mood. Billboards with ghoulish skulls advertised the "Mystery House"; visitors wrote graffiti on the walls and decapitated the statuary. The Browns did what for Sarah had been unthinkable: they flung open the doors of her always too-imperfect home to strangers, for money, who roamed through the house unsupervised and vandalized some of the property. A ghost story that drew down a blood fortune now became the basis of a new fortune, indirectly made off of the Winchester rifle, too. There was no escaping the business. If Sarah was watching, mortified, from Summer Land, she would have seen the mechanism, the magic spring, recoil and release, with ineluctable perfection.[16]

In 1974, Keith Kittle, manager of the Wild West Frontier Village attraction in Santa Clara Valley, left his post there to become general manager of the Winchester Mystery House. The American gun legend and Sarah's gun counter-legend once again converged. In 1993, the house was owned by Edna and Gerard Raney, operating as Winchester Mystery House Associates, and had "sales" of $1.4 million, according to Duns Market Identifier data. The house has been restored and is listed as California Historical Landmark #868. It is still owned by the Winchester Mystery House Associates, but according to one of the house's general managers, it would take "two pages" to list all of those involved in the ownership group, and the management is not forthcoming with those specifics. The house is a tourist attraction, but the management does not share information about the number of annual visitors.[17]

As for the original Winchester factory in New Haven, it declined apace with American industry, falling into decrepitude, its windows shattered, the machinery silenced. It became a fossil of Oliver Winchester's once-breathtaking ambition, and another example of postindustrial blight. Winchester's factory was resurrected in the twenty-first-century fashion for the new economy of the creative class: old industry never dies; it just gets converted to condominiums. A developer bought the factory buildings in 2008 and remodeled them into over a hundred luxury lofts and apartments. "Craft Your Life," the brochure promises. Of the old gun behemoth that armed the world, much of the brickwork and the sturdy beams survive, adding a touch of antique industrial chic. The apartments feature exposed pipes, creating an aura announcing that this was, at one time, a place where something got made. Otherwise, the gun legacy is buried under granite counters and glass-tile backsplashes.

Still, although Llanada Villa became a tourist attraction, advertised by a ghost story that—exactly like the western gun legends—grew more lurid, yet more confidently "factual," with each retelling, this does not mean that there was never a core of truth to it. Having secured a toehold in the legend only whets the appetite to climb higher toward a truth about Sarah's cryptic inner life and her life's work. In 1922, as movers cleared Sarah's house, curiosity-seekers gained access to a mysterious room, the "séance" room, which had been strictly prohibited to visitors, even servants. This room sits at the center of the house physically. Sarah kept the only key to the room's only entrance, although it had three secret exits and trap doors: one in a cupboard; one that dropped several feet down into the kitchen; and one without

The secret exit in Sarah Winchester's "séance room." This space re-sembles a "spirit cabinet," a familiar feature of the medium's craft at the height of spiritualism. Courtesy of the Winchester Mystery House.

a doorknob—once you left through this third door, you couldn't re-enter the room. Sarah had designed it like a spiritualist panic room.[18]

A New Deal Works Progress Administration (WPA) employee who had been tasked with writing a guidebook of California in the 1930s visited the Winchester home years after Sarah's death, and he puzzled over this room. He reported that it was draped from floor to ceiling in white satin during Sarah's lifetime (others say that Sarah had it draped in blue satin, not white). It had thirteen hooks on the wall, and the varnish on the floor was worn in one spot from the pacing of Sarah's slippers. The room is modest, spare, and small. Two windows have iron bars capped with arrow points to keep out prying servants (or malevo-lent spirits, who were thought to be clumsy and accident-prone).[19]

As her arthritis worsened, Sarah sometimes had to ask her servants to help her into the room. Then she would close and lock the door. After some time, often four hours or more, Sarah would summon a servant back to assist her, using the electric intercom system she'd designed. They'd find her silently sitting in her chair, outside of the locked chamber, ready to be helped to the elevator.[20]

In between when Sarah entered the room and left it, legend says, she took a ritualized expedition to outwit the malevolent spirits before settling in for her hours-long meditation. She bolted the door and left by one of her secret passages. Or she disappeared through a hole in the wall and sat for some time until she was confident the evil ghosts had given up their pursuit.[21]

The worldly explanation is to see it not as a "séance" room but as another haphazardly designed and redesigned addition, a place for Sarah to meditate privately, or perhaps to grieve. But it is actually this room, more than any other at the estate, that made me believe Sarah's ghost story the most, because it resembles so closely a popular concept of mid-nineteenth-century spiritualism. It is an ingenuous clue in her labyrinthine estate—the architectural equivalent, perhaps, of that telling phrase Sarah used in her letter to say that her mother-in-law had "passed from mortal vision." In the mid- and late 1800s, when "spirit cabinets" were popular, professional mediums would sometimes recommend that a promising client "sit for development," so that he or she could enjoy manifestations just as miraculous as those the mediums see. To do this, the client was to construct a cabinet in the corner of a room—much as Sarah had built in this room. She was to sit inside the cabinet, alone, "and remain one hour, in as passive a condition as it is possible for you to attain," a book on spiritualism instructed. Mediums recommended that neophytes sit at least "twice per week, always on the same evening and hour," noting that "there is no such thing as failure if you persist." But the new medium must never, ever deviate from the rules, or the schedule. For example, a bell might toll precisely at midnight, or at 2 A.M. It is easy to imagine that if Sarah had seen a wondrous manifestation once, a miracle, she would want the moment back, to see Will once more, by doing the same things that had materialized him with Coombs.[22]

The séance room was said to hold one of the estate's six safes, filled with a dazzling fortune. Every burglar on the Pacific slope knew about Sarah's safes, but they never dared to enter the house, patrolled as it was by hedges, bloodhounds, and spooky rumors. California had grown up on rumors of fortunes hidden beneath the surface, and this was another one. As Llanada Villa was cleared and inventoried after Sarah's death, one of the safes was opened. It contained five items: tangled fishing hooks and lines, a pair of Will Winchester's woolen socks and underwear, a tiny purple velvet box with four strands of blond baby hair, and a yellowed, crumbling, two-line obituary from the death column of the *New Haven Daily Register*: "Died in This City, July 24, 1866, Annie Pardee, infant daughter of William Wirt and Sarah L. Winchester."[23]

She could never buy these things and so in one respect the rumor was true. The safe's treasures were priceless. One day, when "the blues" were running in the East River of New Haven, Will had fished with these lines, and cut these hooks with his hands. He had worn these clothes, and his skin had touched them directly. She had had a daughter, a daughter who took breaths and existed on the earth, who would have been forgotten if not for an obituary, a strand of hair, a headstone—and an involuted two-hundred-room riddle that Sarah invented, by way of eulogy, and perhaps absolution.

CHAPTER 19

THE WEST THAT
WON THE GUN

*The west may need to be seen to be believed, but it must be
believed to be seen.*

—N. Scott Momaday

THE WINCHESTER "WON THE WEST" SEVERAL DECADES AFTER THE
fact, in the 1900s. Everyone knows that the Winchester was the
gun that won the West, not because it happened, but because it was a
twentieth-century slogan in a Winchester marketing campaign. The
slogan was devised by Winchester executive Edwin Pugsley; it was first
introduced in a full-page magazine ad in 1919, and later disseminated
in "French, English, Chinese, Spanish, everything," says Winchester
curator Herbert Houze. "It's a bit of an overstatement. . . . Shall we say,
Winchester did a wonderful marketing job."[1]

In 1959, the company's slogan was, "Winchester: More than a Gun.
An American Legend": by then it could afford to be more abstract and
gestural even than "the gun that won the West." And by 1995, there
was almost a weary, slurred shorthand in how Winchester advertised
the heavy cultural freight of its gun. The company's explanation of its
modern logo, a horse and armed rider, leaves no cliché behind: it conveys "the cowboy, the Indian, the lawman, the pioneer, the mesa, the
mountains, the desert, and the grandeur of the west."[2]

As with the "gun that won the West," much of the history we know about the frontier and guns never happened. The Wild West of the 1800s, recall, was not so wild or gun-violent as it is perceived. There is the gun that won the West, but also the West that won the gun: the social fiction, out of so many contingencies and historical possibilities, which allied to the gun and amplified its cultural mystique. This conquest occurred in the early and mid-1900s, not the 1800s, and most energetically through the braiding of fiction, history, and legend in the mediums of advertisement, film, and story. The gun industry itself helped to deepen its product's mystique, which increasingly traded on the currency of desire and affinity, rather than utility.

The western and the frontier hero dominated movie theaters, magazine stands, bookstores, and televisions in the 1950s before declining as a genre. The body count of gun casualties on the frontier at Saturday matinees far exceeded the number of casualties on the actual frontier. At least 650 westerns were released between 1935 and 1940, and then 501 from 1950 to 1955, and over 250 from 1955 to 1960. Eight of the top ten television prime-time shows in 1959 were westerns, with a total of 39. Publishers sold an average of 35 million paperback westerns a year in the 1950s. Scores of "Old West" magazines, also described as men's magazines, appeared in the mid-1900s, including *Gunslingers of the West*, *True Frontier*, *Outlaws of the Old West*, *Badmen of the Old West*, and *Best of the West*. By one metric of content analysis, the mention of "cowboys" in English printed material peaked in 1939.[3]

In 1969, Ramon Adams compiled an annotated bibliography of 2,491 works on western gunmen. Excluding state and local history guides with only a passing mention of gunmen, or entries without a date, of the 1,951 remaining publications, all but 241 were published in the 1900s; the greatest number of books was published in 1936, followed by the years 1957, 1958, 1960, and 1955, in that order. This is not a precise or exhaustive census of all published material on gunmen, but it roughly quantifies the character's fluorescence in the mid-1900s. This vernacular proliferation extended even to plastic-mold play figurines. The Marx Company debuted its first of 134 Wild West playsets in 1951 and offered more than 400 Wild West figures, with which children in the 1950s played "Cowboys and Indians," Patricia Limerick observed, not "masters and slaves."[4]

In this way we advertised, wrote, filmed, staged, played, and televised our way into a gun culture. As with the earlier example of Buffalo Bill, the West that won the gun was a prematurely postmodern narrative of the fictionalized real: it was important that the truth be asserted, and equally important that it not be told.

———

BUSINESS PROFESSOR DOUGLAS HOLT HAS DESCRIBED HOW commodities that become icons, as Winchester and Colt did in the 1900s, compete and win on a "myth market." The product has intangible value and charisma as a commodity that embodies a powerful cultural myth, contoured through advertisement. The most powerful myths, Holt argued, are those that resolve "acute tensions people feel between their own lives and society's prevailing ideology," and promise to resolve cultural anxieties and antinomies. Like gun legends, the myth flourishes in the space between what happened and what we wish had happened.[5]

Advertisements in the 1900s about the Winchester in the 1800s ran the gamut from international sloganeering to window displays at hardware stores in small towns that were supported by the fledgling Winchester marketing department. The *Winchester Herald*, a company magazine for its sales force, praised a Colorado City window display that created a "lifelike scene of the prairie in the wild days." The window depicted a "treat 'em rough roundup," a "wild show for wild men."[6]

Ad men had discovered the gun's history—or myth. As Colt's concluded in one ad, its gun had been "famous in its past." In the mid-1900s, Smith & Wesson ran an extensive ad campaign under the banner, "Makers of History . . . Arms and the Man." Each ad took a year in American history and airbrushed the gun into the narrative. The year 1891 began with, "Chicago remodels its shore line to prepare for the Columbian Exposition . . . U.S. Patent Office celebrating 100 years of service . . . McKinley races to political prominence . . . Smith

& Wesson startles the hand-arm shooting world with the new .22 Single Shot pistol." These ads, suggestive non sequiturs, placed the pistol atmospherically at the scene of historical events in which it played no part.[7]

Several midcentury Colt's ads rehabilitated the cowboy. Historically a boozy "unmarried lower-class laborer," to quote historian David Cartwright, the cowboy became one of the "lean-jawed, hard riding, fast-shooting men who blasted their way across the pages of a nation's history to the thunder of the guns of Colt." He went from bleary-eyed with drink to steely-eyed with courage: "He can look calmly at danger because he knows he has the advantage," one of the Colt lithographs explained. The most famous and coveted gun industry lithograph, created for Colt's by Frank Schoonover, depicts the austere, sober cowboy "Tex and His Horse Patches," an image for 1926 about 1876.[8]

The WRAC offered cash prizes for photographs and brief histories of early model, historic Winchesters as a form of historical-advertorial promotion. "With many an old-time Winchester is associated some interesting item of history," the company wrote, "some bit of romance, or some story. . . . Perhaps your old Winchester has figured in a real adventure." The article touted the Winchester's role in "push[ing] the frontier of civilization westward," especially. In 1928, the company initiated an Arctic Broadcasting schedule of radio shows to the "polar regions" to convey news and messages to the pioneers and missionaries of the Arctic Circle, inviting listeners to imagine earlier pioneers, to "*see* into their cabins, igloos, huts or ships," and to see therein Winchester rifles and cartridges.[9]

In these ads and other vernacular media, the gun gained a history, in one sense; but it also lost its true history, or at least its historical specificity. Casual assertions held that Americans had "always" loved guns, or that they had a "timeless" tradition of gun fluency, a "priceless tradition" in firearms, or had "long known how to shoot," with "every boy" trained as a marksman. The acceptance of an "inherent love" of the gun, or an "urge to buy" one, whose sources were "mysterious," if not mystified—always there, predating history or the commercial gun culture—elided a great deal. It ignored the changing attitudes toward guns (different guns, for different purposes, in different eras, imbued with different meanings) by which gun interest and fluency has always waxed and waned. It also obscured the gun industry's self-conscious efforts to stoke love for the gun as nothing more than an agnostic imperative of its business as gun utility waned.[10]

In some cases, the gun was retroactively fetishized. Where it had played a role in American history, it was now the star of the show, as numerous articles from the Colt's archives illustrate. In a characteristic symbolic abridgement, the *Savannah Morning News* wrote that "the revolver stands for invention, extension of territories, suppression of lawlessness, influx of wealth and, in general, power." The very "creation of the United States was due to the rifle," it concluded. F. Romer's 1926 book, published by the Colt's company, stated the trend bluntly in its title: *Makers of History: A Story of the Development of the History of Our Country at the Muzzle of a Colt*. Some began to argue that the American long rifle, or Kentucky rifle, had won the Revolutionary War, although antique gun experts consider this notion, in one's terms, "romanticist nonsense." These works transliterated historical narratives that might have been about any number of themes into a story about a gun, which in some cases must have been an easier story to tell. The gun was a historical ellipsis that got Americans from a world before conquest to a settled land after, without contemplation of the contradictions between ideals and realities in the middle.[11]

Historical and biographical interest in the gunman emerged in the 1920s and 1930s with the emergence of "legend-maker" historians, who claimed accuracy, but actually reinforced, or even created, the legends. Biographies of Wild Bill Hickok, Billy the Kid, Wyatt Earp, and others leaned at first toward glamorization of the six-shooters, mirroring in a more high-brow genre the low-brow pulp fiction of the day, and, in the 1960s, toward equally glamorized condemnation.[12]

Popular western stories started off with an emphatic assertion of truthfulness. As early as 1915, Dennis Collins (*The Indians' Last Fight*) worried that Wild West dime novels had created utterly false impressions of the West, inflamed young men's imaginations, and inspired outlawry. But even books marketed as historically accurate were closer to fiction. Widely sold Signet books were largely fictional accounts of actual characters (for example, Ray Hogan's *The Life and Death of Johnny Ringo* in 1963) that were marketed as "actual history." Even works flying under the flag of history continued the gun overkill, exaggerating both the quantity of gun violence and its charisma or "quality"—its moral scaffolding.[13]

Popular fiction and putatively accurate historical narratives of America's gunmen continued farther down the path first trailblazed in the late 1860s. The authentication of the dime-novel fables as fact got a boost in the early 1920s when Dr. Frank O'Brien, a dentist, donated his novel collection to the esteemed New York Public Library. The catalog copy for the collection described dime novels as "realistic novels: it has finally come to be realized that the pictures of pioneer life in the far west, as presented by the Beadle books, are substantially accurate portrayals of the strange era and characters." (Beadle was a publisher.) These novels, said the library, gave a "more accurate and vivid picture" of the West than the work of "formal historians."[14]

This endorsement would have been welcomed by "formal historians," many of whom drew on the dime-novel archive for their accounts. At least two serious historians, in 1926 and 1933, wrote books that "gave respectability" to the legend. If anything, the Wild Bill Hickok gun narrative became more extreme in the fluorescence of western narratives in the mid-1900s, as it was retold under the ennobling flag of nonfiction. In these decades, Hickok became a gun "superman," says an expert on westerns, who killed more people, and killed them faster, with each retelling. Frederick Ritchie Bechdolt (*When the West was Young*, 1922) claimed that Bill had killed eleven at Rock Creek; William S. Hart (*William S. Hart in Wild Bill Hickok*, 1923) said he had killed twenty-five in Abilene; Charles Willis Howe (*Timberleg of the Diamond Trail*, 1949) has Hickok killing "eighty-seven men not including Indians" while he was a peace officer; and O. W. Coursey (*Wild Bill*, 1924) asserted that Bill "never missed," and that he once shot a man who entered the front door with a revolver in his left hand, while with his right he shot a man coming from the rear, although there is no evidence this ever happened. Other accounts simply reprinted the George Ward Nichols or James Buel accounts (*The Great West*, 1958, and Atomic Books, 1946, respectively). Of twenty-five additional books on Hickok published between 1908 and 1968, at least seventeen duplicated the Nichols legend, now asserted more confidently as history. Stories written explicitly for young readers by esteemed publishers such as Random House (Steward Holbrook, *Wild Bill Hickok*, 1952) created a powerful impression for children of an over-gunned Hickok "strapping two revolvers on" before taking down the McCanles gang.[15]

By the mid-1900s, more accurate portrayals of Hickok and other gunmen were available, occasionally acknowledged by authors, and then discreetly ignored in favor of the legend, even with august publishers. Author Glenn Chesney (*Pay Dirt*, Appleton-Century, 1936) mentioned an obscure *Nebraska Historical Magazine* corrective to the Hickok tale, but dismissed it in favor of the tale itself; likewise, a 1949 book published by Bobbs-Merrill tells a corrected version, but the author "writes as though he does not believe it," said a westerns expert.[16]

Stories of dime novels and other mass media of earlier ages found powerful new amplification in the new: movies and, eventually, television. Before Hollywood was Hollywood, it was Oklahoma, a forgotten frontier of the gun culture. Oklahoma's early productions cut a template for depictions of gunmen, outlaws, cowboys, and Indians. The Edison Manufacturing Company produced the first Oklahoma film in 1904, and the genre aspired to documentary realism for an audience that craved nonfiction "actualities." In 1911 a viewer wrote to *Moving Picture World*, "We don't thank you, Mr. Producer, . . . for forcing down our throats the knowledge that this is only a screen. . . . [W]e want to think it's the real thing." Pawnee Bill's Oklahoma buffalo ranch and the 101 Ranch, used for settings in the first western movies, promised authenticity to the filmmaker: "Everything is genuine and true to nature," the ranch promised. "No Jersey cowboys nor painted white men for Indians."[17]

Al Jennings was among the most important figures of Oklahoma's film industry. He made what a cynic might see as a natural progression, from lawyer to outlaw to actor to politician. Apparently, he became a bank robber because of disillusionment with the law after a man who shot his brother to death in a quarrel was acquitted. Jennings was no more successful as a bandit than he had been as a lawyer: his gang perhaps robbed one or two trains and the occasional general store, and in one train robbery left with no more than a few dollars and a jug of whiskey. Jennings spent five years in prison, and when he was released he wandered into evangelism and politics before meeting writers in a New York City club and compiling a "highly romanticized" version of his life, rife with inaccuracies and outright fabrication, which became a *Saturday Evening Post* story, "Beating Back." This account became the basis for a movie in 1915 that was touted as a "bandit story for respectable audiences," and its "*real*" hero as the "Jean Valjean of America," who "beat back at society until it recognized and honored him." Moralists, including the local politician and Congregationalist minister Thomas Harper, obligingly read the new genre as all too realistic—and prescriptive—and wanted to outlaw "any pictures of a bank robbery, train robbery, or any picture of nude forms . . . or any picture whatsoever that would be suggestive of evil thoughts and deeds."[18]

Jennings's movies, like written works on the gunmen, claimed authenticity, promising that actual outlaws, actual Indians, and actual cowboys were playing themselves. They had to be real—but not really real. Historian Richard Slotkin noted that Jennings used actual Oklahoma Indians, and seemed to have a sincere desire to show reality, but the real reality was not the reality audiences craved. In truth, outlaws looked like "city tramps," and Indians lived "in small cabins and dressed like dirt farmers rather than feathered warriors."[19]

Hollywood drew its first gunmen from an obscure book called *Triggernometry: A Gallery of Gunfighters*, by Eugene Cunningham. Filmmaker Nunnally Johnson's researcher used it as his muse for *The Gunfighter* in 1950. The book's introduction would have had obvious value for a scriptwriter. It claimed historical accuracy, and it was atmospherically detailed yet deracinated, easily imagined as a summer movie trailer. It presented a type, "the figure we have come to call the Gunman." His particular place of birth does not really matter, so long as it placed him in the "vast, wild region" of the West, nor his year, so long as it would "set him functioning within the years 1860 to 1900." Killing "would be natural to such men," Cunningham wrote, continuing the tradition of both overstating and naturalizing America's gun pathology.[20]

The movie *Winchester '73* (1950) belongs to the subgenre of what Slotkin defined as the psychological or *film noir* western, which includes *Colt .45* (1950) and *The Gun That Won the West* (1955). These movies, Slotkin said, emphasize the hero's darker, even pathological, aspects, and are characterized by "a particular kind of stylization and abstraction"—indeed, a fetishization of the gun itself. The western noir was particularly detached from historical or social context, with personal motives replacing the social ones, and the line between outlaw and lawman further blurred by their kinship through gun violence. This Cold War gunfighter navigated through dimly lit, claustrophobic, desolate landscapes on a quest driven by his private obsession and desires for justice. This gunfighter, Slotkin brilliantly argued, must be understood in American culture as an idiomatic figure transcending particular historical and social settings.[21]

Winchester '73 is a story of boy meets gun, boy loses gun, another boy loses gun, and so on. Lin McAdam, played by Jimmy Stewart, is on a mysterious quest after "Dutch" Henry Brown. But the Winchester "1 of 1,000" extra special Model 73 rifle is the "main star of the movie," as critics have noted. Today, it would be an impressive example of product placement, since the company was involved in the movie's production.[22]

The first twenty minutes are devoted to a shooting competition to win the coveted rifle. The story, itself a fiction, threads through familiar legends: The competition takes place in Wyatt Earp's Dodge City, on the Fourth of July. Stewart wins the gun, but Dutch steals it from him. As McAdam pursues Dutch across the prairie, the Winchester 73 passes from Dutch's hands to a gun trader's, to an Indian chief's ("This is gun I want," he declares, before scalping and killing the trader), to a shady character named Steve, then back to Dutch. Along the way we discover why McAdam is so intent on pursuing Dutch: he's his brother, and a robber, and had shot their father in the back. McAdam's sidekick, "High Spade," explains to the love interest, Lola Manners, that "the old man sired two sons. One was no good." In a final shootout on a cliff outside of town, waged with repeaters and the 1 in 1,000, McAdam shoots Dutch dead, and he plummets off the cliff. Jimmy Stewart gets the gun—and the girl—in the end, and in that order of priority. The last shot shows only the rifle, the gun version of a close-up.

The Winchester occupies the narrative place that a woman might in another film. It's the object of fevered, discombobulating desire, whose possession is fought over (through the use of other, inferior guns—Dutch complains of the Henry, "this rifle takes too long to kill people"). Lola, like the rifle, changes hands a few times in the movie. Actor Shelley Winters marveled at "all these men . . . running around to get their hands on this goddam rifle instead of going after a beautiful blonde like me."[23]

It is worth noting the particular ways in which the movie transformed the actual biography of the actual Winchester 1 in 1,000 so passionately fought over in the movie. Most significantly, in *Winchester '73*, none of the characters will sell the prized Winchester. Dutch takes it to a gun dealer, but he won't sell it for $300 in gold, and it actually changes hands because of a card game; another character won't give it up until he's shot dead. Another finds it on the battlefield and gives it to another. The next gives the rifle freely back to Dutch, who had stolen it from McAdam. The gun might be won, stolen, given, killed for, or found, but it is not bought or sold. The movie traces the movement of the Winchester, but at each moment when it changes hands, removes it from commerce and subtly elevates it as something more mystical than commercial. This is only one cinematic example of a transformation that had been unfolding in different ways, and places, for decades. The ties between the American gun and the industry and commercial contexts that produced it were getting obscured.

The actual Winchester 73 used in the movie was sold repeatedly, which is unsurprising. Most guns were. It was manufactured in New Haven in December 1873. The WRAC shipped it on November 21, 1876, to a hardware store in Jonesboro, Arkansas. There, a man named Grady bought it. Purportedly, he used it two months later, as part of a sheriff's posse, to kill three cattle thieves. Sometime after that, it was traded in 1877 by an Indian to a man named Wilkes, for three bottles of whiskey. Then in 1893, a man who lived in Scranton bought the rifle in a Montana gunshop.[24]

The movie biography of the rifle exempts it from this quotidian, profane world of commerce. Sale would taint the sense that the 1 in 1,000, like a special totem, belongs with only one person: McAdam. His violence in the movie, and his quest, is perhaps psychotic, but it is also purposeful, almost biblical, in its righteous mission against the patricidal bad-seed brother, Dutch, who plays Cain to McAdam's Abel. High Spade disapproves of "hunting a man," and cautions McAdam ominously, if vaguely, that he's "coming to the end of the trail"; but there can be little doubt that the gun is supporting an odyssey of great consequence and a dark but morally legible quest.

Once the actual Winchester 1 in 1,000 was in the hands of its Scranton owner, a man named Hollis, its use continued in a more prosaically realistic pattern. Hollis used the rifle to kill two men who had "gotten fresh" with his wife, what we know today as a variant of intimate or domestic violence. Presumably he had bought the gun on the secondary market as a good guy and became a bad guy when he killed people with it.

In *Winchester '73*, Dutch mocks his brother after he wins the rifle: "That's a lot of gun to have for just shooting rabbits with." At its next sale, in 1909, the actual Winchester was purchased by Frederick Rogers of St. Louis—who used it for squirrel-hunting.

The next stop of the actual gun before Hollywood was with a Nashville minister who collected antique firearms. He willed it to his son, who in turn lent it to Universal Studios for the movie.

The story of this Winchester 1 in 1,000 got more lethal and morally epic in *Winchester '73*'s rewrite.

Just as the starring gun in *Winchester '73* cannot get sold, backlit by a noncommercial mystique, the gun is today treated as such a hallowed or notorious object, depending on the point of view, and keeps company with such portentous arguments about existential political differences and constitutional law, that it is easy to forget that it is a commodity, produced by a business, designed to make money.

Eventually, it all came full circle: movies and television, shaped by the gun genre of the fictionalized real, became factual certification that Americans had "always" loved guns. The gun's fabularized history was now a part of its material value as well. "It seems that the closer we get to the year 2000," a modern gun ad reads, "the more people need the image of the past when . . . good usually won out in the end . . . and a man's word and his honor meant something real and worth fighting for." Admirers were nostalgic for a past that was not only past but had never really happened.[25]

Television and movies also materially influenced, and still influence, the gun market. "'Good Guys' on TV Stir Interest in Frontier Revolver," a 1956 headline read. The Colt six-shooter reappeared that year as a collector's item, and Colt's was "swamped with orders," especially from NRA convention attendees, whom the article depicted as "gun-hungry guys clamoring for sidearms." Sales of Smith & Wesson's Model 29 .44 Magnum (not a user-friendly gun, with its heavy recoil and loud report) soared for five years after Clint Eastwood's first Dirty Harry movies appeared. Bren 10 gun sales increased after the Miami Vice character Sonny Crockett carried one.[26]

In the 1990s, gun industry magazines urged the business to "reap the profits as shooters relive the old west" in "end-of-trail competitions" and cowboy reenactment shootings, trading on the charisma of American gun violence. Guns & Ammo magazine offered its readers a special edition of the Colt's revolver—"as used by John Wayne in his cowboy films"; and Winchester released a Model 94 memorial carbine in honor of John Wayne at the 1981 NRA convention. It had come to this. The movies and fiction had subsumed history, becoming the real event on which the reproductions were based—as if there were no truth left to tell.[27]

IT IS IMPOSSIBLE TO SAY DEFINITIVELY THAT THE WEST THAT WON the gun in popular media and advertisement stimulated sales on the bottom line, but it is a reasonable assumption, and the two were correlated, at the least. Now part of the Olin Corporation, the Winchester line reached a per capita gun production in the 1950s rivaled only by its production in the first decade of the 1900s. In 1950 it added 384,283 guns to the census (1 per 396 Americans), and production stayed close to this—anywhere from a quarter of a million (252,147) in 1959 to a high mark of 431,055 in 1955—for the rest of the decade, before declining in the 1960s. Meanwhile, Colt's produced 150,296 revolvers and pistols in 1950 (1 per 1,775 Americans) and 209,044 in 1960 (1 per 864). Yearly gun production gives us a rate, to borrow epidemiological terms, but not a (cumulative) incidence of gun ownership, since Winchesters and Colts were built for durability. Each year's production added to a preexisting American gun "load."[28]

As the value of the American gun shifted from utility to mystique, guns with the patina of history became valuable collector's objects. An antique gun subculture and market emerged that still flourishes. This market coincided with some of the first serious histories of the American gun, including Charles Sawyer's *Firearms in American History* (1910) and John Dillin's *The Kentucky Rifle* (1924), followed by Robert Gardner's works in the 1930s. "The collecting of antique firearms is becoming a passion with thousands of persons in the United States," reported the *Savannah Morning News* in 1914, "particularly millionaires and other rich men," as well as the dabbler who hung an old gun on the wall of the newfangled space called a den. In 1914 there were around 5,000 serious collectors, compared to perhaps 500 a few decades earlier. Collectors scavenged through small towns for the rare find, the Harpers Ferry flintlock or a "primordial Colt." The value of the antique firearm was tied to the value of the history (or fable) attached to the firearm. "To the zeal of the antiquarian is added a semi-reverence for these pieces of iron and steel that have won states and empires and contributed to the uplifting and happiness of the race," an article on gun collection breathlessly stated.[29]

Pugsley was an avid firearms collector. When he contemplated selling his collection in the early 1930s, he was assailed by a manic antique arms dealer named Theodore Dexter. Dexter described himself as someone who could "create a demand" and then "blackmail" his public—especially his list of 1,200 collectors—into buying by convincing them that they would be reduced to antique firearms "camp followers" otherwise. As for Pugsley's antique Winchesters, they acquired value as they acquired a richer historical patina in the form of wear and tear. Dexter estimated that the "demand for a '66 Winchester in better condition is almost nil, because the men now in the market for Winchester rifles or earlier models are exhibitors, using Winchesters as part of a 'Western' exhibit, and, as you know, in line with popular ideas that an old gun must look old, the $5.00 model '66 Winchesters serve better than the fine ones." The story of the gun imbued it with value more than its condition.[30]

Books benefited from historical legend as well. In early 1949, Winchester executives wanted to commission an official company history. They eventually secured the services of Yale economist Harold Williamson, who authored a meticulous corporate history. The company thought it might appeal to "gun bugs, cranks, collectors, . . . and arms historians, who regularly buy three or five thousand copies" of any gun book—hinting at the proliferation of gun subcultures. But by this time, the legend of the Winchester held more sway than the history of Winchester as it was: a business. Bantam requested "a rewritten version which would in effect be a 'western.'" An editor explained that it "would be much more interested in the gunmen and peace officers that used Winchesters, in famous battles against Indians and rustlers in which Winchester played a part and in general with the more wild and woolly aspects of Winchester history." With a history in hand, the legend was preferred, or the history implored to act more like the legend.[31]

NINETEENTH-CENTURY AMERICA LEFT TO THE TWENTIETH A diffusion of guns. It also left the beginning of a gun mystique that had been forged on a changeling frontier, annealed with a rifle, and machined into a cultural idiom. That mystique may have been incubated in the nineteenth century, but it flourished in the twentieth, when it acquired the obduracy of fact through repetition in the mediums of advertisement, story, television, radio, history, and film. At midcentury, the gun prevailed on the American myth market.

Its legacy is a simple but profound one for twenty-first-century gun culture and a striking contrast to the gun's reality: the legend conjures a country, and a frontier, imagined as more gun-violent than it was, not less, and a world of gun violence between good guys and bad guys. This Manichean conceptualization—of Hickok facing down a villain on a dusty town plaza—has proven to be almost a cultural narcotic. It is a conceptualization that construes gun violence as a story of crime versus the abstract, cool metaphysics of justice, with the latter achieved by a paramilitary citizen-soldier, when it is more often a story of suicidal self-destruction and intimate, angry, intoxicated impulse. According to the Centers for Disease Control and Prevention (CDC), there were 31,672 gun deaths in the United States in 2010, and 33,636 in 2013. The majority in both 2010 and 2013 (61 and 63 percent, respectively) were suicides. Thirty-six percent in 2010 were homicides, and the rest were accidental. Of the homicides, the majority did not occur between strangers, or by criminals. A study of 400 homicide victims from three cities found that in the 83 percent of cases where the perpetrator was identified, he or she was known to the victim in almost all—95 percent—of these cases (although statistics on homicides committed by known or unknown perpetrators is unavoidably and inherently skewed, because it is based on solved homicides—and it is easier to solve a homicide that involves an intimate or known assailant). The majority of women murdered are killed at home by a family member or an intimate partner—a spouse, lover, boyfriend, or intimate acquaintance (64 percent in 2007, according to the Bureau of Justice Statistics: 24 percent by a spouse or ex-spouse, 21 percent by a boyfriend or girlfriend, and 19 percent by "another family member"). More than half of all female "handgun" homicide victims (57 percent) were killed by an intimate acquaintance. Guns were used in 71.5 percent of spousal murders. Although in theory a gun should equalize and protect women against violence, case control studies have found that having a gun in the home increases a woman's risk for homicide and has "no protective effect."[32]

In the real world individuals often refuse to stay put in one static category. A "good guy," noted by his neighbors as a quiet, upstanding citizen, can snap, becoming a monstrous villain with no apparent warning. We watch horrified as the armed, acting out of mental illness, rage, impulse, sadness, or other unknown and perhaps unknowable causes or motivations, harm others or themselves. It is a grotesque transmogrification, consistently replaced in entertainment media with tropes of the good vanquishing a more comprehensible and ever-fixed evil.

And so every summer night, in Cody, Wyoming, the town reenacts an Old West shoot-out for tourists' entertainment. The audience cheers the reenactment of a murder. Comparable reenactments don't occur for bar brawls or domestic homicides. But this is the seduction of the gun mystique, and some of the cultural tension that the West that won the gun repairs. It refurbishes a story of violence abetted by gun diffusion—careless, serendipitous, often intimate—into a story of justice, radical autonomy, and a compensatory sort of equality. It eclipses the majority of gun deaths, caused by suicide, with the minority of gun deaths caused by honor-fueled homicides. It takes "senseless" gun violence and makes it sensible.

Although the mystique obscures the most prominent facets of gun violence, gun politics still hum with the mystique's early intimations, as Oliver Winchester advertised it, and as it was mightily amplified in the 1900s: a good lone gunman, in danger, against adversaries in a bad world, out there in a wild country.

CHAPTER 20

"MERCHANTS OF DEATH"

WINCHESTER'S HYPHENATED CORPORATE MARRIAGE WITH Simmons did not save the company. After a full, bleak accounting in 1924, fifty-seven years after its first Book of Account was opened, the company went into receivership, with Kidder & Peabody holding most of the stock. Throughout the 1920s, the "dead hand of receivership," Edwin Pugsley recollected, "gradually but inexorably strangled" Winchester, and "the great momentum of the company was slowing down." The company was still paying interest on the money borrowed for the war, and it had only managed to sustain, not grow, its sales. Winchester folded in January 1931, too weak to withstand the Depression, and was bought out of receivership by the rival Olin Corporation. After the war, "had the Company been satisfied with its measure of growth," Winchester gun expert Herbert Houze later speculated, the company might have survived intact as the Winchester Repeating Arms Company that Oliver had conceived. But expansion and over-building was the company's and Sarah's shared hubris. The Winchester ammunition line continues, although Olin stopped US production of Winchester guns in 2006. But in 1931, the family business disappeared into new corporate coverture, a ghost in the machine.[1]

The family names on the most familiar American guns outlasted family control of the businesses. The entrepreneurial fever that burned in the first generation cooled by the third. Remington had been bought by Winchester and Hartley in 1888. Neither Samuel Colt's son nor his nephew wanted to follow in his footsteps, so in 1901, Elizabeth Colt sold the enterprise to New York and Boston interests, at $40 per share, and from there it floated on the open market. By 1908, Newport yachtsman Charles Robinson and other investors had taken financial control. The third generation of Wessons took charge at Smith & Wesson in 1920, but the business languished until it received World War II's British orders. At that war's end, a non-Wesson took the helm: the Swedish toilet valve designer Carl Hellstrom.[2]

As for Sarah Winchester, her legend would prove anachronistic in its ghosts but prescient in its conscience. In the 1920s and 1930s, the matter of gun violence and control emerged as a national issue, and in this atmosphere, Sarah's legend grew apace. Some pacifists, early gun-control advocates, and disarmament activists began to perceive the truth in Sarah's madness and the madness in Oliver's ambition. These critics saw that arms industrialists made fortunes selling lethal weapons, and that perhaps they should feel morally encumbered and accountable. The gun's captains of industry now became "merchants of death"; the armaments trade became the "Bloody International." "I appreciate the fact that the manufacturers of arms and ammunition are not standing very high in the estimation of the public generally," Colt's president meekly demurred in the 1930s.[3]

Gun critic H. C. Engelbrecht rebaptized armaments captains of industry as "merchants of death" in his eponymous 1935 book, which condemned the gun capitalist's "unrestricted methods of modern salesmanship" as "thoroughly anti-social." The phrase stuck. Winchester vice-presidents even used it about themselves. As they contemplated their company history, they wanted to make sure the book was neither a "whitewash nor a 'merchants of death' type of book."[4]

Beverley Nichols was the author whose impassioned bestseller by some reviews was most "effective in inculcating pacifism by its heart-to-heart, unpolitical appeal." Before he penned his indictment of the arms industry, which he called "Death, Inc.," in 1933, Nichols was a wry garden writer who applied his wit to flowers. In characteristic style, he likened those "vulgar, obvious" plants, the cyclamens, to "tiresome women who live in flats with electric stoves and indigestion and a Pekingese snoring in the scullery."[5]

This "sob-brother" British journalist was magnitudes more withering (and unintentionally amusing) toward arms manufacturers than he was toward cyclamens. He began his polemic *Cry Havoc!* with a "shocking fact" that had been there for the seeing since the 1850s: "I knew that guns . . . and all that sort of thing were being made by private firms, but I vaguely imagined that they must be under some sort of government control," Nichols confessed. "I certainly did not realize that the entire business was unfettered and competitive. I did not realize that in our midst were these vast corporations, trading in death . . . owing their very existence to DEATH." For the "trafficker in death," the "more men who are killed, disemboweled, blinded . . . , the better he will be pleased."[6]

Nichols visits "Armsville," a composite of commercial arms manufacturers, and bathes its banalities of commerce—not new, only newly-seen—in a fresh, horrific light. Armsville has a chart of its orders on the wall, and Nichols is shocked to see that the company is supplying two governments engaged in hostilities with each other.

As he tours the factory, the garden-writer in him cannot help but notice the aesthetic discordance of the antiaircraft guns, designed to bring men "down to earth in blazing, screaming death": "[They] looked so nice and peaceful, the sort of thing a woman might put in her hall, if she had a big modern house."[7]

Sarah Winchester couldn't have tormented herself with any more phantasmagoric hauntings than Nichols did when he imagined the arms industrialist, who "congratulated himself on having made a couple of guineas, and went in to have a sole and a glass of sherry . . . and somewhere, somehow, some boy shivered [in] a quick, fleeting agony," as the arms manufacturer's gun shot him dead. Or, when toy soldiers transmogrified, "if you have any imagination," into human limbs "twisting and writhing," and paint running red like blood. Nichols's critique of commercial gun manufacturers was woven through his pacifist and antiwar agenda, a forgotten pathway by which the commercial gun business could be challenged. He saw toy soldiers, romantic war poetry, and history—a "long and wearisome monotone on the things which have died or the things which have caused death"—as "Microbes of Mars" that induced boys to war and violence. He warned parents to avoid these influences "if you do not wish . . . your own son's face . . . 'detached from its skull' to go floating down some drain as yet undug" on a future battlefield.[8]

Following the thread of conscience to its macabre end, Sarah might have asked herself the same question that Nichols did: "When am I going to wake from this hideous nightmare? But it is no nightmare. I am not dreaming. . . . The government of . . . every country, allows vast corporations to trade in death." The gun guilt was his guilt, too. "It needs a strong man to face such a [situation] without hanging his head in shame for the human race"—and Nichols hadn't profited a dime off of it.[9]

The anti-gun conscience was seeing farther into the distance, and into the ways that the gun business was, in the term of the day and movement, antisocial. Writing in *Harper's*, journalist John Gunther imagined that the bullet that might kill him in a war would cost only a "fraction of a cent" to make and could sell for three cents more. It seemed so small an amount, and so distant from the battlefields, but Gunther saw the malevolent totality. He reckoned that in a war, shooting 1 million rounds an hour at $30 per thousand bullets, the profits accumulate for the munitions business, which he deemed "one of the strangest in the world." Gunther reckoned that the dollars spent on armaments in 1933—4,276,800,000 of them—taped end to end, would go around the world 172,169 times.[10]

The tension between commerce and the common good had glimmered from the early 1600s onward, often through the lens of racism and conquest, but increasingly through a nonracial lens. In the postwar mood, what Henry Ford said of war was being applied to guns: "Tell me who profits [from it] and I will tell you how to stop it." Noel Baker, author of the *Private Manufacture of Arms*, saw the tension anew. How could we "reconcile the moral values of patriotism . . . with the moral values of the system of the Private Manufacture of arms"? "The two moral standards are in conflict," he concluded, when some citizens are "allowed to make great profits from selling the arms which their less fortunate compatriots will carry into battle." It is a "revolt of conscience against something which most men feel to be completely wrong." An American somewhere profits from the bullet that kills another American elsewhere. A writer for the *Christian Century* deemed arms production in "the hands of private profit seekers" as a species of "insanity," a deranged form of production that induced "horror" in those who knew of it. "The moral load imposed on the private owners of the arms industry in a profit-seeking order is far too heavy for frail humanity to bear." In June 2015, Pope Francis echoed this view. He condemned "people, managers, businessmen who call themselves Christian and they manufacture weapons," pointing the problem of violence and war back on the gun industry.[11]

There are additional bold examples like this of business-focused approaches in the emerging national politics of gun control, what *The Nation* in 1907 called the remedy of "attacking the tree itself," rather than passing local laws that merely plucked "a few leaves from the evil tree." In 1922, the American Bar Association recommended the closure of factories that made civilian firearms and, specifically, a nationwide ban on the manufacture of pistols, using the slogan, "If nobody had a gun nobody would need a gun." The radical idea of nationalizing the gun industry and doing away with a commercial business altogether even haunted the gala Remington centennial celebration in Ilion. Captain Thomas Marshall spoke out in his speech against the "theory that the Government should own and operate [the] arms and munitions plants. . . . When the Remington company says to the Government, 'we are with you to the finish,'" Marshall remarked, "What better could they ask?" Texas passed legislation in May 1907 that imposed a 50 percent tax on earnings from the sale of revolvers. Others worried about the advertisement of revolvers in detective magazines and popular literature. Representative Thomas Rubey, from Missouri, wanted to ban from the mail publications that carried gun advertisements as "one way we could stop this firearms business." In 1924, Congress openly debated a direct form of gun control. John Miller, a representative from Washington state, introduced a bill to ban the shipment of pistols and small firearms through the US Postal Service. The business-crippling rationale behind the legislation was that since the arms industry was so concentrated in Connecticut, a ban on the shipment of guns would effectively bankrupt it. (The Mailing of Firearms Act passed in February 1927, but the gun industry easily circumvented it by using private shipment services.)[12]

This was an ambitious and far from technocratic vision of gun control that asked foundational questions about the limits of capitalism and free markets (Are all commodities interchangeable, to be treated the same?) and about commercial agnosticism while expanding the idea of collective and corporate responsibility. *Harper's* saw arms firms as "extraordinarily . . . intertwined, lac[ing] the whole world in their net." A 1934 *Fortune* article, "Arms and the Men," conjured a dense web, a "huge and subversive force" at work behind the arming of nations, one that included "holding companies and banks entangled in an international embrace," and controlled by "not more than a handful of men whose power, in some ways, reaches above the power of the state itself." The heavy but invisible "moral load" on the gun and armaments maker was almost too horrible to see in its totality—and so, before, had not been seen at all.[13]

How does a "merchant of death" defend himself? He began to go underground, for one thing, initiating a decades-long process of receding from view. The NRA seeks publicity today, but the gun industry loathes it. Gun captains of industry sought public relations asylum in the other commodities they produced—dishwashers, roller skates, and toilet valves. Arms manufacturers had a newfound sense of "shame" about their business, a 1934 *Harper's* piece concluded. At dinner parties they claimed that they sold guns to support national defense, out of patriotism, or that guns were but "one item in a general iron and steel business." Colt's, for one, "made so many other things."[14]

And, understandably, the gun industry deflected attention to other culprits. Colt's company archive includes a fascinating folder of press releases and dispatches from 1927 to 1930 from the Industrial News Bureau, The Manufacturer, that were pertinent to guns and the gun industry. The bureau supported and defended industry writ large, not just the gun industry, but it did address matters relevant to the gun debate.[15]

Essentially, the bureau voiced the gun industrialist's (i.e., the merchant of death's) point of view. The press releases reveal a "pro-gun" voice materializing into modern, twenty-first-century forms, although even the bureau had to concede that, "in comparison with Europe, our American crime situation is nothing short of disgraceful." The releases argued that gun-control legislation would only restrict the honest gun owner and not the "professional gun toter, the dope peddler, the card shark, the drunken driver, and numerous other lawbreakers." The bureau's strategists construed the gun problem as a problem of crime and law enforcement. This seems an obvious point, that guns are problematic when used to commit crimes. But it was an early example among many of an occlusion, or inflection, in gun politics that would only become more pronounced as the twentieth century progressed: America's emerging gun consciousness was attuned, especially in the 1920s, almost exclusively to homicide rather than suicide. Yet even in the early 1900s, suicides—including gun suicides—were on the rise. Homicide rates actually continued to decline nationally, notwithstanding the lurid, alarming, and politically galvanizing islands of urban Prohibition violence that had sparked much of the soul-searching about gun violence in the first place, and that permanently inflected the discussion as a law enforcement problem—a problem of "organized" crime rather than the more disorganized realities of gun violence. According to the theory of a "suicide-to-murder" ratio, suicides tend to increase while homicides decrease as a society becomes better educated and as employment rates improve. Today, the majority (over 60 percent) of gun deaths are suicides, not homicides. Already, suicide was becoming the hidden violence and tragedy in gun politics, regardless of one's "side" in the debate.[16]

In other releases the bureau wondered why the "inanimate pistol, a piece of harmless metal," should be blamed for crime, rather than a "warped" public consciousness that stimulated the criminal element. We shouldn't "attribute criminality to some . . . commodity." The industry sheltered the gun within the ensemble of ordinary, mundane commodities. It blamed inadequate penalties for crime, the glamorization of violence in the talkies, and graft and corruption in local law enforcement (a pervasive problem in the 1920s). "It is not the instruments of crime which we should legislate against, it is the condition which encourages crime," one of the press releases opined. The bureau dismissed gun-control advocates as "would-be saviors" who perceived themselves as morally superior, and "belittled the old-fashioned American citizen." The gun-control advocates "would make [the average citizen] appear ridiculous and out of step with the times." These statements would feel at home in twenty-first-century fundraising letters against gun control.[17]

As the gun mystique was getting more masculinized with the hunter-citizen, the gun-control idea was getting feminized. Redirecting attention from the gun business, the bureau characterized the gun-control conscience as feminine, irrational, and simple-minded— the germ of an enduring caricature, as mothers and wives of slain victims bring gun control to the political forefront today, and then get marginalized as too emotionally distraught to understand the political, practical intricacies of the issue. The bureau denounced the "ultra-sentimentalists" and the "slobbering sentimentalists" who wanted to prohibit pistol ownership. Anti-pistol laws, it said, were "generally framed by the elements that send flowers and dainties to rapists and murderers," and who "sob over degenerates." In this dispatch the bureau envisioned the empathetic feminine personality both as the victim of gun violence at the hands of "homicidal maniacs and degenerates who butcher women," and the sentimentally addled mastermind of gun control. Gun regulation was the product of a mad "mania" by "fanatics" to control others. In August 1930, the bureau concluded that the United States had failed in solving its crime problem because the right people had not yet been called in to deal with it: the best "scientific and executive intelligence" had been applied to industry (a male realm), while the crime problem had been "given over into the hands of emotional reformers" who were "unable to separate fact from fancy," rather than "logical, experienced thinkers." With gun control, the *Army Ordnance* concluded, history had "given way to hysteria."[18]

IN REALITY, THE EARLY ANTI-GUN CONSCIENCE WAS PROMISINGLY focused on the gun *business*, not the gun owner, or the parsing of criminal and non-criminal customers. It got the notion of business accountability, but with a poor example in World War I. The relevant accounting was never "more death, more dividends," but "more guns sold, more dividends." Winchester wasn't "more pleased" with the grotesque carnage of World War I, even at the hands of armaments that it produced, because, among other things, the war was bad business. An *Army Ordnance* editorial ridiculed the "alleged minister of the gospel" who every Sunday "harangues a thinning congregation with absurd stories" of "merchants of death." It asserted that from 1924 to 1934, more than 90 percent of arms production at Colt's was for the domestic, commercial market, rather than for war.[19]

However, although the early military-industrial complex had proven to be bad business for Winchester, and although it fed a powerful critique of gun capitalists as profiteering vultures, in one crucial respect the US military's dependence on private, for-profit arms makers strongly, if backhandedly, supported arguments for an unregulated commercial market. When the Massachusetts legislature deliberated laws to regulate the manufacture and sale of revolvers and pistols, the War Department retorted that it considered the "continuance in existence of our arms and ammunitions manufactures as vital to national defense," and opposed any law that would prohibit gun sales, thus "forcing such manufacturers out of existence." The department opposed the National Crime Commission's recommendation for fingerprinting of gun owners on the logic that it "did not want to impose any requirement which would seriously handicap manufacturers." A bureau press release summarized the matter bluntly: "American manufacturers of guns and munitions cannot remain in business by waiting for wars. There must be continuous sale of their products, as in any other industry." Colt's vice president, Frank Nichols, testified before Congress that if the company were confronted with gun-control legislation, it might have to stop making and selling pistols, as the profit margins were thin and fragile. "I wonder if you gentlemen want that brought about," Nichols continued. "We were very valuable to the Government during the war. We cannot maintain a plant to assist the Government in cause of war, unless we can stay in business." Gun-control opponents in the 1920s recognized the limits of the American gun market: that the US gun business "must have other than local [national] markets for its products" in order to "stay in business and maintain plants suitable for quantity production." To be prepared to defend the public good, gun men needed to be able to make a private profit, and that required an unfettered commercial market.[20]

Noel Baker, Beverley Nichols, and others in the early 1930s perceived the *system* to be the problem. That system, the gun business writ large, included several features that these chapters have tried to describe: the knotted codependency of the public defense and the private arms market; the imperative to find, develop, and cultivate new markets; the gun's treatment as an ordinary commodity for much of its history; and the banal imperatives of business that drove the gun's production, marketing, and sales. This "system" transcended the villainy or ingenuity of any one gun titan or rifle king. "It is the system, not the failings or misdeeds of individuals, which must be examined," Baker argued. The problem lay "not in the wickedness, hypocrisy, greed or self-deception of the manufacturer of arms. It lies deeper than the weakness of individual men. It is inherent in the system, in which we are all alike enmeshed, a system which leads . . . with the inevitability of mathematics, to a conflict between the public interest . . . and the . . . interest of private individuals and corporations." The problem was gun capitalism, not capitalists.[21]

But when *The Private Manufacture of Arms* was reissued, it was retitled *Hawkers of Death*. A book about a wicked system became a book about a wicked gun capitalist. Likewise, in 1934, Hollywood took Nichols's concept and turned it into *The President Vanishes*, in which diabolical arms manufacturers kidnap the president so they can start a profitable war. In 1938, the first plot of the first superhero cartoon—*Superman*—further adapted Nichols, via *The President Vanishes*. There may be no topic about which we're more inclined to think in cartoon than guns. The Merchant of Death was the gun-control version of the Gunslinger—a fable that occluded the problem of the web in which all of us were implicated, as Noel Baker (and Sarah, by legend) had perceived.

A similar conversion happened in the 1930s, when an otherwise obscure episode from the Civil War was revived as legend: the Hall Carbine Affair. In 1861, with the country in dire need of guns, Chief of Ordnance James Ripley had blundered. He had sold 5,000 Hall arms, made in the 1840s by Simeon North, to arms broker Arthur Eastman. Many of these Hall guns were still in their original boxes, and serviceable, so Ripley perhaps shouldn't have sold them in the first place, but the army had deemed the model obsolete. Eastman tried in vain to resell the guns, until the Union forces realized that the conflict would not end quickly. The ensuing frantic effort to acquire guns, recall, sent Marcellus Hartley on a secret mission to Europe, and substantially inflated the market for Eastman's guns. Simon Stevens, a speculator, agreed to pay Eastman $12.50 apiece for the Hall guns; he borrowed $20,000 from a young banker named J. Pierpont Morgan, who had just started in business for himself, to make the initial payment to Eastman. Morgan took the guns as collateral, Stevens paid him back, and Morgan had no further involvement. Stevens, meanwhile, took the guns that one branch of government, through Ripley, had sold to Eastman for $3.50 each, and resold them to another branch of government, through officer John Fremont, in command of the West, for $22 each.

The Hall Carbine Affair would have remained a wry but obscure footnote of government ineptitude if not for the 1936 publication of an updated edition of Gustavus Myers's *The History of Great American Fortunes*. Myers argued that the Hall carbines had been "condemned" by the government because "they would shoot off the thumbs of the very soldiers using them." He vilified Morgan, who had played an incidental role in the story: Could the Morgan of later years, he wrote, "be the same who started out by successfully palming off . . . five thousand of [the government's] own condemned rifles at extortionate prices? Was it possible that the man who profited from arming the nation's armies with self-slaughtering guns could be the same Morgan? . . . Behold him in the budding of his career." From Myers's opening contribution, the myth *qua* history of the Hall Carbine Affair grew. Publications ranging from the *New Republic* to the *Communist Daily Worker* and the *Saturday Review of Literature* (calling it a "now familiar story"), as well as John Dos Passos's *1919* and Carl Sandburg's *Abraham Lincoln: The War Years*, wrote that Morgan had swindled the United States into repurchasing guns that maimed, killed, and shot off soldiers' thumbs.

R. Gordon Wasson, an author and former vice president of J. P. Morgan, construed the Hall Carbine Affair—and Morgan's apocryphal role in it—as a stock tale on the "morals of capitalism." But the fable satisfied, most likely, because it wasn't actually about the morals of capitalism. It was about the morals of a (gun) capitalist. There is a cultural *desideratum* to have a gun villain—a solitary, lone gun villain—just as there is a cultural *desideratum* to have a gun hero—a solitary, lone gun hero. But the "morals of capitalism" that needed to be told about guns concerned the dizzying "system" that Noel Baker had analyzed, and, by legend, that Sarah had intuited through her own tributaries of guilt, spiritualism, and ghosts.[22]

Baker captured the unexceptionalism at the heart of the gun problem, the extent to which it emerged because guns were interchangeable with other commodities. "Manufacturers of arms," he wrote, "inevitably come to think of their business as similar to other businesses, and this colors all their thinking." H. C. Engelbrecht pondered the arms manufacturer's conscience in similar terms. "He does not see himself as a villain," he wrote: "According to his lights he is simply a business man who sells his wares in accordance with prevailing business practices. The uses to which his products are put and the results of his traffic are apparently no concern of his. . . . Thus there are many naive statements of arms makers which show their complete indifference about anything related to their industry, save its financial success." What Engelbrecht delivered as accusation—that the gun was "just a business" like any other—gun entrepreneurs summoned as exculpation. One of the merchants of death, testifying in 1936 before the Nye Committee, which was investigating the munitions industry and war profiteering, said that armaments were a "practical matter . . . like any other business. It is not different than any other business, sir." This statement was, in short, both true, *and* the problem.[23]

But it also suggested an opportunity: Just as gun owners were becoming more like the "gun cranks," ever more impassioned and emotionally invested in guns, the gun business itself continued along in its disinterested and dispassionate way, looking at the gun as an unexceptional commodity, as it always had, and tending to the bottom line. Yet it was the gun owner, with more political, impassioned, and fervently emotional ideas of the gun, who would become the focus of gun politics and efforts to address gun violence—rather than the rational, bottom-line-driven gun business. Perhaps focusing on the gun industry, and the industrialists who saw it as a business "like any other business," would suggest new solutions to the problems that worried the public and had sparked legislative attention.

Differences between gun owners and gunmakers were evident in the first serious federal debate of regulation, during which gun politics began to assume a familiar, modern form. The early 1930s seemed propitious for gun control. President Franklin D. Roosevelt's attorney general enthusiastically supported gun regulation, and the New Deal had deepened faith in an active federal government that could solve problems. The Depression stimulated a view of the diffuse "social environment" as a culprit in social ills.

Most importantly, gun violence was more visible, and frequent. Researcher H. C. Brearly, who published the first study of homicide in America in 1932, found the American homicide rate in general to be forty-seven times higher than the Swiss rate, ten times higher than the Japanese rate, and seventeen times the English rate. European bellicosity and imperial ambition had kept American gun industrialists in business in the 1800s, but now Europe was enjoying civilian life with comparatively low gun violence. In the United States, the gangster, bootlegging urban violence of the 1920s had raised both gun consciousness and the rate of gun violence. There were 10,050 homicides in the United States in 1928, compared to 520 in France and 284 in Great Britain (France had about one-third of the US population; Great Britain's population was slightly larger than France's, but still less than two-fifths of the population of the United States). The most dramatic change in the data is that, notwithstanding the associations of gun violence with the nineteenth-century West, guns were responsible for the large majority of homicides (71 percent) taking place in the United States by the mid-1920s. In Philadelphia, one researcher found that 64 percent of the homicides from a sample from the years 1920, 1926, and 1932 were committed by gun, in comparison to 25 percent for all of the nineteenth century.[24]

The guns that armed the violence of the 1920s are not actually difficult to trace. They are sometimes identified as machine guns, but the gangster weapon of choice was a Thompson submachine gun, or Tommy Gun. Unlike a machine gun, which was strictly for military purposes and ungainly, weighing from sixty-five to ninety pounds, the submachine gun automatic could fit under a coat, and it had a drum feed that could hold as many as five hundred cartridges (in many respects, it was the distant progeny of Winchester's semiautomatic repeater design). Only one company manufactured this gun: in 1921, Colt's produced 15,000 of them for the Auto Ordnance Company. Colt's vice president, Frank Nichols, explained before Congress that the weapon was "designed for purely a military weapon." "Unfortunately," Nichols confessed, "I think we can state correctly, [Auto Ordnance] was a bit careless in their methods of merchandising [the gun]" once foreign government contracts failed to materialize. The Tommy Gun "got into the hands of dealers, and some of the dealers were not entirely responsible." Nichols asserted confidently that most of those 15,000 guns, either bought or stolen by racketeers, were still in use thirteen years later. No laws restricted their sale or distribution, and for Auto Ordnance, as assistant attorney general Joseph Keenan observed, it was a "pure commercial transaction." They owned a patent on the Thompson, and "sold them to . . . anybody that wanted them. I think there is no mystery about that."[25]

The riddled corpses wrought by these 15,000 guns galvanized national interest in gun control. The National Firearms Act of 1934 is considered the first serious effort at federal gun control, but despite momentum, the act landed meekly into law, defanged during the legislative process. Scholars of this legislation find it more notable for the ways in which it consolidated opposition to firearms legislation than for its impact on firearms themselves.[26]

In the Firearms Act hearings before Congress, NRA representatives agreed with Colt's and other gun manufacturers that they would support any legislation that confined itself to submachine guns and sawed-off shotguns. The NRA voice of the early 1930s was less categorical than it is today, as the organization was "absolutely favorable to reasonable legislation" that targeted submachine guns. Karl Frederick, the NRA president and an Olympian marksman, testified that if three words—"pistols and revolvers"—were removed, the NRA would support the act wholeheartedly. But the NRA was also developing what would become a familiar rationale against gun regulation, delivered through what would become familiar tactics. The group's lobbying was not robustly developed in the early 1930s: Frederick had only been paid his expenses by the NRA for the past two years, and before then he had worked entirely as a volunteer. But the association was developing a direct-mail member mobilization campaign, which irritated congressional committee members, who felt "bombarded" by telegrams, and evidently found this approach novel and strange enough to merit comment and complaint. The NRA sent letters from its headquarters at the Barr Building in Washington, DC, to NRA members in each state, advising them of the hearings and asking them to write in opposition to the bill, but also warning that it would be "harder to kill" than earlier legislation. Representative John McCormack of Massachusetts asked Milton Reckord, NRA executive vice president, if he had advised NRA members about the committee's recommendations, and he replied, "No, except that the legislation is bad." "And they blindly followed it?" McCormack asked. "I would not say blindly," Reckord replied.[27]

The letter argued that the legislation was the leading edge of regulation of sportsmen and all gun owners. It surmised that once the attorney general had this law, directed against pistols and machine guns, he could go to the next Congress and argue for an amendment to include "any firearm," and that "few Congressmen will have time to notice it and within a year . . . every rifle and shotgun owner in the country will find himself paying a special tax and having himself fingerprinted and photographed for the Federal rogues gallery every time he buys or sells a gun of any description." One of the most interesting aspects of this appeal is how the rifle and ordinary shotguns—although explicitly exempt from the proposed legislation—became almost an alibi for the submachine gun, and the hunter-citizen with his Winchester an alibi for the gangster. In other words, the NRA took an all-for-one stance that construed regulation of *any* gun as the start of regulation of *all* guns.[28]

The Industrial News Bureau had for some time been deploying the same strategy—innocence by association—to combat the "anti-firearms frenzy." "The logical outcome of any anti-pistol law," it argued, must be the "prohibition of all fire-arms. It is possible, within a few minutes, to convert any rifle or shotgun into a 'pistol,' such that eventually, all fire-arms" would have to be prohibited. The "free, hunt-loving, self-respecting American"—in short, the "average American," Theodore Roosevelt's hunter-citizen—would pay the price. The bureau warned that the millions of Americans who had "failed to see the writing on the wall" with pistols should consider the question, "Will the rifle and shotgun be next?" The NRA's *American Rifleman* had railed in a December 1924 editorial against the "human conduct governors" who wanted to eliminate war and "deprive people of all fire-arms." The article conceived of all guns as one bundle of sticks—the bundle stronger together than any one stick. "Wisdom dictates the breaking of one stick at a time," the writer said. "Suppose . . . they merely take up pistols, the weakest stick in the bundle? The rifleman is not much interested. It is not his funeral. . . . But hold on, fellows, your stick is the next in the bundle," and the rifle would likely be "the last firearm to go." And the gun industry was only being harassed, the editorial surmised, because "there were too many big sticks in the tobacco bundle" to make cigarettes an enticing target. The president of the

American Game Association reported that the 6 million sportsmen in the United States were "quite perturbed" by legislation that implicated pistols and that might, someday, encompass all guns. The innocence-by-association strategy homogenized eclectic American arms into a single political object, The Gun, with one political fate.[29]

Gun owners who had nothing to do with Al Capone or submachine guns—members of sportsmen's and wildlife organizations, and rifle, pistol, and revolver clubs—put up the strongest resistance. The Winchester sporting rifle customer, Roosevelt's hunter-citizen, although not the target of the legislation, was key to its attenuation.

Significantly, the grassroots appeal for gun regulation and the NRA's response reveal a gender gap in gun politics, or a more deeply gendered view of guns as an explicitly male totem, that had been evident in some gun advertisement since the early 1900s. In explaining the legislation, Assistant Attorney General Joseph Keenan commented that although the committee had not "attempted to generate any propaganda" for gun regulation, it had received "literally thousands of letters from women's organizations and other public-spirited organizations" beseeching that something be done about the "firearms evil." In a sense, these were Sarah Winchester's people, women activists for whom Sarah's ghost story of the American gun would have resonated just as keenly as the cowboy western to the gun enthusiast. Members of the committee took umbrage that the NRA had bombarded them with telegrams opposing the legislation—but Reckord countered adamantly that while Keenan welcomed telegrams from "women's organizations," he "seemed to feel that the receipt . . . of communications from members of men's organizations . . . constituted propaganda." The NRA felt that "it is quite as proper for members of men's organizations to . . . oppose antifirearms legislation of this character as it is for women's organizations to propose such legislation."[30]

As for the merchant of death, it is not clear that the industry shared the NRA's germinal tactics or preoccupations. Materially, the two entities were distinct—Frederick testified that he had never in any way had a commercial interest in gun manufacturing—and the gunmaker likewise spoke for himself, with dispassion. Nichols described himself as a "plain, ordinary business man, and sometimes I think not a very good one." He saw no reason whatsoever that the submachine gun should be manufactured or sold to civilians. As for pistols and revolvers, which were also included in the act, Nichols warned that dealers could not afford to pay the proposed tax, and he doubted whether "under this measure we would be justified in continuing this small arms business." A committee member asked, somewhat incredulously, if the tax and the inconvenience of registration would actually "do away with the demand for a legitimate sale of your goods?" Nichols replied that it would. Nichols was conveying to Congress a lesson that every gun industrialist had learned in every decade: gun markets are fragile, gun demand not always reliable, and profit margins thin, such that a tax and a registration inconvenience, as Nichols argued, would kill their small arms business—and, in turn, their ability to make arms for public defense in times of war. To Keenan, the fact that Colt's and other companies were not making money in the manufacture of small firearms to individuals—indeed, were losing money—meant that legislation would not be destroying "the profits of legitimate industry," because there were no profits to *be* destroyed.[31]

Whatever the case, Keenan drew a sharp distinction between the "opposition to rules and regulations" that came from "those whom we term hobbyists," represented by the NRA, and the gun business, which had "shown a splendid spirit of cooperation." "I cannot overemphasize that," Keenan said, contrary to the impression that the gun industry had selfishly opposed regulations or taxes on the production of certain guns that would effectively "take the profit" out of that line. Rather, their attitude had been "extremely decent and fair." For example, Auto Ordnance had entered into a gentlemen's agreement with the Department of Justice not to sell any of the Tommy Guns they still had without Justice approval. The attorney general commended the gunmaker for its cooperativeness and condemned the "hobbyist" for obstreperousness.[32]

A consequential and profound irony of modern gun politics, germinal in 1934, is that it tends to focus attention and policy on the most fervent, emotionally invested, and politically adamant group—the gun owners—rather than on the most rationalized, bottom-line, agnostic, dispassionate facet of the gun culture—the manufacturers and businesspeople who make the guns. The fact that guns were a business like any other quickened a sense of moral outrage—but it also offered a path not taken to the emerging problem of gun violence.

Just as the 1934 act crystallized opposition to gun control, it suggested new ways that the competitive, secretive, and fractious gun industry might consolidate politically. Immediately after the House hearings, fifteen small-arms manufacturers organized into the Sporting Arms and Ammunition Manufacturers Association, along with 70,000 gun dealers. Roughly the same group of gun manufacturers in 1919 had contemplated and rejected the idea of an association. The American Manufacturers of Small Arms and Ammunition Society first convened in New York on May 17, 1918. It had thirteen members, restricted to companies with war contracts, including, among others, Winchester, Remington, Peters Cartridge Company, New England Westinghouse, Savage Arms Company, Colt's, and DuPont de Nemours and Company. The society's members cooperated in wartime production for national interests in order to ensure that they were standardizing designs across their contracts: for example, so that the over 5 billion cartridges produced for the war could work interchangeably with a variety of firearms.[33]

On February 21, 1919, the society met at the Engineer's Club in New York. With the war over, it was "now considering the advisability of continuing for commercial purposes," the minutes recorded. "Whether we continue commercially or not depends on whether companies can see sufficient [matters] to be done for mutual benefit." In 1919, Winchester and others apparently did not see enough "mutual benefit" in a commercial association. In 1934, they did, and this was part of the gun's political invention, too.[34]

Significant federal firearms regulation would wait until the late 1960s, but much of the gun's political template had been cut by this phase of the American gun business in the 1930s: the provisional unification of the gun industry as one "bundle"; the emphasis on guns-as-a-crime problem and the occlusion of gun suicide by homicide; the gun's place as a commodity with emotional value; the valorization of the average citizen as a hunter and gun owner; the invalidation of the gun-control voice as sentimental and feminine; the regulatory emphasis on the gun owner rather than on the maker; and the demonization of the gun capitalist, rather than the complex web of the gun economy. The gun business *as* a business, its agnostic, bottom-line soul, and its complex interdependency with national defense were recognized and highlighted, but then obscured in cartoonish vilification.[35]

––––––––––

FOR THE LATTER-DAY GUN SALESMEN, THOMAS ADDIS AND OLIVER Winchester's successors, the business continued. The Nye hearings featured letters from Remington dealer Frank Jonas. "The unsettled conditions in South America has [*sic*] been a great thing for me, as I sold a large order for bombs to Brazil and also a fair cartridge order," he wrote. "I also sold very large bomb orders for Colombia, Peru, Ecuador, Bolivia, and now have made up all my losses, and I am back on my feet. It is an ill wind that does not blow someone some good."[36]

In another letter, Jonas stated a feeling that had tormented Sarah and all but eluded the Winchester men—and their historical moments: "We certainly are in a hell of a business." He continued, "A fellow has to wish for trouble so as to make a living, the only consolation being, however, if we don't get the business, someone else will."

But, Jonas concluded, "it would be a terrible state of affairs, if my conscience started to bother me now."[37]

EPILOGUE

"I T OUGHT TO OBSESS US." PRESIDENT BARACK OBAMA MADE THIS
comment about gun violence on September 22, 2013, as he memorialized another mass shooting—this one at the Navy Yard in Washington, DC. There is a tragic inevitability of timeliness when one
writes a book about guns. No matter when it is completed, another
tragedy is likely to bring guns fleetingly to the forefront of attention.
Obama proceeded to call for more federal legislation. By now, this is a
script. It's shocking on its face that political reactions to mass shootings can become cliché, but this is where we find ourselves: an initial
national outpouring of sadness and shock, fueled by stories of the victims, is met with new initiatives, sometimes by grieving family members, to pass federal gun-control legislation, which is momentarily
embraced, only to die in the political process as a casualty of gun-
control opponents as well as political inertia and lackluster interest
from many who initially embraced the proposed legislation. I began
this project after the Sandy Hook Elementary School mass shooting on
December 14, 2012, that killed twenty-six people, all but six of them
children. I finished a draft right after the Navy Yard mass shooting. In
between, no meaningful gun legislation passed, and the issue is mired
in stale tactics, rhetoric, and entrenched, deeply hostile positions.[1]

In this book I have told the history of an iconic American gun as a
history of business and commerce. Today, it would be valuable to shift

attention from the gun owner to the gunmaker, and from gun regulation to corporate accountability. Lawyer and activist Tom Diaz takes this approach, though few others do. Diaz has pointed out that in the old "recycled" political arguments that we hear repeatedly, few people notice the gun industry itself: "[In] finely drawn Constitutional arguments about individual 'rights' and 'responsibilities,' and solemn invocations of cultural symbols from the . . . frontier, any sense of firearms as a profit-making business gets lost. The ultimate fact is that the gun industry is simply a business, and nothing more."[2]

Although still difficult, it is easier to fight a business than a myth. This book is a cultural history of the gun, but it indirectly suggests ways to unthaw the currently frozen field of gun politics with business-focused approaches. A "gun culture" is not synonymous with gun violence, but violence—whether suicide or homicide—is the tragedy that animates gun-control politics. If every American had a gun, but we had almost no civilian gun violence—in other words, if we were more like Switzerland—then we might have a gun culture, but not a gun problem.

The two threads of the Winchester story, Sarah's and Oliver's, suggest new insights about the gun culture and politics. The historical saga of the Winchester corporation points us toward understanding the gun culture as an artifact of ambition, the agonistic, bottom-line legacy of businesses acting like businesses; Sarah's ghost story points us toward imagining guns as a matter of conscience. The gun debate has been mired for so long in rights talk—about what gun owners have a *right* to do and what gun-control advocates have a *right* to force them to do—that it has been forgotten as a business, and also as a matter of conscience. By my definition, shifting from the terrain of rights to conscience and corporate accountability would mean a few specific things: it would mean doing things voluntarily rather than because they are mandated; doing more than is legally required or necessary; doing things for a larger good; and perceiving ways that we are immediately or distantly implicated in and accountable for the problem of gun violence.

A business-focused approach suggests remedies that have nothing to do with "taking guns away" from citizens, federal gun-control legislation, or the Second Amendment. It would shift attention from gun owners to gunmakers, very much as this narrative of the gun's history has attempted to do. Gun corporations, like other corporations, operate by a rational set of concerns that can be mobilized as part, but not all, of the solution to gun violence. They fear liability, they avoid visibility, and despite the "merchant of death" label, they have concerns for public reputation. They also respond to the stark realities of the bottom line. Where the NRA's advocacy for gun owners is famously impassioned, the gun business's concerns are equally dispassionate.

Perhaps the most tantalizing approach would be to incentivize the gun industry to further develop "smart gun" or personalized gun technology, so that a gun would only work in the hands of its authorized user. The idea is loathed, curiously, not only by gun-control foes but also by advocates, although public health researchers argue that it would meaningfully reduce gun deaths. Given how many crimes are committed with guns secured through straw purchasers or secondhand, or through borrowing or theft, or turned and used against their owners, or the rarer tragedy of accidental shootings, this is a promising avenue. The gun industry could develop innovative technology that pushes the design envelope in the direction of greater safety, rather than lethality and power, which Diaz sees as the decades-long trend thus far.[3]

A second business-focused recommendation would be to restore to guns the same civil liability and consumer regulations and protections that apply to almost every other commodity. Imagine that you are a business that mass-produces one of the very few products in the country that is inherently and exclusively designed to be dangerous and lethal, but that you have enjoyed federal protection against civil lawsuits since 2005, exemption from Consumer Protection Safety Commission (CPSC) oversight since 1972, and freedom from any federal agency to oversee your product's design or safety, and that data collection or research that might support legislation damaging to your product is prohibited from federal funding, under law. This is, in brief, the status of the US gun industry. The 2005 Protection of Lawful Commerce in Arms Act prohibits civil liability actions against gun manufacturers, distributors, or dealers for damages caused by their products. As for consumer regulation and protections, guns and ammunition were explicitly exempted from the CPSC, since they fell under the purview of the Bureau of Alcohol, Tobacco, Firearms and Explosives (ATF)—but the ATF does not have quality control authority over the gun industry's product as a product, or anything akin to the CPSC's function. Instead, it is a law enforcement body that focuses on illegal trafficking, use, or sale of guns, and not on design, safety, or features inherent to the gun as a consumer product. This means that a toy gun is subjected to more consumer safeguards as a product than a real gun. Ironically, the gun's very lethality—the fact that it is *designed* to maim, threaten, and kill—makes it an awkward commodity for the CPSC to handle. As for gun research, former Arkansas representative Jay Dickey voiced remorse in October 2015 for his amendment to the 1996 Omnibus Consolidated Appropriations Bill for fiscal year 1997 that prohibited funding from the Centers for Disease Control and Prevention to support research on gun violence that could be construed as supporting or advocating gun control.[4]

The 2005 legislation, or the desire for it, powerfully, if backhandedly, speaks to the effectiveness of tackling gun violence from the business side rather than the side of ownership, and trying to hold corporations, including dealers, responsible and accountable for some of the damages of their products in communities. While opponents of lawsuits argue that they will vaguely, globally, and simplistically hold gun companies responsible for gun harm in general, there are more circumscribed legal actions and strategies that have proven galvanizing and effective in the past. A landmark 1997 Florida case, for example, upheld liability against a K-Mart gun dealer who sold a gun to a man so drunk that he couldn't fill out the required forms. He left the store, went to a bar, and shot his ex-girlfriend, leaving her a quadriplegic. Robert Haas, a Smith & Wesson executive who had pangs of conscience after retirement, testified in 1999 that none of the manufacturers had ever taken steps to screen or supervise wholesalers or retailers, and had "made no effort" to see that their products were sold "properly." In 1999, Wendell Gauthier, a New Orleans lawyer who was dispirited by the ineffectiveness of gun-control politics, started a lawsuit against sixteen gunmakers for failure to install safety devices and take adequate measures to keep guns from criminals. The suit quickly spread to thirty-three other cities. Gunmakers broke ranks, as competitive businesses are wont to do. This action hit them where it mattered. Colt's contemplated abandoning commercial guns to avoid liability; Smith & Wesson wanted to settle, and suffered an NRA boycott because of it.[5]

Under pressure from the 1999 litigation and threat of publicity, Smith & Wesson also drafted its own code of ethics for dealers. The company CEO made it clear that he was attempting to put his 3,500 dealers on notice that they could no longer "turn a blind eye to 'straw purchases,'" and that they could "cut off any dealer accused of questionable business practices," said writer Peter Harry Brown in his account of the lawsuit. This was the first time, from Winchester's day forward, that a gun industrialist had tried to exert control over distribution and sales for the sake of public safety rather than profit. (Smith & Wesson had been a pioneer in gun safety in 1884 as well. The company designed a "safety first" gun, with a strong trigger and a safety feature on the hammer, apparently after D. B. Wesson heard of a child who had been injured by the company's revolver. It manufactured over 91,000 of the model from 1888 to 1902.) For their code of ethics, Smith & Wesson borrowed its approach from automobile manufacturers with their dealers. As part of a proposed settlement, Smith & Wesson's code for their distributors and dealers stipulated that they had to carry enough liability insurance to pay for damages, injuries, and deaths of any person as a result of an illegal sale; bar anyone under eighteen from browsing in gun shops; prohibit the sale of semiautomatic assault weapons; transfer firearms only to people who had taken safety courses; and adhere strictly to the multiple sales prohibitions. In addition, its authorized dealers would be dropped if they sold a disproportionate number of guns used in crime.[6]

Some critics thought the code of ethics lame, if for no other reason than that it came from a gunmaker, but a lawyer who worked on the suit disagreed, pointing out that "Smith & Wesson . . . made unprecedented commitments which far exceed the mandates of federal law and current practices of the gun industry." More likely, the code of ethics was testimony to the effectiveness of setting aside stale policy arguments about federal gun-control regulation and the character of gun owners, and instead thinking about gunmakers.[7]

Repeal of the 2005 legislation would restore the potential for civil liability against the gun industry. Indeed, the 2005 legislation, and the gun industry's exemption from consumer regulation, completes and legislatively formalizes the informal, gradual obfuscation of the gun business *as* a business that this book has traced historically.

Likewise, barriers to the funding of sound and reliable research and data collection to better understand gun violence, or how the gun business works at the most basic levels, should be removed. Such data would point toward more effective policies and approaches. For example, while it is assumed that only federal-level regulations can make a difference in gun violence, this is not entirely true when it comes to the regulation of the gun business and dealers, as opposed to gun customers. Research in 2009 by Douglas Wiebe considered the number of federal firearms licensees (FFLs), stores and individuals licensed to sell firearms, in specific communities related to the gun homicide rate. He found that the data varied a great deal by type of community. In major cities, gun rates were higher where more FFLs were present, but there was no such association in small towns, and in suburbs and smaller cities, gun homicide rates were lower where FFLs were more prevalent. In those specific kinds of communities where a correlation does exist between gun violence and FFL density, one business-focused recommendation would be to use local zoning laws and state-level licensing and inspection legislation to strategically and granularly target problem gun dealers, but currently very few states have or use such simple statutory provisions. Nor do we have solid research on basic facets of gun markets.[8]

This points toward another recommendation for gun politics, which is to consider consumer activism, inclusive of gun dealers. This would also be an approach consistent with the gun's native habitat in business, but the gun consumer, *as a consumer* and a customer, has gotten buried under rhetorical emphasis on gun "owners." Consumers can advocate for workable regulatory frameworks of the gun as a consumer good, like those that govern other dangerous products, from insecticides to automobiles to drugs and pharmaceuticals. If honest gun consumers themselves had data on a dealer or company's record on safety and attentiveness to gun violence, much as a car buyer can find voluminous safety data on different models, then some of those customers might begin to make consumer choices about firearms based at least partly on a gun business's record on safe, responsible, and beneficial practices. This strategy, too, enlists the power of conscience over mandate. Other strategies might include boycotts, or "countermarketing" among gun retailers, a technique whereby businesses repel unwanted demand, and customers, through policies or advertisements. For example, some gun stores today have "members-only" policies, or insist on customer registration, to ward off straw purchasers or a criminal clientele. Or it might mean campaigns that speak to a gun business's or dealer's not insubstantial concern for reputation, and its willingness to do more voluntarily than is required, as a matter of conscience rather than legal compulsion. Walmart, for example, the largest gun seller in the United States, follows a voluntary ten-point code for responsible sales practices. Similarly, after mass shootings in New Orleans and Virginia in the summer of 2015, it voluntarily decided to halt all sales of assault rifles and semiautomatic shotguns, calling the decision a "business," not a "political," one.[9]

At the local level, some dealers have also voluntarily changed their practices to support public safety and the common good, with remarkably swift and positive results. In response to negative publicity—a kind of consumer activism—a Milwaukee gun dealer changed his sales practices when his store was found to be the source for a large number of guns used in crimes. His changes alone contributed to an almost immediate 44 percent reduction in "new crime guns" citywide.[10]

Regulations of gun dealers that focus on sales volume, rather than exclusively on the background, intent, or character of the individual customer, have proven effective. A law in Virginia limiting handgun purchases to one in a thirty-day period helped lead to a dramatic decline in the state's contribution to the crime gun market, as it clogged the pipeline of guns from the South to the Northeast. Dealers had to file multiple-sale reports as well. If this sort of regulation of gun dealers existed at the federal level it might be effective against straw purchasers.[11]

Incidentally, the focus on legislative initiatives directed at gun owners also quickens consumer desire for guns as commodities whose value resides partly in their political mystique today. This was a major shift in the gun's biography, as this book has shown, in the 1900s. In 2013, new gun-control legislation spurred an unprecedented "run on guns." Through August 31 alone that year, Maryland received 85,141, gun purchase applications. The state had received only 70,099 for the entire year of 2012. In these moments, gun-control politics ironically resuscitate a business that has been weakening by commercial forces for decades, driven by demographic changes, waning interest in hunting, and changes in household composition. It is not clear what to do about this unintended effect, but it should at least be understood that the gun as a commodity, today, carries intangible political value, much as an environmentalist might shop organic to express a political affinity. The "need" for guns, as with most other commodities in twenty-first-century culture, has less to do with why customers purchase them than in the past—especially since gun sales have now shifted from self-defense to combat firearms, and to fewer individuals buying more guns—and yet proponents of gun control wonder why a gun owner would "need" more than one.[12]

But there is a final and more nebulous, although vital, recommendation that emerges from the Winchester story. It is to recognize that gun violence and mass shootings are not really technocratic problems, to be most effectively solved through the correspondingly technocratic remedies of legislative campaigns that often fail, and that, in any event, tackle small facets of the problem. This long view of accountability is a prerequisite not only for gun violence but for other twenty-first-century problems. Gary Slotkin's "Cure Violence" project in Chicago, for example, saw tremendous results not by focusing on gun-control legislation, but by treating gun violence like a community epidemic. A Baltimore community leader who organized a "My Corner, My Street" initiative to combat gun violence explained, "We are all stakeholders. It is our problem, whether it directly affects you or not." This is not the easiest or most straightforward path out of a gun-violent culture, but it is probably the most meaningful and lasting one.[13]

When he undertook a sting operation against illegal gun purchases in 1998, an attorney warned Chicago mayor Richard M. Daley that he would never find records that "start with the factory assembly line, and end with the victim's aorta." But this is an accurate, if obscured, chain of causation—an invisible hand that must be made visible. If legend holds, it is a chain that Sarah Winchester understood. And while some swear, as others do about tales of the gunslinger, that Sarah's ghost story is the gospel truth, and others claim it is pure malarkey, it is, apparently, the story that we most want her house to tell us.[14]

Acknowledgments

SINCE THIS BOOK TOOK FORM IN PHASES OVER SEVERAL YEARS, I have accumulated more debts large and small along the way than can be recorded here.

I have received help from many archives over the years, but I would like to single out for thanks Mary Robinson, Karen Preis, and Sean Campbell at the McCracken Research Library of the Buffalo Bill Center of the West in Cody, Wyoming, where I spent pleasant weeks; Mike Disotelle at the Ilion Free Public Library Historical Room in New York, for going above and beyond to pull material; and the many librarians at Johns Hopkins University who were so helpful to their local authorial interloper. Thanks also to Richard Rattenbury at the National Cowboy & Western Heritage Museum in Oklahoma City and to Roy Marcot for archival and photo help.

I received very early and insightful readings and editorial help on this project from Suzannah Lessard, from Richard Todd, and from readers in the vibrant creative nonfiction writing community at Goucher College's creative nonfiction program. Many thanks to John Faragher and Richard Slotkin for their useful and encouraging readings.

My superb agent, Susan Rabiner, has exceeded her job title once again. She has been agent as well as friend, adviser, soothsayer, and all-around genius for getting the story out, and told, as she knows that it can be.

The editors and staff at Basic Books restore my faith that serious and readable nonfiction is still a possibility. I am especially grateful that my editor, Lara Heimert, understood the essence of this project early on and has supported it so enthusiastically. Thanks to Roger Labrie for such a useful and attentive edit, to Kathy Streckfus for equally vigilant copy editing, and to Leah Stecher and Melissa Raymond for moving the ball down the road to production.

I am fortunate to have dear friends who have been co-thinkers, readers, companions, and allies, through this project and other projects of life. I could not hope for a more brilliant, insightful, and delightful posse. In particular, thanks to Shannon Avery, Elizabeth Federman, Haleh Bakhash, Debby Applegate, Christina Klein, Elizabeth McAlister, Kathy Newman, Peter Agree, and Barbara Benham. I'd also like to thank my home-base friends, including Sarah Millspaugh, Lisa Marchetti, Susan Singer, and Jen Parker, for their part in keeping me connected, entertained, and festive through the long and often solitary process of research and writing. Kerri and Taylor Classen helped me get shooting straight, literally, and I am grateful for their efforts.

This book reached completion at a difficult time for my family, and my gratitude goes to my parents Joan and Lloyd Haag, as they enter their ninth decades, for all of their principles and sacrifices over the years, and my sister Carolyn, who still remembers having to drive me to the library on a Saturday morning when I was in third grade so that I could get a jumpstart on a big historical research project.

My son, Quincy, has cheerfully endured the small deprivations that come with having a writer as a parent, including research trips to strange locations, the all-too-familiar refrain, "I'll be in my office, writing," and those very important, jotted-down thoughts on the backs of envelopes scattered through the house. It is good to have a more formal occasion to thank my child for reminding me of the true and enduring things in the world, every single day.

During the final stages of the publication process for this book, my older brother, Stephen Haag, died suddenly, and too early. I miss him every day. I dedicate this book to him, even though the two of us did not agree on much of anything politically, because two things that we did agree on were the importance of constructive discussion in civil society and our impatience for cant. Steve and I were part of a politically mixed family. My father and brother both owned guns, but owned them very differently. My father grew up in Depression-era rural America, and he had rifles most of his life, to shoot squirrels and varmint for the meager dinner pot, or to do occasional target practice. As an adult, living in the city, he donated to gun-control groups. He didn't support the National Rifle Association, although he still owns guns. To him, they had been tools, and I think he was all too happy as an adult to buy his meat in cellophane-wrapped packages in the supermarket rather than having to shoot dinner himself. Steve grew up in the city, had a white-collar job, never hunted, lived in areas without notable crime issues, and did not have a practical need for a gun, but he, too, owned a few guns, in different ways and for different reasons. The gun had political value and resonance for my brother, a libertarian living in the deep blue state of Maryland. In one dimension, this book has tried to trace the history of the American gun cultures that my father and my brother illustrate—the transition from the world of the gun as a tool to the world of the gun as an object with political and cultural mystique or value. My deepest heartache, however, is that Steve and I won't be able to hash all of this out at our next family dinner.

Abbreviations for Frequently Cited Archives

Baltimore, Maryland
> JHUWL: Johns Hopkins University, Welch Medical Library, Special Collections

Cody, Wyoming
> BBHC: Buffalo Bill Center of the West, Historical Center, McCracken Research Library
>> —HH, Herbert Houze Collection, MS70
>> —RMA, Roy Marcot Firearms Advertisements Collection, MS111
>> —SHGC, Schulyer, Hartley & Graham Collection, MS034
>> —WRAC, Records of the Winchester Repeating Arms Company, MS20

Hartford, Connecticut
> CHS: Connecticut Historical Society
>> —BW, Bennett-Winchester Papers, MS528415
>> —SC, The Papers of Samuel Colt, MS28415
> CSL: Connecticut State Library
>> —CC, Colt Collection, RG103

Herkimer, New York
> HCHS: Herkimer County Historical Society
>> —HCHSRM, Remington Material, 1 box
>> —HCHSVF, Vertical Files
>> —SRC, Shepard-Richardson Collection

Ilion, New York
    IPL: Ilion Free Public Library, Historical Room
        —ANRS, A. N. Russell (receiver), Scrapbook, 1864–1904
        —IPLED, Ella Dimmock Collection, Ilion History, box 1,
          vol. 1
        —IPLRA, Remington Arms Folders (2)

New Haven, Connecticut
    NHCHS: New Haven Colony Historical Society
        —DC, Dana Collection (scrapbooks and other material)
    YUMA: Yale University, Manuscripts and Archives, Sterling Library
        —EW, Eli Whitney Papers, MS554

Palo Alto, California
    SUA: Stanford University Archives
        —SUASL, Samuel Leib Papers, SC116

San Jose, California
    HSJ: History San Jose, Research Center
        —SL, Samuel Leib Papers, Sarah Winchester Series
    SJPL: San Jose Public Library
        —CR, California Room, Vertical Files

Wilmington, Delaware
    HM: Hagley Museum and Library
        —RW, Robert Werle Papers, #1885

Notes

INTRODUCTION:
"THE ART AND MYSTERY OF A GUNSMITH"

1. New Haven Colony Historical Society (NHCHS), New Haven, Connecticut, Dana Collection (DC), vol. 122, p. 37, "Biographical Encyclopedia" entry, p. 144.

2. Robert Spitzer, *The Politics of Gun Control*, 2nd ed. (New York: State University of New York Press, 1998), x; James Hamblin, "Why We Can't Talk About Gun Control," *The Atlantic*, www.the.atlantic.com/politics/archive/2014/06/how-to-interpret-the-second-amendment/373664.

3. Buffalo Bill Center of the West, Historical Center, McCracken Research Library (BBHC), Cody, Wyoming, Records of the Winchester Repeating Arms Company (WRAC), MS20, box 11, folder 50, from Edwin Pugsley to Arthur Earle, July 14, 1921.

4. Are we a gun culture today, in the 2010s? Perhaps, by the dual criteria of quantity (we are the most heavily armed civilian population) and quality (the gun is a self-conscious and powerful tool of self-identification, is symbolic and emotional for some Americans, and forms a deep political fault line for all Americans). The United States has an estimated 270 million to 310 million civilian firearms, with most organizations, including the NRA, citing a figure around or upward of 300 million. The *Small Arms Survey* of 2007 (*www.smallarmssurvey.org/fileadmin/docs/A-Yearbook/2007/en/full/Small-Arms-Survey-2007-Chapter-02-EN.pdf*, 39–40) places the number at 270 million; the Bureau of Alcohol, Tobacco, and Firearms has estimated 300 million; and more recent 2012 research by the Congressional Research Service (William J. Krouse, *Gun Control Legislation*, November 14, 2012, www.fas.org/sgp/crs/misc/RL32842.pdf) places the figure at 310 million, a figure cited in Pew Research and other sites as well. The website GUNFAQ (www.gunfaq.org/2013/03/how-many-guns-in-the-united-states) summarizes some of these estimates. *The Small Arms Survey* further reports that there are 875 million combined civilian, military, and law enforcement firearms in the world, of which 75 percent, or 650 million, are civilian owned, with US civilians accounting for 42 percent of those civilian firearms.

But even today, a majority of Americans do not have guns (the trend is toward fewer Americans owning multiple guns), and many lack any fluency with or passion for guns, or even exposure to them. The number of households with a gun has actually declined from 50 percent in the mid-1990s to 34 to 37 percent, by two difference sources, in 2012 and 2013, respectively (2012 results are from the General Social Survey and the 2013 results from Pew, both of which are described in Drew Desilver, "A Minority of Americans Own Guns, but Just How Many Is Unclear," June 4, 2013, Pew Research Center, www.pewresearch.org/fact-tank/2013/06/04/a-minority-of-americans-own-guns -but-just-how-many-is-unclear).

Furthermore, a majority of Americans favor some form of gun control, albeit often unenergetically. Political science scholar Kristin Goss, among others, reasonably questions whether we really are a "gun culture," given these kinds of statistics on gun ownership and support for gun control. See *Disarmed: The Missing Movement for Gun Control in America* (Princeton, NJ: Princeton University Press, 2009). In the 2000s, mass shootings are probably the most visible and tragic catalysts for soul-searching around guns and gun politics, and although there is no good longitudinal data on the frequency of "mass shootings" as a distinct criminal act, a report by the FBI, released on September 25, 2014, does conclude that this form of gun violence has greatly increased in the twenty-first century. US Department of Justice, Federal Bureau of Investigation, *A Study of Active Shooter Incidents in the United States from 2000 to 2013* (Washington, DC: Navy Yard, September 2013, released 2014). While mass shootings inspire the phrase "gun culture" in a pejorative sense, these tragedies do not necessarily a gun culture make.

But to further complicate the question, we should also consider the less obvious, hidden ways in which the heavy presence of civilian arms affects American culture or plays upon our imagination. For example, Philip Cook et al. estimate that gunshot wounds sustained in the single year 1994 produced $2.3 billion in lifetime medical costs, of which $1.1 billion was paid by the US taxpayers. Philip Cook et al., "The Medical Costs of Gunshot Injuries in the United States," *Journal of the American Medical Association* 281, no. 5 (1999): 447. Philip Cook and Jens Ludwig authored what they describe as the first attempt to produce a comprehensive measure of even more "hidden" costs of American gun violence. The authors argue that the "real costs of gun violence come from the devastating emotional costs" experienced by relatives and friends of gunshot victims as well as the "fear and general reduction in quality of life," the reduction in mobility, the increased law enforcement costs, and the lifestyle decisions that the fear of gun violence produces. "One problem," they point out, "is that much of the relevant losses from gun violence are not commodities traded in the marketplace, but rather personal losses such as pain, fear, and life itself." Philip Cook and Jens Ludwig, *Gun Violence: The Real Costs* (New York: Oxford, 2000), 113, 97, 45.

Conversely, supporters of guns might argue for similarly hidden and reverberative— but positive—effects for guns. One could argue from either position that the gun haunts us today in the sense that the impact of "guns in America" subtly extends, for better or worse, beyond the number of Americans who actually own guns, or the number of gun-violence victims, such that we cannot glean whether we are a gun culture simply from counting guns, or even from the subtler exercise of thinking about the cultural impact of guns, or the qualitative dimensions of gun affinity.

I use the term "gun culture" guardedly, but have tried in these pages to suspend the assumption that we are a gun culture, and to treat that concept as a hypothesis rather than a fact, with results that these chapters describe. Among other examples, Roger Lane, a historian of crime, concludes that we were born a gun culture; he is quoted in Lenz, *"Arms Are Necessary": Gun Culture in Eighteenth-Century American Politics and*

Society (Koln: Bohlau, 2010), 12. For a review of the clichés of modern gun politics, from the perspective of both gun and gun-control advocates, see Glenn Utter, "The Evolving Gun Culture in America," *Journal of American & Comparative Culture* 23, no. 2 (2000): 67.

5. Musician and writer Henry Rollins, for example, comments thus at "Joe Cole and American Gun Violence," *LA Weekly*, April 11, 2013, www.laweekly.com/music/henry -rollins-joe-cole-and-american-gun-violence-4168983. Frank Orth, executive vice president of the National Rifle Association from 1959 until his death in 1970, testified before Congress in 1968 about a "very special relationship" between a man and his gun that is "atavistic, with its roots deep in prehistory." Orth's popular touchstone comment is noted at Eugene Hollon, *Frontier Violence: Another Look* (New York: Oxford University Press, 1974), 107. Although Orth refers to "man" and his gun, he was commenting in context on the American male's exceptional relationship to guns.

6. Harold Williamson, *Winchester: The Gun that Won the West* (Washington, DC: Combat Forces, 1952), wrote the corporate history of Winchester and notes, for example, that the "experiences of the Winchester organization were typical of business operations in general between 1850 and 1931 [and] . . . subject to most of the broad influences. . . . Even the more distinguishing features of the company were not unique" (p. x).

7. John Morton Blum, *The Republican Roosevelt* (Cambridge, MA: Harvard University Press, 1954; repr. 1977), 29. The most notable exception is Tom Diaz, a lawyer and gun activist who studies and critiques the gun business today in *The Last Gun: How Changes in the Gun Industry Are Killing Americans and What It Will Take to Stop It* (New York: New Press, 2015), and in *Making a Killing* (New York: New Press, 1999). Addis's sales dispatches on Siam are reprinted in Williamson, *Winchester*, 118–119.

8. So says James Wright in "Ten Essential Observations on Guns in America," in Jan Dizard et al., eds., *Guns in America: A Reader* (New York: New York University Press, 1999), 505.

9. Colonial historians who grapple with this question must contend with spotty, incomplete, and unreliable sources. Still, several studies come up with similar estimates of gun possession in the pre-Revolutionary era. Lenz, for example, a German scholar, in *Arms Are Necessary*, studied a sample of probate records from Massachusetts and South Carolina from 1730 to 1790. He concluded that 42.2 percent listed guns in their inventories, 51.8 percent did not, while readings were inconclusive in another 6 percent. He found that 36.5 percent of Massachusetts homes had guns, and 60.6 percent of South Carolina homes (pp. 88–89). Lenz concludes that guns were not uncommon or universal, and that "those who argue that guns were singularly central to life in the colonies and early states are just as much off the mark" as those who say that they were largely absent in this context (p. 207). A much-respected survey, Alice Hanson Jones, *American Colonial Wealth: Documents and Methods* (Ann Arbor: Consortium for Political and Social Research, 1981), uses 919 probate inventories as her archive. She found that guns were present in 41.6 percent of northern inventories and 61.7 percent of southern inventories. See Robert H. Churchill, "Guns and the Politics of History," *Reviews in American History* 29, no. 3 (2001): 334, for a review, including Michael Bellesiles's *Arming America* (New York: Knopf, 2000), whose count of gun ownership, which he concluded was quite low (19 percent), based on colonial probate records, was subsequently challenged and rejected for questionable sources and technique. Setting aside his gun inventory, this book agrees with one of Bellesiles's conclusions, namely, that the

alliance between the government and the gun industrialist in the antebellum years was crucial to the development of a commercial market. Carole Shammas, in *Wealth, Household Expenditure, and Consumer Goods in Preindustrial England and America, 1550–1800* (Ann Arbor: Consortium for Political and Social Research, 1990), found that gun ownership was far from universal but not insignificant: on the eve of the Revolution, fewer than half the inventories in Massachusetts referenced firearms, and 66 percent of Virginia inventories.

Matthew Ward looked more granularly at two counties in Kentucky in the late 1700s and early 1800s and found that around 66 percent of estate inventories included firearms, although many of these were broken, old, and useless. See his "Guns, Violence and Identity on Trans-Appalachian American Frontier," in Karen Jones, Giacomo Macola, and David Welch, eds., *A Cultural History of Firearms in the Age of Empire* (Farnham, UK: Ashgate, 2013), 23–28.

10. Quoted at Ellsworth S. Grant, *The Colt Legacy: The Story of the Colt Armory in Hartford, 1855–1980* (Providence, RI: Mowbray, 1982), 4–5; William Edwards, *The Story of Colt's Revolver: The Biography of Col. Samuel Colt* (Harrisburg: Stackpole, 1953), 63, 73; K. D. Kirkland, *America's Premier Gunmakers: Colt* (New York: Exeter, 1988), 16; WRAC, series 4, box 11, folder 8, typescript of Winchester history for fiftieth anniversary, June 23, 1959; see also series 4, box 11, folder 50, from Bob McMahon, WRAC, to Connecticut newspapermen, October 8, 1945; Connecticut State Library (CSL), Colt Collection (CC), RG103, business file, series III, box 11A, correspondence, incoming, Allies letter book, 1873–1880, from Hugh Harbison to Allies, October 30, 1877, p. 174 of letter book, for example of "push"; Williamson, *Winchester*, 177, 111; WRAC, series 1, box 6, folder 7, July 7, 1917; series 6, box 13, folder 20, from TG Bennett to "The Trade," 1918, p. 6; series 6, box 13, folder 20, from Win Bennett "To the Trade," p. 22; BBHC, *Winchester Herald*, March 1921, back ad; *Winchester Herald*, April 1921, advertisement, 1.

11. WRAC, series 1, box 6, folder 1, from Henry Brewer, VP of WRAC, to Fowler Manning, February 28, 1918.

12. Williamson, *Winchester*, 209. The very easiest and most concise tables on annual Winchester sales data, which the company itself helped to compile and then verified, can also be found in Williamson, *Winchester*, Appendix D-1 (p. 460). See also 1910 US Census, vol. 8, 487. Utter, "The Evolving Gun Culture in America," 69, writes of two gun cultures—one pro-gun and the other not—that might have developed over the entire history of the United States, but that especially deepened in the twentieth century, not the nineteenth.

13. WRAC, series 1, box 6, folder 7, Sales Department Bulletin, August 2, 1917; see, for example, among many others, "What Every Real Boy Wants for Christmas," *Chicago Tribune*, December 21, 1919; *The Cosmopolitan* 49 (1910): 65 (advertisement); WRAC, series 1, box 6, folder 7, Sales Department Bulletin, July 10, 1917.

14. There is little reliable data on homicide or suicide before the 1930s, or reliable data on the national level for the 1800s. In his review of gun deaths from 1933 to 1982, public health researcher Garen Wintemute finds that suicides accounted for 49 percent of firearm deaths over that half-century, homicides 38 percent, and accidental deaths, 12 percent, but for forty of the fifty years during this timeframe, the firearm suicide rate exceeded the firearm homicide rate, and "excepting the immediate postwar years, the suicide rate was greater by 50% or more for the 25-year period from 1940 to 1964" specifically. Garen Wintemute, "Firearms as a Cause of Death in the United States, 1920–1982," *Journal of Trauma* 27, no. 5 (1987): 532.

15. The lack of attention to the gun business as a business holds true for the historical literature as well. There are very few histories or cultural histories of guns in the United States, and even less historical work on the gun business for the general reader. The historical gun literature is dominated by works of interest to antique firearms collectors, gun experts, and historians of gun technology—with a heavy emphasis on the technical minutiae of historical gun designs—and there is the occasional biography written for audiences already familiar with and interested in guns. I have found it valuable to consult all of this literature, however, in writing this book. Oddly, to my mind, one problem with the cultural-historical literature on guns is that it is most often written either by those who love guns or those who hate them, and not by those who begin with few feelings about them one way or another.

16. Ta-Nehisi Coates, "The Case for Reparations;" *The Atlantic*, June 2014, www.theatlantic.com/features/archive/2014/05/the-case-for-reparations/361631; Jedediah Purdy, *For Common Things: Irony, Trust and Commitment in America Today* (New York: Knopf, 1999).

CHAPTER 1: THE AMERICAN SYSTEM

1. Hagley Museum and Library, Wilmington, Delaware, Robert Werle Papers (RW), #1885, box 4, folder 16, December 8, 1917; Charles C.W. Cooke, discussing "Remington, U.S.A," *National Review* story, C-Span, *Washington Journal*, July 10, 2013, www.c-span.org/video/?313814/charles-cooke-remington-guns.

2. Yale University, Manuscripts and Archives, Sterling Library, MS554, Eli Whitney Papers (EW), series 1, box 1, folder 11, Eli Whitney to Oliver Wolcott, May 1, 1798 (these papers are also available on microfilm); K. D. Kirkland, *America's Premier Gunmakers: Remington* (East Bridgewater, MA: JG Press, 2012), 34, 88; quoted at Edwards, *The Story of Colt's Revolver*, 357.

3. EW, box 1, folder 14, from Eli Whitney to Oliver Tolcott, May 31, 1799; box 1, folder 16, from Eli Whitney to Josiah Stebbins, September 28, 1800; Dean Boorman, *The History of Smith & Wesson Firearms* (Guilford, CT: Lyons, 2002), 25; Columbia, Missouri Historical Society, "The First Requisite of a Military Rifle," letter written to London by Oliver Winchester, August 2, 1869, p. 14.

4. Connecticut Historical Society (CHS), MS28415, Papers of Samuel Colt (SC), box 1, Chris Colt to Samuel Colt, April 27, 1837 (arranged chronologically within boxes); on background, see also Edwards, *The Story of Colt's Revolver*, 24; WRAC, series 4, box 12, folder 18, Winchester genealogy, typescript; series 3, box 8, folder 13, memo from Mary Ellen Winchester to WRAC, February 27, 1941; Glenn Porter, *Merchants and Manufacturers: Studies in the Changing Structure of Nineteenth-Century Marketing* (Baltimore: Johns Hopkins University Press, 1971).

5. Samuel Colt to L. H. Sigourney, May 24, 1853, repr. in appendix, Barnard, *Armsmear*, 349; BBHC, *Winchester Record 2*, "Oliver F. Winchester: Captain of Industry," November 7, 1919, 1.

6. Samuel Colt to Samuel Walker, December 8, 1846, transcribed by the Connecticut Historical Society, *Sam Colt's Own Record: Samuel Colt's Own Record of Transactions with Captain Walker and Eli Whitney, Jr., in 1847* (Hartford: Connecticut Historical Society, 1949), 13–14. In another example, Christopher Spencer spent three years as a gunsmith at Colt's Hartford factory, where he helped install machinery. "Abraham Lincoln and the Repeating Rifle," *Scientific American*, December 1921, 102.

7. SC, box 1, folder 8, from Dudley Selden to Samuel Colt, February 24, 1837; Joseph Bilby, *A Revolution in Arms: A History of the First Repeating Rifles* (Yardley, PA: Westholme, 2006), 68–69; see also Roy Marcot, *Spencer Repeating Firearms* (Irvine, CA: Northwood Heritage Press, 1983), 12; Martin Rywell, *Smith & Wesson: The Story of the Revolver* (Harriman, TN: Pioneer, 1953), 7, 11; Fanny Winchester Hotchkiss, *Winchester Family* (New Haven, CT: Tuttle, Morehouse and Taylor, 1912). Per the custom, young men were apprenticed and Winchester would not have attended school in the farming season.

8. Williamson, *Winchester*, 19; Patricia Cline Cohen, *A Calculating People: The Spread of Numeracy in America* (New York: Routledge, 1982), 121; Alexis de Tocqueville, *Democracy in America*, vol. 1 (New York: Vintage, 1945), 308; Anne C. Rose, *Voices of the Marketplace: American Thought and Culture, 1830–1860* (New York: Twayne, 1995). Rose describes a crucial shift in antebellum America in "how Americans used their minds," moving from an emphasis on the abstract and metaphysical to practical problem solving, science, and mechanics (pp. 84–86).

9. Jeannette Mirsky, *The World of Eli Whitney* (New York: Macmillan, 1952), 289; Denison Olmsted, *Memoir of Eli Whitney, Esq.* (New Haven, CT: Durrie and Peck, 1846 [1832]), 49; SC, box 7, from Samuel Colt to Charles Manby, May 18, 1852. William Hosley, *Colt: The Making of an American Legend* (Amherst: University of Massachusetts Press, 1996), 34, correctly places the gun elite among the "high priests of the new religion of machine-based manufacturing."

It is important to note that the legacy of contract and the emergence of industrial capitalism is complex. These developments shattered many notions of social obligation or bonds of reciprocity, but as Thomas Haskell and others have argued, the contract potentially broadened the humanitarian ethos and philanthropic sense of obligation or social connectivity. Among other things, the instrument of contract posited ironclad obligations to strangers. For a retort by historian David Brion Davis, see Thomas Haskell, "Capitalism and the Origins of Humanitarian Sensibility," Part One, in *American Historical Review* 90, no. 2 (1987): 339–361, and Part Two in *AHR* 90, no. 3 (1987): 547–566.

10. Thomas Carlyle, *Signs of the Times* (New York: Penguin Classics, 1986), 65, 67; in orig. text, "dynamical" and "mechanical," 107; "Course of Mathematics," *North American Review* 13 (October 1821): 364.

11. Jack Rohan, *Yankee Arms Maker: The Incredible Career of Samuel Colt* (New York: Harper and Bros., 1935), 174. Rohan's work was a self-congratulatory, popular account of the Colt's company that the company enthusiastically embraced, and must be read cautiously, although the author did have the advantage of research assistance from Colt's. Also Louisa Tuthill, *Success in Life* (New York: G. P. Putnam,1850), 114; EW, box 1, folder 16, from Wadsworth, inspector of small arms, to Secretary of War, December 24, 1800.

12. "Remington Centennial Programme, 1816–1916," Herkimer County Historical Society, Vertical Files (HCHSVF), #1292, p. 38; Ernest Sits, "When Did Remington Make First Gun? Legend Traced," February 26, 1951, "Ragged Boy Wanted to Shoot Partridges," and Don Perice, "Boy's Desire for Gun Saved Ilion," *Utica Observer-Dispatch*, November 17, 1968," #292; "How a Backwoods Blacksmith Became Famous," *Ilion Citizen*, August 24, 1916, #294; Dimitra Doukas, *Worked Over: The Corporate Sabotage of an American Community* (Ithaca, NY: Cornell University Press, 2003), 58–60; On Remington's healthy, if not inordinate, desire to succeed as a businessman and manufacturer, see Jerry Swinney, "New Notes on Remington's History," *The Gun Report*, April

1997; Roy Marcot, *The History of Remington Firearms* (Guilford, CT: Lyons Press, 2005), 1–11 (Marcot is the foremost historian of Remington); Edwards, *The Story of Colt's Revolver*, 21; Rohan, *Yankee Arms Maker*, 23; *Business Week*, October 19, 1940, 19; US Patent and Trademark Office, O. F. Winchester, of Baltimore, MD, Making Shirts, Specifications of Letters, Patent #5421, February 1, 1848, available online at patft .uspto.gov/netahtml/PTO/patimg.htm.

13. *The Trial of Samuel Colt: Complete Report of the Trial of Samuel Colt v. the Mass Arms Company, Tried June 30, 1851*, in *U.S. Circuit Court, Boston, MA*, transcript, by Martin Rywell (Harriman, TN: Pioneer Press, 1953), 4, 286, 130.

14. Hosley, *Colt*, 74; Herbert Houze, *Samuel Colt: Arms, Art, Invention* (New Haven, CT: Yale University Press, 2006), 20, 73 (Houze also aptly characterizes Colt as "an archetype for the twentieth-century advertising executive," p. 20); Grant, *The Colt Legacy*, 9, 14; Bilby, *A Revolution in Arms*, 234; Williamson, *Winchester*, 23. See also Edmund Lewis, *Volcanic Firearms: Predecessor to the Winchester Rifle* (Woonsocket, RI: Mowbray, 2011), on Winchester as the "consummate entrepreneur," 115. Hosley comments that "what Colt invented was a system of myths, symbols, stagecraft, and distribution" that future mass marketers imitated and rarely surpassed. Biographer Grant, in *The Colt Legacy*, speculates that Colt's success was due more to his "showmanship in telling the world" about his gun. "Far more than his competitors," he writes, "he appreciated the necessity of creating demand through aggressive promotion" (pp. 9, 14). Felicia Deyrup, *Arms Makers of the Connecticut Valley: A Regional Study of the Economic Development of the Small Arms Industry, 1798–1870* (Northampton, MA: Smith College Studies, 1948), 122–123, concludes that Colt understood "the importance of stimulating demand" through "sales promotion."

A prime example of the premodern gun-control celebration of the ruthless gun entrepreneur and his wily, much-applauded efforts to build a market for the gun would be Rohan's *Yankee Arms Maker* (1935), a popular, breathless biography of Samuel Colt, which the company anticipated eagerly.

15. James Whisker, *Arms Makers of Colonial America* (Selinsgrove, PA: Susquehanna University Press, 1992), 16, 17; "Recollections of Half a Century," *Shooting & Fishing* 13, December 21, 1893, 185, bound volume 13 (note: the bound *Shooting & Fishing* series has its own pagination; unless otherwise indicated, here and throughout, pagination refers to the page of the original issue); Lee Kennett, *The Gun in America: The Origins of a National Dilemma* (Westport, CT: Greenwood, 1975), 36. Richard Hofstadter notes Washington's dismay in "America as a Gun Culture," *American Heritage* 21, no. 6 (1970): 5, online; Brown, *Firearms in Colonial America: The Impact on History and Technology, 1492–1792* (Washington, DC: Smithsonian Institution Press, 1980), 126, 226; Whisker, *Arms Makers of Colonial America*, 16, 96; Alden Hatch, *Remington Arms in American History* (New York: Rinehart, 1956), 63 (Hatch worked for years with Remington on his book, although it was written for a broader audience and does not include citations); James Whisker, *The Gunsmith's Trade* (Lewiston, NY: Edwin Mellon Press, 1992), 76; see also Robert Gardner, *American Arms and Arms Makers* (Columbus, OH: College Book Company, 1944).

16. Whisker, *The Gunsmith's Trade*, 77; Brown, *Firearms in Colonial America*, 242, 347, 242–243, 355, 309; Gardner, *American Arms and Arms Makers*, 48–49. Gardner's census of gunmakers is invaluable, and assembled from multiple, eclectic sources.

17. Whisker, *The Gunsmith's Trade*, vi, 145, 158–159, 161, 60, 59; Brown, *Firearms in Colonial America*, 244. Whisker's book is a meticulous re-creation of the census of gunmakers in colonial America. See also Gardner, *American Arms and Arms Makers;*

Whisker, *Arms Makers of Colonial America*, 69. Carl P. Russell, *Guns on the Early Frontier: From Colonial Times to the Years of the Western Fur Trade* (New York: Dover, 2005), notes that many "relics of early gunning in America have been preserved because of the distinctive art work on them, or because they were owned and used in families in which succeeding generations attached sentimental value to them as treasured heirlooms," even if in disrepair (p. 64).

18. Richard Hofstadter, "America as a Gun Culture," 5. Hofstadter quoted Senator Joseph Tydings of Maryland, who in 1968 appealed for gun control and lamented, "It is just tragic that in all of western civilization the United States is the only modern industrial nation that persists in maintaining a gun culture." Whisker, *Arms Makers of Colonial America*, 16, 17; Kennett, *The Gun in America*, 36; Whisker, *Arms Makers of Colonial America*, 133, 19. See, among other sources, Ward, "Guns, Violence, and Identity," which notes the gender relations disruption; James Hanson, *Firearms of the Fur Trade* (Chadron, NE: Museum of the Fur Trade, 2011), 47, 65, 19; Brown, *Firearms of Colonial America*, 157; Calvin Martin, *Keepers of the Game: Indian-Animal Relationships and the Fur Trade* (Berkeley: University of California Press, 1978); Ryan Gale, *For Trade and Treaty: Firearms of the American Indians, 1600–1920* (Elk River, MN: Track of the Wolf, 2010), 1–2; Whisker, *The Gunsmith's Trade*, 87.

19. Brown, *Firearms in Colonial America*, 347; see also Whisker, *Arms Makers of Colonial America*, 202, 54, 34–37; Whisker, *The Gunsmith's Trade*, 71, 168.

20. WRAC, MS 20, series 4, box 12, folder 12, photocopy, *New York in the Revolution Supplement*, 54–55; Deyrup, *Arms Makers of the Connecticut Valley*, 36.

21. Mirsky, *The World of Eli Whitney*, 188–190; Thomas Davidson, "'Instead of the Best Guns in Europe, I Have Sent the Worst': Arthur Lee's Struggle to Buy European Arms During the Revolution," *Dispatch* 26, no. 2 (2012): 4–5.

22. EW, box 1, folder 17, from Elizur Goodrich to Secretary of the Treasury, January 8, 1801; Mirsky, *The World of Eli Whitney*, 143; EW, box 1, folder 16, from Wadsworth, inspector of small arms, to Secretary of War, December 24, 1800; Whisker, *Arms Makers of Colonial America*, 170.

23. Gardner, *American Arms and Arms Makers*, 143; WRAC, unprocessed part of collection, MRL—correspondence, chronological—2003, Edwin Pugsley, folder 2 of 2, "Description of Springfield Armory," typescript, orig. from 1817; Nathan Rosenberg's excellent inquiry into the ambivalent legacy of mechanization, "Why in America?," in Otto Mayr, ed., *Yankee Enterprise: The Rise of the American System of Manufactures* (Washington, DC: Smithsonian Press, 1981), 92, 86, 90–91; Bilby, *A Revolution in Arms*, 68–70; William Hallahan, *Misfire: The History of How America's Small Arms Have Failed Our Country* (New York: Scribner's, 1994), 48–50; Deyrup, *Arms Makers of the Connecticut Valley*, 34–38. For an excellent study of the ways that the unique community and power dynamics of Harpers Ferry affected, and thwarted, adaptation to machine production, see Merritt Roe Smith, *Harpers Ferry Armory and the New Technology: The Challenge of Change* (Ithaca, NY: Cornell University Press, 1977).

24. Whisker, *The Gunsmith's Trade*, 89; Whisker, *Arms Makers of Colonial America*, 128.

25. EW, series 1, box 1, folder 10, from Eli Whitney to Phineas Miller, October 7, 1797. Indeed, historian of technology Merritt Roe Smith has argued that interchangeable processes and the demand for uniformity in arms was very much driven by government and military priorities, and of little initial value, or interest, otherwise. See Merritt Roe Smith, ed., *Military Enterprise and Technological Change: Perspectives on the American Experience* (Cambridge, MA: MIT Press, 1985).

26. EW, box 1, folder 13, from Eli Whitney to Josiah Stebbins, November 24, 1798; Mirsky, *The World of Eli Whitney*, 36–37; EW, box 1, folder 17, from Whitney to Secretary of Treasury Samuel Dexter, January 8, 1801; Mirksy, *The World of Eli Whitney*, 143.

27. EW, series 1, box 1, folder 11, from Eli Whitney to Secretary Wolcott, May 1, 1798; EW, series 1, box 2, folder 42, "The Manufacture of Firearms," memoir, 1812, repr. in Claude Fuller, *The Whitney Firearms* (New York: Standard, 1946).

28. Carolyn Cooper, *Eli Whitney and the Whitney Armory* (Hamden, CT: Eli Whitney Museum, 1980); Mirsky, *The World of Eli Whitney*, 201–202; Olmsted, *Memoir of Eli Whitney*, 67.

29. EW, box 1, folder 18, from Eli Whitney to Dearborn, War Department, June 21, 1801; box 1, folder 12, from Eli Whitney to Wolcott, July 12, 1798; box 1, folder 14, from Eli Whitney to Wolcott, May 31, 1799; Constance McLaughlin Green, *Eli Whitney and the Birth of American Technology* (Boston: Little, Brown, 1956), 174; EW, box 1, folder 14, Eli Whitney to Wolcott, May 31, 1799; box 1, folder 11, from Eli Whitney to Wolcott, May 1, 1798.

30. EW, box 1, folder 16, from Eli Whitney to Josiah Stebbins, April 26, 1800; on industry and the gun crucible, among others, see Alfred Chandler, *The Visible Hand: The Managerial Revolution in American Business* (Cambridge, MA: Belknap, 1977), 72; Brown, *Firearms in Colonial America*, 384; WRAC, unprocessed part of collection, MRL—correspondence, chronological—2003, folder 2 of 2, Edwin Pugsley to Leibold, secretary to Henry Ford, April 10, 1934; Nathan Rosenberg, "Technological Change in the Machine-Tool Industry," *Journal of Economic History* 23, no. 4 (1963): 414–443. See also David Hounshell, *From the American System to Mass Production, 1800–1932* (Baltimore: Johns Hopkins University Press, 1984).

The French philosopher Saint Simon understood early on that industry would monumentally disrupt social relations. He would have seen the arms industry as an "abominable affront to his cherished belief in the innate pacifism of industry," writes Ghita Ionescu. Yet it was precisely through the gun that industry truly began in the United States. Ghita Ionescu, ed., *The Political Thought of Saint-Simon* (London: Oxford University Press, 1976), 52.

31. "The Father of Modern Ordnance: Eli Whitney," *Firepower: The Ordnanceman's Journal*, December 1944, 10–11; photocopy in WRAC, series 4, box 12, folder 12. See also WRAC, series 5, box 13, folder 23, Columbia Broadcasting System, script, "Eli Whitney," March 26, 1944.

32. EW, box 1, folder 16, from Wadsworth, inspector of small arms, to Secretary of War, December 24, 1800.

33. EW, box 1, folder 14, from Eli Whitney to Wolcott, May 31, 1799; box 1, folder 15, from Wolcott to Eli Whitney.

34. EW, box 1, folder 17, from Elizur Goodrich to Secretary of the Treasury, January 8, 1801; "The Father of Modern Ordnance: Eli Whitney," quoted at Mirsky, *The World of Eli Whitney*, 214, 219; EW, box 1, folder 17, from Elizur Goodrich to Secretary of the Treasury, January 8, 1801.

35. EW, box 1, folder 12, from Eli Whitney to Oliver Wolcott, July 12, 1798; box 1, folder 16, from Eli Whitney to Josiah Stebbins, April 26, 1800; box 1, folder 12, from Eli Whitney to Wolcott; box 1, folder 13, from Wolcott to Eli Whitney, October 9, 1798; Joseph Bradley, *Guns for the Tsar: American Technology and the Small Arms Industry in Nineteenth-Century America* (DeKalb: Northern Illinois University Press, 1990), 24–26.

36. See Green, *Eli Whitney and the Birth of American Technology*, 147, 142. Other gunmakers also felt that their survival required special government support and the public

arms market. See documents quoted at Whisker, *The Gunsmith's Trade*, 83, 175–176. Letter from George Bomford, Ordnance Department, December 31, 1823, Doc. #248, 18th Cong., 1st sess., "Contracts Since January 1, 1820, for Cannon . . . Muskets and Other Small Arms," in *American State Papers: Documents, Legislative and Executive, of the Congress of the United States*, vol. 2 (Washington, DC, 1834), 599. The chief of ordnance likewise reported to the secretary of war in 1817: "High wages makes the business unprofitable to the contractors, and ultimately in many instances has occasioned their ruin. A great capital is required for commencing the business, and the returns are slow. . . . Many men [who] are tempted by the encouragements of the government aiding them with the advances of money have totally failed and be[en] reduced to abject poverty or seriously injured in their circumstances," quoted at Deyrup, *Arms Makers of the Connecticut Valley*, 48; Hosley, *Colt*, 49; Chandler, *The Visible Hand*, 51; Green, *Eli Whitney and the Birth of American Technology*, 147. Deyrup, *Arms Makers of the Connecticut Valley*, comments that guns were made on a "very limited scale" beyond government contracts, and that "the [small arms] industry was brought into existence by the federal government only at the expense of great effort" (pp. 43, 45, 215). "Arms manufacture was launched with government aid," she writes, "and through its formative years could not have survived had government support been withdrawn" (p. 3).

37. 1810 US Census, vol. 2, series 4, Tench Coxe, "A Statement of the Arts and Manufactures of the United States of America for the Year 1810," xxii, xlvii. Deyrup, *Arms Makers of the Connecticut Valley*, notes "the sole source of capital in the early . . . arms industry was apparently the federal government," which advanced "considerable amounts" to contractors, as the contractor's sole customer, without requiring interest (pp. 45–46).

38. Hosley, *Colt*, 34; Mirsky, *The World of Eli Whitney*, 201–203; Coxe, 1810 US Census, xxv; EW, box 1, folder 16, from Wadsworth to Secretary of War, December 24, 1800.

39. Chandler, *The Visible Hand*, 73–75; quoted at Bradley, *Guns for the Tsar*, 34.

40. Quoted at Mirsky, *The World of Eli Whitney*, 267, 250.

41. EW, box 3, folder 48, from Eli Whitney to Callender Irvine, November 17, 1813; from Whitney to Irvine, November 11, 1813; from Whiney to Irvine, November 25, 1813; from Irvine to Whitney, November 17, 1813; from Whitney to Irvine, November 25, 1813.

42. Quoted at Mirsky, *The World of Eli Whitney*, 267.

CHAPTER 2: THE CRYSTAL PALACE

1. Henry Barnard, *Armsmear: The Home, the Arm and the Armory of Samuel Colt* (New York: Alvord, 1866), 145–154.

2. WRAC, series 3, box 8, folder 13, typescript, "Oliver Fisher Winchester," n.d.; T. S. Arthur, "The Daguerreotypist," *Godey's Book*, May 1849, 352–355; quoted in Alan Trachtenberg, *Reading American Photographs* (New York: Hill and Wang), 27.

3. *The Trial of Samuel Colt* (describes the mechanical ingenuities of the revolver meticulously); Barnard, *Armsmear*, 166; SC, box 1, from John Pearson to Samuel Colt, March 23, 1836; box 1, from John Pearson to Samuel Colt, April 23, 1836; box 1, from John Pearson to Samuel Colt, May 9, 1836.

4. Hosley, *Colt*, 42; Deyrup, *Arms Makers of the Connecticut Valley*, 55. Hosley writes about how "technologists, capitalists, the army ordnance department," and "opportunists and competitors" flocked to Springfield.

5. Hosley, *Colt*, 40–41; Hallahan, *Misfire*, 60–65; Rosenberg, "Why in America?," 92, 86, 90–91. Hallahan, *Misfire*, 48–50, 62–77. Frenchman Barthelemy Thimonnier almost met the same fate. Outraged tailors burned down his business and almost murdered him for fear that his "sewing machine" would make them obsolete. Jean Granger, *Thimonnier et la machine a coudre* (Paris: Publications Techniques, 1943).

6. Hallahan, *Misfire*, 88; W. W. Greener, *The Gun and Its Development* (London: Cassell, 1910 [1881]), used that phrase to describe the gunsmith turned laborer (p. 284).

7. Hallahan, *Misfire*, 89, 93, 94; Kennett, *The Gun in America*, 89; Deyrup, *Arms Makers of Connecticut Valley*, 128–30, Hosley, *Colt*, 42.

8. An 1830 encyclopedia noted that the gun worker knew only a small part of a gun: ten workmen made one gun, "few of whom can execute any branch of the art but one." *Brewer's Edinburgh Encyclopedia*, 1830, quoted at Barnard, *Armsmear*, 215; HCHSVF, #292, n.d. clipping from Remington publication; WRAC, series 4, box 11, folder 13, from Thomas Hall to John Boone, August 7, 1952; Deyrup, *Arms Makers of the Connecticut Valley*, 91, writes that gunsmiths "were swept away with a completeness similar to the passing of a biological generation." See also Deyrup, *Arms Makers*, 3; Kennett, *The Gun in America*, 89.

9. As Colt testified to Parliament, *Report from the Select Committee on Small Arms, Together with the Proceedings of the Committee, Minutes of Evidence, and Appendix*, House of Commons (Britain), May 12, 1854, pp. 1172–1173; and to a London society of civil engineers, *On the Application of Machinery to the Manufacture of Rotating Chambered-Breech Fire-Arms and Their Peculiarities* (London, 1855), 11–12. "A far flung sales force was a necessity as much as good mechanics," writes Edwards in *The Story of Colt's Revolver*, 37.

10. SC, from Samuel Colt to Dudley Selden, box 1, November 18, 1837.

11. *New York Courier and Enquirer*, December 22, 1837, 4; Edwards, *The Story of Colt's Revolver*, 63, 73; Kirkland, *America's Premier Gunmakers: Colt*, 16; BBHC, Roy Marcot Firearms Advertisements Collection (RMA), *New York Times*, clipping, May 21, 1839.

12. SC, box 1, from Chris Colt to Samuel Colt, March 28, 1837; *The Trial of Samuel Colt*, 264.

13. For example, SC, box 7, folder 9, Samuel Colt to R. W. Latham, July 8, 1858; box 7, folder 9, Samuel Colt to B. R. Floyd, August 8, 1858; box 1, Samuel Colt to B. R. Floyd, October 1, 1858; box 1, folder 1, Chris Colt to Samuel Colt, February 25, 1836; *Sam Colt's Own Record*, from Samuel Colt to Samuel Walker, November 30, 1846, p. 7; from Samuel Colt to John Coffee Hays, March 9, 1847, p. 56–57; Edwards, *The Story of Colt's Revolver*, 118; SC, box 1, from C. F. Pond to Samuel Colt, February 24, 1837. See also Hosley, *Colt*, 19, on Colt's opportunistic character.

14. Quoted in Rohan, *Yankee Arms Maker*, 84, 99–102.

15. SC, box 1, from Chris Colt to Samuel Colt, February 11, 1836; from Chris Colt to Samuel Colt, July 15, 1837.

16. SC, box 1, from Chris Colt to Samuel Colt, September 14, 1836; box 1, from Samuel Colt to Dudley Selden, December 26, 1838; Selden quoted at Grant, *The Colt Legacy*, 4–5.

17. Edwards, *The Story of Colt's Revolver*, 51; SC, box 1, folder 1, Chris Colt to Samuel Colt, February 25, 1836; box 1, Samuel Colt to Dudley Selden, December 26, 1838; box 2, Dudley Selden to Samuel Colt, January 6, 1839.

18. SC, box 7, folder 9, from Samuel Colt to B. R. Floyd, January 1, 1858; Edwards, *The Story of Colt's Revolver*, 68; SC, box 1, from William Harney to Samuel Colt, December 22, 1837.

19. SC, box 1, folder 12, from Samuel Colt to Dudley Selden, February 14, 1838; box 1, folder 12, Dudley Selden to Samuel Colt, February 4, 1838.

20. See *The Trial of Samuel Colt*, 8; Connecticut State Library (CSL), Colt Collection (CC), RG103, box 70A, Roderick Lull, "Colt's: The Story of Small Arms," September 8, 1932.

21. *Report from the Select Committee on Small Arms*, 1104; *New York Evening Star*, January 15, 1841; *On the Application of Machinery*, 11; *The Trial of Samuel Colt*, 8.

22. SC, box 2, from Dudley Selden to Samuel Colt, February 24, 1839; Rohan, *Yankee Arms Maker*, 113; quoted at Houze, *Samuel Colt: Arms, Art, Invention*.

23. New Haven Colony Historical Society (NHCHS), George Dudley Seymour, *New Haven* (New Haven, CT: privately printed, 1942), 262, 283, 256; Horace Scudder, ed., *Connecticut: A Study of Commonwealth-Democracy*, American Commonwealths series (New York: Houghton, Mifflin, 1887), 340, 330; Alexander Johnston, *Connecticut: A Study of Commonwealth Democracy*, American Commonwealths series (New York: Houghton Mifflin, 1887), 339.

24. Hagley Museum and Library, Wilmington, Delaware (HM), *Remington Arms Union Metallic Cartridge Company: The Remington Centennial Book. Some Historical and Human Facts About the Birth and Growth of the Firearms Industry in Ilion, New York* (Ilion, NY, 1916), 8; Ilion Free Public Library, Ella Dimmock Collection, Ilion History (IPLED), box 1, vol. 1, sketch of bridge dropoff, originally appeared in "OD," February 25, 1923; Hatch, *Remington*, 43.

25. WRAC, series 3, box 8, folder 13, typescript, "Oliver Fisher Winchester"; "Winchester & Davies, New Haven Shirt Manufactory, Established 1847," advertisement broadside, circa 1860, reprinted in Herbert Houze, *Winchester Repeating Arms Company: Its History & Development, 1865–1981* (Iola, WI: Krause, 1994), image 3.

26. Williamson, *Winchester*, 9–10; Mary Bellis, "The History of the Sewing Machine," www.inventors.com. Hunt's eclectic mechanical and inventive genius was similar to that of other (gun) inventors of his day. Journalist Julia Keller's insightful study, *Mr. Gatling's Terrible Marvel: The Gun That Changed Everything and the Misunderstood Genius Who Invented It* (New York: Penguin, 2008), details a similar richness of inventive possibility and hope in her subject's career.

27. Lewis, *Volcanic Firearms*, 10–11; Kennett, *The Gun in America*, 36. For a concise description of the muzzle-loader hazards, see Williamson, *Winchester*, 5.

28. Lewis, *Volcanic Firearms*, 10; George Watrous, *The History of Winchester Firearms, 1866–1966* (New York: Winchester Press, 1975), 1; Williamson, *Winchester*, 9–10.

29. WRAC, series 4, box 11, folder 18, typescript, Clinton Nottage Hunt, "A Five Year Plan for Disarmament."

30. *Sam Colt's Own Record*, from Samuel Colt to Sam Houston, February 24, 1847, p. 49; from Samuel Walker to Samuel Colt, February 1847, pp. 42–43; from Samuel Colt to Samuel Walker, December 1846, pp. 10–11; Rohan, *Yankee Arms Maker*, 110.

31. Quoted in Rohan, *Yankee Arms Maker*, 111.

32. *Sam Colt's Own Record*, Samuel Colt to Samuel Walker, January 18, 1847, p. 33.

33. *Sam Colt's Own Record*, Samuel Colt to Samuel Walker, January 18, 1847, p. 31; Samuel Walker to Samuel Colt, March 6, 1847, p. 34; Samuel Walker to Samuel Colt, March 9, 1847, p. 38.

34. *Hartford Courant*, January 20, 1849; from Samuel Colt to Levi Smith, US Navy, quoted in Edwards, *The Story of Colt's Revolver*, 214; letter to Young quoted in Rohan, *Yankee Arms Maker*, 154, 233.

35. *Sam Colt's Own Record*, from Samuel Colt to John Coffee Hays, March 1847, pp. 56–57.

36. Barnard meticulously describes the Cabinet of Memorials in his hagiography of Colt, *Armsmear*, 115–134; see also Houze, *Samuel Colt: Arms, Art, Invention*.

37. Rohan, *Yankee Arms Maker*, 174; "How I Invented Maxim Gun—Hiram Maxim, Outbreak of World War Moves Veteran American to Describe for the Times His Epoch-Making Invention," *New York Times*, November 1, 1914; Bilby, *A Revolution in Arms*, 281.

38. SC, box 6, from George Landers to Samuel Colt, March 22, 1848.

39. Hosley, *Colt*, 25; Rohan, *Yankee Arms Maker*, 175; SC, box 6, from George Landers to Samuel Colt, October 6, 1848; quoted at Grant, *The Colt Legacy*, 8; quoted at Edwards, *The Story of Colt's Revolver*, 256–258, 114; Houze, *Samuel Colt: Arms, Art, Invention*, 185–186; on European foreign agents and Prussia, see SC, box 7, Samuel Colt to Wappenhaus, May 22, 1857; box 7, folder 8, Samuel Colt to Charles Carsoin [sp. illeg.], February 3, 1857; box 7, from Samuel Colt to Wappenhaus, September 19, 1857; box 6, George Law to Samuel Colt, November 27, 1849; *Supplement to the Courant*, "Colonel Colt's Pistols," June 21, 1856, 116. Hosley, *Colt*, 27, notes: "There [internationally], more than in the United States, the reputation and market for his invention grew rapidly."

40. Deyrup, *Arms Makers of the Connecticut Valley*, 45–46, 55; *Report from the Select Committee on Small Arms*, 1173; Barnard, *Armsmear* (where some of Colt's testimony is reprinted), SC, box 1, from Samuel Colt to Dudley Selden, December 26, 1838.

41. "The Manufacture of Firearms: The Armory of E. Remington & Sons, Ilion, New York," *Scientific American*, September 3, 1881, 148.

42. Barnard, *Armsmear*, 162.

43. The Humberger family recalled in 1903 that Henry Humberger had invented a "pepperbox" revolver in his gun shop in Thornville, Ohio, in 1832, and demonstrated it. "When he worked on a gun anyone could visit his shop and watch the progress he was making." Evidently, Colt did just that. The 1903 article concludes that Colt first applied for a patent, but Humberger "was proven . . . as the true inventor" (*Thornville News*, October 1, 1903, reprinted in Gardner, *American Arms and Arms Makers*, 76–77); *The Trial of Samuel Colt*, 129, 130.

44. *The Trial of Samuel Colt*, 4, 9, 10, 286. Colt claimed in 1855, "before London civil engineers[,] that he had first been exposed to other revolvers in 1835, while applying for his first patents . . . [and] felt it would open him to patent litigation to say otherwise." Wayne Van Zwoll, *America's Great Gunmakers* (South Hackensack, NJ: Stoeger, 1992), 55. Italics are reproduced from the original unless otherwise noted.

45. Carlyle, *Signs of the Times*, 83; C. R. Fay, *Palace of Industry, 1850: A Study of the Great Exhibition and Its Fruits* (London: Cambridge University Press, 1951), 14; Nikolaus Pevsner, *High Victorian Design: A Study of the Exhibits of 1851* (London: Architectural Press, 1951), 15.

46. Henry Bessemer, *Sir Henry Bessemer, F.R.S.: An Autobiography* (London: Offices of Engineering, 1905), 125–126; Fay, *Palace of Industry*, 57, 73.

47. Fay, *Palace of Industry*, 58; Pevsner, *High Victorian Design*, 20, 45.

48. Grant, *The Colt Legacy*, 9; Jack Beatty, "The American System of Manufacturing," in Jack Beatty, ed., *Colossus: How the Corporation Changed America* (New York: Broadway, 2001), 34; *Gleason's Pictorial Drawing Room Companion*, "Colt's Fire-Arms," November 12, 1853.

49. *London Daily News*, 1851, reprinted in *New York Times*, September 25, 1851; "Commission to the 1851 London Exhibition," quoted in Houze, *Samuel Colt: Arms, Art, Invention*, 185.

50. "United States: American Labour Profiting by the War-Fury in Europe," *London Magnet*, February 19, 1877, 2; Bradley, *Guns for the Tsar*, 42 (Bradley notes that the New England manufacturers would arm "practically all the governments of the world"); "The Manufacture of Firearms: The Armory of E. Remington & Sons, Ilion, New York," *Scientific American*, September 3, 1881, 148.

51. "The Manufacture of Firearms," 148.

52. *Gleason's*, "Colt's Fire-Arms," 320.

53. "From an Address by Isaac Holden on the Occasion of the Centennial Celebration of the City of Bridgeport, Connecticut, November 12, 1900," in *The American Federationist* 9 (1902): 663; NHCHS, DC, vol. 122, p. 37, *Biographical Encyclopedia* excerpt.

54. "From an Address by Isaac Holden," 663.

55. Williamson, *Winchester*, 20–21; "Among the Nail Makers," *Harper's Monthly Magazine* 21 (July 1860): 163.

56. Robert Henning et al., "The Advertising of E. Remington & Sons: The Creation of an Iconic Brand," *Journal of Historical Research in Marketing* 5, no. 4 (2013): 422; "Winchester & Davies, New Haven Shirt Manufactory, Established 1847," broadside, circa 1860, reprinted in Houze, *Winchester Repeating Arms Company*, image 3.

57. "Surprising Facts in Regard to the Value of Sewing Machines," *Scientific American*, September 22, 1860.

58. Oliver Wendell Holmes, *The Autocrat at the Breakfast-Table* (Boston: Phillips Sampson, 1858), 259.

59. DC, vol. 122, p. 38, excerpt from *Evening Sun*, March 9, 1916, on genesis of the Henry.

CHAPTER 3: "SCATTERING OUR GUNS"

1. 1880 US Census, vol. 2, "Interchangeable Mechanism," 621; *Supplement to the Courant*, "Colonel Colt's Pistols," June 21, 1856, 116; CC, box 70A, clipping from *Ballou's Pictorial Drawing-Room Companion*, "Sketches of Eminent Persons: Samuel Colt," 1852 (likewise called them "the most destructive of weapons of war"); Jacob Abbott, "The Armory at Springfield," *Harper's New Monthly* 5, no. 26 (1852) 146. On the consistent association of the new patented repeater guns with war and warfare, see also, for example, CC, box 70A, *The Daily News* (London), "The New Fashioned Fire Arms," July 18, 1854. Roger Lane, *Murder in America: A History* (Columbus: Ohio State University Press, 1990), 129, finds that "fists, feet, sticks, and bricks still outnumbered guns and knives combined."

2. These numbers come from a bibliography of published literature on murders, Thomas McDade, *The Annals of Murder: A Bibliography of Books and Pamphlets on American Murders from Colonial Times to 1900* (Norman: University of Oklahoma Press, 1961).

3. Russell Gilmore so calls him in "Another Branch of the Manly Sport: American Rifle Games, 1840–1900," in Dizard et al., eds., *Guns in America: A Reader*, 105–107.

4. John Milton, *The Poetical Works of John Milton*, vol. 2, ed. Rev. H. J. Todd (London: 1826), 499; *The Trial of Samuel Colt*, 11; *Hartford Daily Times*, quoted in Hosley, *Colt*, 70–71. Colt was praised on his 1854 European tour for his "contributions towards

peace by the perception of his automatic repeating revolver," as quoted in Grant, *The Colt Legacy*, x. For several additional examples of this logic of the revolver as a "humane improvement" and a way of "annihilating modern warfare," see Samuel Colt, *On the Application of Machinery to the Manufacture of Rotating Chambered-Breech Fire-Arms and Their Peculiarities*, ed. Charles Manby (London: William Clowes and Sons, 1855), 18–19. Colt's first biography, Barnard's *Armsmear*, concludes, "Let him and you be both so well armed that you will destroy each other as utterly as those Kilkenny cats" (p. 184). Rohan, *Yankee Arms Maker*, 297; Hosley, *Colt*, 70, notes that in 1841 the term "peacemaker" was first applied to Cochran's gun, a rival to Colt's.

5. CC, box 70A, "The New Fashioned Fire Arms: A Walk Through the 'Revolver' Factory," *The Daily News* (London), July 18, 1854. In *On the Application of Machinery*, 12, Colt describes his system of "hundreds of distinct operations, involving a great variety of peculiar contrivances and mechanical motions." "Delicate handed little girls," as Dickens called them, had replaced the "brawny gunsmiths." Charles Dickens, "Revolvers," *Household Words: A Weekly Journal* 9 (1855): 354.

6. Roy Jinks, *History of Smith & Wesson: No Thing of Importance Will Come Without Effort* (North Hollywood, CA: Beinfeld, 1977), 159; Marcot, *The History of Remington Firearms*, 22, 44; HCHSVF, #1292, Eliphalet Remington to Philo Remington, June 22, 1857, in "Ilion Centennial Souvenir Programme," p. 45; Henning, "The Advertising of E. Remington & Sons," 437; IPLED, vol. 1, from *Herkimer Democrat*, July 27, 1859, and May 19, 1858; HCHSVF, #1256, copy of letter from F. E. Spinner to E. Remington & Sons, February 11, 1861.

7. SC, box 7, folder 9, Samuel Colt to R. W. Latham, December 3, 1858; box 7, folder 11, Samuel Colt to "Gentlemen," December 3, 1859; box 7, folder 11, from Samuel Colt to William Hartley, December 17, 1859; Edwards, *The Story of Colt's Revolver*, 266.

8. SC, box 7, folder 9, Samuel Colt to R. W. Latham, July 25, 1858; box 7, folder 9, Samuel Colt to R. W. Latham, private and confidential, July 8, 1858; box 7, folder 9, R. W. Latham to Samuel Colt, August 3, 1858; Samuel Colt to Hon. B. R. Floyd, Wytheville, August 8, 1858; from Samuel Colt to Hon. B. R. Floyd, October 1, 1858.

9. Colburn quoted in Bradley, *Guns for the Tsar*, 99.

10. SC, box 7, folder 1, Samuel Colt to Charles Dennet, March 30, 1852; Rohan, *Yankee Arms Maker*, 222; Gino Garibaldi to Samuel Colt and Lieutenant Hans Buck to Colt, reprinted in Barnard, *Armsmear*, 354–364.

11. SC, box 7, folder 1, Samuel Colt to Matthew Perry, March 10, 1852; Matthew Perry to Samuel Colt, April 25, 1857.

12. CC, box 66, folder 3, "Colt's Improved Holster Pistols"; SC, box 7, folder 1, Charles Manby to Samuel Colt, March 5, 1852; box 7, folder 1, Colt to Charles Dennet, March 30, 1852; box 7, folder 1, Colt to Charles Dennet, March 30, 1852.

13. Oliver Winchester considered the "Jennings" gun to be "a connecting link in the history of our gun," the Henry and eventual Model 66. WRAC, series 4, box 11, folder 18, from Winchester to Lawrence, February 10, 1841. Gun experts consider that Winchester was the first to make a commercially successful repeater rifle. See WRAC, series 5, box 13, folder 25, from George Watrous (gun expert) to Edwin Pugsley, on "Winchester Firsts," n.d., 1949.

14. Jinks, *History of Smith & Wesson*, 24, notes that Palmer might have "brought pressure" on Smith and Wesson because of the patents he held. Lewis, *Volcanic Firearms*, 22. Houze believes that the name was first used in a press release prepared by the company. See Williamson, *Winchester*, 11.

15. Quoted in Deyrup, *Arms Makers of the Connecticut Valley*, 122–123; WRAC, additional box 14, folder 7 (unprocessed part of archive).

16. Lewis, *Volcanic Firearms*, 22.

17. Daniel Boorstin quoted in Alan Trachtenberg, *The Incorporation of America: Culture and Society in the Gilded Age* (New York: Hill and Wang, 1982), 83; *Dartmouth College v. Woodward* 17 US 518 (1819); Thomas Holland, *The Elements of Jurisprudence* (Oxford: Clarendon, 1880), 79, 276. See similar ghostly coinage in British jurisprudence, *Lennard's Carrying Co. Ltd. v. Asiatic Petroleum Co. Ltd.* (1915) AC 705. Glenn Porter, *The Rise of Big Business, 1860–1910* (New York: Crowell, 1973), 21; Roger Burlingame, *The American Conscience* (New York: Knopf, 1967), 292.

18. Quoted in Rohan, *Yankee Arms Maker*, 233; Rywell, *Smith & Wesson*, 22.

19. WRAC, Oliver Winchester letter book, to Elisha Root, July 28, 1863; Lewis, *Volcanic Firearms*, 96.

20. BBHC, WRAC, D. H. Veader and A. W. Earle, typescript, "The Story of the WRAC. This Includes Its Predecessors, The Volcanic Repeating Firearms Company and the New Haven Arms Company," 7. On ethnic composition, see Williamson, *Winchester*, 13; WRAC, Oliver Winchester letter book, to Barrow from Oliver Winchester, November 18, 1862.

21. WRAC, series 5, box 13, folder 23, correspondence to Peter Drucker, esq., from Edwin Pugsley, September 1, 1944; WRAC, Veader, "The Story of the WRAC," 13; *New Haven Palladium, March, 1855*, quoted in *Lewis, Volcanic Firearms*; *New Haven Journal Courier*, February 9, 1856.

22. WRAC, Veader, "The Story of the WRAC," 16. Williamson, *Winchester*, 26, notes that his "personal confidence is . . . revealed" in the amount of funds he advanced to the company.

23. This history is told in the greatest detail by Herbert Houze, a former curator of the Winchester records, who describes his book as an alternative business history to Harold Williamson's. See Houze, *Winchester Repeating Arms Company*, 9.

24. Lewis, *Volcanic Firearms*, 67; Donald Jacobus, *The Pardee Genealogy* (New Haven, CT: Printed for New Haven Colony Historical Society, 1927), 244–245. A few sources spell Isabelle's name as "Isabel." Sarah Winchester herself used both spellings, but primarily Isabelle, nicknamed Belle.

25. WRAC, Winchester letter book, to F. Wheeler from Samuel Rogers, Secretary to Winchester, September 11, 1857.

26. WRAC, Winchester letter book, from Winchester to E. B. Martin, October 17, 1862; *Frank Leslie's Illustrated Weekly*, October 9, 1858, quoted in Lewis, *Volcanic Firearms*, 120; R. L. Wilson, *Winchester: An American Legend. The Official History of Winchester Firearms and Ammunition from 1849 to the Present* (New York: Random House, 1991), 5; *Milwaukee Daily Sentinel*, March 30, 1855, quoted in Lewis, *Volcanic Firearms*, 22–23; WRAC, Winchester letter book, from Winchester to J. W. Patterson, April 23, 1858.

27. Lewis, *Volcanic Firearms*, 124; ads reprinted in Lewis, *Volcanic Firearms*, 117, 122; DC, vol. 122, "The Volcanic Repeating Firearms," 26.

28. CC, box 70A/B, "From Stone Hammer to Breech Loader," *Frank Leslie's Popular Monthly* 5, no. 2 (1878): 2; WRAC, Winchester letter book, from Winchester to E. B. Martin, October 17, 1862; WRAC, series 4, box 12, folder 21, Guy Hubbard, "The Beginnings of Smith & Wesson and Winchester," typescript, 14.

29. WRAC, Veader, "The Story of the WRAC," appendix, 11; Lewis, *Volcanic Firearms*, 111, 114.

30. WRAC, Veader, "The Story of the WRAC," 13–14; WRAC, Winchester letter book, from Winchester to G. J. Albright, August 29, 1863; CC, incoming correspondence, box 8, 12/1850 folder, from John Alcott to Samuel Colt, December 16, 1850; box 8, folder 10/1847–12/1847, from Hickman, KY, to Samuel Colt, October 23, 1847.

31. WRAC, Winchester letter book, from Winchester to Messrs. H. D. Clove [sp.?], September 9, 1857; James Wright, "Ten Essential Observations on Guns in America," in Dizard et al., eds., *Guns in America*, 505.

32. Wiley Sword, *The Historic Henry Rifle: Oliver Winchester's Famous Civil War Repeater* (Woonsocket, RI: Mowbray, 2002), 13; WRAC, Winchester letter book, from Winchester to Messrs J. A. [illeg.], January 2, 1858, and Winchester to J. W. Storrs, March 5, 1858; on discounts for volume; see also Van Zwoll, *America's Great Gunmakers*, 128; Winchester letter book, from Winchester to J. A. [illeg.], January 2, 1858; from Winchester to H. Forge, March 4, 1858.

33. WRAC, Winchester letter book, Winchester to J. A. [illeg.], January 2, 1858; Winchester to Wesson and Smith, March 4, 1858.

34. CC, box 70, folder 1, Price List, from Samuel Colt, Hartford, May 1, 1855; box 8, incoming correspondence, 12.1850 folder, from Joseph Grubb to Samuel Colt, December 3, 1850; box 8, 12/1850 folder, from H. W. Donnett, Boston, to Samuel Colt, December 16, 1850; box 8, 12/1850 folder, from Wallis, Philadelphia, to Samuel Colt, December 23, 1850; box 8, 12/1850 folder, from Wm. Smith to Samuel Colt, December 6, 1850; box 8, from Wallis to Samuel Colt, December 20, 1847. On prices too high and volume too small, see also box 8, 12/1850, from Eaton Dun to Samuel Colt, December 31, 1850.

35. WRAC, Winchester letter book, from Winchester to Charles Bradford, Indiana, October 18, 1862; from Winchester to Thomas North [?], October 8, 1862; from Winchester to A. C. Ellithorpe, April 11, 1863. Ellithorpe was actually a prominent politician, so in this case, to build connections, Winchester did fulfill the order. See also Sword, *The Historic Henry Rifle*, 13–15, on Winchester's "refocused marketing strategy."

36. WRAC, Winchester letter book, from Oliver Winchester to E. B. Martin, October 17, 1862; Lewis, *Volcanic Firearms*, 83.

37. WRAC, Winchester letter book, from Winchester to E. B. Martin, October 17, 1862.

38. Jinks, *History of Smith & Wesson*, 10–11.

39. George Madis, *Winchester: Dates of Manufacture, 1849–2000* (Brownsboro, TX: Art and Reference House, 1981), 8; WRAC, Winchester letter book, Winchester to E. B. Martin, October 17, 1862.

40. Lewis, *Volcanic Firearms*, 127; WRAC, Winchester letter book, from Winchester to E. B. Martin, October 17, 1862.

41. Ibid.; "Repeating Fire-Arms," *Scientific American* 19 (October 14, 1868): 245; Hallahan, *Misfire*, 134; Bilby, *A Revolution in Arms*, 226; Ian Hogg, *Weapons of the Civil War* (New York: Military Press, 1987), 37; cited in Sword, *The Historic Henry Rifle*, 31; WRAC, Winchester letter book, Winchester to commissioners Joel Hayden, R. Lee, June 12, 1863.

42. *The Field* review, quoted in John Parsons, *The First Winchester: The Story of the 1866 Repeating Rifle* (New York: Morrow, 1955), 71–73; Ian Hogg, *Weapons of the Civil War*, 38–39.

43. *Scientific American* 3, no. 13.

44. US Patent Office, "B Tyler Henry, of New Haven, Assignor to Oliver F. Winchester, Improvement in Magazine Fire Arms," patent #30,466, October 16, 1860.

45. WRAC, Winchester letter book, from Oliver Winchester to E. B. Martin, October 17, 1862.

46. Ibid. Here and throughout, for parenthetical contemporary equivalents of value, I have followed the economics view that there are a few ways to compare worth historically. For goods and real estate I have used a "standard of living" equivalent, but for comparisons of the Winchester company's worth or value I have used an "economic status value," which measures the relative "prestige value" of an amount of wealth vis-à-vis 2015 standards, i.e., how much money in today's economy would be comparable to the historical figure. See Measuringworth.com, www.measuringworth.com/uscompare.

47. Ibid.

48. Ibid.

49. Ibid.

CHAPTER 4: "MORE WONDERFUL THAN PRACTICAL"

1. Marcot, *The History of Remington Firearms*, 22, notes that "America's peacetime economy of the 1850s meant that the U.S. military had little need for weapons from its own national armories, and even less from private manufacturers," so Remington shifted to "non-military" products to "keep revenue flowing." Van Zwoll, *America's Great Gunmakers*, 129.

2. Beecher quoted in Nancy Koester, *Harriet Beecher Stowe: A Spiritual Life* (Grand Rapids, MI: Eerdmans, 2014), 196; WRAC, Winchester letter book, from Winchester to J. W. Forbes, February 14, 1863; Hatch, *Remington*, 75; Grant, *The Colt Legacy*, 83, xi, 13; Edwards, *The Story of Colt's Revolver*, 357 (in the early 1860s, Colt was, as always, chiefly interested in "making something to sell"; see also pp. 366–368); SC, box 8, 1860, from William Hartley to Samuel Colt, marked confidential, January 13, 1860; CC, box 66, "printed materials / internal advertising and marketing—public," *Sunny South*, Aberdeen, Mississippi, February 21, 1861.

3. A gun manufacturer in Savannah wrote to Colt to propose a southern partnership, "having understood that you were about establishing a Gunn [sic] factory in Richmond." SC, box 7, folder 10, from Mr. J. Gallagher to Samuel Colt, January 5, 1859; SC, box 7, folder 11, from Samuel Colt to William Hartley, Richmond, December 12, 1859; box 7, folder 11, from William Hartley to Samuel Colt, December 16, 1859.

4. SC, box 7, folder 11, from William Hartley to Samuel Colt, December 16, 1859; box 8, folder 1, from William Hartley to Samuel Colt, January 11, 1860; box 8, folder 1, from B. McDonald, Marietta, Georgia, to Samuel Colt, January 26, 1860.

5. "A Word to the People of Connecticut," *New York Times*, January 14, 1861; *New York Daily Tribune*, April 27, 1861.

6. US Congress, Joint Committee on the Conduct of the War, *Part III—Department of the West* (Washington, DC: US Government Printing Office, 1863), 37. Among many others, Kirkland, *America's Premier Gunmakers: Remington*, notes that the union was in "dire straits" for guns (p. 32), as does Dean Boorman, *The History of Colt Firearms* (New York: Lyons, 2001), 69. Gilmore, "Another Branch of the Manly Sport," 105.

7. HM, library, "Marcellus Hartley: A Brief Memoir" (New York: privately published, 1903), 4, 17, 18, 20.

8. *Select Committee on Government Contracts*, 1131 H. Ex. Doc. 67, March 3, 1862, 37th Cong., 2nd sess., letter from Thomas Scott, Acting Secretary of War, to Schuyler, October 2, 1861, p. 229; HM, "Marcellus Hartley . . . ," letter from Hartley to

Stanton, October 7, 1862; from Hartley to P. H. Watson and Secretary of War, October 6, 1862; from Hartley to Stanton, October 8, 1862, pp. 39, 46.

9. Quoted in Kirkland, *America's Premier Gunmakers: Remington*, 31.

10. *Select Committee on Government Contracts*, March 3, 1862, 37th Cong., 2nd sess., Ripley to Simon Cameron, Secretary of War, "Notes on the Subject of Contracting for Small Arms," p. 30. On Ripley's recalcitrance, see also Marcot, *Spencer Repeating Firearms*, 34–48; Sword, *The Historic Henry Rifle*, 41; *Select Committee on Government Contracts*, "Notes on the Subject . . . ," 30; "Abraham Lincoln and the Repeating Rifle," as told by Spencer, *Scientific American*, December 1, 1921; "Breech-Loading Versus Muzzle-Loading Guns," by "O.F.W.," *Scientific American*, March 7, 1863, 150–151; Winchester quoted in Williamson, *Winchester*, 49; Deyrup, *Arms Makers of the Connecticut Valley*, 128 (noting that the US military was content to stick to its "tried and true" methods, and considered patented arms to be fads); Watrous *The History of Winchester Firearms*, 9. Kennett, *The Gun in America*, also notes that the military showed little interest in patented firearms (p. 90).

11. Quoted in Parsons, *The First Winchester*, 69–70; Houze, *Winchester Repeating Arms Company*, 13; "Europe: Our Paris Correspondent," *New York Times*, December 17, 1866, 2.

12. See also Ripley to Simon Cameron, December 11, 1861, reprinted in Marcot, *Spencer Repeating Firearms*, 35; Kirkland, *America's Premier Gunmakers: Colt*, 12; Grant, *The Colt Legacy*, 4–5; Sword, *The Historic Henry Rifle*, 41–43. Hallahan argues in *Misfire* that the Ordnance Department had a deeply entrenched fear of lack of ammunition, a problem that had almost cost the Revolutionary War, and which injudiciously shaped future small arms choices. DC, vol. 122, "The Story of Winchester," corporate history, written during World War I, 28. The memoir reminisces, "One reason, which seems odd to us today, was that it used too much ammunition." Alexander Rose, *American Rifle: A Biography* (New York: Bantam Dell, 2008), also discusses the notion of wasted ammunition.

13. Ripley quoted in Hallahan, *Misfire*, 124; from Samuel Colt to Sam Houston, February 24, 1847, reprinted in *Sam Colt's Own Record*, 49; *The Trial of Samuel Colt*, 38.

14. WRAC, Winchester letter book, Winchester to Andrew Wallace, April 24, 1863; Select Committee on Government Contracts . . . : Ripley to Simon Cameron, p. 30; Ripley to Cameron, December 31, 1861, p. 32; from Messrs. John Gallagher and Co. to Thomas Scott, Acting Secretary of War, October 11, 1861, p. 95; from Gallagher to Thomas Scott, October 30, 1861, p. 96; from Gallagher to Thomas Scott, November 13, 1861, pp. 97–98.

15. Winchester quoted in Sword, *The Historic Henry Rifle*, 53.

16. Bilby, *A Revolution in Arms*, 78, describes Simon Cameron as extremely "reachable."

17. Rep. No. 353, House of Representatives, 33rd Cong., 1st sess., August 3, 1854, "Extension of Colt's Patent," pp. 44, 45, 45–46, 15, 27, 72. On the gun industrialist's appeal to political influence, see also Hallahan, *Misfire*, 118–120; Hosley, *Colt*, 90–94.

18. Gideon Welles to John Dahlgren, June 4, 1861, reprinted in Marcot, *Spencer Repeating Firearms*, 28; "unpublished stockholders . . . ," Marcot, *Spencer Repeating Firearms*, 35; Hallahan, *Misfire*, 148; Bilby, *A Revolution in Arms*, 78.

19. "Abraham Lincoln and the Repeating Rifle"; Marcot, *Spencer Repeating Firearms*, 34–35; Bilby, *A Revolution in Arms*, 68, 76. Other gun industrialists tried for government contracts as well. Smith & Wesson designed the "Schofield" model for Major George

Schofield of the 10th cavalry. The company wanted to interest "anyone who might have influence with the government." Jinks, *History of Smith & Wesson*, 84.

20. Henry expert Bilby describes him as a "shadowy figure," and very much a creation of his own imagination, in *A Revolution in Arms*, 92, 138. Sword, *The Historic Henry Rifle*, 43.

21. CC, box 66, folder 3, "Why Colt's Has Been the Official Sidearm of the U.S. Government Since 1847," n.d., newspaper template advertisement; box 66, folder 3, "Ready for Duty," October 1917.

22. Marcot, *Spencer Repeating Firearms*, 51; Bilby, *A Revolution in Arms*, 86.

23. WRAC, Winchester letter book, from Winchester to John Brown, November 5, 1862; "Indians or," Sword, *The Historic Henry Rifle*, 20.

24. Sword, *The Historic Henry Rifle*, 10. Sword has the best account of Prentice's actions in Kentucky.

25. Sword, *The Historic Henry Rifle*, 10–11; WRAC, Winchester letter book, from Winchester to John Brown, October 17, 1862; from Winchester to Semple and Sons, May 4, 1863.

26. WRAC, Winchester letter book, Winchester to Charles Bradford, October 18, 1862; Winchester to Judge Williams, October 16, 1862; Winchester to John Brown, October 17, 1862; Winchester to Judge Williams, October 16, 1862.

27. WRAC, Winchester letter book, from Winchester to Prentice, October 27, 1862; from Winchester to Prentice, November 4, 1862.

28. WRAC, Winchester letter book, to Philip Vilano [sp.?], December 17, 1862. The erraticism of the war was exacerbated by the company's serious production limitations and hurdles from the start, which boiled down to having to wait for "the machines made at big prices and the hands [paid] at extravagant wages," Winchester said, and wild price fluctuations as well as delays on critical materials such as lead, copper, and steel (letter book, to John Brown, May 23, 1863, and October 9, 1862).

29. WRAC, Winchester letter book, from Winchester to Thomas North [?], October 8, 1862; from Winchester to Kittredge, November 4, 1862; from Winchester to Garrow, December 1, 1862; from Winchester to Vilano [sp.?], December 17, 1862. Among other things, dealers helped manage the gun supply and steadied the erratic pulse of the gun market by returning guns to the factory to apply to current orders, or by sending them to other dealers at Winchester's request. For example, see WRAC, Winchester letter book, from Winchester to John Brown, November 11, 1862; from Winchester to Semple and Sons, April 15, 1862, instructing them to shift unsold rifles to Brown; from Winchester to John Brown, May 7, 1863; from Winchester to Potter and Johnson [sp.?], July 8, 1863; from Winchester to John Brown, December 6, 1862; from Winchester to John Brown, December 30, 1862.

30. WRAC, Winchester letter book, from Winchester to John Brown, May 7, 1863; from Winchester to J. Storer, April 20, 1863.

31. WRAC, Winchester letter book, from Winchester to Judge Williams, March 19, 1863; from Winchester to Kittredge, February 3, 1862; from Winchester to Brown, November 17, 1862; from Winchester to Williams, March 19, 1863; from Winchester to Brown, November 11, 1862; from Winchester to Brown, December 6, 1862; from Winchester to Kittredge, November 14, 1862.

32. WRAC, Winchester letter book, from Winchester to Kittredge, February 3, 1863; from Winchester to John Brown, March 19, 1863; from Winchester to Judge Williams, March 19, 1863.

33. WRAC, Winchester letter book, faithlessness, from Winchester to W. Cleveland [sp.], January 18, 1863; from Winchester to Kittredge, August 4, 1863.

34. WRAC, Winchester letter book, from Winchester to General Alfred [sp.], January 30, 1863; from Winchester to Ellithorpe, April 11, 1863. An 1862 company price list offers the Henry at $42, with additional costs for a leather case, silver plating and engraving, and so on.

35. SC, box 7, folder 1, from Captain [Bervow—sp.?] to Samuel Colt, March 17, 1851; WRAC, Winchester letter book, from Winchester to Judge Williams, December 6, 1862. The *Hartford Courant* in 1856 concluded that the gifting of pistols was a key to Colt's success abroad; see CC, box 70A, "Colonel Colt's Pistols," *Supplement to the Courant*, June 21, 1856, 116. Hosley, *Colt*, 90.

36. David Butler, *United States Firearms: The First Century, 1776–1875* (New York: Winchester Press, 1971), 226. On awareness of Winchester's aggressive sales techniques, see Sword, *The Historic Henry Rifle*.

37. Samuel Colt testified before the British House of Commons and the Select Committee on Small Arms in 1854 that when he began, he intended to make arms for the US government and for "general sale." All "new mechanics think that Government patronage is valuable," he said. "It is an advertisement, if nothing else." British Commons record, p. 1104, also quoted in Barnard, *Armsmear*, 366 (appendix). WRAC, Winchester letter book, from Winchester to Rev. H. Bell [sp.], chaplain, 12th Kentucky Cavalry.

38. CSL, CC, box 70A, "Colt in the Caucasus."

39. WRAC, series 4, box 10, folder 40, "Henry's Repeating Fire Arms, Rifled Muskets, Carbines, Shot Guns, Hunting and Target Rifles, etc., catalog (New Haven: WRAC, 1865), 34–36. Story is also reprinted in Wilson, *Winchester: An American Legend*, 12.

40. Wilson, *Winchester: An American Legend*, 12.

41. WRAC, Winchester letter book, from Winchester to Prentice, December 30, 1862; from Winchester to Captain Wilson, December 30, 1862; from Winchester to Captain Wilson, March 19, 1863.

42. NHCHS, DC, vol. 122, p. 33.

43. WRAC, Winchester letter book, from Winchester to stockholder [illeg.], October 18, 1862.

44. WRAC, Winchester letter book, from Winchester to A. A. Vanwormer, St. Louis, June 8, 1863; from Winchester to John Brown, May 4, 1863.

45. Aaron Pardee, *Genealogy of One Line of the Pardee Family, and Some Memoirs* (Wadsworth, OH: 1896), 66.

46. Ibid., 68.

47. Jacobus, *The Pardee Genealogy*, 244. Sarah Winchester's mother would be one of the original WRAC stockholders; see WRAC, series 3, box 8, folder 13, memo from Henry Brewer, vice president, for "Winchester" file, August 1929. Sarah's one brother, Leonard Jr., joined the carriage-making business. Hokubei Meinichi, "Winchester Mystery House Becomes Tourist Attraction," *North American Daily*, November 13, 1976; Esther Talbot, "Sarah Winchester: Who Knows the Length of a Woman's Shadow?" *The Rosicrucian Digest*, July 1975, 28; Mary Jo Ignoffo, *Captive of the Labyrinth: Sarah L. Winchester Heiress to the Rifle Fortune* (Columbia: University of Missouri Press, 2010), 21.

48. Nancy F. Cott, *Bonds of Womanhood: "Woman's Sphere" in New England, 1780–1835* (New Haven, CT: Yale University Press, 1977); Mary Roth, *Doctors Wanted: No*

Women Need Apply. Sexual Barriers in the Medical Profession, 1835–1975 (New Haven, CT: Yale University Press, 1977), 140; Anne Rose, *Voices of the Marketplace*, describes "greater social distance between husbands and wives" in the early 1800s, and estrangement in their emotional and intellectual lives; see, especially, 60, 72. W. R. Greg, *Why Are Women Redundant?* (London: N. Trubner, 1869), 26.

49. Parsons, *The First Winchester*, 20, 21.

50. Miguel de Cervantes, *Don Quixote* (Philadelphia: Lea and Blanchard, 1847), 354; Dragimirov, quoted and discussed in Bradley, *Guns for the Tsar*, 121–126. I draw on Bradley's excellent discussion here.

51. O. F. W., "Breech-Loading Versus Muzzle-Loading Guns," 151; Hallahan, *Misfire*, 126; Brown, *Firearms in Colonial America*, 166.

52. So wrote Colonel John Wiler of the 17th Indiana regiment, quoted in Butler, *United States Firearms*, 227. Homer Sprague, *History of the Thirteenth Infantry Regiment of Connecticut Volunteers During the Great Rebellion* (Hartford: Case, Lockwood, 1867), 114.

53. The difficulties of using muzzle-loading and earlier rifles are nicely described in Hallahan, *Misfire*, 126–127, and Hatch, *Remington*, 63.

54. Quoted in Bilby, *A Revolution in Arms*, 191, 162; quoted in Sword, *The Historic Henry Rifle*, 64. A Confederate sharpshooter reported that he could fire a Spencer captured in battle so fast that once he had to stop to let the gun cool; see Berry Benson, *Berry Benson's Civil War Book: Memoirs of a Confederate Scout and Sharpshooter* (Athens: University of Georgia Press, 1962), 183. Quoted in Bilby, *A Revolution in Arms*, 194–195.

55. I found Bilby's compilation of battle reports on the Spencer and Henry repeating rifles to be invaluable. Quoted at Bilby, *A Revolution in Arms*, 126, 122. See also Senate, Rep. Com. #257, 31st Cong., 2nd sess., January 30, 1851, "On the Relative Efficiency of Colt's and Others' Repeating Rifles," 2–3.

56. Brown, *Firearms in Colonial America*, 166; Barnard, *Armsmear*, 161; quoted in Sword, *The Historic Henry Rifle*, 14; Bradley, *Guns for the Tsar*, 121–122; Bilby, *A Revolution in Arms*, 217 (describing the Atlanta swap).

57. Advertising broadside, "The Winchester Repeating Rifle: Two Shots a Second," distributed April 1867, reprinted in Houze, *Winchester Repeating Arms Company*, 64; reprinted in Parsons, *The First Winchester*, 79; Missouri Historical Society, Oliver Winchester, "The First Requisite of a Military Rifle," letter written to London by Oliver Winchester, August 2, 1869, pp. 14–15, 4, 15, 5.

58. In the Atlanta campaign from May to September, 1864, the 2nd Division of the 16th Army Corps shot 83,500 Henry .44-caliber cartridges and 11,088 Spencer .52-caliber cartridges. It is also the case that officers' tactical strategies for using the repeater only really began to coalesce toward the end of the war.

59. Winchester, "Breech-Loading Versus Muzzle-Loading Guns," 151. Winchester gravitated often to the term "coolness"; his salesmen in the region swore he sold only to loyal men, but agreed to store his unsold Henrys. Reprinted in Sword, *The Historic Henry Rifle*, 14, and in C. B. Colby, *Firearms by Winchester: A Part of United States History* (New York: Coward-McCann, 1957), 48. This testimonial is reprinted in several sources, including Colby, ibid., 48.

60. Lane, *Murder in America*, 109.

61. Lucian Cary, "The American Rifle," *Holiday*, October 1947, 90; WRAC, series 4, box 11, folder 49, Edwin Pugsley, "Early Winchester Rifles," *American Rifleman*, May 1931, 37; Watrous, *The History of Winchester Firearms*, 9. Even as late as Gettysburg,

battles were fought principally with muzzle-loaders; see Wilson, *Winchester: An American Legend*, 11, on preference for single shot. The Allin, a breech-loading but not a repeating rifle, was chosen after the war as the infantry arm.

CHAPTER 5: MODEL 1866

1. WRAC, series 5, box 13, folder 23, from Edwin Pugsley to Peter Drucker, September 1, 1944. E. Remington & Sons used the contract system as well. Each contractor at Remington would have thirty or so employees that he hired, and each team executed work on one specific part, to exact gauges—one set of gauges kept with the company and the other kept by the contractor in his own office. HCHSVF, #292.

2. Dean Boorman, *The History of Winchester Firearms* (New York: Lyons, 2001), 20–21; Williamson, *Winchester*, 30.

3. WRAC, series 4, box 12, folder 21, typescript, "The Beginning of the Smith & Wesson and the Winchester."

4. Houze, *Winchester Repeating Arms Company*, 22; Bilby, *A Revolution in Arms*, 224.

5. WRAC, series 4, box 10, folder 40, "Henry's Repeating Fire Arms," catalog, New Haven, 1865.

6. The story of the takeover is drawn from Houze, *Winchester Repeating Arms Company*, 22–42. See also WRAC, Veader, "The Story of the WRAC."

7. WRAC, Veader, "The Story of the WRAC."

8. Ibid.

9. The 1876 WRAC board of directors was also dominated by the Winchester family, with Oliver, Will, Sarah Winchester's brother-in-law W. W. Converse, and Jane Winchester's husband TG Bennett. As for the stock, the Winchesters would remain in control for some time. A few months later, on September 6, 1869, of the 4,500 shares of stock, Oliver, Will, Oliver's wife, and Oliver's daughter controlled almost the same amount as in February—2,450. See WRAC, Veader, "The Story of the WRAC," 93, 54.

10. NHCHS, DC, vol. 122, p. 26.

11. Carrie Brown, "Guns for Billy Yank: The Armory in Windsor Meets the Challenge of the Civil War, *Vermont History* 79, no. 2 (2011): 49; Ilion Free Public Library, Remington Arms Folders (IPLRF), folder 1, description from "Atlas of the Hudson River and New York Central Railroads," 1861, p. 93; Mark Twain, "A Glimpse at Hartford," *Alta California*, March 3, 1868; Barnard, *Armsmear*, 54, 55; Robert J. Neal and Roy G. Jinks, *Smith & Wesson, 1857–1945* (New York: A. S. Barnes, 1975), 240.

12. WRAC, box 9, folder 8, correspondence between Oliver Winchester and Smith & Wesson, 1868 to 1873, from Smith and Wesson to Winchester, July 25, 1868; from Smith and Wesson to Winchester, September 10, 1868; from Smith and Wesson to Winchester, September 14, 1868; from Smith and Wesson to Winchester, January 1, 1869; from Curtis (Smith and Wesson attorney) to Winchester, May 31, 1873.

13. On sharps, see Van Zwoll, *America's Great Gunmakers*, 80–89.

14. "Left Valuable Patents: Estate of Benjamin Tyler Henry Probated by Judge Cleveland," *Leader*, June 14, 1898, B13.

15. Nancy Schrom Dye and Daniel Blake Smith, "Mother Love and Infant Death, 1750–1920," in Judith Walzer Leavitt, ed., *Women and Health in America: Historical Readings*, 2nd ed. (Madison: University of Wisconsin Press, 1999), 101, 102.

16. Jacobus, *The Pardee Genealogy*, 244–245; "Obituary" (Ann Dye *née* Winchester), *New York Evangelist*, March, 10, 1864, 35: 10.

17. Johns Hopkins University, Welch Medical Library (JHUWL), Special Collections, Mrs. C. A. Hopkinson, *Hints for the Nursery* (Boston: Little, Brown, 1863), 36; Drs. Elizabeth Garrett Anderson et al., *The Sanitary Care and Treatment of Children and Their Diseases* (New York: Houghton Mifflin, 1881), 100, 243, 108.

18. JHUWL, Charles West, MD, *Diseases of Infancy and Childhood* (Philadelphia: Henry Lea, 1874), 497; Hopkinson, *Hints for the Nursery*, 32–33.

19. West, *Diseases of Infancy and Childhood*, 436.

20. NHCHS, *New England Almanac, Farmer's Friend*; *Beckwith's Almanac*, 1868 ed., describing 1866.

21. WRAC, series 3, box 8, folder 13, typescript, company history; "Oliver Fisher Winchester: Captain of Industry"; BBHC, *Winchester Record* 2, November 7, 1919, 1.

22. On the Joint Stock Incorporation Act as it was perceived in the 1880s, see Johnson, *Connecticut*, 367.

23. WRAC, series 4, box 11, folder 8, typescript of Winchester history for fiftieth anniversary, June 23, 1959; see also series 4, box 11, folder 50, from Bob McMahon, WRAC, to Connecticut newspapermen, October 8, 1945; series 4, box 11, folder 49, draft for *American Rifleman* by Edwin Pugsley, "Early Winchester Rifles," May 1931.

24. JHUWL, Garrett Anderson et al., *Sanitary Care*, 100; West, *Diseases of Infancy*, 479, 497, 529; Hopkinson, *Hints for the Nursery*, 29; Garrett Anderson et al., *Sanitary Care*, 247.

25. Edward Atwater, *History of the City of New Haven to the Present Time* (New York: W. W. Munsell, 1887), 280–281; West, *Diseases of Infancy*, 446.

26. NHCHS, *Beckwith's Almanac*, 1868 ed., for example.

27. Stuart Vyse, *Believing in Magic: The Psychology of Superstition* (New York: Oxford University Press, 1997), 98. On spiritualism's alternative, more "scientific" views of death, see Ann Braude, *Radical Spirits: Spiritualism and Women's Rights in Nineteenth-Century America*, 2nd ed. (Bloomington: Indiana University Press, 2001), 36. On infant death, see Judith Leavitt, *Brought to Bed: Childbearing in America, 1750–1950* (New York: Oxford University Press, 1986), 28.

Thunderstorms are mentioned in a few places, including Lorena Ann Omstead, "The House That Spirits Built," *National Motorist*, July-August 1946, 15; San Jose Public Library, California Room, Vertical Files (CR), Bruce Spoon, Yale University, typescript, "Sarah Winchester and Her House: How a Legend Grows," March 31, 1951, 14; CR, San Jose Chamber of Commerce, "Winchester Mystery House: Four Miles West of San Jose," typescript, 1937; Dean Jennings, "The House of Mystery," *Modern Mechanics*, June 1937.

28. WRAC, 1867 catalog, quoted at Butler, *United States Firearms*, 236; DC, vol. 42, p. 24.

29. Houze, *Winchester Repeating Arms Company*, 46.

30. Ibid.; WRAC, Winchester letter book, from Winchester to Captain Wilson, March 19, 1863; DC, vol. 122, p. 28; WRAC, Vaeder, "The Story of the WRAC," 39.

31. "Spirit Guns: A True Story of the First American Repeating Rifles and Their Use in a Fight on the Western Frontier," *American Rifleman*, February 1929.

32. Ibid.; see also Colby, *Firearms by Winchester*, 4.

33. Adam Smith, *The Theory of Moral Sentiments*, 6th ed. (London: A Millar, 1790), pt. 6, section 2, chap. 2, www.econlib.org/library/Smith/smMS6.html.

34. Alan Wallach, "Colonel Colt's Ambiguous Legacy: Or, When I Hear the Word 'Revolver,' I Reach for my Culture," *American Quarterly* 50, no. 3 (1998): 611.

35. Hosley, *Colt*, 192–193, concludes that Elizabeth was conscious of the ambivalence of Colt's character and family legacy. Thomas McDade, *The Annals of Murder*, 62; Barnard, *Armsmear*, 70.

36. "The Homes of America: VII, Armsmear," *Art Journal*, November 1876, 89 (describing the church); Grant, *The Colt Legacy*, x; Hosley, *Colt*, 200–202; Wallach, "Colonel Colt's Ambiguous Legacy," 619.

CHAPTER 6: "GUN MEN" AND THE "ORIENTAL LECTURER"

1. Spencer Repeating Rifle Company, Catalog of 1866, quoted at Marcot, *Spencer Repeating Firearms*, 90; Alice Williams, *Silk and Guns: The Life of a Connecticut Yankee. Frank Cheney, 1817–1904* (Manchester, CT: Manchester Historical Society, 1996), 99. Deyrup meticulously describes this economy in *Arms Makers of the Connecticut Valley*.

2. WRAC, Veader, "The Story of the WRAC," 36.

3. Herbert Houze calls the market "abysmal" in *Arming the West: A Fresh New Look at the Guns That Were Actually Carried on the Frontier* (Woonsocket, RI: Mowbray, 2008), ix; Boorman, *The History of Smith & Wesson Firearms*, 30; Butler, *United States Firearms*, 235; Grant, *The Colt Legacy*, 29; Bilby, *A Revolution in Arms*, 223; Sword, *The Historic Henry Rifle*, 31; HCHSVF, #292, "Romantic History of the Remington Arms Industry in War and Peace;" "The Remington Works, Ilion, NY," *Scientific American*, April 13, 1872, 240. On the Ordnance Department sales, see *Congressional Series of United States Public Documents*, vol. 1528, *Reports of the Committees of the House of Representatives*, 42nd Cong., 2nd sess., House of Representatives Report #46, "Sales of Ordnance Stores," April 15, 1872 (Washington, DC: US Government Printing Office, 1872), 2.

4. Mass production reduced the unit cost of guns, but it required machines, and the machines were a huge investment that "becomes oppressive when large output is not maintained," explains Deyrup. Furthermore, increased capitalization during the war "demanded a very large increase in the volume of production to keep overhead costs at reasonable levels." *Arms Makers of the Connecticut Valley*, 202; DC, vol. 122, "The Story of Winchester," 28, excerpted from Norris Galpin Osborn's *History of Connecticut* (New York: States History Company, 1925).

5. Hatch, *Remington*, 107, writes that in ammunition, demand would arise and "dazzling profits" accrue; Kirkland, *America's Premier Gunmakers: Remington*, 54; HCHSVF, #293, from A. C. Barrell, "The History of Remington Arms and UMC Companies," *Field and Stream*, 716.

6. Henning et al., "The Advertising of E. Remington & Sons," 427; quoted at Bradley, *Guns for the Tsar*, 106–107; Bilby, *A Revolution in Arms*, 223; WRAC, Veader, "The Story of the WRAC," 42–43.

7. See, for example, Houze, *Winchester Repeating Arms Company*, 36; Kennett, *The Gun in America*, 92; 1880 US Census, vol. 2, "Interchangeable Mechanism," 620. The census elaborates that in 1867 the Danish government visited Remington and contracted for 40,000 arms, with machinery, and the Swedish government contracted for 10,000 arms. Other countries with contracts included Prussia, Spain, Turkey, England, and Russia. Brown, "Guns for Billy Yank," 155–158; WRAC, Veader, "The Story of the WRAC," 153; Van Zwoll, *America's Great Gunmakers*, 94–98; Bilby, *A Revolution in Arms*, notes the "scramble for overseas military contracts" and looking to exploit "whatever American civilian market existed to continue in business" (p. 223).

8. Quoted at Bradley, *Guns for the Tsar*, 108. Deyrup, *Arms Makers of the Connecticut Valley*, aptly calls Colt's entrance into foreign exports "spectacular" in its breadth (pp. 128–130).

9. Boorman, *The History of Smith & Wesson*, 30. Bradley, *Guns for the Tsar*, 115, comments that it "meant the world" to Smith & Wesson to have the Russian contract. Jinks, *History of Smith & Wesson*, 68; WRAC, series 5, box 13, folder 21, letter from WRAC to Mr. Albert Partoll [sp.] on Winchester history, December 7, 1928; WRAC, series 5, box 13, folder 21, correspondence on Buffalo Bill from Thomas Hall to Mr. Albert Partoll [sp.], December 7, 1928; Rywell, *Smith & Wesson*, 75.

10. Rywell, *Smith & Wesson*, 75; Neal and Jinks, *Smith & Wesson*, 166.

11. John Gunther, "Slaughter for Sale," *Harper's*, May 1934, 655; Kirkland, *America's Premier Gunmakers: Remington*, 35. Later, the 1934 Nye Committee on the Investigation of the Munitions Industry found that in "sales methods," "almost without exception, American munitions companies . . . have at times resorted to such unusual . . . methods of 'doing the needful' as to constitute . . . a form of bribery of foreign governmental officials or . . . their close friends." Dealers had broken the spirit if not the letter of the law in selling to belligerents; and, more significantly, other countries, even "belligerent" ones, used the private US arms industry as an auxiliary and sometimes a primary arsenal. John Wiltz, "The Nye Committee Revisited," *Historian* 23, no. 2 (1961). On the Remington aversion to bribes in foreign sales see Ilion Free Public Library (IPL), A. N. Russell (receiver), Scrapbook, 1864–1904 (ANRS), 72; HCHSVF, #293, from A. C. Barrell, "History of the Remington and UMC Companies," *Field and Stream*, 713; ANRS, 71, remarks delivered March 21, 1897, at Ilion banquet.

12. Hatch, *Remington*, 143; Kirkland, *America's Premier Gunmakers: Remington*, 36–37.

13. Remington historian and expert Marcot, *The History of Remington Firearms*, 50, 50–54, comments that it was the sale to foreign governments that brought Remington "unprecedented prosperity." HCHSVF, #1256, *New York Tribune*, May 11, 1871; IPLED, vol. 1, *Army and Navy Journal*, May 6, 1871, notes that the plant was "taxed to the utmost" on the French order. HM, *The Remington Centennial Book*, 18.

14. Kirkland, *America's Premier Gunmakers: Remington*, 36; Hatch, *Remington*, 145; Marcot, *The History of Remington Firearms*, 35, 32.20.

15. IPLED, vol. 1, from *Ilion Citizen*, May 8, 1883; *Herkimer Democrat*, July 7, 1869; *Ilion Citizen*, December 12, 1873; *Ilion Citizen*, January 21, 1881; HCHSVF, #292, from "Romantic History of the Remington Arms Industry in War and Peace." See also IPLED, vol. 1, *New York Herald*, March 9, 1877, on the visit from the Russian grand duke.

16. Hatch, *Remington*, 116–117.

17. BBHC, MS034 Schuyler, Hartley & Graham Collection (SHGC).

18. SHGC, records of Cuban shipments, in box 1, folders 15, 16, 20, 26, 28, 30, 33, 34; box 2, folders 2, 4, 7, 11, 12, 13, 14, 17, 21, 22, 24, 25, 27, 28, 33, 35, 36, 39, 41, 42, 45, 46, 49; box 3, folder 3; box 4, folders 3, 4. E. Remington & Sons itself, however, said it had never sold to insurgents in Cuba. See IPLED, vol. 1, from *Herkimer Democrat*, July 7, 1869.

19. SHGC, records of Mexican shipments, in box 2, folders 33, 50; box 3, folders 6, 9, 10, 12, 18, 37, 48, 53; box 4, folders 7, 8, 17, 18, 19, 27, 35; box 5, folders 10, 14, 17, 21, 28; box 6, folders 4, 35. Dominican Republic in box 2, folders 24, 50; box 3, folders 7, 10, 14, 17, 19, 23, 29; box 5, folders 43, 47, 49, 50, 53, 56. Panama in box 1, folder 10; box 2, folders 1, 34, 38; box 3, folders 42, 51; box 4, folders 3, 22, 24; box 5, folders 10,

18, 29; box 6, folders 37, 38, 40. Curacao in box 1, folders 17, 20, 31; box 2, folders 3, 6, 12, 18. Guatemala in box 3, folders 47, 49, 53; box 5, folder 15; box 6, folder 14. Costa Rica in box 2, folder 22; box 3, folders 13, 47; box 4, folder 34; box 6, folders 5, 56, 57. Haiti in box 2, folder 32; box 3, folders 26, 44. El Salvador in box 2, folder 31; box 3, folder 9; box 5, folder 2. Honduras in box 2, folder 16. Bahamas in box 1, folder 22. Brazil in box 2, folder 30. Ecuador in box 2, folder 36. Chile in box 2, folder 40. Liberia in box 2, folder 40; box 3, folders 18, 48, 52; box 4, folder 9; box 5, folders 1, 24, 31; box 6, folders 11, 38. Japan in box 1, folder 9; box 4, folder 16. Hong Kong in box 1, folder 11. Gabon in box 2, folder 34. Paris in box 1, folder 12.

20. Henning, "The Advertising of E. Remington & Sons," 425, 430, 433–434; Parsons, *The First Winchester*, 82. Winchester's journey from courting US military contracts to foreign contracts is a tale lightly revealed in serial numbers: Henry rifles #1 and #6 went to Secretary of War Edwin Stanton and President Lincoln, respectively; Henry #8909, with Japanese character engraving, sold in 1868 to Emperor Meiji. Sword, *The Historic Henry Rifle*, appendix.

21. Rachel Stohl and Suzette Grillot, *The International Arms Trade* (Cambridge, UK: Polity, 2009), 14. "Up until the 1930s, arms were normally exported as freely as any other civil item," write John Stanley and Maurice Pearton in *The International Trade in Arms* (New York: Praeger, 1972), 5. Alexander DeConde, *Gun Violence in America: The Struggle for Control*, notes the federal government's unactionable embarrassment over shipments to Chile in 1891 (p. 97), for example. *Congressional Series of United States Public Documents*, vol. 1528, *Reports of the Committees of the House of Representatives*, 42nd Cong., 2nd sess., House of Representatives Report #46, "Sales of Ordnance Stores," April 15, 1872 (Washington, DC: US Government Printing Office, 1872), 74.

22. House of Representatives Report #46, "Sales of Ordnance Stores," 13–15.

23. Ibid., 14, 144.

24. Ibid., 5–6.

25. Ibid., 181, 29, 144, 155, 156.

26. Ibid., 216, 8.

27. Arthur Earle, "Thomas Emmett Addis," November 15, 1922, typescript memoir, WRAC, series 3, box 8, folder 13, pp. 2–3; Henry Brewer, "Thomas Emmett Addis," typescript, for *Reader's Digest*, WRAC, series 11, box 1, folder 4, p. 2.

28. Earle, "Thomas Emmett Addis," 2, 9.

29. WRAC, Veader, "The Story of the WRAC," 28.

30. See, especially, BBHC, *Winchester Record* 1, no. 15, "Colonel Tom Addis Carries Winchester into Mexico," February 28, 1919, although the story is told at multiple places in the company archive, including Earle, "Thomas Emmett Addis"; Brewer, "Thomas Emmett Addis"; and WRAC, series 4, box 10, folder 19, typescript, 3 pp., n.d. (noting Addis's foreign contracts).

31. WRAC, Veader, "The Story of the WRAC," 27.

32. WRAC, series 3, box 8, folder 13, and series 7, box 20, folder 19.

33. WRAC, series 4, box 10, folder 19, Brewer, "Thomas Emmett Addis."

34. WRAC, Veader, "The Story of the WRAC," 39, 36.

35. Connecticut Historical Society (CHS), Bennett-Winchester Papers (BW), MS #87108, box 1, folder d, from TG Bennett to Jane Bennett, March 28, 1879.

36. DC, Thomas Bennett obituary, vol. 42, pp. 12–14; Williamson, *Winchester*, 131.

37. BW, box 1, folder d, from TG Bennett to Jane Bennett, from Bucharest, Romania, April 7, 1879; May 14, 1879.

38. Report of the Special Committee on Investigation of the Munitions Industry (The Nye Report), US Congress, Senate, 74th Cong., 2nd sess., February 24, 1936, "The Sales Methods of the Munitions Companies," 3–4; BW, box 1, folder d, from TG Bennett to Jane Bennett, from Bucharest, Romania, March 25, 1879; March 20, 1879.

39. BW, box 1, folder d, from TG Bennett to Jane Bennett, from Constantinople, April 24, 1879.

40. BW, box 1, folder d, from TG Bennett to Jane Bennett, from Bucharest, Romania, March 28, 1879. Here and throughout, I have modernized the spelling in quotations from letters; for example, changing "some thing" to something, "every thing" to everything, and "any one" to anyone.

41. BW, box 1, folder d, from TG Bennett to Jane Bennett, from Bucharest, Romania, March 16, 1878.

42. BW, box 1, folder d, from TG Bennett to Jane Bennett, from Romania, March 28, 1879; March 30, 1879.

43. HCHSVF, #293, A. C. Barrell, "The History of the Remington and U.M.C. Companies," 710–711; Herkimer County Historical Society, Remington Material (HCHSRM), #2015.8.53, "Correspondence from a Correspondent of the New York Press, 1892, Concerning Senator Watson C. Squires and a Daughter of Remington."

44. BBHC, Herbert Houze Collection (HH), MS70, box 1, folder 4, typescript, "A Brief Biography of Benjamin Berkeley Hotchkiss."

45. CSL, typescript, "The Inventors: Andrew and Berkeley [Hotchkiss]," with copies of correspondence and a memoir, p. 71; HH, box 1, folder 4, "A Brief Biography of Benjamin Berkeley Hotchkiss"; HH, box 1, folder 1, "The Hotchkiss Repeater" catalog, May 1, 1879.

46. WRAC, series 11, box 1, folder 4, Henry Brewer, "Thomas Emmett Addis," typescript, October 1944, 7. Boorman notes, in *The History of Winchester Firearms*, 31, that Addis had "unlimited territory and unlimited authority."

47. Blum, *The Republican Roosevelt*, 29.

48. Arthur Earle, "Thomas Emmet Addis," memoir, typescript, November 15, 1922, WRAC, series 3, box 8, folder 13, p. 1.

49. Addis's dispatches from abroad are largely lost in the archive, but these are reprinted in Williamson, *Winchester*, 118–120.

50. Williamson, *Winchester*, 118–120. Smuggling and gun-running were common. See George Madis, *The Winchester Book* (Dallas: 1961), 66.

51. Williamson, *Winchester*, 119; HH, box 1, folder 1, "Terms of Sale."

52. Earle, "Thomas Emmet Addis," 6–7.

53. Van Zwoll, *America's Great Gunmakers*, 134; Henry Brewer, "Thomas Emmett Addis," typescript for *Reader's Digest*, October 1944, HH, series 11, box 1, folder 4, appendix.

54. HH, box 1, folder 4, from London Armory Company to Edwin Pugsley, December 18, 1947.

55. Henry Brewer, "Thomas Emmett Addis," October 1944, typescript, WRAC, series 4, box 10, folder 19, p. 7.

56. Philip Mansel, *Constantinople: City of the World's Desire* (New York: St. Martin's, 1996), 286; Noel Barber, *The Sultans* (New York: Simon and Schuster, 1973), 314, 151.

57. WRAC, Veader, "The Story of the WRAC," 58; *Christopher Oscanyan v. The Winchester Repeating Arms Company, American Law Register* 26, no. 10, new series 17 (October 1878): 626–634, 627.

58. Ibid.

59. "Mr Oscanyan, The Oriental Lecturer, Entered according to Act of Congress in the year 1863, by Charles D. Fredericks & Co., in the Clerk's Office of the District Court of the United States for the Southern District of New York," image retrieved at users.stlcc.edu/mfuller/Oscanyan.html; Johns Hopkins University, Peabody Library, Bound Pamphlets, "International Law Pamphlets," vol. 51, Christopher Oscanyan, "The United States and Turkey," December 1868, 18.

60. Barber, *The Sultans*, 149–150, 151, 152, 154–155.

61. Mansel, *Constantinople*, 284; Oscanyan, "The United States and Turkey," 14, 16, 28, 47. Mark Twain sardonically described the same perilous brew in *The Innocents Abroad*. Phillip Noel Baker, *The Private Manufacture of Arms* (New York: Dover, 1976 [1936]), 137.

62. WRAC, series 5, box 13, folder 21, from Thomas Hall to Mr. J. Forrest, June 27, 1928; BBHC, *Winchester Record* 1, no. 30, May 9, 1919, 2; series 5, box 13, folder 21, from Henry Brewer to Harry Griswald, November 23, 1931; *Christopher Oscanyan v. The Winchester Repeating Arms Company*, 628.

63. *Christopher Oscanyan v. The Winchester Repeating Arms Company*, 628.

64. BW, box 1, folder c, from TG Bennett to Jane Bennett, from Constantinople, December 8, 1877; Kirkland, *America's Premier Gunmakers: Remington*, 54.

65. "The Winchester That Liked the Russians at Plevna," *American Legion*, December 1947, 75.

66. Ibid.

67. From O. F. Winchester to Azarian & Co., May 3, 1870, reprinted in Parsons, *The First Winchester*, 160 (appendix).

68. Herkimer County Historical Society (HCHS), Shepard-Richardson Collection (SRC), item #166, "Handwritten Manuscript of an Opinion as to Matters in Difference Between E. Remington & Sons and Samuel John Norris."

69. Parsons, *The First Winchester*, 161–162.

70. Ibid., 164.

71. Ibid., 155–157.

72. BBHC, *Winchester Record* 1, no. 14, "Early Facts About the Winchester Repeating Arms Company," February 14, 1919; DC, vol. 122, p. 28; WRAC, Veader, "The Story of the WRAC," 82; *Congressional Series of United States Public Documents*, vol. 1528, *Reports of the Committees of the House of Representatives*, 42nd Cong., 2nd sess., House of Representatives Report #46, "Sales of Ordnance Stores," April 15, 1872 (Washington, DC: US Government Printing Office, 1872), 180.

73. Williamson, *Winchester*, 56; WRAC, additional box 22, folder 13, "various correspondence, Edwin Pugsley," October 22, 1873, from Winchester to Malleable Iron Fillings Co., Branford, CT.

74. *Christopher Oscanyan v. The Winchester Repeating Arms Company*, 639, 630.

75. Ibid., 630, 631.

76. "An Exploded 'Torpedo': Adventures of a 'Turkish Nobleman' in New York," *New York Times*, February 4, 1877, 7. Material in the following paragraphs is drawn from this article.

77. BW, box 1, folder d, from TG Bennett to Jane Bennett, from Constantinople, April 15, 1879; Barber, *The Sultans*, 162, 168–170, 162, 174, 170–173.

78. "Turkish Internal Affairs: Charges of Corruption Against a Prominent Official— Refusal of the Minister of War to Explain to the Chamber," *New York Times*, June 19,

1877, 1; BW, box 1, folder c, from TG Bennett to Jane Bennett, from Constantinople, December 5, 1877.

79. BW, box 1, folder c, from TG Bennett to Jane Bennett, from Constantinople, December 8, 1877; December 12, 1877; box 1, folder d, from TG Bennett to Jane Bennett, from Constantinople, April 18, 1879; box 1, folder d, from TG Bennett to Jane Bennett, from Constantinople, January 12, 1878; box 1, folder c, from TG Bennett to Jane Bennett, December 12, 1877; December 21, 1877.

80. BW, MS #87108, box 1, folder c, from TG Bennett to Jane Bennett, from Constantinople, December 21, 1877.

81. Richard T. Trenk Sr., "The Plevna Delay: Winchesters and Peabody-Martinis in the Russo-Turkish War," *Man at Arms Magazine* 19, no. 4 (1997), retrieved online at www.militaryrifles.com/Turkey/Plevna/ThePlevnaDelay.html; "Winchester May Win for Turks Again," *New Haven Register*, October 27, 1971, 4.

82. Trenk, "The Plevna Delay"; "Winchester May Win for Turks Again," *New Haven Register*, October 27, 1971, 4; see also WRAC, series 3, box 8, folder 17.

83. Trenk, "The Plevna Delay."

84. Ibid.

85. WRAC, series 3, box 8, folder 17, tag. no. 123, text on Plevna Delay; quoted in Parsons, *The First Winchester*, 88–91.

86. Clarence Hutt, "Where the Guns Go: On the Trail of the Winchester in Far Corners of the World," *Hardware Review*, April 1920, 17; WRAC, series 3, box 8, folder 18, correspondence from Bangkok, Thailand (sig. illeg.), to WRAC, December 11, 1952; Williamson, *Winchester*, ix; H. C. Engelbrecht and F. C. Hanighen, *Merchants of Death: A Study of the International Armament Industry* (London: George Routledge and Sons, 1935), 42; see also WRAC, series 5, box 13, folder 17, "Stanley Expedition."

87. "Winchester May Win for Turks Again," *New Haven Register*, October 27, 1971, 4. A year later, in October 1878, 74,000 additional arms headed to Turkey; see "Munitions of War for Turkey," *New York Times*, October 18, 1878, 5; "Winchester May Win for Turks Again," *New Haven Register*, October 27, 1971, 4.

88. WRAC, Veader, "The Story of the WRAC," 82.

89. Quoted in Williamson, *Winchester*, 60.

90. Williamson, *Winchester*, 60; WRAC, additional box 10, folder 9, letter to stockholders, March 6, 1872. The consensus is that the Turkish contracts were critical to the company's early survival. WRAC, series 5, box 13, folder 28, from Edwin Pugsley to George Leek, August 9, 1949; DC, vol. 122, p. 28.

91. BW, box 1, folder d, from TG Bennett to Jane Bennett, from Bucharest, Romania, April 28, 1879.

CHAPTER 7: "SPIRIT GUNS"

1. Leavitt, *Brought to Bed*, 23, notes that it is only in the twentieth century that we have a good record of births, live and still, by state and local health departments.

2. Marjorie Pierce, "She Played Musical Houses," *San Jose Mercury News*, July 22, 1973; Millie Robbins, "Millie's Column: The Mysterious Mrs. Winchester," *San Francisco Chronicle*, November 21, 1969, 22.

3. BW, box 1, folder C, from TG Bennett to Jane Bennett, September 26, 1876; box 1, folder c, from TG Bennett to Jane Bennett, September 27, 1876; from TG Bennett to Jane Bennett, July 23, 1878; from TG Bennett to Jane Bennett, May 15, 1884.

4. BW, box 1, folder d, from TG Bennett to Jane Bennett, July 17, 1878.

5. Sinclair House menus and activities, www.whitemountainhistory.org/uploads /sinclair_hop_/1889_lh.pdf; BW, box 1, folder d, from TG Bennett to Jane Bennett, September 8, 1878.

6. NHCHS, Liston Pope, "Rambling Reflections: Profile of Prospect St.," in *Reflections*, Yale Divinity School newsletter, 1966.

7. DC, vol. 42, pp. 12–14; "The Rifle: Hon. O. F. Winchester," *Forest and Stream* 15, no. 21 (1880), 415; DC, vol. 41, p. 2; Grant, *The Colt Legacy*, x.

8. 1870 US Census, 1451, 1515.

9. DC, vol. 42, pp. 12–14.

10. Quoted in Houze, *Winchester Repeating Arms Company*, 23; Kennett, *The Gun in America*, 106.

11. BBHC, *Winchester Record* 2, "Oliver Fisher Winchester: Captain of Industry," November 7, 1919, 1.

12. Ibid.

13. "Uniformity in Time: Work of the Winchester Observatory at Yale—Order for a Heliometer," *New York Times*, May 2, 1880, 2; "A Horological Bureau at Yale," *New York Times*, November 7, 1879, 8; WRAC, series 3, box 8, folder 13, typescript, "Oliver Fisher Winchester"; DC, vol. 122, pp. 36–37; Pope, "Rambling Reflections." The Davies mansion is at 393 Prospect and is one of only four of the mansions from the 1860s and 1870s that survived on the hill.

14. *New Haven Daily Register*, obituaries, March 8, 1881; CR, Spoon, "Sarah Winchester and Her House," 2.

15. CR, "Recluse Heiress Will Enter Court," *Redwood City*, January 9, 1909; *San Jose Daily Mercury*, January 10, 1909, reprinted in "Superstition in Building," *American Architect and Building News*, February 8, 1896, 68; "Winchester Widow Dying: Work on Her Home in San Jose, CA, has Never Ceased," *New York Times*, June 12, 1911, sec. 1, 6; Merle Gray, "Woman of Mystery," *San Jose Mercury and Herald*, July 16, 1911, 6.

16. Ignoffo, *Captive of the Labyrinth*, focuses on the more worldly aspects of Sarah's time in California and calls spiritualism a "mistaken legacy," although to some extent all legends are by nature mistaken, yet, for their own reasons, believed. Emma Hardinge Britten, *Modern American Spiritualism: A Twenty Years' Record of the Communion Between Earth and the World of Spirits* (New York: pub. by author, 1870), 203, 166; Robert Dale Owen, *The Debatable Land* (New York: G. W. Carelton, 1872), 10.

17. Hardinge Britten, *Modern American Spiritualism*, 199; Owen, *The Debatable Land*, 503, 300; Emanuel Swedenborg, *Heaven and Its Wonders: The World of Spirits, and Hell, from Things Heard and Seen* (1758), 460; Andrew Jackson Davis, *A Stellar Key to the Summer Land* (Boston: William White, 1868), 135.

18. Elizabeth Phelps, *The Gates Ajar* (Boston: Fields, Osgood, 1869), 172; Richard Frothington, "How the Spirits Tormented Me," *Galaxy*, December 1867, 1003; Andrew Jackson Davis, *The Philosophy of Spiritual Intercourse: Being an Explanation of Modern Mysteries* (Rochester, NY: Austin, 1910), 296, 298; Davis, *A Stellar Key to the Summer Land*, 143, 181; Hardinge Britten, *Modern American Spiritualism*, 33.

19. In Boston, members of the Putnam and Newton families were spiritualists. John Spear, a Universalist clergyman, had distinguished himself in the temperance and anti-slavery movements before becoming a writing medium. The Lincolns invited spiritualists into the White House to attempt contact with their beloved dead son. See account in Hardinge Britten, *Modern American Spiritualism*, 83–84, 86, 89, 99, 100, 150, 189,

183, 195, 273; Davis, *A Stellar Key to the Summer Land*, 113. A 1919 work, Burton Hendrick, *The Age of Big Business: A Chronicle of the Captains of Industry* (New Haven, CT: Yale University Press, 1919), 21, even contends that Cornelius Vanderbilt "saw visions, and . . . believed in dreams and in signs. The greatest practical genius of his time was a frequent attendant at spiritualistic séances; he cultivated personally the society of mediums" and consulted spiritualists before embarking on new ventures.

20. "4th annual Convention of Spiritualists," *Cleveland Plain Dealer*, September 3–6, 1867; "The First Great Spiritualist Camp Meeting, at Pierpont Grove," *Banner of Light*, September 29, 1866, 3–4; "First National Convention of Spiritualists," *Chicago Tribune*, August 9–15, 1864, accessed at www.spirithistory.com/64chicg.html. This site is a marvelous online archive of primary documents related to spiritualism. It is curated by John Buescher, and I have used it extensively for background.

21. "Convention of Spiritualists—Fourth and Last Day," *Cleveland Plain Dealer*, September 7, 1867; "The Spiritual Convention," *New York Times*, September 2, 1866; "The Spiritual Convention—Loose Ends—Gist of the Proceedings," *Chicago Tribune*, August 17, 1864; "The Spiritual Convention: Adoption of a Platform—Adjournment," *Buffalo Commercial Advertiser*, September 3, 1869; "Seventh Annual Convention of the National Convention of Spiritualists," *Indiana Radical*, September 29, 1870; "National Convention of Spiritualists," *Rochester Daily Union and Advertiser*, August 28, 1868; "The Spiritualists," *Cleveland Plain Dealer*, September 5, 1867; "National Convention of Spiritualists," *Providence Journal*, August 24, 1866; "National Convention of Spiritualists," *Rochester Daily Union and Advertiser*, August 29, 1868.

22. "The Spiritual Convention," *New York Times*, September 2, 1866.

23. Will Winchester patented the reloading tool on October 18, 1874. See Wilson, *Winchester: An American Legend*, 41; Carlyle, *Signs of the Times*, 61; Elizabeth Phelps, "What Is a Fact?" *The Atlantic*, November 1880, 682.

24. Hatch, *Remington*, 80–81.

25. Swedenborg, *Heaven and Its Wonders*, 462, 462–463; 471–473.

26. Hardinge Britten, *Modern American Spiritualism*, 33; Davis, *A Stellar Key to the Summer Land*, 181; Anonymous, *The Harmonium* (London: Culver, Page, Hoyne, 1881), 408.

27. "A Midwinter Feast at Los Altos," *Los Altos Star*, August 5, 1908; Davis, *A Stellar Key to the Summer Land*," 112, 472–473.

28. Carlyle, *Signs of the Times*, 173, writes of the "cogged wheel turned by another" as a metaphor of the mechanized mind.

29. WRAC, series 4, box 12, folder 18, from Robert Winchester to Gene Ball, archivist, May 24, 1980. Articles that identify Coombs or a "seeress" include Josiah Dewey, "Winchester Mystery House," *Yankee*, October 1962, 51; Susy Smith, "Five True Ghost Stories," *The Coronet*, April 1968, 130.

30. 1880 US Census, retrieved online. I draw on the life of the spiritualist medium from a rare but immensely valuable book written anonymously by a successful nineteenth-century medium. This medium revealed the insider terminology, culture, and tricks of the trade. *Revelations of a Spirit Medium, Or, Spiritualistic Mysteries Exposed: A Detailed Explanation of the Methods Used by Fraudulent Mediums* was first published in 1891 by Farrington and Company in Minnesota. The anonymous author claimed to have mastered the trade and successfully converted hundreds to spiritualism, ranging from "day laborers" and the "lowly and the ignorant" to "individuals of great learning," including bankers, lawyers, and professors. The book was "such a crushing expose of the methods of the bogus mediums that it created somewhat of a furor when it first saw the

light," an introduction to a later edition explains (p. xiv). When the book was first released, mediums themselves bought up every copy that they could and destroyed them. The book became exceedingly rare. In 1909 there were only a handful of copies in the United States.

31. "The First Great Spiritualist Camp Meeting," www.spirithistory.com; "Spiritdom Let Loose," *Frederick (MD) Weekly News*, August 2, 1884; "The First Great Spiritualist Camp Meeting: Ten Thousand Attendants!," *Banner of Light*, September 15, 1866, www.spirithistory.com/66camp/html.

32. "Spiritdom Let Loose," *Frederick (MD) Weekly News*, August 2, 1884; Emma Hardinge Britten, "Spiritual Camp Meetings," in *Nineteenth Century Miracles; or, Spirits and Their Work in Every Country of the Earth: A Complete Historical Compendium of the Great Movement Known as "Modern Spiritualism"* (New York: Britten, 1884), 543; *Revelations of a Spirit Medium*, 212.

33. Britten, "Spiritual Camp Meetings," 543.

34. Lake Pleasant Camp Meeting Association, Manager's Circular, 1880, "Arrangements for 1880," www.spirithistory.com/80camps.html; Britten, "Spiritual Camp Meetings," 544.

35. *Revelations of a Spirit Medium*, xviv. Respected magazines ran stories on spiritualism in the 1860s and 1870s. See "The Confessions of a Medium," *The Atlantic*, December 1860, 715.

36. *Revelations of a Spirit Medium*, 131.

37. "Neshaminy Grove Spiritualist Campmeeting," *Bucks County Gazette*, August 7, 1879; "Neshaminy Camp," *Denton (MD) Journal*, August 25, 1883, both accessed at www.spirithistory.com.

38. *Revelations of a Spirit Medium*, 36, 246, lxiv, 90, 246–254.

39. Ibid., 92.

40. Ibid., 108, 107–110.

41. Excerpted and reprinted in ibid., 107–110.

42. Ibid., 196, 199.

43. Ibid., 207.

44. Ibid., 41, 207.

45. David Moore, "Three in Four Americans Believe in Paranormal," June 16, 2005, Gallup News Service, www.gallup.com/poll/16915/Three-Four-Americans-Believe -Paranormal.aspx.

46. BW, box 1, folder d, from TG Bennett to Jane Bennett, September 8, 1878.

47. BW, box 1, folder d, from TG Bennett to Jane Bennett, April 1, 1879.

48. BW, box 1, folder d, from TG Bennett to Jane Bennett, April 13, 1879.

CHAPTER 8: "THE UNHALLOWED TRADE"

1. DC, vol. 42, pp. 22–24; Madis, *Winchester: Dates of Manufacture*. The 1880 US Census noted that "under the stimulus" of heavy military orders, rifles could be produced at the rate of 200 per year per operative employed, working 312 days of 10 hours each, with labor divided among several departments. Wholesale manufacture inverted the man-to-machine equation. There would be two-thirds as many machines as men, versus two-thirds as many men as machines in earlier decades, with "much time . . . wasted" in waiting for machines to finish their work, a problem that "scientific management" and time-motion studies would soon address. 1880 US Census, 621.

2. WRAC, series 4, box 11, folder 50, from Edwin Pugsley to Henry Brewer, on company history, July 9, 1934; RMA, advertisements from *Forest and Stream*, October 21, 1875, and *Rod and Gun*, May 13, 1876 (which uses the same 200,000 figure); ANRS, 71; BBHC, *Winchester Record* 2, "Oliver Fisher Winchester: Captain of Industry," November 7, 1919, 1; report to the board of directors, March 5, 1979, quoted in WRAC, Veader, "The Story of the WRAC," 98; Van Zwoll, *America's Great Gunmakers*, 135.

3. Kennett, *The Gun in America*, 97, 102–103; Hendrick, *The Age of Big Business*, 7, 4; Burlingame, *The American Conscience*, 329; Ron Chernow, *Titan: The Life of John. D. Rockefeller, Sr.* (New York: Random House, 1998), 227; Deyrup, *Arms Makers of the Connecticut Valley*, 203–212 (on disappeared firms in New England); Williamson, *Winchester*, 59.

Meyer Fishbein, "The Census of Manufactures 1810–1890" (Washington, DC: National Archives and Record Service, 1973), cautions that economists consider US Census data prior to 1890 to be prohibitively unsystematic. The 1870 US Census, vol. 3, 434, "General Statistics of Manufactures," reports 709 establishments concerned with firearms and ammunition, encompassing gunsmiths and gunsmithing. These establishments were more dispersed geographically, with 46 in Missouri, 20 in Connecticut, 15 in Mississippi, and so on. The 1880 US Census, vol. 2, 10, reports 39 firearms establishments (no longer making mention of "gunsmithing"), with over half of them in Connecticut (12) and Massachusetts (12). The 1890 US Census, vol. 2, 192, reports 34 firearms manufacturers, including 8 in Connecticut, 13 in Massachusetts, 6 in New York, 3 in Pennsylvania, and 4 in "all other states."

4. He bought the Adirondack Arms Company in 1874. The Strong Fire Arms company sold out to Winchester in 1881, as did C. D. Leet. See WRAC, series 3, box 8, folder 18, and series 4, box 11, folder 8, typescript of Winchester history for fiftieth anniversary, June 23, 1959; Houze, *Winchester Repeating Arms Company*, 63; Deyrup, *Arms Makers of the Connecticut Valley*, 202–205. In 1865, for example, Winchester learned that Isaac Hartshorn, the India Rubber magnate, was filing a patent suit against the Burnside Rifle Company. Burnside manufactured the Spencer repeater, the Henry's chief rival. With what Winchester curator Herbert Houze describes as "pure Machiavellian foresight," Winchester secretly purchased Hartshorn's patent while the suit was in progress because he knew that if Hartshorn won, Winchester could dictate the terms of settlement. When Hartshorn prevailed, Winchester requested payment of damages "made in machinery," thereby elbowing Burnside out of the gun business. Deyrup writes of how other firms lacked Winchester's "absorptive propensity" (p. 202). Rollin Osterweis, *Three Centuries of New Haven, 1638–1938* (New Haven, CT: Yale University Press, 1953), 353; Marcot, *Spencer Repeating Firearms*, 155.

5. Porter, *Merchants and Manufacturers*, 138; Kennett, *The Gun in America*, 110. Deyrup, *Arms Makers of the Connecticut Valley*, notes that the 1870s and 1880s were a "high point" in small arms (p. 7).

6. R. L. Wilson, a gun expert, concludes that "the commercial success of Winchester could have been even greater than it was, had not the president of the firm devoted so much time and energy to going after government contract sales." Wilson, *Winchester: An American Legend*, 158. See also Parsons, *The First Winchester*, 9; Matthew Cragoe, "Cockney Sportsmen? Recreational Shooting in London and Beyond, 1800–1870," in Karen Jones et al., eds., *A Cultural History of Firearms in the Age of Empire*, 79. Britain early on passed civilian gun regulations. WRAC, Veader, "The Story of the WRAC," 43 (appendix). A WRAC salesman's notebook and diary in the archive includes notes on

tariffs and restrictions internationally. WRAC, additional box 2, folder 16, "Alphabetical Notebook of Misc. Information Regarding WRAC, 1890–1910."

7. Kennett, *The Gun in America*, 102; Williamson, *Winchester*, 65. These gun experts also see truth in the idea that arms industrialists came to prefer the commercial market over time. Kennett writes that, "whether by preference or not," arms manufacturers moved toward sales to the public, as government policies left them "little choice in the matter," since its orders and demand would never be adequate. HM, *The Remington Centennial Book*, 20–21; Louis Garavaglia, *Firearms of the American West, 1866–1894* (Albuquerque: University of New Mexico Press, 1985), 128; WRAC, series 4, box 10, folder 50, from J. Movell Hawkins to Manager of Winchester Shooting Promotion Division, January 25, 1923; Deyrup, *Arms Makers of the Connecticut Valley*, also notes that sale and advertisement played an important role, as well as tariffs of 1842, 1846, and 1857 that protected American guns from foreign competition, and that "more than any other arms maker of his day, [Colt] realized the importance of stimulating demand through aggressive sales promotion" (pp. 128, 202, 122–123).

8. This is Henning's conclusion from his meticulous review of advertisements for Remington and other gunmakers, "The Advertising of E. Remington & Sons."

9. Henning, "The Advertising of E. Remington & Sons," 429.

10. *Turf Field and Farm*, March 19, 1875, advertisements in this volume; CC, box 66, folder 3, advertisement, "The Pioneers of Civilization, Colt's Repeating Firearms." The ads here are from the Colt's archive.

11. So writes Rose, *American Rifle*; see also Van Zwoll, *America's Great Gunmakers*, 93; "The National Bundesfest," *Shooting & Fishing* 23, July 7, 1898, 231; Gilmore, "Another Branch of Manly Sport," 117, 107, 112–117.

12. K. D. Kirkland, *America's Premier Gunmakers: Winchester* (East Bridgewater, MA: World Publications Group, 2007), 9; Williamson, *Winchester*, 72; Garavaglia, *Firearms of the American West*, 128; Parsons, *The First Winchester*, 93.

13. HH, box 1, folder 1, "Terms of Sale," 1878 WRAC brochure. Houze, *Arming the West*, describes how from Missouri, guns traveled west along the Union Pacific railroad; north to the Dakota Territory along the Mississippi and Red Rivers; to the northern plains via the Missouri River; and into the southern plains via the Arkansas River. Guns destined for Montana or Idaho and their gold regions came through Fort Benton, Montana, at the headwater of the Missouri River.

14. Parsons, *The First Winchester*, 93.

15. "The Gun Trade in America," *Turf Field and Farm*, March 19, 1875, also in CC, box 70A; Jinks, *History of Smith & Wesson*, 98.

16. HH, box 1, folder 1, "Terms of Sale," 1878 WRAC brochure; Houze, *Arming the West*, 112, speculates that the crates were probably headed for Mexico, given the content; SGHC, box 2, folder 47, November 1–15, 1871, box 19, folder 1, January 1–7, 1897, box 29, folder 31, October 8–14, 1897; US Senate, Congressional Hearings on Revolutions in Mexico, Hearings Before Subcommittee of the Committee on Foreign Relations, September 1912, 62nd Cong., 2nd sess., pursuant to res. 335 (Washington, DC: 1913), 834.

17. CC, business file, series III, box 11A, correspondence, incoming, Allies letter book, 1873–1880, from Hugh Harbison, treasurer, Colt's Co., to Allies, September 28, 1876, p. 132; from Harbison, Colt's, to Allies, July 2, 1874, p. 28; from Harbison, Colt's, to Kittredge et al., November 22, 1875, p. 99; from J. P. Moore & Sons, for Allies, to Colt's Co., January 30, 1874, p. 24; from Harbison, Colt's, to Kittredge et al., July 15,

1874, p. 29; from J. P. Moore & Sons to Colt's, January 30, 1874. On forswearing other guns, see also Deyrup, *Arms Makers of the Connecticut Valley*, 125.

18. CC, Allies letter book, from Schuyler, Hartley & Graham (SHG) to Colt's, June 28, 1875, p. 66; from William Seaver, Secretary of the Allies, to Colt's, September 22, 1876, p. 129; from SHG, for Allies, to Colt's, July 1, 1875, p. 68; from SHG to Colt's, July 2, 1875, p. 69; from Harbison, Colt's Co., to SHG, July 5, 1875; from Colt's Co. to J. P. Norris et al., February 2, 1874.

19. CC, Allies letter book, from Seaver, Secretary of the Allies, to Colt's, December 24, 1874; from Seaver, for Allies, to Colt's, September 22, 1876, p. 129.

20. CC, Allies letter book, from John Norris, "for self and Allies," to Colt's, September 26, 1876, pp. 130–131; Seaver, Secretary of the Allies, to Colt's, September 22, 1876, p. 129; from Allies to Colt's, October 6, 1876, p. 136; from Harbison, Colt's, to Allies, October 9, 1876, p. 138.

21. CC, Allies letter book, from Allies to Colt's, February 27, 1877, p. 157; from Allies to Colt's, October 17, 1877, p. 173.

22. Hanson, *Firearms of the Fur Trade*, 429.

23. Houze, *Arming the West*, vii, 15–18. SHG is one firm, and the figures might reflect different, preferential agreements with other agents. But Houze claims that his numbers show that the real guns of the West weren't Winchesters or Colts.

24. Houze, *Arming the West*, 19.

25. Madis, *Winchester: Dates of Manufacture*, 11.

26. Adam Winkler, *Gunfight: The Battle over the Right to Bear Arms in America* (New York: Norton, 2011), reviews thousands of local and state gun laws. In the 1600s, in some colonies, "bearing arms was restricted to those who would deny the doctrine of transubstantiation," such that Catholics were effectively disarmed. In New York, similar prohibitions applied to Jews, who "remained exempt from the general training and guard duty" because "said nation was not admitted or counted among the citizens." Whisker, *Arms Makers of Colonial America*, 15–16; Lucian Cary, "The American Rifle," *Holiday*, October 1947, 90.

27. An archaeological study of the actual battlefield revealed at least 370 cartridge guns for 1,500 warriors, including 55 Henrys and Model 66 Winchesters and 7 Model 73s. There were enough Winchesters to inspire a sarcastic editorial in the *Army and Navy Journal* saying that the self-interested gun merchants would deal with anyone. "We advised the WRAC to . . . prosecute the Indians for infringement of their patent. . . . The agency people and the traders solemnly affirm that they don't furnish them, so it can only be inferred that the Indians manufacture them themselves." Quoted at Garavaglia, *Firearms of the American West*, 366. John Du Mont, *Custer Battle Guns* (Johnstown, CO: Old Army Press, 1974), 51; Richard Fox, *Archaeological Insights into the Custer Battle: An Assessment of the 1984 Field Season* (Norman: University of Oklahoma Press, 1987), 109–112; Williamson, *Winchester*, 51; US Congress, House, *Report of the Secretary of War*, 46th Cong., 2nd sess., 1879, H. Ex. Doc. 1, pt. 2, vol. 3; United States, Office of Indian Affairs, *Annual Report of the Commissioner of Indian Affairs for the Year 1877*, "Legislation," p. 232 online, p. 628 in orig., "Joint Resolution Prohibiting Supply of Special Metallic Cartridges to Hostile Indians," no. 20, August 5, 1876, 19 Stat. 216; August 15, 1876, Chap. 280; Charles Hanson Jr., "The Post-War Indian Gun Trade," *Museum of the Fur Trade Quarterly* 4, no. 3, (1968): 1, 4; Garavaglia, *Firearms of the American West*, 362; WRAC, series 3, box 8, folder 18, and series 4, box 10, folder 40; WRAC broadside, "Model of 1873, Improvements in Model of 1873"; WRAC, box 10, folder 40,

"Winchester Repeating Fire Arms," 29; Hanson, *Firearms of the Fur Trade*, 425–433. On November 15, 1872, federal agents forbade "Indian Traders" from disposing "in any manner of breech-loading firearms to any Sioux Indians," who nevertheless had the latest repeater rifles. WRAC, series 3, box 8, folder 18, and series 4, box 10, folder 40; WRAC broadside, "Model of 1873," 29; Colonel Richard Dodge, *Our Wild Indians: Thirty-Three Years' Personal Experience Among the Red Men of the Great West* (Hartford, CT: A. D. Worthington, 1883), 422–423; United States, Office of Indian Affairs, *Annual Report of the Commissioner of Indian Affairs for the Year 1877*, Yankton Agency, Dakota, p. 78 online, p. 474 in orig.; Yanctonnais Agency, p. 72 online, p. 468 in orig.

28. United States, Office of Indian Affairs, *Annual Report of the Commissioner of Indian Affairs for the Year 1877*, Apache, New Mexico Agency, p. 158 online, p. 404 in orig.; White River, CO, Agency, p. 46 online, p. 442 in orig.; *Report of the Secretary of the Interior in the Abridgement . . . Containing the Annual Message of the President of the United States to the Two Houses of Congress, with Reports of Departments* (1866–1869), "Sales of Arms to Indians," 748–749.

29. United States, Office of Indian Affairs, *Annual Report of the Commissioner of Indian Affairs for the Year 1877*, "Trade with Indians" (introduction), p. 8 online, p. 404 in orig.; *Report of the Secretary of the Interior*, "Sales of Arms to Indians," 748–749.

CHAPTER 9: THE "MORAL EFFECT" OF A WINCHESTER

1. BBHC, *Winchester Record* 3, no. 3, "Anniversary of Thomas G. Bennett," September 10, 1920.

2. Houze, *Arming the West*, vii.

3. Here and throughout, I draw on the best, most convenient source for Winchester production figures by year, serial number, and model—the meticulous catalog compiled by George Madis, *Winchester: Dates of Manufacture, 1949–2000* (Brownsboro, TX: Art and Reference House, 1981). Madis's painstaking work included not only the WRAC factory records, but also the sometimes more accurate records of inside contractors. When referring to Colt's production figures (see notes below), I draw on the *Blue Book Pocket Guide for Colt Dates of Manufacture*, by gun expert R. L. Wilson et al. (Minneapolis: Blue Book Publications, 2012). Gun owners and collectors who want to identify their gun's age by serial number consult these books. Some of the same limitations concerning production data apply to both businesses, and will be discussed here. To determine an estimate of annual production from 1866 until 1968 I added the numbers of each model produced each year. The overall and per capita figure of Model 73 gun production here is useful to provide a sense of the gun's diffusion and its production history and trends. However, there are several limitations to this production data. Production figures can reveal trends, but cannot be taken as precise.

First, it is impossible to know based on production data how many of any given model stayed within US borders, or to distinguish between national and international sales (although international sales were a small percentage of *overall* sales for Winchester by the early 1900s), so the figure cannot be read too literally as an indication of the addition to the "gun load" within the United States specifically. Second, production figures and sales figures are, obviously, different things, although most often similar. I refer to sales figures in other cases, where indicated, available, and appropriate. Third, for Winchester as for Colt's, not all guns were given serial numbers or numbered consecutively, and some production data is simply lost. For twenty-two of the Winchester models produced between 1866 and 1968, for example, we have only an overall, total production figure, over a series of years, and not an exact annual production (i.e., 105,000 of the 1900 Model were produced between 1899 and 1902; 82,084 of the 59 shotgun were produced between 1960 and 1965). In these twenty-two cases, I have followed the lead of the WRAC itself: when the company lost records on production for its 42 Model from 1955 to 1963, the factory used total production during those years and divided to determine an average yearly production. I have done the same with the models for which specific production data by year is lost. However, this method yields *only* an average production figure—*useful but not specific*—and cannot be taken as a precise description of one year's production for that model. Often, in fact, Colt's and Winchester would have lower production in a model's first year, while tooling up to produce it. My per capita and annual production figures, here and throughout, include averaged production for these twenty-two models.

For the Colt's data, in cases where the serial numbers and the total production figures in Wilson's book are not the same, I have relied on the overall production figure, and averaged, since the Colt's serial numbers were not always consecutive. I have also excluded from this count orders specifically for military contracts, or, in Colt's case, production in his London factory, and eight Colt's models for which experts have no production figures at all.

4. Madis, *Winchester: Dates of Manufacture.*

5. WRAC, series 3, box 8, folder 18, "Model 1873, tag no. 125; series 3, box 8, folder 18, WRAC broadside, "Model of 1873, Improvements in Model of 1873," 2; Wilson, *Winchester: An American Legend*, 41.

6. WRAC, box 8, folder 18, WRAC broadside, "Model of 1873, Improvements in Model of 1873."

7. "The Winchester Repeating Rifle, Two Shots a Second," advertisement broadside, 1867, reprinted in Houze, *Winchester Repeating Arms Company*, 64; reprinted in Parsons, *The First Winchester*, 79.

8. *Sunday Herald and Weekly National Intelligence*, September 24, 1876, editorial.

9. "The Winchester Repeating Rifle, Two Shots a Second," reprinted in Houze, *Winchester Repeating Arms Company*, 64; US Congress, House, *Report of the Secretary of War*, 46th Cong., 2nd sess., 1879, H. Ex. Doc. 1, pt. 2, vol. 3, pp. 569–570 online, p. 326 in orig.; Parsons, *The First Winchester*, 79; Samuel Colt to Sam Houston, February 24, 1847, reprinted in *Sam Colt's Own Record*, 53.

10. Williamson, *Winchester*, 70; WRAC, box 8, folder 18, WRAC broadside, "Model of 1873, Improvements in Model of 1873," 29, 41, 36; Wilson, *Winchester: An American Legend*, 45.

11. Advertising broadside, "The Winchester Repeating Rifle, Two Shots a Second," reprinted in Houze, *Winchester Repeating Arms Company*, 65; draft broadside, reprinted in Parsons, *The First Winchester*, 79; WRAC, series 4, box 10, folder 43, typescript, "Centennial of Firepower," 1962; Madis, *The Winchester Book*, 378; WRAC, series 4, box 11, folder 50, from Edwin Pugsley to Henry Brewer, July 9, 1934; Parsons, *The First Winchester*, 119. The Texas Rangers paid out of their own pockets for the new Winchester because it was better for mounted, mobile warfare.

12. Karen Jones, "Guns, Masculinity, and Marksmanship," in Jones et al., eds., *A Cultural History of Firearms in the Age of Empire*, 47; Julia Cody Goodman, *Buffalo Bill: King of the Old West* (New York: Library Publishers, 1955), 206–208.

13. Hofstadter, "America as a Gun Culture," 2 (online).

14. "Indian, Bear, or Buffalo . . . ," rare Model 66 circular by Oliver Winchester, reprinted in Parsons, *The First Winchester*, 93; RMA, *Army Navy Journal*, August 7, 1875; *Remington Arms Catalogues, 1877–1899*, 6, 10; *Turf Field and Farm*, March 19, 1875, 202, advertisement for Colt's "Peacemaker"; CC, box 66, folder 3, "Colt's Patent Repeating Pistols, Army, Navy and Pocket Sizes," advertisement.

15. Quoted in Wilson, *Winchester: An American Legend*, 32.

16. Greener, *The Gun and Its Development*, 285, 287.

17. Contemporary research on this theme—the extent to which gun ownership makes civilians feel safer—finds interesting results. A 1990 survey found that even a majority of gun owners—58 percent—either felt less safe (2 percent) with a gun, or that it made no difference (56 percent). In the population overall, a 1994 survey found that 71 percent said they would feel "less safe" if more people in their communities had guns, compared to only 19 percent feeling more safe. Opinions among gun owners, specifically, were evenly divided as to whether they'd feel more or less safe, while a large majority (85 percent) of non-gun owners reported that they'd feel less safe. Spitzer, *The Politics of Gun Control*, 62.

18. The engraving read, "One of One Thousand," but the model was referred to more often by "1 in 1,000," or "1 of 1,000." "Extremely Rare Winchester Model 1873 '1 of 1000' Lever Action Rifle, www.icollector.com.

19. WRAC, series 10, box 23, folder 4, from Edwin Pugsley to Angus Macarthur, June 11, 1936.

20. George Ward Nichols, "Wild Bill," *Harper's New Monthly Magazine*, February 1867.

21. Kathy Weiser, "Legends of America," www.legendsofamerica.com/we-wildbill. html; this wonderful site includes newspaper criticisms.

22. Nichols, "Wild Bill"; Ramon Adams, *Six Guns and Saddle Leather: Bibliography of Books and Pamphlets on Western Culture and Gunmen* (Norman: University of Oklahoma Press, 1969), 313, 163; Eugene Cunningham, *Triggernometry: A Gallery of Gunfighters* (Caldwell, ID: Caxton, 1941), 253, 249–262.

23. Quoted in Michael Denning, *Mechanic Accents: Dime Novels and Working-Class Culture in America* (New York: Verso, 1987), 17, 21. Denning's work is a brilliant treatment of the genre. Although I am interested in dime-novel westerns about gunfighters, Denning's work restores both a much more diverse field of dime-novel plots and readers to our understanding of mass-produced fiction.

24. Quoted in Denning, *Mechanic Accents*, 22, 20, 160; Owen Payne White, *The Autobiography of a Durable Sinner* (1941), quoted in Adams, *Six Guns and Saddle Leather*, 689.

25. Adams, *Six Guns and Saddle Leather*, 95, 18, 336.

26. Ibid., 613; Henry Stanley, *My Early Travels and Adventures in America and Asia* (London: Sampson Low Marston, 1895); Cunningham, *Triggernometry*, 249–265.

27. Adams, *Six Guns and Saddle Leather*, 96, 367, 313, 127.

28. Ibid., 356, 289, 172, 468.

29. Cunningham, *Triggernometry*, 249–265.

30. Richard Slotkin, *Gunfighter Nation* (New York: Atheneum, 1992); Goodman, *Buffalo Bill*, 23; Kennett, *The Gun in America*, 119. Eventually 1,700 western and frontier dime-novel titles would be published. John Mack Faragher's brilliant biography of Daniel Boone concludes, aptly, that Boone embodied the "common extraordinary" hero, and that paradox characterizes later depictions of the gunslinging hero. John

Mack Faragher, *Daniel Boone: The Life and Legend of an American Pioneer* (New York: Holt, 1992).

31. Colonel Prentiss Ingraham, *Adventures of Buffalo Bill from Boyhood to Manhood* (New York: Beadle and Adams, 1882), 69.

32. WRAC, series 4, box 11, folder 8.

33. Quoted at Adams, *Six Guns and Saddle Leather*, 98.

34. Quoted at Goodman, *Buffalo Bill*, 219–221; Stella Foote, *Letters from "Buffalo Bill," Taken from the Originals* (Billings, MT: Foote Publishing, 1954), 22. Slotkin's *Gunfighter Nation* remains a classic and monumental study in the cultural stature of the gunfighter as a historically transcendent figure of American mythology and of the "frontier" not as a geographic space, but a trans-historical idiom.

35. Entirely his own man—or woman, in some cases. Historian Laura Browder, *Her Best Shot: Women and Guns in America* (Chapel Hill: University of North Carolina Press, 2006), restores to the narrative the rifle-wielding American pioneer women who were celebrated as defenders of their homes and hearths in the 1800s, so the emerging gun mystique and story in these decades is not entirely about masculinity or male gunslingers—it is more emphatically a story of individual mettle in tough circumstances against tall odds, a narrative that occasionally, although not usually, featured a female protagonist.

36. Ida B. Wells, *Crusade for Justice: The Autobiography of Ida B. Wells* (Chicago: University of Chicago Press, 1970), 62; quoted in Nicholas Johnson, *Negroes and the Gun: The Black Tradition of Arms* (Amherst, MA: Prometheus, 2014), 105. Johnson reviews postbellum African American gun ownership, and I draw on his work here. Thomas Fortune, editor of the *New York Age*, responded to a spate of lynchings by rejecting the "good nigger" moniker in favor of the "'bad nigger with the Winchester who can defend his home, and children, and wife." While he was a professor at Atlanta University, W. E. B. DuBois wrote that he "bought a Winchester double-barreled shotgun and two dozen rounds of shells filled with buckshot. If a white mob had stepped on the campus where I lived I would without hesitation have sprayed their guts over the grass." Johnson concludes that these sentiments were indicative of one substantial stream of public opinion. See also Kevin Yuill, "Better to Die Fighting Against Injustice Than to Die Like a Dog: African Americans and Guns, 1866–1941," in Jones et al., eds., *A Cultural History of Firearms in the Age of Empire*, 213–225, who describes blatant attempts to disarm southern negroes in the early 1900s as well as the positive views of gun ownership among progressive black leaders in the postbellum years.

37. Ida B. Wells-Barnett, *Mob Rule in New Orleans: Robert Charles and His Fight to Death. The Story of His Life, Burning Human Beings Alive, Other Lynching Statistics* (pamphlet, 1900), www.gutenberg.org/files/14976/14976-h/14976-h.htm; Johnson, *Negroes and the Gun*, also tells Robert Charles's story (pp. 114–115).

38. Barnard, *Armsmear*, 185; quoted in Hofstadter, "America as a Gun Culture," 7; Charles E. Cobb Jr., *This Nonviolent Stuff'll Get You Killed* (New York: Basic Books, 2014).

39. The adage " . . . Colt made them equal" was common by the late 1800s and was still used in the 1900s. See, for example, *Real West*, cover of October 1968. Other adages said that a Winchester "could talk fast and with authority in any language," and that "straight shooting is more important than philosophy."

40. In the United States, the greatest homicide danger to a woman comes from those she knows most intimately (64 percent of women murdered in 2007 were murdered by intimate acquaintances, according to the US Bureau of Justice Statistics, including 57

percent of all female handgun homicide victims). Guns were used in 71.5 percent of spousal murders. Although, in theory, the gun equalizes and protects, several controlled studies have found that having a gun in the home increases a woman's risk for becoming the victim of a homicide. "Access to a firearm by the battered woman had no protective effect," concludes one study (Campbell et al., "Risk Factors for Femicide in Abusive Relationships: Results from a Multi-State Control Study," *American Journal of Public Health* 93, no. 7 [1993]: 1089–1097). The US female firearm homicide rate was eleven times higher than that of all other countries combined (D. Hemenway, T. Shinoda-Tagawa, and M. Miller, "Firearm Availability and Female Homicide Victimization Rates Among 25 Populous, High-Income Countries," *Journal of American Medical Women's Association* 57, no. 2 (2002): 101–104. The South historically has been the most heavily armed area of the United States, with guns linked, as Hofstadter, "America as a Gun Culture," noted in his signal essay on the gun culture, to the maintenance of white privilege and control. This association continued after slavery was abolished. See Johnson, *Negroes and the Gun*, 114–115, on convict labor schemes by which African Americans in the late 1800s were arrested on small charges, not infrequently concealed weapons charges, and then "leased out" to whites who could afford to pay their fines. *United States v. Cruikshank*, 92 US 542; DeConde, *Gun Violence in America*, 70–80. On the Colfax massacre, see Charles Lane, *The Day Freedom Died: The Colfax Massacre, the Supreme Court, and the Betrayal of Reconstruction* (New York: Holt, 2009).

41. Yuill, "Better to Die Fighting," 222.

42. Ibid., 227; Gunnar Myrdal, *An American Dilemma*, vol. 2, *The Negro Problem and Modern Democracy*, 7th ed. (New York: Harper and Row, 2009 [1944]), 560. The homicide rate in the mid-1920s comes from H. C. Brearly's study of homicide in the 1930s, *Homicide in the United States* (Chapel Hill: University of North Carolina Press, 1932), the first scholarly treatment of the topic. Cited in Lane, *Murder in America*, 230. In the 1920s, the black homicide rate in southern cities exceeded even that of the late 1900s (Johnson, *Negroes and the Gun*, 118).

43. Alfred Adler, "Billy the Kid: A Case Study in Epic Origins," *Western Folklore* 10, no. 2 (1951): 144; Gary Roberts, "The West's Gunmen, Part I," *The American West* 8, no. 1 (1971): 11; Adams, *Six Guns and Saddle Leather*, 71; B. A. Botkin, *Folk-Say: A Regional Miscellany* (Omaha: University of Oklahoma Press, 1930); Frederick Grey, *Seeking Fortune in America* (London: Smith, Elder, 1912); Olive Woolley Burt, ed., *American Murder Ballads and Their Stories* (New York: Oxford University Press, 1955); Walter Gann, *Tread of the Longhorn* (San Antonio, TX: Naylor, 1949); James Freeman, *Prose and Poetry of the Live Stock Industry of the United States* (Denver: National Livestock Historical Association, 1905).

44. Cunningham, *Triggernometry*, 167–168; Adams, *Six Guns and Saddle Leather*, 183, 399; James Linn, *James Keeley: Newspaperman* (New York: Bobbs-Merrill, 1937).

45. Houze, *Arming the West*, 76, 99, 98, 110.

46. Spitzer, *The Politics of Gun Control*, 10–11; Patricia Limerick, *The Legacy of Conquest: The Unbroken Past of the American West* (New York: Norton, 1987), 71.

47. Winkler, *Gunfight*; Eugene Hollon, *Frontier Violence: Another Look* (New York: Oxford University Press, 1974), 200, 202, 210. Robert Dykstra, *The Cattle Towns* (New York: Knopf, 1968), and Robert Dykstra, "Body Counts and Murder Rates: The Contested Statistics of Western Violence," *Reviews in American History* 31, no. 4 (2003): 554–563, are signal studies that point to lower and more sporadic rates and kinds of gun violence in the West than imagined, as does John Cawelti, *The Six Gun Mystique* (Bowling Green, OH: Bowling Green University Press, 1971). Gregg Lee Carter, *The Gun*

Control Movement (New York: Twayne, 1997), 44. Garry Wills argues that the "west tamed the gun" in *A Necessary Evil: A History of American Distrust of Government* (New York: Simon and Schuster, 2013), 248. DeConde, *Gun Violence in America,* also notes that Texas led one of the first "gun-control" movements in the 1880s (p. 85). Roger McGrath, *Gunfighters, Highwaymen, and Vigilantes: Violence on the Frontier* (Berkeley: University of California Press, 1984), 270; Boorman, *History of Colt Firearms,* 12. In *Six-Guns and Saddle Leather,* Adams wrote that gun legends enliven a process of settlement that was otherwise "dull" (xv). Gary Roberts, "The West's Gunmen, Part II," *The American West* 8, no. 2 (1871): 61; Lane, *Murder in America,* 171.

48. Lane, *Murder in America,* 171.

49. Ibid., 177–178; Hollon, *Frontier Violence,* 196. In his 1869 speech to introduce his Indian "peace policy" of relocation over military action, President Grant mulled the limits of national conscience: "A system which looks to the extinction of a race is too horrible for a nation to adopt without entailing upon itself the wrath of all Christendom and engendering in the citizen a disregard for human life and the rights of others, dangerous to society." Slotkin, *Gunfighter Nation,* 193.

50. David Cartwright, "The Cowboy Subculture," in Dizard et al., eds., *Guns in America: A Reader,* 86, 87.

CHAPTER 10: BALANCING THE LEDGER

1. Summarized in Williamson, *Winchester,* 77–80.

2. "The Rifle," Hon. O. F. Winchester, *New Haven Palladium,* obituary, December 11, 1880, reprinted in *Forest and Stream* 15, no. 21 (1880): 415; Williamson, *Winchester,* 77; DC, vol. 122, p. 37.

3. So concludes Williamson, *Winchester,* 80, who calls them "a matter for conjecture."

4. Williamson, *Winchester,* 76.

5. Boorman, *The History of Winchester Firearms,* 50; Williamson, *Winchester,* 77–78.

6. Williamson, *Winchester,* 84; quoted in Kirkland, *America's Premier Gunmakers: Winchester,* 12; WRAC, series 5, box 13, folder 24, internal correspondence from Peter Smith, Primer Shop, to Edwin Pugsley, July 8, 1946.

7. "Obituary, William W. Winchester," *New York Times,* March 9, 1881, 2.

8. Richard Frothington, "How the Spirits Tormented Me," *Galaxy,* December 1867, 1003.

9. "Niantic Spiritualist Campmeeting," *Denton (MD) Journal,* August 25, 1883, www.spirithistory.com; "Camp Meeting of the First Association of Spiritualists of Philadelphia at Neshaminy Falls Grove," www.spirithistory.com/80camps.html; *Revelations of a Spirit Medium,* 212.

10. "Spiritdom Let Loose," *Frederick (MD) Weekly News,* August 2, 1884, on description of trance state.

11. DC, vol. 42, p. 32; *Revelations of a Spirit Medium,* 179, 120–121.

12. *Revelations of a Spirit Medium,* 120–121.

13. Ibid., 95.

14. Ibid., 47, on how mediums "saw" the spirit.

15. A few accounts of Sarah Winchester lore hold that Will communicated a message about their unfinished house. Dean Jennings, "The House of Mystery," *Modern Mechanics,* June 1937; CR, "Winchester Mystery House," typescript, September 30, 1957.

16. Nathaniel Hawthorne, *Notebooks*, quoted in Larry Reynolds, ed., *A Historical Guide to Nathaniel Hawthorne* (New York: Oxford University Press, 2001), 65.

17. *Revelations of a Spirit Medium*, 292, 293.

18. Ibid., 294.

19. Sam Hurwitt, "Scenes," *San Francisco Chronicle*, September 18, 2005; Dean Jennings, "The House That Mystery Built," *The Coronet*, May 1945, 49.

20. Genevieve Woelf, "Sarah Pardee Winchester: A Driven Woman," pamphlet (San Carlos, CA: Redwood, 1986), 1.

21. Swedenborg, *Heaven and Its Wonders*, 360–361; Talbot, "Sarah Winchester," 28.

CHAPTER 11: SUMMER LAND

1. "Transcontinental Route: Central and Union Pacific Railroads," in Rand McNally, *Pioneer Atlas of the American West* (Chicago: Rand McNally, 1956), 21; WRAC, series 6, box 13, folder 21, photocopy, Guy Hubbard, "The Model 1866 Winchester," *American Rifleman*, May 1931; WRAC, series 4, box 10, folder 43, typescript, "Centennial of Firepower," 1962.

2. BW, box 1, folder e, from TG Bennett to Jane Bennett, December 10, 1883.

3. Union Pacific and Southern Pacific, Passenger Departments, *The Overland Route to the Road of a Thousand Wonders: The Route of the Union Pacific and the Southern Pacific from Omaha to San Francisco, a Journey of Eighteen Hundred Miles, Where Once Bison and the Indian Reigned*, 1908, 10.

4. Ibid., 11.

5. Ibid., 11–13.

6. Ibid., 33–34.

7. *The Lancet* declared the valley as "most equitable" in 1905; see "Los Gatos History: Doctors Prescribed Los Gatos Climate," www.losgatos.com/history/climate.html. Caroline Churchill, *"Little Sheaves" Gathered While Gleaning After Reapers: Being Letters of Travel Commencing in 1870 and Ending in 1873*, "San Jose in June," p. 7, Library of Congress, "American Memory" archive, www.memory.loc.gov.

8. Loraine Immen, *Letters of Travel in California, in the Winter and Spring of 1896* (Grand Rapids, 1896), 38; CR, "Signposts" scrapbook, "Juiciest 'Cot Ever Eaten Gave Moorpark Its Name," November 17, 1972.

9. Churchill, *"Little Sheaves,"* 8.

10. Ibid.

11. Limerick, *The Legacy of Conquest*, x.

12. E. Gould Buffum, *Six Months in the Gold Mines: From a Journey of Three Years' Residence in Upper and Lower California* (Philadelphia: Lea and Blanchard, 1850), 108; William Elsey Connelley, "National Aspects of the Old Oregon Trail," 1915, in Collections of the Kansas State Historical Society, Topeka, Kansas, p. 419; Ben Maddow, *A Sunday Between Wars: The Course of American Life from 1865 to 1917* (New York: Norton, 1979), 108; William Dixon, *White Conquest*, vol. 1 (London: Chatto and Windus, 1876), 154–155, 159, 149.

13. John Baggerly, "Auction Brought Prosperity to Settlers," Los Gatos History, online archive of *Los Gatos Weekly-Times*, www.losgatos.com/auction.html; cited in Dixon, *White Conquest*, 162; Phyllis Filiberti Butler, *Old Santa Clara Valley: A Guide to Historic Buildings from Palo Alto to Gilroy* (San Carlos, CA: Wide World Publishing, 1975), 15–17, 137–138.

14. Butler, *Old Santa Clara Valley*, 32, 85–88; Dixon, *White Conquest*, 146.

15. Ibid., 144.

16. Butler, *Old Santa Clara Valley*, 144.

17. "Death of Mr. William Malcolm," *Shooting & Fishing* 7, March 27, 1890, 425.

18. Ibid.

19. Immen, *Letters of Travel in California*, 38–39.

20. Talbot, "Sarah Winchester," 28.

21. Andrew Jackson Davis, *The Philosophy of Spiritual Intercourse: Being an Explanation of Modern Mysteries* (Boston: Colby and Rich, 1890), 297; Mrs. H. F. M. Brown, "California: Its Ways and Wonders," in *1871 Year Book of Spiritualism*, www.spirithistory.com.

22. Merle Gray, "'The Workshop' of a Woman Architect," *San Jose Mercury Herald*, July 16, 1911, 6.

23. CR, Signposts scrapbooks, "When High Rise in Campbell Was a Barn," May 19, 1972; Winchester Mystery House, "The Winchester Mystery House: The Mansion Designed by Spirits," San Jose, California, Historic Landmark #868 (publication to support historic landmark status).

24. CR, Merle Gray, [title missing], *San Jose Mercury and Herald*, July 16, 1911, 6.

25. Quoted in Sheila Rothman, *Living in the Shadow of Death* (New York: Basic Books, 1994), 137, 147.

26. "The State Fair: Vegetables, Honey, Domestic Manufactures, Plowing Instruments and Machinery, Poultry, Sheep, Swine, Cattle, Fruits and Flowers," *Hartford Daily Courant*, October 13, 1854, 2.

27. CR, "Winchester Mystery House," transcript, radio broadcast on local history, December 4, 1965.

28. Stanford University Archives, Samuel Leib Papers (SUASL), SC116, box 10, folder 5, includes correspondence between Sarah and her lawyer, Leib, in which Sarah shows through a meticulous reading of the abstract of a deed that land she intended to purchase had a muddied provenance, and refused to buy the land with unclear title. See, especially, Sarah Winchester to Leib, March 29, 1906, January 12, 1906, January 22, 1906, February 3, 1906. See also Gene Tuttle, "Title Search Uncovers Strange Facts," *San Jose Mercury News*, April 14, 1979, "Home" section.

29. Clyde Arbuckle, *Clyde Arbuckle's History of San Jose* (San Jose: Smith and McKay, 1985), 55; History San Jose, Research Center (HSJ), Samuel Leib Papers (SL), Sarah Winchester series, box 1, folder 18, "Deeds," description of original lot; SL, box 1, folder 1, correspondence from E. B. Rambo to W. W. Converse, May 8, 1888. On surveying problems, see *Arbuckle's History of San Jose*.

30. Dixon, *White Conquest*, 144; Marion Holbrook, "Sarah Winchester, Woman of Mystery," *Frontier Times*, October 1985, 19; Winchester Mystery House, "The Winchester Mystery House: The Mansion Designed by Spirits," 37. I have also seen the name spelled "Llanda Villa," but follow the Winchester Mystery House spelling.

31. SL, box 1, folder 1, from E. B. Rambo to W. W. Converse, WRAC, April 17, 1888.

32. Arbuckle, *Clyde Arbuckle's History of San Jose*, 100–101; SL, box 1, folder 1, from E. B. Rambo to W. W. Converse, April 17, 1888.

33. SL, box 1, folder 1, from E. B. Rambo to W. W. Converse, WRAC, April 17, 1888.

34. Ibid.

35. Phyllis Filiberti Butler, "Thanks for the Memories: Los Altos' Merriman-Winchester House," *Los Altos Town Crier*, November 27, 1995, www.latc.com/1995/11/27. Two years earlier, Sarah had sold 105 acres to Oliver Hale, but she had no idea that he planned to expand the Southern Pacific "octopus" right in front of the ranch, from Los Altos to Palo Alto. She and Isabelle had fought the "octopus" fiercely. When the surveyors came to lay down the stakes, Isabelle and Sarah pulled them out of the ground, right behind the surveyors. Sarah enlisted her lawyer, Samuel Leib, to battle Hale and Southern Pacific, to no avail. Leib wrote to Sarah on November 17, 1905, that he hadn't succeeded in thwarting the Southern Pacific juggernaut. "My dear Mrs. Winchester," he began, "I am very sorry indeed that I could not carry out your idea in full—namely to prevent the road running through your land at all. . . . The road, I understand, is sure to be built, and when the fences are built, as we will require them to do, it would effectually prevent you from having any access to it, even if you desired[,] which," he hastily added, "I am sure you would not." SL, box 1, folder 1, from Samuel Leib to Sarah Winchester, November 17, 1905.

36. SL, box 1, folder 1, from E. B. Rambo to W. W. Converse, April 17, 1888; box 1, folder 1, from E. B. Rambo to W. W. Converse, April 20, 1888.

37. SL, box 1, folder 1, from W. W. Converse to E. B. Rambo, April 30, 1888; box 1, folder 1, from W. W. Converse to Sarah Winchester, April 30, 1888.

38. SL, box 1, folder 1, from E. B. Rambo to W. W. Converse, May 1, 1888.

39. Cited in "Superstition in Building," *American Architect and Building News*, February 8, 1896, 68.

40. CR, Arthur Fisk, "Mystery House," *Trailblazer*, newsletter, Winter 1971.

41. Ignoffo, *Captive of the Labyrinth*, 119; CR, Amaury Mars, *Reminiscences of Santa Clara Valley and San Jose* (San Francisco: Mysell-Rollins, 1901), chap. 7.

42. Ibid.

43. HSJ, *San Jose Directory*, 1890.

CHAPTER 12:
THE GUN INDUSTRY'S VISIBLE HAND

1. Porter, *Rise of Big Business*, 10–12; Van Zwoll, *America's Great Gunmakers*, 136. Van Zwoll notes that sales troubles also encouraged Winchester and other gun industrialists to lower prices. Quoted at Richard Ohmann, *Selling Culture: Magazines, Markets and Class at the Turn of the Century* (New York: Verso, 1996), 54. Wilson, *Colt's Blue Book*; Madis, *Winchester: Dates of Manufacture*. Williamson, *Winchester*, notes that the company in the 1880s designed jobber discounts to reward volume of sales (p. 115), and that the company worried about its shrinking profit margin throughout the decade (pp. 177–178), but did not feel that it could raise the price of the guns without losing customers. See Williamson, *Winchester*, Appendix F, "Winchester Net Sales, Profits, Profits as Percentage of Sales," 463; RMA, *Forest and Stream*, August 25, 1881.

2. WRAC, series 4, box 10, folder 47, Captain E. Crossman, "With Captain Crossman at the Big Winchester Factories," *Sporting Goods Dealer*, January 1920, 77; WRAC, series 5, box 13, folder 27, internal memo, from F. W. Olin to Edwin Pugsley, n.d.; Williamson, *Winchester*, 111–113; Garavaglia, *Firearms of the American West*, 197–198; WRAC, series 4, box 10, folder 24, typescript for encyclopedia, Thomas Hall, 11; see also Deyrup, *Arms Makers of the Connecticut Valley*, 202; WRAC, series 3, box 8, folder 22, press release from Steve Hannagan, Olin Industries, June 19, 1950. See also Robert

White, curatorial assistant, Cody Firearms Museum, "The Gentlemen's Agreement," Points West online, Spring 2003, http://centerofthewest.org/2014/11/16/points-west -gentlemens-agreement-colt-and-winchester. The Chase National Bank Monies of the World collection included these cartridges in its 80,000 examples of currency.

3. HCHSVF, #1292, "Remington Centennial Programme Book, 1816–1916," 38; Doukas, *Worked Over*, 67. I am indebted to Doukas's illuminating chapter about the 1888 takeover of Remington described here.

4. ANRS, 60, "Industries of Ilion." The Remington Arms Company president and Eliphalet's grandson explained the causes of the company's demise at a 1911 sales convention in HCHSVF, #292, "Minutes of the Convention of Salesmen," *Remington Collector's Journal*, 2nd quarter, 2012, 38; see also HCHSVF, #285, typescript of receiver A. N. Russell's account of the fall, "Ilion and the Remingtons," 12, 14; Hatch, *Remington*, 76–78; Van Zwoll, *America's Great Gunmakers*, 42–49. Chandler, *The Visible Hand*, notes that Remington never built up an adequate sales and marketing structure for new products (p. 308).

5. Henning, "The Advertising of E. Remington & Sons" (notes that the company's attention to martial arms may have "diverted attention away" from civilian sales); Hatch, *Remington*, 180–182; Doukas, *Worked Over*, 87–90; Russell, "Ilion and the Remingtons," 12; "Minutes of the Convention of Salesmen," 38; HM, *The Remington Centennial Book*, 20–21.

6. ANRS, 60, "Sold for 200,000: Second Sale of Remington Armory, Hartley & Graham of New York Again the Purchasers," *Utica Herald*.

7. ANRS, 74, "Ilion Banquet," March 21, 1897 (describing order system); IPLED, vol. 1, "It May Be a Few Weeks or It May Be a Few Months, but the Order System Is Tottering on the Brink," April 9, 1886; "Some Merchants Almost but Not Quite Refuse 'Scrip' or 'Order,'" April 16, 1886; "Orders Are Gone and We Are Glad of It," April 30, 1886, all excerpted from *Ilion Citizen*; HCHSRM, 1 box, items 2015.8.32 and 2015.8.49, annual handwritten financial declarations.

8. ANRS, 40, 39, 60, 61; "The Crash Comes! In the Hands of Receivers—Failure of the Remingtons," *Herkimer Democrat*, April 28, 1886, 3; HCHS, SRC, box 1, item 171, "A Letter to Receivers Explaining the 'Revised Plan' for Reorganization," October 12, 1886; "In the Hands of Receivers," *New York Times*, April 23, 1886, 1.

9. Doukas, *Worked Over*, 83; ANRS, 40, 74.

10. ANRS, 42, from *Utica Herald*.

11. WRAC, Veader, "The Story of the WRAC," 137; "The Long Awaited Sale of Armory Coming," *Ilion Citizen*, January 27, 1888, 5.

12. ANRS, 41–42, 60, "Sold by the Receivers," *Utica Herald*, February 1, 1888; "Spoils to the Victors: Hartley & Graham Get the Property, Again," *Ilion Citizen*, March 9, 1888, 5; "The Armory Sale—Hartley & Graham Buy the Armory 'For a Song,'" *Ilion Citizen*, February 3, 1888, 4; Doukas, *Worked Over*, 84–85; see also "The Result of the Sale," editorial, *Ilion Citizen*, February 3, 1888, 4; "The Remington Sale—Who Bought It—How the Sale Will Affect Ilion—What Our Correspondent Has to Say," *Herkimer Democrat*, February 8, 1888, 12; "The Remington Armory Sale," *New York Times*, February 2, 1888, 5.

13. ANRS, 42, "The Armory Sale—Hartley & Graham Buy the Armory 'For a Song,'" *Ilion Citizen*, February 3, 1888, 4.

14. Ibid.; ANRS, 41–42, "Sold by the Receivers," *Utica Herald*, February 1, 1888; "The Result of the Sale," *Ilion Citizen*, February 3, 1888; "The Remington Sale—Who

Bought It—How the Sale Will Affect Ilion—What Our Correspondent has to Say," *Herkimer Democrat*, February 8, 1888.

15. ANRS, 41–42, "The Result of the Sale," *Ilion Citizen*, February 3, 1888; "The Armory Sale—Hartley & Graham Buy the Armory 'For a Song,'" February 3, 1888.

16. ANRS, 44, "The Remington Armory—Receivers' Report of the Sale," *Ilion Citizen*, February 17, 1888, 1 (transcript of court proceedings); ANRS, 39, "E. Remington & Sons: Meeting of the Creditors," *Utica Herald*.

17. Ibid.

18. Ibid.

19. Ibid.

20. ANRS, 60, "Sold for 200,000: Second Sale of Remington Property, Hartley & Graham of New York Again the Purchasers," *Utica Herald*.

21. ANRS, 60, "Spoils to the Victors: Hartley & Graham Get Property, Again: 200,000 Will Buy You a Million," *Ilion Citizen*, March 9, 1888, 5; "The Remington Armory Sold," *New York Times*, March 8, 1888, 1; WRAC, Veader, "The Story of the WRAC," 138–139.

22. ANRS, 60, "Sold for 200,000: Second Sale of Remington Property, Hartley & Graham of New York Again the Purchasers," *Utica Herald*; "The Final Sale," *Ilion Citizen*, March 9, 1888, 1; "Spoils to the Victors: Hartley & Graham Get Property, Again: 200,000 Will Buy You a Million," *Ilion Citizen*, March 9, 1888.

23. ANRS, 60, "Spoils to the Victors: Hartley & Graham Get Property, Again: 200,000 Will Buy You a Million," *Ilion Citizen*, March 9, 1888; "Sold for 200,000: Second Sale of Remington Property, Hartley & Graham of New York Again the Purchasers," *Utica Herald*; "The Remington Sale: Hartley & Graham Again the Purchasers: The Outlook, as Viewed by Our Ilion Correspondent," *Herkimer Democrat*, March 14, 1888, 1.

24. ANRS, 60, "Sold for 200,000: Second Sale of Remington Property, Hartley & Graham of New York Again the Purchasers," *Utica Herald*; "Spoils to the Victors: Hartley & Graham Get Property, Again: 200,000 Will Buy You a Million," *Ilion Citizen*, March 9, 1888; Doukas, *Worked Over*, 72.

25. ANRS, 60, "Spoils to the Victors: Hartley & Graham Get Property, Again: 200,000 Will Buy You a Million," *Ilion Citizen*, March 9, 1888.

26. WRAC, Veader, "The Story of WRAC," 139. On rival repeater rifles by the 1890s, see Garavaglia, *Firearms of the American West*, 216.

27. Porter, *Rise of Big Business*, 62, 88. In *Titan*, Chernow writes that in the postwar industrial boom, "the most significant revolt against free market capitalism came not from reformers . . . but from businessmen," who improvised the "rules of the game as they went along" and were frustrated by fluctuations and overproduction (pp. 148–149). For example, Winchester had become much more active in the ammunition business. Union Metallic Cartridge was the largest cartridge maker in the world. UMC's Marcellus Hartley was a formidable competitor. Winchester's expansion into ammunition of all kinds brought him into battles with UMC, fought through laborious claims and counterclaims of patent infringements on cartridge design. These skirmishes continued until the two reached an agreement in 1873. They would "cancel and set off one against the other" any patent claims for cartridges, and each party could use the patents of the other if they wanted to. Hartley accepted the agreement partly in exchange for a share of future Turkish orders. For over a decade, the UMC shared with Winchester the bulk of the US ammunition market, and they formed a "community of interest." See Williamson, *Winchester*, 75.

28. Wilson, *Winchester: An American Legend*, 158; Charles Perrow, *Organizing America: Wealth, Power and the Origins of Corporate Capitalism* (Princeton, NJ: Princeton University Press, 2005), 210; William G. Roy, *Socializing Capital: The Rise of the Large Industrial Corporation in America* (Princeton, NJ: Princeton University Press, 1997); WRAC, Veader, "The Story of the WRAC"; WRAC, box 14, folder 1, "Competition and the Marketing of Ammunition," typescript for company history, 230.

29. WRAC, additional box 11, folder 13, draft of Williamson's chapter 17 on the AMA; WRAC, Veader, "The Story of the WRAC," 102.

30. WRAC, additional box 11, folder 13, draft of Williamson's chapter 17.

31. BW, box 1, folder h, from TG Bennett to Jane Bennett, June 12, 1912. On the AMA, see Wilson, *Winchester: An American Legend*, 159–162.

32. WRAC, additional box 11, folder 13, Williamson draft.

33. WRAC, unprocessed part of collection, H. S. Leonard letter book, #1: 1898–1905: from Leonard to Wm. Beers, Philadelphia, September 14, 1901; from Leonard to "Salesmen," November 18, 1905; copy of letter from Vice President (presumably Leonard) to Salesmen, January 28, 1903; from First Vice President to Jobbers, July 18, 1905; from Leonard to Salesmen, re: The Automatic Rifle, August 5, 1903.

34. WRAC, unprocessed part of collection, Leonard letter book from Leonard to Wm. Beers, September 14, 1901.

35. WRAC, unprocessed part of collection, Leonard letter book, from Leonard to "All Salesmen and New York Store, re: Diversion of Association Business," May 1, 1903; from Wm. Odell, AMA, to "gentlemen" (of the AMA), July 17, 1905; from Leonard to jobbers, July 18, 1905; from Leonard to "All Salesmen and New York Store, re: Diversion of Association Business," May 1, 1903; copy of letter to Salesmen, from Vice President Leonard, January 28, 1903.

36. WRAC, unprocessed part of collection, Leonard letter book, from Leonard to all missionaries, April 6, 1903; copy of letter sent by Odell to all houses on special dating list, Texas excepted, January 28, 1903.

37. WRAC, additional box 11, folder 13, from Charles Hopkins to Rusty Casteel, March 28, 1951.

38. WRAC, additional box 11, folder 13, from Sidney Kay to Edwin Pugsley, August 10, 1848.

39. WRAC, Leonard letter book, from Leonard to "A, B, C Gun Houses," October 20, 1905; additional box 11, folder 13, draft of Epilogue, written by Pugsley, p. 4; Leonard letter book, from Leonard to salesmen, September 16, 1905; from Leonard to Athens Hardware and others, October 15, 1905; "Sample," from Leonard to no recipient, February 24, 1903.

40. *Dr. Miles Medical Company v. John B. Park and Sons*, 220 US 373, 374 (1911); *Bauer and Cie. v. O'Donnell*, 229 US 1 (1913); WRAC, Leonard letter book, from President of WRAC to Salesmen, Missionaries, Shooters, New York store and San Francisco store, November 25, 1904; from Leonard to "Gentlemen" [jobbers], December 30, 1906; from President to Salesmen . . . , November 25, 1904.

41. HCHSVF, #292, "That Remington Gun Sale," March 26, 1910, "Remington Co. Sells Shotgun Trade," March 22, 1910.

42. WRAC, Leonard letter book, from Leonard to "Gentlemen" [jobbers], December 30, 1906.

43. Ibid.

44. WRAC, Leonard letter book, from Fred Biffar, Sears, to Augusta, GA [name removed], December 9, 1906; from Biffar to Nebraska gun dealer, March 24, 1906.

45. WRAC, Leonard letter book, WRAC, from President of WRAC to Salesmen, Missionaries, Shooters, New York store and San Francisco store, November 25, 1904; from Assistant Treasurer H. S. Leonard to H. F. Beebe, August 1, 1906.

46. WRAC, series 1, box 5, folder 43, correspondence to W. Sherer Jr., Sydney, N.S.W., Australia, et al., from WRAC first vice president, May 18, 1910.

47. Ibid. Control over dealers for sales continues: Denis Henigan, in *Lethal Logic*, 182–183, describes how Beretta uses contracts with distributors to impose sales requirements to support promotion and volume.

48. WRAC, box 1, folder 24, March 1, 1918, draft letter "to Direct, Indirect and Catalogue Trade"; BBHC, *Winchester Record* 3, March 26, 1920, 7; *Winchester Record* 1, no. 3, September 13, 1918.

49. DeConde, *Gun Violence in America*, 111.

50. WRAC, Vaeder, "The Story of the WRAC," 182; US Senate, Congressional Hearings on Revolutions in Mexico, Hearings Before Subcommittee of the Committee on Foreign Relations, September 1912, 62nd Cong., 2nd sess., pursuant to res. 335 (Washington, DC: 1913), 831–833.

51. SHGC, box 17, folder 31, September 15–21, 1895; box 14, folder 45, June 15–21, 1897; box 15, folder 105, March 1–10, 1897; box 3, folder 49, October 1–15, 1873; box 14, folder 51, September 1–10, 1891; *Congressional Series of United States Public Documents*, vol. 1528, *Reports of the Committees of the House of Representatives*, 42nd Cong., 2nd sess., House of Representatives Report #46, "Sales of Ordnance Stores," April 15, 1872 (Washington, DC: US Government Printing Office, 1872), 181.

52. US Senate, Congressional Hearings on Revolutions in Mexico, Hearings Before Subcommittee of the Committee on Foreign Relations, September 1912, 62nd Cong., 2nd sess., pursuant to res. 335 (Washington, DC: 1913), 178, 118, 120.

53. Ibid., 834, 843, 831, 348, 181, 258.

54. Ibid., 844.

55. Ibid., 844, 846.

56. Peter Harry Brown, *Outgunned* (New York: Free Press, 2003), 52.

CHAPTER 13: LEARNING TO LOVE THE GUN

1. Theodore Roosevelt, *Theodore Roosevelt: An Autobiography* (New York: 1913), 58; Williamson, *Winchester*, 210, ponders whether, "as the 'frontier' yielded to settlement, it might be assumed that the demand for firearms would have declined."

2. "Isolated Riflemen," *Shooting & Fishing* 20, May 38, 1896, 113, bound volume 19 (on the promotion of rifle practice and the NRA, "Another Branch of Manly Sport," p. 116); *Shooting & Fishing* 37, December 15, 1904, 203, bound volume 36; "Legislation for the Promotion of Rifle Practice," *Shooting & Fishing* 37, December 1, 1904, 1; The bill, from Representative Ariosto Wiley of Alabama, would fund a shooting range with government money in every single district (*Shooting & Fishing* 39, January 11, 1906, 292, bound volume 38). The NRA proposed that the government allocate a few million dollars to buy land to ensure that every state had at least a few rifle ranges, even if it meant that "a few creeks are left unimproved in the back country" (like horse farms today, a rifle range might also have constituted an unintended bulwark against real estate development). See "Legislation for the Promotion of Rifle Practice," *Shooting & Fishing* 37, December 1, 1904, 1. In March 1905 and June 1906, legislation passed to allow the secretary of war to sell surplus army magazine rifles to governors for the use of rifle clubs affiliated with the National Rifle Association, and to appropriate funds

annually to provide arms and equipment for the "promotion of rifle practice." "Legislation for the Promotion of Rifle Practice," *Shooting & Fishing* 39, January 11, 1906, 1; "Legislation . . . ," *Shooting & Fishing* 40, July 19,1906, 1; *Shooting & Fishing* 37, March 2, 1905, 1.

3. Roosevelt, *Theodore Roosevelt*, 58; Madis, *Winchester*; Wilson, *Colt's Blue Book*; Williamson, *Winchester*, 209; 1910 US Census, vol. 8, 486. The gun estimate is from US Department of Justice, Office of Justice Studies, "Guns Used in Crime," 1995, 2.

4. Williamson, *Winchester*, 210, 177–178. William Vizzard, *Shots in the Dark: The Policy, Politics and Symbolism of Gun Control* (Lanham, MD: Rowman and Littlefield, 2000), notes that basic firearm design and function has not changed all that much since the early 1900s, "requiring manufacture and dealer to implement strategies to maintain market demand," 24.

5. Richard Rattenbury, *The Art of American Arms Makers: Marketing Guns, Ammunition and Western Adventure During the Golden Age of Illustration* (Oklahoma City: National Cowboy and Western Heritage Museum, 2004), 22, 14, 79. Rattenbury is the curator of history at the museum.

6. Rattenbury, *The Art of American Arms Makers*, 29, 30.

7. HCHSVF, #1256, typescript, "Remington Literature Collecting," 2; HCHSVF, #1256, copy of letter from Remington Arms to wholesaler I. C. Sinen, Philadelphia, November 6, 1920; "The Winchester Calendar," *Shooting & Fishing* 19, January 9, 1896, 249; WRAC produced thirty-four calendars and thirty posters between 1887 and 1930.

8. Rattenbury, *The Art of American Arms Makers*, 85, 102, 121.

9. WRAC, Veader, "The Story of the WRAC," 1–4 (appendix); Van Zwoll, *America's Great Gunmakers*, 141; Williamson, *Winchester*, 183, 117; HCHSVF, #292, "Minutes of the Convention of Salesmen for the Remington Arms Company and the United Metallic Cartridge Company," in *Remington Collector's Journal*, 2nd quarter, 2012, 39.

10. "The Attitudes of Shooting Men," *Shooting & Fishing* 13, December 21, 1893, 182; CC, box 66, last folder, "For Dealers"; WRAC, unprocessed part of collection, Letter book of H. S. Leonard, from Leonard to twenty-two missionaries, named, May 19, 1905.

11. WRAC, Leonard letter book, from Leonard to missionaries and shooters, June 6, 1905.

12. Russell Belk and Janeen Arnold Costa, "The Mountain Man Myth: A Contemporary Consuming Fantasy," *Journal of Consumer Behavior* 25 (December 1998): 218–240. On buffalo extinction and Native American conquest, see Hatch, *Remington*, 155; Karen Jones, "Guns, Masculinity, and Marksmanship," 47–50.

13. "Sportsmen v. Marketmen," *Shooting & Fishing* 19, March 12, 1896, 1; "Proposed Game Legislation," *Shooting & Fishing* 7, March 27, 1890, 1; "The Development of City Markets," *Shooting & Fishing* 7, April 17, 1890, 1.

14. "Proposed Game Legislation," *Shooting & Fishing* 7, March 27, 1890, 1.

15. Editorial, "The Market Hunter," *Shooting & Fishing* 7, January 30, 1890, 1; "The Cause of Decrease of Fish and Game," *Shooting & Fishing* 13, April 6, 1893, 1.

16. "Marketing Game," *Shooting & Fishing* 16, September 20, 1894, 428, bound volume 15.

17. Douglas Brinkley, *The Wilderness Warrior: Theodore Roosevelt and the Crusade for America* (New York: HarperCollins, 2009); Theodore Roosevelt, *Hunting Trips of a Ranchman: Sketches of Sport on the Northern Cattle Plains* (New York: G. P. Putnam's

Sons, 1885), 41; Edmund Morris, *The Rise of Theodore Roosevelt* (New York: Random House, 1979), 278, 324, 417, 570; WRAC, series 10, box 23, folder 6, TR to WRAC, January 29, 1909; WRAC to TR's secretary, February 22, 1909.

18. Theodore Roosevelt, "The Duties of American Citizenship," address before the Liberal Club, Buffalo, New York, January 26, 1893, in *The Works of Theodore Roosevelt*, vol. 15 (New York: Scribner's, 1925 [series 1923–1926]), 6, and *The Wisdom of Theodore Roosevelt* (New York: Kensington, 2003), 98; Roosevelt, *Theodore Roosevelt*, 58, 59; Morris, *The Rise of Theodore Roosevelt*, 570.

19. Roosevelt, *Theodore Roosevelt*, 77, 141; Slotkin, *Gunfighter Nation*, 102–105. In October 1912, Roosevelt would pay with his body when a would-be assassin shot him in the breast as he was en route to a speech in Milwaukee. Remarkably unperturbed and bearing the offending gun no grudge, Roosevelt insisted on delivering a shortened version of his speech. "It takes more than that to kill a bull moose," he told the crowd. Theodore Roosevelt, *Theodore Roosevelt*, 99, 56, 77, 21; Morris, *The Rise of Theodore Roosevelt*, 330. The cowboy and hero-outlaw were male figures by default, but they were most energetically valorized as individuals. See Browder, *Her Best Shot*; Roosevelt, *Theodore Roosevelt*, 123, 125; Morris, *The Rise of Theodore Roosevelt*, 681; Kristian Hoganson, *Fighting for American Manhood: How Gender Politics Provoked the Spanish-American and Philippine-American Wars* (New Haven, CT: Yale University Press, 1998).

20. WRAC, series 10, box 23, folder 5, TR to Win Bennett, May 12, 1909; Morris, *The Rise of Theodore Roosevelt*, 387; Theodore Roosevelt, *Theodore Roosevelt*, 301; Theodore Roosevelt, "African Game Trails: An Account of the African Wanderings of an American Hunter-Naturalist, "On Safari: Rhinos and Giraffes," *Scribner's*, December 1, 1909, 664; WRAC, series 10, box 23, folder 6, Win Bennett to TR, July 6, 1908.

21. "Modern Weapons and Game Destruction," editorial reprinted from Calcutta, India, *Shooting & Fishing* 33, December 11, 1902, 167, bound volume 32; Matthew Cragoe, "Cockney Sportsmen?"

22. WRAC, series 10, box 23, folder 1, from Dr. Danis to WRAC, from Brussels, May 21, 1908.

23. Chandler, *Visible Hand*.

24. This census of production is taken from my review of the manufacturing books for Colt and Winchester, see Chapter 9, note 3. For Carnegie comments, see Andrew Carnegie, *North American Review* (1889), quoted at Porter, *Rise of Big Business*, 101–102. On continuous process production in metal industries, see Chandler, *Visible Hand*, 280–290. See also Rattenbury, *The Art of American Arms Makers*, 19; Susan Porter Benson, "Taylorism: The Cinderella of Occupations: Managing the Work of Department Store Saleswomen, 1900–1940," in Beatty, ed., *Colossus*, 210.

25. Frederick Winslow Taylor, "A Piece-Rate System," *Cassier's*, October 1895.

26. RW, box 4, folder 16, "Winchester Repeating Arms Company," "Time Studies," n.d.; "Drill Press," December 8, 1917.

27. RW, box 4, folder 16, from the Observation Study Section, Cartridge Department, "Writing of Instruction Cards," n.d.

28. BBHC, *Winchester Record* 1, no. 2, "The First Billion: How We Make the .30 Calibre U.S. Military Cartridge," August 30, 1918; RW, box 4, folder 17, "WRAC Cartridge Department, 1917," "Operation A—ROUGHING," n.d.; box 4, folder 17, Gun Department, "New Systems and Forms—General Procedure," n.d.; IPLED, vol. 1, from "Utica Press," January 15, 1916; Theodore Dreiser, "The Making of Small Arms," *Ainslee's Magazine* 1, July 1898, 547.

29. Dreiser, "The Making of Small Arms," 548.

30. Gary John Previts, *A History of Accountancy in the United States: The Cultural Significance of Accounting* (Columbus: Ohio State University Press, 1998), 95, 132; Chandler, *The Visible Hand*, 278–279.

CHAPTER 14: MYSTERY HOUSE

1. Talbot, "Sarah Winchester," 28.

2. BW, box 1, folder b, from Sarah Winchester to Jane Bennett, May 14, 1898. Much of the material in this section comes from this letter. Sarah called Jane "Jennie," but for consistency I will call her Jane here and throughout. Likewise, Sarah was known by the nickname Sallie, but will be called Sarah. See also WRAC, series 4, box 12, folder 18, from Robert Winchester to Gene Ball, archivist, May 24, 1980; Bill Thomas, "Ghosts Are Clever—So I Baffle Them," *New York Times*, May 31, 1970; CR, San Jose Chamber of Commerce, "Winchester Mystery House," typescript, 1937. On Roosevelt's request, see also Charles Hillinger, "'Spirits' Moved Sarah to Build—and Build," *Los Angeles Times*, September 8, 1974; CR, *Heritage West*, March/April 1983, 43.

3. Osterweis, *Three Centuries of New Haven*, 377.

4. Winchester Mystery House, "The Winchester Mystery House: The Mansion Designed by Spirits"; Josiah Dewey, "Winchester Mystery House," *Yankee*, October 1962, 51; Boorman, *The History of Winchester Firearms*, 50.

5. BW, box 1, folder b, from Sarah Winchester to Jane Bennett, June 11, 1898. Much of the material in this section is drawn from this second letter.

6. Talbot, "Sarah Winchester," 28.

7. Snip is referred to as "Zip" at the house, but appears as Snip in the letter.

8. Winchester Mystery House, "The Winchester Mystery House: The Mansion Designed by Spirits," notes that the bell rang at midnight and 2:00 A.M.; Marion Holbrook, "Sarah Winchester, Woman of Mystery," *Frontier Times*, October 1985, 19. On the bell tower and watches, see Bill Thomas, "Ghosts Are Clever—So I Baffle Them," *New York Times*, May 31, 1970; CR, "Mrs. Winchester's Extraordinary 'Spook Palace,'" *San Francisco Examiner*, April 1, 1928; Gerry O'Hara, "Winchester House of Mystery," *San Jose Mercury News*, January 4, 1977; BW, box 1, clippings related to Sarah Winchester, Lloyd Carter, UPI, "Are Tourists Bothering Mistress of Ghost House?," n.d.; "Horological Bureau at Yale," *New York Times*, November 7, 1879, 8; "Uniformity in Time," *New York Times*, May 2, 1880, 2.

9. Gray, "The Workshop."

10. "Superstition in Building," *American Architect and Building News*, February 8, 1896, 68.

11. Ibid.

12. Ibid.; CR, "Mrs. Winchester's Extraordinary 'Spook Palace,'" *San Francisco Examiner*, April 1, 1928; Although stories often refer to a "Chinese butler" living at Sarah's estate, the 1910 US Census (at 66–67) lists two "cooks," R. Ushio and M. Nakimo, and a "waiter," Tomo Ushio, all born in Japan. The census lists a gardener who was born in China, Charlie Yen, and two "servants" and "nurses," young women born in the United States.

13. CR, San Jose Chamber of Commerce, "Winchester Mystery House," typescript, 1937, 1; CR, Sarah Winchester, "Winchester Widow Dying: Work on Her Home in San Jose, CA, Has Never Ceased," *New York Times*, June 12, 1911, sec. 1, 6.

14. Gray, "The Workshop"; Ralph Rambo, "Lady of Mystery" (California, 1967), part of a series on Santa Clara Valley in its pioneer era, 3.

15. Ibid.

CHAPTER 15: "GROTESQUE, YET MAGNIFICENT"

1. BW, box 1, folder b, address from granddaughter of TG and Jane Bennett to the Saturday Morning Club, "House of Mystery," typescript, February 19, 1971, 1.

2. Charles Hillinger, "'Spirits' Moved Sarah to Build—and Build," *Los Angeles Times*, September 8, 1974.

3. Several sources note her sense of culpability, terror, and foreboding after the earthquake; for example, see Winchester Mystery House, "The Winchester Mystery House: The Mansion Designed by Spirits," 26. Karen Smith, "Built to Be Haunted," *Palo Alto Peninsula Times-Tribune*, October 27, 1988; CR, San Jose Chamber of Commerce, "Winchester Mystery House," typescript, 1937 (on cost of construction); SL, box 1, folder 1, from E. B. Rambo to W. W. Converse, May 8, 1888; BW, box 1, folder h, correspondence between TG Bennett and Jane Bennett, April 1906.

4. Ignoffo, *Captive of the Labyrinth*, 154; Karen Smith, "For Halloween: A Haunted House, Ghosts, Spirits," *Palo Alto Peninsula Times Tribune*, October 31, 1983.

5. Ignoffo, *Captive of the Labyrinth*, 155.

6. Weldon Melick, "Sevenscore Gables," *Holiday*, February 1947, 157; Omstead, "The House That Spirits Built," 15. For other details on the earthquake, see John Stark, "Sarah Winchester's Ghostly Penance," *San Francisco Examiner and Chronicle*, August 29, 1976, "Scenes" section, 1; "A Midwinter Feast at Los Altos," *Los Altos Star*, August 5, 1908.

7. SL, box 1, folder 12, 1910 Taxes, list of properties.

8. "Recluse Heiress Will Enter Court"; Millie Robbins, "The Mystery House Puzzle," *Palo Alto Peninsula Times-Tribune*, June 19, 1966.

9. Tom Powell, "Sarah Winchester: Lost in the Legend," *San Mateo Times, The Times Weekend*, May 31, 1969; "A Midwinter Feast at Los Altos," *Los Altos Star*, August 5, 1908; CR, *Heritage West*, March/April 1983, 43.

10. Unfortunately, most of her correspondence, as with the archive of the Winchester Repeating Arms Company, has been destroyed. See Alan Hess, "Sarah Winchester Deserves Recognition," *San Jose Mercury News*, February 15, 1987; Charles Hillinger, "'Spirits' Moved Sarah to Build—and Build," *Los Angeles Times*, September 8, 1974; Rambo, "Mystery House," 12; Ernie Holyer, "The Spooky House That Sarah Built," *Santa Clara Valley Sun Magazine*, July 27, 1977, 3 (recalls that she drew on table cloths); SL, box 1, folder 9, checks written against J. P. Morgan by Sarah Winchester, March 24, 1915.

11. Dean Jennings, "The House That Mystery Built," 49; Ruth Amet, "Winchester House Constructed Like Giant Ant Hill, *San Jose Mercury Herald*, May 27, 1923.

12. Sarah's inventions are mentioned in a variety of places. See George Beronius, "Where Fact Is Stranger Than Fiction," *Los Angeles Times*, May 22, 1977; "Strange World of the Winchester House," *San Francisco Chronicle*, December 11, 1949, clipping in WRAC, series 5, box 13, folder 27; John Stark, "Sarah Winchester's Ghostly Penance," *San Francisco Examiner and Chronicle*, August 29, 1976, "Scenes" section, 1; Marion Holbrook, "Sarah Winchester, Woman of Mystery," *Frontier Times*, October 1985, 19. Although the usual caveats apply to hearsay about Sarah's motives and state of

mind, one of the stories of her building project has an employee commenting, wisely, that Sarah might have been both quite sane and a spiritualist. Woelf, *Sarah Pardee Winchester.*

13. SUASL, SC116, box 10, folder 4, from Sarah Winchester to Leib, box 10, folder 4, November 16, 1905; subseries, Leib Correspondence, box 1, folder 11, Sarah Winchester to Samuel Leib, October 9, 1909.

14. SL, box 1, folder 14, from Sarah Winchester to Samuel Leib, September 18, 1908; from Sarah Winchester to Samuel Leib, October 14, 1908; from Sarah Winchester to Samuel Leib, November 5, 1909; SL, box 1, folder 2, from Samuel Leib to Union Trust Company, July 9, 1909; from Sarah Winchester to Samuel Leib, January 26, 1915; SUASL, SC11, box 10, folders 4 and 5, outline of Sarah's various trust arrangements.

15. Quoted in Woelf, *Sarah Pardee Winchester.*

16. Bill Thomas, "Ghosts Are Clever—So I Baffle Them," *New York Times*, May 31, 1970; Susy Smith, "Five True Ghost Stories," *The Coronet*, April 1968, 130; "Winchester Widow Dying: Work on Her Home in San Jose, CA, Has Never Ceased," *New York Times*, June 12, 1911, sec. 1, 6.

17. Sarah dismissed (but with one year's pay) anyone who saw her face, aside from one of two Japanese cooks who prepared her meals. CR, Joe Custer, "Rich Widow Builds House on Order of Watchful Wraiths Who Dictated Plans," 1936, Scrapbook E; CR, "Mrs. Winchester's Extraordinary 'Spook Palace,'" *San Francisco Examiner*, April 1, 1928. John Stark writes that Sarah Winchester never allowed photographs, in "Sarah Winchester's Ghostly Penance," *San Francisco Examiner and Chronicle*, August 29, 1976, "Scenes" section, 1. CR, Scrapbook E, employee's recollection in Joe Custer, "Rich Widow Builds House on Order of Watchful Wraiths Who Dictated Plans," 1936.

18. CR, San Jose Chamber of Commerce, "Winchester Mystery House," typescript, 1937; Ruth Amet, "Winchester House Constructed Like Giant Ant Hill, *San Jose Mercury Herald*, May 27, 1923; Josiah Dewey, "Winchester Mystery House," *Yankee*, October 1962, 51; "Strange World of the Winchester House," *San Francisco Chronicle*, December 11, 1949; Charles Hillinger, "'Spirits' Moved Sarah to Build—and Build," *Los Angeles Times*, September 8, 1974; CR, "$5,000,000 Spook Home," n.d.; Antoinette May, *Haunted Houses and Wandering Ghosts of California* (San Francisco: Examiner Special Projects, 1977), 52; Bill Thomas, "Ghosts Are Clever—So I Baffle Them," *New York Times*, May 31, 1970; Luise Putcamp, "American Gothic," *New Haven Register*, May 3, 1977; CR, San Jose Chamber of Commerce, "Winchester Mystery House," typescript, 1937; CR, "Mrs. Winchester's Extraordinary Spook Palace," *San Francisco Examiner*, April 1, 1928; Josiah Dewey, "Winchester Mystery House," *Yankee*, October 1962, 51; Winchester Mystery House, "The Winchester Mystery House: The Mansion Designed by Spirits," 18.

19. Rambo, *Lady of Mystery*; Dean Jennings, "The House That Mystery Built," *The Coronet*, May 1945, 49; Alan Hess, "Sarah Winchester Deserves Recognition," *San Jose Mercury News*, February 15, 1987; Marion Holbrook, "Sarah Winchester: Woman of Mystery," *Frontier Times*, October 1985, 19; "Superstition in Building," *American Architect and Building News*, February 8, 1896; Sigmund Freud, *Civilization and Its Discontents* (New York: Penguin, 2002 [1930]), 8.

20. On the discovered room, see Linda Goldstone, "Is Sarah Still Building?" *San Jose Mercury News*, February 23, 1975; CR, *San Jose Mercury News*, "Action Line," column, n.d.; Karen Smith, "Built to Be Haunted," *Palo Alto Peninsula Times Tribune*, October 27, 1988; CR, Edna May Brown, "A History of the Winchester Mystery House," San Francisco, n.d.

21. "Winchester Widow Is Dying: Work on Her House in San Jose, CA, Has Never Ceased," *New York Times*, June 12, 1911, sec. 1, 6; CR, Christopher Fortunato, "A House of Mystery," *Boston Globe*, n.d., 1977, travel section.

22. There is uncertainty as to whether all of these recurrences of the number thirteen were designed by Sarah, or added by the owners of the house after her death, who converted it into a "House of Mystery." Some of the incidences of thirteen appear to me to be of Sarah's own hand, however; for example, the presence of thirteen stones in the exquisite Tiffany glass windows, or the thirteen drainholes, or hooks on the wall. But others might have been added after the fact, and it is impossible to distinguish these from Sarah's with any certainty.

23. Richard Battin, "At Home with Sarah Winchester," *California Today*, June 3, 1973, 22–25; BW, box 1, clippings related to Sarah Winchester, Lloyd Carter, UPI, "Are Tourists Bothering Mistress of Ghost House?" n.d.; Winchester Mystery House, "The Winchester Mystery House: The Mansion Designed by Spirits," 18.

24. CR, San Jose Chamber of Commerce, "The Winchester Mystery House," typescript, 1937. Neither Sarah's employees nor her few callers ever used this stunning entryway. They were admitted instead by an uncomfortable side stairway into a dingy reception room.

25. Author tour of Winchester house, October 27, 2005; Rambo, "Lady of Mystery," 6; Omstead, "The House That Spirits Built," 15.

26. CR, Edna May Brown, "A History of the Winchester Mystery House," San Francisco, n.d.; Richard Battin, "At Home with Sarah Winchester," *California Today*, June 3, 1973, 22–25. On Sarah's play with the number thirteen, see also Rambo, "Lady of Mystery," 4; Winchester Mystery House, "The Winchester Mystery House: The Mansion Designed by Spirits," 18; Bill Thomas, "Ghosts Are Clever—So I Baffle Them," *New York Times*, May 31, 1970.

27. Stephen Greenblatt, *Will in the World: How Shakespeare Became Shakespeare* (New York: Norton, 2004), 300.

28. "'Troilus and Cressida' Will Be Spring Play by Dramat.," *Yale Daily News*, February 22, 1916, 1. See the brilliant criticism by Joyce Carol Oates, "The Tragedy of Existence: Shakespeare's Troilus and Cressida," *Philological Quarterly*, Spring 1967, and *Shakespeare Quarterly*, Spring 1966.

29. CR, San Jose Chamber of Commerce, "Winchester Mystery House," typescript, 1937; SL, box 1, folder 15, Accounting Book, 1878–1885, March 16, 1881. On her insomnia, arthritis, and organ playing, see BW, box 1, folder b, address from granddaughter of TG and Jane Bennett to the "Saturday Morning Club," "House of Mystery," typescript, February 19, 1971, 6.

30. Chandler, *The Visible Hand*, 290, 347; Theodore Dreiser, "The Making of Small Arms," *Ainslee's Magazine* 1, July 1898, 539–540; Captain Crossman, "With Capt. Crossman at the Big Winchester Factories," 77–86; Barnard, *Armsmear*, 214. Dreiser likened the Winchester factory buildings to a "sort of village in themselves," the "exterior plain," and as "safely shut to the stranger as are the walls of a penitentiary"—much like Llanada Villa—yet inside, this contained world was dizzying with thousands of machines. John Stark, "Sarah Winchester's Ghostly Penance," *San Francisco Examiner and Chronicle*, August 29, 1976, "Scenes" section, 1; Jennings, "The House That Tragedy Built," *The Coronet*, May 1945, 49; Omstead, "The House That Spirits Built," 15. Michael Spence, however, in *The Next Convergence: The Future of Economic Growth in a Multispeed World* (New York: Farrar, Straus and Giroux, 2011), asks why an economy should continuously expand and build, especially since this growth does not actually

seem pegged to an improved standard of living. The Winchester Repeating Arms Company ranked 144 overall in US enterprises in 1917. It was one of all but five leading American enterprises that were manufacturing based. The ones that had flourished did so because of size. They were large enough, and their "consumers numerous enough," to handle "high volume flows" for national markets.

31. Dreiser, "The Making of Small Arms," 539, 548.

32. Sarah spent "a great deal of her capital and most of her income building and unbuilding." See "Strange World of the Winchester House," *San Francisco Chronicle*, December 11, 1949.

33. The Winchester Mystery House is in an area that is currently in the midst of real estate madness—Northern California and Silicon Valley. This has been the case since the 1960s and continues today. See "If It's SPACE You Want," *Palo Alto Peninsula Times-Tribune*, June 17, 1961. See also Delia Rio, "Sarah Winchester Goes on Trial: Was She Playing with a Full Deck?" *San Jose Mercury News*, April 1, 1989, 2B.

34. CA, clippings, "Sarah's Winchester's Goal Was to Live Forever: She Thought She Would Never Die if She Never Finished Building," n.d.; Vance Bourjaily, "An Eerie World: The Winchester House," *San Francisco Chronicle*, December 11, 1949; CR, San Jose Chamber of Commerce, "Winchester Mystery House," typescript, 1937.

35. Swedenborg, *Heaven and Its Wonders*, 114–115.

36. DC, vol. 122, p. 41, "The Tale of Winchesters in Figures," data from Osborn's *History of Connecticut*.

37. WRAC, box 11, folder 25, New Haven, CT: "Points of Interest," New Haven Chamber of Commerce, back cover.

38. Dean Jennings, "The House That Mystery Built," *The Coronet*, May 1945, 49; CR, Joe Custer, "Rich Widow Builds House on Order of Watchful Wraiths Who Dictated Plans," 1936, in Scrapbook E; B. L. Coleman, "Winchester House: Victorian Dream or Nightmare?" *Antiques and Auctions News* 8, no. 22 (October 28–November 10, n.d.); CR, Joan Jackson, "Digging in to Restore Sarah's Famous Gardens," *San Jose Mercury News*; Marion Holbrook, "Sarah Winchester, Woman of Mystery," *Frontier Times*, October 1985, 19. On Sarah's gardens, see also Winchester Mystery House, "The Winchester Mystery House: The Mansion Designed by Spirits," 34; SL, box 1, folder 12, 1910 Taxes, list of properties.

39. DC, vol. 122, p. 41, "The Tale of Winchesters in Figures."

40. Karen Smith, "Built to Be Haunted," *Palo Alto Peninsula Times-Tribune*, October 27, 1988; Wilson, *Winchester: An American Legend*, notes that the company was the largest private armory at its peak (p. xi).

CHAPTER 16: OVERBUILDING

1. BW, box 1, folder I, from TG Bennett to Jane Bennett, January 30, 1915; February 14, 1915.

2. DC, vol. 122, p. 36, article from *New Haven Register*, September 1917; WRAC, series 5, box 13, folder 21, from Henry Brewer to Harlay Rogers, November 19, 1928; DC, vol. 42, pp. 20–23, "Bennett Dies, Ex President of Winchester"; NHCHS, Joe Dobrow, "A Farewell to Arms," Yale School of Management, typescript on WRAC, 1922; IPLED, vol. 1, p. 26, article from "Utica Press," January 15, 1916.

3. Dobrow, "A Farewell to Arms"; DC, vol. 42, pp. 20–23, "Bennett Dies, Ex President of Winchester."

4. HH, box 1, folder 23, Personnel Division, Number of Employees, By Department, November 12, 1917; HCHSVF, #292, "Remington Arms Special Makes Its Last Run on Sunday," *Ilion Citizen*, December 19, 1918. Remington also took the dramatic step of employing females in more skilled, mechanical positions, HCHSVF, #292, "May Employ Girls at Remington Gun Plant," *Ilion Citizen*, May 18, 1918.

5. BBHC, *Winchester Record* 1, "The Weakest Link," October 25, 1918, cover editorial; WRAC, additional box 26, folder 6, Winchester Victory Drives, Propaganda Pamphlets, "Guns in Time Will Save Your Boy and Mine."

6. Wilson, *Winchester: An American Legend*, 386, 168; DC, vol. 42, pp. 20–23, "Bennett Dies, Ex President of Winchester."

7. HH, box 1, folder 23, from WRAC to "U.S. War Department, District Board for Division #1," October 1918.

8. HH, box 1, folder 24, "Memorandum of Conference Held at Small Arms Division . . . for the Purpose of Discussing the Capacity of the Country for the .30 cal. Cartridges, Model 1906.

9. Ibid.

10. Harry Hunt, "A Gun Apiece for Every Man 'Over There,' and Here, Too," WRAC, series 1, box 1, folder 2, March 2, 1918; WRAC, series 1, box 2, folder 29, "Speech of Hon. John Q. Tilson of Connecticut, House of Representatives," March 26, 1918. Pugsley anticipated future government dependency on commercial arms; see WRAC, from Pugsley to Henry Brewer, MRL—correspondence, chronological—2003, unprocessed part of collection.

11. SL, box 1, folder 3, from TG Bennett to Sarah Winchester, April 5, 1918; Boorman, *History of Smith & Wesson*, 51–53; Van Zwoll, *America's Great Gunmakers*, 115.

12. WRAC, box 2, folder 9, from J. Otterson to Henry Brewer, February 16, 1918; WRAC, box 2, folder 3, August 24, 1918, memorandum; see also box 2, folder 3, October 28, 1918, memorandum; series 1, box 2, folder 9, from J. Otterson to Henry Brewer, February 16, 1918.

13. HH, series 1, box 1, folder 24, from O. B. Mituham to Chief of Ordnance, Washington, DC, July 28, 1917; WRAC, series 1, box 3, folder 19, personal and confidential, from Win Bennett to Secretary of War Newton Baker, May 6, 1916; series 1, box 3, folder 19, from Secretary of War Newton Baker to Win Bennett, WRAC, June 8, 1916; HCHSVF, #292, "Remington Arms Works Adopt Pass System," *Herkimer Democrat*, January 5, 1917.

14. Brotherhood of Locomotive Firemen, *Locomotive Firemen's Magazine, 1917* (1917), 571; Victoria Morier Wemyss, *The Life and Letters of Lord Wester Wemyss* (London: Eyre and Spottiswoode, 1935), 406; Basil Collier aptly summarizes the feeling after World War I that "only arms manufacturers could expect to profit by continuance of the struggle and that therefore, only arms manufacturers could wish to prolong it." Quoted in Stohl and Grillot, *The International Arms Trade*, 15. John Gunther, "Slaughter for Sale," *Harper's*, May 1934, 655. *The Nation* is quoted in DeConde, *Gun Violence in America*, 106.

John Wiltz, "The Nye Committee Revisited," *Historian* 23, no. 2 (1961): 214, 211. Throughout the 1920s, Americans had blamed arms makers and industrialists for World War I. Historian John Wiltz argues that Nye overplayed to this view at the beginning of the investigation, and "when no evidence emerged to support the hyperbole, he couldn't walk it back." The merchants of death theory and the movement to nationalize the arms trade faded by the late 1930s. But the committee and Nye's speeches contributed to a malevolent atmosphere that hung over the small arms industry as never before.

15. Stohl and Grillot note in *The International Arms Trade* that it has been reasonably argued that there was "no evidence that arms manufacturers expected to profit from war, as they too were tired of the restriction from foreign markets and the burdensome workload that came with the war." In Winchester's case—and Remington's, and Smith & Wesson's—that is true. WRAC, series 1, box 1, folder 24, correspondence from R. C. Swanton, auditor of government accounts, to Lieutenant Jackson, accountant in charge at WRAC plant, April 29, 1918; June 18, 1918; BW, box 1, folder I, from TG Bennett to Jane Bennett, from Ocracoke, North Carolina, June 21, 1916. Among other students of the gun business, Hatch, *Remington*, 62, concludes of Remington that "contrary to the general impression," the company fared better in times of peace than of war, since "the wild flurry of war contracts, the extravagant expansion to fulfill them . . . far outweighs the illusory profits, which are usually lost in the aftermath of reconversion."

16. WRAC, unprocessed part of the collection, correspondence, chronological—2003, uncataloged, Pugsley, "miscellaneous correspondence," from Pugsley to Henry Brewer, October 7, 1921.

17. Browning quoted in Kirkland, *America's Premier Gunmakers: Winchester*, 12; DC, vol. 122, p. 41; Van Zwoll, *America's Great Gunmakers*. Remington raised money to build new facilities by selling company bonds and by securing $13 million in personal loans. WRAC, Veader, "The Story of the WRAC," 183, 191–192.

18. SL, box 1, folder 3, from TG Bennett to Sarah Winchester, April 5, 1918; Browning quoted in Kirkland, *America's Premier Gunmakers: Winchester*, 12.

19. HH, box 1, folder 23, telegram from War Department to WRAC, April 9, 1918.

20. WRAC, series 1, box 5, folder 46, from Henry Brewer to Colonel Charles Black, May 6, 1918, and from Henry Brewer to Mr. Swanton, May 14, 1918; series 5, box 13, folder 24, internal memo from John Otterson to Edwin Pugsley, n.d.

21. WRAC, series 1, box 1, folder 2, Burrell's press clippings, "Guns Enough to Arm 14 Divisions," March 1, 1918 (appears to have been picked up by the *New York Times*, but the name of the paper isn't provided on the clipping); series 1, box 1, folder 2, "Great American Equipment Machine Swings Toward High Tide of Production," February 23, 1918. On Remington's substantial Allied contracts, see Adam Fireston, "Remington's Allied Rifle Contracts During World War I," Luke Mercaldo, ed., *The Remington Collector's Journal*, 2nd quarter, 2012, 22–27.

22. HH, box 1, folder 23, from W. E. Maxon to Henry Brewer, June 15, 1918; WRAC, series 1, box 3, folder 32, telegram from General Brigadier Wheeler to General Manager, WRAC, April 19, 1918; series 1, box 3, folder 32, from A. C. Jewett to M. J. Hammant, July 16, 1918; series 1, box 3, folder 21, telegram from Captain Johnson to WRAC, August 12, 1918.

23. WRAC, series 1, box 6, folder 9, Sales Department Bulletin, July 2, 1918; series 1, box 6, folder 8, Sales Department Bulletin, April 17, 1918.

24. WRAC, series 1, box 4, folder 13, from WRAC to War Trade Board, September 13, 1918; series 1, box 14, folder 13, from War Trade Board, Bureau of Exports, to WRAC, August 7, 1918; series 1, box 4, folder 13, from F. G. Drew to Henry Brewer, July 21, 1919; series 1, box 4, folder 15, from WRAC to War Trade Board, December 2, 1918; series 1, box 4, folder 13, from WRAC to War Trade Intelligence Board of War Trade Board, December 2, 1918.

25. WRAC, series 1, box 4, folder 13, from WRAC Assistant Export Manager to War Board, December 9, 1918; series 1, box 4, folder 13, from R. M. Ames, Ordnance Officer, to WRAC, November 12, 1918.

26. HH, box 1, folder 23, memo from J. D. Cushman re: Burdens and Burden Rate, March 3, 1919; SL, box 1, folder 3, from TG Bennett to Sarah Winchester, April 5, 1918.

27. HH, box 1, folder 24, from Henry Brewer for Colonel Tilson, "Memorandum on All Completed Orders." In its catalog after the war, the company reported producing 700 million cartridges.

28. HH, box 1, folder 24, from WRAC to Lieutenant Jackson, June 18, 1918; WRAC, series 1, box 3, folder 32, memorandum from Edwin Pugsley to A. C. Jewett, "Manufacturing Engineer's Department, "Estimate Covering Costs of Equipping to Manufacture 100,000,000 .30 cal Cartridges per Month," April 1, 1918.

29. From TG Bennett to Samuel Leib, October 2, 1918, reprinted in Williamson, *Winchester*, 262.

30. SL, box 1, folder 3, from TG Bennett to Sarah Winchester, April 5, 1918.

31. "Winchester Widow Dying: Work on Her Home in San Jose, CA, Has Never Ceased," *New York Times*, June 12, 1911, sec. 1, 6; "Mysteryman Kidnaped [sic] to Save His Life," *San Francisco Examiner*, August 13, 1915, 3; Rambo, "Lady of Mystery," 5.

32. Marion Holbrook, "Sarah Winchester, Woman of Mystery," *Frontier Times*, October 1985, 19; Margot Doss, "House of Imaginary Ghosts," *San Francisco Sunday Examiner and Chronicle*, November 5, 1967, 7; CR, Clay Lancaster, *Architectural Follies in America*, 172–177; Barbara Jones, *Follies and Grottoes* (London: Constable, 1953); Gray, "The Workshop"; Ernie Holyer, "The Spooky House That Sarah Built," *Santa Clara Valley Sun Magazine*, July 27, 1977, 3. Apparently the rumors upset Sarah; see "Winchester Mystery House: Fact Sheet," Gardens and Historical Museum, in WRAC, series 4, box 12, folder 18.

33. CR, Talbot, "Sarah Winchester."

34. Robbins, "The Mystery House Puzzle"; "Recluse Heiress Will Enter Court; Gray, "The Workshop"; SL, box 1, folder 2, from Samuel Leib to Sarah Winchester, February 1, 1910; box 1, folder 2, from Samuel Leib to Sarah Winchester, October 8, 1909.

35. Rambo, "Lady of Mystery," 14; SL, box 1, folder 13, order for Renault, from Pierce Arrow Pacific Sales. The bill came to $7,230. Leigh Weimers, "The Grandmother of Winchester Mystery House General Manager Keith Kittle Met Sarah Winchester in San Jose in 1914," *San Jose Mercury News*, August 14, 1994.

36. Talbot, "Sarah Winchester," 28; SL, box 1, folder 3, from TG Bennett to Sarah Winchester, April 5, 1918.

37. SL, box 1, folder 3, from TG Bennett to Sarah Winchester, April 5, 1918.

38. Ibid.; Van Zwoll, *America's Great Gunmakers*, 147. From Bennett's perspective, the War Revenue Act of 1919 would make matters worse. The act would place a tax on firearms manufacture to help defray the costs of World War I.

39. Ignoffo, *Captive of the Labyrinth*, 191.

40. In 1904 Sarah had 2,777 shares; Jane, 2,875; TG Bennett, 32; and Win Bennett, 6, for a total of 5,690 out of 10,000 common stock, so the family retained control. See Wilson, *Winchester: An American Legend*, 163.

41. BW, box 1, folder e, from TG Bennett to Jane Bennett, from London, May 10, 1905.

42. SL, box 1, folder 3, from TG Bennett to Sarah Winchester, August 18, 1918; Wilson, *Winchester: An American Legend*, 171.

43. SL, box 1, folder 3, from TG Bennett to Sarah Winchester, August 18, 1918.

44. Ibid.; Ignoffo, *Captive of the Labyrinth*, 192.

45. From Samuel Leib to TG Bennett, September 23, 1918, reprinted in Williamson, *Winchester*, 262. Apparently, Williamson had requested copies of Winchester correspondence from Leib, and Leib had sent him these original letters, as they are missing from the Sarah Winchester series of his own papers.

46. SL, box 1, folder 3, from TG Bennett to Sarah Winchester, April 5, 1918; from TG Bennett to Samuel Leib, October 2, 1918, reprinted in Williamson, *Winchester*, 264.

47. From Samuel Leib to TG Bennett, quoted in Williamson, *Winchester*, 264. On the payment dispute, see SL, box 1, folder 3, from Samuel Leib to Sarah Winchester, April 6, 1921, and box 1, folder 3, from Samuel Leib to Sarah Winchester, April 6, 1921 (second letter). "As for whatever property you *already* owned, *other* than your interest in the Winchester Repeating Arms Company, you desired to be very fully and clearly protected against paying out any of your money for any liability as a stockholder in the Winchester Company," Leib wrote. He had earned his keep, among many other things, by ensuring that the agreement followed the laws of Connecticut rather than of California, where individual stockholders could still be held responsible for a corporation's debt burdens. See Millie Robbins, "The Mystery House Puzzle," *Palo Alto Peninsula Times-Tribune*, June 19, 1966, for the estimate of $1 million on interior materials, as well as Rambo, "Lady of Mystery," 3.

48. BW, box 1, folder I, from TG Bennett to Jane Bennett, September 24, 1918.

49. BW, box 1, folder I, from TG Bennett to Jane Bennett, September 20, 1918; SL, Sarah Winchester Series, box 1, folder 3, telegram from Sarah Winchester to TG Bennett, September 21, 1918.

50. SL, box 1, folder 3, correspondence between Samuel Leib and Sarah Winchester, April 6, 1921.

51. From TG Bennett to Samuel Leib, March 1919, quoted in Williamson, *Winchester*, 270.

CHAPTER 17: THE SOUL OF THE "GUN CRANK"

1. HH, box 1, folder 23, "Confidential Interdepartmental Memo, Production Program," November 29, 1918; HH, box 1, folder 23, correspondence from K. T. Tredwell, Office of the WRAC vice president, to Assistant Comptroller, February 28, 1919. See also WRAC, series 5, box 13, folder 24, from Edwin Pugsley to C. T. Haven, June 17, 1946.

2. Van Zwoll, *America's Great Gunmakers*, 48–50.

3. Ibid.; Hatch, *Remington*, 222; HCHSVF, #292, "Remington Plant Closed," *Ilion Citizen*, December 23, 1918.

4. Grant, *The Colt Legacy*, 88.

5. Engelbrecht and Hanighen, *Merchants of Death*, 180.

6. WRAC, series 1, box 2, folder 22, from WRAC, no sig., to US Revenue Agent, New Haven, CT, July 25, 1918; series 1, box 6, folder 1, November 19, 1918; Houze, *Winchester Repeating Arms Company*, 194. Making matters worse, the government was acting like a deadbeat customer. Winchester wasn't receiving partial payments for suspended orders after the war ended. Of $3 million the government owed, the company had received only $7,000. The company sent a near-frantic telegram, sarcastically referred to as "our 500 word telegram" by the chief of ordnance, whose staff responded

that such telegrams only "injected bitter feelings." WRAC, series 1, box 2, folder 16, Memo re: Conference of Colonel Franklin and Mr. Charles Graham, September 3, 1919; series 1, box 2, folder 16, "Confirmation of Outgoing Telegram," prepared by Henry Brewer to Major General C. C. Williams, Chief of Ordnance, US Army, September 1919; BBHC, *Winchester Record* 2, no. 15, "Winchester Means Opportunity," February 27, 1920, 1; BBHC, *Winchester Record*, 2, no. 26, "The Winchester Plan," July 30, 1920, 1. Part of the Winchester Plan continued the decades-long momentum away from the jobber and dealer middlemen. The marketing department proposed to establish Winchester retail stores in towns and cities of over 50,000 (the company opened its first retail store in Providence, Rhode Island), and to approach large hardware stores in smaller communities to enlist merchants as exclusive Winchester outlets for their area. The company hosted 1,000 hardware dealers at a "lavish five-day convention," writes Williamson, *Winchester*, but by 1922 both schemes had failed. BBHC, *Winchester Record* 2, no. 15, "Winchester Means Opportunity," February 27, 1920, 1; Van Zwoll, *America's Great Gunmakers*, 145–147.

7. Boorman, *History of Smith & Wesson Firearms*, 54; Jinks, *History of Smith & Wesson*, 265–267; Van Zwoll, *America's Great Gunmakers*, 48–50; Grant, *The Colt Legacy*, 88, 103.

8. Glenn Utter, "The Evolving Gun Culture in America," *Journal of American & Comparative Culture* 23, no. 2 (2000): 67; "The Rifle Crank," *The Rifle* (precursor to *Shooting & Fishing*) 2, April 1888, 501.

9. "Rifle Cranks and Their Hobbies," *Shooting & Fishing* 6, June 27, 1889, 6; "Love for the Rifle Never Dies," *Shooting & Fishing* 8, May 8, 1890, 9; WRAC, series 1, box 6, folder 1, from Henry Brewer, VP of WRAC, to Fowler Manning, February 28, 1918; BBHC, "The Dealer and Organized Shooting," *Winchester Herald*, February 1921, 31; WRAC, series 1, box 6, folder 7, Sales Department Bulletin, November 27, 1917.

10. "Beware the Man with One Gun," *Shooting & Fishing* 37, October 13, 1904, 1; Benson, "Taylorism: The Cinderella of Occupations," 210.

11. HH, box 1, folder 24, from Edwin Pugsley to J. Otterson, January 18, 1919; WRAC, series 5, box 13, folder 23, from Herman and Standard Publishing to Edwin Pugsley, April 26, 1945; WRAC, series 1, box 3, folder 5, from Henry Brewer to J. Otterson, March 28, 1917; HCHSVF, #292, "Minutes of the Convention of Salesmen for the Remington Arms Company and the Union Metallic Cartridge Company," January 9–19, 1911, convention, from *Remington Collector's Journal*, 2nd quarter, 2012, 38. HH, box 4, folder 6, from Henry Brewer to T. C. Johnson, January 14, 1919, refers similarly to the "shooting fraternity in Washington."

12. "Bag Limit on Wild Fowl," *Forest and Stream* 87, March 1917, 142; HH, box 1, folder 24, from Edwin Pugsley to J. Otterson, January 18, 1919.

13. HH, box 1, folder 24, from Edwin Pugsley to J. Otterson, January 18, 1919. On disgust with guns, see Van Zwoll, *America's Great Gunmakers*, 115–122; DeConde, *Gun Violence in America*, notes the "budding anti-gun sentiment" (p. 106). Carol Skalnik Leff and Mark H. Leff, "The Politics of Ineffectiveness": Federal Firearms Legislation, 1919–38," *Annals of the American Academy of Political and Social Science* 455, no. 1 (1981): 48–62, note that gun control emerged as a topic of "marked federal concern" after World War I (p. 49). The gun industry at the time felt the shifting mood. Jinks, *History of Smith & Wesson*, writes that the company after the war faced an "entirely new problem" of "public antipathy toward anything military or associated with violence and killing" (pp. 262–264).

14. BBHC, *Winchester Record* 1, "American Shot Gun Gets Fritz in a Rage," October 15, 1918; WRAC, unprocessed part of collection, Leonard letter book, file no. 1, bound volume, 1898–1905, from Hodson, WRAC vice president, to Salesmen, March 24, 1900; Leonard letter book, ad for "Winchester 'Riot' Gun," February 1903; Leonard letter book, ad for "Winchester Repeating Shot Guns: Protection from Robbers, Home Defense, Safety to Bank Vaults," March 1900; from Griffith to TG Bennett on '97 Riot Gun tests, February 11, 1903; ad, the "Winchester 'Riot' Gun," February 1903; series 1, box 6, folder 1, sales letter, from WRAC to unknown recipients, on plant protection.

15. BBHC, *Winchester Record* 1, "American Shot Gun Gets Fritz in a Rage," October 15, 1918; WRAC, series 1, box 6, folder 1, sales letter, from WRAC to unknown recipients, on plant protection; series 1, box 6, folder 1, letter from WRAC, n.d. (1917–1918), re: Plant Protection; Matt Bai, "Unmaking a Gunmaker: The Fall of an American Icon," *Newsweek*, April 17, 2000, thefiringline.com/forums/archive.

16. BBHC, *Winchester Record* 2, no. 19, "Shooting Is a Sport for Women," April 23, 1920, 1; RMA, *Hunter-Trader-Trapper*, August 15, 1915, *Outer's Book*, October 14, 1914, *The Outing*, August 7, 1907.

17. BBHC, *Winchester Record* 3, no. 2, "American Girls Shoot Their Way into Albanian Hearts," August 27, 1920.

18. WRAC, series 4, box 11, folder 36, from Bill Depperman, WRAC, to Mr. Ad Topperwein, April 6, 1955.

19. WRAC, series 1, box 6, folder 7, July 7, 1917; series 6, box 13, folder 20, from TG Bennett to "The Trade," 1918, p. 6; series 6, box 13, folder 20, from Win Bennett "To The Trade," p. 22.

20. WRAC, series 6, box 13, folder 20, from TG Bennett to "The Trade," 1918, p. 11; Captain Crossman, "With Capt. E. C. Crossman at the Big Winchester Factories," *Sporting Goods Dealer*, January 1920, 86; HCHSVF, #1256.

21. Carter, *The Gun Control Movement*, provides a brief history of the NRA in the interwar years (pp. 66–68). WRAC, series 1, box 6, folder 9, "Equipment Available for Issue to Rifle Clubs," June 26, 1918; series 1, box 4, folder 15, to Fowler Manning, sales agent, from Henry Brewer, December 16, 1918.

22. WRAC, series 1, box 6, folder 9, Sales Bulletin, June 29, 1917; series 6, box 13, folder 20, from TG Bennett to "The Trade," 1918, p. 12; Capper quoted in Kennett, *The Gun in America*, 213.

23. BBHC, *Winchester Herald*, March 1921, back ad; *Winchester Herald*, April 1921, advertisement, 1.

24. WRAC, series 1, box 6, folder 10, October 15, 1918; BBHC, *Winchester Record* 2, no. 15, "Origin and Development of Salesmanship," February 27, 1920, 3; Captain Crossman, "With Capt. Crossman at the Big Winchester Factories," 86.

25. WRAC, series 1, box 6, folder 1, "Confidential Communication from WRAC to Jobbers' Salesmen," June 15, 1917.

26. WRAC, series 1, box 6, folder 1, "Confidential Communication from WRAC to Jobbers' Salesmen," June 5, 1917; HCHSVF, #1256, from Remington Arms to L. C. Siner & Co., August 25, 1917.

27. WRAC, series 1, box 6, folder 7, Sales Department Bulletin, August 2, 1917.

28. So economist Williamson concludes in *Winchester* (pp. 177, 111); HCHSVF, #292, from "Minutes of the Convention of Salesmen for the Remington Arms Company and the United Metallic Cartridge Company," *Remington Collector's Journal*, 2nd quarter, 2012, 39.

29. Porter, *Merchants and Manufacturers*, 213, 225–226; WRAC, series 1, box 6, folder 1, "Confidential Communication from WRAC to Jobbers' Salesmen," June 5, 1917.

30. CC, box 66, last folder, "printed materials / internal, advertising and marketing, broadsides and circulars," "For Dealers: Colt Police Positive Target Revolver"; "Cuts for Dealers," 3; WRAC, Leonard letter book, from Leonard to missionaries, July 3, 1900. Remington started to send "Electrotypes for Jobbers and Dealers" in the early 1900s, from the company's newly minted "Advertising Department" (HCHSVF, #1256).

31. CC, box 66, last folder, "It Pays to Push Colt's"; box 66, folder 3, ad clipping, *National Geographic*, "A Lesson from the Texas Rangers," March 1936; box 66, folder 3, "Colt's Firearms: The New Responsibilities of Peacetime," *American*, November 1919; box 66, folder 3, "Automobilists Be Prepared!"; box 66, folder 3, "Be Prepared Against Country Hold-Ups"; "Automobilists Be Prepared!"; RMA, *National Sportsman*, December 22, 1922. See also RMA, *Outer's Book*, August 11, 1911, which compares a Colt's revolver to the "old" guardian of the home, the bulldog.

32. CC, box 66, folder 3, "Why Colt's Have Been Official Sidearm of the U.S. Government Since 1847," n.d., newspaper advertisement; box 66, folder 3, "Colt's Firearms: The New Responsibilities of Peacetime"; box 66, folder 3, "It's YOUR turn now"; "An Ancient Symbol and a Modern Means of Protection," n.d.

33. CC, box 66, folder 3, "Works Automatically—Requires No Thought," *Everybody's*, April 1912, 36. The parenthetical expression is found in the original ad itself; folder 3, "Automobilists Be Prepared!"; folder 3, "First in War, First in Peace"; "Colt: The Automated Pistol," ad clipped from *McClure's*.

34. CC, box 66, folder 3, ad clipped from *Everybody's*, n.d., 79; folder 3, ad clipped from *Guns*, December 1960, 7.

35. WRAC, series 6, box 13, folder 20, from TG Bennett to "The Trade," 1918, p. 12; series 6, box 13, folder 20, from Win Bennett "To the Trade," pp. 4, 10.

36. CC, box 70, folder 6, no label, "Still Red-Blooded Americans," June 17, 1929. The phrase "real boy" is extremely common in national and local WRAC advertisements and articles. See, for example, "What Every Real Boy Wants for Christmas," *Chicago Tribune*, December 21, 1919; *The Cosmopolitan* 49 (1910): 65, advertisement; "To Every Real Boy Who Loves Real Sport," *New York Times*, Picture Section, advertisement, December 21, 1919; "Talk to Real Boys," *Saturday Evening Post*, advertisement, December 4, 1909, 57; "Three Correct Positions for Earning the 'Sharpshooter' Medal," *Boys' Life*, advertisement, October 1917, 37; *Popular Science*, advertisement, November 1917, 108; *Popular Mechanics*, advertisement, November 1917, 119; WRAC, series 6, box 13, folder 20, from TG Bennett "To the Trade," 1918, p. 12; series 6, box 13, folder 20, from Win Bennett "To the Trade," p. 10. RMA, *The American Boy*, advertisement, June 18, 1918, says, "This is the year for every real American boy to take up" shooting, and Boy Scouts of America, *Handbook for Boys*, advertisement, circa 1920, claimed that "every real boy should be a sharpshooter."

37. WRAC, box 6, folder 7, Bulletin 127, August 9, 1917.

38. WRAC, series 1, box 6, folder 8, June 21, 1917.

39. WRAC, series 1, box 6, folder 8, Sales Department Bulletin, June 23, 1917; series 1, box 6, folder 7, Sales Department Bulletin, July 20, 1917.

40. WRAC, series 1, box 6, folder 1, "Confidential Communication from WRAC to Jobbers' Salesmen," June 5, 1917; series 1, box 6, folder 1, letter from WRAC to Jobbers, n.d. (1917).

41. BBHC, *Winchester Herald*, advertisement, August 1921, 20–21; WRAC, series 1, box 6, folder 7, Sales Department Bulletin, August 2, 1917.

42. BBHC, *Winchester Herald*, "Selling a Winchester Shotgun," August 1921, 20–21.

43. BBHC, *Winchester Record* 3, advertisement, January 1, 1921, 46; CC, box 70, folder 6, no label, "Still Red-Blooded Americans," June 17, 1929.

44. WRAC, box 13, folder 20, "To the Trade," sales form letter, signed by Win Bennett; RMA, *Literary Digest*, December 11, 1920; *National Sportsman*, March 20, 1920; BBHC, *Winchester Record* 3, no. 11, January 1, 1921, 46; BBHC, *Winchester Herald*, Johnson Morgan, "A Line That Made Winchester Famous," February 1921, 29; *Winchester Record* 2, no. 10, December 1919, advertisement, 1.

45. RW, box 3, folder 14, "Outline of Merchandising," draft on the "scientific management" of marketing and advertisement, 5, 2, 12; Oliver Zunz, *Making America Corporate, 1870–1920* (Chicago: University of Chicago Press, 1990), 176; Susan Porter Benson, "Taylorism: The Cinderella of Occupations," 210.

46. Quoted at Richard Ohmann, *Selling Culture: Magazines, Markets and Class at the Turn of the Century* (New York: Verso, 1996), 109. Ohmann's work explains how capitalists tried to manage overproduction by turning to the management of consumption through mass marketing and advertisement.

47. BBHC, *Winchester Herald*, advertisement, June 1921, 21; WRAC, series 1, box 6, folder 7, Sales Department Bulletin, July 10, 1917.

48. WRAC, series 1, box 6, folder 7, Sales Department Bulletin, August 2, 1917.

49. Fred Beard, "Competitive and Combative Advertising: An Historical Analysis," *Journal of Macromarketing* 31 (2011): 390, 393. In an "outline of merchandising," Werle's colleagues observe that "competition exists today not only between producers or distributors of the same type of goods, but many types of goods are competing with an entirely different line of goods." See HM, RW, "Outline of Merchandising," 2.

CHAPTER 18: KING OF INFINITE SPACE

1. CR, *Westward* 8, no. 11 (1955).

2. Author tour of Winchester Mystery House, October 28, 2005.

3. Ibid.

4. Winchester Mystery House, "The Winchester Mystery House: The Mansion Designed by Spirits," 16; "Engineering Firm to Blueprint Winchester Mystery House," *Palo Alto Times*, July 5, 1950.

5. Several articles mention the thirteen palms in Sarah's lifetime, including "Engineering Firm to Blueprint Winchester Mystery House"; CR, Joan Jackson, "Digging in to Restore Sarah's Famous Gardens," *San Jose Mercury News*; Winchester Mystery House, "The Winchester Mystery House: The Mansion Designed by Spirits," 37.

6. Edith Hamilton, *Mythology* (New York: Little, Brown, 2012).

7. Winchester Mystery House, "The Winchester Mystery House: The Mansion Designed by Spirits," 29.

8. BBHC, *Winchester Record* 3, no. 6, "Bennett Day Observed with Fitting Tributes," October 22, 1920, 1; *Winchester Record* 3, "Anniversary of Thomas G. Bennett," September 10, 1920.

9. BW, box 1, folder e, from TG Bennett to Jane Bennett, April [illeg.] 1905; April 12, 1905.

10. On sales conventions, see Zunz, *Making America Corporate*, 186; WRAC, series 4, box 10, folder 15, *Winchester Record* 2, no. 11, "Gun and Ammunition Salesmen Spend Busy Week at Successful Convention," January 2, 1920; series 1, box 4, folder 15, "Draft Program," 1919 sales convention.

11. SL, box 1, folder 3, from Samuel Leib to A. W. Hooper, WRAC, March 2, 1921.

12. BBHC, *Winchester Record* 2, no. 12, "Greetings 1922," January 1, 1922, 4–5; DC, vol. 122, p. 33, from Edwin Pugsley to Arnod Dana, June 7, 1937.

13. "Sarah Winchester Is Summoned by Death," *San Jose Mercury News*, September 7, 1922, 1.

14. "Hospital Gets Funds in Winchester Will," *San Jose Mercury News*, September 7, 1922; "Winchester Millions Go to Charity: San Jose Widow of Rifle Inventor Left But $4,000,000 out of $20,000,000 Fortune," *Palo Alto Times*, October 7, 1922.

15. WRAC, series 4, box 12, folder 18, clipping, "California Living," *Los Angeles Herald*, August 1, 1965; series 10, box 23, folder 20, "Key List"; HSJ, SL, Leib to John Hansen, November 16, 1922; March 16, 1922; Ignoffo, *Captive of the Labyrinth*, 207–208; CR, Millie Robbins, "Mrs. Winchester's Mystery House," *San Francisco Chronicle*, December 2, 1969; HH, box 1, folder 24; CR, "Mrs. Winchester's Extraordinary 'Spook Palace,'" *San Francisco Examiner*, April 1, 1928. Among others who saw the home as "monstrous," see Dean Jennings, "The House That Tragedy Built," *The Coronet*, May 1945, 49.

16. Ruth Amet, "Winchester House Constructed Like Giant Ant Hill, *San Jose Mercury Herald*, May 27, 1923; Gene Tuttle, "Title Search Uncovers Strange Facts," *San Jose Mercury News*, April 14, 1979, "Home" section, CR, "Winchester House of Mystery Fame Proves Real Mystery," 1979, clipping, n.d.; Dean Jennings, "The House That Mystery Built," *The Coronet*, May 1945, 49; David Barry, "Keith Kittle: Mystery Man Keeps Sarah's Legacy Going," *Business Journal*, October 22, 1990, 12; Lynn Ludlow, "The Hammers of Life and Death," *San Francisco Examiner*, September 13, 1964, 36; John Raese, "She Would Like What's Happening to Home," *Palo Alto Peninsula Times-Tribune*, May 1, 1979; Rambo, "Lady of Mystery," 3; CR, Duns Market Identifier, August 18, 1993.

17. CR, Leigh Weimers, "The Grandmother of Winchester Mystery House General Manager Keith Kittle Met Sarah Winchester in San Jose in 1914," *San Jose Mercury News*, August 14, 1994; "Winchester Mystery House Example of Area's Booming High Tech Attractions," February 23, 1997, www.winchestermysteryhouse.com/mediarelationscfm?mode=press&id_press=30&vmode=viewall.

18. Susy Smith, "Five True Ghost Stories," *The Coronet*, April 1968, 130; Genevieve Woelfl, "Sarah Pardee Winchester: A Driven Woman," pamphlet (San Carlos, CA: Redwood, 1986), 11; author's tour of house, October 27, 2005; CR, "Mrs. Winchester's Extraordinary 'Spook Palace,'" *San Francisco Examiner*, April 1, 1928; CR, B. L. Coleman, "Winchester House: Victorian Dream or Nightmare?" *Antiques and Auctions News* 8, no. 22 (October 28–November 10, n.d.).

19. On the reputed white satin room, see several sources, "Winchester Widow Dying," *New York Times*; CR, John Stark, "Sarah Winchester's Ghostly Penance," *San Francisco Examiner and Chronicle*, August 29, 1976, "Scenes" section, 1.; CR, Ernie Holyer, "The Spooky House That Sarah Built," *Santa Clara Valley Sun Magazine*, July 27, 1977, 3; CR, "Mrs. Winchester's Extraordinary 'Spook Palace,'" *San Francisco Examiner*, April 1, 1928; CR, San Jose Chamber of Commerce, "Winchester Mystery House," typescript, 1937. On the séance room, see also Lancaster, *Architectural Follies in America*, 172–177.

20. CR, *Heritage West*, March/April 1983, 43.

21. See for example, CR, San Jose Chamber of Commerce, "Winchester Mystery House," typescript, 1937; "Mrs. Winchester's Extraordinary 'Spook Palace,'" *San Francisco Examiner*, April 1, 1928.

22. *Revelations of a Spirit Medium*, 67–68; Bill Thomas, "Ghosts Are Clever—So I Baffle Them," *New York Times*, May 31, 1970.

23. There were safes in Winchester's house, but not in the "séance room." CR, "Mrs. Winchester's Extraordinary 'Spook Palace,'" *San Francisco Examiner*, April 1, 1928; Bill Thomas, "Ghosts Are Clever—So I Baffle Them," *New York Times*, May 31, 1970; Ed Coonfield, "The Fantastic Winchester Mansion," *Antiques Journal*, November 1975; Millie Robbins, "Mrs. Winchester's Mystery House," *San Francisco Chronicle*, December 2, 1969; CR, *Heritage West*, March/April 1983, 43; Winchester Mystery House, "The Winchester Mystery House: The Mansion Designed by Spirits," 41.

CHAPTER 19:
THE WEST THAT WON THE GUN

1. Don Haar, "The Gun That Won the West: Two Claim Bragging Rights," *Hartford Courant*, January 22, 2006. In another context, Herbert Houze (*Arming the West*, p. vii), the preeminent Colt's and Winchester curator, calls the boast "as much a fiction as the sources from which it's drawn."

2. Quoted at Diaz, *Making a Killing*, 20.

3. Figures on movies and publications at Cartwright, "The Cowboy Subculture," 88–89; Josh Sugarman, *Every Handgun Is Aimed at You: The Case for Banning Handguns* (New York: New Press, 2001), 19; Roberts, "The West's Gunmen, Part I," 12; Roberts, "The West's Gunmen, Part II," 61. Richard Shenkman, in *Legends, Lies and Cherished Myths of American History* (Boston: G. K. Hall, 1990), 112, notes that "many more people have died in Hollywood westerns than ever died on the real frontier." Use of Google Ngram Viewer for search of "cowboys" is an imperfect but interesting metric.

4. My census was based on Adams, *Six Guns and Saddle Leather*. See also Limerick, *The Legacy of Conquest*, 19. Starting in 1895 and going through 1980, fifty different manufacturers sold cowboy, Indian, and Wild West playsets. See www.marxwildwest.com/wildwest.html. Shenkman, *Legends, Lies*, 112.

5. Douglas Holt, "What Becomes an Icon Most?" *Harvard Business Review* 81, no. 3 (2003): 44, 48.

6. BBHC, *Winchester Herald*, January 1922, 36.

7. CC, box 66, last folder, "The Gun That Won the West"; "Famous in the Past," 1960 ad display. The "Makers of History" advertisements are reproduced in Martin Rywell, *Smith & Wesson*, 108–120; See also an interesting sense of history in RMA, a Colt's ad, circa 1908, from *Outdoor Life*, that reads, "Have Been in the Past / Are at the Present / Will be in the Future."

8. Cartwright, "The Cowboy Subculture," 100; "Texas to Honor Colt 'Glory Guns,'" *Hartford Courant*, Sunday edition, clipping, in CC, box 70A; Rattenbury, *The Art of American Arms Makers*, 24–25.

9. WRAC, box 13, folder 20, "Wanted—The Story of Your Old Winchester," *Field and Stream*, April 1919; box 13, folder 20, "What Is the Number of Your Winchester?" *Sporting Goods*; box 13, folder 20, "There's a Great Radio THRILL," *American Rifleman*, December 1928.

10. CC, box 70, folder 5, "What Every Parent Should Know . . . "; Smith & Wesson, *Burning Powder* (1932), 5; CC, box 70, folder 6, "Still Red-Blooded Americans," June 17, 1929.

11. "Fortune Spent in Collecting Antique Firearms," *Savannah Morning News*, January 1914, in WRAC, unprocessed part of collection, MRL—correspondence, chronological—2003 (Pugsley), folder 1 of 2; Romer, *Makers of History*; Brown, *Firearms in Colonial America*, 335. In the Colt's archives, see SCL, RG103, box 70A, Edgar White, "The Colt in History," *Macon Daily Chronicle-Herald*, June 1920; "Marking 100 Years of the Gun That Settled America's West," *Waterbury Republican*, July 16, 1936; "The First Six-Gun Man," *Orlando Sunday Sentennial Star*, D16; John Dicorpo, "The Peacemaker: The Gun That Won the West," *The Sunday Republican*, January 8, 1956; "How the Revolver Won the West from the Fierce Comanches," n.d.; and "Texas to Honor Colt 'Glory Guns,'" *Hartford Courant*, Sunday edition, n.d., typescript of article, which comments that "just three men and their 'glory guns' that were invented by a man a century ago in far-off Hartford brought quiet and order out of chaos to that riot-ridden seaport metropolis."

12. Roberts, "The West's Gunmen, Part I," 12; Roberts, "The West's Gunmen, Part II," 61. Roberts talks of the "legend maker" historians.

13. Dennis Collins, *The Indians' Last Fight, or the Dull Knife Raid* (repr.; New York: AMS, 1972); Adams, *Six Guns and Saddle Leather*, 301.

14. Quoted in Denning, *Mechanic Accents*, 13–14.

15. Roberts, "The West's Gunmen, Part I," 12; Frank J. Wilstach, *Wild Bill Hickok: The Prince of the Pistoleers* (New York: Doubleday, 1926); William E. Connelley, *Wild Bill and His Era* (New York: Press of the Pioneers, 1933); Adams, *Six Guns and Saddle Leather*, 53, 303. I compiled my informal census of Wild Bill books from Adams's meticulous annotated bibliography.

16. Adams, *Six Guns and Saddle Leather*, 118.

17. In 1910, the Edison manufacturing company was producing films in New Jersey, and Hollywood had a population of only about 5,000, but Tulsa and the Oklahoma and Indian territories were thriving. Joe, Zack, and George Miller traveled to St. Louis in 1904 to convince newspaper editors that they should convene their next meeting on the Miller brothers' ranch, where they could feast on buffalo meat and the sumptuary of *real* Indians and cowboys, trick riding, and a "simulated Indian attack on a wagon train." Ranch 101 became a flagship of the early cinema industry. John Wooley, *Shot in Oklahoma: A Century of Sooner State Cinema* (Norman: University of Oklahoma Press, 2011), 15, 21–23, 14–15; Michael Wallis, *The Real Wild West: The 101 Ranch and the Creation of the American West* (New York: St. Martin's, 1999), 249; quoted at Larry O'Dell, Oklahoma @ the Movies (Oklahoma City: Oklahoma Historical Society, 2012), 10.

18. Wooley, *Shot in Oklahoma*, 23–24, 29–30; Oklahoma @ the Movies, 9, 15.

19. Slotkin, *Gunfighter Nation*, 236, 234. Likewise, Henry Starr was a part-Cherokee bank robber and the nephew of the notorious Belle Starr. To salvage Starr's film *A Debtor to the Law*, the director called in a novelist, Patrick McGenney, to fashion something more dramatic out of Starr's real life. Wooley, *Shot in Oklahoma*, 49–53.

20. Slotkin, *Gunfighter Nation*, 383; Cunningham, *Triggernometry*, 1, 3, 5, 8.

21. Slotkin, *Gunfighter Nation*, 379, 380, 382–384.

22. For example, the WRAC printed and distributed over 150,000 posters—"Wanted! Report of Whereabouts of the 123 Rare, Historic Guns of the . . . Winchester '73 Rifles"—to find the 1 of 1,000 rifles, in collaboration with Universal Pictures.

WRAC, series 3, box 8, folder 22, from Steve Hannagan, Press Release, June 19, 1950. Movie Micah, blogspot.com/2014/Winchester-73–1950.html; Bosley Crowther, "Winchester '73: Cowboy Wins, Loses, Recovers Rifle in 'Winchester '73," *New York Times*, June 8, 1950.

23. Martin Chilton, "Winchester '73, Review," *The Telegraph* (UK), March 15, 2015, www.telegraph.co.uk/culture/film/filmreviews/11466703/Winchester-73-review.html.

24. Omar Ranney, "Makes of 'Winchester '73' Used Rifle with a Past," Stage & Screen column, *Cleveland Press*, July 20, 1950, 18.

25. Typical of this expression and trend, a 1932 Smith & Wesson pamphlet notes that the true history of the West had been "multiplied many times by fiction and moving pictures." Smith & Wesson, *Burning Powder*, 5. A Colt's pamphlet points to "movies, television, radio" as proof of America's deep tradition toward guns. CC, box 70, folder 5, "What Every Parent Should Know When a Boy or Girl Wants a Gun," n.d. The gun ad is quoted at Diaz, *Making a Killing*, 177.

26. Diaz, *Making a Killing*, 61, notes that Park Dietz, a forensic psychiatrist, found that Don Johnson's use of a Bren 10 in *Miami Vice* immediately boosted demand. John Dicorpo, "The Return of the 'Peacemaker: The Gun That Won the West," *Sunday Republican*, January 8, 1956, magazine section, in CC, box 70A; Boorman, *History of Smith & Wesson Firearms*, 57. Smith & Wesson struggled to find markets in the 1980s, and a handgun expert recommended that they "could tie into one of these Bruce Willis–type movies and have the good guy win shooting one of these Smith & Wesson revolvers." Quoted at Diaz, *Making a Killing*, 61–62.

27. Cited in Tom Diaz, "Second Amendment Message in Los Angeles," *American Rifleman*, July 1992, 32–33.

28. On my per capita calculations, see Chapter 9, note 3. Also contributing to this load was the fact that the postwar years added new gun manufacturers to America, which further points from the perspective of business to the fluorescence of the gun culture in the twentieth century. An extensive but not exhaustive list of contemporary American manufacturers that have some commercial, nonmilitary, and non-law-enforcement business and website presence includes 102 companies. The years from 1900 to 1944 combined added 4 gunmakers to the 12 gun business survivors from the nineteenth century. In the postwar 1940s, 4 new gunmakers were added; in the 1950s, 4; the 1960s, 4; the 1970s, 12; the 1980s, 11; the 1990s, 23; and the 2000s, 24. (Four other companies on this list do not provide founding dates on their websites.) In contrast, countries that led in gun production before the American System debuted in the mid-1800s have substantially fewer companies today, and they tend to focus on particular niches: two prominent British gun manufacturers, for example, focus on high-end sporting and hunting rifles exclusively. Other countries comparable to the United States simply do not have a notable gun industry—or any of the attendant pressures to sell guns that the industry brings. For example, Canada has a defense industry, but no notable small arms manufacturers.

29. Whisker, *Arms Makers of Colonial America*, 12, notes that "interest in the American rifle and pistol was not expressed in literature until the beginning of the twentieth century"; "Fortune Spent in Collecting Antique Firearms," *Savannah Morning News*, January 1914, in WRAC, unprocessed part of collection, MRL—correspondence, chronological—2003 (Pugsley), folder 1 of 2.

30. WRAC, unprocessed part of collection, MRL—correspondence, chronological—2003 (Pugsley), folder 1 of 2, from Theodore Dexter to Edwin Pugsley, June 12, 1935; from Dexter to Pugsley, June 3, 1936.

31. WRAC, additional box 11, folder 13, from Richard McCloskey to Edwin Pugsley, September 13, 1949; box 13, folder 27, from Richard McCloskey to Harold Williamson, April 1949; series 5, box 13, folder 27, from Richard McCloskey to Harold Williamson, April 4, 1949.

32. Centers for Disease Control and Prevention (CDC), "Deaths: Final Data for 2013," National Vital Statistics Reports (NVSR), vol. 64, no. 2, www.cdc.gov/nchs /deaths.htm; CDC, "Deaths: Final Data for 2010," NVSR, vol. 61, no. 4, www.cdc.gov /nchs/data/nvsr/nvsr61/nvsr61_04.pdf, 11; Arthur Kellermann et al., "Gun Ownership as a Risk Factor for Homicide in the Home," *New England Journal of Medicine* 329, no. 15 (1993): 1084–1091; Peter Cummings et al., "The Association Between the Purchase of a Handgun and Homicide or Suicide," *Journal of Public Health* 87, no. 6 (1997): 974–978; US Department of Justice, Bureau of Justice Statistics, Shannon Catalano et al., "Selected Findings: Female Victims of Violence," September 2009, NCJ228356, www .bjs.gov/content/pub/pdf/fvv.pdf, 3; Jacquelyn Campbell et al., "Risk Factors for Femicide in Abusive Relationships: Results from a Multisite Case Control Study," *American Journal of Public Health* 93, no. 7 (2003): 1089–1097. In terms of the protective effect of guns against domestic violence, it is, again, worth qualifying that these statistics cannot really capture potential violence that is deterred through the brandishing of a gun, or an abuser's or an abused person's knowledge of a gun's presence.

Goss, *Disarmed*, 109, notes the indirect political effects on the gun-control movement of this narrative of crime: "Even though most individuals who are killed by guns die by their own hand," she writes, "or at the hands of someone they know, firearms regulation has long been framed in terms of controlling unpredictable criminal attacks by armed strangers." In turn, this limits the gun-control discourse to law enforcement and criminal behavior experts, which weakens grassroots involvement and enthusiasm. Lawyer and activist Tom Diaz, *Making a Killing*, also discusses the misperception of gun casualties: "The greater part of firearms violence in the United States does not stem from 'guns in the wrong hands,'" he argues, "but the public policy debate remains focused on guns as a "crime issue" (pp. 8–9).

CHAPTER 20: "MERCHANTS OF DEATH"

1. WRAC, additional box 11, folder 13, draft of Epilogue for Williamson Company history; additional box 11, folder 13, from Rusty Casteel to Charles Hopkins, March 21, 1951, on reduced value of company at sale; series 4, box 11, folder 8, typescript of Winchester history for fiftieth anniversary, June 23, 1959, 3; Houze, *Winchester Repeating Arms Company*, 204; see also Van Zwoll, *America's Great Gunmakers*, 146 (on the 1920s slide). Fabrique Nationale began to produce some Winchester gun lines once again in 2010.

2. CC, box 70A, Roderick Lull, "Colt's: The Story of Small Arms," *Branford Review*, March 8, 1932; Van Zwoll, *America's Great Gunmakers*, 75; Grant, *The Colt Legacy*, 15, 78; Boorman, *History of Smith & Wesson*, 54. Historian Roland Marchand writes of how the "pure size" of the corporation, "the magnitude of their production, . . . their national scope in distribution," seemed to dwarf the power of family, church or community, in Beatty, ed., *Colossus*, 130, 176.

3. Historian Peter Brock notes that post–World War I peace and antimilitarist organizations often assigned guilt to profit-seeking commercial arms manufacturers and perceived politicians mostly as armorers' functionaries. Peter Brock, *Pacifism in the Twentieth Century* (New York: Syracuse University Press, 1999), 106, 108. Robert Graves and

Alan Hodge, *The Long Week End: A Social History of Great Britain, 1918–1939* (New York: Norton, 1940), 258; also quoted in Engelbrecht and Hanighen, *Merchants of Death*, 1. Keller, *Mr. Gatling's Terrible Marvel*, observes that the same kind of sudden judgment and condemnation attached to inventor Gatling after his weapon saw action in World War I, although for the most part, he—and the gun—had been ignored for decades before. Gun inventors, like their merchants, were becoming more visible as forces of destruction or villainy, when they had not been so perceived, or even noticed, before.

4. WRAC, series 5, box 13, folder 27, from Richard McCloskey to Edwin Pugsley, April 6, 1949; Engelbrecht and Hanighen, *Merchants of Death*, 6. It was the tendency in the merchants-of-death conspiracy thesis, as with any other, to overestimate the foresight, brilliance, and unity of the conspirators.

5. Graves, *The Long Week End*, 258; Nichols quoted in Christopher Petkanas, "Fabulous Dead People," *New York Times*, blogs, January 12, 2011.

6. Graves, *The Long Week End*, 258; Beverley Nichols, *Cry Havoc!* (Toronto: Doubleday, 1933), 23, 32.

7. Nichols, *Cry Havoc!*, 26, 28.

8. Ibid., 29, 236, 237, 238, 222, 246, 258.

9. Ibid., 32.

10. John Gunther, "Slaughter for Sale," *Harper's*, May 1934, 649; Baker, *The Private Manufacture of Arms*, 55, 84 (for the same expansive thinking).

11. As quoted in Baker, *Private Manufacture of Arms*, 86, 55; Paul Hutchinson, "Profits from Blood—How Long?," *Christian Century*, May 12, 1937, 615, 616; "Pope Says Weapons Manufacturers Can't Call Themselves Christian," June 21, 2015, www .reuters.com/article/2015/06/21/us-pope-turin-arms-idUSKBN0P10U220150621 #9Bqx5vsk7T5D052p.97.

12. *The Nation* and response quoted in DeConde, *Gun Violence in America*, 106, and see also 121–125, 127, 128, for a description of ambitious and business-focused gun initiatives. HCHSVF, #293, "Remington's Centennial Interests Whole Mohawk Valley," *Utica Herald-Dispatch*, August 29, 1916. Senator John Shields, a Tennessee Democrat, had earlier proposed a similar bill, in 1915, to prohibit the interstate shipment of guns. Leff and Leff, "Politics of Ineffectiveness," 59, 49, 50–51.

13. John Gunther, "Slaughter for Sale," *Harper's*, May 1934, 651; "Arms and the Men," *Fortune*, March 1934, 53; See also George Seldes, *Iron, Blood, and Profits: An Exposure of the Worldwide Munitions Racket* (New York: Harper and Brothers, 1934).

14. John Gunther, "Slaughter for Sale," *Harper's*, May 1934, 655; "Facts about Munitions Makers," editorial, *Army Ordnance*, May-June 1934, 361–362; Grant, *The Colt Legacy*, xi.

15. CC, box 70, folder 6 (no label), Industrial News Bureau, *The Manufacturer*. Also printed elsewhere as *The Manufacturer and Industrial News Bureau*.

16. CC, box 70, folder 6 (no label), Industrial News Bureau, *The Manufacturer*, "Aroused Public Consciousness Needed to Combat Criminal," September 3, 1928, "Anti-Pistol Enthusiasts, . . . " December 5, 1927; Lane, *Murder in America*, 86–190, 215, 239. I draw on Lane's work here. He explains that as societies get more educated and urbanized, the rate of suicide tends to increase as the rate of homicide decreases. The suicide rate had begun to climb in the 1900s, and the gun violence of the 1920s was concentrated in cities. Elsewhere in the country, homicide rates were not increasing. Wintemute finds that even for the half-century from 1933 to 1982, "suicide is the

leading cause of firearm deaths," and that availability of firearms increases both firearm homicide and suicide rates. Garen Wintemute, "Firearms as a Cause of Death in the United States, 1920–1982," *Journal of Trauma* 27, no. 5 (1987): 532. The instrumentality effect in criminology holds that the sheer presence of more guns leads to more violent deaths and lethal crime. See Franklin Zimring and Gordon Hawkins, *Crime Is Not the Problem: Lethal Violence in America* (New York: Oxford University Press, 1997). By this argument, the United States does not have more crime than other nations, but it has more lethal crime. "The consistency of findings" about instrumentality "across different populations, using different study designs, and by different researchers is striking," write Daniel Webster and Jon Vernick, eds., *Reducing Gun Violence in America: Informing Policy with Evidence and Analysis* (Baltimore: Johns Hopkins University Press, 2013), 13. John Lott, in *More Guns, Less Crime: Understanding Crime and Gun Control Laws* (Chicago: University of Chicago Press, 2010), argues against the thesis, contending that permissive concealed carry laws reduced violent crime, although Webster and Vernick (p. 39) conclude that the heavy weight of evidence supports the instrumentality thesis.

17. CC, box 70, folder 6, "Why Not Tackle the Real Issue?," April 9, 1928; "Jumping to Conclusions," January 27, 1930; "Certainty of Punishment Deters Crime," December 9, 1929; "An Authority on Crime," June 24, 1929; "Double Penalty for 'Gun-Toting' Criminals," November 28, 1927; "Concentrate on Criminals," January 16, 1928.

18. BBHC, *Winchester Record* 1, no. 16, "Firearms and Crime Prevention," March 14, 1919, 6; CC, box 70, folder 6, "Weeds in the Social Structure," January 1, 1928; "Some Plain Talk on Crime," February 27, 1928; "Women Take to Arms," December 3, 1928; "Making Criminals by Law," August 11, 1930; "Crime Problems and Industrial Problems," August 25, 1930; "Facts About Munitions Makers," 364. Geline Bowman, president of the Business and Professional Women's Association, testified in 1934 that she hoped guns would eventually be treated like narcotics and other "deadly and antisocial things." *Proceedings of the Attorney General's Conference on Crime Held December 10–13, 1934, in Memorial Continental Hall, Washington, DC* (Washington, DC: US Department of Justice, Bureau of Prisons, 1936), 300.

19. "Facts About Munitions Makers," 361.

20. CC, box 70, folder 6, "Anti-Pistol Laws and National Defense," March 4, 1929. See also Nye Report, part 17, 4335–4336. John Gunther made much the same argument from the opposite side of the political spectrum in a 1934 article. The private arms industry, he wrote, was "subtly and formidably connected with the government, to which it pays taxes and in return supplies the means of national aggression or defense." Gunther, "Slaughter for Sale," *Harper's*, May 1934, 651. See also National Firearm Act Hearings Before the Subcommittee on Ways and Means, House of Representatives, 73rd Cong., 2nd sess., on HR 9066, April 15–16, 1934 (pagination in original, throughout), 102, 157; CC, box 70, folder 6, "A Serious Question to Consider," October 2, 1928.

Although it would require more research, and falls beyond the scope of this book, it would be interesting to further explore the dynamic between the US military and the commercial gun business in the Cold War and twenty-first-century contexts. Currently, gun control is most often discussed as if the commercial gun business existed in a vacuum, but this book has shown that there is a centuries-long, complex symbiosis between military and commercial production. Early gun industrialists depended on guaranteed military business to justify their risky initial forays into machine production, and, in this example from the early 1930s, the sporadic needs of war and public defense tacitly supported the drive to maintain unregulated commercial gun sales. Civilian gun regulation and the gun industry obviously interact: countries with tough civilian gun regulation have fewer gun manufacturers, and these regulations are most often cited, plausibly enough, as the reason why Western Europe has lower rates of gun violence. The Tec-9 submachine gun, produced by Intratec, was designed in Sweden as an affordable military weapon, but because there was no market in that country, Intratec formed a subsidiary, Interdynamic, based in Miami, in 1984, to sell the design for the American civilian market, where it became a notorious gun for US crime.

Conversely, however, it should be recognized that the absence of a gun industry, and dependence on gun manufacturers in other countries for defense needs, also made gun regulation easier, as is evident here in the rationale for opposition to gun legislation in the crucial years of the mid-1930s. As the United States became more dramatically the "arsenal to the world," and as it took on a greater burden of defending Western Europe during the Cold War, this perhaps indirectly made civilian gun regulation more difficult, with commercial and military interests interwoven. The unique porousness between US military and commercial business is evident today in the brisk sale of combat firearms to civilians, the advertisement of military weaponry to civilian buyers, and even the military background of some of the founders of twenty-first-century gun companies. One could hypothesize that it is not just that we have more gun industry because we have fewer gun regulations, but that we have fewer gun regulations because we have more gun industry, and we have more gun industry because we assumed more of international defense in the 1900s.

21. Baker, *The Private Manufacture of Armaments*, 15, 52.

22. R. Gordon Wasson, *The Hall Carbine Affair: A Study in Contemporary Folklore* (New York: Pandick Press, 1948), 103.

23. Baker, *The Private Manufacture of Armaments*, 15; Engelbrecht and Hanighen, *Merchants of Death*, 6; Nye Report, part 1, 213.

24. Brearly, *Homicide in the United States*, as described in Lane, *Murder in America*, 229; United States Congress, National Firearms Act Hearings, 73rd Cong., 2nd sess., p. 132; Douglas Eckberg, "Estimates of Early Twentieth-Century U.S. Homicide Rates," *Demography* 32, no. 1 (1995): 1–16.

25. US Congress, National Firearms Act Hearings, 153, 151, 151–152, 154–155.

26. The time also seemed propitious for serious federal legislation because gun control had a powerful and unprecedentedly vehement advocate in FDR's attorney general, Homer Cummings. Leff and Leff, "Politics of Ineffectiveness," 56, 60. The NRA was part of this coalescence. It wasn't exceptionally well-funded in the 1930s, but it was powerful by default, because it had no political counterweight. NRA membership had grown from 3,500 in the early 1920s to ten times that, or 35,000 members.

27. US Congress, National Firearms Act Hearings, 35, 113, 62, 99, 130, 129, 63–64.

28. Ibid., 129. Boorman, *The History of Smith & Wesson*, 57, notes that Smith & Wesson produced a .357 Magnum to combat the gangster violence of Colt's Tommy Gun. US Congress, National Firearm Act Hearings, 5; DeConde, *Gun Violence in America*, 141–144.

29. CC, box 70, folder 6, "Infringing on Citizens' Rights," November 14, 1927; "Will the Rifle and Shotgun Be Next?" September 9, 1929; Captain Askins, "Who Will Be Regulated Next?" *American Rifleman*, December 15, 1924, photocopy in WRAC, series 3, box 8, folder 17. "For the first time [there was] a tendency to attach moral taint to all firearms," writes Kennett in *The Gun in America*, 213. US Congress, National Firearms Act Hearings, 81.

30. US Congress, National Firearms Act Hearings, 92, 113.

31. Ibid., 62, 158, 130, 156, 157, 162.

32. Ibid., 162, 154, 155. Leff and Leff, "The Politics of Ineffectiveness," also observe that "although the Justice Department preferred to put the onus for opposition to gun regulation onto the munitions manufacturers, whose unpopularity as 'merchants of death' peaked between the wars, the most rigorous and effectual resistance came from sportsmen's and wildlife organizations . . . and rifle, pistol and revolver associations" (p. 59).

33. WRAC, series 1, box 4, folder 6, "Minutes of Society of American Manufacturers of Small Arms and Ammunition," May 17, 1918.

34. WRAC, box 4, folder 5, "Minutes of the Meeting of the Ammunition Section of the Society of American Manufacturers of Small Arms and Ammunition," February 21, 1919. On the consolidation of the opposition, see Leff and Leff, "Politics of Ineffectiveness," 59.

35. See Leff and Leff, "Politics of Ineffectiveness," 62, on the emergence of gun control in the 1960s. On contemporary vilification, for example, of the gun owner, see Don Kates and Gary Kleck, *The Great American Gun Debate* (San Francisco: Pacific Research Institute, 1997), 97–100.

36. Nye Report, part 7, 1704.

37. Nye Report, part 4, 781.

EPILOGUE

1. "Transcript: Obama's Navy Yard Shooting Remarks," CNN, September 22, 2013, http://politicalticker.blogs.cnn.com/2013/09/22/transcript-obamas-navy-yard -shooting-remarks. There may be signs that the gun-control movement is moving toward a more emboldened stance, according to Alec MacGallis, "This Is How the NRA Ends," *New Republic*, May 28, 2013, www.newrepublic.com/article/113292/nras-end -real-gun-control-movement-has-arrived.

2. Diaz, *Making a Killing*, 3, 87.

3. Stephen Teret and Adam Mernit, "Personalized Guns: Using Technology to Save Lives," in Daniel Webster and Jon Vernick, eds., *Reducing Gun Violence in America: Informing Policy with Evidence and Analysis* (Baltimore: Johns Hopkins University Press, 2013), 173–181, 178–189. Brown, *Outgunned*, 64, calls the smart gun a "holy grail" in the industry.

4. Diaz, *Making a Killing*, 13, 149, describes the gun's curious status as an inherently dangerous consumer product, "walled" off from consumer regulation or protections, and proposes this regulatory change. "Ex-Rep Dickey Regrets Restricting Laws on Gun Violence Research," National Public Radio, *Morning Edition*, October 9, 2015.

5. Dennis Henigan, *Lethal Logic: Exploding the Myths That Paralyze Gun Policy* (Washington, DC: Potomac Books, 2009), 177. The lawsuit is described in Brown, *Outgunned*, 168, 129, 141.

6. See Jinks, *History of Smith & Wesson*, 134–136, and Neal and Jinks, *Smith & Wesson*, for production numbers. See also Brown, *Outgunned*, 195–211, 54. Journalists referred to the more remorseful and cooperative gun CEOs as "activist gun makers." Vizzard, *Shots in the Dark*, notes that gun manufacturers have "an economic interest in preserving stable markets and limiting costs and risks," which might incline them—as against the NRA—to support "certain market regulations in exchange" for protections against liability (p. 83).

7. Brown, *Outgunned*, 213.

8. Douglas J. Wiebe et. al., "Homicide and Geographic Access to Gun Dealers in the United States," *BMC Public Health* 9 (June 2009), www.biomedcentral.com /1471-2458/9/199.

9. Diaz, *Making a Killing*, 199; G. T. Gundlach et al., "Countermarketing and De-marketing Against Product Diversion: Forensic Research in the Firearms Industry," *Journal of Public Policy & Marketing* 29 (2010): 103–122; Daniel Webster and Jon Vernick, "Spurring Responsible Firearms Sales Practices Through Litigation," in Webster and Vernick, eds., *Reducing Gun Violence in America*, 130; Daniel Kreps, "Walmart Halts Sale of Assault Weapons . . . Calls Move Business, Not Political, Decision," *Rolling Stone*, August 26, 2015, www.rollingstone.com/culture/news/walmart-halts-sale-of -assault-weapons-20150826. See also Vizzard, *Shots in the Dark*, 31; William Weir, *A Well-Regulated Militia: The Battle over Gun Control* (New Haven, CT: Archon Books, 1997), 250; Diaz, *Making a Killing*, 42. Webster and Vernick, in "Spurring Responsible Firearms Sales Practices Through Litigation," 124, argue that policies to hold gun dealers accountable could substantially reduce the traffic to criminals. Phillip Cook et al., "Regulating Gun Markets," *Journal of Criminal Law and Criminology* 86, no. 1 (1995): 59–92, is one of the few studies of gun markets and access. James Jacobs, "Keeping Guns Out of the "Wrong" Hands: The Brady Law and the Limits of Regulation," *Journal of Criminal Law and Criminology* 86, no. 1 (1995): 93–120; David Kennedy, "Youth Violence in Boston: Gun Markets, Serious Youth Offenders, and Use-Reduction Strategy," *Law and Contemporary Problems* 59, no. 1 (1996): 147–196; Julius Wachtel, "Sources of Crime Guns in Los Angeles, California," *Policing: An International Journal of Police Strategies and Management* 21, no. 2 (1998): 220–239; Bureau of Alcohol, Tobacco and Firearms, *Crime Gun Trace Analysis Reports: The Illegal Youth Firearms Market in 27 Communities* (Washington, DC: ATF, 1998).

10. Daniel Webster, Jon Vernick, and Maria Bulzacchelli, "Effects of a Gun Dealer's Change in Sales Practices on the Supply of Guns to Criminals," *Journal of Urban Health* 83 (September 2006), 778–787.

11. Vizzard, *Shots in the Dark*, 155. Weir, *A Well-Regulated Militia*, 253–254, also singles out the Virginia law. It is thought that the gun industry has focused on sales in the South, where gun laws are lax, in order to feed guns into the pipeline headed to the Northeast. Brown, *Outgunned*, 52.

12. Meredith Somers, "Maryland Gun Applications Overwhelm Police, Dealers as Tough Limits Draw Near," *Washington Times*, September 4, 2013. Vizzard, *Shots in the Dark*, notes that the gun market mirrors other consumer markets, in which "practical need" plays less of a role than impulse and desire (p. 24).

13. "Community Leaders Rally for Peace One Corner at a Time in Baltimore City," July 4, 2013, CBS Baltimore, http://baltimore.cbslocal.com/2013/07/04/baltimore-man -rallies-to-stop-recent-spike-in-violence/. Goss, *Disarmed*, concludes similarly that gun-control politics have taken a "rational national," elite-driven approach to pursue comprehensive federal legislation, rather than organizing around "local projects that stood a chance of advancing" and would be conducive to meaningful "movement building" (p. 193).

14. Brown, *Outgunned*, 25.

Index

A. Baldwin and Company, 244–245
A. D. McAusland gun depot, 199–200
Abraham Lincoln: The War Years
    (Dos Passos and Sandburg), 380
abroad, 36–37, 113–114
Acker, Ephraim, 120
Adams, John, 16
Adams, Ramon, 188, 190, 354–355
Addis, Thomas Emmett, 121–125,
    128–130, 166, 388
advertisements, 27, 42–43, 56, 117–118,
    251, 254–255, 373
  "boy plan," 332–333, 334 (fig.)
  Colt's Patent Firearms factory and,
    328–332, 329 (fig.), 331 (fig.),
    356–357
  contracts and gun industry, 74
  guns' mystique and, 337–338
  Henry rifles sales and, 76, 81–83,
    81 (fig.)
  masculinity in, 333
  psychology for desire used in, 336–339
  the West and, 353, 355–357
  WRAC and, 326–328, 333–335,
    355–356
African Americans, 195–198
"African Game Trails," 261
Alexandrovich, Alexei (grand duke),
    113–114, 116
Allies gun dealers, 172–174
Allies Letter Book, 172

AMA. *See* Ammunition Manufacturers
    Association
American Bar Association, 373
American Game Association, 385
American Manufacturers of Small Arms
    and Ammunition Society, 387
American Repeating Rifle Company, 165
American Rifleman, 384
American system, 17–18, 42–43, 52–53
ammunition, 111–112, 116, 226,
    236–239, 369–370
Ammunition Manufacturers Association
    (AMA), 235–239
Armistice Day, 307–308
armories, 20, 23
arms, 13–14, 41–42, 243, 332, 354, 364,
    369–388
  See also magazine fire arms; public
    arms
Armsmear (biography), 37, 107
Armsmear mansion, 35
Arrowsmith, George, 33, 51
"the Art and Mystery of a Gunsmith," 9
Asia
  Chinese transactions in, 129, 135,
    243, 270
  European encroachment on, 50
  gun capitalists' travels to, 113
  international gun market control and,
    243
  Sarah's estate items from, 296

Asia (*continued*)
  Singapore arms smuggling in, 129
  Smith & Wesson Model 3 guns sold
    to, 114
Auto Ordnance Company, 382, 386
Azarian, Aristakes, 133–134, 236
Aziz, Abdul (sultan), 131–132

B. Kittredge and Company, 170
Baker, Lafayette, 74, 112
Baker, Noel, 372–373, 378–380
bankruptcy
  gun mass-production and, 60–61
  Henry's, 99
  multi-firing gun ventures, 56,
    60–61
  New Haven Arms Company
    tottering on, 65
  Paterson company, 30
  Spencer's company, 109, 122
  WRAC tottering on, 121–122
Barber, Noel, 131–132
Barnard, Henry, 37–38, 97–98
Barnett, T. C., 347
bayonets, 19, 71, 87
Beadle & Adams, 189
Beardsley, Arthur, 232
Beaumarchais, Augustin Caron de, 11
Beecher, Henry Ward, 65–66
Belknap, W. W., 118–119
Benedict, Henry, 227
Benet, S. V., 120
Benjamin, Walter, 296
Bennett, T. G., 144, 160–161, 204,
    230, 233, 311, 343–344
  background of, 124–125
  cross-country journey of, 211–212
  gun business and, 124–128, 226,
    304–305
  gun shipment refusal of, 240–241
  post war problems of, 307–308
  reorganization and, 313–316
  Sears' supply cut off by, 241
  Turks and, 139–142
  war and uneasiness of, 299, 303–308
  Winchester, H. marriage to, 124
Bennett, Win, 260, 303–305, 307–308,
    321

Bennett Day, 343–344
Bessemer, Henry, 39
Bey, Rustem, 132–133
Biffar, Fred, 241–242
Billy the Kid, 186, 198–199
Blackfeet Indian Territory, massacre at,
    104–105
Blaine, James, 73
Blockley, Thomas, 10–11
Bomford, George, 23, 27–28
Boone, Daniel, 198
Boorstin, Daniel, 52
"boy plan," 324–325, 332–333, 334 (fig.)
Brewer, Henry, 320, 325
bribery, 28, 72–73, 114
Bridgeport ammunition factory, 116
Bright, F. S., 321
Britain
  gun interchangeability from, 39–42
  gun trade in, 170–171
  gun violence statistics of, 382
  London factory in, 50
  mass-production opinions from, 185
  See also England
Britten, Emma Hardinge, 148–149,
    151, 156
Broadwell, ("the General"), 126
Brough, John, 90
Brown, John, 78–79, 347
Browning, John, 204, 305
Buck, Hans, 49–50
Buel, James, 190
*Buffalo Bill and His Wild West
    Companions* (anonymous), 191
buffalo hunting, 113–114
Buntline, Ned, 190, 192, 194
Burlingame, Roger, 165

Cabinet of Memorials, 35
Caldwell, Augustine, 218
calendars, WRAC lithographic, 252,
    253 (fig.)
California, 213–214, 271–272
Cameron, Simon, 73
camp meetings, spiritualist, 155–156
Capone, Al, 385
Capper, Arthur, 326
Carlyle, Thomas, 5, 151–152

Carnegie, Andrew, 263
Cartridge Department (WRAC), Werle's
    instruction card for, 264–265
Cartwright, David, 201
Case, Augustus, 120
CDC. *See* Centers for Disease Control
    and Prevention
census, 18
Centers for Disease Control and
    Prevention (CDC), 367
Charles, Robert, 195–197
Charleville muskets, 11, 13–14
Cheney, Charles, 73
China, 129
Church of the Good Shepherd, 107
Churchill, Caroline, 213
civil liability, 391–392, 394
Civil War, 65–69, 88, 90–91, 94–99,
    110, 379
clairvoyants, 153, 155, 205–206
    séances and, 148, 157–159, 348–351,
        349 (photo)
    spiritualism and, 147–160, 217,
        284–293, 349–350, 349 (photo)
    See also ghosts
Cody, William ("Buffalo Bill"), 113–114,
    177, 183–184, 186, 190–194,
    193 (fig.), 212
collectors, 365, 366
Collins, Dennis, 357–358
Colt, Amos, 66
Colt, Caroline, 106
Colt, Christopher, 2–3, 26–28
Colt, Elizabeth, 105–107, 296, 370
Colt, John, 106
Colt, Samuel, 1, 3, 5, 23, 30, 80–81,
    145
    backgrounds of gun industrialists and,
        51–60
    Civil War's eve and treason accusation
        of, 67
    Congress and bribery hearings of,
        72–73
    courtroom, patent litigation, 37–39
    death of, 35
    establishment of gun factory by,
        25–26, 66–67, 292
    Florida sales travel venture of, 28–29

flourishing gun business in Europe
    and, 49–50, 113–115
government contracts and, 48–49
gun market and, 26, 181, 225
guns and, 33–34, 39, 70, 82
history and legacy of, 105–107
industry advancement of, 22
as inventor, 7–8
London factory and, 50
as lone inventor of gun, 39, 70
non-profitable ventures of, 33–34,
    37, 110
as out of gun business, 33–37
revolvers and, 2, 6, 22, 27–29, 33–50,
    58–59, 61, 70, 82, 88–89, 106–107,
    114–115, 168–174
scientific amusement of, 21
semiautomatic guns and, 46–47
shotgun as peacemaker and, 196
travels of, 36–37
as visionary, 53
WRAC and, 226
Colt revolvers, 88, 173–174, 330–331,
    331 (fig.), 365
Colt rifles, 88
Colt's Patent Firearms factory, 25–26,
    66–67, 97–99, 145, 226, 263,
    292, 318
    advertising and, 328–332, 329 (fig.),
        331 (fig.), 356–357
Comminge & Geisler, 200
commissions, 134–135, 137–138
Confederacy, 76
"Confronting a Bear," 252
Congress, 11–12, 72–73, 373–374, 378,
    382–384, 386
Connecticut, 41–42, 299–301
Constantinople, 130–139
Consumer Protection Safety
    Commission (CPSC), 391–392
continuous-process production, 263,
    265–266
contracts, 10, 15–17, 28, 71, 74,
    137–139, 387
    control of production and, 68–69
    government, 13–14, 48–49, 299,
        301–308
conventions, sales, 344–346

Converse, W. W., 204, 220–222, 230
Coombs, Ada, 155, 158, 205–210, 285, 351
corporate bodies, 103–105
corporations, 52–53
counterfeiters, 136
courtroom, 37–39, 72–73
"Cowboy Watering Geraniums," 251
cowboys, 201, 353–356, 359–360, 364, 385
Cox, Ebenezer, 23
Coxe, Tench, 18
CPSC. *See* Consumer Protection Safety Commission
Craig, Henry Knox, 23
Crossman, E., 291–293, 325, 327
Crystal Palace, 39–41
Cuba, 36, 95, 135, 171, 243, 270
    armory in, 116
    gun sales and, 114–115
    SHG's shipments to, 117
Cunningham, Eugene, 360–361
"Cure Violence," 396
Custer, George Armstrong, 176–177, 191

daguerreotypist, 21–22
Dahlgren, John, 73
Daley, Richard M., 397
Davies, John, 30–32, 94, 96–97, 104, 145–147
Davis, Andrew Jackson, 154
Day, Horace, 73
dealers, 76–77, 172–176, 240, 243–247, 395–396
Dean, G., 72–73
Deanne, Silas, 11
death, 29, 35, 100–103, 140–142, 268, 367
    Winchester, O., and, 203–204
    Winchester, S., and, 160–161, 343, 345–346
    See also "merchants of death"
"Death, Inc.," 370
debt
    Bennett, T., and WRAC, 311–313
    Bennett, W., and WRAC, 304–305
    Colt, S., and, 29–30, 55
    homicides and gambling, 46

Hunt, W., and, 32
    merger and WRAC, 345
    Winchester, O., and, 55, 61, 63
    Winchester, S., and WRAC, 314, 316
defects, in guns, 9, 56, 60–62, 79, 94–95, 126
"Devil's Pistol," 82
Dexter, Theodore, 365–366
Diaz, Tom, 390–391
Dickens, Charles, 39
Dickerson, Edward, 6–7, 29, 38, 72–73
Dickey, Jay, 392
Diel Ranch, 222
Dillin, John, 365
dime novels, 188–190, 192–194, 193 (fig), 198–199, 251, 357–359
dissolution papers, 228–229
diversification, 319
dividends, 297
donations, Winchester, O., land, 146
Dos Passos, John, 380
Dreiser, Theodore, 265, 293
drill presses, 264
Du Bois, W. E. B., 195
Dunn, Thomas, 23
Dykstra, Robert, 200

E. Remington & Sons manufactory, 24–25, 97, 118–119
    See also Remington, Eliphalet; Remington Arms Company
earthquake, San Francisco (1906), 280–281, 289
Eastman, Arthur, 379
Edison, Thomas, 204
Egypt, 56, 115
Ehlers, John, 30
Eisenhower, Dwight D., 301
electronic voice phenomena (EVP), 160
elite, 4–5, 152
Ellithorpe, A., 80
embargo, 118, 243–244, 247, 306
emotions, 332
empires, 3, 136–137, 268–269, 297, 346
    Ottoman Empire, 35, 131–134, 139
empiricism, 5

"encircle and imprison," 39
Engelbrecht, H. C., 370, 380–381
England
    Buffalo Bill's biography and, 183
    establishing armories in, 16–17
    gunsmith's row in, 16, 41
    importing gunsmiths from, 10–11
    international gun market control
      and, 243
    London factory and, 50
    Smith & Wesson Model 3 guns
      sold to, 114
    starting businesses with dealers in, 26
    war and sales of arms to, 49–50
entertainment industry, 354–355
entrepreneurs, 68
Episcopals, 24
ethics, 4–5
Europe
    as commercial frontline, 68–69
    encroachment on Asia by, 50
    great gun shops of, 41
    gun business flourishing in, 49–50,
      113–115
    gun capitalists' travels to, 36–37, 113
    gun markets in, 171
    gun violence statistics of, 382
    international gun market control
      and, 243
    Remington, S., headquarters
      established in, 114–115
    Smith & Wesson Model 3 guns sold
      to, 114
    starting businesses with dealers in, 26
    tour travels to, 94–99
European gunsmiths
    in Belgium, 41
    England's Gunsmith's Row, 41
    government securing shipments from,
      11–12
    recruiting and importing of, 10–11
    See also gunsmiths
European market, 40–41, 171
EVP. *See* electronic voice phenomena
Exhibition of Industry, 39
exhibits, 39–40, 42
expatriates, 127
expenses, promotional, 27

Falley, Richard, 9
federal firearms licensees (FFLs), 394
Firearms in American History (Sawyer),
    365
firepower, 86–87
Fitzpatrick, William, 245, 246
"Five Year Plan for Disarmament," 33
Floyd, B. R., 49
foreign markets
    Colt, S., abetted by, 37, 39
    in gun business, 166
    gun industrialists and, 112–113
    gun procurement in, 11–20
    SHG shipping to, 175
    Winchester, O., and, 77, 94–95, 116,
      117–118
    WRAF sales in, 242–243
Fort Kearney, 212
Fowler, Horace, 236
France, 119–120, 126
Francis (Pope), 373
Franco-Prussian conflict, 119–120
fraud, 157–160, 207–208
Frederick, Karl, 383
Fremont, John, 67–68, 379
Freund and Brothers, 170
frontier life, 179, 200, 212–213, 249
funding, gun violence research, 394

Gardner, Robert, 365
Garibaldi, Gino, 49–50
Gauthier, Wendell, 392–393
Germany, 119–120, 126, 306–307
ghosts, 280, 285
    Winchester, S., and, 209–210,
      287–294, 343, 347, 349–351, 385,
      390, 397
gifts, guns as, 35–37, 67, 80–81
globalization, 36–37, 41, 113, 129–130,
    141
gold discovery, 214
Goodman, Julia Cody, 183, 192
Goodrich, Elizur, 11
Goodwin, Philip, 251–252
Gorlov, Alexander, 112, 116
government, 34, 67, 135–136, 140,
    176–177, 183–184, 240
    contracts, 13–14, 48–49, 299, 301–308

government (*continued*)
  gun industry and common defense of,
    71–72
  labor increases and, 306
  NRA and surplus weapons of,
    325–326
  sales violation of government to,
    119–120
  Smith & Wesson taken over by, 302
  WRAC's increased labor and, 306
*The Great Plains: The Romance of Western
    American Exploration* (Hough), 191
Greek mythology, 342
Greener, W. W., 185
Greg, W. R., 86
grief, 102–103, 105
"grotesque, yet magnificent," 279–297
gun business, 18, 29–30, 166, 171,
    246, 263
  anti-gun conscience focused on,
    377–388, 392–393
  Bennett, T., and, 124–128, 226,
    304–305
  Colt, S., as out of, 33–37
  Europe's flourishing, 49–50, 113–115
  greed for gain in, 177–178
  gun missionaries deployed in,
    255–256
  history and background of, 1–6, 20,
    367–368, 389–390
  intangible emotional values in, 251
  production efficiency in, 264–265
  public conscience in, 165
gun capitalism, 378–379, 388
gun capitalists, 3, 36–37, 58–59, 71, 109,
    145–146, 203, 317
  as going underground, 374–377
  as "merchants of death," 370–388
  no restrictions on gun sales and, 118,
    124–125
gun cranks, 113, 319–339, 366, 381
gun culture, 2–4, 8, 36–39, 41, 168, 189,
    258–259, 380
  legends in, 198–201
  Ripley and, 70–71
  violence and, 10, 367–368, 370,
    375–376, 389, 392, 396–397
  western, 175

gun depot, 199–200
gun market, 7–8, 59–60, 72, 75–76,
    78–79, 169–172, 176–177
  Colt, S., and, 26, 181, 225
  ending of Seminole War destroying,
    28–30
"gun men," 124, 126
gun ownership, 186–197, 381, 388,
    390–391, 396
gun regulation, 374, 376–377, 383,
    385–386, 395–396
gun shops, 41
gun-control, 370–372, 389, 392–393,
    397
  advocates for, 171
  business-focused approach and, 373
  federal government attempts at,
    176–177, 240
  gun dealers and, 246–247
  gun ownership and, 390–391, 396
  laws, 176, 197
  politics of, 373–375, 394–395
  redirecting gun business and, 376–377
  Tommy Guns and, 373–386
  war and, 387–388
gunfights, 187–189
gunmen, 192–193, 354–355, 360
guns, 35, 41–42, 45, 48, 81, 355, 371, 391
  Addis' selling expedition of, 128–130
  advertising, 76, 337–338
  American, 7–8 16–17, 20
  anti-gun conscience and, 372,
    377–388, 392–393
  barbarity and perfection noted
    of new, 47
  Bennett, T., refusing shipment of,
    240–241
  children and, 326
  Civil War and, 110
  Colt, A., travels to sell, 66
  Colt, S., and, 33–34, 39, 70, 82
  competitions of, 79–80
  custody battle for finished, 30
  defects and, 9, 60–62, 94–95, 126
  designs and patents of, 95
  family closeness to empire of, 3
  foreign market and, 11–20, 94–99
  global lack of demand for, 129

gun capitalists and sales of, 118, 124–125

gun cranks' soul as individuals enamored by, 319–339

Henry's repair of defects in, 61–62

heroism and, 82–83

industry, 66, 98–99

innovation of assembling parts for, 11–16

insanity in production of, 373

interchangeability and, 39–42

inventors, 7–8, 39, 70

legacy and history of, 20, 367–368, 389–390

legends and, 7–8, 368

lobbying, 321–322

low demand for, 110, 129

Marlin as rival, 323

mass-produced, 185–187

mechanics of, 14

Model 3 Army Russian, 114

musket, 87

muzzle-loading shooter, 87–89, 91, 126

need for, 396

New Haven factory of, 163

nineteenth century mystique of, 366–368

as object of commerce, 176

Ordnance Department and, 69–70, 80

patents for, 26, 62–63, 95

phases of, 8–11, 18, 24–25 37–38, 66

pricing of, 25–26

profiting by gifting, 80–81

public, 12

purchases of, 395–397

random freighters used in early shipments of, 31

riot, 322–323

rivals and, 73–74

safety and, 395

sales and, 26–27, 68–69, 76–77, 114–115, 123–125, 140–142

for self-defense, 167–168

semiautomatic, 46–47, 61–62, 69–70, 78–80, 88–91

settlers and expense of, 174

SHG's global sales of, 116–117

shotgun, 196

slander and, 79

spasmodic demand for, 77, 304

spirit, 105

stories, 187–194, 198

Tommy Gun submachine, 373–386

US and, 8–9, 129

uselessness and defects of, 9, 56, 60–62

West as winning, 353–368

Winchester, O., sales of, 83–84, 123–125, 132–133

See also arms; dealers; Henry rifles; magazine fire arms; pistols; rapid-fire rifles; repeater rifles; revolvers; rifles; Spencer rifles; weapons; Winchester rifles

gunsmiths, 101

craft of, 98–99

demise of, 22, 24–25

European, 11–12

Harpers Ferry walk-out of, 23

heirs to, 94

Henry's workshop and, 43

Moroccan, 129–130

patriot, 10–11

pride and merits of early, 12

scarcity of, 9, 25

varied trades of, 9–10

Gunther, John, 372

Hall, John, 28

Hall Carbine Affair, 379–380

Hallahan, William, 87

Hamid, Abdul, II, 139

Hamm, John, 219

handguns. *See* guns; revolvers

Harney, William, 28–29

Harper, Thomas, 360

Harper's, 187–188

Harpers Ferry, 23

Harrison, Guy, 335

Hartford factory, 34

Hartley, Marcellus, 110–112, 115–116, 199, 229–230, 370, 379

Remington Arms Company ownership transferred by, 235

UMC of, 134, 238

Hartley, William, 48, 68–69

Hartley & Graham, 230, 233–234

Hawkers of Death (Baker), 378–379
Hawthorne, Nathaniel, 208
heirlooms, 270–271, 273
Hellstrom, Carl, 370
Hendrick, Burton, 165
Henning, Robert, 167
Henry, Benjamin Tyler, 43, 51–52,
    61–64, 93–94, 98–99, 126
Henry Repeating Rifle Company, 96
    See also New Haven Arms Company
Henry rifles, 61–62, 69–70, 78–80, 86–91
    rebranded as Winchester Model 66,
    104
    sales and advertising of, 76, 81–83,
    81 (fig.)
    Spencer rifles compared to, 95
Herbert, Henry William, 46
*Heroes of the Plains, or Lives and
    Wonderful Adventures of
    Wild Bill* (Buel), 190
heroism, 82–83
Hickok, ("Wild Bill"), 187–190, 357–359
Hicks, W. C., 98–99
Hicks patent, 98–99
history, 1–6, 20, 105–107, 356–357,
    366–368, 389–390
The History of Great American Fortunes
    (Myers), 379–380
*History of Our Wild West and Stories of
    Pioneer Life* (anonymous), 191
Hobbs, A. C., 112
Hofstadter, Richard, 10, 184
Hogan, Ray, 358
Hoganson, Kristin, 261
Hollon, Eugene, 200
Holmes, Oliver Wendell, 43
Holt, Douglas, 355
home improvements, 272, 289
homicide rates, 198, 381–382
Hooper, A. W., 313–314
Hortalez & Company, 11
Hosley, William, 17, 24
Hotchkiss, Andrew, 127
Hotchkiss, Benjamin Berkeley, 127
Hotchkiss, Charles, 127
Hotchkiss repeater, 128
Hough, Emerson, 191
Houze, Herbert, 175, 199

Howe, Elias, 32, 43
Hunt, Clinton Nottage, 33
Hunt, Walter, 32–33, 43, 51
hunting, 46, 256–258, 321–322, 330,
    333, 338
Hunt's Volitional Repeater, 32–33

illicit markets, 246
Immen, Loraine, 216
"In the Gallery of in the Woods," 254, 257
incentives, 58
Incorporation act, 52
Indians, 104–105, 183, 192–194, 212,
    355, 358–360, 366
individualism, 164–165, 184–185, 187,
    194–195
Industrial New Bureau, 375–376, 384
industrial production, 15, 59
industrialists, 62–64
    inventions and, 2–8, 12–15, 26–27,
    32–33, 36–39, 43, 51–53
industry, 22
    See also specific industry
infant deaths, 100–101
Ingraham, Prentice, 190
inheritances, 268–269
interchangeability, 39–42, 40
international arms race, 41–42
inventions, 62–64, 93–94, 282–283, 347
    early industrialists and, 2–8, 12–15,
    26–27, 32–33, 36–39, 43, 51–53
inventories, 295–297, 346–347
inventors, 7–8, 39, 70, 99, 127
Irvine, Callender, 19–20
Isabelle (Winchester, Sarah, sister),
    216–217, 219, 221–222
Islam, 342
Iturbide, Augustin de, 116
Ives, Charles, 102

J. H. Brown Amusement Company, 347
James, Henry, 260
Jefferson, Thomas, 16
Jenkins, Paul, 104–105
Jennings, Al, 359–360
Jennings, Lewis, 51
John Gallagher and Company, 71
Johnson, Nicholas, 195

Jonas, Frank, 388
Juarez, Benito, 122
Junior Rifles Corps, 374–375

Kanzler, Ermanno, 115
Kay, Sidney, 239
Keenan, Joseph, 382, 385–386
Kentucky, 75–76
The Kentucky Rifle (Dillin), 365
Kidder & Peabody, 304, 313, 315,
     317, 369
King, Nelson, 104, 132–133
Kittle, Keith, 347
Kittredge, B., 78–80, 172
Krakauer, Adolph, 245
Krakauer, Zork & Moyer, 245

labyrinth, 285–288
"land of mystery," Nevada as, 212
land purchasing
     Winchester, S., and, 220–222
land speculation
     California gold rush and, 214–216
Landers, George, 36
Lane, Roger, 200
Latham, R. W., 48–49
lawsuits, 43, 47, 61, 137–139, 214, 246,
     391–393
lecturers, spiritualist, 154–160
Lee, Roswell, 18–19, 23, 262
Lee rifles, 227, 244
legacy, 8, 20, 105–107, 110, 348,
     367–368, 389–390
legends, 102–103, 114, 189, 198–201,
     347, 358–359, 379
     lone gun and, 7–8, 368
     of West, 357, 366
     Winchester, S., and, 292–293, 370
legislation, 20, 383, 389, 392–394
Leib, Samuel, 310, 314–315, 345
Leonard, H. S., 237–238, 255
lever functions, 180–181
Lewis, John Woodruff, 198
Li Hung Chang, 126
Lick, James, 215
Lick Observatory, 215–217, 272
Limerick, Patricia, 170, 200, 214
Lincoln, Abraham, 73–74

literature, 357–358, 365–366
lithography, 251–252, 254–255
litigation, 46, 96
Llanada Villa, 220, 342–343, 347
     mansion, 35, 145–146, 267–277
     Mystery House, 284, 286 (fig.),
          308–316, 347–349, 349 (photo)
     Sarah's estate, 273–275, 275 (fig.),
          279–297, 308–316, 341, 346
     upkeep and changes to, 275 (fig.), 280,
          282–297, 341
     See also empires
L&M Oppenheimer, 191
Loaded Paper Shot Shells, 238
loans, 11, 30, 54, 60, 63–64
lobbying, 250, 321–322
Lopez, Narciso, 36

machine production, 15–18, 42, 136
Machinery Hall, 39, 40
machines, 31–32, 62–64
Madero, Francisco, 243
magazine fire arms, 63–64, 93–94, 332,
     354, 364
mail-order catalog
     lack of gun-control in, 240
     Sears and WRAC's pricing policy
          dispute in, 240–242
     WRAC concerns and, 241
Malcolm, William, 216
management, 263–266, 283, 308–316
Manby, Charles, 50
mansions
     Armsmear, 35
     Mystery House, 267–277
     Santa Clara Winchester, 35, 219, 223,
          276–277, 287–288, 294, 309–310,
          315, 346–347
     Winchester, S., and, 145–146
     See also Llanada Villa
Manville, Cyrus, 61
market, 34, 76–84, 94–99, 112–118,
     120–121, 246, 306–307
     myth, 355–364
     See also European market; foreign
          market; gun market; sports market;
          wholesale market
Marketing Game (editorial), 258

marksmanship, 249, 383
Marlin guns, 226, 235, 323
marriage
    Bennett, T., and Winchester, H., 124
    Pardee, S., and Winchester, W.,
        84–86, 144
Mars, Amaury, 223
Marshall, John, 52
Marshall, Thomas, 373
Marston, A. P., 347
martial ecology, 183–184
Martin, E. B., 63–64
masculinity, 333, 376
mass shootings, 389
Massachusetts Arms Company, 38
massacres, 104–105, 113–114, 197
mass-production, 45, 60–61, 185–187
Mauger, Henry, 12
McAusland Brothers, 170
McCanles, David, 188, 190
McCormack, John, 383
McGunnigle, George, 9–10
McKinley, William, 223, 267, 270,
        355–356
mechanical precursors, 37–38
mechanics, 14
mechanization, 5, 39, 52
mediums, 155–160, 350–351
Meeker, John, 321–322
memorabilia
    Cabinet of Memorials, 35
    Winchester, S., safe with, 351
"merchants of death," 369–388
mergers, 345, 369
Merrill, Sarah, 143–144
Merwin, Joseph, 55–56
metaphysics, 154, 156
Metcalfe, Henry, 262
Mexico, 36, 95, 117, 122–124, 244
Middle East, 36
military, 74–78, 166, 169, 175, 227,
        229, 301–302
    weapons, 69, 72
Miller, John, 373–374
Miller, Phineas, 13
Miller, Warner, 233–234
milling machine, 14
Millis, Walter, 318

Mills, A. M., 232
Milton, John, 46
mining, 200–201
missionaries, 255–256
"M'Kandlas" gang, 191
mobile warfare, 182
Model 3 Army Russian gun, 114
Model 1875 revolvers, 115
monopolies, 79, 234
Monroe, James, 16
Monroe Doctrine, 95, 116–117
Morgan, J. Pierpont, 304, 379–380
Morris, Desmond, 261
movie industry, 359–364
murder, 23, 45–46, 257
muskets, 11, 87, 175
muzzle-loading shooter, 87–89, 91, 126
"My Corner, My Street," 396–397
Myers, Gustavus, 379–380
Myrdal, Gunnar, 198
Mystery House, 284, 286 (fig.), 308–316,
        347–349, 349 (photo)
mystique, of gun, 261, 337–338, 354,
        365–368
myths
    easier to fight business than, 390
    gun marketing and, 355–364, 390

National Cowboy and Western Heritage
        Museum, 251
National Crime Commission, 377–378
National Firearms Act, 383, 387
National Police Gazette, 189, 198
National Rifle Association (NRA),
        249–250, 321–322, 325–326,
        391, 393
    gun regulation and, 374, 383, 385–386
Native Americans, 9, 113–114, 176–177,
        196–197, 251, 256
    See also Indians
need, for guns, 396
Nettie (Winchester, Sarah, sister), 216
New Deal Works Progress
        Administration (WPA), 349
New Haven Arms Company, 55, 60, 63,
        65, 94–95, 163
    Henry Repeating Rifle Company
        changed from, 96

Winchester, O., takeover of, 96–97, 99, 101–102
New Haven Hospital Society, 346
New Haven Wheeler & Wilson manufactory, 42–43
Nichols, Beverley, 370–372, 378–379, 382, 385–386
Nichols, Frank, 378, 382, 386
Nichols, George Ward, 187–188
nitrous oxide, 21
North, Frank J., 212
North, Simeon, 28, 379
Nott, Charles, 95–96
NRA. *See* National Rifle Association
Nye, Gerald, 303, 388

Oakley, Annie, 324
Obama, Barack, 389
Odell, William, 238
Oklahoma, 359–360
Olin Corporation, 364–365, 369
One of One Thousand campaign, 186
Ordnance Department, 17, 22–23, 69–70, 80, 119–120
Oscanyan, Christopher, 131–134, 137–140
Osgood House, 233
Otterson, J. E., 345
Ottoman Empire, 35, 131–134, 139
overstocks, 25–26

Palmer, Cortlandt C., 51
paramilitary use, 169
Pardee, Aaron, 84
Pardee, Leonard, 55, 85
Pardee, Sarah L., 84–86
Pasha, Isma'il, 115
Pasha, Osman, 139–140
"Patent Repeating Rifle," 25
patents, 27, 53, 72–73, 94, 152, 175–176
    gun, 26, 62–63, 95
    infringements to, 37
    litigation and, 37–39
    for magazine fire arm, 63
    rifle, 32–33, 51, 55
    right of, 30, 98–99
    sewing machine war for, 32, 43

Winchester, O., and, 38, 96, 128
    See also Colt's Patent Firearms factory
Paterson factory, 25–27, 30
patriotism, 10–11, 183
Paxton, Joseph, 39
"peacemaker," 47
Peacemaker pistol, 184
Pearson, John, 22
penitentiary labor, 66–67
pepperboxes, 37
percussion muskets, 175
perfection, 47, 62, 116
Perry, Matthew, 50
Phelps, Elizabeth, 152
phenomenon, 36–37
Philadelphia Exposition, 128
Pioneer Tales of the Oregon Trail (Hough), 191
pistols, 98, 173–174, 181, 184, 383
    See also guns; revolvers
Pitkin, Waldo, 244
Plevna Winchesters, 141
politics, 373–375, 380, 386–387, 394–395
pomology, 219
Pony Express, 188
Porter, Glenn, 165
Potter, Edward Tuckerman, 107
powder, grains of, 180
precision, 40
Prentice, George, 75–77
The President Vanishes (film), 378–379
pricing, 25–26, 173–174
Prime, William Cowper, 56–57
principle of motion, 105–107
Private Manufacture of Arms (Baker), 372–373, 378–379
production, 47–48, 58, 101–102, 104, 179–180, 301, 373
    continuous-process, 263, 265–266
    contracts and control of, 68–69
    E. Remington & Sons' modernization of, 24–25
    gun business efficiency of, 264–265
    industrial, 15, 59
    machine, 15–18, 42, 136
    mass-, 45, 60–61, 185–187
    Tommy Gun submachine, 382

production (*continued*)
  War Department demands to
    increase, 305–308
  WRAC profits and, 225–226
profit, 33–34, 39, 80–81, 110, 240,
    257, 303–305, 386
promotions, expenses for, 27
Protection of Lawful Commerce in Arms
    Act, 391
Prussian percussion musket, 176
public arms, 10, 16–19, 28
"public guns," 12
Pugsley, Edwin, 304, 345, 353, 365–366
  WRAC and, 101–102, 186,
    321–322, 369
Puritans, 98, 99
putting-out system, 31–32

Rambo, E. B., 220–222
Rambo, Ralph, 282
Randolph, P. B., 150
rapid-fire rifles, 78–84, 87
ratios, 88–89
Rattenbury, Richard, 251
Reckord, Milton, 383
registrations, 386
Remington, Eliphalet, 2, 6, 48, 114,
    135, 227
Remington, Frederic, 251
Remington, Philo, 48, 110, 114, 127, 227
Remington, Samuel, 110, 114–115
Remington Arms Company, 1, 255,
    302–303, 369–370
  bidding on, 230
  commercial market missed by,
    227–228
  debt of, 228–229
  dissolution papers filed by, 228–229
  financial troubles of, 226–227
  Hartley transferring ownership of, 235
  process efficiency in, 265
  Reynolds winning bidding on, 231
  sale set aside of, 231–232
  second auction of, 233
  trade demoralization concerns of, 241
  worker's pool to purchase, 230
  WRAC getting property of, 233–234
Remington rifles, 114–115, 171, 185

Remington "rolling block" rifle, 114–115
reorganization, 313–316
repeater rifles, 25, 32–33, 51–52, 69–70,
    86–87, 140, 185
  breech-loading, 126
  Hotchkiss, 128
  improvements to Winchester Model
    66, 104
  individualism and, 164–165
  Winchester, O., and, 88–91, 203
retailers
  appealing to boy customers through,
    326
  equalizing profits for, 238–241
  inability to visions market and, 228
  sales instructions for, 241–242
  screening and supervision of, 392
  sharing tricks of trade and, 333–335
  tighter control and, 328
  veins of gun market, 170–171
Revelations of a Spirit Medium, 159
Revolutionary War, 9–10
revolvers, 175–176, 182, 364, 383
  Colt, 88, 173–174, 330–331,
    331 (fig.), 365
  Colt, S., and, 2, 6, 22, 27–29, 33–50,
    58–59, 61, 70, 82, 88–89, 106–107,
    114–115, 168–174
  Colt automatic, 330–331, 331 (fig.)
Reynolds, W. W., 126, 230–231, 233
Richard II (Shakespeare), 289–290
riddle, 293–294
rifles, 2, 23, 25–26, 70, 261–262
  Bomford's replacement choices for,
    27–28
  Colt revolving, 88
  Constantinople, Winchester, O., and,
    132–139
  Lee, 227, 244
  as military weapon, 69, 72
  paramilitary use of, 169
  patents, 32–33, 51, 55
  post–Civil War and future of, 94–99
  rapid-fire, 78–84, 87
  Remington, 114–115, 171, 185
  sales dampened by defects of, 9, 56,
    60–62
  semiautomatic, 204

Seminole War and procurement of,
  28–30
Spanish model, 115–116
Spencer, 87–90, 95, 109, 165
sporting and hunting's limited
  prospects for, 46
Springfield, 302
volitional, 32–33, 43
Wesson, 78–80
West won by Winchester, 353–368
Wickham, 19
Winchester, O., and, 6, 51–62,
  94–95
Winchester, O., empire of, 132–133,
  136–137, 268–269, 297
Winchester, S., and empire of,
  268–269, 297, 346
Winchester .30 caliber, 260
Winchester Model 1883, 128
See also arms; guns; Henry rifles;
  magazine fire arms; repeater rifles;
  semiautomatic guns; semiautomatic
  revolvers; Spencer rifles;
  Winchester rifles
rights, 30, 98–99, 390
rimfire .38 revolvers, 173–174
riot guns, 322–323
Ripley, James Wolfe, 23–24, 69–72, 379
Risley, E. H., 232
rivals, 73–74, 165
Road to War (Millis), 318
Robbins and Lawrence, 40, 42, 112–113
Roberts, Gary, 198
Robeson, George, 119–120
Robinson, Charles, 370
Rock Creek story, 188, 190–192
Romer, F., 357
Roosevelt, Theodore, 250, 259, 261,
  333, 381, 384
Rosas, Juan Manuel de, 50
royalties, 94
Rubey, Thomas, 373–374
Russia, 139–141
Rutherford, Sadie, 281

safe
  Mystery House, 351
  Winchester, S., memorabilia in, 351

safety
  data or records of gun, 395
  lawsuits for, 392–393
salary houses, 238
sales, 57, 67, 116–117, 119–120,
  128–131, 328
  Colt, S., Florida travel venture for,
    28–29
  commercial market preferred
    for gun, 304
  conventions, 344–346
  gun, 26–27, 68–69, 76–77, 114–115,
    123–125, 140–142
  gun capitalists and no restrictions on
    gun, 118, 124–125
  Henry rifles advertising and, 76,
    81–83, 81 (fig.)
  lessons to encourage and push,
    335–336
  military as high-volume source for,
    77–78
  poor, 47–49
  rifle's defects dampening, 9, 56, 60–62
  rituals for persuading customers', 336
  Winchester, O., and, 58–59, 74–78,
    83–84, 123–125, 132–133
  WRAC foreign, 242–243
salesmen
  company's sales promises to, 327–328
  continued business of latter-day gun,
    388
  early industry's dispatching of, 27
  incredible folly redemption and
    needed, 121
  network of traveling, 170
  public interest shaped by, 133
San Jose 100, 217
San Juan Hill, 260
Sandburg, Carl, 380
Sandy Hook Elementary School, 389
Santa Clara Valley, 213, 217–218,
  276–277, 279–280, 296
Sarah's estate, 273–275, 275 (fig.),
  279–297, 308–316, 341, 346
  See also empires; Llanada Villa;
    mansions; Mystery House
Sawyer, Charles, 365
Schofield, George, 184

Schofield pistol, 181
Schoonover, Frank, 356
Schuetzenbund (target-shooting
    competition), 168
Schuyler, Hartley & Graham (SHG),
    116–118, 170, 172, 175, 199, 244
Schuyler, Jacob, 68
Scientific American, 62–64, 69–70
"scientific amusement," 21
scientific management, 263–266
Scott, Walter, 335
séances, 148, 157–159, 348–351,
    349 (photo)
Sears, Roebuck and Company, 223,
    240–242, 245, 247
Second Amendment, 169, 176, 197
Selden, Dudley, 25–30
"self-acting machines," 31–32, 45
self-commodification, 190
self-defense, 167–168, 330, 333
semiautomatic guns, 46–47
semiautomatic revolvers, 182
semiautomatic rifles, 204
Seminole War, 28–30
settlers, 174, 183
7-shot pistols, 173–174
sewing machine, 32, 42–43
Shakespeare, William, 289–290, 341
shares, 316
Sharps, Christian, 98–99, 113
Sharps Company, 112–113
Sharps rifle, 26
sharpshooters, 87, 333
Sherer, William, Jr., 243
Sherman Antitrust Act, 236–237, 239
SHG. *See* Schuyler, Hartley & Graham
shipments, 31
shooting competitions, 249–250
shootings, mass, 389
shotguns, 196
Silicon Valley, 294
silk industry, 109, 116
Simmons Hardware, 170
slate-writing, 207–208
slogans, 353, 355
Slotkin, Gary, 396
Slotkin, Richard, 201
Small Arms Division of the Ordnance
    Department, 301–302

small-bore rifles, 261–262
"smart gun," 391
Smith, Adam, 105–107
Smith, Horace, 2–3, 51, 98, 113–114
Smith & Wesson company, 51–53, 110,
    181, 184, 252, 370, 392–393
  government takeover of, 302
  Model 3 Army Russian gun of, 114
  production low for, 47–48
  travels abroad and, 113–114
  West and, 355–356, 364
  Winchester, O., sales proposition to,
    58–59
social issues, 4–5
South America
  Bolivia, 243, 388
  Brazil, 117, 243, 306, 388
  Chile, 115, 117, 124, 243, 306
  Ecuador, 117, 243, 388
  generous buyers in, 242–243
  gun sales in, 388
  international gun market control and,
    243
  Peru in, 115, 124, 243, 306, 388
  sales and peaceful interlude of,
    227–228
  Squires' gun sales in, 126–127
  trailblazing in, 36
Spain, 117, 307
Spanish model rifles, 115–116
Spanish Ordinance Commission, 116
Spanish-American War, 243, 260, 268
Spencer, Christopher, 2–3, 69–70,
    73–75, 109
Spencer Company, 112–113
Spencer rifles, 87–90, 95, 109, 165
Spinner, F. E., 48
"spirit cabinets," 350–351
"spirit guns," 105
"The Spirit Saver of the Carpenters'
    Union," 309
"spirit world," 149, 154, 284
spiritualism, 147–160, 217, 284–293,
    349–350, 349 (photo)
Sporting Arms and Ammunition
    Manufacturers Association, 387
sports market, 46, 168, 226–227,
    258–259
Sprague, Homer, 87, 216

Springfield Armory, 12, 18–19, 23–24
Springfield rifles, 302
Squires, Watson, 118–119, 126–127
stakeholders, 397
Stanford University, 215
Stanley, Henry, 190
Stanton, Edwin, 90
Steam for the Millions, 62
Stebbins, Josiah, 13, 15, 20
Stegner, Wallace, 201
Stevens, Simon, 379
sting operation, 397
stockholders, 52, 55, 63, 83–84, 101,
    142, 312–314
    New Haven Arms Company, 95–96
Straits Settlement, 129
suicides, 367, 375
Summer Land, 149, 154, 205–206
superstitions, 287–288, 342–343
Supreme Court, 197
Swedenborg, Emanuel, 153, 210
systems
    American and corporate, 52–53
    American manufacturing, 17–18,
        42–43
    breech-loading gun, 41
    contract, 93–94
    interchangeable gun, 40
    lack of railroad, 31
    manufacturing and "putting out,"
        31–32

tactics, 383, 385, 389
    Colt, S., business, 106
    pre-auction announcement, 230
    repeaters, muzzle-loaders and military,
        86–91
Taft, William Howard, 243–244
takeovers, 96–97, 99, 101–102, 165
Talcott, George, 69
target-shooting competition
    (*Schuetzenbund*), 168
taxes, 312, 373, 386
Taylor, Frederick Winslow, 263
telescope lens, 216
television industry, 359, 364
"Tex and His Horse Patches," 356
Thompson submachine gun (Tommy
    Gun), 373–386

time studies, 265
time-motion efficiency, 265
"Tinker Dave," 82–83
Tocqueville, Alexis de, 223
Tomlinson, Lizzie, 56
Tommy Gun. *See* Thompson
    submachine gun
Topperwein, Ad, 323
tourism, 139, 347–349, 349 (photo),
    368
trade, gunsmith, 9–12, 22–24, 241
treason, 67
Triggernometry: A Gallery of Gunfighters
    (Cunningham), 360–361
Troilus and Cressida (Shakespeare), 290
The True Life of Billy the Kid (Lewis, J.),
    198
trust, 230, 234
trust funds, 283, 346
tuberculosis, 205, 310
Turkey, 139–142
Tutt, Dave, 187
Twain, Mark, 97–98
Tyler, John, 23
typewriters, 6, 227

UMC. *See* United Metallic Cartridge
the Union, 67–68
unionization, 303
United Metallic Cartridge (UMC),
    111–112, 134, 236, 238, 317
United States (U.S.), 8–9, 120–121,
    129, 132–133, 140, 301–308
United States v. Cruikshank, 197
US. *See* United States
US Model 1822, 176

Van Kleeck, Mary, 302–303
Vergennes, 11
Vest Pocket Pistol, 167–168
Victoria (queen), 39
violations, 95, 119–120, 239, 301
violence, 45–46, 197–198, 200–201,
    244, 381–382
    gun culture and, 10, 367–368, 370,
        375–376, 389, 392, 396–397
Volcanic Repeating Arms Company,
    51–60, 63
volitional rifle, 32–33, 43

volume, 59, 172–173
Vyse, Stuart, 103

Walker, Sam, 33–34
war, 18, 45, 67, 82, 139–141, 387–388
    Bennett, T., and, 299, 303–308
    sewing machine patent, 32, 43
    See also Civil War; Revolutionary
        War; Seminole War;
        Spanish-American War
War Department, 302–303, 305–308,
    377
War Trade Board, 307
warfare
    repeater changing, 86–91, 182
    Winchester Model 73 and, 182
Washington, Booker T., 198
Washington, D. C., 26–27
Washington, George, 9
Wasson, R. Gordon, 380
weapons, 45–47, 175–176, 325–326
Welles, Gideon, 73
Wells, Ida B., 195
Wells Fargo, 123
Werle, Robert, 263, 265
Wesson, Daniel B., 2–3, 51, 98,
    113–114, 393
Wesson rifles, 78–80
the West, 353–368
Western Australia, 129
Wheeler, F. G., 55
"When Action Counts," 252
White, Owen Payne, 189
Whitney, Eli, 2–5, 11–20, 34, 263
wholesale market, 170, 172
Wickham rifles, 19
Wild Bill, The Pistol Dead Shot
    (Ingraham), 190
Wild Jim, The Texas Cowboy (Buntline),
    190
Wild West, 170
Wild West Frontier Village, 347
Wild West show, 183–184, 190–191, 194
"wilderness warrior," 259–260
wildlife, extermination of, 262
Willard Hotel, 74
Williams, P., 231
Williamson, Harold, 239, 366

Wilson, J., 83
Wilson, R. L., 235
Winchester, Annie Pardee, 99–103, 210
Winchester, Hannah Jane, 124, 144,
    160–161, 204, 267–275
Winchester, Jane, 31, 124–126, 139, 142,
    144, 160–161, 310
    control of shares by, 204
    gifts and last holiday of, 271
    letters and, 237, 267–275, 304, 344
    stockholder holdings of, 312–313
Winchester, John, 3
Winchester, Oliver, 2–4, 176, 368
    American system and, 42–43
    background of, 51–60
    business successors of, 388
    changes in private life and family of,
        84–86
    clothing empire and, 30–33,
        53–54, 94
    Constantinople, rifles and, 132–139
    as daguerreotypist, 21–22
    death of, 203–204
    faded dreams of large military sales by,
        74–78
    government and, 71–72
    as gun capitalist, 203
    gun defects and, 9, 60–62, 94–95,
        126
    as gun market inventor, 7–8
    gun rivalry and, 73–74
    gun sales and, 58–59, 74–78, 83–84,
        123–125, 132–133
    Henry and contract system of, 93–94
    Hotchkiss patent for repeater gun by,
        128
    intent to exploit civilian markets, 112
    mansion and character of, 145–147
    misremembered as gun inventor, 99
    New Haven Arms Company takeover
        by, 96–97, 99, 101–102
    patent litigation and, 38, 96
    rapid-fire rifles and, 78–84, 87
    repeater rifles and, 88–91, 203
    rifle empire and, 132–133, 136–137,
        268–269, 297
    rifles and, 6, 51–62
    salesmen search and, 121

Smith and Wesson proposition, 58–59
sports market interest of, 226–227
strategy for ingenious gun marketing
    by, 59–60
tour travels of Davies and, 94–99
Turks and business with, 139–141
vision and ambition of, 31
wholesale markets used by, 170
Winchester Model 66 advertised by,
    184
Winchester, Sarah, 107, 204, 211, 218,
    280, 341–342
    admittance to Llanada Villa refused
        by, 267–268, 276–277
    bad fortune of, 143–145, 147
    business acumen and competency of,
        282–283
    conscience and, 293–294
    Coombs and, 205–206, 208–209
    correspondence and, 267–275,
        311–312
    death and, 160–161, 343, 345–346
    eccentrics of, 279, 314–315
    enigmatic riddle of, 293–294
    estate and, 279–297, 283, 308–316
    exiled life of, 310–311
    ghosts and, 209–210, 287–294, 343,
        347, 349–351, 385, 390, 397
    grief of, 102–103, 105, 205
    houseboat living and ambition of,
        281–282
    land purchasing of, 220–222
    legends and, 292–293, 370
    Llanada Villa and, 282–297, 347
    mediums and, 155, 158, 205–210,
        285, 351
    mysterious mansion of, 223, 267–277
    Mystery House and overbuilding by,
        308–316
    operas played on organ by, 290–291
    pregnancy and, 99, 143–144
    reorganization of WRAC and,
        314–316
    rifle empire and, 268–269, 297, 346
    Santa Clara house and, 213, 219
    spiritualism and, 147–154, 284–291
    See also Pardee, Sarah L.; Sarah's
        estate

Winchester, Will, 96, 100–101, 204–205,
    207, 210
    accountability and, 152
    Coombs' materializing ghost of,
        209–210
    death and, 160–161, 268
    Pardee, S. marriage and, 84–86, 144
    Yale Observatory donation of,
        217–218
Winchester .30 caliber rifle, 260
Winchester '73 (movie), 361–363
Winchester Arms Company, 96–97
Winchester Model 66, 104, 122, 133,
    140, 179–180, 184, 366
Winchester Model 73, 179–181, 186,
    194, 196, 225, 362–363
Winchester Model 1883, 128
Winchester Model 1885, 180
Winchester Mystery House Associates,
    347–349
    See also Mystery House
Winchester Plan, 319
Winchester Repeating Arms Company
    (WRAC), 68, 104, 121, 130,
    133, 145
    Addis' mission and near bankruptcy
        of, 122–124
    advertisements and, 117–118,
        326–328, 333–335, 355–356
    ammunition returns of, 236–237
    beginnings and background of, 164
        (photo), 299–301, 369
    birth of corporate bodies and, 103–105
    "boy plan" and, 324–325
    cartridge board, 111 (photo)
    civilian market of, 166–167, 182–183
    Colt, S. and, 226
    condominium conversion of, 348
    Crossman, E. describing, 291–293
    dealer treatment by, 240
    drill press operation of, 264
    E. Remington & Sons property and,
        233–234
    family disentangled from control of,
        315–316
    firms absorbed by, 165
    first wholesalers of, 172
    foreign sales of, 242–243

Winchester Repeating Arms Company
    (WRAC) *(continued)*
  frontier life closing and, 249
  government contracts and, 301–308
  government increased labor and, 306
  growing competition for, 163–164
  gun dealers and, 243–245
  high-volume consumption needed by,
    165–166
  individualism in, 184–185
  inventory resources and stature of,
    295–296
  jobbers of, 169
  Kidder & Peabody and, 317
  massiveness and impressiveness of,
    299–300
  merger, 345, 369
  One of One Thousand campaign of,
    186
  as overbuilt, 307
  process efficiency in, 265
  production and profits of, 225–226
  promotional calendar of, 253 (fig.)
  Pugsley and, 101–102, 186,
    321–322, 369
  reorganization and, 314–316
  revenue and losses, 109
  richer qualitative value of, 250–251
  rival firms absorbed by, 165
  Roosevelt, T., customer of, 259–260
  as self-contained city, 307, 309
  shares, 312–313
  small-bore rifles of, 261–262
  unionization efforts and, 303
  War Department collaboration and,
    302–303
  Winchester, S., and reorganization of,
    314–316
Winchester rifles, 76–77, 131–132, 174,
    181–182, 195
  death and, 140–142
  as gun that won West, 353–368
  Henry rifles becoming, 91
Winchester-Simmons Company, 345,
    369
Winkler, Adam, 200
Wolcott, Oliver, Jr., 14–17
"Woman Defies Ghosts in Selling her
    House," 280
World Peace Foundation, 33
World War I, 299
WPA. *See* New Deal Works Progress
    Administration
WRAC. *See* Winchester Repeating
    Arms Company
Wright, David Augustus, 72–73
Wright, Henry, 150
Wright, James, 57–58

Yale Divinity School, 146–147
Yale Observatory, 217–219
Yale University, 3, 102, 124, 146, 217,
    219, 239, 263, 268, 274, 299,
    310–311, 366
Yale-New Haven Hospital, 310
Yellow Hand (Cheyenne chief),
    192–194
Young, Brigham, 34

Pamela Haag received a PhD in history from Yale University, a BA from Swarthmore College, and an MFA from Goucher College. She is the author of three books and has published in a wide range of venues, including *American Scholar*, Slate, NPR, *Chronicle of Higher Education*, *Times* (London), *Antioch Review*, and *Christian Science Monitor*. She won a 2012 Sidney essay award and has been awarded several fellowships.